# INTRODUCTION
# TO
# PSYCHOLOGY

# INTRODUCTION TO PSYCHOLOGY

*Editor-in-Chief*
**Arun Kumar**

**INSTITUTE FOR SUSTAINABLE DEVELOPMENT
LUCKNOW**
**&**
**ANMOL PUBLICATIONS PVT. LTD.**
**NEW DELHI - 110 002 (INDIA)**

**ANMOL PUBLICATIONS PVT. LTD.**
H.O.: 4374/4B, Ansari Road, Darya Ganj,
New Delhi-110 002 (India)
Ph.: 23278000, 23261597
**B.O.:** No. 1015, Ist Main Road, BSK IIIrd Stage
IIIrd Phase, IIIrd Block,
Bangalore - 560 085 (India)
*Visit us at*: www.anmolpublications.com

*Editorial Board*

Dr. Arun Kumar, *Editor-in-Chief*
Smt. Laxmi Devi, *Member Secretary, ISD*
Dr. C.P. Yadav, *Member, ISD*
Mr. Arvind Kumar, *Member, ISD*
Dr. L.B. Yadav, *Member, ISD*
Prof. B.L. Sinha, *Member, ISD*

*Introduction to Psychology*
© 2007

[Responsibility for the facts stated, opinions expressed, conclusions reached and plagiarism, if any, in this book is entirely that of the ISD, Lucknow. The Publishers bear no responsibility for them, whatsoever.]

PRINTED IN INDIA

Printed at Mehra Offset Press, Delhi.

# Contents

# Preface

When Psychology first started as an academic discipline; it was thought of as an attempt to study the mind, or mental life. The earliest psychologists were often philosophers who has become interested in how human beings work—what makes them 'tick'. So they spent a great deal of time trying to analyse their own reactions, and to develop ideas about people based on their own experiences, and on examining other people's experiences. But there are problems with introspection as a way of finding things out. One of the main ones is that we are often unconsciously biased—we do not notice things because we do not expect them to be there, or we do not think they are important. And, because our biases often are unconscious, it is very difficult for us to control them. However, it gradually become clear that instrospection, though very interesting as an approach, was not really enough if we wanted to find out about human bindings.

Psychology is the scientific study of behaviour and experience. By including the word scientific, we are saying that our study must be serious and systematic; and also, that we should be able to apply our findings to others, as well as to the people we are studying. Most psychologists use a combination of different approaches and methods, so that they can look at things from several different angles. There's no such thing as a perfect method of study in psychology, but by being aware of the problems, and controlling them as far as possible, we can collect them pretty reliable evidence for many of questions we ask about human beings

Psychologists have traditionally been the keenest critics of their own discipline. This may be one of the reasons why psychology is constantly said to be in a crisis. Self criticism usually originates, however, from comparing oneself with others. Psychology has compared itself with the natural sciences, with psychiatry, with the social sciences, with the humanities and so on, and claims have been raised that psychology should approach its subject matter in the same way as these disciplines. The controversies within psychology can thus be seen as reflections of controversies between the disciplines surrounding it.

Introduction to Psychology, as is obvious from the name, is designed to meet the basic requirement of students and teachers in the field to have an introductory reading of psychology.

We are grateful to all the eminent scholars, whose writings are partially cited or substantially made use of in the present work. Our intention in reproducing the material is to share the fruits of painstaking and erudite researches of these scholars by wider readership. Though every care is taken in presenting the material in logical sequence. We are solely responsible for any shortcoming/omission which may creep in due to inadvertence.

A number of colleagues and friends have provided valuable advice and assistance in putting these volumes together, we are grateful to them all.

**—Arun Kumar**

# 1

# About Psychology

## What is Psychology?

'What exactly is psychology anyway?'. There are many possible answers to this question—by the time you have finished this book you will have some ideas of your own. Perhaps the best way to start, though, would be to try to define psychology in some way.

When psychology first started, it was thought of as an attempt to study the mind, or mental life. The earliest psychologists were often philosophers who had become interested in how human beings work—what makes them 'tick'. So they spent a great deal of time trying to analyse their own reactions, and to develop ideas about people based on their own experiences, and on examining other people's experiences. Trying to analyse your own, personal experience and reactions is known as 'introspection'.

But there are problems with introspection as a way of finding things out. One of the main ones is that we are often unconsciously biased—we don't notice things because we don't expect them to be there, or we don't think they are important. And, because our biases often *are* unconscious, it is very difficult for us to control them. Another problem with introspection as a way of finding things out, is that it is not possible for *other people* to check our observations; that is, we cannot develop any *objective* way of looking at a person's personal experiences and reactions.

So it gradually became clear that introspection, though very interesting as an approach, was not really enough if we wanted to find out about human beings. There were problems, too, with defining psychology as 'the study of the mind', as many people did. One of these problems is that, while we all know what we mean when we talk of the 'mind'. It is very difficult to know if other people mean the same thing. For example: I might talk about my 'mind', and be thinking of that part of myself which engages in thinking and remembering; while you might talk about your 'mind' and be thinking, not just of those parts, but also of your emotions and feelings as well. So although we would be using the same words, we would be thinking of different things, and we would therefore be likely to disagree with what the other person said.

Another problem with talking about the mind—the main one, even—is that we cannot see or touch it; in fact, we have no outward sign that it exists at all, except as it shows through people's *behaviour.* I cannot know what you are thinking, but, if you smile at me and nod your head when I am talking to you, then I may judge that you agree with what I am saying. But the information that I have used to work this out was your *behaviour*—smiles and head—nodding.

Because (If this, there was a change in psychology at the beginning of this century. Psychologists began to concentrate much more on studying behaviour, as a way of finding out about people, than on 'introspection'. Information about people was obtained by studying what they *did,* their actions, speech, and so on. Behaviour is anything which people do that can be observed by someone else; talking, for instance, has been called 'verbal behaviour', and we can also talk about things like 'social behaviour' or 'aggressive behaviour'.

But there are problems, too, with simply studying behaviour. There is more to people than just the behaviour which they are engaging in at any particular time. We all have many memories that may affect the things that we do: we have learned from our *experiences* since we were very tiny Although it isn't possible for someone else to *see* our experiences, they do have an influence on how we act—on our *behaviour.* So the definition of psychology changed: from being the study of the mind, or the study of mental life, it now had a new definition:

"Psychology is the study of behaviour and experience."

This is a much better definition than simple talking of the study of the mind, but it isn't perfect yet! For example if I were to tell you an amusing story about a five year old child that I know, I would probably be describing experience and behaviour. But would you think that you had learned about five-year-olds *in general* from it? Probably not—you would be well aware that five-year-olds are different from each other, and that just because little Jane acted this way it doesn't mean that little Catherine would also act in this same way. Yet I would still have been describing behaviour and experience. But if I were to tell you about a careful study of many different five-year-olds, living in many different types of homes, that would be different. You might well think that you could learn something about five-year-olds *in general* then. So we need to include another word in our definition:

"Psychology is the *scientific* study of behaviour and experience."

By including the word 'scientific', we are saying that our study must be serious and systematic; and also, that we should be able to apply our findings to *others,* as well as to the people we are studying.

**How do We Find Things Out in Psychology?**

Throughout this book, you will find references to studies which people have done, to find out why something happens, or to test an idea which they have had. Finding evidence is a vital part of modern psychology.

There are various stages to doing a systematic study, all of which are important in their own right, and which we will look at. Perhaps the first stage will seem obvious, but it's still important. This is sorting out exactly what the study is *for*. Suppose you were interested in the effects on children of watching television. It's no good just saying 'Oh, I'm interested in what effects it has', because that won't get you anywhere—how are you going to start looking for the effects? As I said at the beginning of this chapter, we need to have a *systematic* approach if we want to find things out which will apply to everyone; it's not enough just to rely on anecdotes, because people are *individuals*, and can behave very differently.

So we need to narrow it down, until we are asking a *definite* question, which we can test out in a systematic fashion. You might say something like: 'Does violence shown on television affect children?' Now, at least, we know what we are looking at—violence on TV—but we still aren't very sure what sort of effects we will look for. Do we mean 'Does it upset children?'. That would be one effect which we could look for. But I don't think it would really be the one which we had in mind when we first asked the question. That would be more like 'Do children behave more violently to each other, when they've been watching violent TV?'. Whatever it is that we are interested in, we have to make sure that we are asking a question which will tell us *that* answer, and not the answer to an entirely different question! This process of narrowing down the questions to which we want answers is a part of the way that we develop the *hypothesis* for the study.

Most studies are designed to *test a hypothesis*. In our example, the hypothesis which we would be testing could be: 'Children who watch violent TV will show more violent behaviour than children who watch non-violent TV.' That would be a kind of statement which we make and then test to see if it's really true. The test, of course, is the study which we now go on to design, but the kind of study we design *depends* on the hypothesis which we are testing—a different hypothesis would need a different method of study. For instance, we might decide that our hypothesis would be 'Teenagers who are violent watch more violent TV than teenagers who are not violent', in which case we would probably do a totally different kind of study to investigate the hypothesis.

There are three main standards which a good psychological study should live up to. The first is that it should be possible to *generalise* from the results. There's no point studying people or animals in detail if we can't hope to find out about people or animals *in general* from it; that wouldn't be much better than an interesting anecdote. It's only if we feel that a study has something more to say, about others as well, that we count it as good evidence.

A second standard is that an experiment should be *replicable*. That means that it should be possible for someone else to copy exactly what the first investigator did, and to get exactly the same results. If we can't do that, then we would say that it's not really very good evidence—the results might just have happened because of some problem in the way that the study was designed, or because the experimenter happened to get very unusual subjects.

The third standard is that whatever is used to assess the effects in the study—the measure—should be *valid*. That means that it really should be measuring what it is trying to measure. For instance, if we were looking at whether violent TV caused violence in children, and we just measured whether they got upset or not, it wouldn't really be valid, because being upset is not necessarily the same as getting violent. So we need to make sure that the study is as realistic and valid as possible.

There are several different methods that we can use to find things out in psychology. Each of these methods is useful for finding out different types of things, but also each of them has its own problems which we have to be very careful about. We will look at some of these methods in turn, and also at some of their problems.

***Experiments***

Experiments are what we do when we are trying to find out if one thing *causes* something else. Because of this, when we are doing an experiment we have to make sure that the results we have got could not have happened in any way other than the one we are trying to investigate. For example: suppose we were trying to find out if students did better at arithmetic tests when they were sitting in a cool room, than when they were sitting in a hot room. Obviously, we would have to test students in a hot room, and also in a cool room. But there are other things we have to take into account too—was it the same room? Perhaps one of the rooms was more comfortable than the other one. The students might have felt more relaxed, and so performed better in the test. If that happened, then we might think that our results showed that the cool room was better than the hot room, but they might really be showing that a comfortable room was better than an uncomfortable one!

There are lots of factors like this which can influence experiments. A good experiment needs to be well-controlled; that is, all these possible influences need to have been noticed and prevented. For example, you could prevent that last problem by making sure that you always used the same room, but heated it differently.

Another factor that we need to be very careful about is the way that our subjects are selected. (This is true of all psychological studies, not just experiments.) A study by Orne, in 1972, showed that volunteer subjects would be much more cooperative and helpful if they knew they were taking part in a psychological experiment, than if they were just being asked to do something in their normal life. Orne asked subjects to add up pairs of numbers on a piece of paper, and then to tear it up. People would refuse to do this unless they thought it was part of' an experiment. If they thought that, then they would do it time and time again!

What this means, then, is that we have to be sure that our subjects are acting realistically, and with many laboratory experiments it isn't possible to be certain of this. Since we also need to make sure that our subjects don't try to be too helpful, and give us the results that we want to get, most experiments will use a *single-blind control*. This means that the subject doesn't know what the hypothesis of the experiment is, so they can't mess it up by trying to be too helpful!

In some experiments it's important to be really careful about subjects guessing the hypothesis. For instance, if we were testing a new type of drug, our subjects might get clues about what we were expecting by little things, like the way that we asked the question, and whether we seemed more interested in some answers than in others. In studies like these, this problem is often coped with by using a *double-blind control*. This means that neither the subject nor the experimenter knows what the hypothesis is. The experimenter is just someone who is working on the experiment but who isn't fully informed about it, so he can't pass on unconscious 'clues' to the subject.

*Standardised procedures* can also be used to prevent these kinds of *experimenter effects*. This means that every step of the experiment is decided beforehand, so that all the subjects get identical experiences. This ensures that the experimenter doesn't unconsciously influence the results by varying the experiment slightly.

*Standardised instructions* are used when subjects might be affected by the way that they are told to do something. So everything that the experimenter says to the subject is decided beforehand, making sure that all the subjects are given exactly the same information.

There are many other ways in which experiments can be influenced, and as I said, a good experimenter will have *controlled* them—so that the results could not possibly have been caused by anything else. As you read through this book, you will find many accounts of experiments: always ask yourself, each time you read about one: 'Could these results have come from anything else?' If they *could*, then we can't take the experiment to be convincing proof of what it was trying to look at.

### Observations

Many subjects in psychology are not suitable for investigation by means of experiments. If we wanted to find out about young children and their playing, for instance, we could not do experiments on the children, for fear that restricting them so much might harm or change their development. So we find out about their playing by *observation*—by watching them carefully, and seeing what we can learn from that.

Again there are problems with relying on observation to find things out. One of the main problems is that, because there are lots of things going on at once, it is very difficult to sort out which thing *causes* something else. The behaviour we are interested in might be caused by several different factors all working together, or it might arise from something that happened before we started watching, and so on. So we have to be content with describing what is happening, and trying to work things out from that.

Other problems, too, arise from possible biases in the observer—especially if they know what the observational study is interested in. For instance: suppose the study was to find out if children in crowded rooms played more aggressively than children with plenty of space. The observer has to note down all the behaviour which the children engage in, and especially aggressive behaviour. But quite a lot of actions that children do can be read two ways: if a child lifts his hand and there is another child standing close by, it could be a threatening action. On the other hand, it might not be—the child might be pointing or even just stretching! But if the observer is expecting the child to be aggressive, then it could be noted down as an aggressive action, even though it wasn't. So observers need to be carefully trained, and it is better if they don't know what the study is about.

Perhaps one of the biggest problems of observational studies, with both humans and animals, is our tendency to act differently if we know that we are being watched. If we go back to the 'children and TV' study, for instance, it's unlikely that we could really get an idea of how violent a particular child or teenager was, just from observation. After all, most violence occurs when people *aren't* watching, not when they are!

But, also, it's very difficult to act naturally when you are aware that someone else is watching you. Try it sometime! So what the psychologist sees may easily not be *valid*—it may have become unrealistic from the very beginning, just by the way it is being studied,

There are three ways that psychologists try to get round this problem. The first one—perhaps the most common—is to try to get the subjects *accustomed* to the observer, so that after a while being watched won't bother them as much, and their behaviour will become more natural. Although this can take a bit of time, it's a method that's quite often used, because it doesn't affect other aspects of the study too much.

Another method is to *conceal* the observer from the subjects—for instance, by using two-way mirrors, or hidden video cameras. But this means that whatever behaviour is being observed has to take place in that particular room or area—if the subjects move away, or just turn their backs to the mirror or camera, the observer isn't able to get a clear view of what they are doing. So this affects the way that the study has to be designed; you couldn't do a very 'natural' study like this.

The third method is known as *participant observation*—where the observer joins in with the group that is being observed. Although this means that the study is often more realistic, it can also mean that the observer gets too involved with what is going on, and so is not as objective as he or she could be. And, also, it isn't very easy for another person to check what the observer is studying, or to replicate it.

***Case Studies***

Rather than trying to collect information from a whole mass of people some studies have concentrated on just one or two individuals, and looked at their experiences and behaviour *in detail.* This is another useful way that we can find things out about how people are influenced, and how different things develop. But case studies, too, have their problems. The most important one of these is the way that only one or two people can be studied at a time. Although this means that we can find out about them in more detail than we could have done otherwise, it also means that we have no way of knowing how *typical* these people are. It might be that the people we have chosen to study are really very unusual, and not like the rest of us at all! In that case, although we might find out interesting things about them, it wouldn't help us much in finding out about people in general.

### *Longitudinal and Cross-Sectional Studies*

A *longitudinal* study is where the same individuals are studied over a long period of time, so that the changes that happen to them can be recorded. For example: if we wanted to compare three-year-olds with nine-year-olds, we could do it by taking a group of each age and looking at them systematically. This would be a *cross-sectional study*. But we would have no way of knowing whether the present three-year-olds were acting in the same way as the nine-year-olds had when they were three. It could be that times had changed slightly—they might have been brought up slightly differently by their parents, or watched different TV programmes, and this could make a difference.

With a longitudinal study, we can control this sort of problem. By looking at the same children when they are three and again when they are nine, we can be sure that we have the same *types* of experience in both groups of children. Also, of course, the individual differences between the children don't matter so much either! On the other hand, as you can imagine, longitudinal studies take a long time to conduct, and are quite expensive too.

The problem of individual differences affecting experiments is one which can be very important. A cross-sectional study is an example of what is known as an *independent-measures design*. This is when we have different people in each of the conditions that we are studying: in this case, for instance, we have *different* people for our three-year-olds and for our nine-year-olds.

But this leaves us with the difficulty that we mentioned before. Experiences in the two groups may be different, and individual differences may affect our results. So if we have an independent-measures design, we need to study a lot of people in each group, in the hope that, with enough people, individual differences will be averaged out and won't affect the study.

One way we *can* control for individual differences, though, is to use a *repeated-measures design*. By doing this, we study the *same* people in the different conditions of our experiment. So any individual differences get cancelled out, and we can simply look at the *differences* between the results that the person had in one condition (like doing an arithmetic test in a hot room) and their results in the other condition (like doing a similar test in a cold room). A longitudinal study is an example of a repeated-measures design, because we are studying the *same* person at different ages.

### *Interviews*

Interviews are another way of collecting useful information to enable us to find out about people. There are many different ways to conduct an interview, ranging from casual chats with people to formal, standardised, set questions which have to be asked in a particular way. Iona and Peter Opie published a study of the rhymes and word-games that school-children use; they collected their data simply by going round school playgrounds and chatting with school-children. On the other hand, George Brown and Tirril Harris's study of depression in a group of London housewives was based on information collected through formal, standard interviews, because in this way it was easier to compare the different women's circumstances.

Each of these methods has advantages and disadvantages. Collecting information by casual, informal interviews means that often the information given is more spontaneous and realistic. But it can also make it very difficult to *generalise*—one person may talk about something so differently from the way that another person does, that it becomes almost impossible to compare what the two people said.

If we use formal, standard interviews, it is much easier to generalise from the results. But if people feel that they are being asked a set of routine and automatic questions from a list they often do not talk as freely as they would in a casual conversation. The interviewer needs to be thoroughly skilled and trained, to make it seem a natural and not an awkward, situation. This can mean that a formal interview study is quite difficult (and expensive) to conduct well.

***Surveys***

Although surveys are often more useful to sociologists than they are to psychologists, they can nonetheless be very helpful. For instance, supposing we were interested in whether violent TV had effects on young people, we might decide If begin our study by a large survey of people's TV watching habits, and their preferred programmes. From the results of this survey, we could pick out extreme groups of subjects—some who watch very violent TV and some who never watch violent TV. Once we had found these people, we could investigate further by using a different method, maybe observations or experiments.

One problem with all psychological methods, but particularly with surveys, is that it matters a great deal just *hop'* the subjects are selected. If we are comparing two groups of people, or wanting to find out about people in general, then it is very important that we have a *representative sample* of subjects. If our sample is biased in some way (for example, only asking very middle-class people about their TV-watching habits, then we are not able to generalise from the results. And in some studies it may even distort the results completely.

In order to get a representative sample, we need to try to make sure that everyone has an equal chance of being chosen. There are two main ways that we can do this: random or stratified sampling

*Random sampling* is when we try to make sure that our choice has not been influenced by anything about that person. For instance, if we stood in a busy street and asked people to answer questions, although we might think we were equally likely to approach anyone, unconsciously we would probably only go up to the ones who looked as though they might answer. But if we approached every seventh or tenth person, say, regardless of what they looked like, that would form a more random sample.

*Stratified or quota sampling* is when we try to select balanced numbers from different *types* of subjects. So, if we wanted to look at how people from different countries thought of

English people, there would be no point in going up to every fifth person in the street. Instead, we would try to get a certain number of people from each different country, and ask for their opinions. In this way, our sample would be more representative.

Both surveys and interviews have the advantage that we are able to study very large samples of subjects fairly easily. However, they have the disadvantage that we cannot really go into things in much detail. Only the more obvious or apparent kinds of human behaviour can be studied using these methods.

Most psychologists use a combination of different approaches and methods, so that they can look at things from several different angles. There's no such thing as a *perfect* method of study in psychology, but by being aware of the problems, and controlling them as far as possible, we can collect some pretty reliable evidence for many of the questions we ask about human beings.

**Why do We Use Animals in Psychology?**

As you read through this book, you will come across many studies which have been made using animals. Many of our findings about how learning takes place, for instance, have been discovered as a result of work with animals, but in the last section 1 talked about psychology as if it were simply the study of human beings.

There are two reasons why we use animals. The first of these is that animals, too, have behaviour and experience. If you see a dog which cringes when you go up to it, you will tend to come to the conclusion that the dog has been badly treated, in the past, and therefore is afraid of you. So the dog's previous *experience* is affecting its *behaviour*. Our definition of psychology did not say 'the study of *human* behaviour and experience'—any kind of behaviour and experience may teach us something.

The second point may need a bit more explanation. It's this: since human beings *are* animals, although very highly-evolved ones, we can learn about characteristics which we share with animals, by studying the animals themselves.

If we are going to learn about ourselves, by learning from animals, then it is necessary for us to be aware of which animals are close to us, and probably most like us in behaviour and reaction to experience. To do this, we have to look at the theory of evolution, and how evolution works.

**Summary**

1. Psychology may be defined as the scientific study of behaviour and experience.
2. Collecting evidence in psychology is important. Formulating the hypothesis is a first stage in most studies.
3. Experiments are performed to identify causes. But they have the disadvantage that attempts to control them carefully may make them become artificial or unrealistic.

4. Observations may be more realistic than experiments, but it is not possible to deduce causalty from them. Also, observer effects may influence the results.
5. Case studies allow the psychologist to investigate things very deeply, but because of the small samples it may not be possible to generalise from the results.
6. Interviews and surveys allow us to study large samples of people, but they are limited in the kind of things which they can investigate.

# 2

# Socialisation

Throughout the world, children are brought up in very different kinds of ways. Throughout the world, also, we find many different kinds of human society. In this chapter, we will look at some of the different methods of the child-rearing, and the effects which they seem to have on the eventual development of the children involved.

First of all, we will look at some child-rearing practices very different from those used in our society.

**Cross-Cultural Studies of Socialisation**

The anthropologist Margaret Mead spent considerable time living with different tribes in the Pacific, observing the way that they organised their society and their lives. She found immense differences between tribes, in their habits and traditions of those tribes. We will look at three of the tribes that she wrote about, and their child-rearing habits.

The Arapesh tribe live in the mountains of New Guinea. They are a very poor people, often struggling to get enough to eat. Their society is very much concerned with co-operation and gentleness, and they are intensely interested in growing things—plants, animals, and children. Their babies, when they are born, are regarded as soft, vulnerable, and precious; they are fed gently, whenever they show the least sign of hunger, and are protected and nurtured by both parents, equally, for an extended infancy period. Throughout childhood, the children are protected, and temper-tantrums, when they happen (usually because there isn't enough food), are appeased, and not regarded as something to be 'dealt with'. Their marriage system reflects the passive dependency of childhood. The husband takes a child-bride, and feeds and protects her, re-playing the role that his parents played for him, when he was a child. In this way, there is no strong break between the support and cherishing that they receive in infancy, and their adult life. The whole society is based around co-operation and gentle interest in others, rather than the self. Aggression and arguments are rare, although adults, will sometimes break out in temper-tantrums. But the emphasis in adult life, as in childhood, is on co-operation and mutual dependency.

By contrast, the Mundugumor tribe are fierce, aggressive, and quarrelsome. The women are is intolerant as the men, and dislike rearing children. Children of the Mundugumor tribe have to struggle for the mother's breast, and she is likely to stop feeding them as soon as they appear the least bit satisfied—they are fed while the mother is standing up, and are never cuddled. Unlike the Arapesh, whose children are carried in soft bags, Mundugumor children have to travel in hard, scratchy baskets, and are always forced to assert themselves, and to fight. At the age of five, when Arapesh children are trailing around the village and playing, Mundugumor children may be sent as hostages to other tribes, knowing that if the war-plans change, their lives will be forfeit. They grow up there, and are expected to learn the language and roadways, in case a future war breaks out with the neighbouring tribe, and they have to be scouts. Because of their upbringing, they are well able to act independently, and to store up hostility against their host-tribe. As adults, although the Mundugumor are arrogant and warlike, they are also full of laughter and energy.

The third tribe which we will look at are the Samoans. They are a society of stable, balanced adults, who all work, and enjoy music, art, and dancing. They do not go in for excesses of emotion, or for laziness and apathy, but lead a life based around work and relaxation. Their children are nursed generously in infancy, and are given food and carried about by all the women in the large household—not just the mother. Later, they are looked after by a child-nurse, a girl of about six years old, whole job it is to look after the baby, and to jet it out of the way if it shows anti-social behaviour, like throwing a temper-tantrum within earshot of the head of the household. Throughout this time, the emphasis is on the natural, gradual development of the child: 'While you may do inappropriate things just now, this is because you are young...you'll grow out of it.' The child is never punished—it is the child-nurse's responsibility to make sure that it doesn't annoy others, by taking it out of the way. IT is fed when hungry, carried when tired, and allowed to sleep when it feels like it. At the age of five or six, this changes, and the children adopt their roles: little girls become child-nurses (a responsible and tough job) while little boys join the other boys, and learn to fish, canoe, climb trees, swim, and all the other skills which the men of the society are required to possess.

When they are adult, Samoan people are gentle, balanced, and serene—with a very stable family structure, and very little mental disturbance in the society.

Freeman, in 1983, suggested that Mead had exaggerated the influence of culture in the development of human personality—particularly in her description of Samoan life. He argued that she had been misled, mainly because she had only been able to stay in Samoa for a relatively short period of time, and also because many of her informants had been adolescent girls, whose information might not have been strictly accurate. Freeman saw the personal etiquette which makes Samoan culture appear so relaxed, as being necessary as a social control over aggressive impulses. He also argued that the society was not as sexually relaxed and open as Mead had suggested.

However, Strathern (1983) has pointed out that Freeman's judgement could also have been influenced by his social contacts—in this case, high-ranking males. As they were strongly involved with political issues, and as virginity is important for girls of high rank, they too may simply have been presenting their side of the case. Although Freeman did spend more time in Samoa than Mead, it is very difficult to obtain a purely unbiased view of any society. Other anthropologists (people who study human societies) have concluded that, although Margaret Mead's evidence may not have been very good, overall her conclusions were probably accurate (R. Ballard 1983).

In 1970, U. Bronfenbrenner published the results of a different cross-cultural study. Instead of looking at people in tribal societies, he looked at the way that children are brought up in modern, industrial societies. His study was a comparison of child-rearing in the United States of America, and the United Soviet Socialist Republics. He found enormous differences between the way that children were brought up in each society. For one thing, the Russians had a much more *planned* approach to the way that children should be brought up—they were very conscious of the fact that their children were going to be the adults of the future, and so the whole society was concerned with bringing them up in the 'right' kind of way.

As with most children, Bronfenbrenner found that the peer group—the other children of the same age which the child associated with—was important in moulding children's behaviour. In America, Bronfenbrenner found, the peer group would often influence the child *against* the society's values: it was considered 'creeping' to work hard in school, or to try to be good. But in Russia, the peer group worked very strongly *with* society's values, and this was deliberately encouraged from an early age. Children worked in 'teams', and were responsible for keeping their own discipline and making sure that each member of their team worked hard in school. If a child was lazy, or dishonest, then it would be the other children in the team who would deal with it, not the adults. Children were very conscious that they would grow up to play a full part in their society, and that their school-days were preparing for that time. It was everyone's *duly* to work hard!

Bronfenbrenner also pointed out that children in Russia are not as 'cut-oil" from the adult world as they are in America. Often, the workers in a local factory would 'adopt' a class at school, and the children would visit the factory, and be taken on educational visits by the workers. And *everyone* seemed to be interested in children. Bronfenbrenner was very surprised one day when he was going down the street with his small child. The child ran on ahead, and coming towards them was a 'gang' of teenage boys. Instead of ignoring the child, as American teenagers would have done, he was picked up, and petted by the lads, before being handed back to his parents.

But in America, Bronfenbrenner said, children-aren't regarded as being so valuable; instead, they often have to take 'second place' to their parents' other interests, and are often left either alone, or with just the company of other children. He said that the average American child watches 22 hours of television a week—as much time as they spend in school! While Bronfenbrenner didn't like everything about the Russian system—the way that children were encouraged to 'tell tales' on each other, for example—he did think that perhaps having children a bit more involved in their society would be a good idea. He thought it likely that insufficient involvement by children in American society was a cause of vandalism and violence among young people.

The problem is, of course, that by taking such a deliberate approach to how children should be brought up, and by making sure that all the influences on the child work in the way that society wants them to, we are getting very close to the idea of children being 'brainwashed' into being just the 'right kind' of people. But Bronfenbrenner was saying that every society influences its children so that they grow up to fit into it, and perhaps people in the Western world should be a bit more aware of what they want their children to grow up to do.

## Child-Rearing Styles

In British society, parents use a variety of different methods for bringing up their children. Some children never receive any physical punishment at all, while others are slapped or spanked for misbehaving. Some children are sent to a playgroup at the age of three or four, others stay at home. Some children are sent to boarding school, some are taught at home, and most go to a day school. All-in-all, it is no wonder that people grow up so widely different, and with such different interests.

### *Independence*

Several studies have been done with the intention of examining different ways that parents deal with their children. Several different *styles* have been found, which represent the different ways that parents would tend to handle their child overall—although, of course, there will be differences for individual events. But, roughly speaking, parents' styles can be sorted into four groups: authoritarian, democratic, permissive, or laissez-faire.

*Authoritarian* parents are those who do not consult their children when decisions are to be made, but go ahead and order their children to do things. All decisions are made by the parent and the child does not have any say in the matter at all.

*Democratic* parents are those parents who consult their children before they make decisions, but who still make the final decision themselves. However, they try to take what the child wants to do into account.

*Permissive* parents are parents who allow the child to make its own decisions. Instead of telling the child what to do, they will ask it to decide, and abide by what the child has said. So, with permissive parents, the child has a great deal of' freedom of action, but not a great deal of guidance from the parents.

*Laissez-faire* parents are those who leave the child to go its own way, entirely. They are not involved in any decisions which the child might make, anti do riot guide that child at all, either by praise or by blame.

It can be seen that these different styles have a lot to do with the amount of independence which the parents allow their child; the authoritarian parents do not allow the child any independence, while the laissez-faire parents allow their child complete independence, and responsibility for its own decisions. Several studies have investigated the effects of these kinds of styles on children, although, unfortunately, they have tended to investigate teachers and youth leaders rather than parents. There is a good reason for this: it might well be that some parents have adopted a particular style of child-rearing *because of their child.* For instance, if their child was continually disobedient, they might have started to use an authoritarian approach, because that was the way that they could keep the child under control, even though they may cave wanted to use a more democratic approach. So when we are looking at parents behaviour, we can't really be sure just which is the cause of a certain kind of behaviour and which is the effect. In the above example, the disobedience might have arisen from the authoritarian approach, or the authoritarian approach might have arisen from the disobedience.

In 1938, Lewin, Lippitt and White studied the effects of different styles of leadership on ten-year-old schoolboys. The boys all attended a club which was held after school, and which was concerned with model-making. The boys were divided into three groups, and each group had a leader who followed a different style—authoritarian, democratic, or laissez-faire. The boys who were in the group with the authoritarian leader were told what models they were going to make, and who they' would be working with. If their work was particularly good, the team leader would praise them, but wouldn't explain his praise, Or, if their work was not so good, the leader would say so, but not explain in detail just why, or how it could be improved. The boys in the group with the democratic leader, on the other hand, were encouraged to discuss what model they were going to make, and who they would work with. If they did well, they were praised, and the leader took pains to point out just what was good about their work; if they did badly, then the leader would try to show them how they could improve it, and discuss it with them. The leader joined in with all the group activities, and was particularly friendly. The group with the laissez-faire leader was not directed at all: the boys chose what they wanted to do with no guidance from the leader who neither praised nor criticised their work. They had to work with no adult support or guidance.

The three groups provided very different results: of the three, the boy's in the group with the autocratic leader worked hardest but when he left the room they would stop working, and they often quarrelled among themselves. Very often, they tried to get the leader's attention, but they were always very polite and respectful to him,

The boys in the democratic leader's group were far more cheerful, and didn't quarrel so much. They were interested in their work and when they spoke to the leader, it was usually to ask questions about it. If the leader went out of the room, they still carried on working; and if they came across a problem they would all try to find the answer to it.

The boys in the group with the laissez-faire leader were very disorganised, and didn't do very much work. If they came across any difficulties, they lust gave up, and they very rarely asked the leader for help. The group itself was noisy and quarrelsome.

In a second part of the experiment Lewin, Lippitt and White changed the boys around, to see it; perhaps, it had just been that some boys were more interested than others. But, after they had sorted them into entirely different groups, they still got the same results, so they could say definitely that it was the style of leadership which was causing them. Unfortunately, there is always the problem with studies like this, that the children are already used to one particular style—the one their parents use—and so they may be reacting to a *change* in style, rather than to the style itself. (Most of the boys had parents who used a democratic approach.) But the study still shows us something about leadership styles, and their effects on children.

Baumrind, in 1967, performed a study which was an attempt to find out if child-rearing styles in the family went along with greater independence, as they had apparently done in the study by Lewin et al., where the boys in the 'democratic' group had worked more independently than the others. By looking at different kinds of approaches from the parents, Baumrind found three categories, which she called authoritarian, authoritative, and permissive. These turn out to be roughly the same as the authoritarian, democratic (authoritative) and permissive styles mentioned before. She found that children of authoritarian parents were fairly self-reliant, but tended also to be withdrawn and mistrustful; while the children of democratic parents were mature and competent, and particularly independent. Children from permissive parents appeared immature and lacked independence and self-discipline. The study was done by interviews with parents, and observations in the home and in the school.

The way that parents bring up their children seems to have quite a lot to do with the independence that they develop. It seems that children become independent as a result of having a mixture of responsibility and guidance; left with no guidance at all, as in the laissez-faire approach, they do not become independent; and if left with no responsibility, as in the authoritarian style, then they also don't become very independent (although they do become more independent than the laissez-faire parents children).

Unfortunately, there are problems with these studies and with other studies which have been conducted by interviewing parents about their child-rearing methods. One of the main problems is that there could be all sorts of things which are influencing the child, apart from the thing that we're interested in. Without getting a full picture of everything that's happened to the child, we can't be sure that our particular variable—for instance the amount of independence a parent allows a child—is exactly the one that's having the effect. Most of these kinds of studies have only investigated one or two things, and not a very wide range.

Another problem is that parents do not necessarily behave in exactly the same way all the time. A parent might be authoritarian about table manners, but democratic about the way that pocket money is spent. When we ask for a single rating of each parent, it could be that we are being much too general; parents act in all sorts of different ways all the time, and this might make our study inaccurate.

A third problem with this kind of approach is the way that information is gathered. Most parents have a good idea of what the 'socially-acceptable' methods of child-rearing are, and what people expect other parents to behave like. So if parents are being asked about how they treat their child, they may be tempted to tell the interviewer how they would *like* to treat their child, or not to mention the bits that they think people won't approve of. So the interview may not get the true picture of how that parent treats that child at all.

Yet another problem is the way that people can jump to conclusions about what *causes* what. If I were to tell you that a good year for strawberries is also a good year for apples, you wouldn't think that the strawberries had caused the apples to grow well, would you? But you might think that perhaps both of them had been caused by something entirely different—for example, by a certain kind of weather. In this case, we'd say that the amount of strawberries *correlates* to the amount of apples, but doesn't *cause* it. In the same way, it could be that an authoritarian style *correlates* of boys 'working hard, but doesn't *cause* it; they might, for instance, be working hard because they have a clear knowledge of what they're doing, and they don't have to stop and think about it much. In most of these studies, it *seems* as if the parents' behaviour causes the child's behaviour, but we don't know that for certain. It might even be the other way round, or it might come from something totally different!

### *Achievement Motivation*

A feature of personality which is similar to independence in some respects, but in other ways quite different from it, is the facet known as *achievement motivation.* This is the way that some children show a strong 'need to achieve' things—they become upset if they can't solve a puzzle, or do well in school, and they will work hard to manage it. Other children, though, don't seem to be that bothered. Although they will do the puzzles that are given to them, and will work in school, they aren't as 'keen' as the children with high achievement motivation, and success isn't as important to them.

Achievement motivation also seems to result hum the way that parents bring up their children. A study by M. Winterbottom, in 1953, looked at achievement motivation in children, and at their parents. The children were given a sentence as an outline, and were asked to tell a story around it. A typical sentence was: "Two children were running a race when one fell over'. The children who had high achievement motivation were expected to tell a story which showed the child being very concerned with winning the race; the children with low achievement motivation were expected to tell a story which wasn't so concerned with the result of the race, but which might, for instance, stress the one child helping another. From the stories that the children told, Winterbottom obtained a score of achievement motivation level for each child.

When the mothers of these children were interviewed, it was found that the children with high achievement motivation had parents who expected their children to manage things earlier (like going to school alone) than mothers of low scorers. They also tended to reward their children with hugs and kisses more; while the mothers whose children showed low achievement motivation did not reward their children very often, but did tend to give them a lot of negative orders ('Don't do that'; 'You can't play with her').

Another study by Rosen and D'Andrade, in 1959, showed that the achievement motivation of children was also connected with what their parents expected of them. If their parents expected a great deal, then the children, also, wanted to achieve very strongly. If the parents didn't expect very much of their children, then the children also had low achievement motivation.

Rosen and D'Andrade asked a blindfolded child to build a tower from building bricks with one hand. The child's parents were watching the child do this, and they were asked how well they thought the child would do. They found that those children with high achievement motivation had parents who expected more from their child; they set high standards of achievement. But they also praised and rewarded their child a lot more, and encouraged it while it was trying to build the tower. Parents of children with low achievement motivation didn't encourage their child much at all, they just watched. So it seems that high expectations from parents aren't the only things which lead to high achievement motivation in children, but praise and encouragement are important too.

### *Conscience*

We have just looked at the effects of parents praising and encouraging their children, but what about punishment? Many people have very strong views about punishment—that you should *never* hit a child, for example, or that some children need a good spanking now and again. But whatever kind of punishment people use, they seem to agree that it should need to be used less and less as the child grows older. As the child grows, it's expected to develop a *conscience* that will tell right from wrong, and that will direct the child's behaviour. There have been several studies that have looked at the connection between punishments, and the development of conscience.

A study by Mackinnon, in 1938, investigated this question. He used college students, and put them in a room with a book of problems which they were asked to solve. The students were told that the answers were in the back of the book, but they were asked not to look at them, but to try to do the problems on their own. By using a two-way mirror, Mackinnon could find if any of them did cheat when he was out of the room. Out of 93 subjects, 43 of them cheated! When Mackinnon asked the subjects later if they had cheated, about half of these 43 confessed, but half didn't. He found that the students with strong consciences—those who had not cheated—were the ones who had parents who relied on *psychological* rather than *physical* punishments. Psychological punishments were the sort where the parent expressed displeasure or hurt feelings at something the child had done, while physical punishments were ones which directly and materially affected the child—like losing pocket money, or being slapped or spanked.

Psychological punishments rely much more on the *relationship* which the child has with the parent or the adult who is doing the punishing. Almost always, the child is expected to perform some kind of action which shows remorse, by saying 'I'm sorry', or by trying to make it up in some way. On the other hand, physical punishment is much more direct and automatic; the child suffers briefly and then the punishment is over. The child isn't expected to do anything special, like apologise, but is expected to avoid doing the offending thing again.

W. Hill said, in 1964, that it is probably the act of remorse which makes the difference between psychological punishment and physical punishment in the building up of Conscience. Since the child itself actually has to do something to express repentance, it is more likely to 'internalise'—to include in its own self-concept—the lesson. As a result of this, the child learns more effectively to avoid doing the 'naughty' act. Since physical punishment can be avoided simply by not being found out, and it makes little difference to any other person, the lesson the child learns doesn't last as long. Once the child is in a position where it won't be punished—when it grows older—then there is no need for it to avoid the 'naughty' behaviour.

If this were true, and it is really the act of remorse which is important, then it wouldn't really matter *which* kind of punishment the parent used, as long as the child also had to apologise, or make recompense somehow. What seems to have happened with Mackinnon's subjects, though, is that they *either* received physical punishment from their parents, in which case that was all, *or* they received psychological punishment from their parents, in which case it was usually accompanied by an act of remorse. It seems that parents who use psychological punishments expect different kinds of behaviour from their children, when they are found out.

Another study, by Sears, Maccoby, and Levin, in 1957, supports this view. They asked mothers about their children's behaviour, and whether they showed strong consciences; and also about the type of punishment which the children received.

They showed that children with strong consciences had parents who not only used psychological punishments, but also tended to make firm demands on their children, expecting them to show a high standard of moral behaviour. They also explained much more than the other parents why they demanded things of their children. Parents who had children with weak consciences tended to be very much more aggressive with their children, and as well as using physical punishments tended not to explain things to them.

So it seems, all round, fairly clear that the way in which children are brought up can have considerable effect on this aspect at least of their later personalities. So what about other characteristics? How far can the way that children are brought up influence other sides of their adult natures?

### Aggression

One characteristic which psychologists are interested in is *aggression*. We know that some people behave very much more aggressively than others, and that people show aggression in different ways—some people seem to 'channel' their aggressive energies into sport, or a competitive job, for instance, while others get involved in fights easily, or hit out at people when they are angry and frustrated. In fact, a very large part of aggressive behaviour seems to arise from frustration, rather than anything else. When playing in nursery school, children become very much more aggressive when they have only a small space to play in, and so are continually interfered with. Also, children behave more aggressively when they have just had a frustrating experience, for instance when they haven't been able to solve a puzzle. In adulthood, some people continue to react aggressively to frustrating events, while others don't. Why is this?

Newson and Newson, in a large study of child-rearing practices in Nottingham, in 1968, found that there were strong class differences in the amount of aggression which children showed. They found that middle-class parents tended to object to their children showing aggressive behaviour, while working-class parents tended to encourage their children to 'stand up for themselves', and to fight back if they were pushed around by other children. When they looked at mothers and infants, they found that, even in the first year of life, infants from working-class homes received more physical punishment than did middle-class infants, and showed more temper tantrums already.

Boys tend to show more aggressive behaviour than girls, and it is sometimes thought that this, too, is a result of parental treatment. A study by Rothbart and Maccoby, in 1966, used tape-recordings of family behaviour. When they analysed the tapes, they found that mothers were far more tolerant of aggressive acts committed by sons, than of aggressive acts committed by daughters. Young boys, it seems, are expected to he aggressive, whereas girls are not.

Another study, by Sears, Maccoby, and Levin, showed that, it children are punished by the parents for being aggressive and particularly if it is physical punishment—aggressive acts can actually *increase*! It seems possible that this comes about as a result of 'modelling'—the parents, by their own behaviour, show the child that aggression can be used—because they, themselves, are using it when they punish the child. Since the children see punishment, and aggression, as being adult-type actions, the children increase their own aggressive behaviour.

## Imitation and Identification

### *Imitation*

Another study of 'modelling', or *observational learning*, was done by Bandura and Walters, in 1963. The children who they were testing observed a real-life, or a filmed, model which was either a child or an adult, performing aggressive actions towards a doll. Later on, the child's own behaviour with the doll was observed, and a note was taken of how much aggressive behaviour the child showed, in its own play with the doll. They found that children were very likely to imitate the behaviour of the 'model' whom they had watched, especially if the model was another child.

In one of these experiments they divided the children into three groups. One group was shown the model being rewarded (by approval from an adult, or by sweets) for showing aggressive behaviour; another group saw the model being punished; and the third group didn't see the model receive any consequences at all. The children's subsequent play reflected what they had seen. Those children who had seen the model being rewarded for aggressive acts themselves showed a high level of aggression in their play. The ones who had seen the model punished showed a low level of aggressive acts, while the no-reward, no-punishment group were in-between.

**Fig. 2.1. Aggressive Behaviour Towards a Bobo Doll**

*After seeing adults act aggressively towards an inflated doll, children were more likely to behave aggressively towards it.*

At this point, Bandura and Walters changed things a bit. They began to reward the children for copying the model, and very soon *all* the children were behaving aggressively with the doll, exactly as the model had done. So, although most of them hadn't imitated the model straight away, when they were in a position where they were rewarded for doing so, they did so easily. All the children were as good as one another in copying the model, and there were no group differences according to whether they had seen the model being punished or rewarded. So the actual *learning* involved must have been the same for all the children, even though their *performance* was different at first.

Bandura connected these findings to the way that children may learn violence from TV programmes. In this study, effectively, he was showing that children can still learn aggressive behaviour, even if they see that behaviour being punished. So perhaps it isn't enough that the 'baddy' should be punished in the end—children could still have learned to imitate the 'baddy' behaviour and if they were in a position where they might benefit from it, then they could imitate that behaviour again.

*Imitation*, like this, seems to be an important way that children learn. It seems to be very much involved in sex-role learning: children learn what kind of behaviour is appropriate for girls or women, and what is appropriate for boys or men, by watching adults (particularly their parents) and how they behave. Later on, they come to *identify* themselves as male or female, and 50 no longer need tis imitate others, but the seeds of this identification are laid down by the first imitative stage.

Margaret Mead has described several different tribes, and their ways of socialising the children. Many of these are completely different, and show, perhaps, just how much sex-roles *are* learned, and may produce completely different societies.

Perhaps the most extreme example of this is among the Tchambuli tribe of New Guinea, in whom the sex-roles which we are used to are completely changed around. The women do the work, make all the major decisions, and control the households, while the men are not regarded as sensible enough to do any practical work, and busy themselves painting, shopping, carving, and dancing. Women are regarded as being strong and capable, involved in serious work. Men are regarded as being fretful, and irresponsible—they wear jewellery and ornaments, and they spend much time gossiping and quarrelling.

From the beginning this difference is expected of the children—in much the same way as the opposite differences are expected in our society—and, by the age of ten or eleven, the little girls are very different from the boys. They are more enterprising and alert, while the boys are timid and unable to concentrate on things.

In the Arapesh tribe, which I mentioned at the beginning of this chapter, the sex-roles are also different from the ones we find in our society, although they aren't as extreme as the Tchambuli. In the Arapesh, *both* sexes are gentle and cooperative, the males taking as much share in child-raising as the females. The kind of differences which we expect between men and women do not show up—the differences appear to lie only in the state of child-birth—and even here the father is considered as involved as the mother.

Among the Iatmul tribe, children of both sexes are brought up together and no differences are drawn until the early teens. Boys will look after children, play with the cooking pots, and go to mourning ceremonies (reserved for women only) with the women and girl children. When they reach their early teens, however, they are withdrawn from women's society, and are ceremonially initiated into manhood, alter which they must associate with the men until they marry. So it is the ceremony of initiation which sets the boys apart, not the earlier upbringing.

As we can see from these studies, human beings are capable of a wide variety of different sex-role behaviour. In our own society, children learn the sex-roles expected of them in many different ways—through their parents' behaviour, through television, through the different toys which boys and girls have to play with (for example, boys' dolls tend to have uniforms and military equipment, while girls' dolls have fashions, and occasionally sports clothes or nursing outfits), through children's books, and many more. From the moment a girl baby is dressed in pink, while a boy baby is dressed in blue, our society says to the child 'you are a girl' (or a boy).

### *Identification*

As it grows up, then, the child is continually presented with models which it can imitate, and which provide information about the sex-role appropriate for it to play. Gradually, it comes to *identify* with its own sex, and to adopt that kind of behaviour. Also, of course, if a child shows the 'right' kind of behaviour, it is often rewarded by approval from its parents, or by getting an appropriate kind of response from another person. So gradually, more and more of the 'right' kind of behaviour is shown by the child, and in this way, too, it learns to behave in the way considered appropriate for its sex. By this process, known as 'operant conditioning', a child may learn the right sex-role behaviour, even if it doesn't have a model present, as might he the case of a boy in a household without a father. In our society, through television and other media (books, films), there are plenty of 'models' from which a child may learn, as they learned in the Bandura and Walters experiments (p. 81).

This isn't to say that there are *no* differences between the sexes in their childhood behaviour. Young boys do tend to engage in more physical, rough-and-tumble play than girls, while young girls tend to be more advanced in learning and using language. Perhaps as a result of this, in our society young girls tend to do better at junior school than boys, "although this changes later on. But, for each kind of sex-type behaviour like this, there will always be exceptions. There will be girls who enjoy rough-and-tumble play, and there will be boys who enjoy and are good at language. When we talk about these kind of differences, we are talking in *general* terms, not laying down hard and fast rules which all children will obey.

In the last century, Sigmund Freud developed a completely different theory of how children come to identify in the appropriate sex-role. We will be looking at Freud's theory more closely in the next chapter.

### *Status Envy*

Some psychologists have said that sex-role learning can be connected with 'status envy'. Status envy is when someone is envied—and therefore imitated—as a result of the things that they own or control. An experiment by Bandura, Ross and Ross in 1963 was set up to demonstrate that status envy may result in children imitating the person who had control over the things which were wanted. The children watched a Film which showed two adults together. One of these adults had a large number of expensive and complicated toys, which the other adult seemed to want. The one who had the toys gave some of them to the other adult. After this, both adults played with the toys, but behaved quite differently.

The children who saw the film were observed, to see which adult they copied. If they were only interested in who had the toys, then, Bandura and the others thought, they would copy both adults equally, since, in the end, both adults had the toys. However, the children copied far more of the behaviour shown by the adult who 'owned' the toys, than the behaviour shown by the other adult. So the experimenters argued, from this, that it was the *control* over he resources which was important to the children—they were demonstrating how *status envy* may lead to imitation.

J. Whiting has suggested that it is the same process which leads to sex-role learning in children. He suggests that, as the child grows up, it sees its father having control over a valuable resource—the mother. As a consequence of this, the young boy imitates the father more, and so learns eventually to *identify* with the father. The child learns its sex-role as a result of status envy.

There are several problems with this argument. The first one, and perhaps the most obvious one, is that it doesn't explain why little girls, too, don't grow up to identify with heir fathers; after all, they grow up in the same family, and see the same things happening. Another problem is that this kind of argument implies that, in a family where the father *doesn't* have control over the mother—where she is more independent, for instance, or where there isn't a father—then the little boys would not grow up identifying with the male sex. Although this is a popular myth (that homosexuals have domineering mothers, for instance), it has repeatedly been shown to *be* a myth. Children from homes where the mother is independent, or where the father is gentle and sensitive rather than domineering, are just as likely to grow up secure in their sexual identity as children from homes with more 'dominant' fathers.

The third argument against this theory is that it doesn't explain Margaret Mead's findings in New Guinea. In many of the tribes she studied, it was the *women* who were envied, for their control of a vital resource—child-bearing. Little girls grew up secure in the knowledge that they, too, would one day have a baby; while the little boys were much more uncertain about their place in the whole scheme of things. And yet most of these tribes (the Tchambuli being the exception) had the kind of sex-role behaviour that we recognise—the women were responsible for child-rearing and preparing food; the men responsible for hunting and fishing. So, in these cases, it certainly can't be status envy on the part of the boys that leads them to identify themselves as male, since child-birth is the envied thing! Rather, it seems to arise from their imitating other males in their society, and being *rewarded* (by praise, or smiles), for doing so.

In this last section, I have talked quite a lot about *social learning*—the way that children gradually learn behaviour appropriate for their society. This is a dual process, which begins with *imitation*, and then, gradually, (perhaps as a result of approval) becomes more deeply engrained, and turns into *identification*. The differences between these two are important ones. When a child imitates another, it is copying an *act*—something that another person has done. But when it comes to *identify* with another, then the process is deeper and more personal. It is saying to itself: 'I am like that person', so instead of simply copying what that person does, it feels itself to *be* like that person—the similarities have become a part of the child's own *self-image*.

There is another, extremely important way that children (and young animals) learn, while they are growing up. It's called *play*.

## Play

Playing is a kind of activity which seems to be limited to mammals. While you may often see young mammals—kittens, lambs, young monkeys, dolphins—playing, you don't see young lizards or young fish doing so. Part of the reason for this lies in the evolution of the nervous system. Essentially, there is a particular part of the brain the limbic system—which seems to control play and those animals which evolved earlier than mammals don't have a limbic system. So the limbic system and play would seem to be later evolutionary developments, which is why only mammals seem to be involved.

What is it, then, about play which makes it special? Well, for one thing, play seems to allow young mammals to practise actions and skills that they will need in adult life, but in such a way that they don't come to any harm if things go wrong, and they haven't mastered the skill properly. If we take this view of play, we can see *why* it would evolve in creatures higher up the phylogenetic scale—if you're going to rely more on learning than on innate behaviour patterns, then you also need a way that you can *practise* that learning safely. If the young cat first tries to pounce on something only when it is actually needing food, then it will get very hungry in the first few weeks! But if, while it is a kitten and still being fed by its mother, it practises pouncing and the other related skills, then by the time it is older, and needs to fend for itself, it will be able to manage relatively easily.

In many ways, children's play serves the same kind of purpose. By practising, and acting out things which it finds in its world, the young child gradually develops its abilities and its understanding of the world around it. Roughly speaking, we can divide children's play into three kinds: motor skills, language, and make-believe.

### *Physical Play*

The kind of play concerned with developing motor skills is very similar to that shown by other mammals. The child practises things—like jumping, skipping, swinging on a bar, or standing very still—until it is good at them. As it gets better at managing the games, the games themselves become more complex: simple chasing games become converted into games where you are 'salt' if you're off the ground; learning to skip a rope becomes converted into an elaborate team game, with chanted songs and special steps. In this way, there is continual challenge and interest for the child, and the level of the game reflects the child's own stage of development of motor skills.

As the child becomes older, those games that develop the motor skills become more 'institutionalised'. That is, they develop more rules, and a definite form—like tennis, or football. But games concerned with the development of motor skills continue into adulthood—darts, for instance, or bowls. In a way, they have developed directly from the playground games which young children learn.

### *Language Play*

Another kind of play which children use is language play infants babble in the cot practising sounds. As they make a noise over and over again, they are *exploring* that sound, and, as they do that, they become more and more practised at it. As the child gradually acquires language, the sound becomes more definite, and the child starts to play with words. Children who have just learned to talk tend to talk a great deal to themselves, while they are playing, and as a part of' their play. In this way they practise using language, and by doing that they are allowing it to develop properly. After a while, they become interested in the language itself—young children are fascinated by rhymes and word-jokes (puns and so on). Very often they make up their own rhymes, as a part of their play.

At first, play with language seems to be a solitary sort of affair. C. Garvey, in a study of children's play in 1977, showed that, at first, the child's playing with nonsense syllables and imaginary conversations is not directed to other children, even if they are in the room, By that time they are three, however, they are more likely to have conversations with other children, and to reflect this in their playing. This goes along with the way that children play anyway—they don't actually start to play *with* other children until they are about that age—although they may well play happily in the same room. After three, rhyming games and acting out parts by using conversations seems to be much more common.

### *Make-Believe Play*

This brings us to the third kind of' play—make-believe. Make-believe means more than games involving imaginary people or places (Let's pretend we're in the haunted wood!); it also means games where the children *act out* rules which they have seen in real life ('I'll be the mummy, you be the baby'), By doing this, the children *practise* their understanding of the world around them, and the way that people act in that world. Make-believe is an important way for the child to come to an understanding of what is around it.

Very often, in make-believe play, the child will express its real-life worries or problems, and in this way, it has an opportunity to sort things out, and perhaps to come to an understanding of them. It is the observation of the way that children do this, which lies behind the technique known as *'play therapy'*. When children are showing disturbed behaviour, and are distressed by something going on around them, they are highly unlikely to tell an adult—or even another child—what the problem is. By giving them time, with an adult present, to play as they want with a variety of toys (which are useful props for this kind of play), the children will frequently express their worries through their play. For example, in a study of one particular child—Dibs—by V. Axline, in 1964, the child repeatedly buried a male doll from the doll's house in the sandbox, which was also in the play therapy room. In this way, Dibs was expressing the hostility he felt towards his father, who was very intolerant of the child. By playing with the models in this way, the child was gradually able to overcome his mixed-up emotions about his family, and to relate to them more positively. (As the child changed, so did the parents—this was an important part of the therapy too, but an indirect result of it). Eventually, the problems of the family were resolved, and the whole home set-up became more relaxed and easy for the child.

Playing, then, is a vital form of learning for the developing child. Whether it plays with toys which are just for children, as happens in our society, or whether it plays with toys that are small copies of the tools used by the adults in its society, doesn't matter. What matters, is that the child is able to imitate, and to practise, skills and roles which it finds in its society, so that it will be able to develop proficiency in them when it becomes adult, and so that it can develop a store of useful skills (in actions or in words), which it can draw on when it needs to.

**Summary**

1. All over the world, children are brought up very differently. These differences seem to lead to strong differences in the adults of a society, too.
2. In our society, we can identify four main *styles* of child-rearing and discipline: Authoritarian, Democratic, Permissive, and Laissez-faire. Each approach seems to produce different results in the children.
3 Independence and achievement motivation have much to do with parents' expectations, and the rewards which parents give children.
4 Punishment may be physical or psychological. Psychological punishment seems to produce children with stronger consciences than physical punishment does.
5. Aggression seems to result from the use of physical punishment by parents, by providing a model for aggressive behaviour.
6. Sex-roles are not always the same in different societies, and seem to be learned by *modelling*, and later, by *identification*.
7. Play is an important part of growing-up. By play, they can practise skills and understanding which they will need in later life.
8. Play may be divided into three kinds; the development of motor skills, the development of language, and make-believe.
9. Play therapy is used to treat children who are highly disturbed—through play, they can express worries, and perhaps solve problems.

# 3

# Social Pressure

In the last chapter, we talked of the way that other people's reactions and responses have an effect on how we think of ourselves. It seems that the quotation 'no man is an island' is true—all of us are affected in some degree by what others do, or by how they react to which we do. Social pressure, then, is something that can be quite important to us as human beings, and is with us all the time, without our even noticing it particularly.

When we say 'social pressure', it sounds as if we are talking about being *forced* to do something, perhaps against your will. But social pressure can be much more gentle and invisible than that. We all like to be accepted by other people—even if we don't go out of our way to seek such acceptance—and often quite unconsciously we will try to go along with things that they say.

## Conformity

### *Sherif's Study*

An experiment by Sherif, in 1935, showed how this sort of thing can happen, how people tend to *conform* to other people's ideas, when they know what those ideas are. Sherif used a phenomenon known as the 'autokinetic effect'. If you sit in a completely dark room—so dark that you can't see anything at all—and are then shown a pin-point of light, that pin-point of light will appear to move about, even though it's completely still. That's the autokinetic effect. Sherif asked people to estimate how much the point of light moved in inches. The answers that they gave were very different, ranging from one to seven inches. Each person, though, tended to make the same kind of judgement whenever they were tested: if someone estimated four inches in one test, in the next test their answer would also be about four inches. And if a subject had estimated the movement as seven inches, then their judgement would also be about seven inches. So they were quite *consistent* in their judgements.

These were the results that *Sherif* got when people were tested on their own. When they sat in the room with other people, however, the results were completely different. Instead of producing a wide variety of judgements, they now tended to go along with each other—even though the hadn't been told to agree at all. Where previously their judgements had ranged from one to seven inches, now they all estimated the movement to be around four to five inches.

Sherif said that this showed that people will always tend to conform. Rather than make an independent judgement, they will come to a 'group agreement' about things, and go by that.

There are problems with this conclusion, though. The first is that Sherif had told his subjects that he was going to move the light. Because of this, the subjects though that they were trying to solve a problem that had a *right answer*, and so they were concerned to find that answer. If they weren't sure of the effect—don't forget, in a dark room you haven't got a background to measure it up against—then they might easily just choose the middle judgement as the most likely, or they might agree with the person who sounded most definite. Although that would be conformity—because they all agreed on a conclusion—it would only show that when people are unsure, they give weight to other people's views. It wouldn't show that people tended to conform to others in any other situation.

Following these criticism, two other experiments were conducted along the same lines, but with a more definite kind of measure. Since the autokinetic effect is an illusion anyway, it is not possible to measure it at all, or to say that someone is right and someone else is wrong. So what was needed was an experiment where there was clearly a right answer and a wrong answer; this would test whether the subject would conform with the group then.

### *Asch's Study of Conformity*

The first experiment was set up by S. Asch, in 1951. He used a simple test, where subjects were shown a line, and asked which of three lines on a test card it matched. The lines were clearly different in length, and when tested on their own, none of Asch's subjects had the least difficulty in giving the right answers.

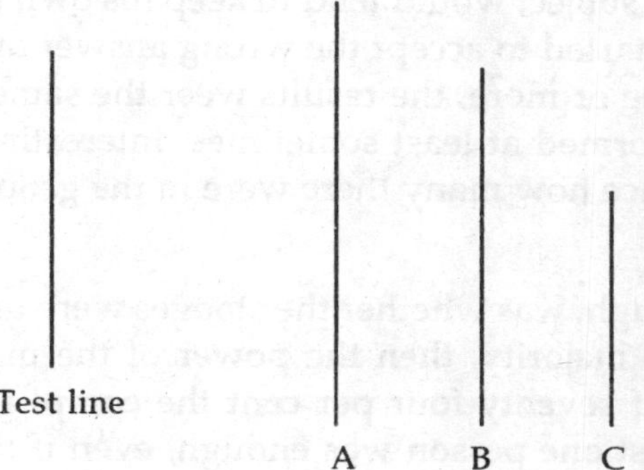


**Fig. 3.1. The Lines Used in Asch's Study**

For the group experiment, Asch used six 'stooges', who were primed beforehand to give certain answers. The subject and the six stooges sat around a table, so arranged that the 'real' subject was sixth to speak. So, before the 'real' subject gave his judgement on whether the line was the same as line A, B, or C on the sample card, he had already heard five of the others give their judgements. (Incidentally, the subject had been told that he was taking part in an experiment in perception.) For the first couple of trials (each trial consisted of showing a line, and asking for the judgement on it), the stooges gave the right answer. I shall quote from Asch's paper for what happened next:

> on the third trial, there is an unexpected disturbance. One person near the end of the group disagrees with all the others in his selection of the matching line. He looks surprised, indeed incredulous, about the disagreement. On the following trial he disagrees again, while the others remain unanimous in their choice. The dissenter becomes more and more worried and hesitant as the disagreement continues in succeeding trials....

Every now and then, the stooges would give the right answer, so that the subject wouldn't suspect that they were in collusion, but sometimes they would all give the same wrong answer in a quite definite manner.

The experimental setup left people with two choices: they could go along with the majority verdict—denying the evidence of their own eyes—or they could keep on with their own independent judgements—going against everyone else. Asch found that thirty-two per cent of his subjects conformed with the majority opinion all the time—against the evidence of their own senses. Another forty-two per cent conformed with the group *some* of the time, but also sometimes made their own judgements as well. Since the test was so easy, and the right answer so clear, this result was quite surprising, but does show the power of group pressure quite convincingly.

Asch performed several variations of his experiment, trying to find out which things were important in getting someone to conform to other views. He found out that the number of people was important: if a subject was only confronted with one other person, who gave a different view, then the subject would tend to keep his own judgement. If there were *two* others, then the subjects started to accept the wrong answer on fourteen per cent of the trials. And if there were three or more, the results weer the same as the ones given above—seventy-four per cent conformed at least sometimes. Interestingly, above three it didn't make a great deal of difference how many there were in the group—the same effect was achieved.

What *did* make a difference, though, was whether the stooges were unanimous or not. If just *one* person disagreed with the majority, then the power of the majority verdict was reduced to a quarter. So instead of seventy-four per cent the compliance went down to eighteen per cent—it seems that just one person was enough, even if they didn't actually agree with the subject! When Asch set things up so that one person agreed with the subject for some of the trials, but then switched to going along with the majority, the subject resisted the group pressure while the 'confederate' was with him, but then, when 'on his own', reached the same levels of compliance as if he had never had an ally.

Although Asch's findings were repeated quite often in the years after they were made, a more recent study, by Perrin and Spencer in 1980, suggested that this high level of conformity might be a 'child of its time'. They replicated the original experiments which Asch had performed, with a wide number of undergraduate students. (Asch's original subjects had been students.) Because Asch's experiment was so well known, they took care to choose their subjects from disciplines like chemistry, or engineering, where they weren't likely to have heard of it. Also, after the experiment, they asked the students if they had heard of this experiment before, and left out those who had from their results.

When they had completed their study, they found that the students just hadn't conformed in the same way as Asch's students. In fact, a subject conformed to the majority verdict on only one trial out of 396. Although their subjects had been just as agitated by the different judgements of the stooges as the previous ones had, they nonetheless stuck to their own judgements and didn't go along with the majority.

Asch (and Perrin and Spencer) attributed this finding to a change in social expectations in the student populations over the thirty years. students were no longer as uncritical towards their tutors and their teaching as they had been, and the social pressure on students to conform was less. Nowadays, people may be expected to rely on their own judgements quite a lot more than they were in 1951. Asch had always explained his findings in terms of the pressures that are around in society, so he was quite prepared to accept that if society changes, then the levels of conformity in a study like this would change too. However, other recent researchers have reported that, unlike Perrin and Spencer, they *have* found that Asch's study still works today. One thing that they have pointed out is that engineering students may be particularly inclined to view accurate line judgements as important, and so they may give the correct judgements because of this, although wishing to conform with the others. We will just have to wait and see what arises from these arguments in the end.

### *Crutchfield's Study*

A experiment similar to Asch's was performed by R. Crutchfield in 1954. He set up a situation where subjects had to choose the right answer from a set of very obvious and easy problems. Unlike Asch, though, he didn't sit his subjects in the same room as the stooges. Instead, they sat in rooms on their own, but with an array of lights which supposedly showed what other people had answered. (The light were 'fixed', of course.) It was possible, Crutchfield thought, that Asch's results had been caused by the *physical presence* of the other people. With his experiment, there wasn't the same kind of *personal* contact, only a more abstract knowledge of what other people had said, shown through the light-display. (Each subject was told that he was the last to answer, so he 'knew' what everyone else had said.) Crutchfield used military officers in his experiment.

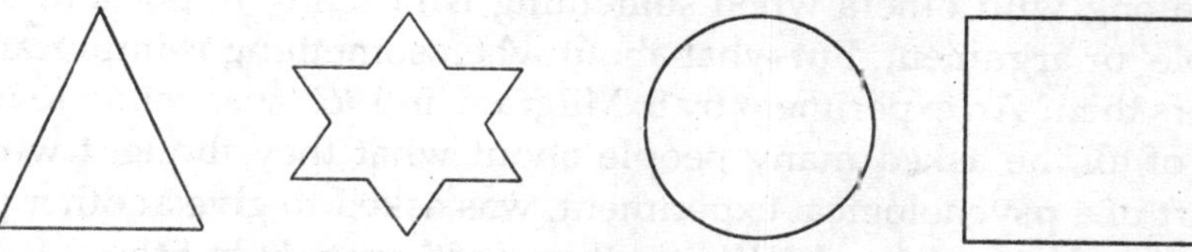

**Fig. 3.2.** Crutchfield's Shapes
Which has the largest surface area?

Crutchfield found a slightly lower level of conformity in his experiment than Asch had found—supporting the hypothesis that it was influenced by other people's physical presence. But, given the simple nature of the problems, the level he found was still considerable at forty-six per cent. None of the subjects had any difficulty with the problem when asked to do it on their own, afterwards.

Crutchfield also found the same sort of effect when opinions were being expressed. When asked privately, *all* the military men said that they thought they would make good leaders; but when asked in the experimental situation whether they agreed with the statement 'I doubt whether I would make a good leader', thirty-seven per cent of them agreed!

Another finding of Crutchfield's was that, if the problem was made more difficult, conformity increased. This would support what we were saying about Sherif's experiment: when people are unsure of the answers, they are more likely to accept other people's opinions than when they known what the answer is.

However, when we're looking at these experiments, it's important to make a distinction between *compliance*—going along with the others; and *internalisation*—actually agreeing with the others. When Asch talked to his subjects after the experiment, many of them were very concerned to explain *why* they had gone along with the majority (or why they hadn't!). Most of them said that they 'hadn't wanted to spoil the results of the perception experiment', and so had gone along with the others. Only a few of them had reached the conclusion that they were wrong and the others were right. These were the ones who would and the others were right. These were the ones who would be said to have internalised the judgement: they had accepted it as being true. Most of the subjects, though, only complied, and didn't internalise the judgements; they suspected that the others were suffering from an optical illusion, or were 'sheep' following the first one.

It's important for us to be clear about this difference, because it would be a mistake to think that people who go along with the majority always do so because they agree with it. In our society, as in most others, we tend to avoid quarrelling, and disagreements; where a decision doesn't seem to be *very* important, we often don't think it's worth it to disagree with someone else. So although we don't internalise the agreement, we still don't openly disagree with it—that is, we *comply* with it.

**Obedience**

The real question, though, is how far will we go in this compliance? As I said before, we may easily go along with others when something isn't really important, for the sake of avoiding 'trouble' or argument. But what about when something *is* important? Will we go along with others then? An experiment by S. Milgram, in 1963, was set up to investigate this question. First of all, he asked many people about what they thought would happen if someone, as part of a psychological experiment, was asked to give another person a set of increasingly strong electrical shocks. Would they do it, or wouldn't they? If they did, what level of shock would they go up to? All the people who were asked said similar things: the subjects wouldn't to beyond quite a low shock level, they would refuse to give any more. All were agreed that less than three per cent of subjects would go to the most extreme shock level—people would stop the experiment well before that.

Milgram then proceeded with the experiment. He advertised for subjects in a local paper, saying that they would be paid to take part in an experiment. When they arrived at the laboratory, they were told that, simply by turning up, they had earned the money, no matter what happened now. (This was to make sure that subjects weren't just doing it for the money.) They were then introduced to another person, and told that they would both take part in a learning experiment—one would be teacher, and the other learner. They drew names from a hat to see who would be which, but in fact the lots were rigged. Both slips of paper said 'teacher', but the other man (who was an actor) sad his said 'learner', and was treated accordingly. In this way, the subjects didn't suspect that the experiment wasn't just a simple learning one.

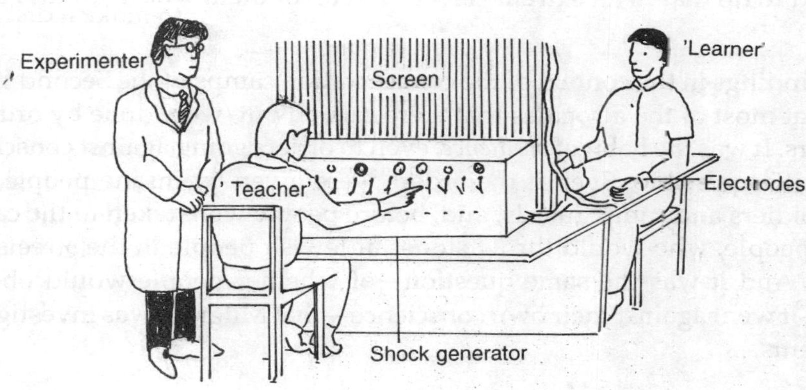


**Fig. 3.3. Milgram's Study of Obedience**

The learner, with the subject looking on, was taken into the next room, and strapped into a chair. Electrodes were attached to his wrists, and the subject was told that they were connected to a shock generator in the next room. (In fact, they were dummies.) The teacher was then put in front of the shock generator, which had a long row of switches, each of which was labelled for a different level of shock. The labels went up by 15 volts each time, until they reached 450 volts. They were also labelled: 'slight shock; moderate shock; strong shock; very strong shock; intense shock; extreme intensity shock; danger; severe shock'; and finally just 'XXX'. So the subjects were well informed about the nature of the 'shock' that they were giving to the learner.

The learning task that they were supposed to be doing was a word-pair one. The teacher would read out a word, and then four possible words which might be paired with it. The learner pressed a button for the answer he chose (A, B, C, or D), which lit up a panel on the teacher's console. If the answer was wrong, the teacher had to give an electric shock—and it had to be increased one step (15 volts) each time. In fact, the wrong answers were all pre-arranged, as were the learner's reaction to the shock. When the shock level reached 300 volts, the learner started to bang on the wall—he had made some vocal complaints before then—but after that he didn't do anything at all. The subjects were told, by the experimenter, to treat no answer at all as if it were a wrong answer; that is, to carry on shocking the subject even though they didn't get a reply to the question, and, of course, increasing the voltage each time.

Milgram's results surprised everyone: instead of the less-than-three per cent who had been predicted to go as far as 450 volts, 62.5% did! And *all* the subjects who took part in the experiments went as far as 300 volts—the point at which the learner banged on the wall. (This was immediately before the 'extreme intensity shock' level.) Despite the fact that our society gives such strong objections to administering violence to others, *must* of Milgram's subjects were prepared to do that to an extreme level. And all of them would do that to one degree or another.

Milgram puts his findings in the context of the concentration camps of the Second World War. He points out that most of the atrocities that were carried out, were done by ordinary people following orders. It was the habit of *obedience*, even to orders going against conscience, which made the atrocities possible. Even if the orders were given by insane people, they were carried out by soldiers and camp guards, and, before people were taken to the camps, by ordinary German people, who would throw stones at Jewish people in the streets, and damage their houses. And it was the same question—of whether people would obey an instruction even when it went against their own conscience—that Milgram was investigating in this set of experiments.

### *Factors Influencing Obedience*

It must not be thought that Milgram's subjects wee all 'latent sadists'—they were not. Throughout the experiment people objected to what they were being asked to do, arguing with the experimenter, and expressing worry about what the learner was experiencing. But very few of them actually got out of the chair, and refused to do any more. when the experimenter said things like: 'The experiment requires that you continue', or 'You have no other choice—you must go on', they went on with the experiment, even though reluctantly. But many were highly disturbed by what they were doing, and, even when they found out that the learner was well and unhurt, they were shocked at their own behaviour: 'I'd never have thought I could do that!'

There were in fact, several things built in to the experiment that made it very difficult for them to stop. One of those was the 'prods' used by the experimenter: 'It is absolutely essential that you continue', and so on. 'It the subjects wanted to know about responsibility, the experimenter would claim responsibility for the experiment.

Another factor was that the amount of shock they had to give was only increased by a little bit each time. This, actually, made it difficult for the subjects to choose a cut-off point—315 volts isn't *very* different from 300 volts, and they'd already given 300 volts! So, on each occasion, it was only a small change from the previous time.

The fact that they had drawn lots to see who would be teacher and who learner was another thing that made it more difficult for the subject to object. As far as he was concerned, it could just as easily have been *him* receiving the shocks, and not giving them.

The learner being in a different room also made a difference. When Milgram repeated the experiment with the learner in the same room as the subject, compliance dropped to forty per cent, which is nonetheless still quite high.

Another possible reason why people were so compliant, Milgram thought, might be because he conducted the experiment at Yale University, where people would expect to find scientists who (a) knew what they were doing; and (b) were responsible. Because of this, he conducted another set of the same experiments, in a seedy set of offices in the centre of the city. Compliance dropped slightly—to fifty per cent—but that is still high, when you think of what it implies about ordinary people.

When Milgram set up a slightly different version of the experiment, where subjects didn't actually press the button themselves, to give the learner the shock, but instead pressed a switch which enabled someone else to give the shock, compliance with the experimenter's request went right up to more than ninety per cent. It seems that, since they didn't actually administer the shock themselves, they didn't feel the responsibility as much either, even though they were the people who made the shock possible.

It is clear from these experiments that, when asked to do so, people will do things that go strongly against their consciences, even though they object at the time. These results weren't just found in America, either. Even in completely different countries, like Norway, the same results were found. So we are talking about a pretty powerful social pressure, which people would go along with, even though they disagreed, and even though they *could* always have walked out of the experiment.

In looking for things that would affect the results, Milgram did find one that had quite a strong influence. If the experimenter wasn't actually in the room when the instructions were given—if he gave the orders by telephone instead—the subject's level of compliance dropped right down to almost zero. Instead of pressing the button, they would only pretend to, or would press the button for a much lower level of shock than the one they were supposed to give. So the physical presence of someone in authority made all the difference.

Milgram linked this to our reactions to people in authority, in general. We *do* tend to obey people who are in authority—teachers, policemen, and so on—indeed, we are trained to do so from when we are quite young. And we also, very often, have the belief that the person in authority knows what they are doing; has been trained for a special job, and often wears a uniform to symbolise their position. Although Milgram's experimenter didn't have any *real* authority—the subjects could have 'disobeyed' at any time, without any bad consequences at all—he *did* have a calm and detached manner, a uniform (a grey lab. coat), and—perhaps most important of all—seemed to know what was going on, and to be aware of possible consequences. All these things served to make him quite a convincing figure of authority, who commanded reluctant obedience from the subjects.

Support for this theory comes from the fact that the subjects were told, if they asked, that the experimenter claimed all responsibility for what was going on. Once they had that reassurance, many of the subjects were visibly relieved. Even though they continued to argue, they didn't do so as strongly as they had before. The experimenter was the 'expert', and so they were able to feel less personally responsible for their actions.

As we talked about 'roles' in terms of the way that the roles that an individual plays in life become a part of that individual's self-concept, and influence the person's development. Milgram's experiments show us an entirely different side of social roles—the way in which a role can influence the behaviour of other people—to an alarming degree.

Throughout Milgram's experiments, the experimenter played his part in a very impersonal kind of way. In order that it wouldn't be his *personality* which caused the effects, everything he said was written down beforehand, and he always used a neutral tone of voice. In this way, Milgram made sure that it wasn't just that the experimenter was an unusually friendly, or persuasive kind of person, as the real person didn't show through at all. Milgram's subjects reacted to the *role* that the experimenter had, and not to the man himself.

We can see from that, that the position of the experimenter—wearing a lab, coat, and directing (or appearing to direct) the experiment—was enough to generate, or to create, *expectations* about that person. In other words, the role the experimenter played led the others in the experiment to decide things about him; for instance that he 'knew what he was doing', or that he was 'responsible and intelligent'. And *because* they had that set of expectations, the subjects in the experiment went on to do what he asked them.

Any social role which we play in life will tend to generate a similar set of expectations. Not the same expectations for teach role—but different people playing the same role will be expected to have things in common with each other. *Any* doctor, for instance, to dress respectably, and so on. *No* doctor would be expected to be found busking with a guitar on a street corner. Similarly, we wouldn't expect to go into the doctor's surgery, and find him or her in tears, saying 'I can't stand it any more!' Although we would probably find it quite difficult to list them, we do have very clear ideas about how someone in a certain role should behave, even though we may only become aware of them when those rules are broken.

**Social Roles**

In 1966, P. Zimbardo performed an experiment which demonstrated just how strong our ideas about roles and role behaviour are. By drawing lots from a pool of subjects (genuine ones this time) he sorted them into two groups. They were to be an imitation of prisoners and guards in a mock jail: one group was to act the part of guards, while the others acted the part of prisoners. The subjects weren't told or guard. *How* they acted these roles was up to them.

After five days, Zimbardo had to stop the experiment. The guards were to clear in their ideas of how prison guards behaved, and so strict with the prisoners, that they wouldn't allow them any rights at all, and often treated them in a humiliating fashion. Although they never used physical violence, they would do things like lining them up and making them count in sequence, with each prisoner saying a number in turn, and not letting them stop until they had said the numbers perfectly in time. When one of the prisoners went on hunger-strike, they locked him in a small closet. The other prisoners were told that they could get him out simply by each of them giving up a blanket (it wasn't cold at all), but by then they were so concerned with their own 'survival' that they thought of the hunger-striker as a 'trouble-maker' and wouldn't help him!

The people who were playing the guards had a very clear idea of just what the role of guard involved. (In fact, it was much stricter than most real prison guards.) By acting that role, they showed how they understood it—and how powerful their expectations were. Similarly once the prisoners had realised that the guards were acting the role out fully, they also adopted the kind of behaviour which they considered appropriate to their role as prisoners. They were anxious not to antagonise the guards—that's why they called the other one a 'trouble-maker'—and wanted just to 'get by' as well as they could. The guards hadn't just got a clear idea of their own role *themselves* but they had also generated *expectations* about themselves from the prisoners.

In part, it could easily have been the prisoners' expectations which helped the experiment to become as extreme as it did. By acting in appeasing ways, they would have strengthened the guards' ideas of their own power, and so caused their behaviour to become more bullying. Of course, it wasn't just that—the guards were well able to become bullying anyway—but the mixture of their own understanding of the role, and the prisoners' expectations, would have been a circular trap, fro which they wouldn't have been able to get out. (Several of the guards said afterwards that they had hated what they were doing.) As I said before, roles don't just influence our own behaviour, but they also cause others to have expectations about what we are likely to do.

### *The Self-Fulfilling Prophecy*

These expectations are very often powerful in influencing our behaviour in all sorts of ways. Sometimes we can get into a kind of circle, where people expect something of us, we try to live up to it, and that strengthens what they expect. For example: supposing a woman was friends who think that she is really witty, and often makes amusing remarks. Because that is their expectation of her, they expect her to make a witty remark when any occasion arises. Because she knows that is what they expect, she tries hard to think of one, and comes out with a fairly witty remark. But, since she has made another one, her friends' belief that she really is witty is strengthened. They now have 'proof' that they were right. So next time, they'll expect her to say something witty again, and the whole process will repeat itself. But notice that the circle is being kept up as much by the friends' expectations, as by the individual's behaviour. And as the reputation is strengthened, the cycle is reinforced—even if she says something which isn't really funny, the friends will make allowances, and still expect her to be amusing the next time. In fact, the whole cycle *might* have even started off accidentally. She might just have said something—once—which her friends found funny, and the whole thing could go on from there.

When we get a cycle like this one, we call it a *self-fulfilling prophecy*. In this case, the friends have made a prophecy—than X is witty—and by their behaviour to X they have made that prophecy come true. In the same way, the girl whom Guthrie reported, changed as the result of a self-fulfilling prophecy (although it was a completely accidental one). The male students had acted as if they had made a prophecy that the girl was good company. And then, by their behaviour towards that girl, the prophecy had come true. She did become good company. This case is a little bit different from the way that most self-fulfilling prophecies work, as the students had made a deliberate decision to change their behaviour, but we can see how their *previous* behaviour must have been a self-fulfilling prophecy for the girl. No-one took an interest in her, so she felt uninteresting. Because she felt uninteresting, she behaved in an uninteresting kind of way, and so no-one took an interest in her. It's a 'vicious circle'.

In 1966, R. Rosenthal performed an experiment which demonstrated just how powerful an influence expectations can have. He used laboratory rats, which had been carefully matched for their abilities, at least in things like running through mazes. The rats were allocated to students, who were told to teach their rats (each student had five rats) to run a particular maze—that is, to take the quickest route through a series of turns and junctions, to reach the goal-box at the end of the maze (where there was food for the rats).

Half the students were told that their rats had been specially bread to be good at running mazes, that they were the result of careful selection and parentage. The other half were told that their rats could be expected, for genetic reasons, to be very poor at maze-learning. When the students proceeded to teach their rats to run through the maze, the self-fulfilling prophecy came true—the rats that were supposed to be 'maze-bright' actually did better than the rats who were supposed to be 'maze-dull'. Some of the 'maze-dull' rats wouldn't even budge from the starting point of the maze. And yet they had all been of similar ability to start with.

On examining these results, Rosenthal found that the students who expected their rats to be bright actually treated them differently to the students whose rats were supposed to be dull. They handled them more, and treated them more gently, and were far more enthusiastic about the whole experiment. The students with the dull rats hadn't liked their rats at all, while those with the bright rats had liked theirs. The difference in handling which this had led to had made a dramatic difference in the way that the rats performed.

In 1968, Rosenthal and Jacobson performed an experiment to see if that same self-fulfilling prophecy would also work in schools. They used a fairly average school in a middle-sized American city, and told teachers there that they were testing the validity of a new test designed to predict intellectual gain in children. In fact, they used a fairly standard intelligence test. By random means, they chose some children from the school who were to be called 'spurters'; in fact these children were no different from their fellows in class, in terms of their work or test results. The teachers were told—as if in casual conversation—that these were children who could be expected to show unusual intellectual gains in the next year. Apart from the teachers being told this, no other experimental treatment was used: the children weren't singled out in front of their classmates, or even spoken to by the experimenters. So the control group of the experiment was the other children in the class; the teachers hadn't been told anything about them at all.

By the end of the year, the 'spurters' had shown considerable changes in their academic work. Their results on schoolwork tests were compared with the results from the year before, and a very strong change showed that by comparison with the other children in their class, they actually had improved. On looking for explanations for this result, Rosenthal and Jacobson found that it *wasn't* just that teachers *talked* to these students more, as they expected, but that their whole attitude—tones of voice, touch, attention—was the thing that seemed to have made a difference to the children. This is quite an important finding, as we tend to be unconscious of these kind of signals; it would be much harder for a teacher to control that kind of influence, than to control something like the length of the spent talking to the children.

Rosenthal and Jacobson found that, in the year of the experiment, it was younger children who showed the most gains; but in the follow-up year, which was the year after that, the older children showed more lasting effects than younger ones did. They thought that this might be because the younger children had changes of teachers, and were more dependent on their teachers' reactions, while the older ones, although initially not so easily influenced, had been able to keep up the improved performance once they had absorbed it into their self-concept. So after a while, they didn't *need* the teachers' encouragement, while the younger ones did.

This experiment has quite strong implications for schools. For instance, if a child comes from a background in a slum area, teachers may well not expect it to do particularly well at school, and may *communicate* that expectation to the child. So a self-fulfilling prophecy would be set up. The teachers would expect the child to be dull at lessons, so they wouldn't give encouragement and help as much as they would to a child they thought more capable, and so the child would fall behind the others. Once it had fallen behind the others, this would be 'proof' that it really *was* dull—at least, it would be proof to the teachers—and so their expectations and treatment of the child as dull would continue. And, because this happens on an unconscious level, it's a particularly difficult circle to break—you can't stop yourself doing something if you don't know that you *are* doing it.

From the studies we have looked in this chapter, we can see that the statement 'Humans are social animals' is perhaps even more true than we think. In the next chapter we'll be looking at another of the influences on our social behaviour work.

**Summary**

1. People tend to conform to what others have said, if they are aware of others' judgements.
2. Conformity is greater when others are physically present, than when they are apart, although people will still conform if apart.
3. Some experiments have shown that people will conform even against their own judgements.
4. There is a difference between compliance—going along with the group for the sake of avoiding argument, but still retaining one's own opinions privately—and internalisation, which means fully accepting the views of the group.
5. Milgram's experiments showed that people will obey others, even when obedience causes them to act against their own conscience and harm another person.
6. Milgram's results link with our behaviour to people in certain *roles*. Roles generate a set of expectations about others, and we expect the people in the roles to conform to those expectations.
7. People's expectations about others can become a self-fulfilling prophecy—the individual lives up to the expectations, and so the expectations are reinforced—thus causing the person to live up to them even more.
8. Studies of the self-fulfilling prophecy have serious implications for education, and for social behaviour generally.

# 4

# Psychology: Evolutions or Revolutions?

Most writers in this section give the historical development of psychology as the basis of their view on its present state and future. Howard Kendler examines what have been taken as shifts of paradigms in psychology and points out that the development can be better understood if a continuity is seen as extending through the turning points, than if they are looked upon as "revolutions" in the Kuhnian sense. In view of this, Kendler pays special attention to cognitive psychology which has been presented as revolutionary against previous outlooks. He points out that if cognitive psychology becomes too detached from previous approaches, it can come to ignore important theoretical problems and omit to deal with central psychological processes.

The writers of this section do not fear a split of psychology into several different disciplines in the future, as has sometimes been predicted. On the contrary, they see different opportunities for psychology to develop into one methodologically unified discipline.

Howard Kendler shows that conscious experience and mentalistic concepts can in principle be fitted into a methodological behaviourism. *Kirsti Lagerspetz* pursues a similar line of thought. She puts forward the idea that academic psychology should attempt to incorporate methodologically not only, for instance, humanistic psychology, but even those peripheral "movements" that call themselves "psychological". Before that, however, some central, essentially philosophical questions should be dealt with.

*Ference Marton* discusses the educational applications of cognitive psychology. His example is the acquisition of learning skills. He reminds the reader of the circumstance, often misunderstood, that the phenomenological method was originally *not* a way to study the inner world. It was the study of how a person experiences his/her environment. It is the investigation of the natural attitude towards the world.

*Martti Takala* also discusses the interaction of the individual with the environment. He thinks that the causation of behaviour can best be studied in a systemic context comprising different levels of proximity to the individual. The activity of the individual should also be considered in a hierarchical context, where more restricted actions are seen as parts of more general activities. The distribution of activities in relation to consumption of time is a way of estimating their importance and meaning in the life of a person.

Behaviour is a constant flow of events. The study of situations is a way of cross-secting this flow, and a study of sequences of situations makes it possible to identify causal relations and developmental trends. Seeing activity as central, Martti Takala considers a new kind of functionalism as the approach to be taken by psychology in the future.

It is true that attempts to describe mental processes structurally have not been so successful in the past. What have been called reliability and validity measures obtained when behaviour has been compared in different situations, have not met the expectations of researchers. This is part of a general neglect in psychological research methodology, taken up by *David Magnusson*. He stresses the importance of studying the same individuals in different types of situations. It is in fact amazing that psychology has traditionally laid great emphasis on the representativeness of samples of subjects, but the importance of sampling over situations has been almost forgotten. This in spite of the fact that the influence of the situation is potentially an equally important source of systematic error. It is misleading to speak of a behaviour trend or a trait without specifying the context where it appears. This leads to a need for systematic analysis, conceptualisation and categorisation of the environment in the future psychology.

Thomas Kuhn's *The Structure of Scientific Revolutions* (1962) has profoundly influenced the contemporary view of the history of psychology. His general thesis is well known. Scientific progress is not based on the accumulation of individual discoveries and theoretical refinements, but instead results from a repetitive historical cycle that consists of two markedly different enterprises: normal science and revolution.

*Normal science* refers to the accumulation of knowledge within a widely adopted global orientation—a "paradigm"—which shapes the kind of research that is conducted and the type of theoretical interpretation that is offered. During the period of normal science, anomalous results usually are discovered which are incompatible with the prevailing paradigm. This initiates the second stage of historical development—the *revolution*—during which time a prevailing paradigm is overthrown by a new one. Revolutions do not occur rapidly because adherents of the dominant paradigm, against which the revolution is directed, resist acknowledging the incompatibility between the new data and their theoretical commitments. The struggle between the old and new paradigms requires many years to resolve, and its final resolution is more a result of the mortality of man than of persuasive evidence or compelling theoretical analysis. With time, the control of science passes from the hands of the older scientists with their outmoded paradigm to the younger investigators with their superior one. A stage of normal science sets in and prevails until a new set of anomalous data is discovered and then the revolutionary era begins again.

For many psychologists Kuhn's analysis has a ring of truth. The history of psychology appears to be a sequence of revolutions against established paradigms. One commonly accepted sequence in America is that experimental psychology began essentially with Titchenerian Structuralism which was overthrown by Functionalism which in turn succumbed to Behaviourism which finally was replaced by Cognitive psychology. In Europe the annals of events were not as orderly but revolutions nevertheless dominated historical changes. Wundtian psychology, soon after its birth, was challenged by ideas that ultimately led to Gestalt psychology. In both Europe and America many psychologists would argue that the paramount upheaval was the psychoanalytic revolution that substituted a relevant psychology for an artificial, ivory-tower conception. Although different sequences of revolutionary changes can be suggested, depending upon the position that one currently adopts, the Kuhnian notion of revolutionary changes followed by a period of normal science, appears to many to be an appropriate description of historical change in psychology. I would, however, suggest that the application is inappropriate, misleading, and incomplete, and damaging to the future of psychology.

### The Relevance of Kuhnian Analysis to the History of Psychology

Although many psychologists have applied Kuhn's historical theory to their discipline, the question can be raised as to whether such application is appropriate. His historical model emerged from the study of the development of physics from the time of Copernicus. Were the revolutions that occurred in psychology similar to those in physics? Psychological revolutions have been primarily methodological in nature. Functionalism overthrew Structuralism by insisting that the subject matter of psychology was not mental content but instead mental activity. Functionalism succumbed to Behaviourism because the direct examination of consciousness did not produce reliable knowledge of the sort that the study of behaviour could. Cognitive psychology was successful in overthrowing Behaviourism because of the prevailing conviction that a satisfactory account of psychology demanded an understanding of the functional organisation of the mind.

Revolutions in physics have obvious substantive implications. The Copernican revolution offered a better interpretation of planetary motion than did the Ptolemaic conception. Although physics from the time of Copernicus has entertained many important methodological disputes, a level of agreement has prevailed about its subject matter, its methods of investigation, and its mode at arriving at "warranted conclusions" that is unmatched in the history of psychology. Thus, "paradigmatic revolutions", of the sort Kuhn described, can only occur in a discipline with a shared conception of methods and goals. Physics therefore can be characterised as a paradigmatic discipline while psychology is assigned by Kuhn to a preparadigmatic status; "Psychology is a multidisciplinary field with different segments employing irreconcilable orientations" (Kendler, 1981).

## HISTORICAL CONTINUITIES AND DISCONTINUITIES

When applied to psychology the Kuhnian model is both misleading and incomplete; historical discontinuities are emphasised at the expense of continuities. A case in point is the mistaken view that Gestalt psychology is simply a revolutionary reaction to the extreme atomism of Wundtian psychology. In actual fact, both positions shared the traditional Germanic passion for wholeness but expressed it in different forms. Wundt proposed the holistic *principle of creative synthesis* which postulated that mental constructions from component processes always produce novel consequences, a position that bears obvious resemblance to

Gestalt notions. The two orientations differed in the manner in which conscious experience was conceptualised. While acknowledging conscious experiences to be "fleeting occurrences, in continual flux and change", Wundt (1910) nevertheless thought it possible to identify the basic processes out of which experience is formed. Gestalt psychology, in contrast, rejected any attempt to analyse consciousness into basic components because of the assumption that conscious experience is formed from integrated wholes which cannot be reduced to their constituent parts.

Limiting Gestalt psychology to its protest against psychological analysis as expressed in its appealing slogan, "The whole is greater than the sum of its parts", ignores the fact that Gestalt psychology shared with Wundtian psychology the conviction that a direct and valid examination of consciousness was possible. This commitment shaped the kind of explanations Gestalt psychologists offered to interpret perceptual phenomena. Principles of perception (e.g., Pragnanz) were considered valid when their experiential qualities could be "shared". Thus, a principle was validated by phenomenological agreement although the criteria for measuring agreement was never clearly spelled out. Kohler, near the end of his career, recognised some limitations in Gestalt explanations: American psychology has "given more attention to methods and strict proof than Gestalt psychology.... In this respect, American psychology was clearly superior. . . ." (Kohler, 1959).

Kohler's admission identifies an unresolved problem among psychologists who employ mentalistic conceptions. What should be the criteria for understanding mental processes? Accurate phenomenological descriptions? Deductive explanations? Some American psychologists who were sympathetic to Gestalt conceptions were obviously dissatisfied with the subjective quality of Gestalt explanations. In the case of the Gestalt principle of Pragnanz (good form) both Attneave (1954) and Garner (1962) reduced the phenomenal quality of good form to the objective characteristic of redundancy; the whole could be predicted from a few parts while poor forms were unpredictable. Their interpretations, expressed mathematically, had clear deductive consequences in contrast to the intuitive Gestalt interpretation.

The important lesson from this brief examination is that both revolutionary and evolutionary changes characterised the transition from Wundtian psychology to Gestalt psychology. An emphasis on discontinuities to the exclusion of continuities leads to an incomplete and misleading historical interpretation. To fully appreciate the influence of Gestalt psychology on modern psychology one must recognise its phenomenological, as well as holistic, commitments.

Another problem of applying the Kuhnian model to psychology is raised by a lack of clear cut distinctions between revolutionary and evolutionary changes. A case in point is the advent of Watsonian Behaviourism. Many consider the shift of the subject matter of psychology from the mind to behaviour to be the most revolutionary notion in the history of psychology. Although Bergmann recognises the "break" that Watson made with the Functionalists (e.g., Angell) with whom Watson studied at the University of Chicago,

Bergmann nevertheless concludes that "Watson is above all a completer and a consummator—the greatest...of the Functionalists" (Bergmann, 1956). As Functionalism was maturing the concern with mental activity was decreasing, while behavioural research steadily increased. Watson merely represented the terminal point in this gradual historical trend.

**The Cognitive Revolution: How Revolutionary?**

Now that the argument has been advanced that a Kuhnian interpretation of the history of psychology can be incomplete and misleading an effort will be made to identify and evaluate what is revolutionary and what is evolutionary in cognitive psychology. The purpose of this analysis will be to illuminate the relationship between cognitive psychology and psychology's past as well as its future.

## COGNITIVE PSYCHOLOGY AND BEHAVIOURISM

Cognitive psychology is usually conceived as a revolt against Behaviourism. So is Humanistic psychology. These two revolutions share little in common, thus raising the question of the target of their respective insurrections. That target, for cognitive psychology, appears to be stimulus-response associationism. More specifically, the revolutionary theme is that behaviour cannot be adequately accounted for by stimulus-response connections even when such a conception is enlarged to include chains of internal associations that mediate between the external stimulus and the overt response. Stimulus-response associations, the argument goes, must be discarded in favor of cognitive processes:

> "The word cognitive, which is derived from cognition, meaning *knowledge,* emphasises mental activities, not just stimuli and responses. It is precisely this shift of emphasis—away from a passive system that accepts stimuli and automatically produces S-R chains, and toward a notion of mental actions—that characterises cognitive theories. According to Neisser, whose book *Cognitive psychology* (1967) gave real impetus to the approach, the focus of cognitive theory is knowledge—how it is acquired, modified, manipulated, used, stored; in short, how it is processed by the human organism. Thus, information processing (a term cognitive psychologists have borrowed from computer scientists) broadly refers to the human being's active interaction with information about his world. Of central importance in this processing are the mental activities that occur between a stimulus and a response." (Klatzky, 1975, pp. 2-3.)

An active mental processing of information (knowledge) distinguishes cognitive psychology from a passive stimulus-response associationism. Or does it? Are the distinctions between *active* and *passive, mentalism* and *behaviourism,* and *knowledge* and *S-R associations,* qualitative or one of degree? Do the distinctions represent evolutionary or revolutionary changes?

*Active vs. Passive models.* Although the active-passive distinction is widely employed, its meaning is not entirely clear. One sometimes gets the impression that the issue is one of whether the organism takes a passive or active role in his own behaviour in the sense that he functions either as a mechanical robot or as a free spirit. Such a distinction reflects more the confusing heritage of the philosophical problem of free will than a meaningful psychological comparison. If we accept a psychological determinism then we cannot conclude that some forms of behaviour are more determined than others.

The passive and active distinction can be equated with the locus of events which initiates behaviour. In a passive model the locus of control resides outside the organism; behaviour is initiated in a machine-like fashion by external stimulation. Behaviour in an active model, in contrast, is self-generated; the organism generates events (e.g., hypotheses) that guide subsequent behaviour. Although the distinction has apparent validity when comparing different kinds of behaviour, such as braking in reaction to a red traffic light as contrasted to searching one's memory for a word that seems to be "on the tip of the tongue", the important question is whether the distinction is theoretically significant. John Watson (1919) in his stimulus-response model, conceptualised food-seeking behaviour of animals as being initiated by stomach contractions which in turn increase the activity level, thus making it more probable that the animal will discover food. Similarly Spence (1952) postulated that rats made observing responses that oriented an organism's receptors toward cues that are correlated with reinforcement. Do these two cases qualify as examples of active behaviour in the sense that they are generated by activities within the organism? Or do they fail to qualify because the S-R model always implies some stimulus, even an unobserved or theoretical one that triggers behaviour? The problem of classifying a theory as active or passive becomes more complicated when mediational processes are considered. One such formulation (Kendler and Kendler, 1962) postulates two modes of behaviour: A "passive" single-unit mode in which an external stimulus triggers a response and a mediational mode in which behaviour is controlled by a covert representational response wherein the representation may entail considerable transformation. Thus, even if the passive-active distinction is accepted as valid, the question remains whether it reliably distinguishes cognitive from stimulus-response formulations.

*Mentalism vs. Behaviourism.* Watson's initial rejection of all mentalistic terms and final flirtation with the denial of human consciousness, contributed a legacy of confusion from which psychology has still to recover. The major thrust of behaviourism was that psychology is a natural science with behaviour as its dependent variable (Kendler, in press). An important corollary is that the *direct* examination of consciousness, either by rigorous introspection or naive phenomenology, could not produce the reliable knowledge demanded by natural science methodology. What Watson failed to realise, along with many of his critics, is that conscious experience and mentalistic concepts are not excommunicated from methodological behaviourism. They can be incorporated within a behaviouristic research program if the requirements of objectivity (inter-subjectivity) are not violated. This can be accomplished when phenomenological evidence is used as a source of theoretical hypotheses and when mental processes are assumed to operate in a theoretical system that is designed to predict publicly observable behaviour.

The strategy of employing conscious experience as a source of theoretical hypotheses can be justified by the past. One example is the conscious attempt to improve memory by encoding meaningless nonsense syllables into meaningful units. Phenomenological evidence of this sort had strategic value in formulating useful encoding hypotheses for theories of memory. Phenomenological evidence, it should be noted, can also be uninformative as well as misleading. Numerous investigators from the time of the famous imageless thought controversy have reported that thinking can occur without any conscious deliberation: "One does one's thinking before one knows what he is to think about" (Boring, 1950, p. 404). Other evidence, both psychoanalytic and experimental (e.g., Latane and Darley, 1968; Latane and Rodin, 1969), indicates that introspective reports can be misleading. Thus, those who believe that introspective evidence can be a rich source of theoretical hypotheses about behaviour must be selective in applying their strategy because of possible discrepancies between the two.

Tolman (1932) demonstrated that a psychological theory could postulate mentalistic activities (e.g., the formation of cognitive maps) without compromising any commitment to methodological behaviourism. By *inferring* the state of a rat's mind from its past experience and its present environment, Tolman was able to make predictions about the rat's behaviour. Cognitive psychology, for the most part, follows the same methodological prescription. The state of the human mind, or more properly its functional organisation, is inferred and then the behavioural output is predicted.

Cognitive psychology, in spite of what some would like to believe, is not at odds with methodological behaviourism. The "revolutionary core" of cognitive psychology is directed against substantive aspects of stimulus-response psychology. But S-R formulations (e.g., Hull-Spence, Skinner, Guthrie) do not share substantive theoretical assumptions; only a commitment to methodological behaviourism and the use of a stimulus-response language (Kendler, 1965) which can be translated into an input-output idiom. The Hull-Spence formulation, it should be noted, rejects the notion that behaviour can be adequately explained solely by stimulus-response associations..Other concepts (e.g., drive) are required even to explain the behaviour of lower animals. When it came to human cognitive behaviour, Spence (1950) proposed a flow-diagram which anticipated later information-processing conceptions, and which radically departed form his own analysis of the discrimination learning of the rat (1936). In his flow diagram he employed concepts (e.g., sense reception, signification, verbal meaning) that referred to the innate organisation of the brain, cognitive expectations, and linguistic meaning. These higher level processes "badly need the attention of all psychologists, cognition, S-R or whatever else" (Spence, 1950).

*Knowledge.* One of the core concepts of cognitive psychology is *knowledge*; an organism processes knowledge (information) which in turn guides his action. The historical significance of this concept depends upon whether it has an existence independent of conscious experience. If knowledge or information refers to "that which is known" or "familiarity gained by actual experience" then the problem becomes one of defining the procedures for measuring it. Does a rat have knowledge of a maze that it has learned? A methodological behaviourist would ignore such a question if an affirmative answer required experiential evidence. The question would have empirical meaning if "knowledge" is considered analogous to Tolman's 's concept of a cognitive map, an inferred state of mind defined in terms of experimental operations that has observable consequences. In the same sense an animal has "knowledge" of a maze if its anticipatory goal responses guide behaviour toward alleys that lead to the goal box.

**Cognitive Psychology: Some Problems**

Does this analysis suggest that cognitive psychology is simply an evolutionary development of stimulus-response psychology? Absolutely not! Differences between stimulus-response and cognitive psychology cannot be denied but neither should the continuities be ignored. Only by appreciating both, and the extent of each, can an appropriate historical perspective of cognitive psychology be gained.

The major obstacle to achieving this balanced view comes from the tendency of converts to revolutionary paradigms, throughout the history of psychology, to exaggerate the novelty and influence of their ideas. Perhaps this is necessary to gain the enthusiasm and dedication required to launch a new orientation. But in the history of psychology this revolutionary zeal has typically created an illusion of a great leap forward that in reality failed to occur. The limitations of one paradigm (S-R associationism) does not automatically validate another (e.g., cognitive psychology). Nor is progress necessarily achieved when research in one empirical domain (e.g., conditioning) is abandoned in favor of investigating another that is considered more basic (e.g., memory). Progress, in the natural sciences, occurs when new evidence as well as existing data, are incorporated into a common theoretical structure.

With these precautionary remarks in mind, an attempt will now be made to discuss briefly three obstacles that cognitive psychologists must overcome in their effort to reach a level of understanding of psychological events not yet attained by other orientations.

(1) The concept of knowledge (information) can function as a double-edged sword. It possesses strategic advantages over stimulus-response associations in interpreting the complexity and variety of human intellectual functioning. At the same time it should be recognised that the intuitive richness of information-processing language can provide a sense of understanding that is not approached by the deductive capacity of the theory (Kendler, 1981). In addition, the attribution of knowledge to an organism tends to impute a level of intelligence which may exceed its capacity. Cognitive psychologists would be well advised not to forget the lessons of Clever Hans nor the famous canon of the mentalistic psychologist, C. Lloyd Morgan, "In no case may we interpret an action as the outcome of the exercise of a higher psychical activity, if it can be interpreted as the outcome of the exercise of one which stands lower in the psychological scale." The best antidote to exaggerating the intellectual functioning of an organism are rigorous comparative and developmental research and theorising, efforts that have only recently interested some cognitive psychologists.

(2) A tendency has been growing among natural-science psychologists to divide their discipline into two independent sub-areas: cognitive science and neuroscience. Cognitive psychology will suffer if its early aversions to physiological psychology and animal

experimentation are allowed to continue. First, it detaches cognitive processes from its biological moorings, most particularly its Darwinian framework. Our cognitive processes are products of our evolutionary past and to ignore that relationship eliminates useful information and ideas. Second,

> "Black-box theories. . .have been plagued by persistent and unresolvable theoretical disputes... One of the main reasons that these theoretical disputes go unresolved is that black-box theories do not provide sufficient constraints to allow for resolutions of theoretical disputes. The environmental operations are too far removed from the underlying biological mechanisms that are responsible for behaviour. As a consequence, numerous theoretical options are available to handle embarrassing data. The result is that core assumptions of black-box theories are able to survive regardless of what results are obtained, thus effectively preventing one theory from achieving dominance over its competitors. In contrast, physiological theories that identify the operation of permanent structures or biochemical reactions as being responsible for given forms of behaviour have relatively' fewer options in defending their truth value when their predictions fail." (Kendler, 1981, pp. 124-125.)

The instrumental value of black-box theories is not being denied; instead a ceiling affect on their explanatory capacity is being suggested.

(3) Emphasising a paradigm's revolutionary message not only ignores its evolutionary background but such an emphasis can also isolate the paradigm from important theoretical problems. Cognitive psychologists have justifiably criticised operant conditioners for ignoring the problems of cognition. At the same time they should recognise the equally justified criticism that they ignore or minimise important psychological processes. Hilgard (1980), for example, argues in favor of a psychological reality that encompasses cognition, affection, and conation.

> "There is always a division of labour, so that someone describing psychological reality is under no obligation to represent at once all of psychology. At the same time, if psychology's major emphasis lies for a time primarily within understanding, or feeling, or the control of action, some components of the total experience are being subordinated, and the account of psychological reality is incomplete." (Hilgard, 1980, p. 116.)

Hilgard's position represents a challenge to cognitive psychology. How will it be met?

**A Final Comment**

Cognitive psychology, in the modern sense, is still young. It can be appropriately characterised as "a paradigm, an approach to constructing theories, a style of theorising. It cannot be correct or incorrect, only more or less productive" (Hayes, 1978). Cognitive psychology's future will depend on its ability to profit from the lessons of history; particularly why the successes of past revolutions in psychology turned into delayed failures. To reduce this possibility, Santayana's warning should be heeded: "Those who cannot remember the past are condemned to repeat it."

## REFERENCES

1. Attneave, F. Some informational aspects of visual perception. *Psychological Review*, 1954, 61, 183-193.
2. Bergmann, C. The contributions of John B. Watson. *Psychological Review*, 1956, 63, 210-214.
3. Boring, E.G. *A History of experimental psychology.* (2nd ed.) Englewood Cliffs, NJ: Prentice-Hall, 1950.
4. Garner, W.R. *Uncertainty and structure as psychological concepts.* New York: Wiley, 1962.
5. Hayes, P. J. Cognitivism as a paradigm. *The behavioural and brain sciences*, 1978, 1, 238-239.
6. Hilgard, E.R. The trilogy of mind. *Journal of the history of the behavioural sciences*, 1980, 16, 107-117.
7. Hull, C.L. *Principles of behaviour.* New York: Appleton-Century, 1943.
8. Kendler, H.H. Motivation and behaviour. In D. Levine (Eds.), *Nebraska symposium on motivation, 1965.* Lincoln, Nebraska: University of Nebraska Press, 1965.
9. Kendler, H.H. *Psychology: A science in conflict.* New York: Oxford, 1981.
10. Kendler, H.H. Behaviourism and psychology: An uneasy alliance. In S. Koch and D.E. Leary (Eds.), *A Century of Psychology as Science.* New York: McGraw-Hill.
11. Kendler, H.H. and Kendler, T. S. Vertical and horizontal processes in problem solving. *Psychological Review*, 1962, 69, 1-16.
12. Klatzky, R. *Human Memory: structure and processes.* San Francisco: Freeman, 1975.
13. Kohler, W Gestalt psychology today. *American psychologist*, 1959, 14, 727-734.
14. Kuhn, T.S. *The structure of scientific revolutions.* Chicago: University of Chicago Press, 1962.
15. Latane, B. and Darley, J. M. Group inhibition of bystander intervention in emergencies. *Journal of personality and social psychology*, 1968, 10, 215-221.
16. Latane, B. and Rodin, J. A lady in distress: Inhibiting effects of friends and strangers on bystander intervention. *Journal of experimental social psychology*, 1969, 5, 189-202.
17. Neisser, U. *Cognitive Osychology.* New York: Appleton-Century-Crafts, 1967.
18. Spence, K.W. The nature of discrimination learning in animals. *Psychological Review*, 1936, 43, 427-449.
19. Spence, K.W. Cognitive versus stimulus-response theories of learning. *Psychological Review*, 1950, 57, 159-172.
20. Spence, K.W. The nature of response in discrimination learning. *Psychological Review*, 1952, 59, 89-93.
21. Tolman, E.C. *Purposive Behaviour in Animals and Men.* New York: Century, 1932.
22. Watson, J.B. *Psychology from the Standpoint of a Behaviourist.* Philadelphia, PA: Lippincott, 1919.
23. Wundt, W. *Principles of Physiological Psychology* (Translated from the fifth German Edition of 1902 by E.B. Titchener), Vol. 2. New York: McMillan, 1910.

# 5

# Psychology and Its Frontiers

In the following, is presented some personal reflections about the problems which psychology is likely to face in the near future. The future development of psychology will firstly be determined by inner reasons, prevalent within the discipline itself and stemming from the different theoretical approaches now prevailing. Secondly, it will depend on certain Philosophical problems these approaches are linked with. Thirdly, it will depend on demands and challenges from disciplines surrounding psychology on different sides, but chiefly the biological and social sciences. Fourthly, it will depend on expectations and pressures coming from society at large. These are discussed at some length, although we do not intend to do this systematically.

**Recent Developments**

Present day psychology still consists of different schools or ways of approaching the problems of mind and behaviour. The schools are not as ill reconciled and as diverse as they are for instance in philosophy, but the split between different systems and theories is still with us. One reason for this is that attempts to understand the human mind and behaviour have had quite different origins and objectives from the outset. Psychology originated partly from the philosophy of mind and thinking, partly from a wish to understand inner experience and emotional life, partly from attempts to look at behaviour "objectively" from the "outside", in the same way as the natural sciences looked at their subject matter, and again in part from the need to develop methods controlling behaviour or using human capacity more effectively. It is little wonder that there has been no satisfactory integration of such divergent aims and methods of approach. The gaps between different claims as to what Psychology is or should be are at the present time still strongly felt.

As readers will surely remember, from about 1967 and for the next ten years a powerful attack on the academic psychology was in progress all over the world. It was connected with student unrest, although the attacks also came from several other quarters such as political movements, professional psychologists in the field, educated laymen in other disciplines (mostly the social sciences and humanities) and, in some instances, even from religious circles.

The target of the attacks was called "behaviourism", "positivism" or "S-R psychology". The terms were used almost synonymously, and we will not go into their different definitions here. The main accusations levelled at psychology concerned the study of problems without useful application, the use of laboratory methods, the neglect of internal experience, excessive operationalism, the study of problems that were not meaningful just because they allowed the use of stricter methods, the denial of free will and initiative, and a view of human beings as merely passive creatures reacting to different stimuli, rather than autonomous individuals (e.g. Grennes et al. 1971).

Although it is often said that scientific debates generally only lead to a strengthening of the previous positions of both parties, in the present case this was not so. On the contrary, at least in the Scandinavian countries, Finland included, the debate had a profound influence on the development of psychology as pursued at the universities. We have discussed this development at some length elsewhere (Lagerspetz 1982). A process of change in the content of both research and teaching was initiated. I believe that most Nordic psychologists looking back at what happened during that time feel that the ensuing development was a beneficial one, and that after all, psychology improved as a result.

In retrospect, this development can be seen for instance in the changing titles of the reports published by the leading Scandinavian departments of psychology and in the Scandinavian Journal of Psychology. The topics investigated changed from being dominated by laboratory experiments to include large numbers of studies belonging to applied psychology.

The reason why academic psychology had to yield, at least partially, to its critics was that the opposition succeeded in uniting forces that had previously been separate and in some cases even mutually exclusive. Such were for instance marxists and the so called "radical psychology", psychoanalysts, humanists, hermeneutists, phenomenologists, plus educated laymen interested in arts and culture. The criticisms were often unjust and used the "straw man technique", where the opponent is depicted as having extreme views which nobody represents, and these opinions are then attacked. Individual research projects were accused of neglecting things they had never intended to study, and not accomplishing aims that had never been set. However, even unjustified criticism, and perhaps often precisely that, can lead to beneficial results.

What changed in academic psychology as a result of the criticisms that went on for approximately ten years was the *type of question* considered appropriate for research. What should be stressed in this connection, however, is that *methodologically* the critics had nothing new or better to offer, except perhaps an increase in the use of introspective techniques. The demands for a change of methods in the direction of less "behaviourism", more subjectivism and more intuition were not followed or, if followed, did not in any case lead to much fruitful research. It may be that these qualities are fruitful and valuable in the work of psychologists with individuals and in human encounters in general, but not as a research strategy.

**The Image of Man Once Again**

We have spoken above of academic psychology as opposed to "all the other ones". This distinction nevertheless recalls the two opposing camps that have characterised psychology almost from its beginning (see e.g. Hempel 1949 (1935), Schlick 1949 (1935), Pratt 1948, Leontjev 1977, p. 71). Beloff (1973, p. 6) called them empiricist-associationist and idealist-antiassociationist psychologists. In this distinction, the neobehaviourists, physiological psychologists, "mechanists", and determinists are on one side and the humanists, hermeneutists, and phenomenologists are on the other. One difference between them is the image of man—or at least as it has been emphasised by the "humanists" For want of better names I have chosen to call the two approaches "mechanist" and "humanist", in accordance with the terms used in the book edited by Chapman and Jones (1980). (See Howarth 1980, p. 144). It is true that "mechanist" has also been used as a derogatory label, whereas the name "humanist" has been taken over by a special school within psychology. Other possible terms, however, also seemed to have connotations that were equally confusing. Admittedly, the distinction is by no means clear, and there are controversies also within these "camps", for instance between neobehaviourists and cognitive psychologists. Nor is it clear where psychoanalysis stands in this dichotomy, since it claims to have a "materialist" and determinist basis. Individual psychologists can probably only rarely be labelled as representing one side only, but I believe that any person acquainted with psychology will feel that the ways to approach the subject matter may well be placed on a dimension ranging between the two poles. The dichotomy is still with us. In later times, humanist psychology proper has become even stronger and has started calling itself "the third force in psychology" (Bugental 1965, p. 10).

There is a good chance that the camps will in the future become integrated within psychology quite well, although this will not occur completely in the 1990's. It is not difficult to predict this, because the process of resolving the controversy is going on and books and symposia have been devoted to it (e.g. Wann 1964, Wheeler 1973). The development described above was a' part of this process. The unification of psychology will emerge as the different camps repeatedly challenge each other to conquer new territories and to correct their methods and language to account for the phenomena the opposing camps are dealing with.

There are some central questions, however, which must be agreed upon before reconciliation at the theoretical level is possible. These questions are essentially philosophical, and have been thoroughly discussed in now classic philosophical articles written forty years ago or more, now forgotten by the debating parties [Schlick 1949 (1935), Hempel 1949 (1935), University of California Associates 1949 (1938)1 It is true that these treatises are in some respects out of date and even erroneous, but the main points made are important, and useful for the solution of the controversies within modern Psychology. I agree with Westland (1978, p. 58) that psychologists more than Students of Some other disciplines, have avoided considering Philosophical questions.

One such question is freedom *versus* predictability of behaviour. It seems to lie at the bottom of all the now so popular discussions of "the image of man". The academic Psychology, or the psychology that we have here chosen to call "mechanist", has been accused of looking upon man as a passive creature upon which different forces act (for instance Kelly 1969, May 1962, p. 184, Leontjev 1977, p 72-77, Eskola 1982, p. 52). The causal model has been considered inadequate for explaining the actions of a free individual. To quote Rogers (1964, p. 130): "Man has long felt himself to be a puppet in life—molded by economic forces, by unconscious forces, by environmental forces."

When taken Superficially, this accusation is correct. In search of variables to explain human behaviour, the psychology originally inspired by the natural sciences has in the past often led to trivial, superficial and uninteresting research designs, attitudes and explanations. This is particularly true within the psychology of personality and within social psychology; the "causes" arrived at have often been too crude and simplistic to account for the details of more refined mental, social and emotional phenomena.

The criticism may partly be due to the fact that talk about "control" of behaviour has often made people to think of *social* control, or "ruling" behaviour from the outside. On a deeper theoretical level, however, psychology can not just rest content with noting that "the image of man" has to be changed, and say that hereafter man should be seen as "free".

Firstly, it is obvious that a position seeing humans as reacting only to *outer* stimuli is untenable (Wheeler 1973). The criticism of the so called "mechanist" psychology has also implied, however, that man should not be seen as only reacting to *outer and inner* stimuli either, as was evident for example from the quotation from Rogers above. This is difficult to accept on a theoretical level, without invoking the old idea of the "ghost in the machine" (Blakemore 1977, p. 35). If the humans act neither because of outer nor of inner stimuli, why do they act at all? I do not think that the humanists have really answered this question. They have been stressing freedom of choice (Rogers, 1964, p. 130), without analysing how it is related to explanations based on a causal determination of behaviour.

The view of a so called mechanist would be clear in this case. He would claim that it is possible in principle to predict the behaviour or the experience of a human being at a given moment if we know all of the factors that can affect it, such as his history of reinforcements, heredity, the forces and stimuli of the situation, images, motives, plans and intentions, and so on. Since the concepts of plan and intention have occupied a key position in the controversy, the "mechanist" would cite the analysis by Braithwaite (1953) who writes (pp. 324-325): "Teleological explanations of intentional goal-directed activities are always understood as reducible to causal explanations with intentions as causes." (See also Kari Lagerspetz, 1959, pp. 18-20).

Another point, however, is that the question of *predictability* is not quite the same as that of *free will* at least in principle. Predictability is a practical question, whereas freedom of will is a philosophical one. In practice, there is no danger of psychologists or any other people ever being able to predict precisely what somebody is going to do or to think next, because a complete knowledge of all the relevant circumstances will probably never be available.

There may also be behaviour that is quite *predictable* even if we assume that the individual is acting out of *free will*. For instance, he chooses an action that can be predicted assuming that he acts *rationally*. We can go further, however, and say that acting rationally means to maximise one's own benefits. This is psychologically equal to pursuing one's own needs. The needs, in turn, can be seen as causal determinants of behaviour.

But, the humanist would say, people definitely have the feeling of possessing a free will; they feel that they can do what they please. This has been a common argument against causal and determinist accounts of behaviour. A person can think that the actions of *others* are causally determined, but this does not apply to himself/herself. Therefore it cannot apply to others, either (Chein 1972; quoted from Westland 1978, p. 64). This is, however, a false deduction. It is quite possible to have a *feeling* of free will, and still in reality be determined by inner and outer causes. The feeling of free will is probably even an important causal factor in shaping the mental life of human beings.

I do not attempt to solve these old problems here, but merely to show how psychological and Philosophical problems are connected and should perhaps be solved together, and not within the two disciplines separately. The question of free will is often said to be one that should be left to philosophers. I do not know why this should be so. On the contrary, psychologists are probably in a better position to investigate under which circumstances people feel they are acting out of free will, and when not. For instance, when a person is pursuing his strongest needs, he may feel that he is acting out of free will, whereas other people might find his behaviour to be causally determined. On the other hand, when a person is choosing between equally valid alternatives, his behaviour is difficult for an outsider to predict, but his own feeling of free will may not be especially strong.

There is, however, yet another important side to the problem of the image of man in psychology, especially to that most central question, the freedom of the will. The view that science holds on such matters has an impact on the feelings and conduct of people. If psychology sees man as not being in Possession of free will, people, on reading and hearing about this, will feel discouraged and deny responsibility for their doings (cf. University of California Associates, 1949). Psychologists are generally aware of such questions (e.g. Jahoda 1980, p. 279), and this awareness can, consciously or unconsciously, rebound on them when they formulate their views on the nature of man. Scientific inquiry into the nature of man should, however, be kept separate from considerations as to how the knowledge should be conveyed to the public. It is clear that psychologists, especially since they are psychologists, should take responsibility for how their views influence people. Maybe the public should be told for instance that the behaviour of human beings is causally affected by what they think of themselves.

It may be also important to bear in mind that even a determinist view of human nature does not imply "passivity", as has sometimes been claimed. Neither does it mean that humans are "submitted to the circumstances" (Kelly 1969), or that "rules" are imposed on them from the outside. It only implies that the human mind is a *process* which has its *own* rules. The description of these rules is one of the tasks of psychology.

These rules can be described in different terms on different levels of psychological science. For instance, cognitive psychology has likened the human mind to the functioning of a computer. On the other hand in the study of human relations, mental health problems and the individual as a part of society, it is probably an expedient model to assume that humans act autonomously, and have initiative and free choice. But in reality this is perhaps just a "shorthand description" of causal processes. On a deeper level I do not think that scientific psychology can accept *without analysis* such notions as autonomous activity, free will, initiative and the like, as qualities of humans. The subject matter of psychology is precisely research into this kind of thing.

Although different terminologies must be used at different levels of research, it is to be hoped that these will become more easily translatable to each others' language. There are some older and well known examples of this type of integration. In their book "Personality and psychotherapy" (1950) Dollard and Miller succeeded in combining learning theory and psychoanalysis. Another example is "Plans and the structure of behaviour" by Miller, Galanter, and Pribram (1960) which managed to make the concepts of expectation and plan acceptable within the neobehaviourist psychology.

It seems that the mechanist explanations have not hitherto been detailed and refined enough to account adequately for those phenomena studied by other types of approach. I believe, however, that they may do this in principle. Something to this end was recently expressed by Howarth (1980, p. 147): "The more adequate the mechanist's attempts to deal with complex behaviour, the more difficult it is to distinguish mechanist and humanist language in operational terms."

My prediction is that in the psychology of the future, the mechanists will take over in two ways, in the sphere of methodology and in the sphere of language. The humanists and psychoanalysts, on the other hand, will point out the problems and problem areas that need to be studied. Below, under the heading of "Borderline cases", I will make the point that even peripheral "movements", now appearing outside the discipline, could contribute to a broader and more unified psychology.

**"Borderline Cases"**

At present very different opinions prevail in society about what psychology is or should be. The psychology department of any university receives through the mail plenty of announcements of courses and congresses or advertisements for literature dealing with parapsychology, transcendental meditation, yoga, transpersonal psychology, music therapy, "demonology", and so on. These movements vary greatly in how scientific" they are and what prestige they have. Many of them call themselves "psychological". What is typical for all of them is that they purport to have solutions to problems which one thinks should typically be solved by psychology proper, like anxiety, peace of mind, human relations, lack of concentration, and so on. Academic psychologists usually feel uneasy when confronted with these peripheral movements. They feel that they should be able either to account for them or to dismiss them, or in any case to know what aspects in them should be taken up by psychology proper and what parts should be rejected.

This is one of the things which I anticipate as being among the tasks of future psychology. The reason why it should be done is not only to make psychology a unitary science, but also to make use of the potential ideas and skills inherent in the more marginal systems and movements. It has been said that "crazy" people can be "geniuses" in some special way, although otherwise disturbed. In the same way, borderline movements can contain useful or even ingenious ideas when translated to the system and language of scientific psychology. Moreover, the very fact that a certain type of movement has developed, tells us something about human experience and human needs. In some of the marginal movements, the theory upon which the movement is based may be found to be basically wrong, although some of its ideas or ways of functioning may be useful. It can also be worthwhile to study the movements "from the outside" to see what it is in them that appeals to people, if "translated" to the language of ordinary psychology. Writing about the "usefulness" of psychology, Westland (1978) mentions that psychology has often been useful in a "negative" way, that is, by showing that something is *not* the case. In connection with the marginal movements, academic psychology will probably have to function frequently in this manner. For instance, if it is shown that so called supernatural phenomena do not exist (as seems likely from much of the recent literature, e.g. Taylor 1980), it still remains for psychology to study why and under what circumstances people experience things as being "supernatural". What happens in a spiritualist seance, how does the "medium" experience her/his own functioning? What makes the others believe or not believe? Why do people think it important to explain what they are experiencing, on the basis of other forces, than those known within science and everyday life? In addition to providing explanations, the task of psychology will in such instances be to *rule out* certain ways of thinking.

What has been said above about marginal systems and movements also pertains to some extent to applied psychology. What is nowadays called applied psychology is often in reality not any practical application of the theories or results of academic psychology. It is rather a kind of common sense which has been found useful. The same state of affairs has existed and often still exists in medicine: some drug or treatment has been found useful in curing a disease, although it is not known on what mechanisms its effect is based. The physiological mechanisms have been discovered later.

It is highly desirable that this kind of integration of different practices into the bulk of psychology should gradually take place in the future.

**Sociobiology and the Frontiers of Psychology**

Psychology will, however, also be challenged from other quarters. The two watchdogs of psychology are the social sciences on one hand and physiology with the rest of biology on the other. The recent expansion of so called sociobiology is an example of such a challenge, although it has not been sufficiently met by psychologists. Sociobiology is an attempt to connect the level of society with the level of biology, without paying attention to psychology lying between these fields. Psychologists have interfered remarkably little in this attempt, although the biological and the social can in reality only be connected through the behaviour of individuals, which is the subject matter of psychology.

Sociobiologists have invented a concept called "gene altruism" (Wilson 1975, p. 3-4). This means that individuals are prone to help their relatives and make sacrifices for their benefit more. than for others because the relatives carry the same genes. In evolutionary terms this tendency is thought to lead to a better preservation of one's own kin.

Such a tendency, if it were true, is bound to be manifested in the behaviour of *individuals*. It would be a kind of hereditary motivation which would probably be shown in behaviour independently of conscious control. It is not enough to point out that in society people generally do help their relatives more because, for historical reasons, the family is a unit in the social system, and it is considered ones duty help one's relatives. (It is interesting that this feeling of duty extends to adopted children and pet animals, which are not relatives.) Psychologists should devise designs and carry out research to investigate this assumed tendency. (For examples of such studies see Snowdon 1983.)

Furthermore, a considerable amount of psychological research has already been conducted on the functioning and development of altruism and helping behaviour (Krebs 1970). This literature ought to be taken into account when the idea of "gene altruism" is studied and discussed by sociobiologists.

Another example of how Sociobiologists have bypassed Psychology is in the claim that wars are caused by human aggression (Lorenz 1963, Wilson 1978). This idea has posed as an application of *biology* to the level of human Society. Later in this article I will try to make a case for that the idea in itself is basically wrong. However, in this connection I wish merely to pay attention to the fact that the sociobiologists imply without scruples that human aggression is a *biological* phenomenon. This may be so to the extent that all human emotions or, in fact, all psychological phenomena are "biological". The point is, however, that virtually all study of aggression in humans has been carried out within psychology and by Psychologists although the sociobiologists do not seem aware of this bulk of research. The situational variation of aggression, as well as the variation of aggressiveness as a personality characteristic, can be largely accounted for by factors that are essentially psychological by any definition of the word. An attempt to "explain" collective violence on the basis of biological factors implies a disregard of the main information available about human aggression. It is no wonder that the attempts to do this so far have not reached a level that survives scientific scrutiny.

Sociobiology has been discussed and heavily criticised for different reasons (see e.g. Breuer 1982). My contribution to these criticisms lies just in pointing out that sociobiology cannot be very successful as long as it tries to take a short cut from biology to the social sciences without taking psychology into account. Psychology lies between the two areas occupied by these disciplines 'and has empirical research results for the same issues that sociobiologists try to "explain". It would be better, of course, if psychologists themselves in the future took care of their relations to neighbouring sciences.

**Reductionism and the Integration of Psychology with the Social Sciences**

Sciences are often regarded as forming a hierarchical ladder on which the humanities and social sciences occupy the "highest" and chemistry and physics the "lowest" rungs. Explanations, which explain phenomena on a higher level as phenomena belonging to the subject matter of a discipline at a lower level are called reductionist. Such, for instance, are explanations of behaviour, i.e. psychological phenomena, on the basis of physiology, or of biological phenomena on the basis of biochemistry. Reduction has often been a successful way of accounting scientifically for phenomena which have previously proved difficult to understand. Reductionist explanations, however, have also been heavily criticised (Rose and Rose 1974, Ayala and Dobzhansky 1974, pp. vii-viii), especially when the social sciences have provided the level to be explained, and psychology or biology the level from which the explanations have been found. These may be called "reductions downwards". (Lagerspetz and Lagerspetz, 1979)

Sometimes, however, "reductions upwards" are used, i.e. phenomena lower on the ladder are explained by higher level facts. One such example is the explanation of somatic disease, for instance coronary illness or gastric ulcer (biological level), by emotional unbalance or disturbance (psychological level). This type of reduction is also employed when the psychology of individuals is accounted for by their being part of society.

As Mats Bjorkman points out in his chapter in the present volume, psychology has traditionally been the science of individuals more or less detached from their environment. In later times, however, psychology has more commonly also taken into account social and other environmental variables in the explanations of behaviour. Societal factors are seen both as situational determinants and as influencing the development of recurring behaviour patterns, such as habits and personality traits. For instance, emotional disturbance, like mental illness, is no longer explained only on the basis of factors within the individual such as inherited personality characteristics or deviant metabolism, but is seen mainly as a result of special kinds of social interactions. The conduct of criminal offenders has been explained on the basis of social influences within "subcultures" of society (Wolfgang and Ferracuti, 1967). These are examples of what are here called "upward reductions":' the psychological phenomena are accounted for as instances from the level of the social sciences. Such explanations are likely to become more common as an understanding of social factors increases among psychologists in the 1990's, and psychology integrates better with its neighbours higher on the hierarchical ladder of the sciences.

What is wrong then with "downward reductions", that is, attempts to explain collective behaviour on the basis of the psychology of individuals? After all, society consists of individuals who, in turn, are the study objects of psychology. My belief is that the reductionist "explanations" offered have frequently been far too crude and oversimplified to be scientific. One phenomenon or characteristic from the psychology of individuals has been "generalised" to account for behaviour on the level of organisations, as when the women's liberation movement is "explained" as being caused by penis envy, or wars on the basis of individual aggression. Collective behaviour never results from one type of motive only on the individual level. Saying this does not mean, however, that what happens on the collective level could not in principle be also accounted for at the individual level, if necessary. But the explanation then involves many different variables and their complex interactions.

Let us examine in some detail the latter example, i.e., the idea that aggression on the individual level is what causes wars on the collective level. As I mentioned above, the sociobiologists have taken this as a reduction from the level of society to the level of biology. But, in fact, it should be seen as an instance of reduction from society to *psychology*.

One way to test this proposition is to study the motives and the psychological characteristics of people who initiate and takes part in wars. Is aggression the motive or aggressiveness the personality trait that mostly accounts for their behaviour? My guess is that an empirical study with any acceptable methods and design would not show aggression to be the most prevalent motive of either soldiers taking part in a war or of politicians deciding to start one.

It is true that war propaganda to some extent tries to appeal to aggression and this may influence the attitudes of people. The propaganda appeals more, however, to the emotion of *fear*. It is mostly the enemy that is depicted as aggressive. Fear is surely a more prevalent emotion than aggression in people taking part in a war. Soldiers come to the front in the first place because they obey commands. *Obedience* and *suggestibility* are more necessary human personality traits for war than aggression. Important prerequisites are also *idealism, sociality,* and *altruism,* even to the point of complete sacrifice of oneself for the benefit of others. It is generally assumed that the efficiency of an army depends to a great extent on such characteristics.

Political leaders and decision makers, in turn, do not usually start wars because they are aggressive, although popular belief tends to suggest this. Since war is used as an extension of the policy of a government, the leaders can see it as their *duty* to engage in war. *Ambition, self-assertiveness,* and *fear of failure* are important motives in war leaders, in addition to fear of disapproval by supporters, only to mention some of the psychological forces involved.

The motives of people engaged in producing weapons for wars can be analysed in a corresponding way. The workers in the arms factories are afraid of unemployment, and they think that it is the responsibility of politicians to decide what their products are used for. The scientists who invent and develop the weapons tend to think in the same way, and they are similarly afraid of unemployment, and motivated by the pursuit of their scientific careers. It should be noted, then, that most people working for war are doing so for other motives, than giving outlet to their aggressive impulses.

There are many other motives and psychological characteristics without which wars could never have begun as a social institution. For instance, *intelligence* is necessary for planning and manufacturing weapons, and for the strategy and tactics of war. Language, enabling an effective communications system, is required to conduct any major military operations, and so on.

In sum, to account for *war* on the collective level by psychological motives and characteristics on the individual level, it is not sufficient or pertinent to mention only *aggression* as an explanation. Above we have mentioned fear, suggestibility, idealism, altruism, sociality, sense of duty, self-assertion, fear of failure, intelligence, and language; and other characteristics might also be mentioned.

Elsewhere I have discussed the relation of aggression to war in more detail (Lagerspetz 1982b) and aggression in animals and man (Lagerspetz 1981). The point I want to make here is that a social level phenomenon cannot be accounted for on the psychological level as the expression of one single psychological trait. "Explanations" of this type have fostered a negative attitude towards all attempts at explaining phenomena in social life in terms of psychology. This negative attitude towards psychology as a basis of reductionist explanations may have encouraged sociobiologists to make "reductions" from social level to the level of *biology* instead. I believe, however, that if done properly, psychology could contribute to a deeper understanding of social phenomena. The reverse, of course, is also true, namely that the behaviour of individuals, which is the subject matter of psychology is better understood when variables from the social level are taken into account.

## Conclusion

It is often said that since psychology consists of many types of problem areas, different types of research methods or paradigms should be used in their study. Those advocating this believe, for instance, that religious experience should preferably be studied using a hermeneutic or phenomenological approach and visual perception, say, should be studied with a behaviourist approach. This is indeed mostly the case at present. However, linking problem area and method together further adds to the segregation of psychology into separate areas. It would perhaps sometimes be useful to do quite the opposite: study religious experience in a "behaviourist" way (this has been done by Bjorkqvist, 1982) and approach for instance visual perception hermeneutically. As far as this is done, it will facilitate understanding between research workers in different areas of psychology and force them to use a common language.

Psychologists have traditionally been the keenest critics of their own discipline. This may be one of the reasons why psychology is constantly said to be in a crisis. Self criticism usually originates, however, from comparing oneself with others. Psychology has compared itself with the natural sciences, with psychiatry, with the social sciences, with the humanities and so on, and claims have been raised that psychology should approach its subject matter in the same way as these disciplines. The controversies within psychology can thus be seen as reflections of controversies between the disciplines surrounding it.

Psychology constitutes an important point of contact between disciplines that are otherwise far from each other, for instance between what has been called "the two cultures", science and arts (Hempel 1949, p. 375, Snow 1961). As far as psychology succeeds internally in conciliating the different approaches, it could constitute a general model for how different types of disciplines can be combined at a theoretical level.

## REFERENCES

1. Ayala, F.J. and Dobzhansky, T. (Eds.) *Studies in the Philosophy of Biology*. Berkeley: University of California Press, 1974.
2. Beloff, J. *Psychological Sciences. A review of modern psychology*. London: Crosby Lockwood Staples, 1973.
3. Bjorkqvist, K. Ecstasy from a physiological point of view. In N.G. Holm (Ed.), *Religious Ecstasy*. Scripta Instituti Donneriani Aboensis XI, Stockholm: Almqvist and Wiksell, 1982.
4. Blakemore, C. *Mechanics of the Mind*. Cambridge: Cambridge University Press, 1977.
5. Braithwaite, R.B. *Scientific Explanation*. Cambridge: Cambridge University Press, 1953.
6. Breuer, G. *Sociobiology and the Human Dimension*. Cambridge: Cambridge University Press, 1982.
7. Bugental, J.F.T. *The Search for Authenticity*. New York: Holt, Rinehart and Winston, 1965.
8. Chapman, A.J. and Jones, D. M. (Eds.) *Models of Man*. Leicester: The British Psychological Society, 1980.
9. Dollard, J. and Miller, N.E. *Personality and Psychotherapy. An analysis in terms of learning, thinking, and culture*. New York: McGraw-Hill, 1950.
10. Eskola, A. *Socialpsykologins grunder—en kritisk granskning*. Stockholm: Almqvist and Wiksell, 1982.
11. Grennes, C.E., Johansson, A., Johansson, M., Katzenelson, B., Kvale, S. and Willert, S. *Psykologi och praxis. Uppsatser i psykologins dialektik*. Malmo: Bo Cavefors Forlag, 1971.
12. Hempel, C. C. The logical analysis of psychology. In H. Feigl and W. Sellars (Eds.), Readings' in philosophical analysis. New York: Appleton Century Crofts, 1949. (First appeared in French in *Revue de Synthese*, 1935.)
13. Howarth, C. I. The structure of effective psychology: man as a problem solver. In Chapman, A.J. and Jones, D. M. (Eds.), *Models of Man*. Leicester: The British Psychological Society, 1980.
14. Jahoda, M. One model of man or many? In Chapman, A. J. and Jones, D. M. (Eds.), *Models of Man*. Leicester: The British Psychological Society, 1980.
15. Kelly, C. A. Personal construct theory and the psychotherapeutic interview. In Maher, B. (Ed.), *Clinical Psychology and Personality*. New York: Wiley, 1969.
16. Krebs, D. L. Altruism—an examination of the concept and a review of the literature. *Psychological Bulletin*, 1970, 73, 256-302.
17. Lagerspetz, K.M.J. Combining aggression studies in infrahumans and man. In Brain, P.F. and Benton, D. (Eds.), *Multi-disciplinary approaches to aggression research*. Amsterdam: Elsevier/North-Holland Biomedical Press, 1981.
18. Lagerspetz, K.M.J. Teoria ja sovellus psykologiliiton tahanastisena elinaikana. *Psykologiuutiset* 1982 a, 7, (6), 4-6.
19. Lagerspetz, K.M.J. Are wars caused by human aggression? *Adult Education in Finland*. 1982 b, 19 (1), 21-29.
20. Lagerspetz, K.Y.H. Teleological explanations and terms in biology. *Annales Zoologici Societatis Zoologiae Botanicae Fennicae Vanamo*, 1959. Tom. 19, 6, 1-73.
21. Lagerspetz, K.Y.H. and Lagerspetz, K.M.J. Ajatuksia reduktion ongelmasta. *Psykologia*, 1979, 14, (3), 3-7.
22. Leontjev, A.N. *Toiminta, tietoisuus, persoonallisuus*. Kuopio: Kansankulttuuri, 1977. (Dejatel'nost. Cozonanie. Litshnost. Moscow, 1975.)
23. May, R. *Love and Will*. New York: Norton, 1969.

24. Miller, C. A., Galanter, E. and Pribram, K. H. *Plans and the Structure of Behaviour.* London: Holt, Rinehart and Winston, 1960.
25. Pratt, C.C. *The Logic of Modern Psychology.* New York: MacMillan, 1948.
26. Rogers, C. R. Toward a science of the person. In Wann, T. W. (Ed.), *Behaviourism and phenomenology. Contrasting Bases for Modern Psychology.* Chicago: The University of Chicago Press, 1964.
27. Rose, S.P.R. and Rose, H. "Do not adjust your mind, there is a fault in reality"—ideology in neurobiology. *Cognition*, 1973, 2, 479-502.
28. Schlick, M. On the relation between psychological and physical concepts. In H. Feigl and W. Sellars (Eds.), *Readings in philosophical analysis.* New York: Appleton Century Crofts, 1949. (First appeared in French in *Revue de Synthese*, 1935.)
29. Snow, C.P. *The Two Cultures and the Scientific Revolution.* Cambridge: Cambridge University Press, 1961.
30. Snowdon, C.T. Ethology, comparative psychology, and animal behaviour. *Annual Review of Psychology*, 1983, 34, 63-94.
31. Taylor, J. *Science and the Supernatural. An investigation of paranormal phenomena.* London: Granada, 1980.
32. University of California Associates. The freedom of the will. In H. Feigl and W. Sellars (Eds.), *Readings in Philosophical Analysis.* New York: Appleton Century Crofts. (First published in *Knowledge and Society*, 1938.)
33. Wann, T.W. (Ed.) *Behaviourism and Phenomenology. Constrasting Bases for Modern Psychology.* Chicago: University of Chicago Press, 1964.
34. Westland, G. *Current Crises of Psychology.* London: Heinemann, 1978.
35. Wheeler, H. (Ed.) *Beyond the Punitive Society.* San Francisco: Freeman, 1973.
36. Wilson, E.O. *Sociology. The New Synthesis.* Cambridge, Mass.: Harvard University Press, 1975.
37. Wilson, E.O. *On Human Nature.* Cambridge, Mass.: Harvard University Press, 1978.
38. Wolfgang, M.E. and Ferracuti, F. *The Subculture of Violence. Towards an Integrated Theory of Criminology.* London: Tavistock Publications, 1967.

# 6

# Towards a Psychology Beyond the Individual

Johnny von Wright, discussed the possible contributions of cognitive psychology to educational practice. Cognitive psychology should, he said,

> "...offer tools, both intellectual and practical, which may help the teacher better to understand his own work and his students' ways of thinking and learning. However, ultimately these analyses have to be made, and the tools used, by the teacher himself: each teaching situation has its unique and individual features, and that is true of each teacher and each pupil as well. Hence I think it is more useful for the teacher to try to understand these tools and their use, rather than to look to cognitive psychology for generalisation and ready-made recipes." (von Wright, 1980, p. 18)

As it has been suggested that psychology in the future must be the common theme for this *Festschrift* and educational applications of cognitive psychology, will in the future be exactly of the kind hinted at by von Wright in the above quotation, we intend to develop here in our own way the point he has made.

Looking for "...generalisations and ready-made recipes" has indeed been the dominating view of what scientific contributions to the improvement of educational practice may look like, since empirical psychology was founded during the second half of the 19th century. Since then, there have been expectations that psychology, by establishing law-like relationships, would be able to point out certain preferable courses of action to be used in the context of school. The basic idea has been that once we have managed to reveal the fundamental characteristics of learning, the insights thus attained can be applied to the unlimited variation of every-day school life and suggest how educational reality is to be dealt with. The notion of fundamental characteristics of learning refers to the question of *what* is learned, on the one hand, and to the question of *how* that which is learned is learned, i.e. which factors facilitate or inhibit learning, on the other. (The answer to the first question has been phrased in terms of stimulus-response bonds, cognitive maps, response-reinforcement connections etc. and to the second in terms of exercise, insight, reinforcement etc.)

This way of formulating questions has not proved entirely successful. The most important reason far the failure (or at least partial failure) of the find-the-fundamental-mechanisms-first-and-apply-them-to-various-contents-and-contexts strategy can be found in the excessive variation we face both with regard to the content of learning and to the personal history of the human beings whose learning the researcher aims at characterising. (It is exactly this that von Wright refers to in the above quotation, I think, when saying

> "...each teaching situation has its unique and individual features, and that is true of each teacher and each pupil as well.")

The approach, adopted by "main-stream" psychological research, on which I am trying to cast some doubts, accords perfectly with accepted canons of "the scientific method": try to isolate the essential characteristics of the phenomenon, abstracted from its various appearances in the different situations of every day life and apply the knowledge thus gained, later on, to those situations from which the phenomenon was abstracted. Such a strategy can be extremely successful, assuming that the variation itself is not an essential characteristic of the phenomenon in question. As regards learning, I think it is.

This claim will not he logically justified, only illustrated and used as a starting-point for a description of the various steps in conceptual development which could lead to the establishing of a cognitive psychology capable of providing teachers with "intellectual and practical tools" in their work. As an example of the not too infrequent case of the untenability of too broad a generalisation, I have chosen the most frequent of all educational tasks, the acquisition of reading skills.

**What Does it Take to Read?**

To oversimplify this extremely complex question unwarrartedly, there are two competing views of reading and thereby of learning to read. In the first case, the communicative function of reading is taken as the point of departure. The reading skill is simply seen as the extension of the skill to understand spoken language; text is written speech in this perspective. In the second case, the opposite of this view is held. Reading is seen as the specific technical skill of translating (decoding) letters to sounds. This capacity of "breaking the code" is considered to be the heart of the matter. Text does not appear as written speech from such a perspective. On the contrary, the teacher's task is to reinforce the children's linguistic awareness, so they become conscious of the fundamental difference between written and spoken language. In one case, reading is conceptualised as an analytic process going from the whole to the parts, in the other case the reverse is held to be true; reading is conceptualised as a synthetic process going from the parts to the whole. In the jargon of modern cognitive psychology this distinction brings to mind (or rather: is identical with) the distinction between top-down and bottom-up processes. The difference between these two antithetical ideas of reading has highly important practical implications for elementary reading instructions. Either one stresses the communicative function, the continuity between spoken and written language and uses the pupils' interest in the context as a basis or one aims at developing the decoding skills by means of carefully designed—but from the content point of view, rather meaningless—texts and exercises. Needless to say, the second one has always been the dominating approach and it is not very likely that any radical change will take place in the immediate future, even if the alternative paradigm for reading instructions seems to be gaining increasing support both from researchers and practitioners (at least in Sweden). Such a development in Sweden is, without any doubt, largely due to the unstinting work of a brilliant primary school teacher, the late Ulrika Leimar. She developed a method, or rather, an approach to reading instructions, where speech is used as a basis. The children start with "their own words", words which they suggest themselves, and which when written down by the teacher, form the link between the spoken and the written language and constitute a starting-point for the analysis into their constituent parts (see Leimar, 1974).

Ulrika Leimar apparently had no knowledge of the work of Sylvia Ashton-Warner, who had developed a very similar way of reasoning many years earlier. In New Zealand, Ashton-Warner (1963) who worked with Maori children, invented, when faced with the failure of the traditional method, what she called organic reading, which meant that reading instructions were based on a "key vocabulary", consisting of words central in the children's world. These words were suggested by the children and they usually revolved around two basic emotions; fear and sex, as did the two most powerful words that were found in the children's vocabulary; ghost and kiss.

> "First words must have an intense meaning. First words must be already part of the dynamic life. First books must be made of the stuff of the child himself, whatever and wherever the child."

says Ashton-Warner (1963, p. 32). By means of the organic reading method the Maori children learned to read like other children do, but unlike other Maori children subjected to other teaching methods. Obviously, these children, belonging to an illiterate culture were not aware of "the idea of reading". And it was exactly this missing insight that was arrived at by means of the teaching method which used their "lived reality" as the point of departure and which clearly stressed the communicative (and not the technical) aspect of reading.

Such a line of reasoning about reading was developed further into systematic research by Edfeldt (1982) who came to the conclusion that there is a great deal of evidence in cognitive psychology that strongly supports a communicative, top-down view of reading.

Lundberg (1982), on the other hand, in a review of recent research into reading, concluded that the most important thing in reading instruction is to facilitate the development of linguistic awareness, the training of the skill of phonological decoding.

In a highly interesting study, Hazel Francis followed ten children during their first three years of reading instruction. On the basis of her observations, the conclusion could be drawn that the children may spontaneously develop different strategies for reading. And not only did their ways of setting about the task of learning to read accord with one or the other of the two main alternative views of reading described above, but also different children reached the same level of reading proficiency by means of either of the two alternatives (Francis, 1982).

A doctoral student of mine, Dagmar Neuman, with many years of experience as a primary school teacher and as a teacher for pupils with special reading difficulties, wrote a letter to me recently after attending a public discussion between the two above-mentioned proponents of the two approaches to reading instruction, Ake Edfeldt and Ingvar Lundberg. She describes how she had successfully used something like "the organic teaching method" to teach school beginners to read and how she, when trying to help secondary school students with reading difficulties, realised that she had to train their decoding skills systematically.

> "In the previous special instruction classes, far too many of my upper secondary school pupils had been given a book (which they had often chosen themselves) in order to train their reading skill. They told me that nobody had listened when they tried to explain that they could not read the book given them, although they knew that it was a book they liked. They were all very positive towards finally being allowed to start working on their decoding problems. Before the end of the school year, they had begun to look for literature in the library. We first read together (I read one page then the pupil reads half a page, etc.) and, after a while, the pupil reads alone (finally at home as well, after which she would tell me the most important things that had "happened since last time"). It was meaningful to start practising to read when practising no longer reinforced the faulty decoding patterns previously used by the pupils."

The conclusion to be drawn from this, one which seemed to be shared by most of the teachers with whom I have informally discussed this matter, is that one should not overgeneralise; in different cases and under different circumstances the answer to the question of what is the basic problem in reading instructions may vary, and accordingly, the appropriate instructional strategy may too.

The extremely oversimplified picture I have chosen to illustrate the thesis that generalisations about "the best teaching methods" may not be the best thing for cognitive psychology to aim at when it comes to its educational applications, can thus be summarised in the following way. There are two basic components of skills that can be identified. One is being able to grasp the idea of reading, the understanding of the communicative function of reading, of the fact that someone writes something in order to make it known to someone else. In this case, similarities between written and spoken language are focused on, the sense in which text is "speech in a written form" is central. The other component is the technical skill of translating visual signs into sounds, this is the "breaking of the code", the increase of linguistic awareness (of, for instance, in what way spoken and written language differ).

When pointed out and explained, both these components seem to be acknowledged by most researchers of reading and by the practitioners of the domain of skill, i.e. by primary school teachers. In most cases, however, one of these two components has been taken for granted, i.e. it has not been thematised. It has then been tacitly assumed that the child acquires only one of the components, the other follows automatically. Opinion does indeed differ as to which of the components should be used as a point of departure. Some argue that once the children have understood what reading is all about, they will more or less develop the technique by themselves. Others argue that once the child has acquired the technical skill of phonological decoding, understanding will follow. Both of these views are true in many cases, neither of them is true in all. In actual fact, both components are necessary but not sufficient conditions for being able to read. The understanding of the idea of reading is always implicitly presupposed when the technical training of the skill starts. This assumption is frequently justified, but sometimes it is not. In such cases, one should concentrate one's efforts on developing the missing insight, as did Sylvia Ashton-Warner. On the other hand, understanding the idea of reading and being given the opportunity of analysing self-chosen words and self-invented texts is often sufficient when learning to read, but many times it is not. In such cases one must concentrate one's efforts on training the specific skills that are lacking, as did Dagmar Neuman.

This line of reasoning concerns inter-individual differences, or rather: the contextuality of interindividual differences. We can, however, also speak of a contextuality of intra-individual differences. It is simply not the case that once one has learnt to read, the skill is executed in the same way, with the same *ease* and smoothness, on all occasions. It is a commonplace observation that when we face difficult words, especially new words, we have to use our decoding skills in a controlled, non-automatic fashion, even if we never do so otherwise. Even more important, however, is perhaps the fact that highly literate adults in certain contexts may almost completely forget about the communicative aspect of reading. Saljo (1982) has demonstrated in a most illuminating investigation that many adults, when reading a next in a situation which they define as a "learning situation", completely disregard the message the author is trying to get across to the reader and focus entirely on trying to memorise the wording of the text instead.

In most cases, the contextuality of reading (or of other capabilities) both from the inter— and the intra-individual point of view can only with great difficulty be included in the thinking about reading (or about other capabilities). This is, I think due to a certain absoluteness of the conceptualisation of the transmission of skills.

It is often thought to be possible to characterise the skill in a more or less unique way, the teacher is often thought to possess the skill and have the goal of handing it over to or developing it in the pupil who, after having acquired it, is thought to have it as a self-evident property. Both for logical and for empirical reasons it appears, however, that a conceptualisation of skills in relational terms (i.e. as an aspect of the relation between a person and a task in a certain situation) is to be preferred.

**From Pre-Aristotelian to Post-Galilean Modes of Thinking**

Inspired by Kurt Lewin's (1936) writing, several decades ago, Reiser (1939) drew attention to certain, more or less universal changes in modes of thinking that have taken place in the history of science. Lewin had argued that psychology had still to go through that highly significant change in the way of thinking which, in Physics, was initiated by Galileo. Before that, the Aristotelian mode of thought had dominated. Its most characteristic feature is the inclination

> "...to find explanation of events in terms of the individual as such, in some inner motive or emotion, whereas the Galilean view demands that we no longer seek the "cause" of events in the nature of the single, isolated object, but in the relation between an object and its surroundings..." (p. 152)

It was exactly such a shift in thinking that Lewin intended to bring about by introducing the notion of "topological psychology" according to which behaviour is always seen as function of *a person in an environment*. The *field* concepts were introduced in topological psychology to set organism and environment in relation with each other.

In addition to the Aristotelian and the Galilean views, Reiser identified two other ways of thinking. Firstly, there is a pre-Aristotelian mode of orientation, characterised by Levy-Bruhl (1923) in his study of "primitive mentality". Secondly, there is a post-Galilean way of thinking, in which man and world are seen as united again. Here, we cannot describe anything, except in relation to something else. This state of affairs—Reiser argues—characterises modern physics. As I understand it, the difference between Galilean and post-Galilean ways of thinking is one of giving explanations in terms of relations between entities on the one hand and using relational terms in the descriptions themselves, on the other. This distinction seems to be congruent with the distinction between external and internal relations, i.e. relations between separately defined entities, on one hand, and on the other, relations which stem from the fact that the entities are defined in relation to each other, without having any separate meaning.

**Phenomenology As A Basis for A Psychology of Internal Relations**

The unity of man and the world is the basic tenet of phenomenology. As the distinguishing feature of psychological phenomena, Franz Brentano introduced the concept of intentionality in 1874. Psychological phenomena—he says—are characterised by an orientation towards an object, by a reference to a content. Love is always the love of someone and learning is always learning of something. Edmund Husserl, the founding father of the phenomenological movement laid this idea as a cornerstone for his philosophy. There are two aspects of the experience of an object, the act of experiencing, the "noesis", and that which is experienced, i.e. the meaning of the object towards which one's attention is directed, the "noema". These two aspects jointly form the whole, the experience of the object in question. (For a highly readable presentation of the basic concepts in phenomenology, see Ihde, 1977.)

The relational character of modern physics—in Reiser's above—mentioned discussion—concerns the different parts of physical systems; in actual fact the relatedness applies to the whole universe. And not even the human observer stands outside the system, he is certainly a part of it. The dependence of the description on the one who describes, and the dependence of the measurement on the measuring instrument draws attention to the fact that man-world relations, too, are of an internal character, as are those between different entities of the physical world. The physicist's search for truths about the physical world has thus led him to recognise the subjectivity of our knowledge about the physical world.

The phenomenologist, on the other hand, starts by reflecting on our conditions for gaining knowledge about the world and it is in this way he is forced to realise the subjective nature of our knowledge. Both the physicist and the philosopher are thus led to face subjectivity because of their interest in saying something about "the real world". In contrast to this, for the psychologist—at least for the psychologist with such an orientation—subjectivity is the starting point, the subject matter, the content of his discipline.

One would perhaps expect phenomenological: thinking to lend itself easily as a basis for psychological research. This is not, however, the case. There is a common misconception that phenomenologically inspired psychology is confused with introspection (see, for instance, Greeno, 1982). But as intentionality implies orientation towards the world, introspection is in actual fact its antithesis. As, for instance, thinking is always thinking about something, you cannot observe your own thoughts, what you can do is to describe what you are thinking about. Phenomenological research was originally meant to describe--as truthfully as possible—a first-person experience of something in the world. The experience described is thought to be of a radically different kind to our everyday experiences. The aim is to free ourselves—by means of the "Phenomenological reduction"—from our preconceived ideas, to shift from a "natural" to a "phenomenological attitude" in order to gain access to the "essence" of that which our experience is an experience of.

The phenomenological method is thus an alternative to the empirical method, or rather,—as Husserl expressed it—the former is propedeutic to the latter. What he meant was that we must clarify the foundations, on which we build our knowledge about the world. If subjectivity in itself is the subject matter, as may be the case in psychology, we must study someone else's subjectivity. (This follows from the above remark about introspection.) Thereby we enter, however, the field of empirical research, to which, as was pointed out above, phenomenology is an alternative. In order to apply phenomenology to psychology, we must thus transcend the realms of phenomenology. What we have to do is in a phenomenological frame of mind (on the researcher's part) to investigate the natural attitude (on the subject's part).

Such a step has indeed been taken, for instance, by Amedeo Giorgi of Duquesne University in Pittsburgh, USA. One of his main projects has been to collect interview protocols from people relating some everyday experience of learning. Giorgi (1975) has developed a rigorous procedure for qualitative analysis of protocols and by applying this method to various cases of learning as experienced by laymen, he aims at revealing the essential structure of learning as it exists in contemporary America.

**Behaviourism As A Basis for A Psychology of Internal Relation**

In addition to the above mentioned confusion of phenomenology and introspection, there is another common misconception about phenomenology, also clearly articulated by

Greeno (1982), namely that phenomenology does not deal with action, only with experience. Once the above-mentioned step from first-person (eidetic) phenomenology to third-person (empirical) phenomenology is taken, it becomes obvious, however, that man-world relations, in the sense of the person's experience of the world, can be expressed not only by words but also by behaviour. In this way we can, in actual fact, find a common element in phenomenology and behaviourism. Merleau-Ponty (1965) says that Watson, the founder of behaviourism held the view

> "...that behaviour is not located in the nervous system, that it resides between the individual and the environment, that consequently the study of behaviour can be made without a word about physiology, and finally that it is concerned with a stream of activity which the living being projects around itself...." (pp. 225-226)

What Watson had in mind, Merleau-Ponty says, was "...what others have called existence".

Kvale and Grennes (1975) in a surprising comparison between Skinner and Sartre find remarkable similarities 'in their views, the most important of which is their objecting to the common-place dualism between man and world in psychology, to "the illusion of the double world". This dualism refers to the idea that there is, on the one hand, an objective, outer world and on the other, a subjective representation of it, inside man, a kind of inner world to which the person reacts. However, frequently this notion is taken for granted, it leads inevitably to an infinite regress: Who, in that case, does the reacting? Though both reject the dualistic picture of man-world relations, the alternatives offered by Skinner's radical behaviourism and by the phenomenological-existential tradition to which Sartre belongs differ most considerably. Skinner's solution of this dualism is to reduce what seems to be two kinds of entities to one kind only. The physical world is all there is: "Watching a person behave...is like watching any physical or biological system" (Skinner, 1961, p 206). Though undercutting one dichotomy, that between "the real world" and its representation, Skinner preserves another one, namely that between the acting person and the world which he is acting on. In fact, he explicitly denies intentionality; "...seeing does not imply something seen" (Skinner, 1964, p. 89). As Kvale and Grennes (1975) point out, though Skinner is quite right in dismissing the introspectionist's "...considering a thing-like content as the essential aspect of perception", he makes the opposite mistake of only considering the behavioural aspects of perception.

The alternative solution lies in neither accepting the dualism, nor the reduction of one aspect to the other. The act and that which is acted upon, the experiencing and that which is experienced, the perceiving and that which is perceived cannot be separated, according to this view. Heidegger's (1962) term "being-in-the-world" has been used to express the view that man exists and acts directly in the world. Kvale and Grennes (1975) say:

> "Being-in-the-world is simply man's concrete behaviour in the world, his mode of relating to things and man. Behaviour is no mere indication of an inner state, man is behaviour to the world." (p. 42)

In spite of these fundamental differences between radical behaviourism and the phenomenological-existential tradition, they have—as was said earlier—their reflection of the dualism between "real" and "represented" world in common, and this position separates both from the most dynamic research approach within the field which constitutes the starting-point for the present discussion, i.e. the field of educational applications of cognitive psychology. This approach, the commonplace form of which is said to be antithetical to both Skinner and Sartre, is called cognitive science.

**Cognitive Science As A Basis for A Psychology of Internal Relations**

In models of the human mind that have been inspired by computer analogies, (and it is exactly this kind of model that the cognitive science approach stems from), it is absolutely fundamental to see the behaviour of a person as a function of his representational system and of the procedures operating on it (and thus doing the "reasoning"). It is therefore surprising, to say the least, when one of the most prominent figures in the field, Terry Winograd (1960) questions this basic idea underlying models of cognitive science.[1]

Having worked on programs that make the computer "understand" natural language, he was influenced by arguments against the dualism between the "real" world and its representation, the "inner" world, which had been put by the phenomenological-existentialistic tradition, and which he came across during a series of cross-disciplinary seminars at Berkeley about the nature of language and cognition. Among the (non-phenomenological) works discussed there were those of the biologist Marturana (1977) who, starting from an entirely different point, ends up with a view remarkably similar to the anti-dualist line of argument briefly developed above.

The error in describing cognition frequently takes the following form, Marturana says:

1. The scientist observes some recurrent pattern of interactions of an organism.
2. He or she devises some formal representation (for example, a set of generative rules or a "schema") that characterises the regularities.
3. The organism is assumed to "have" the representation in order to be able to exhibit the regularities.
4. (Depending on the particular sub-field.) The scientist looks for experiments that will demonstrate the presence of the representation, or designs a computer program using it to see whether the behaviour can be generated by the program. (Winograd, 1980, pp 226-227)

The error is committed by taking the third step. Though a phenomenon may appear, from the observer's point of view, to reflect representation, it can very well be understood as the activity of a system with no mechanism for a representation. Marturana points to a simple example:

"...we might watch a baby successfully getting milk from its mother's nipple and argue that it has a "representation" of the relevant anatomy, or the activity of feeding.

On the other hand we might note that there is a reflex that causes it to react to a touch on the cheek by turning its head in that direction, and another triggers sucking when something touches its mouth. From the viewpoint of effective behaviour it has a "correct representation", but it would be fruitless to look for neurophysiological mechanisms that correspond to reasoning that uses facts about breasts or milk". (Winograd, 1980, p. 227)

From this, Winograd continues the line of reasoning and extends it to include the way in which computers are used, and especially the reasons for programs breaking down. Why programs fail to achieve what they are supposed to is frequently due to the fact that they are not used in accordance with the underlying assumptions made by the programmer. Winograd argues for a shift of interest from the logic of cognitive processes to a logic of argument. "We need theories"—he says—"that can help in understanding the properties of dialogues in which a person tries to elucidate the background assumptions that may have led to a breakdown" (Winograd, 1960, p. 236).

This view certainly represents a change in focus from the representation of the outer world *in* the information processing system (man or machine) to the course of events that takes place *between* information processing systems (man and man or man and machine).

**Distinguishing between Conceptions of the World Around Us and the Categories Used to Describe Them**

Differences in underlying assumptions appear to be just one instance of the principle that for each phenomenon we can find, there seem to he a number of qualitatively different ways in which people experience, conceptualise, understand it. ("Conception" stands here for the more generally sounding term "man-world relation" used above. The possible distinctions between experience, conception, understanding will not be elaborated on here.) Studies which aim at mapping such variation can be seen to form a special domain of knowledge, and this discipline has been called phenomenography (Marton, 1981). The mapping is done in terms of sets of distinctive categories of description, where each category corresponds to a special conception of a certain phenomenon. Theman (1983) has argued, in a way which parallels Husserl's characterisation of the experience of something, that each conception can be seen as a correlation of a *noematic* and a *noetic* aspect (the former referring to the *what*, the latter to the *how* of the conception).

An important component of the phenomenological method is *the* imaginative *variation*, a play with possibilities. Its counterpart in a phenomenographic investigation (as in other kinds of empirical-phenomenological investigations) is the factual variation obtained.[2] The phenomenologist, however, transcends the level of imaginative variation, he aims at the invariant, he aims at essences.

There are (at least) two different interpretations of the term "essence". According to one interpretation, it is used in an inductive sense: that which a number of things have in common (e.g. the common denominator of varying experiences of the same object). The second alternative is to see the underlying structure of the factual or possible variation as being the invariant or essential aspect of the experience (or conception) of something.

As in phenomenography, the variation in itself is the object of investigation, it is only in the second sense that we can look for invariance in a set of varying conceptions. Once we have managed to reveal the underlying structure we can find, however,—as a rule—logical relations existing between conceptions of one phenomenon and conceptions of another phenomenon. The discovery of such relations is an important task for phenomenography, the mere listing of conceptions of one phenomenon after the other can hardly be found sufficient.

In empirical investigations, we often find variation in conceptions not only between, but also within individuals. Depending on the context, e.g. the question asked, they may exhibit qualitatively different conceptions of the very same phenomenon. The conceptions are thus frequently not characteristics of the individual, rather, they are characteristic of ways of functioning. Instead of seeing the different conceptions as representing different groups of individuals, the intraindividual variation found invites us to think in terms of an abstract system of description, a gigantic space of categories, in which the individuals move—more or less freely—back and forth.[3]

This implies, that we make a distinction between the "lived" or articulated conception, on the one hand, and the category of description used to signify it, on the other. This lends a certain degree of autonomy to the latter and reflects the fact that the way in which we describe how a phenomenon is conceptualised is by no means self-evident; it is not a question of simply "reading-off" what is in front of us. On the contrary; categories of description are important results, in phenomenography the most important ones.

By not seeing categories of descriptions as integral parts of the very act of experiencing or conceptualising, we make it possible to apply these categories to contents when conceptions are expressed not by persons but by man-made artifacts. The law system may, for instance, tell us a great deal about prevalent ideas in a certain society, and how we build new cities may very well reflect our way of stratifying the life-world.

**Embodied Conceptions**

"Lifting out" the categories of description from the context in which they have been discovered makes it possible for us to apply them to other contexts and to see structural similarities between different kinds of entities. We shall illustrate this by means of an example from Leif Lybeck's research into proportionality reasoning. He used interviews on simple problems of proportionality, such as "if a cube which has a volume of 4 $cm^3$ weighs 6 g, how much would a cube made of the same material weigh if its volume were 6 $cm^3$.

On the basis of thorough analysis of the interview data on several similar problems, Lybeck (1979) identified eight qualitatively different ways of dealing with the problem of proportionality, eight qualitatively different conceptions of the structure of the problem. Each one of these eight conceptions could be seen as having two different aspects, the function and the quantification aspect in Lybeck's terminology; we would perhaps say the noetic and the noematic aspect respectively. The former—the only one which is of interest here—refers to whether the student sets the different qualities or different variables (volume and mass in the example above) in relation to each other or whether his reasoning is based on the relation between specific values of the same variable. The difference is between saying (and thinking): "The weight is 1.5 times greater than the volume (6/4), it must then be g (6 x 1.5)" on the one hand, and saying (and thinking): "6 $cm^3$ is 1.5 times more than 4 $cm^3$ (6/4), it must then be g (1.5 x 6)" on the other. Subtle though the difference may seem (especially as I chose a case where the numbers are the same), it is of fundamental importance. All quantification is namely based on the first one of these two forms of thought, which represents a disregard of the difference in quality when these are set in relation to each other. A student of physics must necessarily think in this way not only in order to be able to think as the physicist does.

To reason in terms of different extensions of the same quality seems to be a far more natural way of thinking. Millions of young people in schools around the world have to take this step from one mode of thinking to another each day, without their teachers even being aware of the difficulty.

Indeed, this mostly unnoticed difference represents a gigantic step in the history of science. In a very informative study of the development of numbers from a historical perspective Thompson (1983) says that Creek mathematics was a theory of proportions and not of proportionality. Euclid expressed the view in book V that we should only compare homogeneous magnitudes by forming their quotient. We could compare, for instance, $W_1$ and $W_2$ (which are, let us say, weights) and $L_1$ and $L_2$ (which are, let us say, lengths) in the form

$W_1$ is to $W_2$ as $L_1$ is to $L_2$,

but it was impossible for the Greeks to form products

$W_1 L_2$ is equal to $W_2 L_1$

or quotients between inhomogeneous magnitudes:

$W_1$ is to $L_1$ as $W_2$ is to $L_2$.

John Wallis, in the 17th century, was the first mathematician to divide heterogeneous magnitudes. It was with him that the formula for defining velocity was born

$v = s/t$, where s is distance and t is time.

By analysing systems of mathematics during various historical periods Thompson was thus able to identify important differences in modes of thinking, just as Lybeck did by interviewing secondary school students of our time. These two kinds of independent findings prove each other's significance.

From the point of view of the present line of reasoning, it is essential to realise that a scientific system can be seen as a sedimentation of ways of thinking, or, put in more general terms, of "man-world relations". Traces of societies of the past as well as different physical, regulative and scientific ways of arranging our existence today in actual fact reflect the ways in which we think or have thought about the world around us. Society embodies conceptions. This idea—which is by no means an entirely new one for a sociologist of the Durkheimian school (see, Halbwachs, 1980)—certainly opens up a new field for psychological research. This kind of research is, furthermore, likely to provide teachers with the kind of intellectual tools which, I think, von Wright had in mind in the introductory quotation. By analysing our present society and its history we may become aware of that which is taken for granted, but which is by no means obvious to our students. It is this possible shift in focus of psychological research from individual to society (not so much as a determining force, but as a source of data about how the world is conceived by us) that motivates my choice of title for this chapter. But if we can regard arrangements as embodiments of conceptions, can we not reverse the principle and deliberately embody a conception which we want to develop in our students in some kind of arrangement? This is, of course, a question of inventing a technique which facilitates the development of a certain conceptualisation. The use of special research-based techniques in educational contexts has long been associated with an intructional process aiming at clearly defined *behavioural* objectives, but there are, of course, no reasons for claiming that there could never be any technical solutions to the problem of changing the student's ideas about some topic.[4]

By "technique" we mean a reasonably well-defined procedure, regardless of how technically advanced it is. Freudenthal (1978) gives an example of how a technically extremely simple technique is highly effective in inducing fundamental conceptual change.

> "In the first grade a few lessons on probability are given, without, of course, even mentioning the word. They play with a big die in front of the class and by chance and unintentionally the teacher asks questions like: Is it easier throwing an ace or a six? Is it easier for me throwing a six than for you? Unanimously and without any hesitation the pupils give the wrong answer. They know from Ludo how difficult it is throwing a six: and they also know that adults are more adroit than children. After these introductory exercises, each pupil is given the cardboard networks or a cube to be cut out, to be stuck together and to be painted with the dice symbols. It takes a lot of time—the poor lefthanded with righthanded scissor, the glue sucked up by the cardboard, the dice collapsing when painted—I bitterly regret the waste of time. Some children knew that opposite sides must add up to seven; others did not. All start playing again, noting down the results, and comparing them, and casually the teacher asks once more: Is it easier throwing an ace or a six? Is it easier for me throwing a six than for you. Unanimously the pupils give the correct answer—they even find the question ridiculous. The gain proves transferable, in other instances in the same and the next lesson the magic of the dice is gone—how they behave next Sunday when they play Ludo I cannot tell.

*Though I have observed other sharp discontinuties in learning processes this has been the sharpest, this complete reversion from a convinced 'yes' to a convinced 'no'* and even then in a period where no proper instruction took place. The actual and troublesome construction of the dice is more convincing an argument than the tongues of men and of angels could be." (pp. 185-186)

Of course, bearing in mind the rapid development in the educational use of computers one would expect that programs bringing about sudden insights (conscious or unconscious) of a similar kind as in Freudenthal's example will become available. To what extent this will turn out to be true depends entirely on whether the taken-for-granted conceptions that are embodied in the authorised system of knowledge can be revealed and then embodied again in the programs.

**Concluding Summary**

The way in which this paper deals with psychology in the future is probably not very obvious. We will thus very briefly summarise what has been said above in terms of an attempt to uncover the underlying logic of argument.

First of all, the topic of my paper is much more narrow than psychology in the future. Instead, we have tried to outline some ideas about the way cognitive psychology will contribute to educational praxis in the future. As a point of departure, I chose a quotation from Johnny von Wright in which he says that instead of generalisations, psychology should aim at supplying teachers with intellectual and practical tools. The obvious reason for my doing this is that I think that future contributions of cognitive psychology to educational praxis will have the form of intellectual and practical tools.

Having exemplified the limits of generalisations with a discussion about research into reading instructions, I have tried to reconstruct the path of conceptual development along which psychology must travel in order to be able to produce the kind of contributions von Wright was referring to. This strategy is based on the view that the future of a discipline is to a very great extent based on and foreshadowed by its past.

Reiser's discussion of four distinctively different possible modes of thinking in psychology offers a frame of reference here. The first level is a *pre-Aristotelian* way of reasoning, aptly described by Levy-Bruhl under the name of "primitive mentality". The *self* is not separated from the not-self, everything is everything else, as Reiser says. In the *Aristotelian* logic, which is the distinguishing feature of the next level we find sharp distinctions, explanations are given in terms of the inherent characteristics of each conceptually isolated entity. On the third level, which is the *Galilean* mode of thinking, explanations are given in terms of relations between entities. On the fourth level, which may be called *post-Galilean* orientation, we return to the idea of unity between man and world; in this case the entities are not only seen as being related to each other, they are also described in relation to each other.[5]

Reiser's article, published in 1939, was inspired by Kurt Lewin who had argued that psychology should proceed to a Galilean mode of reasoning. Reiser himself thought that we should go further than that and he pointed out the fourth level.

I have tried to show that we are now on the way towards a convergence on that level. In widely differing approaches, like phenomenological psychology, radical behaviourism and cognitive science, relational descriptions are applied. My point is, however, that again we must take another step. We must distinguish between the man world-relations (or conceptions) described and the categories used to describe them. This is necessary in order to reach what may be seen as an additional level of progression. Only when we have sectioned off the categories of description from what is described can we extract our categories from the sedimentation of the man-world relations, only then can we see all the taken-for-granted conceptions embodied in contemporary society as well as in traces of the past. And only then can we embody these taken-for-granted conceptions in techniques which have the function of bringing them out in our students.

And the categories of description pointing out what is taken for granted by us, but not by our students, are the intellectual tools, and the techniques that make our students share our understanding of the world are the practical ones.

## NOTES

1. I thank Seth Chaiklin of the University of Pittsburgh who drew my attention to Winograd's excellent article. On a more general level, Chaiklins most insightful questions about the relationship between contemporary cognitive psychology and the research approach developed by our group in Goteborg were indirectly a main source of inspiration to the outline of this chapter.
2. Here, I will only mention one of the several important aspects in which phenomenography differs from phenomenology. The former is substantively oriented while the latter has a methodological form. In consequence, Phenomenography "Points away from itself", it is always the phenomenography of something.
3. There are other similar movements. Feldman (1980) and Biggs and Collis (1982) have independently argued in favor of using Piagetian levels for describing the progression through learning cycles related to specific capabilities. In both works, a case was made for abandoning the ontological assumptions (about general cognitive structures) and for "lifting out" the categories employed to characterise the levels from their specific psychological context and using them as a system for description.
4. This point has, of course, been made in many other quarters. Personally, I benefited very much from a recent discussion I had with Graham Gibbs of Oxford Polytechnics.
5. In actual fact, Reiser deals with levels 3 and 4 as subcategories of a more general *non-Aristotelian* mode of thought.

## REFERENCES

1. Ashton-Warner, S. *Teacher*. New York: Simon and Schuster, 1963.
2. Biggs, J.B. and Collis, K.F. *Evaluating the quality of learning: the SOLO-taxonomy*. New York: Academic Press, 1982.
3. Edfeldt, A. *Lasprocessen*. Stockholm: Liber, 1982. (The process of reading.)
4. Feldman, D. *Beyond universals in cognitive development*. Norwood: Ablex, 1980.
5. Francis, M. *Learning to read*. London: George Allen and Unwin, 1982.

6. Freudenthal, H. *Weeding and sowing. Preface to a science of mathematical education.* Dordrecht: Reidel, 1978.
7. Giorgi, A. An application of phenomenological method in psychology In Giorgi, A., Fischer, C. and Murray, F. (Eds.), *Duquesne studies in phenomenological psychology II.* Pittsburgh: Duquesne University Press, 1975.
8. Greeno, J. G. Response to "The hegemoney of natural scientific conceptions of learning". *American Psychologist*, 1982, 37, 332-334.
9. Halbwachs, M. *The Collective Memory.* New York: Harper and Row, 1980. (Published originally in French, 1950.)
10. Heidegger, M. *Being and Time.* New York: Harper and Row, 1962.
11. Ihde, D. *Experimental phenomenology.* New York: Dutnam, 1977.
12. Kvale, S and Grennes, C. F. Skinner and Sartre: Towards a radical phenomenology of behaviour? In Giorgi, A., Fischer, C. and Murray, F. (Eds.), *Duquesne studies in phenomenological psychology II.* Pittsburgh: Duquesne University Press, 1975.
13. Leimar, U. *Lasning pa talets grund.* Lund: Gleerup, 1974. (Reading on the ground of speech.)
14. Lewin, K. *The Principles of Topological Psychology.* New York: McGraw-Hill, 1936.
15. Levy-Bruhl, L. *Primitive Mentality.* London: George Allen and Unwin, 1923.
16. Lundberg, I. *Lasprocessen i Ijuset av aktuell forskning.* Stockholm: Skoidverstyrelsen, 1982. (The process of reading in the light of recent research.)
17. Lybeck, L. Some real pictures from the class-room based research in physics teaching at Goteborg. *Reports from the Department of Education, University of Goteborg,* no 88, 1979.
18. Marton, F. Phenomenography—describing conceptions of the world around us. *Instructional Science,* 1981; 10, 177-200.
19. Marturana, H. R. Biology of language. In R. W. Riber (Ed.), *The Neuropsychology of Language.* New York: Plenum Press, 1977.
20. Merleau-Ponty, M. *The Structure of Behaviour.* London: Methuen, 1965. (Originally published in French, 1942.)
21. Reiser, 0. Aristotelian, Galilean and non-Aristotelian modes of thinking. *Psychological Review,* 1939, 46, 151-162.
22. Skinner, B.F. *Cumulative record.* London: Methuen, 1961.
23. Skinner, B.F. Behaviourism at fifty. In T.W. Wann (Ed.), *Behaviourism and Phenomenology—Contrasting Bases for Modern Psychology.* Chicago: Chicago University Press, 1964.
24. Saljo, R. *Learning and Understanding.* Goteborg: Acta Universitatis Gothoburgensis, 1982.
25. Theman, J. *Uppfattningar av politisk makt.* (Conceptions of political power.) (Unpublished manuscript)
26. Thompson, J. *Talbegreppets historia fran pedagogisk synpunkt.* (The history of the concept of number from a pedagogical point of view.) (Unpublished manuscript)
27. Winograd, T. What does it mean to understand language? *Cognitive Science,* 1980, 4, 209-241.
28. von Wright, J. Cognitive processes and educational research. In J. von Wright: Two papers on learning in school age children. *Reports from the Institute of Psychology,* University of Turk, no. 51, 1980.

7

# Towards a Neofunctionalist Theory of Psychology

The development of any branch of science is determined by two kinds of factors. First, one can speak of the internal dynamics of a discipline. New ideas and theoretical results, original methods and empirical results direct the next steps in the accumulation of knowledge. Second, scientific progress is regulated by *external conditions and pressures.* These forces are gradually growing in importance owing to the technical and financial prerequisites which are essential for the continuity of large scale research. They are, certainly, intimately related to the problems and demands arisen in various sectors of society. An attempt to predict the future progress of psychological science should consider both of these factors.

The closing session of the 19th International Congress of Psychology in London 1969 consisted of a symposium, Psychology in the Future (Proceedings, 1971). The papers of the three scientists covered their expectations of the period from the immediate future to the year 2000 and further until a very distant future.

The first speaker, professor Pribram, emphasised the significance of internal dynamics. The biological and physiological orientation on the one hand and the cognitive and information-processing approach on the other seemed to provide the most promising avenues for both theoretical and empirical research in the next decade, and their integration with each other was deemed essential for understanding symbolic activity. Professor Kay, again, assumed that the orientation of psychological science would be radically and beneficially influenced by some of the new nations and their cultural traditions. He listed social pressures which seemed to require new emphases of research: problems created by new technology, increased need to control human activity, increased internationalisation, population problems, etc. According to Pribram and Kay psychological knowledge would provide man of the future with necessary equipment for controlling both social change and his own activity.

The position of psychology in the very distant future was discussed by professor Toda. He examined the conditions for the survival of man and concluded that psychology must become the master science or mankind will perish. Psychological knowledge would be decisive for releasing international tensions and improving intergroup understanding.

Accordingly, recent ideas and promising findings guide the prognoses of tomorrow's psychology, while the assumptions concerning the more distant future are chiefly based on external factors, such as expected social changes, or on beliefs of the destiny of man and its determinants. The contributors ascribed to psychological science a central role among all the disciplines. Their view of the impact of an in- creasing level of knowledge was rather optimistic. Such an attitude was common among scientists about 10 to 15 years ago. For instance, Campbell and Converse (1972) maintained that "we live in an age when confidence that man can eventually control and shape the social forces about him has risen significantly". It also implied an increased ability to manipulate the physical and biological environment. The model of rational man comprised clear cognizance of some ultimate goal, intelligent control, and repeated checking on progress. What was neglected in these contributions, was the latent impact of social pressures on the theoretical orientations: on the ways of posing questions and constructing explanatory frameworks. The conventional research tradition was at the same time criticised by researchers who emphasised the social responsibility of psychologists (e.g., Korten and al., 1970).

**Traditional Schools and Actual Trends in Psychological Research**

The classical debates reflected inherent problems of any psychological explanation: the choice of the units of analysis, the nature of explanation, the relationship between subjective and objective data, etc. Yet, it would not be relevant to describe the present trends merely in terms of classical systems and theories. The theoretical significance of general explanatory systems has decreased or, at any rate, their function is different; the highly abstract conceptual distinctions which seemed to involve insurmountable obstacles between competing theories are less relevant. The traditional theories, when generalised to various sectors of psychological research, tended to use the same term to cover distinctly different referents. More accurate description and analysis of psychological phenomena is required for the present discussions. The new theoretical orientations reflect the specific content of data and the complexity of psychological phenomena. From the point of view of the present paper a brief discussion of the outgrowth of the functionalist way of thinking within psychology will be provided in the following:

The first attempt to create a genuine psychological theory at the end of the 19th century, which is usually called *structuralism*, looked for the unique qualities of mental processes, the elements which could be used for construing the structure of consciousness. It was thought that these elementary units can be discovered and classified by introspection. The modern structural theories also endeavour to interpret the internal processes and especially the mental representations which remain relatively independent of time and situation. The similarity with early structuralism is, however, very limited, because the basic structures are sought in general patterns and not on the basis of elementaristic analysis, as was stressed already by Gestalt psychologists. To account for the construction of cognitive structures or motivational systems we must appeal to the subject's acts; 'lived experience' is not sufficient. Construction of models for analysing actions represents a way of thinking which has manifested itself in biology, in linguistics and the study of communication, etc.

(Piaget, 1968). Structural orientation may be considered a general paradigm rather than a theory.

Structuralistic thinking is frequently, and for historical reasons, contrasted with *functionalism.* The early functionalist school (James, Dewey, etc.) was dissatisfied with the limitations of introspection and the isolation of the mind from organismic and environmental connections. It considered the function of the mind as mediating between organism and environment. The empirical study was directed to activity, the functions of activity, and its relationship to the conditions of consciousness. The concept of function remained, however, vague and vacillating, and functionalism cannot be considered a homogeneous school. It expanded the scope of psychological science noticeably but was to a considerable degree replaced by the more systematic and simplifying behavioural methodology, while the problems of meaning and intention were neglected.

The functional thinking in *cultural anthropology* and *sociology* represents a somewhat different tradition than the psychological functionalism. The general model implied that all major social patterns operate to maintain the integration of the larger social system. Persistence of any state of the system was explained by the adaptive or integrative effects of acts and patterns. The functionalist position stressed the existence of general patterns of adaptation and integration without bringing in historical and psychological factors. To avoid the *ex-post* and circular functional explanations it was necessary to specify the nature of explanation. The difficulty of defining adaptation and of finding general patterns encouraged the study of small systems under specified conditions. It turned out necessary to abandon the focus on adaptation and to consider the prerequisites of any state of the system. All functional systems can be described as sets of interdependent variables, the values of which determine whether a certain effect will be attained (Cancian, 1968). Such a 'liberalised' version of functionalist analysis no more differs from scientific analysis in general. Finally, no basic theoretical conflict remains between structuralism and functionalism. The difference is revealed from the point of departure for description (Levy, 1968) as well as from the explanatory concepts applied at the level of empirical theory. -

In psychological theory, the *'probabilistic functionalism'* constructed by Brunswik (1956) revived the original functionalist orientation but it also implied some novel aspects which have been important for later theoretical discussions. First, behavioural laws were not assumed to be universal or uniform. According to Brunswik, they are necessarily limited to probabilistic expressions because of the restrictions imposed by a great variety of interacting factors in behaviour. Second, the environmental factors relevant to the activity of an organism can be ordered along a 'proximal'-'distal' dimension. These factors range from the temporally/spatially most remote factors to physical objects and further to outer physical areas of an organism. The most proximal factors are intraorganismic functions and states. A similar arrangement is found on the response side. Both distal and proximal factors should be considered in explanations. Brunswik considered that the emphasis of psychological research should first be on the distal relationships.

Except for the systematic arrangement of environments, no theory of their relationships was included in Brunswik's model. The physical, ecological, social and cultural variables were treated separately from each other. Brunswik was more interested in the formal aspect of his model, and it has acted as a framework for the multilevel explanations of complex social, historical and psychological processes.

To sum up, the present functionalist orientation emphasizes

(1) activity and its meaning, and

(2) organism-environment relationships,

and the conditions of activity patterns in particular. Accordingly, the study of action and activity may be regarded as the continuation of the classical functionalism. It comprises subfields which vary in their complexity and which, therefore, are often treated apart from each other.

**Levels of Examining Human Activity**

The contemporary study of human activity comprises all the levels of description from simple psychomotor acts to global patterns of activity and to an individual life process as a whole. At the lowest level it is concerned with the elementary psychological units of activity and motor learning (single acts and episodes). The division of activity into units corresponding to the everyday interpretation of human action and interpersonal perception in daily life represents the second level of description. The highest level of description is concerned with the stages of life and with the stability and change of the life process.

Action-oriented theories may be characterised as partial reactions to the ambiguous and intricate inferences of the traditional psychodynamic theory on the one hand and to the classificatory trait psychology on the other. The theory of action does not postulate any fixed conceptual scheme of personality structure. Nor does it accept the quasi- explanation of activity in terms of highly abstract traits or dimensions of personality. Rather, it aims to examine the network of activities, their meanings and conditions, and may finally arrive at a hierarchic model of the structure of activity.

Three levels of describing activity, mentioned above, are distinguished for the present discussion. Although they differ greatly with regard to their explanatory power and conceptual framework, they comprise common points of view. Activity pattern(s), individual goals, and situations, environments or other conditions are examined together. In spite of the fact that they cannot be always assessed independently of each other, the interrelationships among these aspects are essential for interpretations. Another common characteristic may be found in the systemic approach to the 'levels' or 'layers' of situations, environments and other conditions which provides opportunities for an integrated outlook, instead of regarding these merely as heterogeneous 'background variables'.

## Theory of Action and Interaction

The recent theory of action which is mainly concerned with the lowest level of description has originated from two sources. First, the analysis of intentional action is essential for the psychology of *work* Intentional action consists of goals and subgoals, main decisions and subdecisions. The goals of a task to be executed are usually explicit. The subgoals and decisions which are necessary and/or available to a person must be assessed from the successive stages of performance. Checking on the results of an act constitutes a particular step of the process. A task consists of a number of acts. The description of the progress of per- the goals and intentions involved, as well as of the working conditions and antecedent stages provide material for the explanation of action. Interpretation may require the conceptualisation of the internal representations or scripts and processes which cannot be directly, observed. Evidence for the correctness of such interpretations is provided by, e.g., learning programmes designed according to the theoretical n odel (Hacker, 1977). The analysis of work activity is mainly restricted to actions in which both the goals and the constraints are evident and the performer represents a rational man.

Second, the structure of action has been studied in *social psychology*. Description of interpersonal interaction involves additional problems to be considered. Harre and Secord (1972) distinguished three types of social episodes: formal episodes, causal episodes, and enigmatic or unique episodes. One can also discriminate between intentional actions, overlearned routine actions, and externally guided actions. This classification partly overlaps with that by Harre' and Secord. A sharp distinction is sometimes made between intentional actions and mere behaviour, or between 'things people do and things which merely happen to them (Brenner, 7980). In the writer's opinion such distinctions are necessary in connection with specific research problems but they cannot be considered universal, because the same episode may represent an over- learned routine and externally guided behaviour, and be simultaneously a phase of an intentional action, Intentions and meanings can be described at different levels, depending on the purpose of analysis and the choice of units (Rommetweit, 1980).

So far the structure of action has been mostly examined in interaction situations, and research is still in its infancy (e.g., Forgas, 1979; Lamb, 1979; Hooff, 1982; Lyytinen and al., 1982). The observation and time sampling studies carried out in the thirties in the USA resulted in disappointments, mainly due to the non-theoretical and mechanical procedures adopted.

More recently, the analysis of interaction episodes has followed two lines. According to the first alternative an interaction episode is divided into acts and sequences of acts (e.g., Raush, 1965; Patterson and Cobb, 1972). The probabilities of a particular type of later act — for instance, of an aggressive, dominant or cooperative act — are predicted from the immediate antecedent acts or from consecutive antecedent acts. The *conditional probabilities* of various categories of antecedent acts are assessed to predict the following steps of interaction and examined separately for groups differing in their resources of choosing alternative reactions in different situations. The explanation of the regularities of (e.g., aggression, dominance or cooperation) episodes is accordingly provided in terms of the conditional probabilities and environmental settings. In addition to the conditional probabilities, other statistical techniques, e.g., the lag sequential analysis and the Markov chains, have been applied to interaction sequences (Lewis and Lee-Painter, 1974; Sackett, 1979). The aim of these studies is to elucidate universal patterns of action, characteristic to given types of task.

Statistical analysis of sequences is most suitable for the 'causal episodes'. According to Harre' and Secord (1972) causal analysis of sequences does not, regardless of the size of the unit, pertain to the most important aspects of social interaction. In connection with formal episodes, the explicit *social rules* are sufficient to account for the sequences of action. Some rules are universal in nearly all situations: they prevent aggression, guard against temptation or help with common difficulties. In other cases, information on the *roles* displayed by the interactants may be necessary for understanding the process. It should, however, be pointed out that rule-following may be similar to an activity sequence determined by purely external conditions. Identification of latent rules and roles is essential for understanding the enigmatic sequences. Yet, such functional interpretations are rather weak, unless independent evidence is available of what the goals actually are in each situation (Furnham and Argyle, 1981, p. 58).

Argyle and others (1981) have listed *other factors* which may be essential for analysing the laws and regularities of action. The contextual characteristics of situation, the skills and repertoires of the alternatives available at a fixed time guide and constrain activity. The relationships among various types of explanations are intricate. Harre and Secord (1972) and others have regarded the conflict between the "causal" model and the "rule-role" model as a controversy between general scientific paradigms. In the writer's opinion, different types of explanations are necessary for various kinds of action, and they do not exclude each other. They should rather be regarded as complementary interpretations.

This circumstance is perhaps most clearly indicated in the series of studies carried out by the team of von Cranach (von Cranach and al., 1980). The researchers studied children's play and its outcome. First, they examined the main patterns of dyadic conflicts in preschool children. Second, they indicated the roles and rules which were essential for these patterns and those which were irrelevant. The analysis has been restricted to intentional acts and to the hierarchies of structured action. The experiments showed that the network of routes toward a concrete goal, for instance, toward reaching a toy, was very simple in some interpersonal conflicts, while various alternative routes were available in others. The development of a successful act followed a consistent pattern, and also the process ending in a failure was rather uniform. In a sample of children playing under the presence of adults the social norms and rules were more important determiners of the sequence than the social roles. For instance, social justice (the right of retaining the toy) was more important than power. Von Cranach examined the development of interaction patterns and combined the qualitative description of episodes with a quantitative analysis of sequences.

### Socio-ecological Study of Activity Structure

Two large groups of problems are essential to the future progress of the "action-in-context" research: systemic description of situations and environments, and holistic approach to individual activity structures. Traditionally, environmental and ecological psychology have studied the cognitive, emotional and behavioural responses of people to the physical features of their environments (Argyle and al., 1981). What was regarded as "social environment" consisted of heterogeneous sets of factors with no theoretical linkages (Takala, 1983 b).

*Situations and environments.* Global models of the relationship between various environments have been first presented in cultural anthropology and cross-cultural psychology. McClelland-(1961) and Whiting and Whiting (1975) elaborated models to describe the processes by means of which the cultural and societal systems are mediated through micro-social environments to an individual and his or her activity. The linkages between the systems which are superimposed on each other are extremely complicated for any causal explanation. Nevertheless, systematic ordering of environmental inputs is necessary. While environmental and ecological psychology preferred to describe environments as objective factors, environments and situations are now construed according to their objective and subjective meanings (to both functional and experienced meanings).

In the present discussion of personality theory it is customary to maintain that the objective qualities of environments are not important as such. It is the subject's interpretation only which counts. Accordingly, the environmental systems are reduced to one level, to that of the recipient's understanding. Such a position means that the problems of multilevel mediation are forgotten or neglected. According to the socioecological point of view essential aspects of psychological explanation and understanding are curtailed, if "environment" is conceptualised as "the subjective meaning of environmental inputs". What is needed, is a comprehensive theory of the multilevel relationships. Multilevel interactional models, comprising the environmental systems, a temporal dimension, and the intervening concepts required for understanding the process of mediation, have turned out to be fruitful for the systemic treatment of complex environmental—situational data. The distinction between more and less "distal" or "proximal" aspects is not enough. Theoretical links of macro- and microsocial factors are fundamental for explanations (Takala, 1983 b). These problems have been thoroughly discussed by social psychologists who have made attempts to integrate sociological and psychological explanations (e.g., Andereeva et. al., 1978).

Such models have been constructed mainly for interpreting family interaction and child development. Previous investigations have shown that family environment is an important factor in the development of personality, but they can be criticised for failing to specify the processes through which the environment affects the child. The description of environments and situations proposed by Bronfenbrenner (1979) represents a new approach for integrating cultural, ecological, social, and interpersonal systems of description. Yet, it is not sufficient for the theoretical understanding of the relationships among various levels. It has been realised that more specific information is needed about how family environments differ from each other and what additional environmental aspects should be accounted for. A couple of recent examples may suffice. Parke and Lewis (1981) examined the conditions of child abuse and analysed both the levels of environment/situation and the mediators explaining the process of transmission at each level. Laosa (1981) maintained that advance in causal-inference methodology would make it possible to test theoretical models that involve complex networks of causation: The models should specify variables and relations out of the universe of psychological and social reality. The variables should be arranged according to their hypothetical causal linkages and advanced statistical techniques should be used (cf. also Makinen, 1982).

Social and historical data concerning the parents and the family comprise the most "distal" level of explanation. The second level consists of the parents' personality characteristics. The following level of environmental inputs includes both parental attitudes, expectations, or strategies, and such objective aspects of home environment which indicate the amount and the nature of stimulation provided to the child. The child's behaviour vis-a-vis parental actions is also included in the model. The prediction of children's intellectual achievements or gross problems in adjustment which were considered in the studies by Laosa and Lewis and Parker is relatively simple as compared with other aspects of personality formation in which the reciprocal relationships between the child and the parents should be specified. The oversimplified empirical studies cannot allow estimation of the correctness of any model at once. A long series of partly overlapping experiments is needed.

*Activity structure.* In addition to the systemic treatment of environment discussed above, *activities* should be described in a systematic way. The concept of behaviour setting was coined by Barker (1968) as an "ecobehavioural concept" to describe behaviour occurring under certain (specified) conditions. He listed a number of settings and demonstrated the changes in the number and the structure of settings caused by cultural, ecological, and interpersonal conditions.

The categories of behaviour settings proposed by Barker were not integrated into a description of activity structure. The everyday structure of activities has been studied in the sociological investigations concerning the *way of life* or life *style*. At the theoretical level it involves the consistent pattern of activities characteristic of people or groups living under certain conditions in the society (Rutkevich, 1975). Groups living under approximately similar material and physical conditions are assumed to display roughly similar patterns of activity. Most sociological studies have paid attention to the socioeconomic aspects of life style, e.g., to the use of public services or to consumption patterns (e.g., Zablocki and Kanter, 1976; Ryvkina, 1979). Detailed comparisons of life styles of people differing with regard to some social or individual characteristics are more relevant for psychological research (Willmott and Young, 1972; Yadov, 1979).

The study of activity in relation to personal goals and living conditions corresponds to the point of view developed in connection with life style, in spite of the fact that it has been connected with a different theoretical framework. Psychological analysis of way of life should emphasize the meaning of activity and individual activity structures (Takala. 1977, 1983 a, b). A person facing a particular situation is compelled to choose among alternatives, and the choices have an impact on his or her future activity. He tends to adopt routines to solve everyday problems in a more or less consistent manner.

A hierarchic view of activity is required. The use of time provides a general framework for understanding the structure of activity. Everyday activities are categorised into main spheres, and both their importance and their frequency (or total time consumption) are assessed. A rough typology of life styles can be constructed in terms of dominant activities (Zetterberg, 1977). The particular problem of the study determines the categories used in the detailed description. In a study of family interaction, for instance, a distinction was made between activities involving interaction between parent(s) and child(ren), between the parents, between active interaction and passive contacts between verbal and motor interaction, etc. Further, the interpersonal meanings of mutual contacts have been registered (e.g., Takala, 1979). The personal value orientations as components of the way of life have been thoroughly analysed by Yadov (1979).

Two alternatives can be expected to prove fruitful for the future research on life styles and activity structures. Description and comparison of activity structure formed under specified environmental conditions provides ample opportunities. Some recent Finnish studies have described and compared activity structures of internally homogeneous groups or particular extreme groups: the family life style of sporting children (Vanhalakka-Ruoho, 1981); the life style in families of children with chronic heart disease (Heiskanen et al., 1981); the life styles and family interaction of some occupational and ecological groups (Lerber et al., 1979; Takala et al., 1979). The other alternative consists of restricting to single aspects of activity, while varying the environmental conditions (at different levels of description).

## The Study of Complex Life Processes

Most longitudinal studies of life processes have considered personality development and change in terms of trait-life characteristics. They can be completed with other types of strategy which stress a more complex description of activities and conditions.

First, they include life styles as persistent *routines.* The network of accumulated habits forms the framework for an individual's activity programme, and they tend to become more central, when the life conditions remain unchanged and when he or she has reached a later stage of life span. The significance of daily routines was traditionally neglected in the psychology of personality because they were considered a peripheral and not a personally motivated sector of activity. Nevertheless, the daily routines cover a great portion of activities. They also determine the freedom of an individual to make genuine choices in a definite life situation. The person himself remains unaware of many important decisions which are being made continuously as products of everyday activity.

The second type of data which are important for the study of life process consists of *critical changes* in a person's total programme of activity. Such changes may originate from shifts of life conditions, as for instance, in connection with the acquisition of economic independence, retirement, or with the change of family structure. The effect of critical life events is usually interpreted in terms of individual coping responses in clinical psychology. The interpretation comprises information on the objective changes in life conditions, the subjective meanings of these changes, their impact on individual life goals and beliefs during the crisis and in the subsequent coping stage, as well as on the changes of activity structures. Some objective life events may not cause any significant change in life goals or activity structures, while other events disrupt the usual patterns and necessitate the person to reconsider the meaning of previous goals and the importance of activities (e.g., Heiskanen et al., 1981).

Regardless of whether the study of life process is based on stable conditions or critical changes, simultaneous examination of activity structures, life situations and conditions, and personal goals is important.

One of the most important studies of the life process in which both macro- and microsocial aspects were considered has been that carried out by Elder (1974) in connection with the longitudinal Oakland project. He examined the historical change caused by the Great Depression in 1930 and compared the life experience and personality of adolescents who grew up in economically deprived and non-deprived families. Economic loss produced changes in the life patterns, family relationships, and sharing of domestic work and responsibility, and caused social strains. Owing to the unique nature of the original data and careful follow-up procedures Elder was able to draw conclusions on the impact of critical life changes on family process and personality development until adulthood.

**Conclusions**

The predictions presented in the paper about the orientation of psychological theory and research in the 1990's are based on the writer's interpretation of the present trends and the internal dynamics of science. The orientation is also associated with external factors: with the emphasis on the "quality of life" and corresponding social reforms.

The psychology of action represents a renewed attempt of solving traditional problems. In addition, it pays attention to such aspects of everyday activity and conditions which have been largely neglected in the theory of personality. It suggests an accurate and rich description of action rather than new abstract distinctions which may lose contact with psychological reality. The orientation may be called neofunctionalism providing no general theory is implies by this label. The approach consists of

1. multilevel examination of activities and environments/situations
2. consideration of activities (activity structures), personal goals/intentions and environments in relation to each other
3. recognition of the heterogeneous nature of explanations required for the interpretation of complex phenomena involved.

In conclusion, we may return to the old problem of structural vs. functional explanations. In psychological explanations the structures are inseparable from action, as was stressed already by Kaila (1934) in his theory of personality. According to the terminology of Piaget (1968) the function chiefly credited for the formation of structures is assimilation. Assimilation is a process whereby a function reproduces its own activity and produces first a schema, and the generalised schemata are called structures. The functional explanations tended to criticize the structural concepts and avoided them as far as possible. The attempts ended with failures. What remains, is the emphasis on action, and especially on intentional activity, and some reluctance in the construction of model in the abstract.

## REFERENCES


1. Andreeva, G., Bogomolova, N. N. and Petrovskaia, L. A. *Sotsial'naia psihologiia na zapade.* Moscow: Moscow University Press, 1978.
2. Argyle, M., Furnham, A. and Graham, J. *Social Situations.* Cambridge: Cambridge University Press, 1981.
3. Barker, R. G. *Ecological Psychology.* Stanford: Stanford University Press, 1968.
4. Brenner, M. *The Structure of action: Introduction.* In M. Brenner (Ed.), The structure of action. Oxford: Blackwell, 1980.
5. Bronfenbrenner, U. *The Ecology of Human Development.* Cambridge, Mass.: Harvard University Press, 1979.
6. Brunswik, F. Perception and the representative design of psychological experiments. Berkeley: University of California Press, 1956.
7. Campbell, A. and Converse, P. E. Social change and human change. In A. Campbell and P. E. Converse (Eds.), *The human meaning of social change.* New York: Russell Foundation, 1972.
8. Cancian, F. M. Varieties of functional analysis. In D. L. Sills (Ed.), *International Encyclopedia of the Social Science;* vol. 6. New York: Macmillan and Free Press, 1968.
9. von Cranach, M., Kalbermatten, U., Indermuhle, K. and Gugler, B. Zielgerichtetes Handeln. Bern, Huber, 1980.
10. Elder, G. *Children of the Great Depression.* Chicago: University of Chicago Press, 1974.
11. Forgas, J.P. *Social Episodes: the Study of Interaction Routines.* New York: Academic Press, 1979.
12. Furnham, A. and Argyle, M. (Eds.), *The Psychology of Social Situations.* Oxford: Pergamon Press, 1981.
13. Hacker, W. *Allgemeine Arbeits- und Ingenieurpsychologie.* Berlin: VEB Deutscher Verlag der Wissenschaften, 1977.
14. Harre, R. and Secord, P. F. *The Explanation of Social Behaviour.* Oxford: Blackwell, 1972.
15. Heiskanen, M., Koskinen, P.-L., Myllyla, M., Ramstedt-Lipponen, S., Ratilainen, P. and Taipale, L. *Sydanvikainen Lapsi ja hanen perheensa.* (Child with heart disease and his/her family, in Finnish). M. Soc. Sc. Thesis. Department of Psychology, University of Jyvaskyla, 1981.
16. van Hooff, 3. Categories and sequences of behaviour: methods of description and analysis. In K. Scherer and P. Ekman (Eds.), *Handbook of Methods in Nonverbal Behaviour Research.* Cambridge: Cambridge University Press, 1982.
17. Kaila, F. *Persoonallisuus.* (Personality, in Finnish). Helsinki: Otava, 1934.
18. Korten, F. F., Cook, S. W. and Lacey, J.I. (Eds.), *Psychology and the Problems of Society.* Washington: American Psychological Association, 1970.

19. Lamb, M. Issues in the study of social interaction: An introduction. In M. Lamb, S. Suomi and G. Stephenson (Eds.), *Social Interaction Analysis.* Madison: University of Wisconsin Press, 1979.

20. Laosa, L. M. Families as facilitators of children's intellectual development at three years of age: a causal analysis. Princeton: Educational Testing Service, 1981. (To be published in L. M. Laosa and I. Sigel (Eds.), *Families as learning environments for children.* New York: Plenum).

21. Lerber, E.-L., Malkavaara, E., Paatola, S. and Takala, M. Perheen elamantapa toimintojen ja ajanktiytdn avulla kuvattuna: Vertailua maanviljelija, •myyja- ja teollisuustydntekija Perheiden kesken. (Family's life style, described in terms of activities and time consumption: comparison between farmers, salesmen and industrial workers, in Finnish). *Reports from the Department of Psychology, University of Jyvaskyla,* 216, 1979.

22. Lewis, M. and Lee-Painter, S. An interactional approach to the mother-infant dyad. In M. Lamb and L. Rosenblum (Eds.), *Friendship and Peer Relations.* New York: Wiley, 1974.

23. Levy, M.J., jr. Structural functional analysis. In D. L. Sills (Ed.), *International Encyclopedia of the Social Science*; vol. 6. New York: Macmillan and Free Press, 1968.

24. Lyytinen, p., Rasku-Puttonen, H. and Takala, M. Vuorovaiku-tuksen en tasoisia anal ysoint i menetelmia. (Techniques for different levels of interaction analysis, in Finnish.) *Reports from the Department of Psychology, University of Jyavaskyla,* 250, 1982.

25. McClelland, D.C., *The Achieving Society.* Princeton: van Nostrand, 1961.

26. Makinen, R., Teachers' work, well-being and health. *Jyvaskyla Studies in Education, Psychology and Social Research,* 46, 1982.

27. Parke, R.D. and Lewis, N.G., The family in context: a multilevel interactional analysis of child abuse. In R.W. Henderson (Ed.), *Parent-child interaction.* New York, Academic Press, 1981.

28. Patterson, G.R. and Cobb, J.A., Stimulus control for classes of noxious behaviours. In J.F. Knutson (Ed.), *The Control of Aggression.* Chicago, Aldine, 1972.

29. Piaget, J., *Le structuralisme.* Paris, Presses universitaires de France, 1968.

30. *Proceedings, XIX International Congress of Psychology.* London, British Psychological Society, 1971.

31. Raush, H., Interaction sequences. *Journal of Personality and Social Psychology,* 1965, 2, 485-499.

32. Rommetweit, R., On 'meanings' of acts and what is meant and made known by what is said in a pluralistic social world. In M. Brenner (Ed.), *The Structure of Action.* Oxford, Blackwell, 1980.

33. Rutkevich, M.N., Sotsialistichesky obraz zhizni i ego razvitie. *Voprosy Filosofii,* 1975, 11, 46-58.

34. Ryvkina, R.V. *Obraz zhizni sel'skogo naseleniia.* Novosikirsk: Nauka, 1979.

35. Sackett, G., The lag sequential analysis of contingency and cyclicity in behavioural interaction research. In J. Osofsky (Ed.), *Handbook of Infant Development.* New York: Wiley, 1979.

36. Takala, M., Elamantapa ja persoonallisuus. (Way of life and personality, in Finnish). *Psykologia,* 1977, 12, 26-38.

37. Takala, M., Alanen, L., Luolaja, J. and Polkki, P. Perheen elamantapa, Vanhempien kasvatustietoisuus ja lasten sosiaalinen kehitys. (Family's way of life, parental awareness of parenthood and children's social development, in Finnish). *Reports from the Department of Psychology, University of Jyvaskyla,* 219, 1979.

38. Takala, M., Family way of life and interaction patterns. Manuscript, 1983 (a). (To be published in W. Doise and A. Palmonari (Eds.), *Social interaction.* Cambridge: Cambridge University Press).

39. Takala, M., A socioecological approach to personality and the problem of situations. Manuscript 1983 (b). (To be published in H. Bonarius, G. van Heck and N., Smid (Eds.), *Personality psychology in Europe: theoretical and empirical developments.* Hillsdale: Erlbaum).

40. Vanhalakka-Ruoho, M., Perhe ja urheileva lapsi. (Family and the sporting child, in Finnish). *Reports from the Department of Psychology, University of Tampere*, 123, 1981.

41. Whiting, B. and Whiting, J.W.M., *Children of six cultures.* Cambridge, Mass.: Harvard University Press, 1975.

42. Willmott, P. and Young, M., *The Symmetrical Family.* Harmondsworth, Penguin, 1972.

43. Yadov, V. (Ed.), *Samoregulatsiia i prognosirovanie sotsial'nogo povedenii lichnmosti.* Leningrad, Nauka, 1979.

44. Zablocki, B.D. and Kanter, R.M., The differentiation of life-styles. *Annual Review of Sociology*, 1976, 2, 269-298.

45. Zetterberg, H.L. *Arbete, livstil och motivation.* Stockholm, SAF, 1977.

# 8

# Brunswikian Psychology for the 1990's

In his classic book *The Conceptual Framework of Psychology,* Brunswik (1952) tried not only to describe the history of psychology up till about 1950, but also to dissect the general trends of development in psychology, trends which would make it possible to predict where psychology was going.

In his analysis, Brunswik found a general trend of development from an "encapsulated psychology" towards a more "functionalistic psychology'. By encapsulated psychology, Brunswik meant a psychology which focussed exclusively upon the organism, i.e., a psychology concerned only with the nature of the "psychological machinery" without reference to the environment. According to Brunswik, such a psychology missed the point, that psychological mechanisms have a specific use to the organism and must be studied in use. Psychological mechanisms have evolved to play a part in the organism's adaptation to the environment and they exist because they have increased the organism's chances of survival. They can only be understood in that context. Psychology, therefore, must turn functional; it must be concerned with the organism's ability to reach important goals in its ordinary environment. Consequently, the primary datum for psychological analysis should be achievement of goals under natural circumstances and further analysis should be directed at finding the strategies and tactics employed by the organism to reach its level of achievement. In short, a proper psychology should be a science of organism-environment relations, rather than a science of the organism (Brunswik, 1956), and its principal aim should be to study how the organism comes to terms with its environment.

From his analysis of the history of psychology, Brunswik concluded that it was moving towards such a functionalistic analysis, with his own psychology of perception as one example of where psychology was headed. It is now 31 years since *The Conceptual Framework of Psychology* was published and we should therefore be in a position to ascertain whether Brunswik was correct in his prediction about where psychology was going.

Generally speaking, it is clear that psychology *has* become increasingly functional since the 1950's (see, e.g., Beilin, 1982 for a general discussion of "neofunctionalism" in modern cognitive and developmental psychology). Thus, one might be tempted to conclude that Brunswik was correct in his prediction. However, even though psychology has become more functional, it has not become functional in exactly the sense advocated by Brunswik.

In the remainder of this chapter, 1 will discuss two important aspects of Brunswik's brand of functionalism which have not become a general part of present day psychology and argue that incorporating these principles would constitute an important task for psychology in the 1990's. However, we start with a discussion of some of the general characteristics of Brunswik's functionalism.

**General Characteristics of Brunswikian Functional Psychology**

Brunswik's thinking about psychology grew out of his analysis of visual perception. As for most perceptual theory, the fundamental point of departure for Brunswik's theory was the distinction between distal and proximal stimulation, i.e., the distinction between the objects in the real world (the distal stimuli) and the information available to the organism about these objects (the proximal stimuli). Adopting a traditional cue theory, Brunswik concluded that the relation between proximal and distal stimuli was at best a probabilistic one (hence his theory was called "probabilistic functionalism"). The process of perception was therefore seen as a process involving inference, where imperfect proximal data are used to draw conclusions about the state of the distal object. What saves these inferences is that the proximal stimulation is highly redundant, and contains a number of intersubstitutable cues. Thus, even though the relation between each cue and the distal object may be imperfect, stimulation under normal circumstances is so rich in cues that perceptual inferences are normally highly accurate, as Brunswik (1944) was able to show in his classic study of perceptual achievement under natural circumstances. This finding was, of course, in sharp contrast to laboratory results on perception which did not provide such rich stimulation, and where perceptual achievement was often found to be quite low, as well as influenced by various irrelevant factors, such as set and motives (see, e.g., Bruner and Postman, 1949).

According to Brunswik, the fundamental task for a psychology of perception is to ascertain the level of perceptual achievement and to account for this achievement in terms of the proximal cues. To do so, the psychologist needs to know two things: the relations between the proximal cues and the distal variable, i.e., the *ecological validity* of the cues, and the relations between the cues and the perceptual response, i.e., the *utilisation of the cues.* Knowing the validity of the cues is important because it gives information about the upper limit of achievement. If the cues do not have perfect validity, perceptual achievement cannot be perfect: it can only be as good as the validity of the cues allows. Imperfect achievement, therefore, does not necessarily mean that the process of perception functions suboptimally. It may simply mean that the perceiver has not had access to information which allows perfect achievement. To analyse perception, therefore, (and this is of course true of analysis of all kinds of cognitive functions, not only of perception) one needs to pay as much attention to the perceptual task as to the perceptual process.

A Brunswikian psychology of perception, and cognition generally, thus requires a double focus with equal attention to the task and the psychological process.

Analyses of achievement would, of course, be completely pointless if undertaken under conditions that were not representative of the organism's ordinary environment. If one were interested in the perception of size, one would, of course, not investigate only how the subjects were able to perceive the height of a one meter stick. Instead, one would present a sample of sticks varying in length so as to be representative of the lengths usually seen by the subject. If one is interested in the perception of people, one should not have one's subjects judge only one stimulus person. This principle is generally recognised in studies of the perception of physical quantities; there does not seem to be any studies of size perception using only one object. There is, however, certainly no dearth of person perception studies using a single stimulus person (see, for example, Nisbett and Wilson, 1977, where 118 subjects rated a single person). Since no one person is likely to be representative of all persons, such studies do not allow any inferences about people's ability to perceive other people, or about the process of person perception generally. The same unfortunate tendency of neglecting to sample tasks representatively is seen in other areas of cognition. This is especially true in the area of judgment and decision making where far reaching conclusions about people's ability to make judgments and decisions are made on the basis of a very narrow range of tasks (see Nisbett and Ross, 1980, for examples). Indeed, the situation in the field of judgment and decision making now seems to close to that in the field of perception at the height of "new look in perception" in the middle fifties when accurate perceiving seemed next to impossible, at least if one were to believe the accounts emerging from psychological research. Considerable effort is now being spent to developing models which will explain why man is such a bad decision maker, models which also lead to recommendations as to how decision making should be improved. Yet, we do not really know whether man is a bad decision maker because we have not studied decision making under representative conditions.

The need to study a representative set of cases arises not only because one needs to know achievement for the kinds of distal objects that the organism has learned to "come to terms with", but also because one needs to measure achievement under conditions where the organism has access to the kind of proximal stimulation it customarily uses. That is, one should measure achievement under the conditions of rich redundant proximal stimulation which prevail in natural life, rather than under the impoverished conditions of the psychological laboratory, where an object may be represented by a line drawing, or a person by one of two sentences on a piece of paper. What could we possibly conclude about, say depth Perception, from experiments using line drawings rather than moving objects for which shape, colour and light distributions change as they move providing rich redundant information? And what could we conclude about how our subjects perceive people whom they may have known for years from experiments which only provide information in the form of a sentence on a piece of paper. Clearly, most psychological experiments provide information of very low validity. Consequently, they are not likely to lead to any trustworthy estimate of perceptual achievement under normal circumstances. This is not without consequence, for such estimates of achievement set the stage for subsequent theory development, leading to attempts to explain why perception is bad, rather than to attempts to explain why it works well.

The use of unrepresentative experimental conditions is often defended on the ground that the primary interest is to study psychological process, rather than achievement. However, it does not take much reflection to realise that the choice of experimental conditions has important effects on our understanding of the nature of psychological processes, and not only upon our conception of achievement. The psychology of learning and memory provides some clear examples of this.

For the first six decades of this century, associationism was the dominant theory of learning and memory, seemingly verified in thousands of experiments. These experiments hardly constituted any real challenge to the theory, however. If we look at the structure of the tasks used in learning and memory experiments, we can see why this is the case.

Take the paired associates task, for example, which in one form or another was the dominant kind of task in learning and memory experiments during the first half of this century. Lists of paired associates actually *consist* of a set of associations between stimulus and response items. Consequently, learning such a list cannot be anything but the acquisition of a set of associations. Furthermore, the procedure in these experiments resulted in data which consist of associations between stimuli and responses. No wonder that the concept of association was found useful to explain these results of these experiments, and that there was no room for alternative conceptions. However, this explanation is clearly circular. New conceptions of learning and memory did not emerge until new tasks were being introduced, e.g., when lists with words belonging to different categories were introduced, memory was suddenly found to be categorical and hierarchically organised. That theory of memory was, however, only a recollection of the new kind of memory task, and the results obtained with these tasks do not constitute a critical test of associationistic theory. Clearly, a very different conception of memory would have emerged if memory researchers had started with a survey of memory performance under more representative conditions. It should at least have saved tens of thousands of subjects the drudgery of learning lists of CVC's. Such a survey of "natural memory" still remains to be done (see Neisser, 1982) condemning subjects in psychological experiments to continue to learn lists for many years to come. This brief discussion must suffice to illustrate the importance of two of the basic principles of Brunswikian functionalism:

1. Psychological processes must be studied in context to provide basic data on achievement.
2. In psychological research, equal attention should be given to the environment (the cognitive task) and to the psychological process proper.

We now turn to a discussion of each of these principles.

### Psychological Processes Should be Studied in Context to Provide Data on Achievement

The general principle that psychological processes should be studied in context has two aspects. The first is that psychological processes should be studied under representative conditions. We have already discussed that aspect above, and we will therefore concentrate on the second principle, the so called *Behaviour-Research Isomorphy Principle* (BRI-principle).

*The BRI-principle.* This principle (Brunswik, 1952) asserts that research should focus where behaviour is focussed. This means that researchers should be concerned with what organisms do under ordinary circumstances. They should not construct experimental tasks that differ in fundamental aspects from the tasks of concern to the organism under natural circumstances. Most important, researchers should not attempt to build a general psychology upon such tasks. Thus, even though normative decision theory may require people to make judgments of probability, it makes little sense for a psychologist interested in decision making to study how people estimate probabilities, if the estimation of probabilities is not part of decision making as it ordinarily occurs. At the present time, we do not know whether people estimate probabilities when making decisions. Yet, important conclusions about people's ability to make rational decisions are made on the basis of experiments that require estimation of probabilities (e.g., Kahneman, Slovic and Tversky, 1982).

To take another example, if we are interested in memory, the BRI principle requires that we start our research by surveying how people actually use past information in solving whatever kinds of tasks they encounter in their everyday lives. We should then try to assess whether they do so successfully, or unsuccessfully, i.e., we should assess their achievement. We should, of course, also note whether or not they use various memory aids, and how these aids are used. Such aids, and how they are used, will presumably reflect long experience with memory and failures, and they may thus tell us something important about memory. At the very least, they will provide a rich source of hypotheses about the nature of memory.

Data from such a survey would, first of all, give us an estimate of memory achievement, and we would thus know whether a theory of memory should explain a predominantly good performance or a predominantly bad performance. Indeed, surveys of this kind might very well indicate that one should not develop separate theories of memory at all. First, it may very well be that the use of past information takes place in so many and varied contexts, that a general theory is just not viable. Second, it may be, that pure memory performances are not observed, but that the use of memory always is part of some other activity. Furthermore, it may be heavily dependent upon that activity, that a separate theory of memory cannot be used to predict any interesting form of behaviour.

As we all know, this is not at all how research on memory has been conducted, and as a consequence, we do not know whether memory is good or bad. Nor do we know whether there is one or many forms of memory. Indeed, we do not know whether it is possible to develop a general theory of memory performance at all. However, the problems with the psychological research on memory are now receiving attention, and the research is being criticised by Neisser (1982) on exactly the grounds discussed in this section. The book edited by Neisser also presents a number of studies of memory under natural circumstances. The results of these studies indicate that laboratory based memory theory is of little use in trying to understand memory performance under natural conditions (Neisser, 1982). Yet, these studies suggest that, at least in the field of memory research, things are moving in the direction predicted by Brunswik.

Although these remarks concerned research on memory, they were not made just to criticise memory research. Memory research was chosen because it illustrates the consequences of not following the BRI-principle so clearly, and because it highlights a general problem of modern psychology: that the research problems are derived from old faculty psychology rather than from an empirical analysis of what people actually do. This points to one of the most urgent problems for psychology in the 1990's: to survey and classify the tasks that people actually perform in their everyday lives. Without such a survey, we are likely to remain in the firm grip of the dead hand of tradition, which stems from old faculty psychology. There is much to be gained from such an analysis, because it would, in one stroke, put an end to tedious and embarrasing discussions about the relevance of psychological research.

### Equal Attention of the Task and the Organism

We have already discussed the reasons why we need to pay attention to the nature of the tasks facing the organism: The first reason is that the nature of the tasks determines the level of achievement for that task, and we need to know this limit to evaluate the organism's actual level of performance. The second is that the nature of the task determines what we will be able to learn about the psychological processes from the experiment. If we study judgment by means of linear additive tasks (such as the MMPI) we will find that the judgment process follows a linear additive model, but if we use configural judgment tasks, the judgment process will be configural as well (Brehmer, 1969).

As a necessary first step in psychological studies, therefore, we need a thorough analysis of the nature of tasks facing organisms in the ordinary environment. Brunswik underlined the importance of studying the environment as a prolegomenon to psychology. He thought that this study could be carried out by means of physical measurement *alone* without reference to the organism, recommending "a psychology without a subject" (Brunswik, 1956).

Today, it seems that Brunswik overestimated the powers of physical measurement. Physical measurement will just give information about those aspects of the environment that we choose to measure, and the, measurements we take will reflect our theory about the nature of the psychological processes that we study. This is clearly demonstrated by a comparison between the stimulus descriptions used by Brunswik and those sought by perception psychologists following the Gibsonian tradition. Thus, those working in the Brunswikian tradition end up with a set of cues each of which is imperfectly related to the distal object. These cues have then to be combined into an estimate of the distal state by means of some model, e.g., multiple regression. Gibsonian psychologists, on the other hand, look for so called "higher order variables" which are combinations of the simple variables analysed by the Brunswikians. These "higher order variables" are said to specify the distal objects completely, doing away with the need for probabilism and inference in perception (Gibson, 1979). Clearly, the task descriptions resulting from analyses by Brunswikians and Gibsonians will differ, and they will differ because Brunswikians and Gibsonians have different conceptions of the nature of perception. This is brought home very clearly by the new concept of "affordances" suggested by Gibson (1979).

The concept of "affordance" refers to the fact that the ecology of, say, places to sit is very different for a short person and a tall person, and very different for a human and a cat. When the organism wants to sit, it has to react to that aspect of the stimulations that gives information about whether a place is "sitable" or not, and this information will be very different for a cat and a human. These are clearly the important aspects of stimulation; an organism needs to know where it can sit and walk, where it can pass, and where it has to turn, and it needs to pick up the information that allows it do whatever it intends. This information will obviously be very different for different organisms. Indeed, the description of the perceptual task will have meaning only in relation to a given species, thus it makes no sense to think of a "psychology without a subject". The description of the environment and the tasks facing the organism must be made with reference to the organism who has to cope with these tasks. Consequently, the study of the environment cannot be a prolegomenon to the study of psychology as Brunswik (1956) thought. The description of the environment has to be made for a given organism, and it will be as accurate as our understanding of the organism allows it to be. That does not make an understanding of the nature of the task any less important; the behaviour of the organism still has to be understood in relation to the nature of the task it is trying to solve. This, then, just gives added emphasis to Brunswik's dictum that equal attention must be paid to the organism and the environment, for just paying attention to the one of these terms of the organism-environment relation will not suffice. However, it will not be possible to study only the relation between the task and the organism, the reverse relation will have to be studied as well.

This is brought home very clearly in Piagetian psychology. From a Brunswikian point of view, one of the virtues of Piagetian psychology is its thorough task analysis in terms of levels of logic required for their solution. An important point emerging from Piaget's analyses is that a given task must be seen in different ways, depending on the cognitive level of the subject working on the task. Thus, the typical conservation task (Piaget, 1952) is very different for a four year old who can only take one dimension into account at a time, e.g., the height of the liquid in the beaker, than it is for an eight year old who is able to consider both height and width of the liquid at the same time. We can understand the difference in performance between the four and eight year old children only if we realise that the tasks facing them are very different from a psychological point of view.

Piagetian research is just one of the indications that the importance of task analyses is beginning to be realised more and more in modern cognitive psychology. For example, Newell and Simon (1972) in their monumental monograph on human problem solving advocate task analysis along Brunwikian lines as a necessary first step in research on cognition. Hopefully, others will follow their lead.

**Conclusions**

According to Brunswik, psychology should be concerned with organism- environment relations, rather than with the organism. Therefore, it should move from its initial encapsulated state towards a more functional analysis of behaviour. This would involve an assessment of the organism's achievement under natural conditions, and then proceed to explain achievement in terms of the validity of the information available to the organism, and how this information was used. This requires that achievement be assessed under representative conditions, and that not only the strategies and tactics employed by the organism be studied. The task facing the organism also has to be studied.

It is clear that, generally speaking, psychology has not become functionalistic in the sense predicted by Brunswik. We still do not know what achievement is under natural conditions for very many important psychological activities. Instead, psychologists form opinions about achievement from highly nonrepresentative experiments. This leads to extravagant statements about, for example, the capacities of people as decision makers, that are without foundation (although they may, of course, be true).

Furthermore, it is clear that we do not find thorough analyses of the nature of the tasks employed in psychological experiments, and that this leads to false pictures of the nature of the psychological processes being studied. For example, the widespread belief that human judgment follows a linear additive model is probably due to that the tasks employed in studies of judgment have usually been linear and additive, but this has not been recognised because the tasks have not been analysed (Brehmer, 1969).

There are, however, hopeful signs. Thus, there is general concern about the lack of ecological validity of psychological findings (e.g., Bronfenbrenner, 1977; Neisser, 1976, 1982), and it is being realised that this lack of validity sterns from a neglect of what amounts to the Brunswikian principles of representativeness and the Behaviour-Research Isomorphy. In addition, there is growing concern with task analysis in cognitive psychology. Thus, there seems to be light at the end of the tunnel. The 1990's may very well be the time for Brunswik's ideas to come.

## REFERENCES

1. Beilin, H. The new functionalism and Piaget's program. In E. Kofsky Scholnick (Ed.), *New Trends in conceptual representation: Challenges to Piaget's theory?* Hillsdale, N. J.: Lawrence Earlbaum, 1983.
2. Brehmer, B. Cognitive dependence on additive and configural cue-criterion relations. *American Journal of Psychology,* 1969, 82, 490-482.
3. Bronfenbrenner, U. Toward an experimental ecology of human development. *American Psychologist,* 1977, 32, 513-531.
4. Bruner, J.S. and Postman, L. On the exception of incongruity: A paradigm. *Journal of Personality* 1949, 18, 206-223.
5. Brunswik, E. Distal focussing of perception: Size-constancy in a representative sample of situations. *Psychological Monographs,* 1944. Whole No. 254.

6. Brunswik, E. *Conceptual Framework of Psychology.* Chicago: University of Chicago Press, 1952.
7. Brunswik, E. *Perception and the Representative Design of Psychological Experiments.* Berkeley, California: University of California Press, 1956.
8. Brunswik, E. Scope and aspects of the cognitive problem. In H. Gruber, R. Jessor and K. R. Hammond (Eds.), *Contemporary Approaches to Cognition.* Cambridge, Harvard University Press, 1957.
9. Gibson, J.J. *The Ecological Approach to Visual Perception.* Boston: Houghton-Mifflin, 1979.
10. Kahneman, D., Slovic, P and Tversky, A. *Judgment under Uncertainty: Heuristics and Biases.* London: Cambridge University Press, 1982.
11. Neisser, U. *Cognition and Reality.* San Francisco: Freeman, 1976.
12. Neisser, U. (Ed.), *Memory observed.* San Francisco: Freeman, 1962
13. Nisbett, R. E. and Ross, L. *Human inference: Strategies and Shortcoming of Social Judgment.* Englewood Cliffs, N.J.: Prentice-Hall, 1980.
14 Nisbett, R. E. and Wilson, T. D. The halo effect: Evidence for unconscious alteration of judgments. *Journal of Personality and Social Psychology,* 1977, 35, 250-256.
15. Newell, A. and Simon, H. A. *Human Problem Solving.* Englewood Cliffs, N. J.: Prentice-Hall, 1972.
16. Piaget, J. *The Child's Conception of Number.* London: Routledge and Kegan Paul, 1952.

# 9

# Culture in Psychology

There is a discrepancy between a premise of contemporary mainstream psychology and a characteristic of its subject matter. The premise is that psychology should, ideally, be independent of culture. One should try to observe objectively and theorize freely. The characteristic of the subject matter is that both psychologists and subjects are constituted by their common culture, and that they must share and live with the indigenous psychology embedded in the culture. Scientific psychologists try to ignore and eliminate what cannot be eliminated, and, hence, the discipline cannot progress.

As a first Step, let us move the psychological researcher to the village of a newly discovered stone age tribe. Let us suppose that the psychologist has so far escaped being cooked for dinner and that relations for the moment appear to be peaceful. Two natives are standing in front of a stone upon which lies a fruit of a species unknown to the psychologist. One of the natives utters something which to the psychologist sounds like "uage" and the other one immediately afterwards makes a sound that the psychologist hears as "eiage". In this situation, the psychologist cannot be said to recognize any definite psychological phenomena in the persons observed. She does not know whether the natives are addressing her or each other, whether they are agreeing or disagreeing, whether they are discussing her suitability for dinner or, perhaps, the fruit in front of them. If the latter alternative is true, she has no idea of whether they are referring to the ripeness, skin quality, colour, size, or shape of the fruit, to the question of ownership, to ways of preparing it, its suitability for a religious Ceremony, etc. They may even be referring to distinctions for which the psychologist has no words. She does not have an inkling of whether the persons in front of her are honest or deceitful in their displayed intentions (whatever they may be), calm or excited, friendly or unfriendly, decided or undecided, etc. There is no need to prolong this example. Let me merely add that in order to perform psychological experiments in general, and, hence, also with these people, at least three conditions must be fulfilled:

1. One must establish a *contract* of some sort, according to which the participants are obligated to perform honestly and conscientiously as instructed.
2. There must be a set of *introductions* (mediated verbally or nonverbally, directly or indirectly through situational arrangements), and it must be possible to take for granted or to establish that the subjects understand these instructions in exactly the way intended by the experimenter.

3. It must be possible for the experimenter to understand correctly the performance of the subjects with respect to the topics investigated. It should be clear that, in the situation described above, there is no immediate prospect of achieving any one of these three criteria.

The following simple conclusion appears inescapable: *Psychological research is impossible unless the researcher participates in the culture of the persons involved.* In the example given there is unobstructed physical access to what goes on, including perfect conditions for tape- and videorecordings, yet no definite psychological observations can be described. Something additional is needed, namely to participate in the culture. What does this mean?

In order to illustrate this, let us move the psychologist back to her own culture. She is now standing in a market place in a village in her home country. A saleswoman and a customer are looking at a melon and the customer asks: "What do you charge for this one?" The saleswoman gives a price. The customer says "outrageous!" and leaves. The saleswoman mutters something about "stupid tourists."

In this case, the psychologist has witnessed a perfectly intelligible exchange between two persons, and has got a definite impression of what the participants wanted, thought and felt. Obviously, this has been possible because the psychologist understands the language and the culture. Understanding the language means understanding what is meant by what is said under the assumed circumstances. Understanding the culture here means, among other things, recognizing the setting — a market place — and what it involves, recognizing the roles of salesperson and customer and what they involve, etc.

The preceding does not mean that the psychologist cannot be mistaken. However, a mistake is not likely to involve faulty knowledge of what words and clues mean under given circumstances. A mistake more likely stems from an error in recognizing the relevant context. Just after having watched the episode described above, the psychologist may hear the words "cut — ten minutes break!", discover some hidden cameras and come to realize that she has watched the taking of a scene in a film. The meaning of the episode now changes completely. The saleswoman and the customer now appear as paid actors, the emotions are recognised as only apparent, etc. However, even this shift in interpretation can only occur as long a the psychologist participates in the culture. She must know about films, actors, and what this involves.

With the given example as background, let us now formulate more abstractly what is meant by participation in a culture.

Human babies are socialised into adults. Occasionally older individuals are socialised into a new culture too. In both cases this is, among other things, a process of becoming able to describe, explain and predict the behaviour of others in given situations, and to become describable, explainable and predictable oneself. The outcome of the continuous socialisation of newcomers is the maintenance of a society in which the behaviour of members is mutually describable, explainable and predictable to a high extent, and where cooperation is therefore possible. The system allowing this description, explanation and prediction (language and nonverbal situational clues) is *common* to the members and, hence, allows the individuals to take a number of things for granted in interacting with each other. It is this commonality of what is taken for granted (the meanings of statements and situations) that makes understanding and communication, and, therefore, also psychology, possible. Only to the extent that you can take for granted what is meant by words and nonverbal situational clues in a given context, can a message be understood.

On the basis of the preceding, let us now assume that we can achieve access to psychological phenomena in other persons only through participation in the culture. Let us, furthermore, assume that the task of scientific psychology is to describe, explain and predict psychological phenomena. Something very interesting happens when these two assumptions are combined.

Consider the episode in the market place. A *description* has already been provided, in terms of ordinary English. Such a description can usually be shown to be reliable in the sense that other bystanders, as well as the participants themselves, will subscribe to it. It may also serve as a guide to a reconstruction of the scene for persons who did not witness it. A set of *explanations* of the events follows directly from the description. The saleswoman stands there *because* she wants to sell the melon and the customer is there *because* she wants to buy it, provided the price is right. Therefore, the customer wants to know the price. The saleswoman understands this and states the price. The customer thinks the price is unjustifiably high and is irritated because she wanted the melon, but is prevented from buying it by what she sees as the saleswoman's greed. The saleswoman is angry at being accused (by implication) of being greedy, is also frustrated by not being able to sell the melon, and thinks that the tourist is stupid, since she does not understand what is a reasonable price, given the costs of fertilizers, etc. Finally, given the description and the ensuing explanations, a set of *predictions* can be made. We may predict that the saleswoman will try to sell to other customers, will always give the price when asked, will be pleased when she sells and frustrated when she fails to sell, etc. Similarly, we may 'expect persons who are potential customers to buy when they want something and when the price is right. Also, we may predict that customers will be frustrated when — the price is felt to be too high, and pleased when it is right or lower, etc. We may expect both saleswoman and the customers to become angry when they are insulted, etc. Finally, we may predict that the customer will be very surprised and suspicious if the saleswoman offers the melon for free, and we may predict that the saleswoman will try to prevent the customer from taking the melon without paying the required price, etc.

All the mentioned descriptions, explanations and predictions, as well as innumerable others, are more or less *shared* by all the persons participating in the episode, including the bystanders. Furthermore, when sharing is less complete, the differences in viewpoints can often be successfully communicated between the participants, relying on meanings that *are* shared.

The conclusion is that the persons whose activities are to be described, explained and predicted by scientific psychology, already *have* a system of psychological description, explanation and prediction. Whatever the merits of this shared system, it is at least efficient enough to allow people to live their entire lives together and to cooperate sufficiently well to maintain their society. I have tried to describe parts of this *indigenous* psychology of Western culture (Heelas & Lock 1981) in several recent publications. See e.g. (Smedslund 1978, 1980, 1981, 1982a, 1982b, in press). It would appear, then, that scientific psychology should try to describe, explain and predict the activities of persons who already have and live with an implicit, culturally determined psychology. The challenge involved in this rather curious situation has not generally been met.

The main attitude of scientific psychology towards our already existing indigenous psychology has been to *ignore it*. In so far as this is true, the situation reminds me of the old proverb "the fish do not know the ocean": The psychologists do not know culture. More precisely, the fish do not know that they tacitly know the ocean, and they do not know exactly what it is that they know tacitly. Analogously, psychologists frequently do not know that they tacitly know their culture and take it for granted in their research, and also they do not know exactly what it is that they know tacitly.

An auxiliary strategy has been to treat everyday folk psychology as a sort of inferior theory, full of inconsistencies, ambiguities, and frequently as being wrong. Textbooks often begin with a brief dismissal of common sense.

The most serious aspect of this ignorance or rejection of indigenous folk psychology (common sense) is that it involves a failure to recognize that the common meaning system quite literally is part of what *constitutes* what we call a person. To be a person *is* among other things to describe, explain and predict one's own and others' behaviour according to the indigenous psychology embedded in one's culture.

*Human beings have made themselves describable, explainable and predictable to each other and to themselves through socialisation.* The social order within which we exist is what *makes* us describable, explainable and predictable. It also makes-it possible to communicate our individual differences and, hence, enables us to gain some understanding of the individuality of the other person.

The preceding means that the psychological researcher is faced with a very peculiar dilemma. She can gain access to her subject matter only through participation in the culture involved. Furthermore, her scientific descriptions, explanations and predictions must account for the descriptions, explanations and predictions that her subjects make. These latter, taken together, make up the indigenous (common sense) psychology of the culture involved. In other words, scientific psychology must account for common sense psychology. How this can be done is a fundamental problem in psychology.

Any attempt to formulate a scientific account which contradicts (deviates from) the common sense account adhered to by the subjects investigated, appears doomed to failure. Let us use the example of the market place, described above. The persons involved react to and describe the commodity for sale as a "melon". A scientific account of what the people are referring to must also describe the object as a "melon". Any other description would introduce distinctions not responded to and not relevant for the persons involved, and, hence, would be useless. Similarly, the explanation of why the customer asks "what do you charge for this one?" must be that she wants to buy the melon if the price is right. Everyone involved takes this for granted and a scientific explanation of why the person asks this question cannot deviate from this. Finally, everyone involved will predict that if the customer attempts to take the melon without payment, the saleswoman will react strongly. The scientific psychologist, having access to the same background information must predict the same outcome, or be wrong.

It appears, then, that within a wide range of ordinary situations, scientific description/explanation/prediction and common sense description/explanation/prediction *must* coincide, but with the difference that the former are *explications* of the latter, which are often *implicit* in form. As I have tried to show elsewhere (Smedslund 1982a, 1982b) the psychologist's explications can be presented to the persons investigated for comments and can be revised to fit these comments. As a final outcome of such dialogues with other members of the culture, a high degree of consensus may be reached as to the adequacy of the explication, and, hence, it may be regarded as provisionally validated. Given a sufficiently broad set of such validated explications, one may be said to have an explicit (scientific) formulation of the indigenous psychology associated with the given culture. Finally, since people have been *socialised* into culture and its psychology, it may be said that the order explicated by scientific psychology is entirely man-made.

## Conclusion

We have not, in psychology, embarked upon an exploration of the unknown, but upon an explication of the well-known. And, as we gradually achieve our goal of lifting the veil of the obvious, the outcome will be as depicted by Novalis (1977, p. 110):

"Emem gelang es - er hob den Schleier der Gottin von Sais. Aber was sah er? - er sah - Wunder des Wunders, sich selbst."

Getting to know ourselves explicitly will change us. But that is another story.

## REFERENCES

1. Heelas, P. and Lock, A. (Eds.), *Indigenous psychologies. The anthropology of the self.* London, Academic Press, 1981.
2. Novalis (Fr. von Hardenberg). *Schriften, Erster Band,* Darmstadt, 1977.
3. Smedslund, J. Bandura's theory of self-efficiency: a set of common sense theorems. *Scandinavian Journal of Psychology,* 1978, 19, 1-14.
4. Smedslund, J. Analysing the primary code: from empiricism to apriorism. In D. Olson (Ed.), *The Social Foundations of Language and Thought. Essays in Honour of J.S. Bruner.* New York: Norton, 1980.

5. Smedslund, J. The logic of psychological treatment. *Scandinavian Journal of Psychology*, 1981, 22, 65-77.
6. Smedslund, J. Seven common-sense rules of psychological treatment. *Journal of the Norwegian Psychological Association*, 1982, 19, 441-449 (a).
7. Smedslund, J. Revising explications of common sense through dialogue: thirty-six psychological theorems. *Scandinavian Journal of Psychology*, 1982, 23, 299-305 (b).
8. Smedslund, J. What is necessarily true in psychology? *Annals of Theoretical Psychology*, in press.

# 10

# The Research Object of Psychology in the 1990's

## Introduction

What kind of man will we be studying in the 1990's? Which kinds of changes will occur in the content of life activities, life careers and values? How will these changes determine the aspect of the human being we will study — our research object? These questions are discussed in this chapter, both theoretically — by asking what actually changes in man — and in the light of some findings of a longitudinal study made among Finnish students. When considering new trends in psychological research, we seldom remember that the object of research, man living with his social relationships, is constantly changing. The expectations of people regarding psychology and the problems it should solve are rising. The change may be ambiguous and controversial, but it still influences the way in which psychological problems will be formulated.

The history of science proves that new approaches emerge when the object of research is defined in a new way: in a wider context than before, or by the stressing of different aspects. Physicists have recognised the fact that the methods they use in the analysis of physical reality do mold that reality. The independence between the researcher and his object appears today to be a myth. In psychology, although a human science, it is common to look upon the subjects of our study as passive beings, who await the analysis of the researcher with "ready-made" qualities. The essential components of personality and behaviour have, it seems, already been discovered; therefore one would not expect any dramatic changes in these properties (cognition, motivation, self-awareness, abilities, temperament, and interests). This conception may actually be true: the structure of man's activity does not change over time in its formal elements. If the TOTE model of Miller, Galanter and Pribram (1960) is basically valid, its components—the "Plan" and the "Image" — can be identified in the behaviour of medieval people and of workers in an automated factory as well. But the content and meaning of the life processes do change, in respect to historical changes. This process will be subjected to a closer inspection in a later section of our essay.

In his recent essay, Shames (1982) states that since the days of Wundt, psychology has been based on a naturalistic picture of man. Psychological processes are seen as faculties of biological man, the "homo sapiens" organism. This creates the impression of psychology as a study of the abstract individual, whose properties are readily available for examination. Shames claims that human processes are modelled, in psychology, according to technological and biological ones. The specific nature of "human" remains thus unrecognised. The study of specifically human processes, concludes Shames, would require a psychology based on the objective, historical conditions of these processes. Understanding the dialectical connection between social evolution and the development of the individual — expressed in Marx's thesis about human existence as a totality of man's social relationships — will be, then, the key question in the analysis.

The role of social evolution is not ignored in present life-span theories, and was also inherent in the works of such classical psychological thinkers as Wilhelm Wundt and Pierre Janet. But social evolution is commonly understood to be a separate dimension of development, external to the individual. This creates a picture of man as passively adapting to social changes (Sabour 1982). The internal unity of the social changes and the development of the individual is thus not recognised (cf. also Shames 1982); the discontinuous nature of human development, stressed by the French psychologist Henry Wallon and his student Rene Zazzo, is ignored (Sabour 1982a; cf. also below: the methodological problems of longitudinal studies). Theories concerning life careers, vocational development, and generation changes during the last decade focused psychological discussion on the historical bases of man's development. Still, there is a need to contemplate the bases on which new psychological properties — new modes of motives and abilities — are formulated; the processes through which our relationships with various social objects are transformed. One may think that these relationships are the problem of sociologists and not psychologists. But if this were the case, the analysis of internal personal relationships and meanings in the context of historical change would be neglected. This would make our psychology rather sterile.

**A Macropsychological Question**

In studying change, the first task is to discriminate between phenomena of a primary nature and those of peripheral importance. It is not a crucial question to ask whether individuals in the 1990's will be more extrovert, neurotic, complex, alienated, or competent in intellectual operations than persons today (they probably will be), but we should know what the actual content of alienation, intelligence, or extroversion in that period will be and how it will be related to the individual's position in the spheres of work, leisure, or community life. This problem-approach has been called macropsychological (Hayrynen, 1980). The macropsychological study is not only confined to a general analysis of how the individual and the society are related to each other, but attempts to discover, by means of historical, longitudinal, and interdisciplinary methods, how these relationships are manifested in society at a specific time, in the context of its economic development, political struggle, etc.

The writing of this essay has been especially stimulated by the problems we have faced in a longitudinal study, in which we are investigating the later life courses of students who in 1965 applied to study at Helsinki University and participated in a survey about their value-orientations, self-concepts, and vocational interests (Hayrynen et al., 1982). Some of the measurements were repeated in 1982, for those then professionally employed as scientists, artists, teachers or in other academic posts. The study also contains a comparison of the university applicants of 1965 and those of 1982, which offers an opportunity to examine the trends revealed in cohort variation. This research thus allows an analysis of changes in psychological relationships over a period of 17 years (1965-1982), a period equal in length to that between 1983 and the year 2000.

Although our research team had no major objections towards using sophisticated statistical procedures, it was soon realised that a total picture of changes would entail the consideration of several historical factors, whose influence is best reflected in individual life histories. The specific nature of the university of the 1960's, the economic crisis of capitalism in the 1970's, the change in the structure and content of professional activities and the decline of traditional academic roles are related to the life courses of the subjects we are studying, not as direct "variables", but as new conditions for their life responses.

The trends affecting life content of the individual in the present period appear to be linked to a culmination of trends in the Western type of society: the increase of bureaucracy, the overgrowth of organisations, and an increase of the general level of knowledge which widens the individual's conciousness about the world, but also makes him aware of new risks and dangers. The problem of individuals in the present period is that they have not yet developed the forms of action by means of which they would be able to respond to the new risks and challenges; above all, the risk of nuclear war, general violence, and the challenge of maintaining peace. According to the sociologist C. Wright Mills, the persons of the post-war period faced their problems — in contrast to those of the 1930's—without a clear awareness of their values. This was connected to the general rise of apathy and anxiety characteristic of the 1950's (Mills 1959). Even now, the determinants of anxiety and passivity are related to the macrosocial development, which culminates in the features already present in the 1950's, and represents at the same time new types of problems. The final consequences of this social development depend on how people will respond and act — privately or collectively, passively or actively, with irrational thinking or with a help of a rational synthesis. The task of psychology would be to deliver the theoretical means for a closer analysis of these alternatives.

## How is Man Changing?

What can change in man? Not all fluctuations of traits are tied to -historicai change. On the other hand, historical changes are manifested in different ways in different individuals. Differences in temperament, experience or styles determine how people act in changing circumstances. But styles of acting are not the most important level of the human system since they do not express the motives of activity and the relationships between individuals and their environments. Instead of defining a human "basic nature" we should try to define the quality of the psychological relationships which are transformed historically.

A typical psychological relationship could be a person's judgement of himself, his self concept. As stated by S. L. Rubinstein, one of the central theorists in Soviet psychology, social consciousness is not born from a person's self-conceptions, but self-concept develops to the extent the person becomes an independent subject. It is thus a product of social development and reflects an emergence of specific historical conditions; when early men worked together with the same social goals and motives, they did not actually need a self concept. The fact that self-awareness arises from controversies is analysed from a different perspective by the American psychologist R. A. Wicklund, who has developed a theory of "objective self-awareness" (1982). It seems that self-reflexion grows in situations in which the original bond between a person and his group is somehow disrupted. Not only the content of self-image, but also the function of self-concept seems to alter during the social development. This might occur in a changed relationship between self-concept and professional choice, or in the new role self-consciousness plays in the processes of learning and work (cf. Shames: the increasing self-control of human processes).

Starting from the ideas of L. S. Vygotski, A. A. Leontjev (1977) has developed the concept of objective or goal-orientated activity. External, objective activity is the primary layer of man's development, from which the internal psychological processes grow. This occurs through a process called interiorisation of the external conditions of activity. The theory is rather general in certain of its aspects and does not fully explain now *new motives and types of personality* are generated, exclusive of previously established social models. Nevertheless it enables the asking of interesting questions regarding the development of the human mind: e.g. in which situations is the psyche — or the "Image" — actually needed (Galperin 1977), how personality originates, or what are the historical and phylogenetic conditions which have created the human mind (Davydov and Zinchenko 1982)? The psychological relationships which connect-man with his objective environment can thus be seen as the results of his activities: social change does not influence persons directly, but forms new frames for their activities. Since activities are not mechanically determined by external conditions of living, the final consequences of the social alterations depend on how persons respond to these changes.

We may now consider how new social conditions actually enter our conscious awareness. First, vague feelings and experiences arise which demonstrate a controversy in the present disposition of life. What is known as creativeness is activated when these controversies are explored and handled. In the second phase, the altered conditions of life are expressed in new technological, political, aesthetic or scientific meanings which, in fact, are products of human goal-orientated activities. The altered situation requires people to arrange their psychological relationships, what Leontjev calls the *"personal meanings"*, in a new manner. One of the fundamental aspects of change is just this re-arrangement of personal meanings. Leontjev notes that the *structure of activity* is not changed historically: it obeys the motives which have stimulated it and is realised in conscious acts ("Handlungen") What does change dramatically are the ways in which motives are related to these objective goals; the ways in which people comprehend their position in the world, the extent to which they master the new skills and mental operations necessary for their personal fulfillment. (Leontjev 1977, 198.)

The dynamic aspect of social change is stressed when Leontjev analyzes the discrepancy between personal meanings and the objective conditions of persons in class society (1977, 201). In the context of class society personal meanings — reflecting the motives originated in life — may fail to find objective meanings which fully express them. In this case people are guided by stereotypes, established in individual or mass communication, which do not offer real solutions for their courses of life. These stereotypes of a "happy life", "enemies to be destroyed", etc. replace, in a way, the real social aims and models of life. It is just the threat to these stereotypes, concludes Leontjev, which causes anxiety and disaster in persons, subjected to conditions they cannot sufficiently explain by means of the acquired stereotypes. In this Leontjev appears to formulate the alienation syndrome as expressed *in the level of controversial psychological relationships* (cf. the definition of the anxiety syndrome by C.. Wright Mills). Thus we cannot speak of personal meanings and psychological relationships as a neatly organised system, but as a system which is in a continuous state of transition. This is reflected in the *sedimentary nature* of Psychological relationships, which often contain elements of the earlier phases of life histories, "memories" as related to the anticipatory images of the future. This occurs especially in people who live in countries which have gone through rapid social transformation, such as Finland. The layers of the old rural culture may exist in the memories of individuals together with a conception of what is new and modern. Different layers of personal meanings may be conflicted with each other, as reflected in the controversies of the personal life goals.

We may ask how persons respond to the changes occurring in the objective conditions of their life: how they revise their goals and react to the new standards of action? In principle, there are four types of potential *life-responses*.. One is the attempt to *fulfill the norms* reflecting the new conditions of life: to re-learn, study, transform oneself. develop new mental abilities. Creativity in the collective scale occur just in this emergence of new mental abilities and new patterns of life among great masses of people (cf. Hayrynen, 1977). Some persons may be contented with the minimal achievement or *withdrawal,* in which they minimize the personal risks and avoid facing the controversies. This often means limiting one's self and one s scope of personal meanings. Still others take the *initiative* and try to overcome the contradictions of their circumstances by means of creative re-molding, either through organisational mastery, through intellectual production, or through new ideological solutions. And there may be the conflict-ridden individuals who neither possess an external strategy for coping with the situations nor can resolve their controversies through internal adjustments. The typology of the "life responses" which is outlined here resembles, in many respects, the analysis of personality types by Abulhanova- Slavskaja (1983). The young Finnish clinical psychologists Kari Lahtela and Reijo Pehunen have, starting from similar theoretical premises, developed the concept of "life strategy", which can be used to study how persons react towards aging or towards illnesses limiting their scope of action. We shall introduce in the next section a chart of the life responses of the subjects of our longitudinal study, in which we outline the types of change observed in different persons belonging to the finnish educated class.

**Study of Change—Two Conceptions**

Any longitudinal study faces the problem of a qualitative, historical change in the psychological relationships it studies. It is not an easy task to define whether a change occurs, or how it may be attributed to different sources of influence. Although formulating the general scheme for the relationships to be analysed, Leontjev's theory gives little help in defining the actual contents of psychological processes (cf. Davydov 1981, 25). Kalleberg and Loscocco's study (1983), focusing on age differences in job satisfaction, illustrates quite well the complex nature of the interplay of various factors — work, self, social relationships etc. — which produce changes in the course of life. Doubts have been expressed, however, as to whether the changes in the course of life can be principally attributed to separate factors such as developmental aging, cultural evolution, and the divergence in the patterns of socially determined life careers. In order to preserve the unity of the individual life course it has been suggested that the survey methods be complemented with softer, biographical studies (e.g., Rosenmayr 1980). R.W. White, who has demonstrated the value of studying individual lives as a whole (White 1975), claims that the use of correlative procedures, however sophisticated, has added little if nothing to our knowledge about the determinants of life processes. He agrees with the argument according to which the attempt to study separate factors and the underlying cause-effect model is badly misplaced in the study of lives (White 1981, 15).

One of the arguments against the quantitative approach is that it does not reveal the *internal* aspects of change. On the other hand, our macropsychological scheme suggests that *both* quantitatively observed trends *and* internal transformations in the subjects are important and should be studied in their mutual relationship. Against this background it is interesting to recall the critique of the longitudinal method presented by Rene Zazzo in 1966 at the World Congress of Psychology (ref. by Wall & William 1970, 14-18). Zazzo makes a radical distinction between two ways of studying change. One is the *predictive study,* which is concerned with the stability of psychological traits over a longer period, and aims to study how these traits are modified by environmental factors. This is the usual model of correlative research, which occurs as a series of cross-sectional analyses of the same sample, using standardised scales. In contrast to this is the *study of genetic changes* in which the basic problem is to reveal the types of change and the quality of different responses which may occur in individuals. The work of Jean Piaget — owing nothing to longitudinal studies, remarks Zazzo — illustrates the latter approach. If one aims to illuminate the typology of personality changes in a certain historical period the logic of the study may come close to the genetic approach.

It seems self-defeating for a person conducting survey-type research to refer to the critiques of Zazzo and White. However, the statistical analysis of life changes approaches the problem of qualitative change from another angle. It can illuminate the external modes in which values and other orientations change over time. Statistical macrodata also offer an opportunity to reveal, within a given population, the typical and the extreme cases which can then be subjected to a deeper biographical analysis.

## Chance in the Models of Vocational Choice—Shifts in the Object of Research

It sometimes appears that during a longitudinal programme a researcher alters his *particular object of research;* the angle from which he studies the behaviour of his subjects, will be changed. This has happened in our present study of academic careers; our focus has shifted from the model of choice to the types of personality change among the present academic workers. In order to demonstrate how the object of research can change and lead to an alternative explanation of the phenomena investigated, we will characterize the theoretical background of our earlier research programme.

In 1965, the study was chiefly aimed at reporting the model of vocational choice among the students who applied to different fields of study. The assumption was that students anticipate various academic cultures and professional environments when making their life choices, which are then reflected in the pattern of interests, values and self- evaluations typical of students making a similar choice. This theoretical view emphasised the selection of the life course as a process based on values and other orientations which are readily developed before the student enters the stage of vocational choice (cf. Rosenberg, 1957; Super & al., 1963; Holland, 1962, 1973). There is empirical evidence that individuals really attempt to implement their personal motivational goals (their "personal meanings") when selecting vocations. The problem is, whether these trends also determine the later course of life.

The self-selection model clearly stresses a static, reproductive nature of the processes through which the vocational choices of individuals occur — interests and anticipatory images reflecting the existing stratification of jobs. M. L. Kohn and C. Schooler contrast the selection model — according to which "personality is formed before occupational careers begin, with people fitting into and perhaps molding their jobs, but not being affected by them" — with the argument that work affects all facets of personality (Kohn & Schooler 1978, 24-25). The former conception can, according to the writers, be traced to the ideology of personnel selection and the ideas of Frederic Taylor, and the latter to the writings of the early Marx Walker and his research group state that these different directions of explaining value-orientations lead to different explanations of the reasons why men and women differ in their orientations at work (Walker & al., 1982). If these differences are attributed to the variation of work offered to both sexes, the primary concern would be for the equal distribution of meaningful jobs. It can be said that the previous stage of our research programme related its findings to the self-selection model, while at the later stage the life-activity model appeared more relevant. The paradox that certain findings seem to support both of these models nevertheless requires closer attention.

The study of university applicants in 1965 revealed certain fundamental modes of vocational orientation which largely resemble the self-selection models defined by Holland

(1962), and even show similarities with the factors of interests identified by Thurstone in his early factor experimentations. On the basis of this, it would seem that the dimensions along which young people select their vocations would not alter much over the decades. When factors related to the choice of a profession with a well-established role-image and stable position were studied more carefully, the results were presented in the form of a static selection-circle which also summarised the findings concerning the students' vocational stereotypes:

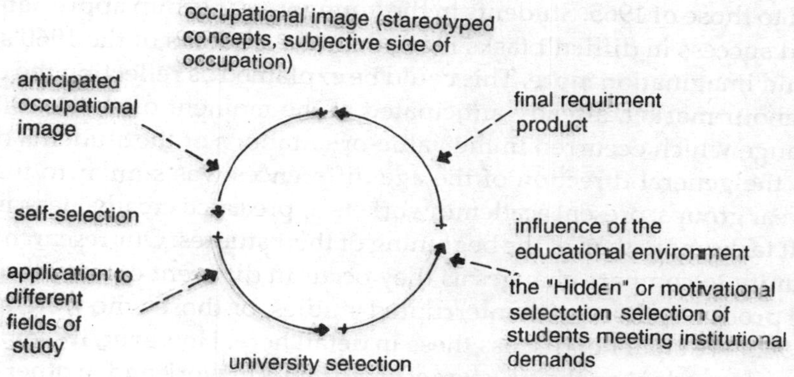


**Figure 10.1.** Selection-circle model

The selection-circle model actually demonstrates the tendencies which aim to support the traditional academic career system and resist the trends that change the professional image. This circle appears most clearly in the selection of Medicine, Law, and Architecture. It may be that this selection-circle influences the later phases of the professional career, too: this could be manifested as the duration and rigidity of vocational interests in later professional life, as the "inertia" of the selection trend. In fact, the vocational interests of different professional groups appear to be rather stable aspects of personality (cf. Strong 1951). One may ask, however, whether this stability reflects the static structure of these academic professions more than any internal property of the interests. What would happen if no resemblance exists between interests and the later occupational position, and if there are trends in the present occupational structure which would break down the "circle", i.e., change the model of self-selection?

In fact, contradictory tendencies were observed in the 1960's in the selections and the development of the educational atmosphere in several fields of higher learning. An anomalous selection process-related to the uncertainty of vocational choice — appeared in the Social Sciences and the Humanities, in which the connection between studies and the future prospects of work was small. A new trend which emerged in the 1970's was the decrease in the relative number of student places at universities available for grammar school leavers; less than one-fifth were immediately able to secure a place at university. Hannu Perho has shown in his doctoral dissertation at the University of Joensuu that the strategy of the applicants is now geared more towards getting admitted to university than to specific personal values (1982). The result is that entrants into a certain field of study do not necessarily possess the motivation for this particular study; in Leontjev's terms this "motivational dilemma" represents the circumstances in which students' motives and their goals of action diverge from each other.

The findings of our longitudinal study, as far as they have been analysed; have indicated an increase in expectations concerning the "ideal occupation" of the university applicants of 1982 as compared to those of 1965. Students in the younger year group appreciate creativity, self-direction, and success in difficult tasks more than the students of the 1960's, and value their willpower and imagination more. This could be explained as reflecting the competitive situation in the labour market, already anticipated at the moment of choice. But when we examined the change which occurred in the value-orientations of the students of 1965 over the past 17 years the general direction of the age differences was similar to that observed between the two year groups: present academic workers appreciated creativeness, independent work and difficult tasks more than at the beginning of their studies. Our research disposition offers an opportunity to compare changes as they occur in different career groups: persons with eminent life products, those with interrupted studies, or those who were not accepted to university in 1965. We shall not discuss these in detail here. However, it seems that value changes are indeed dependent on the *structure of life activities* in work and in other community life. There are professional women who show a sharp increase in their self-rated motivation for leadership and independence, and in their general ability to deal with practical problems. These findings support the hypothesis concerning the primary importance of work activities. Preliminary findings also indicate that particularly interests in leadership and in humanitarian work may change contextually, depending on work experience (for example, "leadership" may serve, in some people, altruistic and not prestige-related motives).

The increase in the level of demand, manifested both in the year group differences and in the developmental changes appears to express a more fundamental trend in the socio-cultural change. The growth in the expectations of students who are selecting their educational career appears to conflict with the conception of decrease in self-directed educational choice (a finding of Dr. Perho). There is, however, a contradiction in the altered premises of choice. The higher level of demand among the students of the 1980's appears to reflect a shift towards *personality-based* occupational values. For example, male students who in 1982 applied to study medicine were, compared to the applicants of the year 1965, more concerned with the intrinsic aspects of the physician's work than with the. prestige. On the other hand, the students of 1982 rated their overall vocational preferences generally lower than the students of 1965, the preference for the field they had selected notwithstanding. This may reflect the changing role of vocational interests in the system of vocational choice. Since it is difficult to maintain a vocational interest, students do not appear liable to pattern their personal orientations into the form of lasting and firm occupational preferences. Furthermore, the bureaucratisation of selections and careers in the public sector (social service, medical care, teaching, administration) generally diminishes the range of autonomous occupational choice. For this reason, individuals may be more concerned, in the future, about how work is divided and what the contents of their jobs are, than with developing static vocational interests. This may support a breaking-down of the fixed selection models, as they were manifested in our study of 1965.

It seems that interests, too, change their content and function in the system of life orientations during the individual's life course. At the moment of educational choice, the function of interests is to direct all young people towards one place or another in the division of labour. Interests then express *both* the personal meanings of these individuals, *and* the stereotyped conceptions about job stratification and men's and women's work. In a static occupational structure — which dominated academic professions before the "crisis of professionalism" in the 1960's — these stereotypes are powerful (cf. above Leontjev's analysis of personal meanings). The problem emerges when work experience contradicts with stereotypes. People may, in that event, develop new orientations which indicate their changed personal needs, or they may be directed toward the wrong stereotypes, developing wrong ideas about their positions. This leads us to contemplate the typology of life responses among the people of today as the final issue in this paper.

**Towards a Typology of Life Changes**

The theme of different courses of personality development has been approached by Jack Block, who in his longitudinal study compared the different stages of the individual's life course by means of the Q-sort diagnostic procedure (1971). Though Block related some of the types to cultural changes in American society, he has not particularly studied the social trends which produce personality changes during a certain period. This requires a consideration of the challenges which, in different social classes and in the whole society, reflect the principal model of social change. In this process, the new forms of attitudes, motives and creative action are born. For example, women have created, in recent years, new ways of life which exceed the boundaries of the earlier "sex role stereotypes".

We do not aim here to define any of the basic types of life course of this period, but attempt to demonstrate how various objective directions of change may be reflected in different individuals. The question is, how the ways in which our subjects express their perspectives, life outcomes, and links with different social processes fit into the theoretical scheme of life responses previously outlined. These responses have been tentatively classified by evaluating the whole content of a questionnaire or an interview transcript and also through the analysis of available documents indicating life outcomes: lists of publications, activities or other merits, etc. (About 900 of our follow-up sample have returned the questionnaire and 30 are participating in the complementary interviews.) It seems that these persons are chiefly engaged in three alternative kinds of social relationships: organisational and interpersonal relations; professional culture and the work-process, with the related development of knowledge; and universal cultural relations, with reference' to national or global aspects. These form the fields of "personal meanings" or the types of life goals our subjects have selected. In so doing, they have also defined the objective contexts in which they will define their successes and defeats.

Another aspect of our typology is the *level of life response* classified in the previous section: how the individuals innovate, fulfil, are affected by or contradict the social relationships they have chosen as the goals of their actions. When the three types of life models (the "capitalism affirmative", showing the middle class life context; the professional culture model; the universal intellectualist model) are contrasted with the degree of life outcome, there are twelve sub-types produced, as indicated in Table 10.1.

**TABLE 10.1**

**A Typology of the Life Models and the Level of Life Responses Among the Educated Class in Final and**

(the scheme for the biographical study of the Academic Careers Research Project 1965-1982)

| | The Life Model: the type of relationships the individual is chiefly engaged on; the focus of "personal meanings" | | |
|---|---|---|---|
| The Level of Life Response | Organisational and interpersonal relations (the middle class context) | Professional culture and the model of the specific intellectual | Universal culture; national or global relations |
| Initiative-productive | Entrepreneur orientation<br>— top careerists<br>— mastery of current affairs | High expertancy<br>— inventive-productive | Universal intellectual<br>— productive-critical |
| Fulfils the norm; antipating and aware of values | Community orientation<br>— local status<br>— interpersonal mastery | Commitment to occupation professional mastery<br>— enjoyment of work | Creative-participating<br>— adjusting to new cultural norms and anticipating consequences |
| Minimal achievement: conformism or withdrawal | Withdrawal to middle-class private life<br>— life without risks<br>— guided by stereotypes | Orientated towards work without personal ideas<br>— work stress or other factors of dissatisfaction | Contemplative intellectual<br>— escape to ideas or estheticism<br>— exclusive rationalism |
| Conflicted desires; threat to identity | Resentment<br>— fixation to petty-bourgeois values<br>— diffuse anxiety | Acute crisis of professional identity<br>— lack of career alternatives or perspectives on work | Confused intellectual<br>— ideological and political withdrawal<br>— turning to subjectivism |

The typology shows certain *abstracted variants* of a large individual variation in our longitudinal sample. Compared with classifications based on occupational position or on vocational personality type (cf. Holland, 1973), the types which are formulated here represent the way in which the subject defines his position towards different social objects or meanings of the period. A person may utilize his high organisational position in different ways: he may represent the "Enterprising personality" (Holland), i.e., an inclination towards middle-class careerist values, or may utilize the same position for pursuing certain collective, political or intellectual, goals. In this context persons test the interests and value-orientations which have guided their choices and may reject some of the underlying stereotypes. Persons may also discard their earlier ideals — there are scientists and professionals who, after a certain career sequence, will be more attached to a business-like way of life than to the ideals of a "specific intellectual" (this term was introduced by Michel Foucault in 1977 as an opposite to the "universal intellectual" representing traditional intellectualism).

The typology which is formulated will prove its general acceptability only when we study how it applies to the analysis of different "developmental trajectories", showing how individuals have arrived at a certain life outcome. We should also ask how the life trajectory of a person who now represents one of these types will be developed further; what his alternatives are. It seems that each individual represents a set of more or less mutually conflicting psychological relationships, or facets of personality. There are productive personalities who, at the same time, feel a powerlessness or a confusion of values in some of their "life sediments", and conforming, indifferent ones, who are still developing new skills and values, under the pressure of their life conditions. The generation of new "objective meanings" often leads to sudden changes in the psychological relationships which presently appear static. Therefore, typologies as presented above are linked with a certain period and with the responses characteristic of a given class of people. They nevertheless direct psychological research towards analyzing the emerging modes of activities.

**Conclusions**

Two trends appear to have the largest effect on the purposes of future psychology: the changes in the aspect of man, which in psychology is defined as the object of research, and the transformation occurring in the position of different groups of people, in their *psychological relationships*. To analyze that transformation, psychology must develop new concepts, in which social evolution is related to the development of the individual. Cultural historical conceptions in Soviet psychology — based on the ideas of L. S. Vygotski — have opened new perspectives, although they may remain at a general level concerning the real contents and the actual dynamics of the social changes. It seems that a study of these transformations during a certain period should cornbine the use of statistics and empirical methods, as well as concrete socio-historical and biographical analyses.

The above paper may have succeeded in indicating that a macropsychological perspective also opens new views for practical psychology. While an important field of psychology has been the study of disorders in the regulation of behaviour, a "psychology of normality" — the study of the syndromes which reflect the social dynamics in the individuals of a certain period, the forms of their anxiety, confusion, or creative productivity — may be lagging behind. The analysis of "life responses", as related to the emergence of new social meanings expressed as ideological conceptions, products of arts, new professional competencies etc., may prove an important aspect in the study of concrete life courses.

The longitudinal study reported above created an impression that people of the 1980's, although facing new types of social tensions and risks, are still developing higher "personality-based" needs; they may prove more oriented towards the contents of life than people of earlier decades. This may also generate certain new pressures on the *relationship between the researcher and the research subject* in psychology. People apparently want to know more about the premises of psychological research, especially if they are supposed to participate in it as examinees, the research subjects. On the other hand, the researcher may try to give the subjects an organised picture about the objectives of the research. This may lead to a *dialogue* between the investigator and the subjects of the research and change the relationship which nowadays — especially in abstract empiricism — emphasizes a mechanical, non-subject nature of man as the source of psychological information. At least our longitudinal study indicated, when we offered persons an opportunity to comment on and criticize the procedure and the aim of the study, that they often actually raised points and questions which the investigators had not foreseen in their plans. Life is even more complicated in reality than in psychology.

It seems that the social changes which occur, re-form, in many ways, the psychological relationships between the individual and society; they influence the individual's position towards other people, arts and sciences, work, politics, as well as toward himself — all the relations of personality (cf. Rahmani 1973, Lomov 1981: on the formulations of Myasichev). This offers new ways to study these relationships, be they called interests, personal meanings, attitudes, or social interactions. An alternative to the present type of research is one in which the subject and the investigator form a collective, with the common purpose of creating knowledge. In this context, psychology should reevaluate the bases of the researcher-subject relationship, as well as its own image of the subject it studies (cf. also Riegel, 1975).

## REFERENCES

1. Abulhanova-Slavskaja, K.A. Typology of personality activity in social psychology. In Helkama, K. (Ed.), *Proceedings of the 2nd Finnish-Soviet Symposium on Personality.*
2. Block, J. *Lives through Time.* Berkeley, Bancroft Books, 1971.
3. Davydov, V.V. The category of activity and mental reflection in the theory of A.N. Leontjev. *Soviet Psychology*, 1980, XIX, 3-38.
4. Davydov, V.V. and Zinchenko, V.P. The principle of Development in psychology. *Soviet Psychology*, 1981, XX, 22-46.
5. Foucault, M. The political function of intellectual. *Radical Philosophy*, 1977, No. 17.
6. Galperin, P. Ya. *Johdatusta Psykologiaan* (In Finish; Introduction to psychology). Helsinki, Kasankulttuuri, 1977.
7. Holland, J.L., Some explorations of a theory of vocational choice: 1, One- and two-year longitudinal studies. *Psychological Monographs*, 1962, No. 26, Whole No. 545.
8. Holland, J.L., *Making vocational choice: a theory of careers.* New Jersey: Prentice-Hall, 1973.
9. Hayrynen, Y.-P. *The flow of new students to different fields of study.* Educational choice, career motivation and discriminating effects of university admission. Helsinki: Finnish Academy of Sciences and Letters, 1970.
10. Hayrynen, Y.-P., Formation and use of mental abilities as a psychological and social phenomenon. *Acta Psychological Fennica V*, 1977. Helsinki: Psychological Society, 1977, (In Finnish)
11. Hayrynen, Y.-P., A small community interested in macro-psychology: a report form the psychological Institute in Joensuu. *Acta Psychologica Fennica VII*, 1980. Helsinki: Finish Psychological Society, 1980.
12. Hayrynen, Y.-P., Hayrynen, L., Jaakkola, R. and Tormulainen, T., Academic careers study—a framework for a 17 years longitudinal study. *University of Joensuu, Section of Educational Sciences*, Bulletin 31/1982.

13. Kalleberg, A. and Loscocco, K.L., Aging, values, and rewards: explaining age differences in job satisfaction. *American Sociological Review*, 1983, 48, 78-90.
14. Kohn, M.L., and Schooler, C., The reciprocal effects of substantive complexity of work and intellectual flexibility: a longitudinal assessment. *American Journal of Sociology*, 1978, 84, 24-52.
15. Lomov, B.R., Persoonallisuuden tutkimuksen metodologisia ongelmia. (In Finnish; Methodological problems of research into personality). *Publications of the Committee on Scientific and Technical cooperation between Finland and the USSR*, Helsinki, 1981.
16. Miller, G., Galanter, E. and Pribram, K. *Plans and the structure of behaviour*. New York, Wiley, 1960.
17. Mills, C., Wright, *The sociological imagination*. Oxford University Press, 1959.
18. Perho, H. The nature and significance of vocational and study orientation in class teacher education. (English summary). *Publications of the University of Joensuu, Series A No. 23*, 1982.
19. Rahmani, L., *Soviet psychology*. New York: International Universities Press, 1973.
20. Riegel, K.F. Subject-object alienation in psychological experiments and testing. *Human Development*, 1975, 18, 181-193.
21. Rosenberg, M.J., *Occupations and values*. Glencoe, III.: The Free Press, 1957.
22. Rosenmayr, L. Achievements, doubts, and prospects of the sociology of aging. *Human Development*, 1980, 23, 46-62.
23. Subour, M'd. The career theory from the past to the future. *University of Joensuu, Department of Psychology*, mimeo, 1982.
24. Sabour, M'd. The Developmental psychology of Henry Wallon — an overview. *University of Joensuu, Department of Psychology*, mimeo, 1982.
25. Shames, C. The application of dialectics to the theory of personality. In A. Kossakowski and K. Obuchowski (Eds.), *Progress in psychology of personality*. XXIInd International Congress of Psychology. Amsterdam: North-Holand Publishing Company, 1982.
26. Strong, E.K., Jr. Permanence of interest scores over 22 years. *Journal of Applied Psychology*, 1951, 35, 89-91.
27. Super, D.E., Starishevsky, R., Matlin, N. and Jordaan, J.P. *Career Development: Self-concept Theory*. New York: College Entrance Examination Board, 1963.
28. Walker, J.E., Tausky, C. and Oliver, D. Men and women at work: similarities and differences in work values within occupational groupings. *Journal of Vocational Behaviour*, 1982, 21, 17-36.
29. Wall, W.D. and Williams, H.L., *Longitudinal Studies and the Social Sciences*. London, Heineman (Social Science Research Council), 1970.
30. White, R.W. *Lives in progress*. 3rd ed. New York, Holt, Rinehart and Winston, 1975.
31. White, R.W., Exploring personality the long way: the study of lives. In A. I. Rabin, J. Aronoff, A.M. Barclay and R.A. Zucker (Eds.), *Further explorations in personality*. New York: Wiley, 1981.
32. Wicklund, R.A. How society uses self-awareness. In J. Suls (Ed.), *Psychological Perspectives of Self*. Vol. 1. Hillsdale, N. J., Lawrence Erlbaum, 1982.

# 11

# Psychology in the 1990's: Trends, Threats and Challenges

## Introduction

"It is 1996, the XXV World Congress of Psychology was held. Upon consideration, however, it is decided that, for several reasons; the meeting might just as well be cancelled. Why? What could have happened in the world and in the field of psychology during these thirteen years?"

This is one of the instructions or "scripts" I have used in gathering from different groups images and impressions of trends in development in the world in general and in the sphere of life important to the respondents in particular. In some of the instructions there is a World Congress, but "it has to be broken off". The respondent is asked to enter the spirit of the 1996 scene and to tell us why the meeting has to be discontinued: "What has happened?" Some of the instructions picture a congress where everything "goes smoothly, with no disputes whatsoever". Again, the respondent is asked: "What has really happened in the world and in the field of psychology during these thirteen years?"

In some sub-samples the respondents are people actively involved in sport, not psychologists. The event that is now cancelled, or has to *be* broken off, or is a great success is the Olympic Games. When the' sample consists of specialists in adult education, the event is the "V Unesco Conference on Adult Education". The setting has been altered according to the interests of the respondents because it is believed, as Allport (1943) suggests, that meaningful, consistent response patterns (e.g. "traits") can be found only when the subject has a deep interest at stake ("ego-involvement").

In studying life stories of French bakery workers, Bertaux and Bertaux-Wiame (1981) found that the group studied did not need to be very large or "representative" in the traditional sense to give a relatively permanent result. If cases were added, every new story confirmed what the preceding ones had shown. The authors call their finding a process of saturation."

Something along the same lines was discovered here, too. A certain structure that was found in the responses of, say, a few dozen persons, remained unaltered when new cases were added, and the surface spectrum of the answers gained more saturation. This structure consists of three broad categories of threats or problematic tendencies:

(1) Dangers originating in the social systems developed by man suddenly threaten the action (psychology, sport, adult education, etc.) *from outside.* A scientific congress or the Olympics have to be broken off or they cannot be held because of a world war, a nuclear catastrophe, or some comparable politico-military or technical-economic catastrophe.

(2) Some problematic tendencies in the large social systems have slowly penetrated the field of action in question and now threaten it *from within.* Such serious politically based disagreements arise between Eastern and Western sportsmen that the Olympic Games have to be cancelled. Or the conference on adult education is no longer worth arranging because ready access to computers and new information technology have rendered adult education useless.

(3) The origin of the threats is not outside the field of action but in *its own internal logic.* The Olympic Games, for instance, are not worth staging because the limits of human performance have been reached and results can no longer be improved. Or differentiation in the field of psychology has drawn the different branches so far apart that they no longer understand each other.

Besides these three categories, a fourth distinctive feature of this basic structure can also be noted. The respondents have difficulties in imagining a situation where the Olympic Games or a scientific congress run smoothly and without discord except by assuming that *something extreme* has happened: a nuclear war has been waged, desolating most of the Earth; a unified world-state reaching all the corners of the world has been declared; or a utopian invention doing away with all contradictions and conflicts has been made (e.g. a "pill"). Contradictions and unsolved problems would seem to be part of the normal cycle of things; abolition of these is something which requires very special reasons. Today, pessimism seems more realistic than optimism.

Naturally, the answers of different individuals were not uniform. Two interpretations may be proposed to explain the variation. First, if opinions on some matter are evenly divided, for example, a purely social contradiction may lie behind the division: half of the people strongly support the matter and the other half oppose it. But the division may also be accounted for by a contradiction within each person's mind: every individual finds equally good reasons to be for or against it (see Coleman 1964, 381-383).

The variation in the explanations our respondents proposed for the imaginary events of 1996 was congruent with the latter interpretation. Real interindividual differences (e.g. in optimism towards the world situation) can, of course, be found within the group; more distinctive, however, is that every respondent plays, in his or her consciousness, with several possibilities. This is evidenced by the several alternative explanations most of the respondents give. In one and the same answer we may have elements from all the three categories mentioned.

## Dangers Threatening Psychology From Outside

In the following I will not give a mechanical presentation of the results of these inquiries; rather, I intend to use them as a heuristic instrument in considering how psychology will have developed by the 1990's. In what way, for instance, will psychology react to or be moulded by the fact that developments stemming from systems created by man turn to threaten him and his actions?

Peculiar to these dangers is that they seem to arise from rational action aimed at positive goals. We want to raise our standard of living, we want to build a "good society", a "good life". The outcome? Increasing air and water pollution, more poison in almost everything we eat. Or again, nations wish to secure peace and protect their people by a build-up of nuclear weaponry, but what results is an ever greater threat of war and increasing insecurity.

To explain this paradox, psychologists have often argued that humans are led by some irrational innate forces into war and destruction, despite the rationalism and regard for life in how they try to act. Although these explanations have met severe criticism, it is most unlikely that we will see them disappear in the future. On the contrary, if the atmosphere in the world grows more tense and the threat of large-scale destruction grows, we can expect mystifying and irrational talk of these threats and catastrophes to increase.

But besides this loose talk, we can also expect a more rational approach to these problems to gain ground. The international movement of physicians for the prevention of nuclear war, concerned with both investigation of the consequences of a nuclear war and informing people of these consequences, is a good example of such rationality. Psychologists have in some countries also founded similar movements.[1] This would seem to suggest that, in the 1990's, psychology is ever more oriented towards studying those odd *mechanisms of rationality* that often make the outcome of man's action something other than was intended or, as Deutsch (1983) calls them, the malignant social processes.

More specifically, focus will probably be on the relationship between individual and collective rationality. The best known paradigm of this relationship is the "Prisoner's Dilemma" (see Barry and Hardin 1982, 24-25; 73-74), introduced and named in the early 1950's. The rational decisions made by both prisoners separately do not lead to collective rationality, to the best possible result for both of them. The problem has been much studied by more or less mechanically arranged laboratory experiments, but it seems as if all researchers had not, in full depth, understood the great theoretical importance of this problem.

It is perhaps easier to see the links of this problem with the great problems of the world if it is presented in the form known as "the commons problem" (Edney 1980). A commons problem arises when a group of people who share one single indivisible pool of resources arrive at a point where their rate of consumption threatens to exhaust it. The drain on the world's nonrenewable natural resources would be a typical "commons problem". As far as the individual actor is concerned, it would be rational to appropriate as great a share of these resources as possible before they are exhausted; but it would also be rational to cut down on consumption to ensure future access to these resources. In the long run, then, "collective rationality" or provident use of common resources would, even from the individual actor's view-point, be rational.

The time dimension is thus an important aspect in the paradox of individual and collective rationality. This we see clearly when the problem is conceptualised as a "social trap" (Platt 1973). The general logic of this mechanism is shown in figure 11.1. For the individual, every act brings, in the short term, positive consequences. Every step in the arms build-up taken by a state, for example, adds to its feeling of security or seems to boost the national economy. But in the long run, the outcome has negative consequences for the whole group of actors; the arms race as a whole produces an immense feeling of insecurity and a real threat of' the extinction of mankind. Man is caught like a fish in a trap; we launched ourselves in a certain direction, which soon proved to be lethal. Yet no-one seems to be able to pinpoint where the crucial mistake was made.

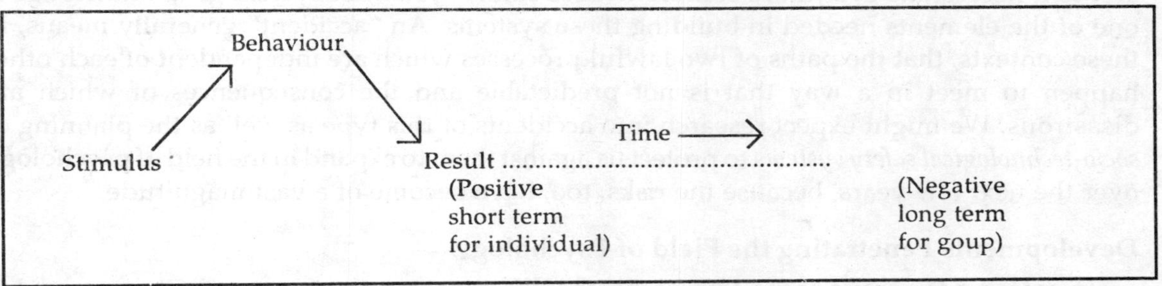


Figure 11.1. Elements of a Social Trap (Edney 1980; based on Platt, 1973).

### *How, Then, Could Collective Rationality Become Possible?*

Olson's (1965) analysis of "the logic of collective action" gives some clues as to where and how we might find the answer. He analyses a situation where a group of rational and self-interested individuals have some interests in common. Now we would be inclined to think that, inasmuch as these individuals are rational and self-interested, they would without doubt act on behalf of their common interests.

But this is precisely what does not happen, according to Olson. Unless the number of individuals in the group is quite small, or unless coercion or other such devices are used to bring about collective action, rational self-interested individuals will not act to further their common or group interests, not even if they are agreed on the existence of a common interest and of the methods to achieve it. Conversely; If, within a large group or organisation, people act to achieve their common interest, they do so for other reasons than as an automatic consequence of rationality. They may, for instance, find extra pleasure or advantages from participation, they may adapt themselves to the pressures coming from their immediate environment, or they act as driven by a moral or ideological norm they have appropriated.

In analysing the mechanisms of rational action, the psychologist obviously cannot confine himself to the form of action Max Weber (1947, 115-118) describes by the concept *"zweckrational"*. Collective rationality, i.e., action maintaining and preserving common values, can well be found where action is still, in Weber's terms, "traditional". For instance, people respect and protect nature as long as they hold the strong belief that nature is sacred, the abode of God.

Collective rationality can also be found where action is based on Weber's *Wertrationalitat*, i.e., persistent orientation to specific absolute values. Today, such values might be peace or sustaining life on earth. If psychology wishes to meet today's challenges, it must therefore break loose from the bonds of *Zweckrationalitat* and dig into the significance of moral, religion, and ideologies as from the viewpoint of rational collective action.

Catastrophes threatening us from outside give occasion to another kind of prediction, too. Threats such as accidental nuclear explosions or a nuclear war occurring by pure accident necessitate ever more comprehensive safety systems. Psychological knowledge is one of the elements needed in building these systems. An "accident" generally means, in these contexts, that the paths of two lawful processes which are independent of each other happen to meet in a way that is not predictable and the consequences of which are disastrous. We might expect research into accidents of this type as well as the planning of *socio-technological safety systems* to protect us against them to expand in the field of psychology over the next few years, because the risks, too, have become of a vast magnitude,

**Developments Penetrating the Field of Psychology**

In entering the spirit of the 1996 scene, the different groups of respondents proposed at least three different lines of societal development that may also penetrate the field of psychology, adult education or sports, paralysing these activities or rendering them useless. First, it is Possible that *external coercion* begins with an ever tighter grip to determine human behaviour, whereby analysis of psychological determinants becomes meaningless. Secondly, especially in the case of sports, such changes in *personality* and people's *motivation* were surmised to have taken place that people in the future were no longer willing to make the efforts sports required. One of the psychologists interviewed had, in his own way, a very similar idea of the future: the "normal" or "sane" personality will tomorrow be what we today call a narcissistically disturbed personality. Those engaged in the field of adult education, then, were afraid of such developments in *information systems* that render adult education unnecessary. Computers and innumerable TV channels provide people with all the information they need easily, without any trouble necessary in acquiring it.

The fear of increasing external coercion or necessities would seem to a great extent to be based on the trend that man is, as it were, drifting further apart from the object of his needs, as new social mediations are growing between him and that object. Take man's relation to food.[2] What mediations has civilisation brought between food and man?

In the first place, contrary to primitive man, we prepare our food. Cooking, heat, the pots and pans are one mediation which has drawn man further away from his food as compared with the hunter-gatherer who dug out roots and worms from the ground and gobbled them up. But today we also eat increasing amounts of "fast" food, which means a new link in the chain of mediations: the fast food industry and the related advertisement industry.

When we go shopping for foodstuffs, we can rarely smell them, taste them, or touch them. If we want to know' what this or that packaged food product contains, we have to read the declaration of contents on it; we have to be satisfied with this linguistic-theoretical mediation instead of concretely sensing. We eat our meals with design cutlery, observing table manners, keeping an eye for anything "not good" for us, instead of stuffing down our food with gay abandon.

New mediations are growing at the other end of chain too, in foodstuff production. Production has became ever more synthetic and mechanised. Agricultural policy, production contracts, fertilisers and insecticides, hog factories and poultry factories, and a science developing the related technology—all this has come between man and the food nature yields.

The increase in coercion and necessities can be seen in that production to an ever greater extent determines what we can eat and in what form. Few of us eat what we really want to but what's on special offer. We know that our food is adulterated with additives and poison, but there's nothing we can do about it. The feeling of powerlessness increases; it is difficult to understand what is happening with common-sense knowledge. The world is full of coercion and necessities, ruled and understood only by experts. When the expert says that something is necessary to "guarantee national security" or to "boost industrial competitiveness", there's nothing more to be said.

Solutions to these problems are sought in two opposite directions, and psychologists, too, seem to be far from unanimous as to where the solutions lie. Some believe that man, by means of science, is capable of gaining rational control over those complex mediations, even if just now they seem to have got out of hand. In psychology, this belief strengthens *scientistic tendencies.* Psychology oriented towards natural sciences is in particular expected to come up with inventions that would decisively add to man's ability to take rational control over his environment.

Others, then, believe that the only solution is to shorten and simplify the social chains of mediation. Power must be decentralised, direct action must be increased, small units of production must be brought back. In political life, the "green" movement represents this solution. In psychology, we find *action research* in this direction, with its emancipatory objectives and "soft" methods.

Changes in the structure of personality and motivation here mean those types of problems that e.g. Albee (1977) has dealt with. His concern is that "the self-contained, inner-directed, career-oriented, middle-class individual disappears from the contemporary scene and is replaced with the status-seeking lotus eater". Psychologists become gurus "who argue that learning to feel is far more important than learning to think and that teaching students to be therapists and encounter-group manipulators does not require, indeed may be inhibited by, a library".

Behind these fears are obviously some real changes in late-capitalist society. Socialisation mechanisms no longer produce such a Protestant ethics of work as in the early stages of capitalism. With mass unemployment thriving, work cannot be something that shapes one's personality or anchors one's way of life in the same way as previously. Riesman's (1953) "inner-directed" person turns into an other-directed person or a "narcissistic" personality as depicted by Lasch (1978) and others.

However, the consequences psychology faces need not be as disastrous as Albee fears. On the contrary, the outcome may well be that the psychology of the 1990's is more conscious of man's historical conditions and developments, and that *historical psychology* rises to the position it deserves.

"Man" is then no longer identified with the man of early capitalism, but psychology unfolds into three directions. In the first place, it begins, with ever greater determination, to explore the developments in society that are presently changing the psychology of man in advanced capitalist countries. Secondly, following Bronfenbrenner's (1970) pioneer work, it gives an interest in how socialism has affected the personality of the generations that have grown up under it. And thirdly, it starts investigating the immensely rich laboratory that the developing countries in Africa, Asia and Latin America form, no longer from the Western ethnocentric perspective, but from that of the real circumstances and cultures of those countries.

Developments in information systems also open our eyes to what in psychology belongs to a specific historical time, as well as make us examine how the general validity of psychological knowledge could be improved. In traditional society, man learns rules tied to specific situations: how this or that job is done, how to act in this or that situation. As societal change speeds up, such knowledge soon becomes obsolete. Of importance, therefore, become such general skills as reading, writing, and arithmetic and such operations upon which ability tests have traditionally been based. With computers, electronic gadgets, television and music gaining a more central footing in our culture, psychology is forced to shift its focus to even more general matters: from testing permanent "skills" or "traits" to the study of *cognitive processes* and *internal representations* in general, as indeed has happened over the last few years. This development will probably continue and strengthen in the *1990's*, because the revolution of new information systems is still in process.

## The Internal Development of Psychology

"Despite all the efforts to improve the comprehensibility of conceptual systems used in psychology, we have come to a point where different schools have drifted so far apart that it appears impossible to hold one unifying congress." In specifying why they believed a World Congress of Psychology is no longer feasible in 1996, a good many of the psychologists who participated in our experiment made up this kind of explanation.

In effect, the continuous expansion of Psychological research is believed to create several kinds of problems. First, the very number of psychologists in the world is getting so high that, even from the technical point of view, staging a congress is becoming more or less impossible. Second, the exponential growth of scientific knowledge cannot continue forever. But what, then, will happen within science when it starts to approximate its limits? Will it stagnate into "normal science", unable to bring about scientific revolutions, as has been predicted (Verronen 1983)? Will this already be the fate of psychology in the 1990's? Third, the drifting apart of different branches and theoretical lines of thought following from the growth of the field of science threatens its unity.

Let us take one example. What might be a common field of interest for psychology used as an *aid to social technology* and, on the other hand, psychology that aims at influencing *through* people's *consciousness*?

A typical example of social technology is Taylor's (1903) "scientific management", the objective of which is to regulate, up to the slightest movement of the hand, how the worker uses the labour power he has sold to the employer. The scientific planning of this use is detached from the actual use, to be separately undertaken by researchers. Skinner's (1971) idea that all planning initiative concerning man's action must be removed from the individual himself and transferred to "designers of a culture" is an extreme example of socio-technological thinking.

Of little socio-technological use, then, are the numerous glorified social psychological experiments. For instance, it is hardly possible to develop techniques and socio-technological systems based on social influence from Sherif and Asch's famous experiments that would not be familiar to us from everyday life. The same must be said of Milgram's experiments on obedience. An extreme form of social technology based on obedience is a soldier who upon command is prepared to kill a person called an enemy. Mankind has not needed Milgram's experiments to work out this application of obedience.

The significance of this kind of research lies in the influence it has on the person who reads about the experiments and their results. The average middle-class person has appropriated an ideology of individualism, which, according to Lukes' (1973) analysis, includes amongst other things a belief in man's autonomy and human dignity. Experiments dealing with social influence are an embarrassing reminder of the fact that man, in effect, is not as autonomous as the ideology of individualism tries to claim. Milgram's experiments make us restless, as they question the credibility of the doctrine of individualism in suggesting that man can easily be made to wound another person's dignity—by causing intolerable pain to him, for instance. The studies influence through consciousness; this is where their significance lies.

Those psychologists who give their knowledge and skills to the use of social technology and those who try to achieve something by arousing consciousness may in the 1990's be even farther away from each other than at present—both scientifically and politically. Such differentiation will probably also produce countertendencies: more determined attempts to bridge the gaps between different branches and lines of thought in psychology and-to search for a common object of research for this science. This would imply the strengthening of research into the *philosophical grounds of psychology* and the *history of psychology*.

Psychology as a whole would also be strengthened if *social psychology* were able to break loose from narrow-minded—and often rather naive—laboratory experiments and turn towards a wider perspective, as suggested over the last few years by, for instance, Archibald (1978), Doise (1978), Israel (1979) or Tajfel and Fraser (1978), in works that as such differ quite radically from one another. The present author has also, in a recent book (Eskola 1982), tried to introduce social psychology, in Brickmanls (1980) words, as "a point of confluence for the human sciences". The development of psychology will not, however, automatically take us to this or that point in the 1990's. Much depends on how we, as researchers, wish to develop our science.

## NOTES

1. The psychologists' peace committee was founded in Finland in the spring of 1982. Its first Chairman is professor J. M. von Wright.
2. This example has been influenced by Sten Andersson's (1980) delightful book on "the roles of food", or "sociological gastronomy".

## REFERENCES


1. Albee, G. W. The protestant ethic, sex, and psychotherapy. *American Psychologist*, 1977, 32, 150-161.
2. Allport, G. W. The ego in contemporary psychology. *Psychological Review*, 1943, 50, 451-478.
3. Andersson, S. *Matens roller—sociologisk gastronomi.* Stockholm: Almqvist and Wiksell, 1980.
4. Archibald, W. P. *Social Psychology as Political Economy.* Toronto: McGraw-Hill Ryerson, 1978.
5. Barry, B. and Hardin, R. (Eds.), *Rational Man and Irrational Society?* Beverly Hills: Sage, 1982.
6. Bertaux, D. and Bertaux-Wiame, I. Life stories in the bakers' trade. D. Bertaux (Ed.), *Biography and Society.* Beverly Hills: Sage, 1981.
7. Brickman, P. A social psychology of human concerns. R. Gilmour and S. Duck (Eds.), *The Development of Social Psychology.* London: Academic Press, 1980.
8. Bronfenbrenner, U. *Two Worlds of Childhod: U.S. and U.S.S.R.* New York: Russell Sage Foundation, 1970.
9. Coleman, J.S *Introduction to Mathematical Sociology.* London: Collier-Macmillan, 1964.
10. Deutsch, M. The prevention of World War III: a psychological perspective. *Political psychology*, 1983, 4, 3-31.
11. Doise, W. *Groups and Individuals: Explanations in Social Psychology.* Cambridge: Cambridge University Press, 1978.
12. Edney, J. J. The commons problem. Alternative perspectives. *American Psychologist*, 1980, 35, 131-150.

13. Eskola, A. *Socialpsykologins grunder—en kritisk granskning.* Stockholm: Almqvist and Wiksell, 1982.
14. Israel, J. *Om relationistisk socialpsykologi.* Goteborg: Korpen, 1979.
15. Lasch, C. *The Culture of Narcissism.* New York: W. W. Norton, 1978.
16. Lukes, S. *Individualism.* Oxford: Basil Blackwell, 1973.
17. Olson, M. *The Logic of Collective Action.* Cambridge: Harvard University Press, 1965.
18. Platt, J. Social traps. *American Psychologist,* 1973, 28, 641-651.
19. Riesman, D., with Glazer, N. A Denney R. *The lonely crowd.* Garden City, N.Y.: Doubleday, 1953.
20. Skinner, B.F. *Beyond Freedom and Dignity.* New York: Knopf, 1971.
21. Tajfel, H. and Fraser, C. (Eds.), *Introducing Social Psychology.* Harmondsworth: Penguin, 1978.
22. Taylor, F. W. *Scientific Management.* New York: Harper, 1947 (originally 1903).
23. Weber, M. *The Theory of Social and Economic Organisation.* New York: Oxford University Press, 1947.
24. Verronen, V. Tieteen kehityksen sisallollinen ja kvantita-tiivinen aspekti. *Kirjastotiede ja informatiikka,* 1983, 2, 3-10.

# 12

# What Will Psychology Be Like in the Future?

Cohen (1977) interviewed thirteen renowned psychologists about their discipline. He concluded—among other things (p. 335)—that psychologists appeared to exercise their "need for power" in fighting over what psychology should be about. Each of them seemed to be of the opinion that the research area he himself represented was the most important one in psychology. The rest of the discipline, which did not deal with those particular problems, was said to have "accomplished nothing".

Such has not been the case with the authors of the present volume. They are quite willing to see the merits of other areas of psychology, and think that their own speciality might be improved by a broadening of its prevailing views. Furthermore, reading the articles gives the impression that the views presented in most of the contributions can be fitted together quite well on at least some level of generalisation. This latter state of affairs may perhaps justify the validity of the outlook emerging from this book.

The present epilogue cannot of course give due credit even to all the main ideas presented by the different contributors. Some general themes and ways of thinking may, however, be mentioned as common to many of them.

One such general trend is to consider a kind of *process orientation* as the way psychology will and should take in the future. A couple of authors speak explicitly about a new functionalism, having in mind both a study of processes and a pragmatic attitude. Both behaviour and mental life are continuously ongoing processes. Even when attempts are made to organise this flow of events into structure-like entities such as mental faculties or traits, the process character of the study object must not be relinquished. Psychological "structures" can never be structures in the same sense as anatomical ones for instance are, but are comprised of successively occurring instances of behaviour or mental states.

Related to the pragmatic attitude is an emphasis on behaviour as an *interaction between the individual and his/her environment*. Methodological questions concerning this interaction and its description are discussed in several contributions. The relationship between the individual and the environment is accounted for more adequately when the behaviour is studied in its ecological context. The idea of *ecological validity* of research settings and methods is conveyed explicitly or implicitly by many contributors. It is also felt that *unobtrusive methods* should be used which do not interfere with the natural processes or the behaviour of the persons under study.

Present day psychologists in general, and perhaps especially the contributors of this volume, are skilled in using sophisticated statistics and experimental methods. It is remarkable that in spite of this, they do not particularly emphasise the importance of rigorous experimentation, strict controls, objectivity of research or other such things. They rather seem to take them for granted, and call for methods that grasp the meaningfulness and genuineness of behaviour. Although most of the writers do not subscribe to the phenomenological movement, many of them feel that more attention should be paid within academic psychology to how people *experience* their environments and their own actions.

It is true, as one of the contributors points out, that the *unity of science* is not in itself necessarily valuable. At its worst, a striving for unity may blur the sight for differences which cannot be explained by common principles. How, then, can one not miss the wood for the trees and, yet preserve the identity of details? The history of psychology includes many turns and reorientations which have aimed at increasing clarity and coherence. In retrospect, however, they mostly reflect methodological innovations rather than theoretical advances. These have been strongly polarised in such terms as structuralism-functionalism, introspection-objectivity, ideographic-nomothetic, correlative-experimental, molecular, and so on. At the present time, one of these, i.e. structuralism vs. functionalism, is readily observable. The question is now whether we are only witnessing the old pendulum swinging again, this time in the direction towards functionalism? It might be recalled that a thoughtful functionalist critique of the present information processing psychology has already been provided by Garner (1980).

A somewhat unexpected feature of his presentation is its resemblance to the ideas presented by Osward Kulpe and his associates when criticising Wundt's approach about eighty years ago (see Boring, 1950, 401-410). Are we, then, at the mercy of a crude logic of pairs of mutually exclusive alternatives? This prospect is frightening because a dialectics of this kind is surely not the best catalyst for the growth of knowledge. Our impression from the present volume is that, fortunately, such a state of affairs no longer exists. The above-mentioned theoretical positions were mainly formulated at one level of psychological inquiry. Hence there was much debate on the image of man, reductionism, etc. In contrast to this, psychology is now evolving to a multilevel enterprise including different complementary methods which do not claim priority over each other. Attempts to fit together pieces of knowledge attained within different areas of a discipline, or within different disciplines, force researchers to regard the latter from new angles. New aspects of phenomena may emerge and must be dealt with.

This is what is aimed at in many contributions to the present volume where the forecast of a more unified psychology is made. The writers suggest, for example, that psychology and the neurosciences, psychology and the social sciences, and different areas of psychology should be linked together in a more exact and detailed way than has been the case before, so as to form a less incoherent and less controversial outlook on human mind and behaviour. This is the task for a *systemic approach* to psychology to which some of the writers refer. Its main contribution will be the liberation of psychological thinking form the locked chambers of narrowly defined positions, while simultaneously preserving the traditional scientific rigour.

## REFERENCES

1. Boring, E.G. *A History of Experimental Psychology.* New York: Appleton-Century-Crofts, 1950, (2nd ed.)
2. Cohen, D. *Psychologists on Psychology.* New York: Taplinger, 1977.
3. Garner, W.R. Association lecture: Functional aspects of information processing: In Nickerson, R.S. (Eds.), *Attention and Performance VIII.* Hillsdale, N.J.: Erlbaum, 1980.

# 13

# Psychology's Place in Science

Psychology has been short on both history and historians. As time passes, so will the shortages. There are several signs indicating that the history of psychology is emerging into robust health; The *Journal of the History of the Behavioural Sciences* started publication in 1964 and continues to provide an outlet within psychology for articles on our history. The International Society for the History of the Behavioural and Social Sciences, established in 1969, holds annual meetings. It is called Cheiron after the wisest of the mythological centaurs. Division 26 of the American Psychological Association is the Division for the History of Psychology; it first met as a formal division in 1966. There is now an archive for the history of psychology at the University of Akron. Finally, the first American Ph.D. awarded on the basis of a dissertation on the history of psychology was awarded to Dr. Barbara Ross of the University of New Hampshire under the guidance of Dr. R.I. Watson, editor of the *Journal of the History of the Behavioural Sciences.* Thus nearly all the marks of professional maturity have come to the history of psychology only since 1964.

There are also some encouraging signs that professional historians, rather than professional psychologists, are beginning to pay attention to the history of psychology. For example, Sokal (1971) has written on one of America's leading early psychologists, James McKeen Cattell.

Even before the history of psychology showed these signs of maturity, psychologists were fascinated by their own past. Solso (1971) studied the lists of books recommended by graduate departments of psychology in the United States and found that Boring's *A History of Experimental Psychology* was among the exclusive group of books most recommended in 1953, and has remained there since. There seems to be no doubt that psychologists, like other scientists, regard the study of their history as an extremely important subject. We now turn to a very brief sketch of a little of that history and to some of the lessons that seem to derive from this overview.

The schools of psychology can be better understood with these lessons clearly in mind. Accordingly, this chapter sketches several ideas relevant to the understanding of psychology's emergence and its position in science. First, we discuss the growth of some general philosophical ideas which seem critical to the emergence of science. Then some more specific problems which contributed to the emergence of psychology as a separate-science are outlined. Third, the initial subject matter of psychology is compared with its contemporary subject matter. We next turn our attention to psychology's place in the corporate organisational chart of science. Three topics help in this assessment: psychology as a part of the hierarchy of science, pure versus applied science, and special problems related to the subject matter of psychology.

### The Growth of Scientific Ideas

Table 13.1 presents, for ready reference, a summary of the contributions of some of the men who helped to develop the scientific ideas that finally led to a science of psychology. Their birth and death dates are approximate both because the historical record may be incomplete and because calendar changes often make interpretation of existing records difficult.

Many historians have noted the apparently stepwise progress of the sciences, beginning with those farthest from man and moving toward those closest to him and his immediate affairs, and the consequent late development of the science of psychology. Astronomy and physics were the first sciences to develop. Archimedes, in the third century B.C., was in some ways a sophisticated physicist. In the early seventeenth century, Kepler's mathematical description of the motions of the planets around the sun was already the culmination of a long line of astronomical discoveries. The body of man was investigated long before there was a science for the "mind" of man. Harvey, in 1628, described the circulation of the blood, about 250 years before Ebbinghaus did his pioneer work on memory.

Two reasons have been suggested for this long-time neglect of the behaviour of man. One is the sanctity of the human being as maintained by human institutions. The other is the complexity of the human being as proclaimed by those who have tried to study him. We might add that it is often easiest to be objective about the things that concern us least.

The foregoing statements, of course, are ruthlessly selected to make the general point. We know that philosophers and laymen have long wrestled with explanations of the human being, but there was not a formal *science* of behaviour, as there were other sciences. Some of the contributions of these men will be discussed in more detail in the text to follow, but it will be helpful if the reader has an overall view of them before examining certain key concepts.

#### *Explanation: External and Internal*

There was a time in the history of man when events were typically explained in terms of forces outside the scope of observable natural events. For example, Norse mythology explained storms by saying that the Warrior of the gods was angry, and Homer explained victory in war in terms of the favoritism of the Greek gods. From the scientific point of view, there are two very basic things wrong with these explanations: (1) they refer the explanation to unobservables, and (2) the events used as explanations do not fit within the same context as the events to be explained; there is thus no apparent logical connection between the alleged causes and their consequences. Such explanations are therefore called *external,* as opposed to *internal*.

**TABLE 13.1**

**Summary of Major Contributions to the Development of Psychology**

| Philosophy | | |
|---|---|---|
| *Man* | *Approximate Birth and Death Dates* | *Contribution* |
| Thales | Sixth century B.C. | Naturalistic explanation; universe composed of water. |
| Socrates | C. 470-399 B.C. | Idealistic philosopher; essentially antiscientific. |
| Democritus | c. 460-370 B.C. | Universe composed of atoms; reductionistic account of complex phenomena. |
| Plato | 427-347 B.C. | Rationalistic, dualistic approach. |
| Aristotle | 384-322 B.C. | Rationalistic and observational methods; classification systems for biology; laws of associative memory. |
| Roger Bacon | c. 1214-1 294 | Emphasis on free empirical observation. |
| Francis Bacon | 1561-1626 | *Novum organum:* gave philosophical support to empirical science. |
| Descartes | 1596-1650 | Dualistic interactionism; action of body mechanistic. |
| Leibniz | 1646-1716 | Activity as basic; degrees of consciousness; co-invertor of calculus. |
| La Mettrie | 1709-1751 | Mechanistic explanation applied to man's behaviour. |
| Kant | 1724-1804 | Importance of native abilities in ordering the data of experience. |

| Physics and Astronomy | | |
|---|---|---|
| *Man* | *Approximate Birth and Death Dates* | *Contribution* |
| Archimedes | c. 387-212 B.C. | First well-known experimental physicist. |
| Ptolemy | Second century B.C. | Alexandrian astronomer; his view of earth as center of universe held for centuries. |
| Copernicus | 1473-1543 | Polish astronomer who placed sun at center of solar system; changed man's view of his own importance. |
| Galileo | 1564-1642 | Reestablished observation as final court of appeal; made astronomical and physical discoveries. |
| Kepler | 1571-1630 | Mathematical description of planetary orbits. |
| Newton | 1642-1727 | Co-inventor of calculus; set pattern of physics for 200 years. |
| Bessel | 1784-1846 | Astronomer at Konigsberg; worked out personal equations and thus posed a problem for psychology. |

| Biological Science | | |
|---|---|---|
| *Man* | *Approximate Birth and Death Dates* | *Contribution* |
| Hippocrates | c. 460-380 B.C. | "Father of medicine"; an excellent observer; naturalistic view or man. |
| Herophilus and Erasistratus | Third century B.C. | First inference of distinction between sensory and motor nerves. |
| Galen | Second century | Famous physician and anatomist; performed animal experiments. |
| Vesalius | 1514-1564 | First thorough treatise on human anatomy. |
| Harvey | 1578-1657 | Demonstrated the circulation of the blood. |
| Van Leeuwenhoek | 1632-1723 | First effective microscope; discovery or identification of protozoa, bacteria, and human sperm. |
| Linnacus | 1707-1778 | Binomial system of biological classification. |
| Darwin | 1809-1882 | *The origin of specks:* primary publication on organic evolution. |

| Emergence of Modern Physiology | | |
|---|---|---|
| *Man* | *Approximate Birth and Death Dates* | *Contribution* |
| J. Mueller | 1801-1858 | Comprehensive *Handbuch der Physiologie des Menschen:* doctrine of "specific energies of nerves." |
| Bernard | 1813-1878 | Concept of the internal environment. |
| Helmholtz | 1821-1894 | Eminent physiologist; first experimental measurement of speed of nerve impulse; theories of hearing and seeing. |

| Emergence of Psychology | | |
|---|---|---|
| *Man* | *Approximate Birth and Death Dates* | *Contribution* |
| Weber | 1795-1878 | Pioneer physiologist; formulated law: $dR/R = C$; really a psychological law. |
| Fechner | 1801-1887 | *Elemente der Psychophysik:* believed by some to mark beginnings of experimental psychology; modified Weber's law into Weber-Fechner form: $S=C \log R$. |
| Galton | 1822-1911 | work in eugenics, statistics, individual differences; set many problems for psychology. |
| Wundt | 1832-1920 | Founder of first psychological laboratory, at University of Leipzig. |

It is not always easy to tell whether a particular explanation is internal. The extremes are easy: theological explanations of natural events are clearly external, and accepted scientific accounts are usually internal. Paradoxically, some of the most sophisticated scientific explanations are the most difficult ones to classify. These sophisticated explanations often depend on postulated but initially unobserved entities like genes, stimulus elements, or Omega Minus particles. Most scientists accept explanations couched in terms of such concepts as internal because they or their effects are potentially observable, are "observed" indirectly, or have implications for observations at another level. Questions arise, however, if it is not clear that the concept is formulated so that it is potentially observable, if the supposed indirect observation can be accounted for in other ways, or if the implications from the deductive system containing the concept are not clear.

Although there are still people who explain disasters in terms of "the wrath of God," scientific explanation does not have recourse to such descriptions. Thales, a Greek philosopher of the sixth century BC., is sometimes given credit for Initiating attempts to explain natural events in terms of other natural events; he explained the nature of matter in terms of a single basic *natural* element, water. Democritus soon after explained matter in terms of basic particles called *atoms*, and modern man still holds to a similar conception. Whether these men really deserve credit for the swing toward internal explanation, however, is not important; the important thing is that science as we know it depends on the use of explanations which refer to observables within the same natural framework as the observables to be explained.

The Greek culture that developed this idea eventually disappeared. The idealistic skepticism of Socrates and Plato, ingenious as it was, may have contributed to its disappearance. The ensuing Middle Ages showed little concern for internal types of explanations or for scientific problems; perhaps the attitude was that great interest in natural events was bad for the soul. Such science as there was during the medieval period was largely in the East. It remained for the Renaissance, beginning (by the most common convention) with Galileo and his contemporaries, to renew European interest in natural science. An example of the external thinking that was predominant in the Middle Ages is the typical treatment of convulsions by flogging; such action was thought to drive out of the body the demons or evil spirits that were considered to be responsible for convulsive behaviour. Today, of course, such treatment is not used because convulsive behaviour is generally viewed as determined by organic conditions within the body (an internal explanation). Convulsive electroshock is used in the treatment of psychosis with explanations of its effectiveness which are probably less satisfying than if we still believed in evil spirits; however, it may be significant that we are *seeking* an internal explanation.

In denigrating external explanations, we are not assuming that the implications of the explanation *necessarily* lead to ineffective treatments. People are frequently "right for the wrong reasons." For example, recent work in behaviour modification would lead us to believe that flogging, systematically administered every time the "evil spirit" was seen at work, might eliminate the undesirable behaviour in some cases. R. I. Watson (1963) gives an example which shows that a more nearly correct conclusion may follow from a kind of evidence which we would find altogether unacceptable today, while an inferior conclusion about the same issue derives from an attempt at "internal" explanation. Watson says of Aristotle's views (1963, p. 52):

> In identifying life with the *psyche* and this, in turn, with the heart, he also rejects the Platonic doctrine of the brain as the organ of the soul. He used as one argument for doing so the fact that he found the brain to be insensible to direct stimulation. It is ironical that Plato was right for the wrong reasons. Plato assigned reason to the brain on the basis of several irrelevant reasons typical of which is the fact that the brain was the part of man nearest the heavens. Aristotle; on the other hand, was wrong for the "right," *i.e.*, naturalistic reasons.

If some right decisions follow from the wrong theories, the theories have a greater life expectancy than if all decisions turn out badly. Phrenologists recommended practicing algebra for those who had an inadequate bump in the area responsible, according to their system, for algebraic proficiency. If this "treatment" both followed from the theory and produced algebraic ability, the theory could be regarded as "confirmed"; as a matter of fact, it did take phrenology a long time to disappear.

Such examples bring home the fact that observations cannot logically confirm theories; they can only disconfirm them. In scientific practice, theories are seldom rejected because of a single disconfirmation. They can almost always be saved by finding a flaw in the observation or in the relationship between the observation and the theory. Even if these modes of rescue fail, most theories are complex enough so that a change in a part will bring the theory into line with the observation, and the bulk of the theory can be saved. On the confirming side, too, the dictates of pure logic are not followed. If an observation occurs as a theory says it should, confidence in the usefulness of the theory increases, despite the illogic of the increase in confidence. Certainly the illogic is not without reason; the theory, after all, has been demonstrated to be "right" with respect to the observation.

### *Reliance on Observation*

Parallel with the use of internal explanation was an increasing reliance on observation. Most of the earlier Greek thinkers relied more on rationalistic methods than is the case in the modern era. For example, Euclid early developed a deductive geometry, and Pythagoras and his followers had a mystic belief in the efficacy of numbers. Socrates and Plato lent support to a rationalistic approach, Socrates with his logical questioning procedure and Plato with his emphasis on the importance of the ideal world, which he somehow regarded as above and beyond the real world. Both tended to suspect the evidence of the senses as the source of truth and thus helped to turn the tide against what is now regarded as an essential feature of scientific method—a primary reliance on observation.

Aristotle was one early thinker who used observation as well as rational methods. He was an advocate of logic and reasonableness, but not and respecter of authority. His own authority, however, was accepted during the Middle Ages at the expense of observational methods. Galileo was important in renewing the scientific attitude toward observation and authority. He relied, for example, upon *observation* of the time of fall of bodies of unequal weight, rather than upon the authoritative statement that heavy bodies fall faster than light ones. Francis Bacon, in his *No Vum organum* of 1620,. made one of file most famous appeals for empiricism. He felt that science should work strictly by induction, piling observation upon observation until general facts emerge from specific facts.

The English empiricists who came after Bacon tried to follow his approach to its logical conclusion. Locke denied the innate ideas attributed to man by thinkers like Socrates and Descartes. Berkeley denied that we could be sure of the existence of the external world, since we have only experience to go on Though he returned the external world to us only slightly used, with the help of the assumption of the existence of God, his skeptical position was more convincing than his retreat, and has been more influential. Finally, Hume applied empiricistic thinking to the notion of causality and maintained that all we really know is that some events are invariably contiguous in space and time. Our notion of causality is based on this observation.

Kant reacted to the empiricists, particularly Hume, and proposed a compromise type of theory in which experience remains the teacher, but needs a student with a certain native endowment. Kant's specific statements about what is known prior to experience have been rejected, but his general point that the attainment of knowledge requires certain prior abilities is still accepted.

Despite the contrast between the extremes of empiricism and rationalism, there is no such thing as a *purely* rationalistic or *purely* empiricistic approach, nor is there a clear-cut line of demarcation between the two approaches. Francis Bacon, in his "discarding" of the rationalistic approach, had to use rationalistic methods in his arguments. The most empirically minded, "hardheaded" scientists eventually make general statements based on their observations—and hence depend for their application on the use of the rationalistic method. On the other hand, the rationalistic philosopher very probably takes the plausible assumptions with which he begins from some kind of empirical observations. The scientific usefulness of his rationalistically derived conclusions depends on their consonance with observations. Though there is no pure approach and no clear method of classifying the techniques of particular individuals as more rationalistic or more empirical, we believe it is reasonable to say that science has tended to emphasise the empirical more than the national. The final arbiter of truth for a scientist is not what rationally *ought to be* but what observationally *is.*

### *Simplification*

Thales and Democritus tried to simplify the apparent complexity of nature by appealing to simpler elements and to assumptions which allowed them to derive the observed complexity from the assumed simplicity. Their attempts were also *reductionistic,* since they reduced complexity by explanations depending on the existence of phenomena at a different, "lower" level; for example, Democritus supposed man to be built of particles much like those which compose other forms of matter. Physiological psychologists make similar reductionistic statements when behavioural data are explained in terms of physiological events, which again are at another level of observation. It does not follow that a reductionistic account wilt also necessarily be a simple account, or even the simplest available at a given level of explanation. Science seeks and accepts not only simple hypotheses but also the simplest overall theory which adequately explains all the observations made.

Reductionistic explanations offer at least a potential economy of concepts, since a single concept can serve at more than one level of explanation. These economies may serve as the basis for choice between otherwise equivalent theories Turner says (1967, pp. 178-179):

> When we turn to the ideá of a hierarchy of explanation, we especially realise that there is a guidance implicit within scientific invention. One seeks not only an explanation of a particular set of events but also a theoretical construction that itself is derivable from within some still more basic science. Chemical explanations, for example, were conceived in terms wholly unique to the phenomenology of chemistry itself. But the advantages and the guidance of atomic constructions are now all too apparent. Geneticists could have continued to think in terms of the gross characteristics of genotypes, but the molecular model of biochemistry offered explanations of the duplicative powers of the genes. And psychology can continue to build hypothetico-deductive models in learning theory, knowing (perhaps unconsciously) that issues of alternative theories will be resolved by developments in neuropsychology.

In his later book (1971), Turner continues to favor reductionism but discusses the issues in much greater detail. For example, he considers various alternative routes that might be taken in a reductionistic program: linguistic reduction, mechanical reduction (through computer simulation), and neurological reduction.

### *Placement of Man in Nature*

The Greeks seem to have regarded man as having no special status apart from the rest of nature. Many of the Greek philosophers would probably have agreed that the behaviour of man is lawful and predictable, just like the behaviour of inanimate nature. The Middle Ages, however, took a different view of man. He was regarded as a creature with a soul, possessed of a free will which set him apart from ordinary natural laws, subject only to his own willfulness and perhaps to the rule of God. Such a creature, being free-willed, could not be an object of scientific investigation. Even the body of man was regarded as sacrosanct, and dissection was dangerous for the dissector. These strictures against observation hindered the development of anatomy and medicine for centuries, and misconceptions that are today considered incredible persisted for over a thousand years. A science of man could not flourish in such an atmosphere.

Today concern for the rights of the living has superseded concern for the rights of the dead. However, if the reader is tempted to believe that performance of research is no longer an issue, he should familiarise himself with the current, continuing, and often acrimonious controversy surrounding the treatment of animal and human subjects. Wolfensberger

(1967), for example, discusses the use of human subjects. Related battles have raged around psychological testing. The entire issue of the *American Psychologist* for November, 1965, was devoted to an examination of the testing issue. The basic conflict involved is between the right of the human individual to privacy and the need of other-scientists and government agencies particularly—to get information about him. We do not wish to prejudge such issues; ethical matters are not yet decidable by scientific methods, so we shall limit ourselves to pointing out that problems in the ethics of science may always be with us.

Descartes started a trend which again favored psychological, or at least human, research. A predictable system is a researchable system. Descartes regarded the body of a man as a machine which will move and behave in predictable ways if we know what the "inputs" are. He salvaged free will for man by possessing him of a soul which was free and which decided the actions of the body. Such a view made at least dead (soulless) bodies accessible to scientific investigation; animals, since Descartes regarded them as soulless, were also accessible.

The idea that man might be an object of scientific study was furthered by La Mettrie. He was convinced, apparently largely by the deterioration of his own thought processes during a fever, that man was *altogether* a machine, dependent in mind as in body upon physical events. He espoused this view, despite strong opposition, until his death.

The man-machine analogy to which Descartes and La Mettrie contributed is a good example of the kind of partial analogy which starts persistent controversy. It is clear that man is not identical to any existing machine either in his construction or in his mode of operation. Descartes and La Mettrie, both brilliant thinkers, cannot seriously be considered stupid enough to have overlooked this glaring fact. Neither can other mechanistic thinkers. All of them are supporting a limited likeness between man and machine. Machines are constructed and fairly well understood by man, and their behaviour can be predicted. Man, although neither constructed nor understood by himself, seems also to be a creature of his construction and should in principle be predictable like machines. Critics of the "mechanistic" position attack the complete, unintended analogy of the mechanist as often as the partial analogy he intends.

There was still much resistance to viewing man within a deterministic, natural framework when Charles Darwin advanced his theory of organic evolution. Evolution itself was not a new idea, but Darwin buttressed the evolutionary theory with so much evidence that it to the scientific community by storm. Evolution restored the continuity between man and other animals which Descartes had denied when he attributed a soul to man alone. It also contradicted the Biblical account of creation. The theologically based opposition aroused a heated controversy which persisted into the twentieth century and was heard around the world. Today there is little questioning of the correctness of the general outlines of evolutionary theory. Evolution is a fact for the scientific community, if not for all the lay community. Its acceptance has made the science of psychology more acceptable by making it more plausible than ever to view the behaviour of man as lawful. It has also made the study of animals an important part of that science; the assumed continuity between animals and men supports the belief that knowledge gained in the study of animals will have significance for the behaviour of men.

## Psychology's Legacy of Problems

Finally, then, the behaviour of man came to be regarded as lawful, and a science of psychology was possible. But the basic scientific and philosophical assumptions prerequisite for the development of a science were not all that psychology found in its legacy when it began as a formal science. Psychology also inherited certain problems that developed within science and philosophy before it won its independence. Problems, as well as necessary assumptions, must exist before a new science will arise. Some of the problems passed on to psychology were phrased in such a way that their scientific resolution through experiment was impossible, but they nevertheless stimulated research as attempts were made to find those elusive answers. We shall consider four problem areas: the mind-body problem, the physiology of perception, the reaction-time problem, and questions related to individual differences.

### *The Mind-Body Problem*

The ghostly apparitions of dreams may first have convinced man that there was more to him than met the physical eye. The writing of Plato shows that the thinking of his time divided man into two components. Descartes's dualistic views did not differ greatly from Plato's. Both systems fit into the Christian theology; some unobservable component is necessary if the immortality of man is logically to be maintained, since the observable portions of man are mortal. Even today, the thinking of the layman separates man into two components.

If man has both a mind and a body, then the question naturally arises: "what is the relationship between the two parts?" A long tradition of thought made the question inevitable. Before psychology ever had a formal beginning as a science, a German physicist, Theodor Fechner, started work on the problem. It was his intention to write equations that described the functional relationships between the psychic and the physical realms. The result which he believed he found is the Weber-Fechner law, so named because E.H. Weber had already expressed much the same psychophysical relationship in a simpler, more primitive form. Boring (1950, p. 483) has questioned whether Fechner really intended to take a dualistic position, but certainly his problem was stated in dualistic terms. For example, in his *Elemente der Psychophysik* (1860), Fechner said he was concerned with "the exact science of the functional relations or relations of dependency between body and mind." In order to demonstrate these functional relations, it is necessary to measure mind and body separately and therefore to have two separate things to measure. Fechner thought he was measuring two different things. On the one side he had the stimulus, which acted on the body. On the other side he had the sensation, which he thought of as a mental event. Fechner wished to demonstrate the identity of the two kinds of events, but it was difficult to reunite the two aspects that had been separated by assumption. He wanted to demonstrate empirically an identity that philosophers, using rationalistic methods, had been alternately proving and disproving for hundreds of years.

**TABLE 13.2**

**Major Philosophical Solutions to the Mind-Body Problem (An early important exponent of each position is identified in parentheses, with the approximate date of his contributions.)**

| | |
|---|---|
| | Dualism* |
| Cartesian interactionism (Descartes, 1641) | Two separate and interacting processes assumed. |
| Psychophysical parallelism (Spinoza, 1665) | Two separate, independent, but perfectly correlated processes assumed. |
| Occasionaslism (Malebranche, 1675) | Two separate and independent processes assumed; correlated by the intervention of God. |
| | Monism** |
| Materialism (Democritus, 400 B.C.) | A single underlying physical reality assumed. |
| Subjective idealism (Berkeley, 1710) | A single underlying mental or spiritual reality assumed. |
| Phenomenalism (Hume, 1740) | There are neither minds nor bodies as far as can be known; only ideas resulting from sense impressions exist. |
| | Compromises |
| Double-aspect view (Russell, 1915) | Two processes assumed to be a function or one underlying reality. |
| Epiphenomenalism (Hobbes, 1658) | Mind assumed to he a noncausal by-product of body. |

* Any point of view implying a basic difference between mind and body and therefore a relationship to be explained.

** Any point of view ignoring either mind or body or subsuming both under the same rubric.

The major mind-body positions that have been taken by philosophers are classified and summarised in Table 13.2. The reader should familiarise himself with the general outline presented here, for the "solutions" reappear in the following chapters. There is no scientific method for deciding among them. Early psychologists, as we shall see, nevertheless felt it necessary to take some stand on the mind-body problem. Then, for seven' decades it became fashionable to reject the problem altogether as meaningless. Today, whether it is meaningless or meaningful, soluble or insoluble, it seems to be coming back to the front as a topic of psychological conversation. We shall return to the problem in more detail later.

### *The Psychology of Perception*

Other scientists, notably physiologists were interested in another relationship,' that between physiological processes and perception, Hermann Ludwig Ferdinand von Helmholtz is the most famous of those interested in this relationship; he modified Thomas Young's color theory and developed his own theory of hearing. Helmholtz, along with the English empiricists, believed that all knowledge depends upon sense experience. If this is our assumption, then the problem of sense physiology is also the problem of epistemology—the problem of the origins, nature, and limitations of knowledge. Physiological findings in this area of study have philosophical implications. Helmholtz tried to refute Kant's statement that there is innate knowledge. Kant had believed that the axioms of geometry are known independently from any experience of them, Helmholtz asked whether we would have developed the same geometry if we had inhabited the inside surface of a hollow sphere. He discussed non-Euclidean geometries in a spirit which is surprisingly modern.

If the views of Helmholtz and Kant are viewed only in broad outline, however, the two differ less than they may have thought. Although Kant is categorised with nativists and Helmholtz with empiricists, Kant did admit the role of experience, Helmholtz recognised the need for some basic mental faculties to exist in 'order that the mind be able to develop the concept of space out of the raw materials of experience. There is, of course, a considerable difference in emphasis. The empiricist, by virtue of his philosophy, wants to observe and thus wants observable things to be as important as possible. The nativist tends to be a rationalist, and it is convenient for rationalists if the uncertain stuff of experience can be assigned as small a role as possible.

***The Reaction-time Problem***

The new science of psychology look over a second problem with epistemological implications. F.W. Bessel, the astronomer, noticed an account of the firing of an assistant at Greenwich Observatory. The assistant's readings did not agree with the readings of the head astronomer, and it is easy to guess whose readings were assumed to be wrong. Bessel recognised the possibility that the error might have been due to a difference in the time; required for the two observers to react to information presented to different senses, rather than being the result of carelessness. He checked his hunch by comparing the times at which he recorded star transits with the times at which other astronomers under the same conditions recorded the transits. There were discrepancies in-nearly all cases. Bessel then tried to write personal equations, or correction terms, which would reduce all the readings to a common basis. However, it was obvious that there could be no absolute standard of correctness where the human observer was concerned. Our knowledge was once again shown to depend upon observers and their methods of observing and recording. If the determination of the time at which a star crosses a line is subject to error, then it seems logical that more complex judgments and observations must be even more subject to error. It was not the philosophical point, however, which was important; it was the fact that the theoretical problems of epistemology were shown to be real, practical problems that stimulated Bessel and others after him to action.

Donders, a physiologist, further developed the problem, and Wundt took over the subtractive procedure from Donders. The subtractive procedure was supposed to reveal the time for psychological functions; the time for a high-level function was the total time for the activity, minus the time for some lower-level activity which was a part of the total. Wundt and many other early psychologists believed that by making the reaction required successively more difficult, the time for sensing, perceiving, apperceiving, discriminating, and the like could be found by subtracting the time for the next simpler reaction from that for the just more complicated reaction. Few psychologists would still hold this view; for example, it is not clear that perceiving involves sensing plus perceiving. The whole nature of the process being timed may change as the task is progressively complicated. The subtractive assumption is invalid.

### *Individual Differences*

Two fields of study that have remained extremely important up to the present day are individual differences and statistics, which was initially taken over and developed by psychology as a method for studying these differences. Much of the American acceptance of psychology may be attributed to the effectiveness of aptitude testing, which is part of the study of individual differences.

Sir Francis Galton pioneered in the development of both statistics and the study of individual differences. He developed the technique of correlation in connection with his inheritance studies. He was, led to it by the observation that children typically *regress* toward the mean relative to their parents in such characteristics as height and intelligence; that is, children of extremely tall or short, or bright or stupid, parents *tend* to be closer to the norm in these characteristics than their parents. Correlation is symbolised by *r*, for regression, and Galton is remembered for his early perception of the importance of statistics.

The major factor underlying the development of these interests was the Darwinian theory of evolution. Galton, who was Darwin's cousin, was himself interested in a practical problem—the improvement of the race through eugenics. In order to practice genetic manipulation, he needed to know how traits were inherited. This type of practical concern was in the direct line or conceptual descent that led from evolution to American functionalism. Stress on the organism's adjustment to the environments as a determining condition of survival or nonsurvival became a primary concern of psychology. The intellectual ferment produced by the theory of evolution raised questions that led directly to Galton's interest in individual differences, mental testing, and the statistical evaluation of differences and to the flourishing school of functionalism in the United States.

The theory of evolution also had implications for man's view of the philosophical controversy between rationalism and empiricism. Previously, most rationalists had to buttress their positions by postulating some kind of farfetched preestablished harmony between the constitution of the world and man's ideas about it. How could it happen that man possesses correct innate ideas about the world in which he lives? It is not scientifically convincing to suggest that God gives ideas to man. From the evolutionary point of view, however, it could be suggested that the rational (physiological?) side of man has been *pushed into harmony with the world* by the pressures of evolution. We can, according to this argument, count on the outcomes of rational analysis because man, through evolution, has come to think the right things about the world. Men who were mistaken about the world presumably took the wrong course of action and died. Those who were "rational" survived. Evolution solidifies the effects of the world on man into a kind of physiological rationalism.

## Psychology's Initial Subject Matter

We now turn from our discussion of prepsychological scientific developments to a discussion of psychology's beginnings. The prepsychological problems that we have discussed were all taken over as experimental problems, but the systematic framework imposed on psychology by Wilhelm Wundt at the University of Leipzig in Germany was not exactly what one would expect.

It seems natural that psychology should be experimental, physiological, and interested in problems of sensation and perception. Since it came out of philosophy, one would also expect it to be interested in epistemological problems. Physiology actually played a very small direct role. Although Wundt called his psychology an experimental physiological psychology, there was almost no physiological experimentation; R. I. Watson (1963, p. 249; 1971, pp. 275-276) does note that pulse and breathing rates were monitored in studies of feeling. The minimisation of physiology is doubly surprising because Wundt was himself a physiologist. However, psychology needed primarily the name of physiology. Physiology had prestige, which the young science of psychology wanted. Accordingly, physiology was often invoked to illustrate the scientific respectability of psychology in general and of specific theories in particular.

Physics and mathematics have served similar functions and controversies have raged about whether the alleged dependence of psychology on older disciplines is good or bad. In the case of physiology, at least, much progress has been made. Psychologists today are muck more prone to practice physiology and much less prone merely to invoke it. It is interesting that, despite his training, Wundt refused to tie his infant science to the tail of physiology 100 years too soon.

Wundt was able to justify avoiding physiological experimentation because of his philosophical position on the mind-body problem. He believed that the mind and body run parallel courses but that one cannot say that bodily events *cause* mental events; external events simply give rise to certain bodily processes and, at the same time, to parallel mental processes (cf. Table 13.3). He thought the primary task of psychology was to discover the elements of conscious processes, the manner of their connection, and the laws determining their connection. Since mind and body are parallel, the simplest way to do this, in Wundt's opinion, was to make a *direct* study of the mental events through the method of introspection. Psychology might later turn to the question of just what bodily processes accompany given mental processes, but that problem was secondary. This aspect of Wundt's thought has a modern parallel. Skinner, among others, has insisted that the *direct* study of *behaviour* is more likely to be profitable than the attempt to relate it to physiologic*al* processes.

Wundt thus brought a kind of problem of dualism to psychology. He also brought a strong belief in the experimental method. His research was laboratory inspection, not armchair introspection. He intended to rule metaphysical specula`tion out of psychology. He was constantly looking for experimental ways to attack mental processes. Wundt's experimentalism implied that he had accepted the necessary ideas which developed within science and which had to be accepted before a *science* of psychology could become a reality: the necessity for internal explanation, the reliance on observation, and the placement of man within the realm of the scientifically knowable. His search for the elements of consciousness also showed his attempt at simplification, or his reductionism, if one prefers.

The Leipzig laboratory, officially founded in 1879, also took over many of the specific problems that were waiting for a psychology. The reaction-time problem has already been mentioned. Problems in sensation and perception were taken over from Helmholtz, Fechner, and others.

There was less at Leipzig to remind one of psychology's predecessors on the other side of the channel. Only through a brash American student, James McKeen Cattell, did the Leipzig laboratory turn out any work on Galton's problem of individual differences. Wundt, with prophetic accuracy, called Cattell's interest *ganz amerikanisch* (typically American). It has indeed turned out to be America's armies, schools, and industries that have placed the greatest emphasis on testing individuals for most efficient placement.

It would be interesting to trace the beginning of psychology further than this passing glance allows, but our present purpose is simply to place the field of psychology in some kind of perspective relative to its history and role in modern science. Therefore, we now turn to an examination of the subject matter of psychology as it appears from a modern viewpoint. This will give us a basis for comparing what we bow to be the subject matter of our field with the more limited views of the proper subject matter of psychology usually adhered to by the members of various of psychology's older schools. We shall also see later bow the emergence of each new school tended to add breadth to the prior conceptions of the subject matter of psychology.

## Modern Psychology's Subject Matter

There is no way to define the subject matter of psychology so that the definition will please all psychologists. Any definition turns out to be either too exclusive to be useful or too general to be meaningful. Yet it is possible to sketch in some approximate lines of demarcation.

First, there is practically universal agreement that psychology studies the behaviour of organisms. There are those who hotly contend that psychology also studies experience; they are opposed by methodological behaviourists, who believe that experience is *used* by the psychologist in his study, but has no special status as a subject matter for psychology. We choose to skirt this issue here, and shall take it up in more detail in connection with the chapter on behaviourism. Meanwhile, we shall consider some possible limitations on the type of behaviour studied by psychologists.

Many definitions of psychology stipulate that the behaviour to be studied must be emitted by an intact organism or that it must be studied in terms of large, molar units. With this latter restriction, the swinging of a bat would be considered an appropriate unit for psychological study, while the flexion of the left arm would not. Others might exclude the smaller, molecular units on the grounds that there is no purposefulness in such responses, although this criticism is now less frequently heard. In fact, neither the restriction to intact organisms nor the restriction to molar units seems justified in terms of what psychologists are now studying. Although it is true that most studies are concerned with large units of behaviour, sonic theorists (e.g., Guthrie, 1952) believe that the most effective conceptualisation and experimentation will be in terms of more elementary units of behaviour, such as flexions of individual muscles. Some recent studies have used the contraction of individual *motor units* as the dependent variable. No one denies that the men who do these studies are psychologists. Therefore, it seems meaningless to deny that what they are studying is psychology. We agree with Bergmann and Spence (1944) that the choice of units of study is a matter of convenience.

Similarly, we see no reason to stipulate that psychology, by definition, can study only intact organisms. That stipulation would exclude from psychology much interesting experimentation, for example, that on brain-damaged monkeys (e.g., Harlow, Davis, Settlage, and Meyer. 1952). The line between intact and nonintact organisms would have to be carefully drawn; recent work on the effects of electrical and chemical stimulation of tiny areas of the brain (N.E. Miller, 1958a; Olds, 1955) would have to he brought before the court for a ruling on whether the damage done was sufficient to disqualify the organism from intactness. There is no point in suck quibbling. If the man who calls himself a psychologist study whatever he pleases. We can best discover what psychology is by seeing what he studies.

Science (and psychology as a part of it) studies relationships. What, then, does psychology study in relation to responses? The answer seems to be: "Nearly everything that *can* be related." Stimulus-response (S-R) psychology has today become so popular that it obscures the fact that many of the relationships studied by psychologists are relationships between responses made at two different times; for example, the responses made on an intelligence test, or the resulting "IQ," may be related to other response-determined numbers assigned in a scholastic or industrial situation. This is an important part of psychology. Certainly we do not deny that stimulus-response relationships are important. Historically; these became an object of study very early. Bessel became interested in the time relationships between stimuli and responses and initiated 'the reaction-time experiment. Helm-holtz, with his interest in the relationship between the stimulating situation and the contents of perception, was actually studying a functional relationship between stimulus and verbal response. Thus it hardly seems necessary to reiterate the importance of such laws relating stimulus and response.

There are, in addition, many experiments relating behaviour to antecedents which are neither stimuli nor responses. These antecedents may usually be characterised as *state variables* (see Skinner, 1938); for example, we may change the state of an organism by injecting certain drugs, by extirpating part of the brain, by administering electroshock, or by starving the organism. We might study individual differences in behaviour; this would mean a study of the effects of different initial conditions of unknown nature and origin upon behaviour. We might, of course, enlarge the conception of stimulus to include all these instances of antecedents, but this would simply make "stimulus" equivalent to "any antecedent condition that we do not call a response." We may as well preserve the orthodox general definition of a stimulus as a physical energy impinging upon a receptor and note that the above-mentioned state variables do not exclusively affect receptors.

A rough initial definition of psychology then might be: "Psychology is the science which studies the relationships between antecedent events or conditions and the behaviour of organisms." This is admittedly a broad definition, but psychology has become a broad field. Even this definition excludes much work actually being done, unless our definition of "behaviour" encompasses nearly anything, including changes in brain size or composition, for example. A narrower definition might more cleanly excise psychology from the rest of the body of science, but we feel that it should not be so excised. Even as the physiologists initially found themselves studying psychological problems, so the psychologist finds himself studying physiology in order to understand psychology better. Some of the first psychological studies were psychophysical. Modern psychologists still find themselves making physical measurements in describing stimuli, and so some overlap with physics remains. Certainly the overlaps on the other end of the scale, with sociology and anthropology, are equally siting and equally important. Fortunately, psychologists show no evidence of knowing the definition of their science. Their intellects and experimentation go whether their previous work leads them. They have not restricted their interests, and it will hardly advance psychology (or any other science) to be prescriptive and say, "As a psychologist you shall study only." The early systems of psychology might have served their purpose better and lasted longer had they been less prescriptive of psychology's subject matter.

Instances of studies undertaken by psychologists could be multiplied indefinitely. Their scope is awesome, ranging from pure to applied, from physiological to sociological, from experimental to clinical, and from the five-hour to the fifty-year observation time. These activities include fitting simple mathematical models to learning curves for white rats, fitting space-suit requirements to astronauts, determining the effects of radiation on behaviour, studying the cultural impact of racial integration, and specifying the roles to be played by men and by computers in very complex industrial and military systems. These are just a few of the diverse areas which fall within the boundary of psychology's subject matter. Today's psychology refuses to be bound to a narrow subject matter by formal definition or systematic prescription.

### Psychology and A Hierarchy of Science

A hierarchy of science is diagrammed in Table 13.3. The major scientific fields are ordered in terms of their dependence upon those below them in the table: the things taken as elements at one level of the table may be themselves explained in terms of variables at a lower—that is, a more basic—level. For example, a biologist might employ the behaviour of single cells as a basis for explaining more molar behaviour, while the cell's internal functions may be explained in chemical and physical terms by referring to the variables studied at the next lower level; the psychologist may stop his analysis with a reflex which is itself explained in terms of physiological variables.

**TABLE 13.3**

**A Hierarchy of Science and Scientific Occupations**

| | Scientific Field | Practitioners | Technicians |
|---|---|---|---|
| Social: | (Political science | City manager | |
| | Economics | Certified public accountant | Bookkeeper |
| | Sociology | Social worker | |
| | Social psychology | Probation officer | Police officer |
| Behavioural | Psychology | Clinical psychologist | Psychometrist |
| | Ethology | Zoo director | Zoo worker |
| | Physiology | Physician, surgeon | Technician |
| | Embryology | | |
| | Genetics | | |
| Biological: | Zoology | Veterinarian | |
| | Botany | Horticulturist | |
| | Biophysics | | |
| | Biochemistry | | Pharmacist |
| | Astronomy | Navigator | Sailor |
| | Geology | | |
| | Chemistry | Engineer | Draftsman |
| Physical: | Physics | | |
| | Physical chemistry | | |
| | Mathematics | Statistician | Comptometer or calculator operator |
| Tool: | Logic | Programmer (computer) | |

The so-called tool sciences are placed at the base of the hierarchy. Mathematics and logic are shown separately, although the former may be subsumed under the latter. Neither mathematics nor logic has any empirical content of its own, but each may serve all the empirical sciences. The most fundamental natural sciences, physics and chemistry, are placed immediately above the tool sciences, since they deal with the basic structure of nature.

Biological sciences are shown next at a higher level of organisation; they deal with the structure and function of a special kind of physical material—that composing plants and animals.

Behavioural science, with psychology here included as the major example, is interpolated immediately between the biological sciences and the social sciences. These disciplines all deal with living organisms in varying degrees of relationship—and hence complexity. If psychology has its feet planted in biology, its upper regions clearly extend into the more complex realm of social science. The extent to which the various major social sciences are accepted as science varies, but they are shown here in increasing order of complexity. Scientific techniques may change to some extent with the progress of science, and the latitude within which a study may remain a science is a matter of individual preference.

The hierarchy of the sciences might well be arranged in a circle rather than along a line, for, one might ask, which sciences are basic to mathematics and logic? The answer, if there is any, must be that psychology and the social sciences underlie these most basic of sciences, since mathematics and logic are constructions of men, and therefore the sciences that study man must provide an explanation of their construction. It follows from this view that the sciences should be arranged in some sort of magic circle, like the colors in a color wheel, or we should regard the sciences as essentially unitary.

It should be clear from this discussion of a circular rather than a linear arrangement of the sciences that it is not a simple matter to relate the various disciplines. A closely related issue is seen in debates between mechanists and vitalists or, more generally, between reductionists and emergentists. The reductionist would argue for a linear arrangement of the sciences and for an eventual reduction of the tither, more molar disciplines to the concepts and principles of the lower, more basic disciplines. The emergentist would argue that new principles emerge in more molar, complex arrangements of matter, and a molar discipline must recognise this emergence if it expects to make progress. For example, the emergentist becomes a vitalist if he argues that new' principles are necessary to describe life—that it is not reducible to physical-chemical principles; the emergentist becomes a mentalist if he argues that the operation of mind involves unique emergent principles. Probably neither an extreme reductionist nor an extreme emergentist position is satisfactory. The issue is too complex for us to attempt to work it through here; Turner (1971) devotes the whole of his very sophisticated book to the issue.

The only adequate way in which a given field, or subject matter, of science can be differentiated is in terms of the kinds of variables that are treated. This kind of distinction underlies the hierarchical arrangement shown in Table 13.3. Interdisciplinary fields, such as biochemistry, biophysics, and social psychology, are indicated in the hierarchy to call attention to the fact that the old boundaries of fields are quite arbitrary, often having been fixed by historical accident, and do not represent immutable lines of cleavage. Some of the most interesting and important research is being done in the interdisciplinary fields. As research progresses in any interdisciplinary field, the new field becomes established and is increasingly recognised as a subject matter, or discipline, in its own right (e.g., biochemistry and biophysics). Increased differentiation occurs as the body of science grows larger and justifies progressive specialisation.

As the borders become filled in with interdisciplinary fields, science becomes more integrated as well as more differentiated. The relationships between traditional fields become better understood. An excellent example would be the well-established fields of physics and chemistry. An interdisciplinary field, physical chemistry, came into being. However, even as it became differentiated as a field of study, the distinction between physics and chemistry became so blurred that they are no longer clearly distinguishable fields.

As an adjunct to this arrangement of sciences, the most closely related fields of application of some of the sciences are shown at the right in Table 13.3. These are placed under the rubric *practice,* and the personnel involved in their pursuit are called *practitioners* (a term which has most often been associated with the medical field). These persons are not, in any strict sense, scientists. They are *not* applied scientists, although that term might seem logically to apply to them. They are the *users* of scientific knowledge and technological developments. There is no reason why they cannot also be engaged in scientific work. To the extent that they are so engaged, they are scientists. That would imply that they are actively engaged in attempting to discover, through scientific methods, new knowledge, since this is the distinguishing characteristic of the scientist.

Generally at a somewhat lower level of training and competence are the various technicians. Theirs is a more circumscribed service. They do not, as technicians, make diagnoses or prescribe treatments, but instead provide important technical information and service to the practitioner. The medical laboratory technician and the psychometrician are familiar representatives. Other examples, listed are less clear-cut, since many of the jobs at the technician level may be filled by persons without real technical training and since it is difficult to classify certain occupations. For example, is a pharmacist a practitioner or a technician? This debatable point accounts for the gaps in the last column of Table 13.3. There is no reason why such technicians cannot also be practitioners or even scientists. But they are usually handicapped in this regard by the specialised nature of their professional training, as compared with the more extended training of scientists and practitioners. The heavy service requirements demanded by their conditions of employment limit the time they can devote to other pursuits. This is also often an important factor limiting clinical psychologists (not to mention teachers in some colleges!) in their ability to do scientific research.

In considering the three types of professional activities outlined here, it is necessary for the reader to remember that the distinctions are often blurred in real life. Not only may a given individual serve in more than one role at the same time, as suggested above, but he also may shift from one role to another as his training progresses or his job changes. Blurring of the distinction between scientist and practitioner has been most pronounced within recent years in the various engineering fields, as physicists and engineers have rubbed elbows in all sorts of enterprises in new areas, such as the development of nuclear energy. Nevertheless, most individuals can be clearly placed in a single category.

A fourth type of professional person, less closely connected with the academic world than the others, is the inventor. His main objective is the development of new kinds of gadgets and devices. He may be considered a special kind of engineer. He may also have scientific interests and make important scientific discoveries, but these need not necessarily be a part of his role as an inventor. In practice, in sometimes may be impossible to make a new device until some relevant scientific advance has been made, and the inventor may turn applied scientist and try to produce the needed advance.

**Pure and Applied Science**

No firm line can be drawn between *pure* and *applied* scientists. The only way they can be separated is in terms of their motivation, and this is a trkky problem, as students of psychology should know. Nevertheless, a rough but bask distinction can be made. Pure scientists are persons who are concerned primarily with the discovery of new facts and the development of theories without immediate regard for the utility of such knowledge. Applied Scientists are persons who have the same primary objective but who are immediately concerned with the application of such knowledge. There does tend to be some difference in the kinds of problems with which each type of scientist works, but no hard-and-fast distinctions of problem types are possible. The applied scientist chooses for investigation variables and relationships that appear immediately relevant to some practical problem.

Many apparently applied scientists have made for contributions to basic knowledge. For example, Pasteurs primary interest was in the production of vaccines, but he was also instrumental in, and is today possibly best known for, the development of the germ theory of disease. On the other hand, many apparently pure scientists have discovered facts and produced theories which have then been more or less directly applied to practical problems. The most recent and spectacular example of this is the contribution of the host of mathematical physicists whose work in one way or another was utilised in the development of atomic energy. This example of collaboration between the scientific and the engineering professions is characteristic of many less striking cases and illustrates the fact that the ultimate utility of new knowledge cannot readily be predicted in advance (Bronk, 1954).

**Special Problems Related to the Subject Matter of Psychology**

***Controls***

We have emphasised the fact that control is essential to the development of science. Only through appropriate measures can we be sure that hypothesised relationships between variables really hold. Fundamentally, psychology is no different from any other science in its need for control. It is different in its ability to impose the necessary controls, especially when the object of our curiosity is human behaviour. For example, we may wonder whether form perception in the human being is highly dependent on early experience with the visual world. In order to investigate this problem, we might like a supply of human infants who can be deprived of all visual stimulation for varying periods of their early life. Where is our supply of such infants? Our value system does not condone treatment of this kind. We may wonder whether social isolation in childhood is really conducive to the development of schizophrenia; here we have the same problem of unavailability of subjects. We may wish to study the effects of mating individuals with certain characteristics on the behaviour patterns of the offspring, but who will engage in this carefully controlled mating? Examples could be multiplied indefinitely. There are quite obviously limits to the manipulations we can perform with human subjects. It is true that if we wait long enough, the events we desire may happen by chance, or we can piece together isolated cases that represent something of the kind of treatment we need. But the progress of science is slowed when it must wait for the desired events to occur.

Psychology and astronomy are in similar positions in this regard; the astronomer has had to wait, for example, until Mars comes close to Earth before he can make the most useful observations of that planet. With the availability of inter-planetary vehicles, the astronomer may be somewhat better off. With the increasing concern for the protection of the rights of subjects, the psychologist may be somewhat worse off!

It is largely this kind of limitation which has turned many psychologists to the study of animals. The limitations of control with animals are much less severe, so the psychologist need not wait for the chance occurrence of the situation he wishes to observe.

Psychology, like physics, has a problem with its observations. In physics, the Heisenberg principle sets clear, mathematically stated limits on the accuracy with which elementary particles can be observed. In psychology, the problems of observation cannot be so clearly formulated, but they nevertheless are quite serious in practice. The recent work of Rosenthal (1966, 1968a, 1968b) is currently the best known among the investigations of the effects of the experimenter on the outcome of the experiment. Obvious types of effects involve the conscious or unconscious attempt to influence the outcome so that it will conform better to the experimenter's hypothesis and the recording of results in such a way that they will hear out this hypothesis. Less obvious examples of biasing by experimenters would include acting differently toward male and female subjects (Rosenthal, 1968b). Some types of errors in experimentation could be avoided by having the experiment conducted by computer. Others can be avoided by the usual "double-blind" procedures, in which persons conducting the experiment do not know which condition any subject is in until the data are obtained and recorded. Still others—like smiling more at female subjects if the experimenter is male—must be specifically guarded against even in double-blind procedures, if a human experimenter is involved. These problems arise because people, like particles, are extremely sensitive to the effects of observation. Even lower animals clearly reveal this property at the overt behavioural level; every rat-runner who has used a clear plastic operant chamber has noticed the rat observing the experimenter for long periods of time, seemingly preferring this exploratory activity to what the hungry animal is "supposed" to be doing-pressing the bar for food. The rat's sensitivity to the experimenter's preconceptions has also been documented (Rosenthal and Lawson, 1964).

### *Quantification*

Mathematics is a specialised language. It is closely related to logic: Both are abstract, both are somewhat remote from the language of everyday life, and both have a grammar which is restricted and precise. These characteristics have made specialised symbolic systems useful for the well-established sciences, especially physics and chemistry. However, mathematics and logic are *only* symbolic systems, and no magic inheres in either. Empirically they are abstract systems which are thus testable only when given some observational content. From this viewpoint, the scientific usefulness of such systems depends on their ability to produce empirical predictions. These predictions must then hold within the empirical events to which the mathematics or logic has been coordinated through more or less precise definitions

Different types of mathematics are useful for different problems even within physics. For example, the complex number system is useful for problems in electric circuitry, and non-Euclidean geometry is useful for relativity theory. We saw in the previous chapter that the "eightfold way" required still another type. An inappropriate type of mathematics would lead only to confusion' in any given case. The only way one can discover whether a given mathematics or logic or geometry is useful for testing a given empirical system is to try to set up definitions relating the symbolic system to the empirical system. These rules are rules for measurement. It may not be possible even to finish the definitional step. If it is, one can then see whether the predictions made on the basis of the permissible deductions' within the symbolic system lead to empirical sense or empirical nonsense.

Psychology has not yet been as successful as the older sciences in its attempt to apply mathematical treatment to its problems. However, there are many recent books on mathematical developments in psychology, and the *Journal of Mathematical Psychology is* devoted exclusively to such developments. These developments indicate that strong efforts are being put forth and substantial progress is being made in this direction.

Before we can use mathematics, we must establish the required relations between the empirical object of study and the mathematics we wish to use. We call this process *quantification* when we are using the ordinary mathematics of real numbers. A more general word for the establishment of the required relationship to the elements of any mathematical system is *scaling.* Stevens (1951), among others, has discussed the different types of scaling. Psychology has usually had to be content with coordinating its subject matter to weaker kinds of systems than the mathematics of real numbers; the bulk of our subject matter is treated only with the language of the everyday world, and probabilities are assessed with statistics that may or may not be appropriate.

Does the subject matter of psychology lend itself to traditional measurement and traditional mathematics, or are some different symbolic systems necessary? It is too early in the history of our science to know the answers to these questions. On the one hand, Weitzenhoffer (1951) has suggested that psychologists persist in their attempts to measure in the traditional fashion, and Reese (1943) has recommended that we go ahead and use mathematics as though we were justified in doing so, being always careful to remember just what our measurements mean and assigning them no meaning beyond the operations performed. On the other hand, Stevens (1955) has stated that the weakness of psychology's measuring operations invalidates many of the statistical tests performed. Nevertheless, Burke (1963) has argued that our statistics are appropriate in many cases, despite the weakness of our measurements, and some studies (Box, 1953) do indicate that statistical tests are approximately correct in many cases, despite violations of the assumptions on which they are based (that is, the tests are "robust").

Stevens (1968), who has been an advocate of limiting statistical operations according to the measurement operations which produced the numbers, has extended and clarified the dialogue. He points out, as we have, that science is in the business of relating empirical structures to symbolic structures. Statistics can indeed proceed with its manipulations regardless of the character of the measurements which produced its numbers. The critical question is, however, what the effect of this will be on the whole "schemapiric" endeavor-that is, on the whole attempt to map empirical domains with symbolic domains. Burke has been arguing for maximum freedom for the statistician, and Stevens for maximum caution. In his 1968 article, Stevens argues for calculation rather than debate in order to find out how likely it is that an inappropriate statistic will lead to a deviant conclusion. (Burke would add that, paradoxically, there are cases in which an inappropriate statistic is less likely to lead to a deviant conclusion than is an appropriate statistic.) At any rate, Stevens seems willing to submit questions about measurement and its relationship to statistics to the judgment of time, and so are we.

In view of this rather confused state of affairs, we cannot say for sure that quantification is unusually difficult for psychology or even more difficult than for the other sciences; at the present stage, it *seems* more difficult. Certainly psychologists need to become more sophisticated in handling mathematics, measurement, and logic. Then they can use or develop appropriate systems, appropriate coordinations of existing systems to psychological problems, or both. Psychologists must concern themselves with the use of deductive systems before psychology will be a finished science. We cannot say whether enough empirical data are available to make extensive attempts of this kind profitable at present.

Some have argued against the desirability of quantification. These critics say that attempts at quantification tend to interfere with the meaningfulness of the phenomena in question. Others argue that the attempt to quantify is an instance of the tail wagging the dog, of the method unnecessarily restricting the problem. These critics hold that quantification can succeed only if the problem dealt with is so restricted as to lose all significance. None of these arguments can be refuted, but the usefulness of quantification in the other sciences argues against their ready acceptance. Quantification is a tool and is not an end in itself, and we believe that most psychologists recognise that fact clearly.

Quantification and mathematical treatment have at least two advantages: The statements are precise and clear, and the richness of deductive possibilities is greatly increased. The reasons for increased clarity are the explicit statement of rules for deduction within mathematical systems and the necessity, before measurement can occur, for rules of correspondence between events and the numerical symbols used. "Richness of deductive possibilities" can be illustrated by an example using psychoanalytic language. Suppose it is said that all neurosis is caused by the symbolic expression of intrapsychic conflicts. The implication of (deduction from?) this statement seems to be limited to the expectation that wherever we find neurosis, we shall also find the symbolic expression of intrapsychic conflicts. We would probably ask many other questions, answers to which are not supplied by the nonquantitative form of the statement. How much neurosis will we find for how such intrapsychic conflict? Are the measurement operations for neurosis different from those for intrapsychic conflicts? (If not, the statement is circular as well as Limited.) What is the mathematical statement of the quantitative relationship between the two studies? (For example, if neurosis is symbolised by $N$ and intrapsychic conflict by $C$, it could he that $N$=$C$, $N$-½$C^2$, or $N$-¼$C^3$ + a constant.) If we have measurement operations and the functional relationship; for example, $N$ ½$C^2$, we can make an infinite number of precise predictions, either from values of $N$ to values of $C$ or from values of $C$ to values of $N$, depending upon which we measure first. Such deductive possibilities are certainly "rich."

Deutsch, Platt, and Senghass (1971) have concluded that two-thirds of all the major advances in social science between 1900 and 1965 involved a quantitative component. Psychology, which was among the sciences considered, was a leader in contributions. If these authors have evaluated the situation correctly, there can be no doubt that quantification has been profitable *already* in psychology, and one cannot reasonably expect anything other than ever-increasing profit froth the endeavor as psychologists increasingly equip themselves to engage in it.

### *Subjectivism*

Psychology involves the study of living organisms, often people. It seems to be more difficult to achieve the unbiased scientific attitude toward this subject matter than toward any other. The medical student studying anatomy doubtless has certain qualms when he pulls his first cadaver out of the formaldehyde, and part of this qualm doubtless comes from the realisation that the object of his investigation and dissection bears a marked similarity to himself. Psychology has had some difficulties on the same score; as the analysts would say, there have been resistances to the acceptance of certain ideas, among them the basic one that man's behaviour can be studied scientifically—especially if the man is oneself.

Beyond this, the psychologist himself has difficulty in achieving objectivity award his field. Since psychologists are people, they have a tendency to anthropomorphise. The objects of psychological study seem especially receptive objects for the projection of our own ideas, even though sober evidence may be lacking. The call of common sense, too, is particularly strident when we feel that we understand humankind simply by virtue of being human. Yet the facts may be exactly otherwise; we might achieve undreamed-of insights were we but Martians studying man in the cool light of an earth day.

### *Complexity*

There are certain senses in which the subject matter of psychology seems to be more complex than that of many sciences. From a reductionistic point of view, for example, one would have to understand much of chemistry in order to understand the nature of nerve transmission, which people think one would have to understand before one could understand behaviour completely. However, the biologist might argue that his field is equally complex on this score, and the sociologist might argue that his field is even more complex, since an understanding of individuals would presumably be necessary before one could understand social behaviour.

Another, and perhaps more fundamental, way in which complexity can be defined is in terms of the number of interacting variables that are effective in the determination of some consequence. Certainly behaviour appears to be influenced by a large number of such variables. But the same thing can be said of many other sciences, and how many important variables operate in behaviour determination remains to be discovered.

The degree of complexity a subject matter is judged to have may depend upon the stage of development of the science that deals with that subject matter. At the beginning, the subject matter may look simple. As some facts are gathered, however, problems develop, and the field begins to look complex. The development of special instrumentation may reveal new complexities even as it solves old puzzles; for example, the microscope literally brought to light a bewildering array of microscopic life, at the same time that it made diseases comprehensible. In physiological psychology, equipment to record bioelectrical potentials has played a similar role. As theories are developed, they play a similar role in relation to complexity. At first, the theory seems to solve problems, though it suggests additional observations for its own evaluation. The initially reduced complexity seems always to return as soon as some disconfirmatory observations are made. The degree of manifest complexity may fluctuate, in this way returning to the high side after having seemed to be lower for a while. At present, psychology seems to be in the process of immersing itself in a complex welter of facts, and this may account for its apparent complexity.

Thus, the common argument that the subject matter of psychology is more complex than that of the other sciences does not rest on perfectly firm ground. Nonetheless, psychologists agree that the subject matter is sufficiently complex for them, in many instances downright confusing. Perhaps another 100 years of study will give a better indication of relative complexity. In our present state of ignorance, the argument that many of psychology's difficulties can be explained in this way is appealing.

Our general thesis throughout has been that the criteria that apply to science in general also apply to psychology. The discussion of problems that seem to be accentuated because of the nature of the subject matter is not to be construed as meaning that psychology is in these respects apart from science. It follows that psychology shares the general problems and will find its special solutions as the other sciences have done. Perhaps the only problem which cannot be circumvented is that science can advance only through work, and work takes time.

Psychology has not existed long enough to solve its problems. The weaknesses that we shall see in its systems and theories exist partially for that reason.

## Summary and Conclusions

Several scientific ideas had to develop within science before psychology could emerge. Prominent among these were the following propositions: that explanation of an event should be sought within the same system as the one within which the event occurred, that observation is the arbiter of scientific truth, and that man is a part of the natural order. It follows that man's behaviour can be studied scientifically to determine the laws governing that behaviour.

Certain problems were willed to psychology because of its immediate prehistory within science and philosophy. Among them were relating the mental and physical aspects of man, explaining the physiology of perception and the contents of perception, determining the basis for the "personal equation," and analysing individual differences and heredity. The effects of these problems upon experimental psychology as it was conceived by its founder, Wilhelm Wundt, have been examined.

The subject matter of modern psychology has been defined broadly. The intensification of certain scientific problems as a result of the nature of the subject matter has been pointed out: the difficulty of controlling conditions is enhanced, the problem of quantification is rendered more difficult, the subject matter disposes the psychologist toward subjectivism and the subject matter is complex. These problems are not unique to psychology but they seem to be exaggerated there.

## *Further Readings*

For the general historical background of psychology, the student can consult Boring's *History of experimental psychology* (1950) or Murphy's *Historical introduction to modern psychology* (1949). The five volumes of autobiographical material edited by Murchison (1930-1936), by Boring et al. (1952), and by Boring and Lindzey (1967) are extremely 'valuable in providing insight into some of the personal factors, ordinarily out of sight or in the background, in the careers of many historically important men in the field. *A source book in the history of psychology* (1965), edited by Herrnstein and Boring, provides selected classics ranging from Aristotle to McDougall for the student who likes his history firsthand. For a general orientation to the history of science, the following classic works may be recommended: Conant's *On understanding science: A historical approach* (1947) and *Harvard case histories in experimental science* (1957); Butterfield's *Origins of modern science: 1300-1800* (1957); and Sarton's *Guide to the history of science* (1952). A variety of works in the philosophy of science are available for the reader who wants to delve into this area. Particularly relevant to the mind-body issue is *Concepts, theories, and the mind-body problem*, edited by Feigl, Scriven, and Maxwell (1958) and published as Volume 2 in the *Minnesota studies in the philosophy of science.* Volume I in that series, edited by Feigl and Scriven (1956) and entitled *The foundations of science and the concepts of psychology and psychoanalysis*, also contains many informative papers. Feigl and Maxwell's *Current issues in the philosophy of science* (1961) contains papers and rebuttals read at symposia in the 1959 meetings of the American Association for the Advancement of Science. Several books of readings *in* this field are available, for example, Danto and Morgenbesser's *Philosophy of science: A reader* (1960); P.P. Wiener's *Readings in philosophy of science* (1953), Feigl and Sellars' *Readings in philosophical analysis* (1949); and Feigl and Brodbeck's *Readings in the philosophy of science* (1953). The best introduction to the problems of mathematics, measurement, and their relationship to statistics can probably be gained by reading Stevens's chapter entitled "Mathematics, measurement, and psychophysics," in his *Handbook of experimental psychology* (1951); Burke's "Measurement scales and statistical models," which appears in Marx's *Theories in Contemporary Psychology* (1963), should be read to round out the picture.

# 14

# Systems and Theories

Our intent in this chapter is to set the stage for a critical evaluation of systems and theories. Terms will be defined, the nature of systems and theories will be outlined, and some requirements will be proposed. Though many of the issues raised will be controversial, we hope to provide a background that will make the controversies meaningful.

## DEFINITIONS OF BASIC TERMS

### Definition

*Webster's Third New International Dictionary* gives the following as one meaning of the word *define:* to "determine with precision or exhibit clearly the boundaries of... to make distinct in outline or features." This definition *of define* is *in* perfect agreement with a geometric representation of the classification process given by Sebestyen (1962). Since it seems that this kind of classification procedure is a formalisation of the usual less formal, more intuitive approach to definition, we shall describe a simple version of what classification is. We think that substantial gains to understanding may come from this formal approach.

#### *Simple Geometric Representation*

Sebestyen's procedure starts with a simple geometric representation. Membership in a class is determined by noting whether a particular event to be classified falls within a geometric region. If there are only two "characteristics" or "measures" of objects considered, the geometric representation can be in two dimensions, and the defining regions can be areas in two-dimensional space, one dimension for each characteristic under consideration. Figure 14.1 is an abstract representation of a classification space with two regions outlined, one for each of two classes. Each class is centered on a point which represents the class best. Note that the "best," or "prototypical," example of a member of class 2 has a value of 2 on characteristic 1 and a value of 2.5 on characteristic 2. Anything which falls within the range of I to 3 on characteristic 1 and within the range of 1.5 to 3.5 on characteristic 2 is "defined" to be within class 2. Class 1 is defined within the same "classification space," but differs in definition.

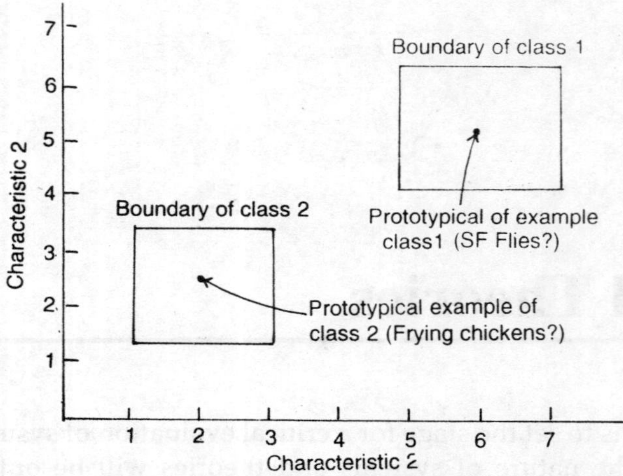


**Fig. 14.1** A classification scheme which formalises the properties or definitions.

If characteristic 1 were number of legs and characteristic 2 were number of pounds, then class 2 would include frying chickens. Baby monkeys might also fit. The reader may think of other interesting examples. Class I is more difficult to populate. Science-fiction flies come to mind; 5- or 6-pound six-leggers are (we think fortunately) rare among terrestrial creatures.

In setting up a definition, the definer is free to use whatever characteristics he chooses. This type of formalisation is not limited to two characteristics; an indefinite number of characteristics can be accommodated. The two-dimensional geometric representation can handle only two characteristics; for three characteristics, three-dimensional space can be used. The class definition will be represented by a volume within the three-dimensional space. If the representation of the element in question, within the character space, falls within the volume, it is a member of the class. If more than three characteristics are used, the situation must be represented algebraically rather than geometrically.

### *Algebraic Representation*

The algebraic representation of the specific example already given would be as follows. The relevant characteristics are number of legs and weight in pounds; in that order. The prototypical example of class I would be written (6, 5); the prototypical example of class 2 would be written (2, 2.5). The class definition for class I would be ($5 < C_1 < 7$; $4 < C_2 < 6$). This means simply that any object for which characteristic I is between 5 and 7 and for which characteristic 2 is between 4 and 6 is within class 1. Definitions which depend on any number of characteristics can be handled in approximately this way, simply by increasing the number of characteristics for which a prototypical number and limits are stated.

A more economical method for stating class limits, which may be used in many cases, involves establishing a boundary on each class by stating a "distance" from the prototypical element within which an element to be classified may be considered a member of the class.

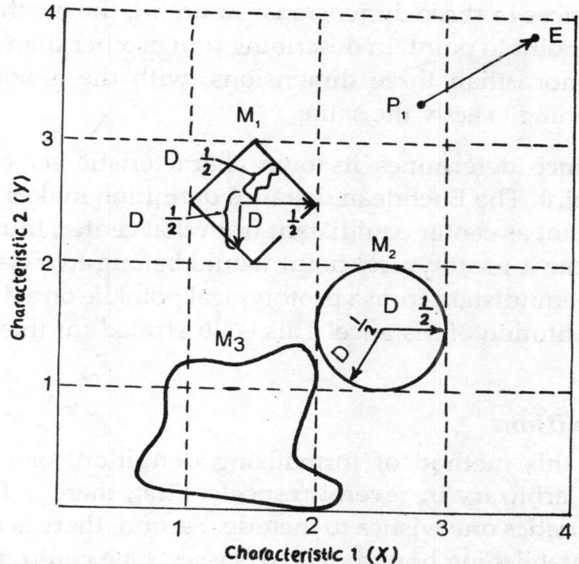


**Fig. 14.2.** Illustration of classes defined by distance—measures.

Figure 14.2 illustrates the relevant concepts. In the upper right-hand corner are two points connected by a line; the line is the distance between the two points $P_1$ and $E$. $P_1$ represents the prototypical value for some class. *E* represents an element whose distance from the prototypical point is to be determined. We ordinarily think of distance as being defined in the Euclidean way implied by drawing the straight line. The Euclidean definition of the distance between two points in a two-dimensional space is the square root of the sum of the squares of differences between the coordinates, that is, $D_E = \sqrt{(X_1-X_2)^2 + (Y_1-Y_2)^2}$. Here the coordinates of the first point are $X_1$, $Y_1'$ and the coordinates of the second point are $X_1$, $X_2$. The class labeled $M_2$ is a class defined by using the Euclidean distance measure; all points lying within the circle of points one-half unit away from the prototypical point are defined to be within the class.

The class labeled $M_1$ is defined by using a different definition of distance. The distance is defined as the sum of the absolute differences, on each individual dimension, between the prototypical point and any point under examination; in this case, $D_{CB} = | X_1 - X_2 | + Y_1 - Y_2 |$. This distance has been called the *city-block distance* because it is like the distance one has to go if one must travel on city streets, rather than being able to "cut across." If someone lives one block north of you and one block west of you, he is two blocks away in practice, and this is exactly what the city-block definition of distance would tell us. The straight-line (Euclidean) distance would be the square root of 2, a little over 1.4 Units.

Either definition of distance is easily extended to any number of dimensions; ore simply has to work with an additional *difference* for each additional *dimension*. If, for example, one lived in one of the vertical cities that we may inhabit in the future, it would become habitual to compute city-block distances in three dimensions, summing the north-south, east-west, and vertical distances from point to point. In describing things other than physical position, it may be helpful to use more than three dimensions, with the general procedure for determining distance remaining exactly the same.

Any definition of distance determines its own characteristic set of points that are equidistant from a given point. The Euclidean distance definition makes the points that lie on a circle with the given point as center equidistant from that center; thus all points within a circle of a given radius from a prototypical point would belong to a class, according to a Euclidean definition. Points equidistant from a prototypical point lie on a diamond, however, according to a city-block definition of distance! This is illustrated for the case of class $M_1$ in Figure 14.2.

### *Arbitrary Features of Definitions*

Careful thought about this method of formalising definition, or class membership, reveals that definitions are arbitrary in several respects. First, there is freedom to choose whatever defining characteristics one wishes to include. Second, there is freedom to choose any available method for establishing boundaries to classes. One could, for example, draw a freehand figure around the prototypical point, as illustrated by $M_3$ in Figure 14.2. Even if a distance measure is used, there is freedom to define distance in any of several ways. We have not discussed more complex ways to define distance, but several are available (and it should be clear that some dimensions can be weighted more heavily than others by multiplying "more important" dimensions by some constant). Third, the bound- flies on the class can be made very exclusive by including only those elements which are very close to the prototypical point) or very inclusive (by including elements a greater distance away). Definitions can be changed by changing any of the above properties. It is often the case that an event to be classified falls within the limits of more than one class. One then might want to construct a "cleaner" definitional scheme for that context.

### *Illustrations of Definitional Problems*

Whittaker (1969) furnishes an interesting example of such an attempt at definitional and classificatory sharpening. Most of us have asked the question "Animal, vegetable, or mineral?" so many times that the classification of living things into plants and animals seems almost a fact of nature rather than a classification scheme imposed by man.

Whittaker, however, finds the definitions of plants and animals inadequate to determine clearly the - membership of some living things. The prevailing definitional scheme is also inadequate to reflect what is known or suspected about the evolutionary relationships between families. He considers a four-category classification system, but prefers a five-way system, which he believes better corrects the above deficiencies. Whittaker (1969) makes his definitional bases quite explicit: "A five-way kingdom system is proposed here, based both on levels of organisation and on types of organisation as evolved in relation to three principal means of nutrition—photosynthesis, absorption, and ingestion" (p. 158). Whittaker also explicitly recognises the fact that definitions are not, despite superficial appearances, completely arbitrary. He states (1969): "Revised broad classifications deserve wide consideration, for they may better express major relationships in the living world and more effectively classify the phyla than the two-kingdom system" (p .158).

Willems and Raush (1969, p. 47) provide an example which is of more direct relevance to psychology and which happens to use the same kind of definitional formalisation we are proposing here. A "space" is established for describing research activities. The two dimensions which establish the space are the degree of manipulation of antecedent conditions by the experimenter and the degree of imposition of units on the subject matter by the investigator. It is suggested that research low on both dimensions is prototypical of naturalistic research and that research high on both dimensions is experimental research. Once the space is established, it becomes obvious that research may also be intermediate on either or both dimensions, or it may be low on one dimension and high on the other. This fact provides an illustration of the gains that sometimes follow the systematic, formal specification of what we are really" doing; in the present case, new possibilities are nearly forced to our attention by the formal framework.

### *Summary*

Let us summarise our discussion of definition: (1) A geometric description of classification—which is intimately related to definition—is general and precise and therefore has advantages over a purely verbal description of definition. (2) Both the dimensions of description and the borderlines of the classes defined within these dimensions can be chosen arbitrarily, but some definitions will turn out to be better than others because they make better theory possible, provide for cleaner distinctions between classes, or direct attention to more useful facets of the things defined. (3) Definitions are flexible, not permanent; those which play a role in useful laws will last longer than those which do not. (4) There is therefore an intimate but often overlooked relationship between definition and theory. Definitions are very important and deserve more emphasis than they usually receive.

## Terms: Primitive and Defined

Within theories and systems' two kinds of terms will occur: ***defined terms,*** which are completely expressible within the framework of a given system, and ***primitive terms,*** which are not (see Achinstein, 1968, pp. 68-49). A primitive term may be connected (by semantic rules) to something which is more familiar and which is external to the theory. That is, it may be defined by pointing to some observable operation, event, or object. In some cases, primitive terms are left undefined:

Hull's system (Hilgard & Bower, 1966) is one of the better-known attempts at axiomatisation in psychology. One of his postulates states that the relationship between habit strength ($_sH_r$) and number of trials (*N*) is:

$$_sH_r = 100(1-10^{-iN})$$

${}_sH_r$, then, is defined in terms of $N$. From the context of the preceding discussion, it can be seen that habit strength, as a term in Hull's system, takes its definition from number of trials, which is also a part of the system ($i$ is a constant defined by Hull). However, number of trials is defined on the basis of a reading on a counter, a tally on a worksheet, or a quantity determined by some other appropriate measuring device, which is *not* part of the Hullian system. $N$, then, is a primitive term.

Many theories are not as structurally explicit as Hull's, making it difficult to ascertain which theoretical terms are primitive and which are defined. Psychoanalytic theory is an example of this; Freud did not clarify the relationships between many of his terms, so that those which are expressible completely within his system are not always distinguishable from those which are not.

There is no logical hindrance to defining any term of a theory by relating it to terms or events outside the theory. If a term is defined externally, we may wish to distinguish between the meaning of the term as defined externally and its meaning as defined internally. In the case of variables, the externally defined variable might be called an *experimental variable,* and the theoretically defined variable might be called a *theoretical variable.* If a theory is "correct," the value determined through the theoretical definition will be the same as the value determined by making empirical observations. The primitive term, having no theoretical definition, can have at most an external definition. It may simply be left undefined. Scientists prefer theories with the fewest possible undefined terms, but a theory may be acceptable provided every term makes at least indirect contact with empirical observations.

**Constructs**

A construct is a special kind of concept. It is less simple than a concept like "man" or "house" or "boat." These are named correctly because they, as objects, share with other members of the class the properties which give them membership (see our discussion of definition). Some concepts may be more complex than the examples above, and constructs are always more complex. Constructs represent relationships between objects or events. Common psychological constructs such as "anxiety," "fear," and "habit" are in this respect similar to more general constructs like "patriotism," "school spirit," and "justice." Thus, responses alone are insufficient to define the concept of fear or habit; some reference to the stimulus situation as well's to the response situation must be given. In defining habit, we must know the probability that a certain response will occur to a given stimulus situation, not just that a response has occurred. Constructs, therefore, are a subclass of concepts, including some of the more complex concepts. English and English say (1958): "As compared with concept, a construct is a planfully designed model, with full awareness of the relationships between the data and the model" (p. 116). However, these authors point out that the distinction between the two terms seems to be a matter of degree.

Constructs are useful in summarising relationships succinctly, and they may also be helpful in generalising from some sets of observed relationships to other, as yet unobserved sets. However, many difficulties in psychology stem from a failure to define constructs unambiguously. The development of simpler and more empirically meaningful constructs is an important objective of contemporary psychology. This is the area in which the simple, basic proposition of the operationist—that we should make clear the empirical referents of our complex terms—has the most to offer.

MacCorquodale and Meehl (1948) made a much-cited distinction between two "kinds" of constructs: hypothetical constructs and intervening variables. Constructs vary along several dimensions, but the MacCorquodale and Meehl distinction emphasised one important dimension more than the others. Their emphasis was on the degree to which a construct is operationally clear in meaning. The intervening variable, as they used the term, is a construct with a clear, limited, operational meaning. The hypothetical construct has "excess meaning" in the sense that it has meanings beyond those justified by its operational definition. An example of such excess meaning would be the assumption that some particular physiological changes underlie the behavioural changes that occur as habit strength increases. Another kind of excess meaning would be the kind brought to a construct by its role in a deductive system (theory or model).

Although MacCorquodale and Meehl were arguing for intervening variables and against hypothetical constructs, it seems to us that both kinds of constructs are important. One cannot give a blanket endorsement of either type, or a blanket condemnation of either type. The initial negative attitude toward hypothetical constructs probably came about because some horrible examples of this type had no clear operational meaning, no clear place in a formal theory, no physiological meaning, and hence no useful role to play in science. However, constructs with sound operational meaning, a dear theoretical definition, and potential physiological meaning would seem to be ideal-more interesting than concepts whose meaning is exhausted by the observations already made. If we limited ourselves to constructs of this latter type, we would need to establish a new construct for every new set of operations. Scientists do not, because they could not, proceed in this way. Such "exhausted" constructs have never been used, and we discuss them only as a hypothetical pure case. We are *not* against the clear identification of the source and operational meaning of constructs. We do, however, believe that constructs are fruitful only when they are embedded in a larger theoretical context.

This term has two major usages. First, it is used to refer to a fundamental assumption which is not to be directly or intentionally tested. The assumption may be essential to the pursuit of science for example, the assumption that the world is consistently orderly and that the order is discoverable by man. The assumption may be of more restricted importance, as in the case of the early behavioristic assumption that all behaviour can be analysed into stimulus-response relationships. As is true of this example, most such postulates are informal, natural-language statements. It is generally held that such assumptions, which are often on a philosophical level, should be as few, simple, and carefully set forth as possible.

The second type of postulate is a theoretical proposition which is intended to be more directly tested by means of empirical work. A set of these propositions, in the case of a deductive theory, could be used within a given logical framework to yield further propositions implied by the original set. The further propositions (theorems) derived will depend upon the rules for deduction as well as upon the original statements. Within mathematics or logic, theorems are "true" or "valid" by definition, given the original statements and the rules for deduction. Asking whether a theorem which follows from the postulates and rules for deduction is true is exactly like asking whether a chess move that follows from the rules is true. The answer is "yes" to both in the sense that the theorem and the move followed from the rules. Both the theorem and the move might be silly, useless, or false as descriptions of some empirical state of affairs.

Within science, theorems must at some stage make statements about empirical observations if they are to have any scientific utility. The postulates of a system are thus tested indirectly by observing the concurrence or lack of it between theorems and observations. The best example of an extensive and highly formalised set of postulates within psychology is afforded by the work of Hull (1943, 1951, 1952; Hull, Hovland, Ross, Hall, Perkins, & Fitch, 1940). His system suffered from logical weaknesses not shared by more recent, less extensive efforts.

**Hypotheses**

Experimental. The hypothesis is a guess about the explanation of some natural phenomenon. Its elaboration may take many forms. One important dimension along which hypotheses vary is their degree of specificity. The most specific hypotheses apply to a particular situation. The best example is the experimental hypothesis, which is the particular prediction that is made about the outcome of an experiment. Such particular hypotheses may come from a more general theoretical framework or from more general hypotheses.

***Public Versus Private***

In one form or another, the hypothesis plays a central role in the advance of science. Two different types of hypotheses, with quite different roles, should be carefully distinguished. These are what we shall call *public* and *private* hypotheses Public hypotheses are those which have been formally explicated and publicly advanced, usually in published form. Private hypotheses are those which have been entertained by some investigator or thinker, but have not been publicly expressed.

Although it is the public, or formally explicated, hypothesis that receives most of our attention, a little reflection quickly reveals the more pervasive nature of the private hypothesis. For every public hypothesis there are uncounted numbers of private hypotheses. In scientific thinking these undergo almost constant revision, and the point at which they are made public varies with the investigator and as a result of many situational factors. Charles Darwin, for example, worked on his private hypotheses about the theory of evolution for more than twenty years before the appearance of a competitive manuscript containing the same basic idea stimulated him to make his hypotheses public. Had Wallace's manuscript not come into his hands, there is no way of knowing how long the eccentric Darwin might have held his hypotheses to himself. The unpublished hypothesis is in the somewhat peculiar position of being critical to scientific progress, but worthless in itself. For science to move ahead, it is, indeed, eventually a matter of "publish or perish," when hypotheses are being considered.

We may think of the mass of all scientific hypotheses as being like an iceberg. It is only the top one-tenth (or much less) of the total thought that is open to the criticism and empirical attack of the scientific public. Publication of a hypothesis invites such attack, and it is only through such attack that effective scientific evaluation can be made. Unfortunately, psychologists do not always recognise that it is necessary to publicise their hypotheses in this way. Public formalisation of a hypothesis for empirical attack does not require the investigator to stop thinking and revising his hypotheses, but it is a necessary step if the product of his thinking is to be tested by others.

### *Conscious Versus Unconscious*

Another distinction can be made between conscious and unconscious hypotheses. Sidman (1960) argues that many significant experiments are done to satisfy simple wonderment, as it might be expressed in "I wonder what would happen if...." The implication is that hypotheses need not precede experimentation. Others might argue that an unconscious hypothesis is being tested and that the hypothesis can be inferred from the behaviour of the investigator. We cannot settle this disagreement and shall state only that it seems safe to say that some investigators believe strongly in formulating hypotheses, and others do not.

The source of hypotheses—and why some persons are so much better than others at producing them—is a fascinating problem. Little progress his been made to date toward its solution. About all we can say is that as a person becomes more ad more thoroughly immersed in his subject matter, he tends to develop more and better ideas. More specific rules of thumb for developing effective scientific ideas await future investigations.

A scientific law is generally held to be a well-established empirical relationship; for example, under certain conditions, water freezes at 32°F. Laws consitute the a anchorage points for theories, and sometimes the backbone of the theory itself. Laws are generalisations of an empirical sort that have the greatest degree of factualness. The science of physics has developed a large number of lawful relationships. Many observers believe that psychology must develop a larger number of such laws before it can develop effective theory.

The term *law* is also used to refer to an especially well-established theoretical proposition. The proposition becomes well established because it successfully plays its part in the derivation of predictions which are empirically tested. It is often hard to draw the line between the two kinds of usage of the word *law*. The step from the concrete observation to its verbal statement always involves some degree of abstraction. There is thus no purely empirical law in the strictest sense of the word. On the other hand, the most abstract proposition may rest on some kind of informal observation of nature by the proponent of the proposition. In spite of the difficulty of making this distinction, we should recognise the dimensions of abstractness and of generality when speaking of scientific laws.

## THE NATURE OF SYSTEMS

### Characteristics of Systems

Part 2 of this book consists of descriptions and discussions of psychological systems; in this section we are discussing some of the general characteristics of systems. Psychological systems are closely related to those of philosophy. One important similarity is that both philosophers and psychological systematists tend to give great scope to their systems; a system is thus a set of very general statements. McGeoch (1933) writes about systems as they might ideally be. His definition of a system makes them sound highly desirable: "By the term 'psychological system' is implied a coherent and inclusive, yet flexible, organisation and interpretation of the facts and special theories of the subject" (p .2).

This definition makes it clear that a system is a large order. It is inclusive and organises theories, which themselves possess generality. The definition leaves a good deal of room for ambiguity; words like *coherent*, *flexible*, *organisation*, and *interpretation* come from the lay language and are not themselves clearly defined. These words seem to be as much an attempt to sell systems as to define what they are.

According to McGeoch, we cannot have systems until we have facts and theories, since systems are organisations of these prior elements. We have few real theories in psychology, in the strict sense of the term; most psychological theories are better viewed as programs or as informal or preliminary theories. One can thus question whether psychology has ever had a system in McGeoch's sense of that word. But certainly there have been plenty of systems of some kind.

Edna Heidbreder, one of McGeoch's contemporaries and fellow psychologists, said (1933): "Psychology, especially in the United States has risked everything on being science; and science on principle refrains from speculation that is not permeated and stabilised by fact. Yet there is not enough fact in the whole science of psychology to make a single solid system" (p. 3). We shall see that her statement is still true today.

### Functions of Systems

What, then, was the function of the systems that did exist? If they did not have the facts that Heidbreder said science requires or the predictive power implied by McGeoch's definition, what power did they have? Heidbreder (1933, p. 9) felt that they had a sort of comforting power; in the absence of real knowledge, they served in its place. We would put it in a somewhat different way. A theory, or *a finished* system of the kind McGeoch described, would tell a scientist or a layman what to expect as a result of any given manipulation of the subject matter of psychology; it would provide for the prediction, and perhaps for the manipulation, of the events within the scope of the system. According to this usage, a system would be a supertheory. Unfortunately, there is a time in the development of any science when the information for such prediction and manipulation is simply not available. The chief problem then is to *direct the scientist in his study of the subject matter* so that his efforts will be most efficiently used to further knowledge. When this is the state of affairs, a system for directing his efforts tends to appear. Thus, one aspect of the philosophy of science is an attempt to describe the scientific process as it is and ought to be and thereby to direct scientists in general in what they should do. A system of psychology does the same thing partially, except that it is concerned with psychologists rather than with scientists in general. Such systems contain statements about what the subject matter in question is or ought to be. They tell the psychologist what problems ought to be studied, by providing a purpose for the scientists. They tell him how he ought to go about studying the suggested problems. These directive statements, however, are not couched in a form which makes their functions obvious. They are not directed to the scientist in the form of orders, and yet his behaviour is influenced by them.

We can make this last point by rephrasing some of the key contentions of some of psychology's systems in a form which makes their influence more obvious:

*Structuralism.* As psychologists you ought to study the contents of consciousness through the method of introspection.

*Behaviourism.* You ought to study stimulus-response connections through strictly objective methods.

*Gestalt psychology.* You can arrive at useful formulations only through the consideration of large units of both stimulus and response; you should study configurations or fields.

*Functionalism.* Prime concerns of psychology' should be the study of the function of behaviour in adapting to the environment and the formulation or mathematical functions relating behaviour to antecedent variables.

*Associationism.* The psychologist should study the principles of association of ideas (or of words or stimulus-response connection), analysing complex events into simpler ones.

*Psychoanalysis.* The core of psychology is motivation, much of which is unconscious and must be studied through its manifestations in dreams, errors, symptoms, or free association.

There is a continuing interplay between the systematic philosophical prescriptions of a particular school and its empirical findings. Gestalt psychology, for example, became a formal school after particular findings had been interpreted in a unique way by its founders. The empirical, theoretical, and systematic statements tend to be stirred together, and the amalgam then is the system. We tend to use the words *school* and *system* almost interchangeably, but the word *school* implies people, and the word *system* implies their findings and beliefs (see the Glossary).

A word which applies roughly to the directive or superordinate aspects of a system is *metatheory.* A metatheory in general is a set of methodological considerations used in constructing or evaluating a theory; it is, so to speak, a theory about theory. A metatheory differs from a psychological system in being more highly formalised. A loose, informal metatheory can usually be sifted out of a school or system, but there wilt be a large remainder of empirical and philosophical statements.

**Proposed Prescriptions for Psychology**

R.I. Watson (1967) has taken a position similar to the one outlined above. He proposes a set of prescriptive, directive dimensions which he thinks are critical for systematic psychology. A system of psychology can be described by checking its position on each of the eighteen dimensions listed by Watson. The eighteen dimensions then constitute an eighteen-dimensional space like the definitional spaces discussed earlier in this chapter. The list of dimensions given below is taken from Watson (1967, pp. 436-437):

***The Prescriptions of Psychology Arranged in Contrasting Pairs***

*Conscious mentalism-Unconscious mentalism* (emphasis on awareness of mental structure or activity—unawareness).

*Contentual objectivism-Contentual subjectivism* (psychological data viewed as behaviour of individual—as mental structure or activity of individual).

*Determinism-Indeterminism* (human events completely explicable in terms of antecedents—not completely so explicable).

*Empiricism-Rationalism* (major, if not exclusive source of knowledge is experience—is reason).

*Functionalism-Structuralism,* (psychological categories are activities—are contents).

*Inductivism-Deductivism* (investigations begun with facts or observations—with assumed established truths).

*Mechanism-Vitalism* (activities of living being completely explicable by physiochemical constituents-not so explicable).

*Methodological objectivism-Methodological subjectivism* (use of methods open to verification by another competent observer—not so open).

*Molecularism-Molarism* (psychological data most aptly described in terms of relatively small units—relatively large units).

*Monism-Dualism* (fundamental principle or entity in universe is of one kind- is of two kinds, mind and matter).

*Naturalism-Supernaturalism* (nature requires for its operation and explanation only principles found within it—requires transcendent guidance as well).

*Nomotheticism-Indiographicism* (emphasis upon discovering general laws- upon explaining particular events or individuals).

*Peripheralism-Centralism* (stress upon psychological events taking place at periphery of body—within the body).

*Purism-Utilitarianism* (seeking of knowledge for its own sake—for its usefulness in other activities).

*Quantitativism-Qualitativism* (stress upon knowledge which is countable or measurable-upon that which is different in kind or essence).

*Rationalism-Irrationalism* (emphasis upon data supposed to follow dictates of good sense and intellect-intrusion or domination of emotive and conative factors upon intellectual processes).

*Staticism-Developmentalism* (emphasis upon cross-sectional view-upon changes with time).

*Staticism-Dynamicism* (emphasis upon enduring aspects—upon change and factors making for change).

**TABLE 14.1**

**Standard Deviations of Twenty-three Student Judgements of Six Psychological Systems on Each of Watson's Eighteen Prescriptive Dimensions**

| *Watson's Dimensions* | *Systems* | | | | | |
|---|---|---|---|---|---|---|
| | *Associationism* | *Structuralism* | *Functionalism* | *Behaviorism* | *Gestalt theory* | *Psycho-analysis* |
| Mentalism: conscious versus unconscious | 0.84 | 0.62 | 0.70 | 1.29 | 1.10 | 0.95 |
| Content: objective versus subjective | 1.05 | 1.11 | 0.72 | 1.12 | 0.75 | 1.27 |
| Determinism-indeterminism | 0.86 | 0.85 | 1.08 | 0.94 | 1.00 | 1.22 |
| Empiricism-rationalism | 0.88 | 0.99 | 0.83 | 0.80 | 0.87 | 1.07 |
| Functionalism-structuralism | 1.12 | 1.06 | 0.83 | 0.94 | 0.93 | 0.71 |
| Inductivism-deductivism | 0.63 | 1.23 | 0.85 | 0.16 | 0.79 | 1.25 |
| Mechanism-vitalism | 1.05 | 1.18 | 0.57 | 1.19 | 0.66 | 1.26 |
| Methods: objectivism versus subjectivism | 1.25 | 1.23 | 0.94 | 0.91 | 1.17 | 1.13 |
| Molecularism-molarism | 0.57 | 1.25 | 0.94 | 1.17 | 1.11 | 1.10 |
| Monism-dualism | 0.68 | 1.01 | 1.01 | 0.68 | 0.54 | 0.77 |
| Naturalism-supernaturalism | 0.74 | 1.08 | 0.70 | 0.13 | 1.01 | 1.26 |
| Nomotheticism-idiographicism | 1.05 | 1.25 | 0.87 | 1.15 | 1.18 | 1.45 |
| Peripheralism-centralism | 1.03 | 0.94 | 0.79 | 0.39 | 0.73 | 0.52 |
| Purism-utilitarianism | 0.87 | 1.16 | 0.63 | 0.37 | 0.41 | 0.52 |
| Quantitativism-qualitativism | 1.03 | 0.58 | 0.82 | 0.95 | 0.83 | 0.55 |
| Rationalism-irrationalism | 1.00 | 0.81 | 0.90 | 1.00 | 0.93 | 1.61 |
| Staticism-developmentalism | 1.04 | 1.17 | 1.10 | 0.99 | 1.24 | 1.35 |
| Staticism-dynamicism | 1.01 | 0.80 | 0.72 | 1.10 | 125 | 1.19 |

Any list like Watson's is bound to have some component of arbitrariness, and the dimensions are not necessarily independent of one another. Nevertheless, this list represents a thoughtful analysis by one student of psychological systems, and it should help to direct the attention of other students to some of the important issues. As with any dimensions, it is of interest to know whether the values of psychological systems on these dimensions can be judged reliably by persons presumed to be somewhat familiar with the systems and with the dimensions.

In order to make a rough assessment of the reliability of judgment of values on these dimensions, twenty-three graduate students in a course in advanced systematic psychology were asked to rate the six systems treated in this book on each of Watson's eighteen dimensions. A five-point scale was used for the ratings. The number 1 represented the extreme left-hand position on a dimension, while 5 indicated the extreme right. For example, if psychoanalysis were rated on the staticism-dynamicism dimension as being *extremely* dynamic, it would be assigned a 5. The students also chose and ranked the three dimensions thought to be most heavily emphasised by each school. Most students might be expected to choose methodological objectivism-methodological subjectivism as one of the dimensions most heavily emphasised by the behavioristic school.

Although the instructions for rating did not require it, most of the students used only whole numbers — 1, 2, 3, 4, or 5. If students knew absolutely nothing about the positions of the systems on the dimensions and assigned the numbers with equal probability, the standard deviation of the numbers so assigned would be 1.414. If the standard deviation of the numbers actually assigned is less than this, it means that the students responded on the basis of some information they had about the dimensions. Table 14.1 shows that the standard deviation of the judgments of the twenty-three students was nearly always below what would be expected on the bas.. of random assignment of the values, although there were some exceptions.

It is interesting to examine the adequacy of these dimensions a definitional scheme, at least in a crude way. The students' mean rating were taken as defining the "prototypical points" for each of-the six psychological systems. Then two "experts" (the authors) also rated the six systems. Each of them used a 4-inch line for each dimension as a rating aid and indicated the position of each system on each dimension on one of the lines. The extreme left was labeled 1, and the extreme right was labeled 5. The number assigned a system was then determined by measuring its position on the line with a ruler. The students' and the authors' mean ratings are shown in Table 14.2.

The authors' ratings were averaged for each dimension for each system. Then the city-block distances of the eighteen authors' means from the eighteen students' means were determined for each system. The sum of the differences gave the city-block distance.

The distance of our own structuralism from structuralism, functionalism, associationism, behaviourism, Gestalt psychology, and psychoanalysis, as rated by the "mean student," was computed. It was closest to the students' prototypical point for structuralism and hence

**TABLE 14.2**

**Mean Judgments by Twenty-three Students and the Authors of the Positions of Six Psychological Systems on Each of Watson's Eighteen Prescriptive Dimensions**

| *Watson's Dimensions* | *Mean Ratings* | | | | | | | | | | | |
|---|---|---|---|---|---|---|---|---|---|---|---|---|
| | *Associationism* | | *Structuralism* | | *Functionalism* | | *Behaviorism* | | *Gestalt Theory* | | *Psychoanalysis* | |
| | *Students* | *Authors* | *Students* | *Authors* | *Students* | *Authors* | *Students* | *Authors* | *Students* | *Authors* | *Students* | *Authors* |
| Mentalism: conscious versus unconscious | 2.9 | 2.2 | 1.2 | 1.2 | 2.4 | 2.5 | 3.3 | 4.4 | 2.7 | 2.3 | 4.4 | 4.8 |
| Content: objective versus subjective | 2.3 | 3.2 | 4.1 | 4.9 | 2.3 | 2.1 | 1.6 | 1.1 | 3.8 | 3.8 | 4.1 | 4.2 |
| Determinism-indeterminism | 2.0 | 1-3 | 2.8 | 2.2 | 2.9 | 2.2 | 1.4 | 1.1 | 3.0 | 2.2 | 1.9 | 1.1 |
| Empiricism-rationalism | 1.8 | 1.1 | 1:7 | 1.7 | 2.6 | 2.2 | 1.4 | 1.3 | 3.0 | 3.2 | 2.8 | 3.6 |
| Functionalism-structuralism | 2.6 | 2.4 | 4.5 | 4.8 | 1.4 | 1.1 | 1.9 | 1.5 | 3.5 | 3.7 | 3.7 | 3.1 |
| Inductivism-deductivisrn | 2.3 | 1.5 | 2.6 | 3.2 | 1.9 | 1.9 | 1.7 | 1.7 | 3.4 | 4.1 | 3.4 | 4.3 |
| Mechanism-vitalism | 2.5 | 1.4 | 2.9 | 2.0 | 2.8 | 3.0 | 1.4 | 1.1 | 2.8 | 2.9 | 3.4 | 2.3 |
| Methods: objectivism versus subjectivism | 1.5 | 1.9 | 3.0 | 5.0 | 2.4 | 2.0 | 1.7 | 1.1 | 3.8 | 3.7 | 4.2 | 4.6 |
| Molecularism-molarism | 1.9 | 1.2 | 1.7 | 1.6 | 3.3 | 3.2 | 1.9 | 1.3 | 4.6 | 4.8 | 4.2 | 3.3 |
| Monism-dualism | 2.7 | 3.3 | 3.6 | 1.6 | 2.6 | 4.1 | 1.1 | 1.1 | 3.6 | 4.1 | 3.5 | 4.2 |
| Naturalism-supernaturalism | 1.5 | 2.3 | 2.1 | 1.6 | 1.8 | 1.4 | 1.1 | 1.1 | 2.2 | 2.4 | 2.4 | 1.9 |
| Nomotheticism-idiographicism | 2.4 | 1.3 | 2.6 | 1.2 | 3.2 | 2.9 | 2.3 | 1.0 | 2.6 | 4.1 | 3.3 | 3.1 |
| Peripheralism-centralism | 1.8 | 2.5 | 3.6 | 4.4 | 2.7 | 2.2 | 1.2 | 1.1 | 3.9 | 4.7 | 4.4 | 4.6 |
| Purism-utilitarianism | 3.6 | 1.6 | 1.4 | 1.1 | 4.2 | 4.9 | 3.5 | 3.2 | 2.6 | 2.2 | 4.1 | 4.6 |
| Quantitativism-qualitativism | 1.8 | 1.9 | 3.4 | 3.2 | 2.6 | 2.1 | 1.2 | 1.6 | 4.1 | 4.7 | 4.7 | 4.6 |
| Rationalism-irrationalism | 2.2 | 1.9 | 2.0 | 2.0 | 2.4 | 3.1 | 3.0 | 4.0 | 4.0 | 2.8 | 3.0 | 4.8 |
| Staticism-developmentalism | 3.2 | 3.3 | 2.7 | 1.3 | 3.2 | 4.1 | 3.0 | 2.8 | 3.9 | 2.3 | 2.7 | 3.6 |
| Staticism-dynamicism | 3.1 | 2.6 | 1.9 | 1.4 | 3.7 | 4.6 | 3.7 | 2.6 | 3.0 | 4.2 | 3.6 | 4.6 |

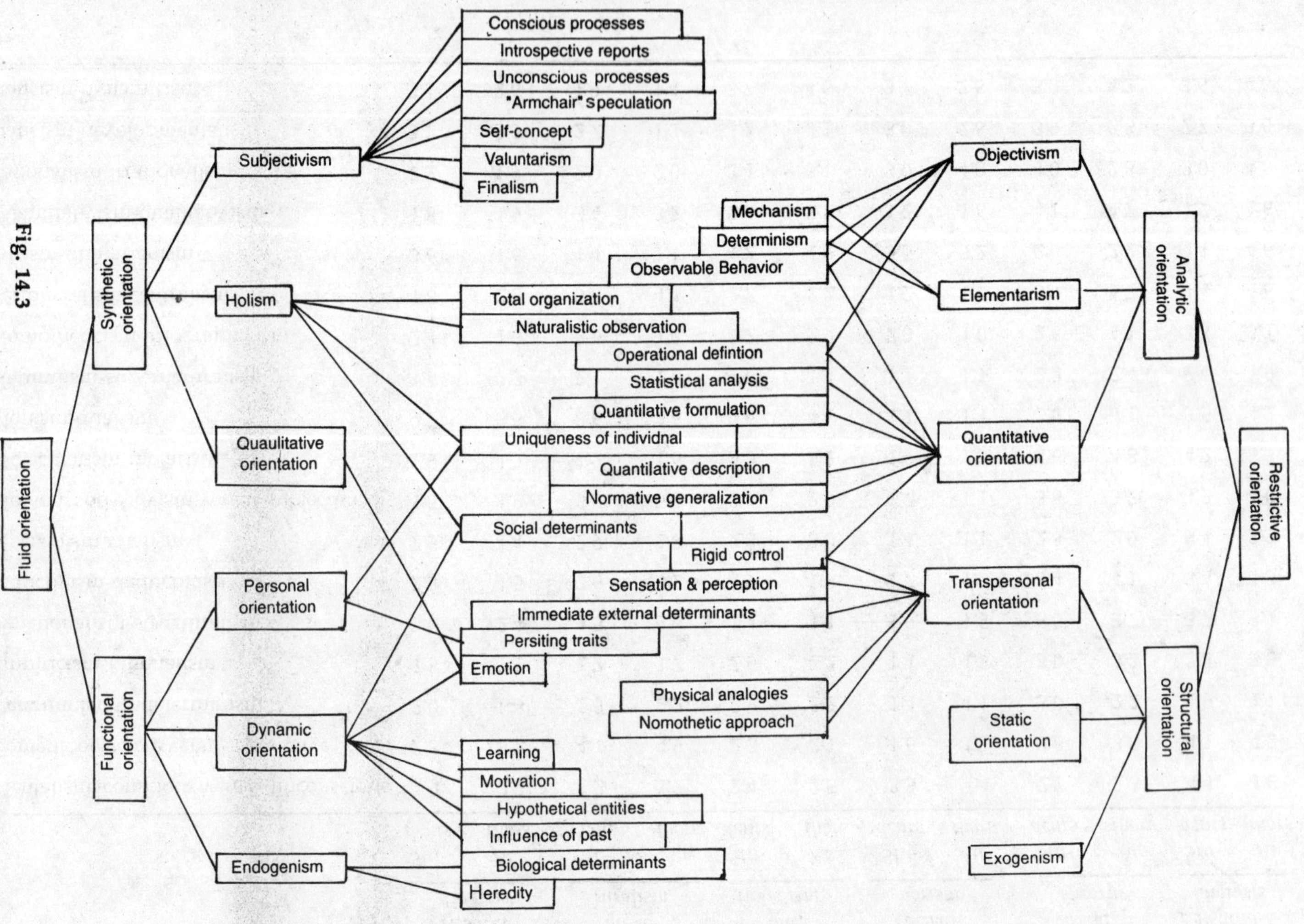


**Fig. 14.3** A bipolar hierarchy of theoretical variables. (The variable shown in the middle are relatively specific while those on the left and right sides represent more general and mutually opposing trands). (From Coan, 1968, 720).

would have been correctly identified as a set of ratings for structuralism, had its identity been unknown. Table 14.3 shows all the intersystem distances. In five out of six cases, the classification bard on this definitional system was correct. In the sixth case—Gestalt psychology-the system misclassified it as psychoanalysis. It thus appears that the system based on Watson's criteria is a promising definitional scheme for systems of psychology, and we shall refer the student back to the positions of various systems of psychology on these conceptual dimensions as each system is discussed. Relating one system to another on these dimensions should help the student to obtain an integrated picture of all systems.

## Empirically Derived Characteristics of Systems

Watson's dimensions, though based on a careful study of history and philosophy, were conceived by a single individual. Coan (1968) found a systematic procedure for tapping the judgments of a *roup* of experts in the history of psychology. He asked 232 correspondents to rate 54 carefully selected famous psychologists as to their emphasis on 34 characteristics, such as nomothetic emphasis. All rating was done on a five-point scale ranging from positive emphasis on the characteristic to rejection of the characteristic. What this study uncovered, then, was the opinions of 232 expert judges as to whether and to what degree 54 psychologists had emphasised 34 variables in their theorising and/or experimentation.

**TABLE 14.3**

**City-block Distances between Authors' Mean Rating of Each System and Students' Mean Rating of Each System**

| | | *Students* | | | | | |
|---|---|---|---|---|---|---|---|
| | | *Associationism* | *Structuralism* | *Functionalism* | *Behaviorism* | *Gestalt theory* | *Psychoanalysis* |
| **Authors** | Associationism | 12.4 | 16.3 | 17.9 | 15.5 | 23.8 | 27.9 |
| | Structuralism | 25.5 | 12.3 | 29.4 | 32.8 | 23.3 | 24.6 |
| | Functionalism | 12.7 | 24.0 | 8.8 | 16.4 | 21.1 | 22.6 |
| | Behaviourism | 15.6 | 30.3 | 22.7 | 8.3 | 32.0 | 32.9 |
| | Gestalt theory | 24.9 | 18.6 | 21.2 | 32.2 | 10.4 | 10.2 |
| | Psychoanalysis | 27.8 | 26.3 | 22.7 | 31.5 | 16.2 | 11.9 |

Coan derived six specific factors from the judgments. Factor 1 is labeled *subjectivistic* versus *objectivistic*. According to Coan's findings, subjectivistic theorists would be exemplified by McDougall, Piaget, and Jung, while the latter type include Estes, Hull, and Watson. Factor 2 is labeled *holistic* versus *elementaristic*. Holistic theorists are Goldstein, Kohler, and Koffka Elementaristic theorists are Spence, Titchener, and Ebbinghaus. Coan calls factor 3 *transpersonal* versus *persons'*, and factors 4 to 6 he labels *quantitative* versus *qualitative*, *dynamic* versus static, and *synthetic* versus *analytic*, respectively.

Coan finds that these specific factors are themselves interrelated, with subjectivism, holism, and a qualitative trend tending to go together to make up a synthetic trend opposed to an analytic trend composed of the objectivistic, elementaristic, and quantitative trends. A second general factor at this level is the structural orientation (transpersonal, static, exogenistic) versus the functional orientation (personal, dynamic, endogenistic). Finally, the analytic and structural orientations relate to a general restrictive orientation, with the synthetic and functional orientations relating to a general fluid orientation.

Coan's system thus provides an interesting additional way to organise the views of particular systematists and theorists. There is a surprising and comforting amount of overlap between the issues raised by Watson's prescriptions and Coan's factors, despite the great differences in detail.

**Paradigms**

The reader should now be better equipped to relate psychological systems to Kuhn's paradigms. Kuhn thinks of paradigms as *accepted* examples of scientific practice, including all its elements: law, theory, application, and instrumentation. The paradigm must stimulate research by defining the problems of a field and by being revolutionary enough to attract individuals away from other fields of, or approaches to, scientific inquiry.

R.I. Watson (1967), cited above, dubbed psychology a prescriptive science because he wanted to distinguish it from the more advanced sciences, which more clearly have paradigms. Psychology has never been "of one mind" enough for Watson to feel that any one approach can claim paradigmatic status. The reader will recognise that an argument about whether psychology has any paradigms would be an argument about whether psychology has any paradigms would be an argument about definition; the settlement of such an argument must be arbitrary. Certainly if we drop the "universality of agreement" dimension from our definitional space, we might think of several candidates for psychological paradigms: the classical conditioning paradigm, operant conditioning, verbal learning, and others. All have the kind guiding function Kuhn attributes to paradigms.

Contemporary Skinnerian psychology-what might be called the *operant conditioning paradigm*—seems an especially strong candidate. It has fairly wide acceptance and includes law, application, instrumentation, and a kind of theory. It has been revolutionary enough to attract many strong adherents and stimulate research. "Normal science," of the everyday puzzle-solving type emphasised by Kuhn, is busily working out unfinished business within the confines of this paradigm..

Krantz (1972) found some evidence that operant psychologists form a school. The *Journal of the Experimental Analysis of Behavior*, for example, cites itself quite often; this high rate of self-citation is some evidence, admittedly rather weak, of isolation from other aspects of psychology. After evaluating this and other evidence, Krantz answers with a qualified "yes" the question whether operant psychology is a school. Most students of operant techniques, however, do not see themselves as members of schools. This is probably true of nearly any psychologist, past or present; we all tend to see ourselves as psychologists and dislike admitting that we have been too much influenced by any single point of view.

Psychology thus might or might not be said to have paradigms, depending on how one wishes to restrict the definition. Whether it has or not, Watson (1971b) finds his prescriptive approach to the study of the history of psychology very useful. Through it, he believes one can avoid both excessive emphasis on the exclusively antiquarian view of the past and, at the same time, avoid excessive distortion of the past because it is viewed too much in terms of present conceptualisations. Fuchs and Kawash (1972) have used Watson's prescriptions as a starting point for a factor analytic approach similar to Coan's and have used the factors to describe five schools of psychology. The systematic approach to the study of the history of psychology is well on its way.

## Criteria for Systems

We will now turn the calendar back about forty years to find out how systems were seen by psychologists when systematic issues were still extremely prominent. It will be clear that the questions asked were less systematic and detailed and that there was no attempt at quantitative treatment. However, the level of analysis was close to the same level of sophistication as the systems being analysed. McGeoch (1933) presented six criteria which he felt should be met by a system of psychology. Table 14.4 is adapted from McGeoch's criteria.

**TABLE 14.4**

**McGeoch's Criteria for a System**

| | |
|---|---|
| I. | The system must contain a definition of the field of psychology |
| II. | The system must make its postulates explicit |
| | A Postdates should be as few as possible |
| | B The postulates should be necessary |
| | C The postulates should contain little of the finished system |
| III. | The nature of the data to be studied must be specified |
| | A Objective-subjective |
| | B Qualitative-quantitative |
| | C Units of description |
| | D Provide genetic starting point |
| IV. | A mind-body position must be taken |
| V. | The organisation of the data, its principles of connection, must be accounted for |
| VI. | Principles of selection must be given |

Source: Adapted from McGeoch, 1933.

The criteria are consistent with our contention that the systems of psychology have served chiefly to direct the behaviour of psychologists in their pursuit of scientific knowledge about psychology. Why should McGeoch require a system to provide a definition of the field? Because the definition functions to tell psychologists what to study. The postulates McGeoch is talking about also have at times a directive function. McGeoch's postulates are not the type from which theorems in the formal sense are derived; they are the underlying assumptions that direct or justify the behaviour of the man who accepts them. The nature of the data to be studied must be specified with sufficient clarity to direct scientific investigation. Requirements IV to VI specify problems that McGeoch felt must be dealt with. To meet the last two requirements-accounting for the organisation of the data and giving the principles of selection-the system would have to consist of at least some empirical information, unless the principles were based completely on rational guesses.

Modem psychologists, unlike McGeoch, are likely to be casual about the definition of psychology. They recognise that boundaries of fields are always shifting and that new disciplines arise along the boundaries as fields become more specialised. Certainly few psychologists would refuse to study a promising new problem simply because it didn't look like "psychology."

McGeoch's requirements for postulates, if applied to *formal* postulates, are certainly reasonable. However, they may not be so important if intended to apply to the informal assumptions or hypotheses which were developed—and may be discarded-in connection with the development of the formal postulates.

Psychology today uses all kinds of data. A given psychologist uses whatever data are helpful in attacking a problem. While we like to feel that our data are objective, the distinction between objective and subjective is difficult to make. We require that our data be such that they can be gathered again by any investigator who wishes to check the validity of our results. Beyond this, we can say little. Units of description are chosen for the sake of convenience, and if the data cannot be quantitative, qualitative data are used.

It is clear that McGeoch made an arbitrary choice of the mind-body problem as one on which a system had to take a stand; he might have chosen the nativism-empiricism question or any one of a number of others. Although McGeoch's criteria are somewhat incomplete and unrealistic, they do include the kinds of factors that actually, were considered important when systematic issues were of great interest, and their level of sophistication is similar to the level of sophistication reflected in the systems themselves.

McGeoch himself said of the mind-body position (1933): "The problem need not, of course, be stated in traditional metaphysical fashion.... The point is that the problem is there and must be treated (or avoided) somehow if an adequate system is to be constructed" (p. 8). He thus left open the alternative of avoiding the problem. Many psychologists today choose this alternative and would argue that the problem is *not* there until someone poses it and that it is not a useful problem to pose, at least at present. We shall discuss these issues at greater length when we consider the attack of the behaviourists on consciousness.

The last two requirements are still legitimate. They require for their fulfillment the statement of relevant variables and the statement of the functional relationships between them. Much of science is concerned with such statements.

These criteria provide a sample of what psychologists of over three decades ago felt a system should be. The requirements are stated without great attention to detail. No attempt is made to apply them to a particular theory or system. The desired characteristics are generality and scope of attempted coverage rather than predictive power.

## THE NATURE OF THEORY

### Pure Versus Practical

Often the word *theory* is used in contrast to *practice* or *application*. This usage is correct in that it implies that theories involve some use of abstraction. It is not correct if it is taken to imply that theories are impractical, or not applied. Theories, observations, and applications usually arise in intimate interactions. Rarely does the investigator find a handy mathematical or logical system and then go looking for data that it might fit. Theories and areas of investigation grow after applications are demonstrated; who would doubt that the military applications are partly responsible for the billions that have been spent on particle physics in the last twenty-five years?

### Degrees of Confirmation

Some authors use the word *theory* to refer to a hypothesis that has received a considerable amount of empirical support. When *theory* is used in this sense, the term *law* is used for the most thoroughly tested and verified propositions (Warren, 1934, p. 128).

In its more general scientific usages, the word *theory* refers to some proposition from which a large number of empirical observations can be deduced. For example, Bergmann (1957) defined a theory as a "group of laws deductively connected" (p. 31). If he limits the components of theory to laws, then he must be using a broad definition of the word *law*. Theories can certainly be built from postulates which are not well demonstrated empirically or which are incapable of empirical demonstration, or even from analogies whose parts are known not to correspond to the phenomena covered by the theory. An example of the latter would be the hydraulic analogy with electric currents. We arc quite sure that there is no water in the wires, and yet predictions can be made from such an analogy if the appropriate mathematics is used.

Bergmann's requirement for any theory, then, is that the key components be "deductively connected." This means simply that there must be a method of arriving at new statements from the original statements; there must be appropriate operations which result in deductive statements.

### *An Abstract Theory*

Since there is considerable emphasis on deduction in any theory, let us construct and examine an extremely simple postulate set, using a rule for deduction to derive theorems.

*Postulates*

1. *'*-"
2. " ' "-+

*Rule for Deduction*

1 If a symbol or symbols appear in any postulate on opposite sides of the symbol -, all symbols on one side of the - may be substituted for all symbols on the other side of the -, wherever they appear in any postulate or theorem.

What theorems can we derive in this simple system? Starting with postulate 2, we might replace," wherever it appears, with its equivalent from postulate 1. We then have *'*'*'*.+ (theorem 1).

We can operate on theorem 1 in one direction to produce theorem 2-+-+- and in the other direction to produce theorem 3–*'*'*'*.*'*'*'* (We could as easily have derived theorem 2 from postulate 2).

The student who has a strong stomach and a high threshold for boredom may proceed to discover a few additional theorems, like "-". Others will already be won de ring what the point of this construction is, especially in view of the meaning less and abstract nature of the "statements" made. The system was made intention ally abstract so that the student could look at our "theory" as a kind of game, free of the distractions that empirical interpretation brings, and see in stark outline the nature of such abstract games.

The theory can be given empirical interpretation by letting * stand for one apple," for two apples, and + for four apples. The operation plus, as usually understood for apples, can be indicated by', and equals by - We can now interpret our theory as being about apples, making wise statements like "One apple plus one apple plus one apple plus one apple equals four apples" (theorem I). If our operations on empirical apples are described by a statement that agrees with this interpretation of our abstract theorem, we have a successful theory about apple combinations. Our little exercise, which started life as a rudimentary abstract system, would become a rudimentary scientific theory, since it would then say something about apples. It has all the necessary elements of a scientific theory abstract formal statements, rules for manipulating these abstract statements, and a "dictionary" which relates the terms of the statements to empirical observations.

**Motivation for Theory Construction**

The abstract portions of a theory may be developed because the theorist has either of two motives: He may wish to deal with the empirical world more effectively and want an abstract system to help him do so, or he may just be playing a mathematical game and develop the system as a matter of curiosity. Euclid's geometry was probably based, ultimately, on problems of surveying. Many modern mathematicians deal with symbols at a very abstract level and do not much care about any possible correspondence between the mathematical system and an empirical system. There are therefore many extant mathematical systems available for new scientific applications if the scientist has the necessary sophistication to find them and to set up appropriate relationships between his subject matter and the mathematical system. Kurt Lewin (1936), for example, took advantage of a relatively new mathematics (topology) in developing his psychological theory, and he even developed a new mathematics (hodology) to deal with his conceptualisation of directionality (vectors) in behaviour. Estes (1959) used standard mathematics in developing his mathematical model of learning.

## Dimensions of Theories

Scientific theories may differ in many ways. They yield deductions about different *subject matters*. They differ greatly in *generality;* Hull's theory (1952) dealt with all simple mammalian behaviour, while Estes' theory (1950), as he originally proposed it, dealt only with the probability of a certain type of response. Theories differ in *precision* of statement; some make predictions that are at best qualitative, while at the other end of the scale are the very precise quantitative statements. Even within the same degree of quantitativeness of prediction, theories may differ as to the degree of *rigor* of the predictions; sometimes the argument, though involving quantitative statements, is loose and relatively informal, and in other cases the processes of derivation and prediction may be better formalised and more rigorous logically. Theories differ in the *origins* of their component statements, or postulates; some theories are combinations of empirically based statements, which are verifiable or potentially verifiable, and other theories are composed of statements arrived at rationally rather than empirically. No theory, whatever its qualities, is ever final, even though all the predictive statements made from it have been verified perfectly. There always remains the possibility that any given theory will be replaced by another theory which is simpler, more general, or more consistent with other relevant theories.

On the other hand, theories are seldom discarded simply because they are too specific or even because some of the predictions made from them are wrong. Rather, they are discarded when they are replaced by something better. A theory will generally be modified and used as long as it is the only thing available within some problem area.

## Models

A model is a particular subclass of theory, as we have defined theory. Some authors. separate them completely, and others treat them as synonyms, but we prefer to make models a subclass of theories, since both function in the derivation of theorems and in making predictions. Boring summed up the difference between the two succinctly (1957, p. 191):

Today we hear less about theories and more about models. What is the difference? The theory claims to be true, even though we all know that assurance about the validity of these claims varies greatly from theory to theory and from time to time for the same theory. The theory is an *as*, whereas the model is an *as-if.* The theory is indicative; the model, subjunctive.

The model is a pattern to be abandoned easily at the demand of progress.

By an *as,* Boring means that the theorist expects to observe, or has observed, empirical referents for the terms of his theory. The postulates of the theory are, or can become, empirical laws. The postulates of a model are not expected to become laws. The model builder bows that his postulates are purely abstract and cannot be coordinated with the empirical observations at the postulate level. We might draw an example from psychoanalysis. Freud's thinking with regard to the id, ego, and superego was probably *as-if* thinking; these elements functioned in a model. Yet labeling the functions or aspects of personality in this way (drawing diagrams of them, etc.) led many to believe that these words represented actual, observable entities; that is, these people believed that Freud had a theory, not a model.

A mathematical model, then, would be a "computational device." The mathematical function clearly does not reflect reality. A physical model is computational in a non-mathematical sense; that is, it behaves analogously to the thing modeled, and like the mathematical model, it serves as a basis for making predictions. A man is *not* a machine, nor is an atom a collection of billiard balls; yet machines and billiards may be useful analogies (models), and they can "be abandoned easily at the demand of progress."

The model may be differentiated from the metatheory in terms of its closer relationship to the structure of the empirical measures and the observations. That is, the metatheory provides general guidelines for the kind of theory to be developed; the model provides more specific guidelines for the empirical research and thus for the laws that are developed.

**Criteria for Theories**

Estes, Koch, MacCorquodale, Meehl, Mueller, Schoenfeld, and Verplanck (1954) presented an outline for the criticism of learning theories. In comparing this outline with McGeoch's criteria, several contrasts strike us. The questions asked in the outline are specific and logically sophisticated. They concern the ability of the theory to make predictions. There are no questions or requirements which *demand* any directive statements regarding the behaviour of the investigator. There is one question about generality ("range of data for which interpretation or explanation in terms of the theory has been claimed"), but there is no implication that the range must be great. The authors' first concern seems to be with the *language* of the theory. This implies a growing recognition that much of science is verbal behaviour. The outline deals with theories rather than with the more inclusive systems' and thus would not be expected to parallel McGeoch's discussion exactly; however, this dealing with smaller problems is itself a significant trend in psychology. Initially, all sciences tend to present "big," general problems. These problems usually are not amenable to experimental attack until they are broken down into smaller problems and perhaps rephrased completely.

Some attitudes of Estes et al. toward the evaluation of theory are given in a quotation from their discussion of the outline (1954, pp. xiv, xv):

We believe wide agreement would obtain among current writers in the logic of science that an adequate review of any scientific theory must include essentially the same features. . . . Scientific theories are evaluated not on some absolute scale of "theoryness," but with respect to what we expect them to do. Some of the functions of a useful theory are: (I) clarifying the description of the world possible in ordinary language, (2) summarising existing knowledge, (3) mediating applications of our knowledge to new situations, (4) leading to fruitful lines of experimental inquiry.

Table 14.5 presents the outline in full. The student should study every point very carefully. As we write, more than fifteen years after this outline was prepared, we still find the questions useful. The issues raised are still issues, and our hopes for theory are now as they were then.

## TRENDS IN SYSTEMS AND THEORIES

### Increasing Explicitness

We can now look back on what has been said and see what has happened and is happening to systems and theories. First, they are growing more limited and more explicit.

**TABLE 14.5**

**Outline for Reviews of Theories**

I Structure of the Theory

A Delineation of empirical area

1. Data language

   Is the data language explicit and theoretically neutral?

   How does the theorist relate his empirical variables to the data language?

2. Dependent and independent variables

   How does the selection or variables compare with those of other learning theories?

   What influence does the choice of variables exert upon the form of the theory?

B Theoretical concepts

1. Primitive terms

   Are primitive terms of the theory reducible to physical or object language? Is the usage of primitive terms fixed by implicit or explicit definitions?

2. Principal constructs

   Do these serve only a summarising function or are they related by definition or by hypothesis to terms of other disciplines (e.g., physiology)?

3. Relations assumed among constructs

   How are the major theoretical variables interrelated in the foundation assumptions of the theory?

   How are such interrelations constructed from the observation base of the theory?

4. Relations assumed or derived between constructs and experimentally defined variables

| II | Methodological Characteristics |
|---|---|
| | A. Standing of the theory on principal methodological "dimensions" |
| | 1. Explicit axiomatisation |
| | 2. Quantitativeness |
| | 3. Consistency and independence of principal theoretical assumptions |
| | 4. Use of physical or mathematical models |
| | B. Techniques of derivation |
| | Are the empirical consequences of the theory developed by informal arguments or format derivations? |
| **III** | **Empirical Content and Adequacy** |
| | A Range of data for which interpretation or explanation in terms of the theory has been claimed |
| | B Specificity of prediction demonstrated |
| | C Obvious failures to handle facts in the area III-A |
| | D Tour-do-force |
| | Has it been possible to predict new experimental phenomena? |
| | Have any predictions of this sort been confirmed? |
| | Does the theory account for facts not predictable from competing theories in the same area? |
| | E Sensitivity to empirical evidence |
| | F Programmtaticity |
| | G Special virtues or limitations. Techniques which may prove useful outside the context of the specific theory |

Source: Estes et al., 1954, pp. xiii, xiv.

Theorist: are no longer content with superficial statements that have no real predictive value; even the most sophisticated-appearing theory is subjected to careful examination and may at times be found lacking. For example, Cotton (1955) has shown that Hull's learning theory really is not adequate for making some predictions that it purports to be able to make. Psychologists are no longer content with comfortable generalities that allow labels to be tacked on to results after they occur; they want theories or systems to say what is *going* to happen and to say it clearly and exactly. They want theorists and systematists to show exactly how they know and how they predict. It follows from these demands that any contemporary system that fulfills them must be a miniature system, covering only a very small range of behaviour, perhaps only for a single kind of organism in a single simple situation. We still have too few facts to build full-scale systems.

## Laboratory and Field

The demand for increased rigor and precision has led to a growing concern for measurement and for mathematical statements. The same demands have led to two trends that at first glance seem opposed: a trend toward the laboratory and ever more carefully controlled experimentation and a trend toward a greater amount of naturalistic observation. The trend toward better-controlled experimentation is intended to ensure that the statements made are correct; inadequacies in past experiments, and hesitancy to accept results because of lack of control, have led to the laboratory. The trend toward naturalism arises partly out of a similar concern; the "naturalist" recognises that it is as illegitimate to generalise when the base situation failed to include all relevant *variables* as when the base situation did not include all the relevant *controls.* It seems to us that both trends are desirable and are occurring because of increased sophistication on the part of psychologists. However, some psychologists of the less tough-minded variety have objected to the increasing abstraction and artificiality which often characterise the laboratory experiment. Skinner is one of many who have defended the position of the laboratory worker. (1957a, p. 370):

> Have we been guilty of an undue simplification of conditions in order to obtain this level of rigor? Hive we really "proved" that there is comparable order outside the laboratory? It is difficult to be sure of the answers to such questions. Suppose we are observing the rate at which a man sips his breakfast coffee.... It is unlikely that we shall record a smooth curve. But although our behavioural curve will not be pretty, *neither will the cooling curve for the coffee in the cup.* In extrapolating our results to the world at large, we can do no more than the physical and biological sciences in general. Because of experiments performed under laboratory conditions, no one doubts that the cooling of the coffee in the cup is an orderly process, even though the actual curve would be difficult to explain. Similarly when we have investigated behaviour under the advantageous conditions of the laboratory, we can accept its basic orderliness in the world at large even though we cannot there wholly demonstrate law.

There are two other divergent contemporary tendencies, which are related to a demand for more rigor. On the one hand, there is a greater tendency to regard theoretical statements as *as-ifs,* that is, a tendency to use models rather than theories. If the psychologist is ignorant of what physiological events correlate with his behavioural observations, rigor dictates that he should not couch his theory in physiological terms. Many psychologist simply ignore physiology on these grounds mid point out that the predictive value of a model does not depend on any assumptions about the existence of components of the model. On the other hand, there are many psychologists today who feel that ignorance of physiology is deplorable. However, they generally *do not* "physiologise"; that is, they do not talk about physiological explanations in the complete absence of physiological knowledge. Physiologising in this sense is, we hope, disappearing from psychology.

Despite all the changes, parts of the old systems still persist in the "foundation assumptions" that we saw mentioned by some of our leading modem theorists (see Table 14.5). R.I. Watson (1967) sees these attitudes as very important, as does Koch (1959). These orientative attitudes are still defended and attacked, and the struggle still generates friction, heat, and, we may hope, experimentation. Psychology's systems may be dead, but the remnants are still with us. It is a fascinating business to study their modern rearrangements and modifications. If systems are regarded chiefly as specialisations of the general philosophy of science for application to a particular discipline, then some kind of system will always be found in every science.

**Summary and Conclusions**

A working idea of what a system is, and should be, is necessary for our later evaluation of systems. The origins of systems were largely philosophical. They may be loosely defined as organisations of facts and theories. Yet psychology's systems have not really been exemplifications of our definition; they have been less statements about the subject matter of psychology than statements about the way that subject matter ought to be approached. They have had some usefulness in motivating people to perform experiments and to be cautious and critical; they have hindered by turning attention too much to big questions that at present are answerable only on the basis of rational guesses. There is a growing tendency to replace the traditional system with a more limited type of theory, to use models as well as theories, and to demand far more precision, logical development, and explicitness of the more limited type of statement. Yet the basic orientative attitudes of the old systems live on in modem psychology.

# 15

# Varieties of S-R Theory

Anyone who tries to define S-R psychology should be prepared for an exercise in tolerance of frustration and ambiguity. It seems clear that we must first define stimulus and response if we are ever to define a stimulus-response psychology. Unfortunately, no agreed-upon definitions are available. We are in no position to legislate usage, but we can at least point to some of the alternative possibilities. The alternative chosen will determine what is taken to be S-R psychology.

One issue concerns whether the stimulus is to be defined independently or is to be only "that which produces a response." We have already seen that Dewey in 1896 deplored the artificial analysis of the reflex into stimulus and response. Skinner (1938) agreed in the sense that he thought it useful to consider a stimulus and a response to be any situational and behavioural aspects of a context that could be town to enter into an orderly functional relation. J.J. Gibson (1960) was critical of this kind of formulation and pointed to the possibility that it would lead to circularity in some cases (that is, the stimulus might become whatever was needed to bring about the response, leaving no independent term to explain the response). Hocutt (1967) defended the meaningfulness of relational terms of this type. Among Hocutt's examples of such concepts are those of man and wife, neither of which earn be defined independently of the marriage relation. Despite their lack of independence, it remains meaningful to speak of a wife as something like the "female partner in a marriage relationship." Even if a stimulus is conceptualised initially as independent of responses and is defined in terms of physical energies, it will be of eventual interest only if it does enter into some relationship with a response. It would seem, then, that the S-R psychologist need only be careful to have a means of identifying stimuli and manipulating them; he can then ascertain whether the independently identified stimulus enters into relationships with independently identified responses.

A second important question concerns the relative level of molarity of definition of stimulus and response. On the stimulus side, we have encountered a version of this problem in the contrast between the molecular view of the stimulus taken by the structuralists and the molar view taken by the Gestaltists. Brunswik's lens models and his scheme of the organism in its surroundings are clear expositions of some of the possibilities both for stimulus and for response definition. Brunswik's general argument tends toward molar definition for psychology, at least at the outset. The typical S-R psychologist is probably more molecular than Brunswik would wish and is in this respect a descendant of the more molecular and analytic associationistic school.

A third definitional question concerns what should be included in the definition of stimulus and response. The molar-molecular issue is related to the problem of inclusiveness, but more is involved than that. Specific questions related to the general issue would include, "Is deprivation a stimulus?" and "Is an injection of androgens a stimulus?" Because he believes that such things are *not* stimuli, Skinner does not think of himself as an S-R psychologist (Evans, 1968, p. 20; Skinner, 1966, p. 12). On the other hand, Kimble, because he uses the terms *stimulus* and *response* more inclusively, concludes (1967): "Thus the facts of psychology turn out to be Ss and Rs, a state of which suggests with a certain insistence that the laws of psychology must be reducible to these terms and that an S-R psychology is an inevitability" (p. 76).

It is clear that there is disagreement about whether one must be an S-R psychologist because there is disagreement about what an S-R psychologist is. The latter disagreement follows, in turn, from the fact that stimulus and response are defined differently by different people. We shall leave this problem at this point and turn to an examination of some theories which are usually agreed to be S-R theories. This examination will reveal some of the properties generally shared by such theories. Contemporary S-R theory can be divided into two broad classes which differ in the role accorded the *reinforcement*, or response-strengthening, process.

The first of these classes may be called *S-R reinforcement theory.* Both of the two major subtypes of this theory afford reinforcement a central role, but they interpret the nature of this role differently. Many psychologists, like Hull, have interested themselves in the mechanism of the reinforcement process; some form of "need reduction" has been most often identified as the necessary and sufficient condition for reinforcement. Others, like Skinner, have stressed the importance of reinforcement without commitment to the underlying nature of the process. This view may be classed as *descriptive* S-R theory, since the fact of reinforcement is accepted in a descriptive or theoretically neutral sense.

The second class of modern S-R theory is generally called *contiguity theory.* Following Guthrie, contiguity theorists hold that all that is essential to learning is contiguity of stimulus and response. Reinforcement, in the sense of presentation of a so-called reinforcing stimulus such as food or money, is important only because it changes the stimulus situation and so preserves associations already established. From a historical point of view, modern contiguity theory is a highly refined associationism.

Several writers have suggested combinations of these two major views. These two-factor theories are treated briefly. With the exception of Mowrer's (1960a) version, they present few new theoretical position, but rearrange the basic points already present in the two major positions.

All the different S-R theories have a great deal in common, probably more then theories of perception or personality. For one thing, they are all primarily *learning* theories.

Nearly all S-R theories now distinguish between learning and performance (Kimble, 1961) with some variables affecting only the latter, but learning remains central. Because of the important role that learning has played in these theories, it is often very difficult to distinguish between learning theory and general behaviour theory. Hull, for example, considered himself a general behaviour theorist and thought of learning constructs as central but not exclusive determiners of performance. To most psychologists, however, Hull has been a learning theorist because he has been concerned primarily with behaviour *modification*. Similar statements could be made about most of the other theorists discussed in this chapter.

A second characteristic common to all S-R theorists is their neobehaviourism. The most marked difference between modern *neobehaviourism* and Watsonian behaviourism is the greatly increased theoretical sophistication of the former. Watson, Weiss, and Holt had to be content with making gross generalisations based on very limited empirical evidence. Today, however, detailed logical justification as well as empirical evidence is demanded by and of neobehaviourists.

## S-R REINFORCEMENT THEORY: THE HULL-SPENCE SCHOOL

The main lines of modern S-R reinforcement theory were laid down by Clark L. Hull. In the development of this systematic effort he had the assistance of many psychologists, notably Kenneth Spence and Neal Miller. Both were associated with him for many years at Yale University, and both helped to determine the way in which Hull's theory developed. Spence especially has been consistently interested in the form of the theory and has trained and sent forth a large number of theoretical devotees. For these reasons we refer to the "Hull-Spence school." Miller not only worked directly with the theory but also extended it to the explanation of personality.

### Hull's Career

Clark Hull (1884-1952) was born in New York and reared in Michigan. Throughout his childhood and early adult years, he was beset by illnesses, and he suffered from very poor vision all his life. Polio left him crippled in one leg, and he himself believed that much of his motivation derived from his handicap; however, there is some reason to doubt that this is the whole story. His own "idea books" refer to a possible future greatness seven years before he contracted polio (Hays, 1962).

Hull's education was interrupted both by these physical problems and by lack of money; he had to teach both in one-room rural schools and in a Kentucky normal school for various periods. Nevertheless, he managed to earn his bachelor's degree at the University of Michigan, where Pillsbury was a dominant influence, and to complete his doctoral research at the University of Wisconsin. His dissertation was a study of concept formation (Hull,

1920). He was thirty-four by the time he completed his own personal obstacle course that led him to a Ph.D. His idea books (Hull, 1962) show that he was often concerned that his late start might prevent him from achieving the greatness to which he aspired. At one stage he expected to have only six creative years left; then he raised the estimate to eleven upon reading of the advanced ages at which men like Kant and Leibniz had created great works. When he made the eleven-year estimate, he actually had twenty productive years left!

After receiving his Ph.D., Hull stayed on at Wisconsin as a member of the psychology staff. One of his early research efforts concerned the effects of tobacco smoking on efficiency of behaviour. These much-cited experiments (Hull, 1924) were marked for their especially good control of the sensory factors involved in smoking (such as the warmth of the air produced by a pipe). The control of suggestibility by concealing whether tobacco was actually present presaged Hull's later concern with the general problem of suggestion.

As a result of being assigned a course in tests and measures, Hull surveyed the literature in that field and eventually published an important early text, *Aptitude testing* (1928). He did not continue these activities, however, because of what he has called his "pessimistic view as to the future of tests in this field" (1952b, p. 151). Here again Hull himself provides us with good justification for doubting his assessment of his own motives; since he says in an idea book of 1929 that he still plans to do "a grand experiment on a huge scale" (1962, p. 827) with the intention of constructing a universal aptitude battery. Hull's discussions there convey the clear impression that the aptitude work was merely being deferred until later because he thought of it as the kind of work that an older and less creative man than he then was might successfully do.

Hull's next persistent research interest was in suggestibility, hypnotic and otherwise. He became involved because he had to present academic lectures and laboratory work to medical students. He spent ten productive years in research on suggestion, supervising a large number of senior theses. By his own count, some twenty persons engaged in the research, which was reported in thirty-two papers. He has stated that his interest in hypnotic research was not encouraged after he moved to Yale because of medical opposition, which he had not encountered in the Middle West (1952b). His publication of the book summarising the research, *Hypnosis and suggestibility* (1933), marked the end of this phase of his research career. The book remains a classic in the field of hypnosis.

Hull's third and final major research interest was learning theory. He studied Anrep's translation of Pavlov's *Conditioned reflexes* (1927) and became progressively more interested in learning and general behaviour theory. In 1929 he became a research professor at Yale's Institute of Psychology (which was shortly to become the Institute of Human Relations). Thenceforth he turned to the development of behaviour theory on a full-scale basis. He continued zealous and devoted work on this most important part of his contribution to psychology, despite declining health during the last few years of his life, until his death in 1952. He left behind a band of students as devoted to him as he had been to them.

### Development of Hull's System

The focal point of Hull's theoretical thinking was the conditioned reflex, as conceptualised by Pavlov. Hull regarded it as a kind of simplified learning situation which was admirably suited for experimental analyses. The findings could then be extended to other, more complex phenomena. Hull made the extension by basing the axioms of his system on experimental findings from conditioning experiments. For example, Hull's postulate II in his final system states the value of the "molar stimulus trace" as a function of time since stimulation.

**Postulate II. Stimulus Reception**

A. When a brief stimulus (5) impinges upon a suitable receptor there is initiated the recruitment phase of a self-propagating molar afferent trace impulse (s′), the molar stimulus equivalent (S′) of which arises as a power function of time (ṭ) since the beginning of the stimulus, i.e.,

$$S' = 465{,}190 \times \underset{\cdot}{t}^{7.6936} + 1.0,$$

S′ reaching its maximum (and termination) when ṭ equals about .450″.

B. Following the maximum of the recruitment phase of the molar stimulus trace, there supervenes a more lengthy subsident phase (S′), the stimulus equivalent of which descends as a power function of time (ṭ′), i.e.,

$$S' = 6.9310\ (\underset{\cdot}{t}' + .01)^{-1.0796}$$

where $\underset{\cdot}{t}' = \underset{\cdot}{t} - .450''$.

C. The intensity of the molar stimulus trace (s′) is a logarithmic function of the molar stimulus equivalent of the trace, i.e.,

$$s' = \log S'.$$

This postulate shows very clearly some characteristics of Hull's theory. It is stated formally and carefully. Symbols are introduced and defined, and they make mathematical statements possible. The mathematical statements are frequently quite precise, although the precision may be misleading in view of the uncertainty of the statements and the relative crudeness of the data which justify the postulates.

Postulate II, like many of Hull's postulates, arose rather directly out of the empirical relationships observed in conditioning experiments. Koch (1954, pp 70ff.) has discussed the problems connected with inducing postulates from data; he believes that mill erred in basing postulates too directly on data. Data may, of course, be limited or invalid, but that is not the main issue here. The more serious question is whether postulates based directly on data from particular experiments have my reasonable chance of being useful in a general theory. The history of science would suggest that the probability that such postulates would prove ultimately useful in a general abstract theory is extremely low. The more abstract postulate is usually several steps removed from the function forms seen directly in the data.

Such use of conditioning experiments as a source of axioms is a distinct and critical change from previous behaviouristic practice; Watson, for example, used the conditioned reflex grossly, as an element from which complex behaviour could be directly constructed by chaining elements together. It is dear that Hull's theorising was a great leap forward within the behaviouristic tradition, at least in sophistication of theoretical methodology.

In justifying his procedures, Hull published a series of brilliantly conceived theoretical papers on conditioning during the 1930s. Perhaps the best known of these was his presidential address before the American Psychological Association, entitled "Mind, mechanism, and adaptive behaviour" (1937). The general purpose of these papers, exemplified in the title cited, was to show how basic conditioning principles might be extended to complex behavioural processes. As a methodological, rather than a metaphysical, behaviourist, Hull did not deny the existence of mental phenomena. However, he thought mental phenomena *needed explaining*, rather than themselves being useful as explanatory devices. He therefore proposed to give as complete an account of action as possible, and he hoped that this account would someday help to account for consciousness. Hull thought that the behavioural approach to mental phenomena had not had a thorough trial. He wanted to give it a trial that would either succeed or show that the approach could not work.

A brief excursion into the field of verbal rote learning followed this early theoretical work. Here Hull enlisted the aid of a set of mathematicians and logicians, as well as psychologists, and attempted a rigorous quantitative analysis of the kind of rote verbal learning fiat studied by Ebbinghaus. Although the book that emerged from this effort has been hailed as a landmark in the development of scientific psychology, it has been seldom read, less often under. stood, and unproductive of research. *Mathematico-deductive theory of rote learning* (Hull, Hovland, Ross, Hall, Perkins, and Fitch, 1940) thus remains an idealised but relatively fruitless model of psychological theory construction.

Hull's next major publication, *Principles of behaviour* (1943), had quite the opposite effect. Its appearance marked the beginning of an era of psychological research in which Hull became the unquestioned leader of learning research in this country and one of the most controversial figures in the field. In *Principles of behaviour* Hull attempted to lay down the framework for a comprehensive theory of all mammalian behaviour. He outlined a set of postulates and corollaries, logically interlaced in the hypothetico-deductive style that he had come to consider a model of scientific theorising.

Although many psychologists did not think the book fulfilled the great promise of Hull's early theoretical papers, *Principles of behaviour* nevertheless had enormous influence on research in the learning area. Hull became by far the most cited writer in the field. Untold numbers of master's theses and doctoral dissertations dealt with tests of various of the implications of Hull's theoretical system. Up to the time of his death in 1952, Hull remained the dominant figure in the field of learning theory.

A major factor in the success of *Principles of behaviour* in stimulating research was its detailed spelling out of the postulate-corollary set. Hull deliberately laid the system out in as explicit a manner as possible in order to expedite continuous and persistent empirical checking. This characteristics was probably the most important feature of his systematic endeavour.

In terms of content, perhaps the most important aspect of Hull's theorising was its attempt to reconcile the basic Thorndikian notion of effect with the conditioning paradigm and methodology of Pavlov. In essence, what Hull attempted to do was to incorporate the effect principle—now called *reinforcement*—into a conditioning type of framework. Unlike Watson, he did not think that frequency and recency of response were sufficient principles to account for learning. The emphasis on effect was evident in the last organisation of his postulate set. Hull began with introductory postulates that dealt with "unlearned stimulus-response connections" (postulate I) and "stimulus reception" (postulate II). He then stated the key principle of reinforcement, first described as the *law of primary reinforcement* (1943, p. 80), as follows (1952, pp. 5-6):

> **Postulate III. Primary Reinforcement**
> Whenever an effector activity (R) is closely associated with a stimulus afferent impulse or trace(s) and the conjunction is closely associated with a rapid diminution in the motivational stimulus ($S_D$ or $S_G$), there will result an increment ($\Delta$) to a tendency for that stimulus to evoke that response.

Immediately following were corollaries dealing with secondary motivation and secondary reinforcement. Postulate IV stated the law of habit formation, utilising the variable of number of reinforcements.

Hull's last books were *Essentials of behaviour* (1951) and *A behaviour system* (1952). The latter work attempted to extend the application of quantitative methods within the system and to extend the system to problems of individual behaviour. A final contemplated work on social behaviour was never begun. As a matter of fact, Hull, who was very ill during his last years, did not live to read the galley proofs of *A behaviour system*.

Most of the modifications of the original (1943) system in Hull's final works were relatively minor, consisting mainly of rearrangements of postulates and corollaries and changes in details. The most important modification was the shift in the relationships of antecedent stimulus determinants to the constructs ${}_SH_R$ and ${}_SE_R$. This shift left the habit construct ${}_SH_R$ a function only of number of reinforcements and gave the reaction-evocation construct ${}_SE_R$ increased importance in that it was directly determined by the stimulus factors formerly held to affect ${}_SH_R$ (see Figure 15.1). After the shift, a relatively simple derivation of latent learning was possible (see Hilgard and Bower, 1966; Koch, 1954). Latent learning had been the most important of the experimental results produced by cognitive non S-R theorists and advanced as especially embarrassing for Hullian S-R theory.

## Hullian Methodology

### *Objectivity*

Hull was first and foremost a behaviourist. He rejected metaphysical behaviourism, with its denial of consciousness, but fully and enthusiastically endorsed methodological behaviourism. Hull was considered the arch-objectivist of the 1940s by both his followers, who reveled in this identification, and his opponents, who chose it as a point of attack. In pursuing his behaviouristic program, Hull tried to use concepts reducible, at least in principle, to physical terms.

Hull (1943) gave physicalistic definitions of stimulus and response; stimulus was defined in part as "stimulus energy in general, e.g., the energy of sound, light, or heat waves, pressure, etc." (p. 407). Koch (1954) does a nice job of showing that Hull's operations with stimuli did not at all conform to his definition. In practice, a stimulus was a part of the environment which the experimenter discriminated and responded to. Thus Hull, like most objectivists, did not really follow physicalistic definitions in his experimental work. However, even his critics have typically found Hull's data language objective enough.

Hull, with his more sophisticated behaviourism, was intensely concerned with some methodological problems not considered by Watson. Hull's theory contained a number of explicit intervening variables, while Watson's theorising involved implicit intervening variables at most. Hull's intervening variables were functions of antecedent conditions like number of reinforced trials, stimulus intensity, or hours of deprivation. These intervening quantities then entered further equations that determined what the properties of the observed response should be (cf. Figure 15.1). It is often tempting in a psychological system to postulate intraorganismic variables whose quantity is appropriate to predict the response properties needed in the system. Hull was very careful to avoid this kind of trap; he insisted that every intervening variable be anchored in both antecedent and response conditions. To the extent that the anchoring was successful, the intervening variables were assured of having a clear meaning. If the predictions generated coincided with observed data, the intervening variables could be said to "summarise" the observed relationships.

### *Hypothetico-deductive Form*

Hull was greatly impressed by the elegance of the formal mathematical and physical systems, such as those developed by Euclid and Newton. As his interest in developing a general behaviour system grew, he determined to model it upon these examples. The result was that he attempted to build a highly formalised and comprehensive behaviour theory in a hypothetico-deductive framework. Formal postulates and corollaries were advanced, together with theorems laid down as deductive consequences. Such a system is hypothetico-deductive because it begins with *hypotheses* which are sufficiently well connected in a logical system so that their consequences can be *deduced*. The deductions (theorems) are related by the theorist to statements of empirical observations which should be made under the conditions specified by the theorem. The validity of the empirical statements is then checked by the experiment. If the statements are true, the hypotheses are retained; if they are false, the hypotheses require modification or rejection.

In *Principles of behaviour* (1943) Hull laid down sixteen primary principles, as postulates, and a large number of corollaries; in the revision of the system (1951) a total of eighteen postulates and twelve corollaries was produced. In accordance with the hypothetico-deductive procedure that Hull intended to follow, these primary principles were to be used deductively to predict secondary principles, such as the goal gradient and latent learning.

A single relatively simple example will serve to illustrate the way in which Hull used some prior empirical knowledge, one or more primary principles (postulates or corollaries), and some deductive derivation combined with a little quantification to produce theorems that could be tested empirically. Consider the problem of the order of elimination of blind alleys in maze learning, as by a rat. It had long been known that the blind alleys closest to the goal are eliminated first, a principle called the "goal-gradient hypothesis" by Hull (1932). Hull incorporated this empirical fact into a logical postulate by assuming that the response potential of any response is a function of its distance, in time, from the reinforcing event (in this case, the reaching of the food incentive in the goal box). Thus his corollary iii, delay in reinforcement (J), reads (1952): "A. *The greater the delay in reinforcement of a link within a given behaviour chain, the weaker will be the resulting reaction potential of the link in question to the stimulus traces present at the time*" (p. 126).

This principle, the logical derivation of which was given (1952), led to a number of empirical predictions, stated as theorems, for multidirectional maze learning (1952). Among these, for example, were the propositions that a long blind alley, since it entails a greater temporal delay of reinforcement, will be eliminated more quickly than a short blind alley (theorem 104, p. 282) and that the rate of locomotion through the maze will become progressively faster for the later, compared with the early, parts (theorem 110, p. 286). Now it is important to note that neither of. these two predictions could be generated directly from the first empirical result itself, the observation of a gradient of error elimination, but could be logically derived from the general principle concerning temporal delay of reinforcement which was developed from the empirical data. Such logical deduction of many new and different empirical predictions from a smaller number of key principles is considered to be a major contribution of a hypothetico-deductive system. Hull's *Behaviour system* is full of such derivations, with quantitative calculations, and so represents a much closer approximation to hypothetico-deductive methodology than the more programmatic *Principles of behaviour* does.

To Hull's credit, it must be said that he did not attempt to hold to a static or fixed system; indeed, his thinking was extremely fluid, and his formal theory went through an almost continuous series of revisions. He thus used the hypothetico-deductive system in the way it was intended. An indication of the extent to which he practiced the methodology he preached may be seen in his systematic writing of "idea books" and his distribution of mimeographed memorandums for criticism. His first idea book covered the period from 1902 to 1906, when he stopped writing until January, 1916. After that, he continued to write regularly until eighteen days before his death (Hays, 1962). There Is an interesting disagreement about the number of these books; Hull stated (1951, p. 120) that there were twenty-five volumes, and Hays has said that at Hull's death in 1952, there were seventy-three! Perhaps Hull did not think that some of his handwritten notebooks were of high-enough quality to be considered among his idea books.

### *Quantitative Character*

Hull felt very strongly that theoretical progress in psychology would come as a consequence of the successful extension of quantification. His own theory was supposed to be a primarily quantitative one. In *Principles of behaviour* Hull's quantification was largely programmatic, and more apparent than real. Many postulates had no mathematical form or lacked numerical values for the constants. Hull was acutely aware both of the shortcomings of his 1943 system and of the difficulties associated with genuine quantitative statements. He immediately set out to achieve genuine quantification and published five articles which reported on this work. The basic experiment (Felsinger, Gladstone, Yamaguchi, and Hull, 1947; see also Koch, 1954) was a study of latency of response to a manipulandum; latency was measured from the time that a shutter was removed to make the manipulandum available. Thurstone's method of paired comparisons was used to estimate the amount of ${}_{S}E_{R}$. (reaction potential) giving rise to the response.

Whenever intervening variables which cannot be directly observed are involved in a theoretical chain, rational decisions involving an element of guesswork must be made as to the quantitative interrelationships between all the variables in the theory. There seems to be no escape from this conclusion. Guesses which produce a useful general theory require a high degree of creativity, plus some luck. Logan (1959, pp. 303-306) has given a concise example of the general method by which Hull proceeded to combine empirical observations with rational guesses to produce his version of a quantitative behaviour theory.

### Summary of the System

Essentially, as an S-R system, Hullian theory deals with three types of variables: the stimulus (antecedent or input), the intervening (intraorganismic), and the response (consequent or output). The following highly abbreviated account is intended to give something of the general, nature and flavour of the system. The basic system is represented diagrammatically in Figure. 15.1. For a more detailed exposition the reader is referred to one of the original sources (e.g., Hull, 1943, 1951,1952) or to a secondary explanatory source (e.g., Hilgard and Bower, 1966; Spence, 1951a, 1951b).

The input, or stimulus, variables are such objective factors as number of reinforced trials, deprivation of incentive, intensity of the conditioned stimulus; and amount of reward. These various factors are directly associated with resulting processes hypothesised to function within the organism: intervening variables of the first order. Examples are habit strength (${}_{S}H_{R}$) as a function of number of trials *(N)*, drive *(D)* as a function of drive condition such as deprivation of incentive ($C_D$), stimulus-intensity dynamism *(V)* as a function of stimulus intensity *(S)*, and incentive reinforcement *(K)* as a function of amount of reward *(w)*.

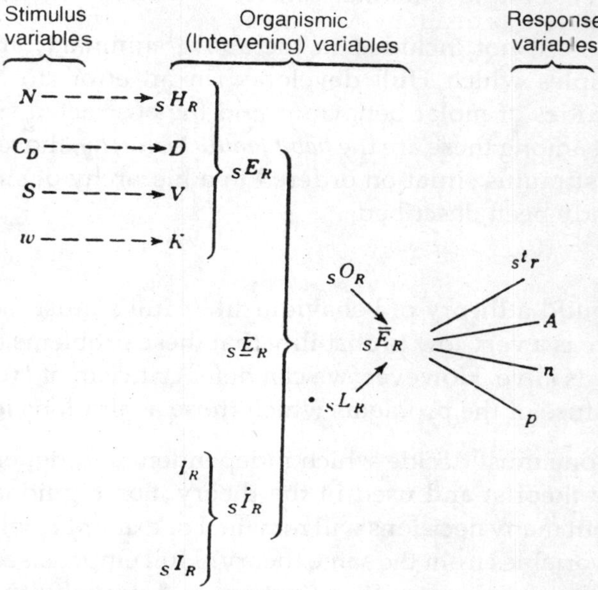


**Fig. 15.1.** Simplified diagrammatic representation of the Hullian system. See text for explanation of symbols and relationships.

Certain of these direct, or first-order, constructs are assumed now to coalesce into a smaller number of second-order intervening variables. The major construct is reaction potential or response evocation ($_SH_R$.), which is a joint function of $_SH_R$, D, V, and K. Also to be considered at this level are generalised reaction potential ($_SH_R$.), which is a function of the amount of similarity of the present conditioned stimulus to ones previously experienced for which habit strengths have been established, and the aggregate of the negative reaction tendencies ($_SI_R$). The latter construct is a function of reactive inhibition ($I_R$) and conditioned or learned inhibition ($_SI_R$), both of which are the direct consequence of work performed in the response.

At the final level, the higher-order intervening constructs then are net reaction potention ($_SE_R$), a function of the two excitatory factors and the one inhibitory factor just mentioned, and two more speculative and less well-specified constructs which modify its action. These are the oscillation ($_SO_R$) and threshold ($_SL_R$) of reaction potential. Finally, on the output side, there are four major measures of the effectiveness of response: latency ($_St_R$), amplitude *(A)*, number of responses to extinction *(n)*, and probability of response *(p)*.

Supplementary to the above descriptive account are a number of stimulus-trace concepts, such as the **drive stimulus** ($S_D$) and the fractional goal response ($S_G$) which are of primary importance in the system and also in more recent modifications of it, especially that of

Spence (1956); these were omitted from the summarising description so that the essential system could be presented in as simple a manner consistent with its character.

Also of great importance, but not included in the above summary, are a number of secondary or derived principles which Hull developed in an effort to bridge the gap between the normal complexities of molar behaviour and the abstracted simplicity of his postulate set. Most important among these are the *habit family hierarchy,* the total set of habits which may occur in a given stimulus situation ordered in a hierarchy of strength, and the *goal gradient,* which has already been described.

**Systematic Issues**

Anyone who aspires to build a theory of behaviour like Hull's must face a number of very difficult problems. There is a very low probability that these problems could be solved today, let alone when Hull was alive. However, we can defer criticism of Hull's aspirations until later and look at the nature of the problems which those aspirations led him to face.

Fairly early in the game, one must decide which independent and dependent variables will be discriminated by the theorist and used in the theory. Some guidance is available from experimental practice. but many decisions will remain. For example, will it be profitable to try to predict all response variables from the same theory? Hull emphasised the prediction of latency, amplitude, number of responses to extinction, and probability of responding. skinner believes that rate of response is the best measure to we; he studies primarily free operants, responses which the animal is free to repeat "at will." Hull studied primarily controlled operants, wherein the experimenter controls opportunities for response emission, as in a runway. His decision to relate his final intervening variable—net generalised reaction potential—to four response measures made it legitimate to ask whether these measures were actually correlated as the theory said they should be. Hull could have avoided embarrassing issues of this kind by making predictions of only one response measure—but he would have lost a great deal of generality in so doing.

Similar problems had to be faced at the level of the intervening variables. For example, there is Hull's decision to have essentially only a single excitatory learning construct, ${}_SH_R$. If a theorist were working today, he might feel it necessary to have distinct constructs (or distinct theories) for different kinds of learning; for example, food-motivated learning might be distinguished from sex-motivated learning within the theory.

A very general problem connected with the intervening variables concerns what we might call their *reality status.* Hull and his colleagues no doubt had hundreds of discussions about whether it was wise to give the constructs of the theory a physiological interpretation. We have been characterising Hull's intervening variables as organismic," which implies some physiological commitment. A more neutral description would be simply that the intervening variables are intratheoretical—which they indubitably are—rather than intraorganismic, which they may or may not be. We shall discuss the characteristics of constructs in more detial, since there are many facets to the problem.

Even after the constructs of a system are isolated and their general type decided upon, there remain problems concerning the definition of each construct and the specification of construct interrelationships. As an example of such problems, we might take the innocuous-looking *N*, the number of reinforced trials. What is a reinforced trial? Both Hull's earlier concept of reinforcement as need reduction and his later emphasis on drive-stimulus reduction as the necessary condition for reinforcement failed to eliminate the possibility of circularity. Thus, one could proceed to look for the need or drive-stimulus reduction *after* observing that behaviour was strengthened in situations in which the experimenter did not intentionally reduce any need and in which no obvious drive stimulus was reduced. Hull's difficulty with the concept of reinforcement shows how hard it is to construct good definitions. The way in which looseness in the definition of reinforcement makes the concept of *N* imprecise illustrates the way in which problems with one definition can affect other concepts throughout the theoretical effort.

The specification of construct interrelationships is at least as fertile a source of problems. The habit construct $_{S}H_{R}$ can again serve as an example. In Hull's early theory, several variables, including drive *(D)* and incentive *(K)*, influenced habit. Habit then influenced reaction potential. Since habit changed slowly and continuously, it was not possible to derive sudden shifts in performance from the theory. Since such shifts occurred in the latent learning experiments (Hilgard and Bower, 1966), a change in the theory was obviously needed. Hull changed the construct interrelationships so that *D* and *K* affected $_{S}E_{R}$ rather than $_{S}H_{R}$ and the rapid change in response strength following changes in deprivation or incentive became possible. We are not implying that Hull changed the construct interrelationships *in order to explain* latent learning. Both Hilgard and Bower (1966) and Koch (1954) believe the change was made so that $_{S}H_{R}$ could more easily be quantified. It is clear, however, that the change in construct interrelationships did make it possible to explain some latent-learning phenomena, at least qualitatively.

The more precise statement of the relationship between constructs itself created additional controversies. Let us take $_{S}H_{R}$ as an example again. Its mathematical relationship to number of trials (*N*) was postulated to be as follows:

$$_{S}H_{R} = \text{I} — 10^{-aN}$$

Trials were assumed to be evenly spaced, and the constant *a* was thought to be approximately 0.03 in numerical value (Hull, 1951, p. 32).

This clear mathematical statement implies that each trial imparts an increment to the strength of $_{S}H_{R}$ and thus indirectly to the tendency to respond. Although this is not truly a continuous function, since *N* takes only discrete values Hull's theory was called a *continuity* theory to distinguish it from the view that learning is a basically sudden, or an all-or-one process. The latter view would be exemplified by the Gestalt position, which was that learning is sudden and insightful and thus noncontinuous. The starkness of Hull's mathematical statements made disagreements stand out nakedly and resulted in controversies like the continuity-noncontinuity controversy and the latent-learning controversy and led to questions about the generality of drives in activating habits.

## Criticisms of Hullian System

Few psychologists have met such searching and often vehement criticism as Hull *has.* As a leading neobehaviourist, he inherited the kind *d* criticism that had earlier been accorded Watson. Much of this criticism has been polemic, or based on fundamental methodological or theoretical differences of opinion, and much seems to have been trivial or even personal in nature. Nevertheless, the solid critical points persistently lodged against Hull merit our attention.

### *Synthetic Approach*

As we have seen, Hull attempted to work out a complete and comprehensive theoretical account of mammalian behaviour almost at a single stroke. His systematic venture was essentially a synthetic one. He endeavored to fashion and put together the pieces of his puzzle in advance of much research. In Hull's defense, however, it must be said that he started with such empirical evidence as he could find and persistently tried to build up additional evidence.

Hull attempted to emulate the formal elegance of the systems of Euclid and Newton within a much shorter time than these beautifully integrated formal systems required for their development. The neatness and elegance of the final product in the case of such formal theory hide the fitfulness of actual development; it may be that theoretical progress is expedited by less ambitious efforts at the start. It is now generally conceded, even by many of those sympathetic to the Hullian brand of psychology, that his efforts represented an overly optimistic approach to an exceedingly complex set of problems.

### *Particularistic Approach*

Perhaps the most persistent criticism from sympathetic sources has been that Hull relied too much upon certain particular values of critical variables within special experimental circumstances. The problem of generality, always a knotty one in behaviour theory, was noted early by Koch (1944, p. 283) in his review of *Principles of behaviour;* the point has more recently been made by Hilgard and Bower (1966, p. 186), who have cited the dependence of Hull's system upon particular constants from rat bar-pressing and human eyelid experimentation.

An indication of the extreme particularism of certain aspects of Hull's theorising, in the sense of dependence upon particular experimental setups, may be seen in his provisional definition of the *wat* (honouring *Watson)* as the unit of reaction potential (1951, p. 100):

The wat is the mean standard deviation of the momentary reaction potential $({}_{S}E_{R})$ of standard albino rats, 90 days of age, learning a simple manipulative act requiring a 10-gram pressure by 24-hour distributed trials under 23 hours' hunter, water available, with reward in the form of a 2.5-gram pellet of the usual dry dog food the mean being taken from all the reinforcement trials producing the habit strength from 75 to .85 habs inclusive.

The improbability of successful generalisation from such particular values of food weight and manipulandum pressure to other variables in animal behaviour itself, let alone more complex behavioural functions of higher mammalian forms such as humans, should be quite evident. Thus while Hull's specificity is in some respects admirable, the aspirations of his theorising seem rather far removed from the actual achievements. Reservations concerning the generality of his theory were made increasingly by Hull in his later writings (cf. Koch, 1954, pp-I 67ff.) and are especially evident in the more restricted tone of his final work (Hull, 1952).

The only reasonable answer to these criticisms is simply that the results will determine the efficacy of the approach. More important, this is also the only answer to the more general criticism made of S-R theorists: that they oversimplify complex behavioural problems. Until we try, we cannot really be sure whether an approach such as Hull's will be adequate to account for the complexities of mammalian behaviour, and the only scientific way to be sure is to try.

### *Logical Weakness*

Probably the most telling critical attack upon Hull's theory involves the demonstration that his system was not at all the tightly knit, logical one that he intended it to be and that many for awhile after its publication believed it to be. Hull sometimes failed to build in logically necessary connections between his constructs. A number of careful critical attacks have appeared. Koch's (1954) critique is particularly devastating because of its extremely detailed documentation and logical sophistication (in spite of his unsympathetic and some times unfair attitude). The easy testability of construct relationships that Hull envisioned is now seen to be largely illusory. Cotton (1955) gives a persuasive and beautifully worked-out demonstration of the impossibility of making predictions from Hull's theory as it was presented. Difficulties remain even when "friendly" assumptions are made in the attempt to make derivations possible. We are forced to conclude that Hull's theory was not finished even in the logical sense.

Two reactions to the growing realisation of the logical inadequacy of Hull's theorising are typical: first, a marked swing to a purely descriptive kind of positivism, such as that provided by Skinner; and second, an intensification of the attention paid to so-called miniature systems, whereby more limited problem areas are more thoroughly attacked. Hull himself showed signs of limiting his approach in *A behaviour system (1952)*, where he systematically explored problem areas and emphasised the overall system less than previously.

## Hull's Contributions

### *Objective Terminology and Methodology*

Hull's own life was that of a scientist and scholar, a life of the mind. But in his psychology he determined to start with action, stay with action, and see how far action could carry him. His terms, therefore, were not new names for old concept. *Inhibition, habit strength, reaction potential*—these words had some of their creator's active vitality, ringing forth with the promise of carrying out the evangelical behaviouristic programme thrust upon the incredulous world at Watson's psychological revival meeting. The type of methodology implied by these terms will not be forgotten, whatever the fate of the theory in which Hull embedded them.

We believe that Hull's most important contribution to psychology was his demonstration of the value of setting one's sights upon the ultimate goal of a thoroughly scientific and systematic behaviour theory. He lived his own scientific life in pursuit of that goal and thereby influenced even those who disagreed most vehemently with the details of his work. Few psychologists have had so deep and enduring an effect on the professional motivation of so many researchers. He popularised the strictly objective behaviouristic approach as it had never been popularised previously.

***New Problem Areas***

Hull opened new problem areas in a rather peculiar sense. He did not develop important new pieces of apparatus or initiate research in previously untouched areas. Rather, he reconceived ways of viewing problems and suggested new relationships to be studied. He was a theoretical psychologist, as some physicists are theoretical physicists. Unfortunately, he was a theoretician Preceded by no Einstein, Newton, Copernicus, or perhaps even Archimedes in the field of psychology. Nevertheless, when he formulated a postulate or derived a theorem from his postulate set, other investigators were prone to perform experiments to test the stated relationships; for example, after Hull stated his belief about the shape of the generalisation gradient, research focused on the empirical determination of the gradient. The very attempt to formalise a theory of behaviour forced Hull and his followers to see what must be known before the formalisation could be completed. Key concepts, such as stimulus, and processes, such as reinforcement, had to undergo intensive examination.

Although Hull was most strongly attacked by cognitive theorists and field theorists, in one respect his system was more fieldlike than the typical field theory. Hull specified as many of the relevant variables as he could reasonably conceive and also stated their hypothesised mode of interaction (cf. Figure 15.1). Not only is this high degree of theoretical specificity a far cry from the largely speculative utilisation of conditioning by the early behaviourists, such as Watson, but it is also a good deal more concrete than anything offered by Hull's critics who were more prone to counter the Watsonian speculation with their own speculation than to provide specification of the composition of the psychological field (cf. Estes, 1954b).

Finally, Hull has been criticised by some psychologists of other persuasions for giving too much direction to research effort. He and his system concentrated effort on the solution of those theoretical problems which he believed had to be solved before behaviour theory could make significant advances. However, some have felt that we cannot, at the present time, afford to decide the direction of research on formal theoretical grounds. Rather, those empirical areas should be studied which are producing results that are interesting in themselves. We believe that there is value in both views and that it is fortunate there are large number of psychologists available to take both paths; Hull made a great contribution in providing one kind of guidance.

**Hull's Place in History**

Clark Hull's place in psychological history seems to be assured. He may have been one of those rare men who actively influence their times to such an extent that they can redirect a science. On the other hand, one may prefer the alternative view that this apparent influence is an illusion resulting from a man's merely moving within the historical steam of events and so actually moving *with* the times. The latter point of view is one that Boring (1950) has particularly emphasised (as stressed in the concept of *Zeitgeist*, or spirit of the times), in contrast to Carlyle's "great man" interpretation of history.

Whatever the causation, it is true that Clark Hull found psychology still wrestling bard with broad systematic issues, and he left large segments of it wrestling with criticisms of his postulates and theorems. In a sense both kinds of wrestling are misspent. The systematic issues were elusive foes for the psychologist, and Hull's system revealed gaps to the serious student that made criticism almost superfluous. Yet Hull taught psychology a new type of game, one so enthralling that now all but the strictest of positivists want to play.

It is paradoxical that Hull changed metatheory by being concerned with theory. His predecessors, the earlier behaviourists, had done their utmost to turn psychology away from verbal issues and toward more empirically meaningful problems. But this never quite came off. Hull brought it off with a positive effect. Hull was certainly deeply and intelligently concerned with metatheory, and his system is the grandest ever attempted in the behaviouristic tradition. His distinction and his influence are based on the fact that he did not stop there. His attempt to push on into the tangled unknown where specific issues are resolved was largely unsuccessful. That has inevitable at the time. He did not come back with maps that were likely to be serviceable, but none before Hull had even given psychological explorers much of a feel for what a psychological theory should be.

Another paradox is Hull's lack of rigor. His system had the appearance but not the reality. He never had time to smooth out wrinkles. In this he is in the company of all of psychology's greatest men. If there is in psychology a man excessively afraid of being wrong, that man has published no extensive theory. Hull, even while striving for a rigorous statement, had to stand with those who had no such fear. In this rather peculiar way, he carved his niche in history between the systematists and those following him who will construct more lasting behaviour theories.

For a time, it seemed that hull had made of psychology his own private yard. In the early fifties, he was cited far more often than any other psychologist in the *Journal of Experimental Psychology* (Ammons, 1962), and his *Principles of behaviour* or (1943) was the most frequently cited publication, with its nearest rival cited less than a fourth as often in the *Journal of Experimental Psychology* and three other journals included in the tabulation. Between 1930 and 1950, Hull was regarded as the leading psychological theorist (Coan and Zagona, 1962, p. 319). Recently, however, ever, it would appear that his fall from favour has been rapid. The pendulum of theoretical style has swung rapidly toward primarily inductive procedures, but there are signs that it is swinging back. Mathematical modeling of a less grand scope is becoming popular, and there is no denying Hull's priority and early dominance in this type of endeavor.

**Hull's Students**

Kenneth W. Spence (1907-1967) was the most important successor to Hull, as far as the type of theory Hull was trying to develop is concerned. He took his doctoral training at Yale, where he was strongly influenced by his association with Hull, although he. took his degree under Yerkes, and he worked for four years at the Yale Laboratories of Primate Biology in Orange Park. From 1938 to 1964, he was at the University of Iowa, where he worked very actively in research on learning and motivation. In 1964 he moved to the University of Texas, where he remained until his death at the relatively early age of 59. While at Iowa he published a number of theoretical papers with Gustav Bergmann, the philosopher. Spence's major works are *Behaviour theory* and *conditioning* (1956) and *Behaviour theory and learning: Selected papers* (1960). The former was based on the 1955 Silliman lectures at Yale; Spence was the first psychologist to be honored by an invitation to deliver these lectures.

Spence's first important research and theorising dealt with the problem of discrimination learning (1936; 1937a, 1937b). He produced a classic demonstration of how a conditioning theory involving positive and negative reaction tendencies interacting algebraically can account for the primary data of discrimination and transposition. His tilt with the Gestaltists on the explanation of these phenomena is an excellent illustration of opposing approaches to psychological explanation. On one side we see Spence operating in the reductive mode characteristic of associationistic psychology, of S-R psychology as a more modern version, of Hull, and of Spence himself. Lloyd Morgan's canon is one of the first principles of theorising for this tradition. Spence's theorising on discrimination and transposition serves as an inspiring model of simplicity and clarity for exponents of this general approach. Hull's early work on the derivation of complex behaviours from conditioning was similar in this respect.

While recognising his debt to basic Hullian theory, Spence was careful to point out the differences between his own theoretical efforts and those of Hull (cf. especially his 1956 book). He was less concerned with the comprehensive formality with which Hull endowed his work and more concerned with the quantification of variables. He did not share Hull's enthusiasm for physiological suggestions and speculations, feeling that until physiology has more to offer psychology, it can most profitably be kept out of behaviour theory. He said (1956, p. 57) that he had not accepted the Hullian emphasis on need reduction as the essential component of the reinforcement process; he nude no specific physiological assumption about the nature of action of a reinforcer. Finally, he was much more cautious (1956) than Hull in regard to "hazarding a set of theoretical postulate: on the basis of a minimum of empirical data" (p. 58). Spence also pointed out that, on the related question of generality, he intended his own work to be restricted to the particular experimental situations from which hi: data came. Spence adopted the basic Hullian apprcach and many of the theoretical constructs, but put less emphasis on the postulational approach and modified some of the postulates that he did accept.

Spence treated the key motivational variables somewhat differently from the way Hull did. Both men assumed that there was a multiplicative relationship between motivation and habit in the production of response (reaction potential). Spence, however, theorised that incentive and deprivation factors added to produce motivation; Hull had incentive and deprivation in a multiplicative relationship. Spence's formulation allowed for the occurrence of a response even when either incentive or drive was at zero, as long as the other factor was nonzero. Hull's multiplicative relationship called for a zero value of *SER* when either incentive or drive was zero; it is difficult to embarrass Hull on this point, however, since it is not easy to be certain that drive is completely absent. Neither is it easy to choose between the additive and multiplicative assumptions by doing a parametric study in which $D$ and $K$ are varied. The reason is that $K$ is assumed to be related to fractional anticipatory goal responses and the stimuli produced by them. Thus motivation has come to have a learned component, and the relationship between drive, incentive, and reaction potential is further complicated. The two theories have, in a sense, been given a "side chain" which must be taken into account when making predictions. That is, suppose we are computing ${}_SE_R$ for a response after several trials. Its amount will depend on $K$. The amount of $K$ will in turn depend on the ${}_SE_R$ of the fractional anticipatory goal responses conditioned to the cues present. Thus we must compute ${}_SE_R$ twice, the first time in the theoretical side chain that determines a value for $K$.

Spence also took quite a different view of reinforcement from that of Hull. In his later work, he assumed that habit formation was not dependent on reinforcement. He suggested a two-factor learning theory which is precisely reversed from the usual one. Usually, contiguity factors are assumed to account for classical conditioning, and reinforcement for instrumental conditioning. Spence's contiguity explanation for instrumental conditioning does not necessitate any change in the basic form of the theory; it simply changes the definition of what constitutes a trial for the purposes of the theory. For Hull, a trial was a *reinforced* trial. For Spence reinforcement did not matter; it mattered only that the response was performed in the presence of the stimulus. On this matter, Spence's position resembled Tolman's; Spence was interested in Tolman's competing theory and was dose to Tolman in some of his methodological attitudes (Kendler, 1967).

Following his early development of theory applicable to simple discrimination learning, Spence directed or supervised research projects on eyelid conditioning, latent learning, transposition, secondary reinforcement, and "anxiety" as measured by a questionnaire technique (see Spence, 1960). His work, much of it in collaboration with Janet Taylor Spence, on the relationship between anxiety and learning is widely quoted in articles on personality.

One of Spence's preoccupations in his later work was with the disentanglement of cognitive factors from the results of human eyelid conditioning studies. Earlier work had demonstrated apparent qualitative differences between eyelid conditioning in animals lower than man and in man. Human subjects typically extinguished conditioned eyeblinks in a very small number of trials, typically one or two, while animals might continue to make conditioned responses for hundred; of trials. Spence and his students used an ingenious masking task to conceal the true nature of the experiment, thereby apparently eliminating the influence of Inhibitory cognitive factors and obtaining extinction behaviour in human subjects that paralleled the behaviour typically seen in animal subjects (see Spence, 1966).

This last work of Spence's ties in with the history of psychological systems in an interesting way. For one thing, the experimental situation is especially designed to reduce one aspect of the human subjects' functioning to the level of animal functioning. After Darwin, those working in a reductive tradition had often had to face the charge that they were in general trying to reduce human capabilities to the level of animal capabilities. Spence's work on eyelid conditioning thus exemplifies at the experimental level a reductive tendency which too frequently took place only at a theoretical level. At the same time, the attempt at reduction forced a clear recognition of a qualitative difference between human and animal functioning. The differences, like the similarities, have too often remained nebulous and theoretical. In following up on Hull's reductive program, Spence found factors which, at least at this time, cannot successfully be accounted for reductively. He thus, like many honest scientists, made a kind of contribution to those who hold opposing view-points about the nature of man.

Hull had a number of other students who became important theoreticians in their own right. We shall single out only two of them: O.H. Mowrer, who will be discussed briefly later in this chapter because of his development of a two-factor theory of learning, and Neal Miller (1909—), who has been almost incredibly productive, largely in empirical investigation but also to some extent in theoretical developments that grow rather directly out of the data. He worked with John Dollard to integrate learning theory with psychoanalytic theory in *Personality and psychotherapy* (Dollard and Miller, 1950). This work probably grew out of Hull's seminars of 1936 and 1937 on the relationships between these apparently diverse areas of psychology. In turn, there is little doubt that it helped to pave the way for more recent developments in behaviour modification.

Miller has also done more than enough work to constitute a successful, complete career in physiological psychology. Some of these studies, and many of his behavioural studies, are reviewed in his article in the Koch series (N.E. Miller, 1959).

Some of Miller's experiments have involved electrical stimulation of brain centers; some, the effects of fistula feeding; and some, preloading the stomach with different substances before eating and engaging in instrumental behaviours. Still other studies were examination of feeding without any nutritive consequences, and several have involved various behavioural effects of drugs.

It is not surprising that Miller has been led to a careful and sophisticated consideration of the starting and stopping of behaviour. For one thing, he was aware of the fact that, under certain conditions, electrical stimulation of centers in the brain will be alternatively started and stopped by rats free to do both. For another, he knew that feeding may sometimes be started by brain stimulation or stopped by stomach loading and that feeding may *not* stop when it "should" after hypothalamic brain lesions.

Thinking about "go" and "stop" mechanisms may in turn have helped to lead Miller to his theoretical views on the nature of reinforcement. He was also exposed in 1954 to some of Sheffield's ideas (Haber, 1966, pp. 98ff.). Sheffield suggested that an *increase* in drive, produced directly or indirectly by reward, might account for learning better than the decrease in drive or drive stimulus typically assumed by earlier theories. Hull and Miller would both have, at one time, embraced the view that reinforcement is effective because it reduces the intensity of drive stimuli. It is reasonable to assume that Sheffield was instrumental in changing Miller's theory of reinforcement.

Miller suggested (1963) that reinforcing operations are effective because they activate a "go" mechanism. Responses occurring when the mechanism is activated are intensified and increase in frequency, according to Miller's view. Learning requires only contiguity between stimulus and response, but learning is increased by increases in the intensity or frequency of the pairing. Reinforcement (activation of the "go" mechanism) indirectly increases learning by increasing the opportunity for contiguity to produce learning.

This ingenious proposal is similar to the suggestions of several other theorists. It bears a striking resemblance to Guthrie's theory in that contiguity alone is supposed to suffice for learning (see the discussion later in this chapter). Thorndike's "confirming reaction" is something like Miller's go mechanism; the latter, however, is supposed to affect learning indirectly through increasing performance (which is the way Tolman would also have seen the problem), rather than directly through strengthening connections, as Thorndike had suggested.

Recently, Miller has been involved in a number of studies on whether autonomic responses can be conditioned through operant techniques (N.E. Miller, 1969). This work treats a problem which was central for Hull; we have seen that Hull accepted the Thorndikian principle of effect as a basic condition for learning. Hull had rejected his own earlier tentative commitment to contiguity (as in classical conditioning) as a sufficient condition for learning. Miller's work, which shows that the autonomic system is surprisingly susceptible to modification via effect learning, supports Hull's later formulation, albeit indirectly.

Ironically, at about the same time that Miller was enlarging the scope of behaviour which could be modified through; reward learning, Brown and Jenkins (1968) reported that key pecking could be shaped simply by illuminating the key prior to food delivery, that is, through a procedure very much like classical conditioning! It may be that we are about to lose one of our traditional distinction, that between classical and operant conditioning. It may emerge rephrased as a distinction between response-independent and response-dependent schedules (Staddon and Simmelhag, 1971).

## REINFORCEMENT THEORY: SKINNERIAN POSITIVISM

### Skinner's Career

B.F. Skinner (1904—) has had a most remarkable career. It is similar to that of Sir Francis Galton in its demonstration of great breadth of interest and exceptional ingenuity of empirical operations. Skinner's contributions have been kaleidoscopic. His lively intellectual curiosity has refused to be contained within the narrow confines of a specialised area. He has concerned himself with an analysis of verbal learning, with missile-guiding pigeons, with teaching machines, and with the control of behaviour by scheduled reinforcement. The ingenious apparatus to his credit includes an automatised baby-tending device, used with one of his own children and later marketed commercially. In his leisure time, Skinner has even managed to write a novel on a utopian theme, *Walden two* (1948b).

Skinner received his doctoral degree from Harvard in 1931. Following several years of postdoctoral fellowships he taught at the University of Minnesota (1936 to 1945) and at Indiana University (1945 to 1947), where he was chairman. He returned to Harvard in 1947. During the 1930s and 1940s Skinner's influence was less than that of Hull and Tolman, but it is now far greater (Coan and Zagona, 1962). His influence on younger psychologists has been especially impressive. Part of the reason for his ascendance is disillusionment with comprehensive theory of the Hullian type. Skinner's Positivistic inclinations are at the opposite pole from Hull's fondness for the development of formal theories.

### Methodological Emphasis

Skinner is best known for his insistence upon a strictly descriptive, atheoretical approach to behaviour research. He has long felt that the state of knowledge in psychology is inadequate to justify elaborate, formal theorising. Skinnerians often state that when theories are developed and espoused, personal satisfactions from confirmations and disconfirmations, rather than acquisition of facts, tend to become the issue. Skinner believes that more effective progress toward the prediction and control of behaviour can be obtained through a careful collection of data. The "functional analysis of behaviour" has been his objective. In this, experimental techniques are to be utilised, and the relationships between variables are to be established. Eventually, Skinner holds, sufficient empirical relationships will be established to justify the formation of some limited theories or more comprehensive generalisations, but these must be prepared with caution. Such integrative principles should be allowed to develop, not forced prematurely.

Skinner is not against all theory, and it may be that he believes psychology is more nearly ready for theory now than it was forty years ago, when he entered the field. At any rate, he has said (Evans, 1968): "But I look forward to an overall theory of human behaviour which will bring together a lot of facts and express them in a more general way. That kind of theory I would be very much interested in prompting and I consider myself to be a theoretician" (p.

88). In fact, Skinner has taken pains to emphasise his interest in theory, subtitling one of his hooks (1969) *A theoretical analysis* and detailing in its preface the numerous theoretical articles he has written. It is dangerous to overgeneralise with Skinner, just as it is with a Titchener or a Thorndike—or with any great figure in the history of psychology. Brilliant men seldom take positions as extreme as the positions ascribed to them by incautious critics.

A second important methodological emphasis of Skinner has been his insistence upon a thorough analysis of the behaviour of a single organism and his disinclination to use large groups of subjects. Large numbers of subjects have too often been used, he contends, to cover up lack of experimental controls; with adequate controls, a single subject, or a very small number of subjects, should be sufficient. The use of large groups, he says, also leads indirectly to other difficulties. When a large group is used, the experimenter usually attends primarily or exclusively to certain statistical properties of the group, rather, than to the behaviours of the individuals within it. Individual variations may then" be lost, and the statistical measures may not describe the characteristics of any of the individuals within the group (Sidman, 1960). Skinner does not believe that such experiments are likely to lead to a Science in which prediction and control of the behaviour of individual organisms are possible. On the other hand, when large amounts of data from a single animal are collected under stringently controlled conditions, the results will be clearly replicable with other individuals. No statistical techniques will be necessary.

Third, Skinner has objected particularly to physiological speculation in the guise of theory. He has been against what he has considered excessive and futile physiologising; when physiological data have more concrete points on which behavioural observations can turn, they should be permitted to influence psychology, but not before. This generally aphysiological attitude has been shared by Spence, and together they have contributed to the prominence of the so-called empty-organism era in recent psychological thinking. Even on this issue, it is easy to overdramatise Skinner's attitude. His opposition to too much physiologising seems to be largely a matter of self-discipline. He says (Evans, 1968): "I have never said anything against the study of physiology, and I feel that I have done my best to facilitate it by clarifying the problems that the physiologist has to deal with. At the same time, I don't want to borrow support from physiology when my formulation breaks down" (p. 22).

A fourth major methodological Characteristic of Skinner has been his emphasis on operant, as compared with respondent, behaviour. Skinner early distinguished between responses made in direct response to stimulation (such as classical conditioned responses of a Pavlovian sort) and those emitted by the organism in the absence of any apparent external stimulation (the operant). The eliciting stimuli for the operant are unknown. The free operant is an operant whose emission does not directly preclude successive emissions of the same response; its study has been especially favoured by Skinnerians. The free operant is best exemplified in the case of the bar pressing of rats and the key pecking of pigeons. Both animals usually respond in the Skinner box. These boxes are insulated against noise, and temperature and lighting are closely controlled. Data gathered under such controlled conditions tend to be more uniform than the data that are usually available. Skinner has typically used the rate of emission of a response as his dependent variable; the response is a simple one, and the measure, therefore, is relatively uncomplicated. A cumulative recorder which directly produces a cumulative frequency curve of responses, rather than the typical learning curve, has been used to record the data.

The free operant as the object of study, the use of rate as the primary datum, and the cumulative recorder as an instrument—these three, in Skinner's view, constitute a unique combination that makes for progress. Rate becomes a meaningful measure only when free operants are being studied, and the cumulative recorder shows rate characteristics over a long period of time. The experimenter can see what is happening to rate almost as soon as it happens, and he can change his procedures if that seems appropriate. Skinner (1966, p. 16) points out how important it was in chemistry to use dull, colourless weight as a measure in order to bring chaos to order in that field of study. He thinks the use of rate as a measure may have similar effects in psychology.

**Major Contributions**

Perhaps the most significant feature of Skinner's research and thinking has been his continuing work on the problem of reinforcement scheduling in operant conditioning. His early emphasis on intermittent reinforcement (1938) culminated in the exhaustive volume *Schedules of reinforcement* (Ferster and Skinner, 1957). He worked first with the rat in the Skinner box, subsequently with the pigeon in a comparable chamber, and ultimately with human subjects. Use of children as subjects in operant conditioning studies involving various reinforcement schedules has become a very important feature of behavioural research, involving psychologists of varying degrees of adherence to Skinnerian principles.

This research with children shades over into applied work with children (Risley, 1968); in the work cited, Risley and his co-workers wed operant conditioning techniques to teach verbal and other behaviours to culturally deprived children. Ullman and Krasner (1965) present a host of cases in which behaviour was modified in children and in adult psychotics by the application of operant techniques. Their book is only one of the earlier ones reporting what is happening in the behaviour modification movement. The primary tool used by workers in this tradition is reinforcement systematically applied. This systematic application usually involves depriving the patient of the reinforcer and establishing a schedule in which reinforcement is strictly dependent on the behaviour of the patient.

A number of examples may be cited from everyday-life situations to illustrate the effectiveness of intermittent reinforcement in controlling behaviour. One of the most apt is the control of behaviour exercised by the occasional payoff of the slot machine or by other gambling devices. Examination of other situations indicates that reinforcement is characteristically scheduled intermittently, rather than continuously, as it has more typically been scheduled in framing experiments. Thus the child's behaviour produces approbation in the parent, but not invariably; the student succeeds on examinations, but also falls or misses particular items; and the typical fisherman returns home empty-handed from a very large proportion of his trips.

In laboratory investigations of the effects of different schedules of reinforcement, four major types have been used. These are *fixed interval* (FI), in which the first response made after some fixed period of time is reinforced; *variable interval* (FI), in which the first response made after some variable period of time is reinforced; *fixed ratio* (FR), in which the first response made after some fixed number of responses is reinforced; and *variable ratio* (VR) in which the first response made after some variable number of responses is reinforced. The two variable schedules (VI and VR) and the fixed-ratio schedule (FR) characteristically produce remarkably steady and high rates of responding. The FI schedule ideally produces more cyclical cumulative performance curves featuring bursts of responses just preceding the usual reinforcement time, with pauses or very low rates of response immediately following reinforcement. This pattern of responding gives the cumulative curve its so-called scalloped appearance.

Skinner's research with control of animal behaviour is another long-standing contribution. He developed the method of *shaping*. Shaping is accomplished by giving an animal a reward if his response approximates the desired response. For example, if a rat is to be taught to climb a ladder, he would first be given food if he simply approached the ladder; then he might be required to reach up the ladder, then to get on it, and finally to climb it in order to receive his food reward. Skinner's method has been taken over by a large number of animal trainers. One of his early students, Keller Breland, left the academic field to become an animal trainer and has been very successful (Breland and Breland, 1951, 1961).

The observations made by the Brelands in the course of training many species of animals led them to depart in some respects from the Skinnerian views on operant conditioning. The Brelands noted (1961) numerous incidents of failure to teach the operant behaviours desired. For example (see Breland and Breland, 1966, pp 67-68), raccoons, pigs, squirrel monkeys, and other animals often have trouble letting go of a token which they are learning to insert into a food dispenser, much as humans insert coins into machines. The Brelands believed that more primitive behaviours were activated on earlier trials and that these more primitive behaviours interfered with the performance of the operant response. They described this "instinctive drift" as follows (1961, p 684):

> The general principle seems to be that wherever an animal has strong instinctive behaviours in the area of the conditioned response, after continued running the organism will drift toward the instinctive behaviour, to the detriment of the conditioned behaviour and even to the delay or preclusion of the reinforcement.

The Brelands, although they were nurtured by Skinner in the environmentalistic tradition which has been a common feature of the behaviouristic outlook, have been prominent among psychologists partly responsible for the swing toward nativism, which the ethologists initiated and which is evident in American psychology today. Lockard (1971) has documented that part of the nativistic trend which is most closely related to animal behaviour, detailing some of the contributions of the Brelands and of ethologists like Lorenz and Tinbergen. Lockard's conclusions come through dearly in statements like the following (1971, p. 171):

> Scientifically Sneaking, only two piece of information were needed to bring behaviour into the modem synthesis of the new biology: the fact that behaviour has a genetic basis, thus making it heritable and therefore subject to natural selection; and the fact that behaviour, or rather, particular behaviours, are adaptive—that the bear intimate relationships to particulars of the environment such that some kind of advantage results. The genetic. basis of hundreds and hundreds of particular behaviours has been demonstrated beyond doubt, and the adaptive significance of particular behaviours has been demonstrated in hundreds of cases.

During World War II Skinner conducted applied research on animals under the auspices of General Mills in Minneapolis. Apparently he was well along in the development of a training programme whereby pigeons could be used in the guiding device in a bomb when the development of atomic weapons ended the war and removed the immediate urgency from this research. The project has been declassified, and a fascinating account given by Skinner (1960).

One of the most striking of Skinner's demonstrations of the potency of shaping in control of animal behaviour is his research on "Superstitious behaviour" in pigeons (1948a). He demonstrated that clear-cut and uniquely individual responses could be quickly developed in hungry pigeons when they were given food at regular intervals regardless of their behaviour. Such an arrangement, with the delivery of food not contingent on the animal's pressing a bar, pecking a key, or engaging in any specified behaviour, constitutes a *noncontingent* schedule (also Sometimes called an *incontingent* schedule). In such a situation some response, which just happens to precede a reinforcement early in the session, will generally be fixated and will predominate in the behavioural repertoire of the animal during the experimental period. This occurs because one or two early reinforcements increase the rate at which the particular response is emitted, thus making more and more likely its occurrence just prior to subsequent reinforcements. The particular response Strengthened, such as wing flapping, neck craning, leg raising, etc., varies from one animal to the next. Probably the outcome of this procedure depends on the interaction between the animal's initial repertoire in the situation and the particular schedule of reinforcement delivery. Herrnstein (1966) reports on a study in which the animal is first taught a responses on a fixed-interval schedule and then is shifted to a non contingent schedule; this procedure gives the experimenter control over the animal's repertoire, at least in that it allows him to specify which response dun be of highest frequency when the noncontingent condition is initiated Under these conditions, Herrnstein found that the high-frequency response was maintained at a rate well above the operant level over the course of many seasons. This result, however, probably depends on the relationship between the contingent conditions and the noncontingent conditions, since Edwards, West, and Jackson (1968) found that response rates fell fairly rapidly when noncontingent conditions were instituted.

The concept of superstitious behaviour has been generalised to explain some aspects of the behaviour that occurs under contingent conditions. For example, a number of different stereotyped responses may occur in different subjects, even though no particular topography is necessary to produce the reinforcement. It seems likely that some of the topographies are more effortful than necessary. The topographies may be said to be conditioned superstitiously because of their adventitious pairing with reinforcement.

Skinner has pointed out the fact that the connection between response and reinforcement in most operant work is simply a temporal relationship; as he says (1966): "The response produces food only in the sense that food follows it—a Humean version of causality" (".14). He is also aware that superstitious behaviours arise from response-reinforcement relationships not specified by the experimenter, and he has generalised this thinking to contingent conditions (1966): "It is characteristic of most contingencies that they are not precisely controlled, and in any case they are effective only in combination with the behaviour which the organism brings to the experiment" (pp. 20-21). Schoenfeld, Cumming, and Hearst (1968) have suggested a classification scheme for schedules of reinforcement which characterised them in terms of strictly temporal variables; the critical properties of schedules dealt with were the length of the period during which reinforcement was available and the total "cycle length," which included the period of unavailability as well as the period of availability. If the animal responded during the period of availability, the reinforcement was delivered; during the remainder of the period, responding produced no results. They found a general response-rate increase when, for a fixed cycle time, reinforcement availability time was increased. Conversely, rates tended to decrease when the reinforcement availability time decreased.

This work and Skinner's own thinking would seem to be pointing toward a description of contingencies couched in more basic terms than those currently used. Describing a schedule as "fixed-interval fifteen-seconds" leaves out critical properties of the relationship between reinforcement delivery and the organism's behaviour. It also encourages a distinction between such a schedule and a fixed-ratio twenty-five-response schedule, whether or not such a distinction is important in a particular context. Finally, the similarities which may exist between intermittent reinforcement schedules and free food delivery on a noncontingent basis may tend to be obscured. A general description in terms of more basic properties of the various schedules as they relate to the organism's responses should make it possible to describe all the types of schedules in a common framework with noncontingent reinforcement delivery.

The first factor that comes to mind is the probability that a reinforcement will follow any specified response under study. For example, it is easy to specify these probabilities in a bar-pressing experiment with a traditional fixed-ratio five-second schedule, at lent for the bar-pressing response. The probability that each of the first four responses following reinforcement will be itself reinforced is zero. The probability that the fifth response will be reinforced is 1. It is obvious that any desired distribution of probabilities could be scheduled for each cycle of five responses. Any such schedule based on five responses could be called a *cycle-five* schedule to express the fact that the same set of five probabilities repeats throughout a session. The five probabilities could be 0.2, 0.4, 0.6, 0.8, and 1.0, or they could be 0.92, 0.30, 0.61, 0.00, and 0.24. Similar reasoning applies to interval schedules, except that responses are described in terms of the *time* since the last reinforcement rather than in terms of the number of responses since the last reinforcement. In the typical schedule, these probability relationships with the response are kept simple and are specified only with respect to the response being recorded. In a general descriptive scheme, there should be no limitations on the probability distributions, on the property of the response of which the probability is a function, or on the number of responses to which the probability distributions can be attached. In the noncontingent situation the experimenter does not ordinarily specify in advance these probability distributions, but they nevertheless exist in the sense that the animal comes to the situation with various responses occurring at various rates. These rates, in conjunction with the noncontingent rate of delivery of the reinforcer, determine the probability that each of the responses in the repertoire will initially be the one that precedes reinforcement delivery. The delivery of the reinforcement would be expected to change the rates of all the responses in the repertoire and thus to affect the probability that each would precede the second reinforcement.

Two recent papers seem to bear out the expectation that the study of superstitious behaviour may be particularly instructive and that it is revealing to consider all the responses in the animal's repertoire, or at least more than one. Staddon and Simmelhag (1971) studied the occurrence of a number of behaviours in a noncontingent reinforcement situation. They found, among other things, that highly characteristic sequences of behaviours occurred; component responses of the sequences never occurred "out of position." These authors compare the results of response-independent and response-dependent schedules and suggest a new view of the modification of adaptive behaviour as a result of the comparison of multiple responses in the two situations.

Dunham (1971) uses a somewhat similar multiple-response base-line procedure to examine what happens to several responses in an animal's repertoire when punishment is introduced into an ongoing situation. His study enables him to question the dominant version of punishment theory: that responses are suppressed by punishment because alternative responses are strengthened and compete with them. Dunham also shows that only one of the several alternative responses is usually the beneficiary of the weakening of the punished response. There seems to be little doubt that much future progress will be made through more careful and detailed examination of the relationships between reinforcements or punishers and the animal's ongoing repertoire of behaviour.

The average delay time between the reinforced response and the effective reinforcement would also seem to be an important property of a schedule of reinforcement. This delay time is usually held fixed and low in studies of schedules of reinforcement. This delay time is usually held fixed and low in studies of schedules of reinforcement. When there is a response-reinforcement contingency, the delay would be constant from trial to trial, except for minor variations due to variable equipment operating time or to variations in the time the subject takes to respond to the presence of the reinforcer. However, the response-reinforcement interval would be more variable when noncontingent reinforcements were being delivered and would be longer on the average than in the usual contingent case. It should be clear, however, that only the experimenter knows whether a contingency exists or not. To the animal, the whole situation might look like a game of "find the contingency, if one exists." He could be regarded by us as a casuality-detecting machine which examines response-reinforcement relationships to determine whether any qualify as causal relationships. The characteristics of these relationships (which are assumed above to be described by the probability of reinforcement, and the properties of response-reinforcement delays) are *all* the experimental subject has to work with to inform him of the contingency.

The rat, like David Hume, cannot be certain that casuality exists. Neither, in the superstitious case, can he be certain that causality does not exists. If Skinner has reduced the relationship to a temporal contiguity, how can the animal know that pressing a bar is more likely to be connected to the delivery of food than standing on his hind legs is? Let us consider the dilemma of our philosopher-rat "thinking" about a serious shock which he just received. At the time of shock onset, he was urinating leisurely in a quiet corner, having begun two seconds previously. The offset of urination was immediate, but the shock persisted while the rat leapt several times about the cage, and it stopped one second after he scratched desperately at the southwest corner. If the rat is well versed in the lore of psychology, he knows that the experimenter could be trying out shock as a punishment for urinating in the corner (and the definition of that response class might be very broad or very narrow). On the other hand, the shock might be serving as a negative reinforcer for the behaviour of scratching the southwest corner. Only a further trial, or many trials, will give him the information about response-reinforcement relationships that he needs to sort out the various possibilities. The only difference between the aversive case and the positive-reinforcement case is that both onset and offset are dramatic for aversive stimuli, while we limit our interest for the most part to the *delivery* of positive reinforcement.

If the probability-delay descriptive scheme described above were accepted, the current distinctions between types of schedules might fall into disuse and be regarded as special cases within the more general framework. Precise realisations of such schedules might require computer control of reinforcement delivery and the use of brain stimulation as a reinforcer in order to bring delay under exact control. The reduction of schedules to the status of special cases within a more general framework might be a precursor of the development of a more comprehensive theory of operant behaviours.

Another of Skinner's central and persistent interests has been research and systematic thinking about verbal behaviour. His conceptualisation of the important human behavioural problems of language has been influential in the field. This interest culminated in publication of a major work, *Verbal behaviour* (1957b). According to Skinner's interpretation, language as verbal behaviour is basically similar to other behaviour and can be best understood when viewed in this general conceptual framework.

Skinner characterises verbal behaviour as behaviour whose reinforcement is mediated by another organism that has been specifically conditioned to mediate such reinforcements. Verbal operants, like other operants, are recognised because of a relationship to an antecedent condition, typically a controlling stimulus. An example of a functional relationship between an antecedent variable and a verbal response would be one's writing "chair" as a response to the object on which he sits. Such responses are called *tacts* by Skinner because their controlling variable is *contact* with an object, event, or property of an object or event. If one says coffee" because one is deprived of that substance, he is to Skinner emitting a *mand* because of his *demand* for the appropriate reinforcer. Skinner believes that the appropriate course of investigation of language involves just the functional analysis of the relationship between antecedents and verbal behaviour. The organism makes no real contribution to verbal behaving, but is best regarded as a locus through which variables act.

Skinner usually receives credit for the great contemporary interest in programmed learning, much of which he probably deserves. We might consider the following, quoted in Boring and Lindzey, 1967, p. 322:

> In a window of the little apparatus showed a four-choice question to which the student responded by pressing the key corresponding to the answer he thought right. If it was, the next question turned up, but if not, he had to try again until he did find the right answer—meanwhile a counter kept a cumulative record of his tries. Moreover (two features no device since has had) if a lever were raised, the device was changed into a self-scoring and rewarding testing machine: whatever key was pressed, the next question turned up, but the counter counted only rights; also when the set on a reward dial was reached, a candy lozenge was automatically presented....

This quotation is not from Skinner's autobiography, but from Pressey's, and the machine described was exhibited in 1925. However, teaching machines did not catch on until much later. It is interesting to ask why. The machines themselves have undergone changes, but some highly successful ones are very simple—no more complex than Pressey's much earlier machine. Modern exponents of programmed learning would probably insist that the materials are now better organised and that the technical features of this organisation are responsible for the current much greater success of programmed learning

It is, nevertheless, interesting to contemplate the possibility that the reason for Skinner's success in popularising this approach to learning, where Pressey had failed thirty years earlier, is that Skinner had better reasons to believe that the technique ought to work. Further, he had a cohesive and enthusiastic group of followers, and Pressey did not. The principles of operant Conditioning were working in the control of animal behaviour, and concurrent efforts indicated that they would work for the control of human behaviour. Thus a *Zeitgeist* was developing within which programmed learning could thrive. It was probably Pressey's fate to be a little too far ahead of his time in 1925.

Most recently, Skinner's latest book; *Beyond Freedom and Dignity* (1971), threw down the gauntlet to our society. Vice-president Spiro Agnew picked it up (Goodall, 1972). Judging by the fact that the book has been high on the best-seller lists for a long time, the individual members of society are also picking it up. Skinner was no doubt issuing a deliberate challenge when he implied that freedom and dignity, two of our most holy cows, are in the way of progress toward a better world. Agnew, the prototype of a good American Hindu, is hardly ready to eat those cows, though the world starve. Your authors have no comment on whether those cows belong on the street or on the table; however, it seems likely that society is going to take psychology more and more seriously, and Skinner's book is one of the most important events in getting society's attention. It may be that, in the future, psychology will get support more commensurate with the importance of the problems we must deal with.

**Criticisms of Skinner**

The most persistent attacks have been concentrated on Skinner's positivism. Critics have maintained that Skinner is deluding himself if he believes theory has no value. Theory is inevitable. Every experiment and observation is in some way planned, based on hunches or ideas; therefore, say the critics, it is better to bring the presuppositions into the open and formalise them. Then they can be recognised and critically evaluated rather than hidden. In addition, formal theory in the older sciences has afforded a generality which Skinner's fact gathering alone can never achieve.

Skinner has several replies available. First, he is not antitheoretical; he is only against certain types of theories, either those which are premature or those which are attempts to avoid the necessity for empirical work or for genuine explanation. He does believe that theories may guide investigators into unprofitable efforts to confirm or disconfirm theories, when they might better devote themselves to the exploration of interesting empirical situations. Theories should be primarily inductive, not based on logical guesses. Theories *should* be an end product of scientific endeavor, but they should be proposed only as the data are ready to support them. Second, Skinner would probably insist that presuppositions need to be kept to a minimum. Premature speculation, even if it is not misleading, is a waste of time. In the worst cases, it will be misleading, a waste of time both directly and indirectly, and a source of personal involvement and controversy.

Skinner has also been criticised for his peripheralism. This kind of argument has two major facets. One involves his aphysiological bias; this is largely a matter of taste. If one prefers not to think in physiological terms, surely this is his privilege. The other involves his refusal to posit intervening processes of a psychological sort (such as Hull's habit strength or inhibition, Spence's incentive motivation, and the like). Here too the issue is one of personal preference, but difficulties arise when one side attempts to force its views on the other.

We have already noted in passing Skinner's own contention that he is not against real physiological psychology. He is against only the practice of taking refuge in physiological terminology when behavioural accounts break down. The use of merely verbal explanations, whether physiological, mentalistic, or anything else, is discouraged by Skinner.

In some cases, Skinner or his followers may have waxed too enthusiastic in their efforts to purify psychological language by eliminating terms like *emotion*, *motivation*, and *perception*. These much-abused terms may be highly variable in meaning and yet might still have some core of useful meaning. If so, the critics would have a legitimate claim that certain problems were being neglected because of a positivistic insistence on purity of language. The reply might be that the problems of nature eventually insist that attention be paid to them. Meanwhile, there are plenty of problems suggested by concepts with demonstrated meaningfulness. Would the critic rather devote time to issues that are assuredly meaningful or to problems with no clear meaning?

Skinner has been criticised for extrapolating well beyond his data (cf. his proposals about complex human problems in *Science and Human Behaviour,* 1953a). On this issue he seems to be somewhat vulnerable. The whole spirit of his methodology seems to revolve around the notion of sticking close to already observed facts. Yet his generalisations to human behaviour very clearly go far beyond the observations of the laboratory.

There is a reply to this kind of criticism too. Bem and Bem (1968), in discussing the relationship between Skinner's *Verbal behaviour* and Lenneberg's *Biological foundations of language,* indicate the direction such a defense might take: "Both works, in short, constitute plausibility arguments for particular views of verbal behaviour" (p. 497). Skinner clearly stated that this was the way in which he viewed his analysis of verbal behaviour, and he could easily extend this argument to his other extrapolations. If they are accepted as merely suggestions stemming from his conceptual framework, they may serve at least as an intellectual stimulant. The extent to which simple principles can be applied to apparently complex situations and processes is an empirical problem and cannot be safely prejudged.

With regard to Chomsky's attack on Skinner's treatment of verbal learning, MacCorquodale (1969) has published a long and detailed defense and an explanation of Skinner's effort.

All the preceding criticisms involve. broad methodological or attitudinal characteristics of Skinner's Position. It is about as difficult to score heavy against Skinner on such points as it would be to criticise him effectively because he prefers a behaviouristic approach to an existential one. These are flit kinds of issues about which it is often said that the opponents "talk through" one another without making contact.

There are some issues which can be more closely joined, one of which concerns the use of statistics. Skinner and his followers are usually not interested in statistical tests; their attitude is probably best presented by Sidman (1960). Skinner himself says (Evans, 1968): "No student of mine to my knowledge has ever 'designed an experiment'" (p. 89). The Skinnerian methodology typically involves intensive and carefully controlled investigation of a small group of subjects. The search is for reliable functional relationships, and reliability is established by demonstrating the same functional relationship in several *individual* organisms, preferably under several different conditions. The Statistical approach more typically uses larger groups of subjects and examines quantitative indices of the group's performance. Skinner does not believe that we are likely to arrive at laws which will help us predict and control the behaviour of the individual unless we look at individuals. The issue is, like the more general issues, debatable, but the Skinnerians have certainly forced some important questions into the spotlight, where they can be more carefully considered. Some aspects of operant methodology are unquestionably useful, and on some issues concerning the relationships between group and individual functions the Skinnerians can be demonstrated to be correct. Those who advocate an overtly statistical approach are probably correct when they maintain that Skinnerians must make some statistical decisions, for example, about whether rate of responding has stabilised and about whether experimental manipulations have reliably been shown to have produced an effect.

The efficiency of the atheoretical approach has been questioned The book *Schedules of reinforcement* (Ferster and Skinner, *1957)* has been used as an example of the dangers of too inductive and Positivistic an approach. It summarises about seventy thousand hours of continuously recorded behaviour of individual pigeons, during which time the pigeons emitted approximately one-quarter of a billion responses. The data are presented in a total of 921 Separate figures with almost no interpretive, or even surmmarising, comment. This procedure accords well with Skinner's (1959a) belief that the scientist should be brought into direct contact with data, but it does not agree so well with the scientific temperament of those whose immediate interests are in general principles.

Cook (1963) has criticised Skinnerians for too literal an application of techniques appropriate in the operant conditioning chamber to programmed learning. For one thing, there is a great deal of evidence that humans need *not* make an overt response in order to learn, and in fact often do better if no overt response is required (Hillix and Marx, 1960; Rosenbaum and Hewitt, 1966; Rosenbaum and Schutz, 1967). Further, they often do as well when they are told in advance what the correct response as prompted) as they do when they are reinforced after making the correct response. Both these errors in the application of operant techniques to humans are specific instances of the general criticism of premature extrapolation.

The best-known criticism of Skinner's extrapolations is by Chomsky (1959). In his famous thirty-two-page review of *Verbal behaviour*, chomsky analyses Skinner's formulation with great care and criticises it with great effectiveness. He devotes a great deal of attention to the terms *stimulus. response*, and *reinforcement,* since these are critical terms in Skinner's account of verbal behaviour. Serious problems arise with the use of each of the three terms as they are employed in the analysis of verbal behaviour. We shall note here only some difficulties with the use of *reinforcement.*

Chomsky notes that, in bar-pressing experiments, the reinforcer is an identifiable stimulus and that statements about reinforcement therefore have a meaningful referent, which in turn makes it meaningful to use the concept of reinforcement in the explanation of behaviour. Chomsky contends that the extension to the explanation of verbal behaviour is, however, completely unjustified. In support of his argument, he cites from Skinner a number of examples in which *reinforcement* does *not* refer to an identifiable stimulus. Skinner often uses automatic self-reinforcement (not identifiable as a stimulus!) as an explanation of why verbal behaviour is maintained. Future reinforcements are also appealed to, as when a writer is said to be reinforced because of the effect his work will have upon future generations. Chomsky says of such usage (1959): "In fact, the term is wed in such a way that the assertion that reinforcement is necessary for learning and continued availability of behaviour is likewise empty" (p. 37).

Chomsky's review is reminiscent of Koch's review of Hull's work. Both are extremely sophisticated, careful, and thorough reviews. Both attack specific issues with great force and accuracy. Yet from one point of view both reviews are unjust. The reason is that Hull and Skinner were both being programmatic. Neither believed that he was correct in detail; in fact, it was Hull's explicit intention to set up hypotheses which could be proved wrong by others. However, chomsky would probably rejoin that the defects in detail in Skinner are so great that the whole programme becomes meaningless. At this time, the pendulum of history seems to be swinging in the direction of a verdict for Chomsky.

However, Skinner himself seems confident that the pendulum will, in the end, swing back and award the victory to him (M.H. Hall, 1967, pp. 69-70):

> What the Psycholinguists miss is any conception of a functional analysis as opposed to a structural analysis of verbal behaviour.... They lean very heavily on the mentalistic psychology, and they are going to be let down because there is no such psychology. But as I said earlier, now they are postulating innate ideas, and that is next to worthless, if nota little bit comical. But I am in no real hurry, I have had my say. I am not interested in arguing with them at all. When all their mythical machinery finally grinds to a halt and is laid aside, discarded, then we will see what is remembered fifty or a hundred years from now, when the truth will have all been brought out in the open.

MacCorquodale (1969) agrees with Skinner. After chastising Chomsky for what he sees as misunderstanding Skinner's purpose, MacCorquodale says (1969, p. 841):

> Unfortunately for his purposes, Chomsky did not grasp the differences between Skinnerian and Watsonian-Hullian behaviourism, and his criticisms, although stylistically effective, were mostly irrelevant to *Verbal Behaviour*.
>
> He was simply wrong. This is a *great* book.

**Skinner's Role in Contemporary Systematic Psychology**

The extent of Skinner's systematic contributions to modern experimental psychology is nicely summarised in the formal citation accompanying the American Psychological Association's Distinguished Scientific Contribution Award granted him in 1958. This citation is as follows (*American Psychologist*, 1958):

> An imaginative and creative scientist, characterised by great objectivity in scientific matters and by warmth and enthusiasm in personal contacts. Choosing simple operant behaviour as subject matter, he has challenged alternative analyses of behaviour, insisting that description take precedence over hypotheses. By careful control of experimental conditions, he has produced data which are relatively free from fortuitous variation. Despite his antitheoretical position, he is considered an important systematist

and has developed a self-consistent description of behaviour which has greatly increased our ability to predict and control the behaviour of organisms from rat to man, Few American psychologists have had so profound an impact on the development of psychology and on promising younger psychologists.

Whereas in the period 1945 to 1950 there was no more enthusiastic band of psychologists than those working actively within the Hull-Spence systematic framework, today the same thing can be said of the Skinnerians, as they are often called. In addition to the group with Skinner at Harvard, there has been for years a tightly knit group trained under Fred Keller and William Schoenfeld at Columbia University. Skinnerian psychologists, resenting the orthodox restrictions of the American Psychological Association's journals particularly the unwritten regulations concerning sample size and statistical tests), established the *Journal for the Experimental Analysis of Behaviour* as their journal in 1958. Skinnerian techniques are almost universally accepted for some purposes even by opponents of the Skinnerian viewpoint. Young psychologists eager to help make the study of behaviour an exact science continue to flock to the Skinnerian banner, often to the discomfiture of those holding opposing views. The popular press is coming to recognise Skinner as the greatest contemporary behaviourist (e.g., *Time*, 1969) and his theoretical views as a serious competitor to Freud's. He has revivified and extended the strictly behavioural position. As one reviewer put it (MacLeod, 1959): "Watson's spirit is indestructible. Cleansed and purified, it breathes through the writings of B.F. Skinner" (p. 34).

## CONTIGUITY THEORY: GUTHRIAN ASSOCIANISM

### Guthrie's Career

Edwin Guthrie (1886-1959) was for several decades the leading exponent of a simple contiguity principle of learning. Throughout a long period, while first one and then another opposing school developed, Guthrie held steadfast to a small number of strict associationistic principles. This patience has finally paid off in the modern appearance of statistical models of learning based largely upon the Guthrian pattern. However, Guthrie's own contribution has remained that of a prophet and overseer more than that of an active experimentalist or detailed theorist.

Guthrie remained at one school, the University of Washington, throughout his entire academic career (1914 to 1956). He had less than the usual formal training in psychology, having been trained instead in philosophy and mathematics. He took his doctoral degree in 1912 at the University of Pennsylvania after having earned degrees earlier at the University of Nebraska. With one major exception (Guthrie and Horton, 1946), he preferred writing and argumentation to experimentation. His several books, especially *The psychology of learning (1935,* rev. 1952) and *The psychology of human conflict* (1938), are full of persuasive anecdotal supports for his general associationistic principles, but contain little controlled evidence.

Watson's doctrines so influenced Guthrie that he became a thoroughgoing behaviourist, although he differed from Watson on many points of theory. Guthrie's interest in psychology was apparently kindled during his graduate training by the philosopher E. A. Singer. He has stated that his year's collaboration on a textbook with the psychologist Stevenson Smith (S. Smith and Guthrie, 1921) gave him "invaluable training" in psychology. He retained his early interest in problems of philosophy of science throughout his career; his final major work (Guthrie, 1959) shows a continuing interest in general methodological questions, such as the relationship between logic, language, and scientific progress.

**Guthrie's Basic Principles**

Guthrie believed that a small number of primary principles are sufficient to account for the fundamental facts of behaviour modification. His most famous principle is popularly referred to as *one-trial learning*. Guthrie held that S-R associations, as the basis of learning, are established by contiguity per se in a single pairing of stimulus and response. He early stated this principle as follows (1935): "A combination of stimuli which has accompanied a movement will on its recurrence tend to be followed by that movement" (p.26). A related principle is (1942): "A stimulus pattern gains its fun associative strength on the occasion of its first pairing with a response" (p. 30). Guthrie offered final simplified union (1959): "What is being noticed becomes a signal for what is being done" (p. 186). This statement reflects his concern with the active role of the organism (the old problem of attention). In his final paper he also placed increased emphasis on the problem of patterning in stimulus complexes (cf. Guthrie, 1959, pp. 186ff.).

His early distinction between acts and movements enabled Guthrie to hold to his basic one-trial-learning principle and still account for the fact that behaviour modification typically requires repeated pairings of cue and response before it can be reliably predicted that the response will occur in the presence of the cue. According to Guthrie, the basic connections are between stimuli and movements, but *acts,* rather than movements, are usually measured. An example of an act would be serving a tennis ball into the service court; every separate muscular movement which was necessary would serve well as an example of what Guthrie means by a movement. While observable in principle, these movements are not easily noticed and are generally overlooked in theorising. However, anyone who has ever had tennis lessons is aware of the fact that these movements must sometimes be considered and carefully learned, especially when complex coordinations are involved.

This does not mean that movements are equivalent to the contractions of individual muscles. In a sense, what Guthrie means by movement is itself a kind of behavioural result; it is a result in terms of what is happening to a part of the organism, but it is not a result in terms of the environment. It is not the most molecular level of description which could be used. As Guthrie says (1959): "A description of the action of the individual muscles concerned would be hopeless confusion" (p.183).

The situation is similar on the stimulus side Guthrie regarded a complex stimulus as a collection of a great many stimulus components, with not all components present on every occasion. The net results of this complexity of stimulus and response components is that a large number of presentations of the gross stimulus and occurrences of the gross response (the act) are required before satisfactory regularity can be found in the behaviour being measured. This is so because large numbers of the stimulus and response components need to be involved in the conditioning process. If exact replications of stimuli and responses could be achieved, single presentations would be sufficient to produce perfect conditioning.

For Guthrie, the process of conditioning is as follows: Aspects of the total stimulus situation present on a given trial become associated with a successful movement, that is, one which is part of the sequence constituting the successful "act." The successful movement causes movement-produced stimuli, which, along with external stimuli present in the environment as it may be altered by the movement, are associated with a subsequent successful movement. This chain of movements linked by movement-produced stimuli constitutes an act. When the act is terminated, it must result in the removal of the relevant stimuli if it is to be retained. Otherwise, other movements would become associated with the same stimuli.

On a subsequent trial in which different aspects of the total stimulus situation are present, the subject will engage in random behaviours until he again performs the act successfully. The movements constituting the act on that occasion are consequently associated with the stimulus complex present during the second trial. This associative process will recur on additional trials until successful movements are conditioned to all aspects of the stimulus situation. When this point is reached, conditioning is complete, and the act will occur smoothly, whatever aspect of the stimulus situation happens to be present.

Finally, it should be noted that Guthrie thought learning occurs through pure contiguity of stimulus and response. This might be considered a misguided view of the process of forming associations, since it is obvious that reinforcers have an important role in learning. Guthrie had no need to deny that rein forcers are effective; his theory simply accounted for their effectiveness in an ingenious and different way. The reinforcer was presumed to change the stimulus situation in which the response had just been made. The original stimulus situation (prereinforcer) therefore cannot be disconnected from the response just made and connected to a new response; the connection is thus preserved because of the stimulus change produced by the presence of the reinforcer. Unlearning, or extinction, is really the learning of different responses to the same stimulus, according to Guthrie. He is therefore able to present a beautifully parsimonious and consistent picture of the totality of behaviour modification.

**Evaluation of Guthrie**

Guthrie's views have been most directly supported in the laboratory by his own investigation of stereotypy in the cat's behaviour in the puzzle box (Guthrie and Horton, 1946) and by two investigations of Voeks (1948, 1954). Guthrie did not himself present any highly formalised theory; he stated (1959) that he did not think psychology was yet advanced enough to justify such theory. Voeks *(1950)* has nevertheless published a useful formalisation of Guthrie's position. Her postulate of postremity, or recency, for example, states that only the last response made to a stimulus remains conditioned. Guthrie had said the same thing, but had made no effort to state it formally or to combine it with other postulates to form a system from which deductions could be made.

Although Guthrie did not leave any comprehensive theory, it is interesting to examine some experiments designed to test his statement that the last response made is the one that will be preserved and made again on the next presentation of the same cue. Voeks (1948) found that human subjects learning mazes made the postreme response far more often than the response which had previously been made most frequently. Postremity won out over frequency in predicting responses for fifty-six out of fifty-seven subjects, in cases where the two principles made opposing predictions. Seward, Dill, and Holland (1944); however, found that subjects in a multiple-choice situation usually made the response made earliest, rather than latest, to a particular cue (colour). It would thus appear from these two studies that the principle of postremity works sometimes, but not always-a statement which is true with disturbing frequency when applied to psychological principles.

The most searching criticism of Guthrie's theory has been offered by Mueller and Schoenfeld (1954). They have indicated that the simplicity of Guthrian notions is more apparent than real and has been achieved only at the expense of failure to we explicit about key problems. They have also suggested that Guthrie has developed no real system at all, in clear contrast to many of the leading alternative theorists. He has been satisfied merely with repeating, over the years, certain of the key assumptions with which he started. Finally, they have raised some serious questions concerning the interpretation of the Guthrie and Horton (1946) data on stereotypy of behaviour. Their treatment should be consulted, along with Guthrie's final authoritative paper (1959), by anyone interested in an evaluation of Guthrian theory.

Guthrie's success in maintaining his position as a leading learning theorist is uprising in view of the relative paucity of experimental support his theory reviewed. This success has probably been due to a combination of several factors. Foremost among these is the apparent simplicity of his theory compared with the leading alternatives, such as Hull's. There is no difficulty in grasping at least the basis of Guthrie's views, and this simplicity appeals to many psychologists. A second factor has been the difficulty experienced by opposing theorists in presenting evidence which clearly contradicts the Guthrian theory. Finally, there is the fact that Guthrie and some of his adherents, notably Sheffield, have been consistently able to point to weaknesses and contradictions in the alternative accounts. Hull's need-reduction principle has been a special target (e.g., Sheffield, 1948; Sheffield, 1949; Sheffield and Roby, 1950; Sheffield, Wulff, and Backer, 1951). The fact that these successful attacks depend upon the greater predictive specificity of the alternative accounts does not seem to have reduced the effectiveness of the Guthrian attack. A consequence of this success in criticism has been that Guthrie's theory has remained a formidable alternative account, even though its laurels may have been won on largely negative grounds.

Despite these limitations, Guthrie has been more than merely an astute critic and propounder of simple generalisations supported by fluent anecdotal stories. He is one theorist who has stood by his theoretical guns, consistently espousing a contiguity principle as the basis of all learning. He has supported his emphasis on movements as the theoretical response elements by experimental studies of stereotypy and has shown how well stereotypy observed by other experimenters can be subsumed by his theoretical analyses. Guthrie has demonstrated the theoretical roles that can be played by mediating mechanisms like movement-produced stimuli. This ingenious mechanism is much like Hull's fractional anticipatory goal response in that both serve as the forgers of links in the chain of behaviour. Finally, Guthrie has not said much because he did not believe he had enough information to say much. Thus he has made a small target. In 1958, the year before his death, Guthrie, the consistent psychologist, received the American Psychological Foundation Gold Medal Award in recognition of his distinguished contributions. These contributions have not stopped with his death; William K. Estes has modeled his statistical association theory on Guthrian principles.

**Two-Factor Theories**

It has been clear for a very long time that the Throndikian and the Pavlovian procedures for studying learning differ in the operations employed. In the Pavlovian procedure, the unconditioned stimulus follows the conditioned stimulus, whatever the subject in the experiment does. In the Thorndikian procedure, the reward is presented only if the subject has Previously engaged in the behaviour required by the experimenter. This basic difference in procedure implies some corollary distinctions. In the Pavlovian paradigm, the conditioned stimulus, which comes to elicit the conditioned response if learning occurs, is an identifiable stimulus and is manipulated by the experimenter. The unconditioned stimulus elicits an identifiable unconditioned response. The unconditioned response in the Pavlovian studies was always, or nearly always, an involuntary response mediated by the autonomic nervous system. The conditioned response typically bean a close relationship to the unconditioned response, if it is not identical to it as measured in the experiment. The Thorndikian procedure is different in all the above respects: There is no experimentally identified conditioned stimulus; the response elicited by the reward is not of great interest, nor do the experimental arrangements "force" the performance of the unconditioned response to the reward; the response to be learned may not be at all related in form to the response made to the reward; and the responses of interest are mediated by the "voluntary" nervous system.

A consideration of these operational differences between Pavlovian (classical) conditioning and Thorndikian (instrumental) learning leads one fairly naturally to question whether different laws of behaviour modification are involved in the two situations. For example, one might ask whether stimulus associations, as in Pavlovian conditioning, and stimulus-response associations, as emphasised by the Thorndikian procedure, are formed by different basic processes. Rescorla and Solomon (1967), in their review of the literature on two-factor learning theories, state that three different sets of variables are usually implicated by those who think there are two basically different processes. The three sets are the class of responses affected by the process, the effective reinforcers involved, and the results of the learning process. The most Common distinction based on response characteristics has been that classical conditioning involves autonomic responses, while instrumental learning involves somatic (skeletal) responses, but a number of other distinctions have also been suggested. It is more difficult to find a basis for distinguishing the kinds of reinforcers, but it has been suggested that the "rewards" used in instrumental learning have to have an affective character, while Pavlovian reinforcers do not; again, several bases for a distinction between the reinforcers have been proposed. Finally, among die several Possible distinctions between the "products" of learning is the suggestion that classical conditioning involves stimulus-stimulus connections, while instrumental learning produces stimulus-response connections. There is no highly convincing empirical evidence that compels adherence to any of these theoretical distinctions, but there is not sufficient evidence to reject them either.

The most popular theoretical Strategy has been an attempt to reduce the two operationally different procedures to a common theoretical framework which can explain both. Hull, for example, accepted the laws of Pavlovian conditioning as basic, but modified the most common conception of the process in his emphasis on the necessity for drive reduction to occur if learning is to be successful. The more complex, and therefore less popular, solution is to assume that there are two different processes involved and to propose a theory which relates the two processes. If this approach is chosen, it is natural to assume that classical conditioning involves contiguity as a basic Process and that instrumental learning involves reward as a basic component.

Kimble (1961) reports that Miller and Konorski presented an early version of two-factor theory in 1928, and that they were followed into the field by Schlosberg (1937) and by Skinner (1938). Skinner's distinction between type S and type R conditioning has since. become part of the jargon of our discipline; the former was essentially Pavlovian, and the latter Thorndikian. Skinner was far more interested in the Thorndikian, operant variety, and he held the evidence for pure Pavlovian conditioning to be questionable.

Mowrer later became, and has remained, the best-known two-factor theorist because of the tightness of his reasoning, the empirical work which buttressed his suggestions, and the length and number of his publications on the subject (1947, 1951, 1954). He contrasted conditioning and solution learning. The acquisition of emotions, meaning, attitudes, and the like is mediated through simple contiguity of stimuli-conditioning. Overt instrumental learning—solution learning—occurs through reinforcement, or law-of-effect learning. Since Mowrer was originally a strong Hullian reinforcement theorist, his shift was an important one. His interpretation was criticised by his earlier collaborator, Neal Miller (1951), among others.

A suggestion for a different kind of two-factor theory has been made by Spence in his Silliman Lectures (1956). As he pointed out, one might develop his suggestions into a two-factor theory "exactly the opposite of the well-known two-factor theory espoused by Schlosberg, Mowrer, and others" (p. 151). Reinforcement would thus be accorded a determining role in the case of classically conditioned responses, which are emphasised in Spence's systematic theorising, rather than in that of instrumental behaviour.

By far the most ambitious effort at a two-factor theory has been provided by Mowrer (1956, 1960a, 1960b) in a drastic revision of his earlier two-factor theory. Actually, this theory is no longer "two-factor" in the original sense; Mowrer has come to accept now only conditioning or sign learning as the single basic learning process; solution learning is regarded as a special, derived case of conditioning. It is still a two-factor theory, however, in the sense that it stresses two *types of reinforcement. Decremental reinforcement* refers to the need-reducing type of process stressed by Thorndike and Hull in their theories; *incremental reinforcement* refers to the growth of "fear" with consequent avoidance behaviour from excessive stimulation.

The present theory was developed mainly by means of an extension of the secondary-reinforcement principle. Mowrer assumes that when a hungry animal contains food, response-produced stimuli become conditioned as secondary reinforcers—as "promising" stimuli which arouse "hope." In this "feedback theory of habit," as Mowrer calls it, hope is thus conditioned in fundamentally the same manner as fear is conditioned in aversive learning. The parallelism is stated by Mowrer (1960b): "A conditioned stimulus not only makes the subject salivate: it also makes him *hopeful,* just as surely as a stimulus which has been associated with the onset of pain makes a subject *fearful*' (p. 8).

It is too early to say whether learning will eventually be subsumed under a single set of laws, under two sets, or under several. Rescorla and Solomon (1967) cite a number of empirical studies which demonstrate interactions between classical and instrumental conditioning. Changes in rate of instrumental responding can be produced by the introduction of conditioned stimuli previously used in the Pavlovian context. Such empirical demonstrations obviously do not prove that there are two kinds of learning, but they do show that it is profitable to study the relationships between situations in which stimulus *contiguity* is arranged (Pavlovian) and situations in which a response-reinforcement *contingency* is arranged. Two-factor theories may not turn out to be "correct," but they at least have the virtue of encouraging the study of such relationships.

**Summary and Conclusions**

In this chapter we have surveyed some theoretical positions loosely called S-R. In the main, these are neobehaviouristic and concentrate on the problem of learning. They are distinguished on the basis of their treatment of the problem of reinforcement.

The reinforcement theory of Clark L. Hull represents a combination of the Thorndikian law of effect and the Pavlovian conditioning paradigm. This hypothetico-deductive system is highly formalised. It is by far the most ambitious theoretical and systematic effort of its kind. Compared with Watson, Hull was a sophisticated theorist, much concerned with logical as well as experimental specifications and empirical tests; he was a methodological, rather than a metaphysical, behaviourist. In spite of, or even perhaps partly because of, his high aspirations, Hull's direct systematic influence has declined markedly in recent years. This decline has been a function both of the fundamental faults found in his system and of the increasing popularity of a more positivistic psychology of the kind advanced by B.F.

Skinner. Today Hullian psychology is represented mainly in the theoretical efforts of Kenneth W. Spence and his associates and, in much more modified form, in the work of Neal E. Miller.

Skinner has been much less interested in formal theory than Hull. He believes that theory should develop inductively and be determined by data, rather than from postulates which then determine what data are gathered. Skinner does seem to have either moderated or clarified his position, beginning from what seemed to be an antitheoretical position and developing toward a positive attitude toward certain limited types of theory.

In keeping with his metatheoreticil belief, Skinner has maintained an atheoretical, descriptive view of reinforcement. His research has been some of the most provocative and stimulating to be found in psychology. His interests have ranged freely from baby boxes to utopian communities.

The major opposition within the S-R camp to the various reinforcement theories has been provided by the contiguity theorists, who hold to some kind of associationistic principle. They argue that reinforcement operates mainly to protect S-R connections formed through contiguity per se. E. R. Guthrie has been the most influential contiguity theorist over several decades. Within the past decade, however, the basic Guthrian contiguity principle has been cast in mathematical form by W. K. Estes and his associates. Their use of mathematical models has given a strong impetus to empirical research as well as to theoretical development.

A number of two-factor theories have also been developed. These have historically attempted to combine the reinforcement and contiguity positions. The most recent of these, by O.H. Mowrer, does offer something of a novel approach. It involves two kinds of reinforcement, both based upon the conditioning or contiguity principle.

An important conclusion to be drawn from the wide variety of theoretical approaches outlined is that no one procedure can be guaranteed in advance to be more productive than any other. Rather, all kinds of empirical and theoretical endeavors are to be encouraged, as long as the fundamental requirements of scientific procedure are met. Each approach that is given a thorough trial will help to motivate and organise research. Which kind of research will eventually be seen to be most significant must await the verdict of history.

# 16

# Varieties of Field Theory

Several psychological theorists have been called *field theorists* because of a supposed analogy between their theories and the field theories of physics. Robert Oppenheimer, who presumably understood the nature of field theory very well, questioned the usefulness of the analogy. In the published version of his speech to the American Psychological Association, he put the matter quite politely (1956, pp.133-134):

> But probably between sciences of very different character, the direct formal analogies in their structure are not too likely to be helpful. Certainly what the pseudo-Newtonians did with sociology was a laughable affair; and similar things have been done with mechanical notions of how psychological phenomena are to be explained.... I know that when I hear the word "field" used in physics and in psychology I have a nervousness that I cannot entirely account for.

As psychologists, we shall of course be quick to consider the possibility that we have here simply the case of an effete physicist throwing up a defense of his own territory. However, we might quickly find ourselves unduly swelling the ranks of the effete if we put all those who question this particular analogy into those ranks. For example, one of our own (psychologist William K. Estes) said in connection with his examination of Kurt Lewin's theory (1954b, pp. 318-319):

> Now we may ask what are the distinguishing characteristics of the enterprises which claim or at least permit the appellation field theory? It should be noted first of all that most of the attributes claimed by field theorists and sympathetic reviewers tend to vanish or at least become non-differentiating upon critical scrutiny. It is not clear to the present writer in what technical sense the term field theory is especially applicable to the systems of Lewin, Koffka, Kohler, or Tolman. The term field has been taken over from physics, but it is not easy to find a basis for the presumed analogy between field theories of physics and the so-called field theories of psychology.

Estes goes on to point out that many of the adjectives that are supposed to describe field theories in psychology apply equally well to S-R theories, for example, *dynamic* and *multiply determined*.

Two points can be extracted from the objections of Oppenheimer and Estes. First, there is no close technical or formal relationship between the field theory of physics and the field theory of psychology. We shall see that Lewin developed the most formalised field theory in psychology and that it used an altogether different formal system and an altogether different set of variables from those used by any extant field theory in physics.

The second point is that the metatheoretical programme which was supposed to direct the efforts of field theorists in psychology did not produce theories which bore the distinctive marks of the metatheory. A detailed examination of this point would carry us too far from our purpose here, and Estes (1954b) has already documented this assertion.

What, then, is there left to discuss about field theory? There are two things. First, we can examine the analogy at the *metatheoretical* level between the field theories of physics and those of psychology, since there seems to be no valid analogy at a more technical level. Second, we can discuss the nature of the theories which have been called *field theories* in psychology, regardless of whether they are really any more fieldlike (in the sense of physics) than their competitors. We shall therefore be taking a friendly look at field theory, trying to assess it more in terms of its own aspirations than in terms of those of an outside critic. We believe that field theorists in psychology have made extremely important contributions to our methodology and that this justifies a close look at their suggestions and criticisms.

## THE METATHEORETICAL ANALOGIES

Einstein's special relativity theory of 1905, and his general relativity theory of 1915, had unparalleled impacts on the view of the world held by physicists and philosophers alike. Related developments in quantum theory have further revolutionised man's world view. The awe with which these contributions are sometimes viewed is revealed by Gillispie (1960), who says: "And Lorentz lacked only that ultimate quality of something like divinity in Einstein's mind, which would take the same evidence and quite transform the shape of the world that physics sees in nature" (p. 506).

Even before the formulation of Einstein's special theory, Maxwell's field theory evoked great admiration. Under the circumstances, it was natural and desirable that the developing science of psychology try to emulate its more established fellow scientists by borrowing the lessons learned in the transformation from classical physics to relativity theory, the most prestigious representative of physical field theory.

The philosophy of relativity theory is a sea in which every man can find water beyond his depth. We must, nevertheless, try to extract from it those features which were taken over in the metatheoretical attitudes of field theorists in psychology.

Einstein's relativity theory, as modified by Minkowski, places events in a four-dimensional space-time field. The description of events is holistic" in this and in other field theories in the sense that the theory inextricably interrelates the variables in describing the "trajectory" of events through this four-dimensional field. This general holistic property of field theories is taken over by field theorists in psychology as part of their metatheoretical equipment, whether or not it ever becomes visible as a characteristic of their theories.

A second supposed property of physical field theory, its dynamic character, is more controversial; that is, it is not agreed that relativity theory, at least, is really dynamic in the sense that it admits of change in a degree greater than the more "mechanistic" theories of classical physics. It has been argued that relativity theory provides for a complete and *static* view of existence, with past and future stretched out along the temporal dimension just as the sun and stars are arrayed in the spatial dimensions. Whether or not one agrees with this position (see Fraser, 1966, pp. 417-454, for both sides of the argument), it is hard to see why field theories in physics might be regarded as more dynamic than non-field theories. In psychology, "dynamic" has come to have a quite different connotation involving motivation, especially unconscious motivation, in addition to the more nearly physical meaning emphasizing change.

Field theories in physics do generally provide for continuity, for example, in space and time. The field properties may therefore change continuously, and this continuity of change—a mathematical continuity-may somehow connote dynamicism. It is, at least superficially, peculiar that Gestalt theory gave rise to a noncontinuity view of learning despite the close relationship of Gestalt metatheory to its precursors in physical field theory.

Einsteinian theory set sharp limits to the range of causality. Events which were too distant in space-time could not interact; no causal factors could propagate faster than the speed of light in a vacuum. The paths of the planets were reconceived as being along the shortest paths in the curved space produced by the presence of other bodies. There was no longer a gravitational attraction per se, since in some cases that attraction would have to take place instantaneously over vast distances. The field in which the planet moved at the time produced the movement of the planet. Action at a distance was no longer required. Psychological field theories seem generally to have taken over this view; they generally accept the "contemporaneity principle," which states that only conditions actually present at a given time can affect events occurring at that time.

There is a rather strange and contorted relationship between positivism and relativity theory. Mach was the positivist physicist and philosopher who furnished Einstein with the skepticism he needed to reexamine the foundations of physics and to eliminate, through his brilliant synthesis, the Newtonian notions of absolute space and absolute time. It was in the positivistic spirit that Einstein asked how one would determine, from two platforms moving with respect to each other, whether not two events occurring somewhere else were simultaneous. It was therefore an outgrowth of Mach's thought that led Einstein to the conclusion that two honest md right-thinking men on the two platforms would necessarily arrive at opposite conclusion about the order of succession of events, provided certain conditions obtained.

Further, it was in the positivistic tradition when Heisenberg asked how one could go about determining the velocity and position of an electron; logic drove him to conclude that there was an irreducible uncertainty produced by the interaction of the electron with the measuring system. The electron, therefore, *does not have,* from the point of view of the positivist, a determinate position and velocity at the same time.

Now the contortions begin. Einstein, who started as a son of positivism, did not find it possible to remain an altogether loyal son. He did not wish to accept a basic indeterminacy at the heart of physics, even though it had been demanded by the same kinds of questions he had asked about the universe on a very large scale. Relativism could reign through the vast reaches of space, as long as its shady younger brother left the atom its determinate existence.

Another contortion comes from the fact that positivism, which started as a quest for *positive* knowledge, led inexorably to the conclusion that there are stringent limitations on what can be known. Some have concluded mistakenly that this means that subjectivism is now justified because of relativity or the indeterminacy principle. This is not true; the "facts" are perfectly objective in both cases, and will be agreed to by everyone making observations under the same physical conditions. Field theory in psychology seems to have, at least in some cases, substituted a version of subjectivism for relativism; we shall see that Lewin, like the Gestalt psychologists, accepts the causal efficacy of the "psychological field" of the individual; this psychological field seems to be insufficiently objectified for scientific purposes.

Apart from these metatheoretical considerations, there has been a high degree of commonality of theoretical content among field theories. Most important here are the widely shared interest in problems of perception and cognition and the correlated tendency to utilise perceptual and cognitive processes as explanatory factors. This is hardly surprising in view of the close relationship between modern field theories and classical Gestalt psychology, which was concerned primarily with similar emphases.

Principally, but by no means exclusively, field theory as used in psychology has come to refer to the metatheory of Kurt Lewin; his system is therefore the first of the several versions described in the present chapter. The unique combination of behaviourism and Gestalt psychology achieved in the purposivism of E. C. Tolman is included as the second important specimen of field theory. The theoretically more circumscribed but increasingly influential thinking of Egon Brunswik is next described. Then we turn to an examination of some of the contributions of Roger Barker, who combines some ideas of Lewin with those of Brunswik in some unique investigations. Finally, other systematists (K.S. Lashley, J. R. Kantor, and R. H. Wheeler), whose work may be classified as falling within some kind of field-theoretical classification, are more briefly described.

## VECTOR FIELD THEORY: LEWIN'S LIFE SPACE

The contributions to psychological theory made by Kurt Lewin (1890-1947) have been among the most significant of recent decades. On the one hand, Lewin was a brilliant researcher. Even his severest critics recognise him as a most ingenious experimenter; the series of experimental studies which he directed while at the University of Berlin in the

1920s is a model of theoretical creativity and imagination combined with sound experimental methodology. On the other hand, throughout his career he remained a strong advocate of the primacy of directive theory in research, and he is best known for his development of the motivational, or vector, system of psychology, most commonly referred to as *field theory*.

Although Lewin was associated with an active center of Gestalt psychology at Berlin, he retained little identification with the orthodox group, and his systematizing went well beyond the usual confines of the school. As a matter of fact, there was no formal relationship between his theories and those of the Gestaltists. Lewin's early efforts were concerned largely with motivational problems of the individual subject, which led to an interest in problems of personality organisation; his later efforts were concerned mainly with a wide variety of problems in social psychology, including his initiation of the group-dynamics movement and his assistance in the development of *action research* (i.e., research directed at producing social changes). In between, he was peripherally concerned with problems such as the nature of learning, cultural factors in personality structure, and child development. But in all these diverse areas Lewin brought to bear on critical issues the same fundamental approach: an emphasis always upon the psychological, rather than the simple environmental, factors in the situation (or field). This emphasis is comparable to the earlier Gestalt distinction, most explicitly made by Koffka, between the "behavioural" and the "geographical" environment. The crux of the distinction is that the effective meaning of the environmental conditions depends upon more than merely physical attributes; that is, a description in terms of such factors alone is inadequate. It is the individual's *perception* of the physical attributes which determines how he will react.

**Lewin 's Career**

Kurt Lewin was born in Prussia and received his higher education at the Universities of Freiburg, Munich, and Berlin (Ph.D., 1914). He was thus present during the early, formative years of the Gestalt movement. After a five-year interlude of military service, he returned to Berlin and remained in various academic capacities until 1932, when he came to the United States. He spent that year as visiting professor at Stanford and the following two years at Cornell. The decision to establish permanent residence in this country was made as a consequence of the rise of Nazi power in Germany, where his Jewish ancestry became a handicap. Lewin went to the child Welfare Station of the State University of Iowa as professor of child psychology in 1935 and finally to Massachusetts Institute of Technology in 1944. In this last appointment he was director of the Research Center for Group Dynamics, a movement which he had only fairly well started at the time of his death in 1947.

Lewin's major publications were in the form of journal reports and contributions to various collections of papers. His own papers have been collected in four small volumes. The first two of these, *A dynamic theory of personality* (1935) and *Principles of topological psychology* (1936), represent the earlier European phase of his career; the last two collections, *Resolving social conflicts* (1948) and *Field theory in social science* (1951), relate to the later American phase.

## Topology and Hodological Space

Lewin selected topology, a relatively new geometry, as providing a mathematical model upon which he could base his conceptual representation of psychological processes. In brief, topology is a geometry where spatial relationships are represented in a strictly nonmetrical manner. Positional relationships between areas or legions are maintained in spite of various kinds of changes in size and shape. The primary concern is with the connections between bounded regions and with their spatial relationships; for example, one area will remain inside another throughout a wide variety of stretchings and distortions. (See Brown, 1936, for a relatively simplified introduction to Lewin's use of the topological geometry.) Lewin felt that such positional relationships were the best way to conceptualise the structure of psychological relationships. There was, however, one serious limitation to topology: its lack of directional concepts. To represent the psychological concept of direction, Lewin then invented a new qualitative geometry (1938), which he named *hodological space* (from the Greek *hodos,* translated as "path"). He developed the characteristics of such a space that he felt were necessary for an adequate representation of the dynamic factors, usually called *vectors,* in psychological relationships.

Cartwright (1959, pp. 61-65) reports that recent researchers have substituted a new mathematical tool, the linear graph, for Lewin's topology plus hodology. On the planar maps which Lewin usually used to represent his life spaces, no more than four regions can have mutual boundaries. This limits the complexity of structure which can be represented on a two-dimensional, planar map. On a linear graph, an indefinite number of points (which replace regions in the life space) can be mutually interconnected. The linear graph also allows for the representation of asymmetrical relationships, as when movement can occur from region A to region B, but not back. There is no natural way to represent these asymmetries on the map.

## Life Space

Lewin's objective in adapting and even inventing such geometries was to clarify his conceptualisation of the psychological field, or *life space.* The life space is most simply

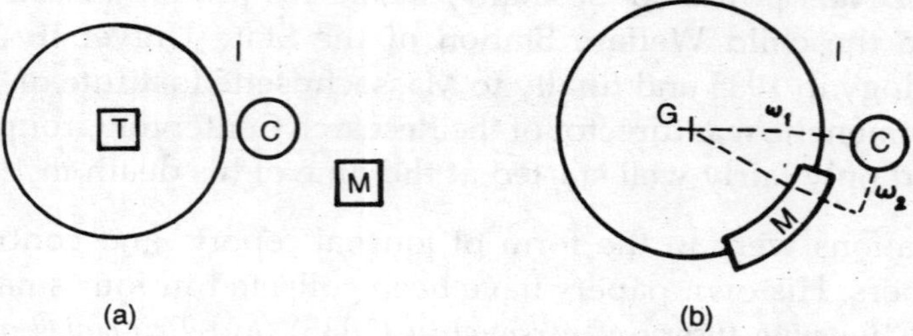


**Fig. 16.1.** Situation in which a young child wishes to reach a toy which lies inside a circular barrier. (a) Physical situation; (b) psychological situation. C, child; T, toy; I, barrier; M, mother; G, goal; $w_1$, $w_2$, paths. (From Lewin, 1936, p. 147).

defined as the totality of effective *psychological* factors for a given person at some particular time. It consists of a number of differentiated *regions,* which represent significant conditions in the person's life. Although the totality of factors is emphasised in definitions such as the above, in actual practice only the most relevant ones are ordinarily included in diagrammatic presentations of the life-space concept.

Let us illustrate Lewin's distinction between physical and psychological representations by a relatively simple example from his writing. Figure 16.1a shows the physical situation, and Figure 16.1b shows the psychological representation, where a goal object (toy) is placed out of reach within a circular area Direct physical approach to the goal via path $w_1$ is not possible, but psychological locomotion, via path $w_2$, is effective if mother can be persuaded to obtain the toy. Although the example pictured involves a physical barrier, the same psychological situation might obtain with a barrier produced by verbal restriction involving the toy, especially for an older child. Or, in somewhat similar situations, the barrier might consist of more strictly personal or intraorganismic factors such as politeness in a child trained not to take things without asking or timidity or even fear in some other child. In these cases the physical picture would show no barrier, but the psychological representation, for this slice of the life space, might look very much like that shown in the figure.

A somewhat more comprehensive example of a typical life space is shown in Figure 16.2. Here Lewin depicted a series of locomotions involving a particular occupational choice for a young man. Lewin (1936) pointed out that the passing of the college entrance examinations, while not a physical locomotion, represents a "real change of position in the quasi-social... life.... Many things are now within his reach which were not before" (p. 48). It is this kind of crossing from one region to another that is emphasised in the life-space schema.

Important dimensions of the life space, as lewin conceptualised it, are its temporal and reality characteristics. As the child grows older, not only does his life space become increasingly differentiated into regions as a function of his maturity and expanding personal problems, but it also develops temporal and reality-irreality dimensions. For example, the child begins to plan for the future as well as to respond more effectively in longer time units. Further, he begins to use imagery and fantasy and thus to live, in some degree, on an irreality level; there he is less restricted in his behaviour by the usual barriers of the real world.

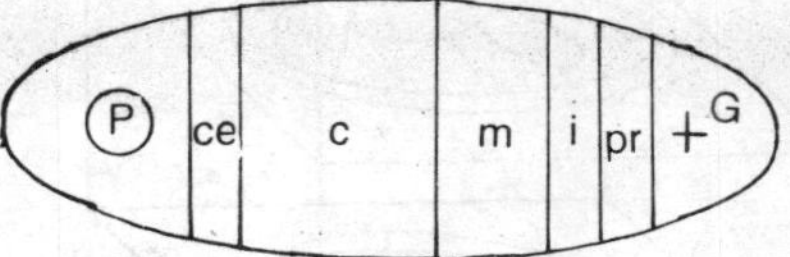


**Fig. 16.2.** Situation of a boy who wants to become a physician. P, person; G, goal; ce, college entrance examinations; c, college; m, medical school; i, internship; pr, establishing a practice. (From Lewin, 1936, p. 48)

The reality dimension is illustrated in Figure 16.3, in which Lewin showed three levels of this variable in the life space.

This dimension Lewin considered a prime significance in a psychological analysis, and so it was given considerable attention in his work. Lewin did not believe that an absolute reality or irreality dimension was tenable because of the continually changing field of experiences; that is, what at one instance may be considered absolute reality may be altered by new events and experiences. Furthermore, as the individual matures, the reality-irreality dimension broadens and becomes more differentiated (1936, p. 204).

Perhaps the most widely known Lewinian contribution within the life-space framework is his conceptualisation of conflict. He stated that there are three basic types of conflicts producing frustration: approach-approach, approach-avoidance, and avoidance-avoidance. Approach-approach conflict occurs when an individual desires to achieve two goals, only one of which is obtainable (e.g.,' one has two invitations for the same evening). Approach-avoidance conflict is characterised by a goal which is both desired and undesired (e.g., one desires the money but not the effort entailed in a proffered job). An avoidance-avoidance conflict is present when anticipated consequences are both undesirable (e.g., one must accept an unwanted invitation or offend an esteemed friend). This type of conflict is characterised by a vacillation between the alternatives or by an attempt to escape the situation ("leave the field").

**Lewin's System**

It is impossible to describe any single integrated system constructed by Lewin . This is mainly because Lewin never attempted to produce such an integrated system; when not concerned with methodological problems in field theory, he worked on a variety of different problems. All of them involved somewhat the same general type of working assumptions and procedures and to a great extent the same constructs. However, no serious attempt was made by Lewin to coordinate these concepts into one systematic framework (cf. Cartwright, 1959).

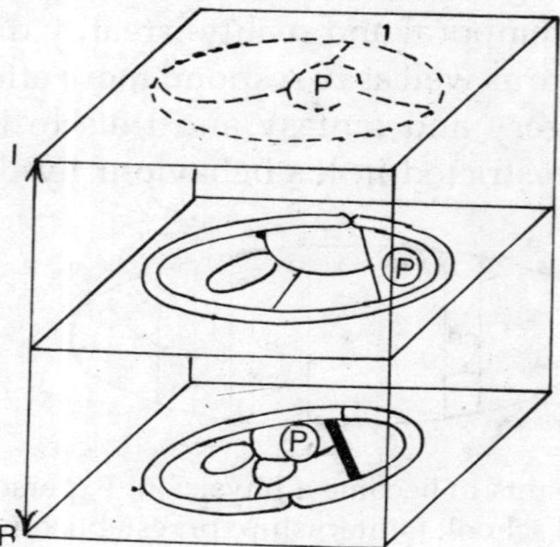


**Fig. 16.3.** Representation of different degrees of reality by an additional dimension of the life space. R, more real level; I, more real level; P, person. In a level of greater reality the barriers are stronger, and the person P is more dearly separated from his environment. (From Lewin, 1936, p. 200.)

The coordinated series of researches involving Lewin's assumption of the *tension system* has been selected as the best example of his work; in some respects it comes close to being an integrated system. A continuing series of experimental studies, some of them described below, were all based upon implications of this central concept. Lewin himself has provided a theoretical account of these researches, emphasizing the formal assumptions and derivations (Lewin, 1940, pp. 13-28; 1944, pp. 4-20). Our treatment follows this account as well as the more informal description given by Deutsch (1954, pp. 199ff.).

The background for Lewin's development of the construct of the tension system goes back to his first psychological research (1917). He was interested in refining sore of Ach's (1910) earlier research on the strength of the will. The general procedure here was to establish associations of nonsense syllables through repeated pairings and then to evaluate the strength of the voluntary factor, manipulated by instructions, by opposing it to the habitual tendency. (See Hilgard, 1956, pp. 258ff., for a description of this research and the theoretical rationales.) Lewin finally rejected Ach's attempt to supplement the association factor with such new constructs as set and determining tendency, in the tradition of the Wurzburg school, to which Ach belonged. He felt that Ach had not gone far enough in his interpretation. Rather than accept both association and voluntary factors, Lewin concluded that the best conceptualisation was to assume that there are simply two voluntary factors. He pointed out that association per se provided no motive power. As he later put it (1940, p. 14):

> Dynamically, an "association" is something like a link in a chain, i.e., a pattern of restraining forces without intrinsic tendency to create a change. This property of a need or quasi-need can be represented by coordinating it to a "system in tension." By taking this construct seriously and using certain operational definitions, particularly by correlating the "release of tension" to a "satisfaction of the need" (or "reaching of the goal") and the "setting up of tension" to an "intention" or to a "need in a state of hunger," a great many testable conclusions were made possible.

The first formal effort to test the tension-system proposition thus developed by Lewin was the doctoral-dissertation research done by Zeigarnik (1927) under his supervision. Her experiments were based on the assumptions that (I) tension systems would be established in a subject when he was given simple tasks to perform and (2) if such tension systems were not dissipated, as would normally occur with the completion of the tasks, their persistence would result in a greater likelihood of subsequent recall by the subject of the names of the tasks. Her results in a variety of experiments substantially confirmed this prediction, since interrupted tasks were generally better recalled by subjects than completed tasks. There has been an extensive experimental literature (cf. Alper, 1948; Deutsch, 1954) concerning this interesting phenomenon, the so-called Zeigarnik effect.

The next experimental test of the tension-system construct was performed by Ovsiankina (1928). She showed that subjects would voluntarily resume interrupted activities more often than they would return to activities that had been completed.

Following the confirmatory results of these first two studies, a large number of further experimental tests were performed. Among the better known of these are the studies of Lissner (1933) and Mahler (1933) on the role of substitute activities as effective dischargers of tension; of Hoppe (1930) and J. D. Frank (1935) on success and failure, especially as these are related to the "level of aspiration" expressed by the subject; and of Karsten (1928) on "psychical satiation," which concerns the problem of the reduction in performance of an activity as a function of the continued repetition of the activity. A summary of these and other related studies is provided by Lewin (1935, pp 239ff.). Although we do not have space here to present a further development of Lewin's contributions to research and theory via the tension-system construct, its fruitfulness is well attested by the manner in which these concepts and problems have been utilised in personality theory (cf. Deutsch, 1954).

Lewin's later concern with systematic problems of social psychology may be illustrated by his interesting, and somewhat unusual, wartime research on food habits of people (Lewin, 1943b; see also Lewin, 1951, Ch. 8). Here Lewin raised first the question of why people eat what they do. Interaction of psychological factors (e.g., cultural tradition, individual preference) and nonpsychological factors (e.g., food availability, cost) was investigated in the framework of a so-called channel theory. According to this viewpoint, most of the food that appears on the table is eventually eaten by someone or other in the family group, so that the primary question reduces to one that concerns the particular channels by which food is obtained for family use. The two major sources of food in this country during World War II were store purchases and gardening (minor channels were country buying, home baking and canning, and the like). Lewin emphasised the role of the "gatekeeper"—ordinarily the housewife—as the individual who determines for each channel how much of each foodstuff shall be procured and taken through the various stages of preparation for consumption (in the case of home gardening, of course, a larger number of steps are necessary before the final usable products are available for the table).

The psychology of the gatekeeper, as Lewin phrased it' thus became a focal point of this research. Although a large number of interesting questions were asked in the pursuit of the problem, we shall outline only one that received considerable empirical attention. That is the question of the most effective procedure for changing opinions. Here attention centered on individual versus group procedures. Lewin pointed out (1951, Ch. 10) that an a priori expectation might well be that single individuals, being "more pliable" than groups of like-minded persons, should be easier to convince. An opposite conclusion, however, is supported by the preponderance of much research (on a variety of social problems, such as alcoholism and prejudices, as well as food habits). Once the group standards themselves are changed, as by group rather than individual discussions, individual opinions are much more readily altered.

One illustrative study concerned increased consumption of fresh milk. No pressure was used in the individual or group discussions, and equal time was spent in each case. The results showed clearly that compliance by housewives with the requested change was greater following the group procedure. Similar results were found for other types of foodstuffs (such as evaporated milk and orange juice) and for quite different social problems (such as increased productivity among factory workers). A public commitment to a new course of action seems generally to produce more permanence of changed attitudes or behaviours. In some cases, the degree of change may even increase over a period of time following the experimental manipulations; when this happens there is said to be a "sleeper effect."

This research is a good example of the way in which Lewin's work combined theoretically important questions with practically significant problems and procedures. Food acceptability was of practical importance when Lewin started this research during wartime, and as the world's population increases, the problem promises to become of permanent practical significance. More generally, group processes are important to man's sense of well-being, and to his very survival. The contemporary upsurge in interest in T groups, etc., can be traced, to a very great extent, directly to the work of Lewin (see, for example, Bradford, Gibb, & Benne, 1964).

**Criticisms of Lewin**

Most of the critical objections to Lewin have been methodological ones, centering around his development and use of the field-theoretical approach.

One persistent criticism has involved Lewin's alleged misuse or misappropriation of topological concepts (London, 1944). The charge here is that Lewin has merely borrowed the terminology and certain of the gross conceptualisations from this geometry and has failed to utilise anything like the full set of fundamental topological relationships. In answer to this objection, Lewin has argued that all that can legitimately be required of a psychologist who attempts to apply a mathematical model is that he coordinate some of the conceptual relations with empirical processes (1951): "There can be no other meaning and no other proof of the applicability of these geometries to psychology than the fruitfulness' of predictions based on such coordination" (p. 22). If one accepts this modest objective as legitimate and sufficient, one can hardly argue with Lewin's appropriation and invention of geometries, at least as far as this aspect of his methodology is concerned.

Another criticism, voiced even by some who are strongly sympathetic to Lewin (Deutsch, 1954) as well as by less friendly critics, has been that he has failed to specify which of several possible interpretations he in tended for key terms, such as *person*, or key relationships, such as *person* to *life space*. A related but much more fundamental criticism (Estes, 1954b) has been that Lewin has generally failed to indicate the empirical basis of his psychological concepts, such as life space, in spite of his admirable emphasis upon the necessity for strict operational coordinating definitions among concepts.

A corollary to the above stricture is the objection that Lewin in his emphasis upon the central cognitive aspects of behaviour has tended to ignore the motor aspects. Field theorists generally, with their perceptual or cognitive orientation, have tended to undervalue the response side of the S-O-R formulation.

In a much-cited criticism, Brunswik has gone even further, holding that Lewin's "encapsulation into the central layer" means that his life space "is post-perceptual and pre-behavioural" (Brunswik, 1943). Lewin's reply to this particular comment has been that he did not think that psychology needs to study the objective physical and sociological factors which do not have implications for behaviour. However, he was willing to include the study of those objective factors which are potential determiners of the life space; this kind of study he called *psychological ecology* (Lewin, 1943a). Cartwright's paper contains a carefully detailed formulation of this problem of the "boundary zone" of the life space (1959, pp. 69ff.).

Other critical evaluations of the more technical aspects of Lewinian field theory may be found in Leeper (1943) and Cartwright (1959). Comprehensive reviews by Deutsch (1954) and Escalona (1954) cover the contributions of his work to social psychology and child psychology, respectively.

Finally, a serious objection to Lewin has been that he failed to make his general conceptual system sufficiently precise and specific so that it can be disconfirmed by experimental test. To quote Estes (1954b, p. 332):

> This informal development of coordinating definitions in use enables the theorist to give plausible accounts of concrete situations, but with no possibility of having the theory refuted by the outcome of the behavioural situation, since the correspondence between theoretical and empirical terms is adjusted in accordance with the empirical findings and is never formally incorporated into the system. Flexibility is obtained at the cost of testability?.

It is necessary to recognise the important distinction between Lewin's effective experimental-theoretical research on specific problems, emphasised in the following section, and his theoretical efforts of a systematic sort, criticised in the preceding paragraph for their lack of adequate empirical specification. In particular, the life-space schemata seem to be of very limited value in setting up experiments. They serve as pedagogic devices and perhaps provide a general stimulating effect for the experimenter. Although it is impossible to identify the sources of a man's influence with certainty, it seems likely that Lewin's tremendous contemporary influence stems less from his formal theorizing than from his informal theorizing and the associated empirical work.

## Lewin's Contributions

Lewin has few peers as a creative conceptualiser *and* an ingenious experimenter. It was largely this ability to implement his theoretical insights with concrete empirical situations that accounts for his preeminence. This ability was apparently based, at least in part, upon insightful observations of the everyday-life scene. For example, his conceptualisation of the tension system in relation to memory (cf. the Zeigarnik effect, described above) is said to have been suggested by his observation that waiters in Berlin restaurants had a remarkably accurate memory for the detailed amount of each bill-until after it was paid (G. W. Hartmann,

1935, p. 221). Similarly, in his later career, his interest in problems of social interaction, such as the role of a social minority, was at least partially stimulated by his own keen awareness of the tragedies which he observed in the real world (Deutsch, 1954).

Second, Lewin's specific contributions to psychological theory were of great scope and depth. He developed concepts and experimental techniques, such as level of aspiration, that have enjoyed widespread acceptance in the fields of personality and motivation. These contributions to personality theory have had a strong, continuing influence.

Finally, Lewin's pioneering efforts in the field of social psychology would be sufficient to guarantee him a lasting and prominent place in the history of psychology. His early research in social psychology in this country is exemplified by the pioneer studies (Lewin, 1939; Lippitt, 1940; Lippitt & White, 1943) on behaviour in social climates that were experimentally manipulated. For example, leadership techniques were experimentally varied in boys' clubs (laissez faire, democratic, autocratic), and various behaviours, such as aggression, were correlated with different social climates that resulted (Lippitt & White, 1943). These studies not only opened up an important new area of social research but also had some influence upon educational and social practices (Cartwright, 1959).

The final phase of Lewin's research, concerned mainly with group dynamics, found him taking more of an administrative and supervisory role and leaving to others the detailed working out of hypotheses and collection of data. In *Resolving social conflicts* (1948), Lewin reported on various experimental efforts to change social behaviour in real, everyday-life situations (such as interracial factory workshops). It is unfortunate that his relatively early death prevented further contributions to this kind of research programme.

The lines of work started by Lewin certainly did not stop with his death. He was one of those rare individuals who are in tune with the times twenty-five to fifty years after they are no longer alive. The problems connected with social influence and leadership are still under active study. Field observations, which so often gave Lewin his inspiration, are fast gaining respectability as a source of psychological information (Willems & Raush, 1969). His concern, late in life, with psychological ecology must have provided part of the impetus for Barker's work resulting in a book on precisely that topic (1968). Even his attempt to find parallels between different fields, best seen in his general attitude toward field theory and his attempt to use mathematical formalism, may have, at the least, provided part of the general background for the development of general systems theory (see Buckley, 1968, for papers in this area). To say that Kurt Lewin was one of the germinal figures for modem psychology is praise too faint.

## COGNITIVE FIELD THEORY: TOLMAN'S PURPOSIVE BEHAVIOURISM

The most important contribution of Edward C. Tolman (1886-1959) to the development of behaviourism has already been noted. The emphasis which he early placed on a *molar* interpretation of behaviour as *purposive* (1932) persisted throughout his long and illustrious career. Although Tolman cannot be said to have developed a definitive theory, his system of psychology, with its primarily cognitive, or S-S, position on learning, has been extremely influential. He has been the most acceptable of the major avowed behaviourists to nonbehaviouristically oriented psychologists. His system represents the seemingly paradoxical combination of important elements of behaviourism and Gestalt psychology. His primary orientation has been stimulus-entered, or cognitive, rather than S-R; in his later papers especially (e.g., 1949a) he has not only professed a deep-seated admiration for the field-theoretical views of Kurt Lewin but also adopted an essentially Lewinian position with regard to fundamental theoretical problems. For these reasons Tolman is treated here as a kind of field theorist.

**Tolman's Career**

Edward Tolman was born in Massachusetts and took an engineering degree at the Massachusetts Institute of Technology. He switched to psychology and received his M.A. in 1912 and his Ph.D. in 1915 from Harvard. He served as an instructor in psychology at Northwestern University from 1915 to 1918. Tolman then moved to the University of California, where he established a rat laboratory. During World War II he served for two years (1944 and 1945) in the Office of Strategic Services. In' 1950, at the age of sixty-four, Tolman demonstrated his patriotism in a different way by leading the fight against the state loyalty oath. During the next three years while the issue was being resolved, Tolman held appointments at the 'University of Chicago and at Harvard. His humanness, which made him beloved by his students, shows through even in the conclusion to his final published statement (1959, p. 152):

> I have liked to think about psychology in ways that have proved congenial to me. Since all the sciences, and especially psychology, are still immersed in such tremendous realms of the uncertain and the unknown, the best that any individual scientist, especially any psychologist, can do seems to be to follow his own gleam and his own bent, however inadequate they may be. In fact, I suppose that actually this is what we all do. In the end, the only sure criterion is to have fun. And I have had fun.

Tolman the man was thus something of a maverick and a dissenter. We shall see, too, that the system produced by this man refuses to fit itself easily into the usual categories.

**Tolman's System**

The foundation of Tolman's purposive behaviourism was present in his first and major book, *Purposive* behaviour *in animals and men* (1932), in a loosely formulated manner. Until recently, little effort was expended to organise the major ideas into anything like an integrated system. Predictions about experimental outcomes were not related to one another in any logically rigorous manner. In a word, Tolman has long been considered a programmatic theorist. A detailed attempt at a more definitive formalisation of his major principles was made by MacCorquodale and Meehl (1954), and in a final work Tolman himself (1959) has endeavored to present a somewhat more organised picture of his system. We shall present here a summary of certain of his most salient principles.

The primary principle in Tolman's systematic thinking about behaviour is that in its purposive or adaptive activities, the organism utilises environmental objects and develops *means-end readinesses* with regard to them and their role in relation to his behaviour. This phrase is but one of many awkwardly compounded terms which Tolman coined early in his career and used consistently in his writing; this one is particularly emphasised in his "Principles of purposive behaviour" (1959). The term is roughly synonymous with *cognitions* or *expectancies*. It refers to the kind of learning which Tolman felt was central to behaviour-sign learning. Briefly put, the organism learns "what leads to what." Like the Gestalt theorists, Tolman felt that the actual behaviour is relatively unimportant; the primary determiners of action are central, not peripheral, as the typical S-R theorist would hold.

A more formal structure in Tolman's system was developed in his final comprehensive statement (1959). There he presented a systematic schema for each of five representative situations: simple approach to food, simple escape from electric shock, simple avoidance of electric shock, choice-point learning, and latent learning.

Without going into a detailed explication of these paradigms and the notation system used by Tolman, we may note several salient considerations suggested by the scheme. First; a somewhat superficial similarity to the Hullian system is evident. To some extent this logical interrelating of concepts was induced by the form of presentation requested by the editor of the book for which this particular paper was prepared; to some extent, perhaps, this kind of formalisation was encouraged by the earlier effort of MacCorquodale and Meehl to put Tolman's thinking into Hullian form. In any case, it should also be mentioned, in fairness, that a somewhat comparable, though much simpler, tabular arrangement was early used by Tolman (e.g., 1936, 1938).

Second, and more important, Tolman's final formulation illustrates the centre role played in his theory by the cognitive constructs. Here a little explanatory detail is in order. Two major cognitive constructs are involved. The means-end readiness is a relatively pure acquired cognitive disposition—pure in the sense that it endures independently of the present motivational state of the organism; that is, he may know where food is whether or not he is hungry. The expectation, on the other hand, is the concrete product of the means-end readiness—a cognitive event that applies directly and specifically to the present situation. Tolman summed up the two concepts (1959, pp. 113-114):

> A means-end readiness, as I conceive it, is a condition in the organism, which is equivalent to what in ordinary parlance we call a "belief" (a readiness or disposition) to the effect that an instance of this *sort* of stimulus situation, if reacted to by an instance of this *sort* of response, will lead to an instance of that *sort* of further stimulus situation, or else, that an instance of this *sort* of stimulus situation will simply by itself be accompanied, or followed, by an instance of that *sort* of stimulus situation. Further, I assume that the different readinesses or beliefs (dispositions) are stored up together (in the nervous system). When they are concretely activated in the form of expectancies they tend to interact and/or consolidate with one another. And I would also assert

> that "thinking" as we know it in human beings, is in essence no more than an activated interplay among expectancies resulting from such previously acquired readinesses which result in new expectancies and resultant new means-end readinesses.

Tolman conceded the weakness of this formulation in terms of specific empirical measures. He recognised the difficulty of implementing such constructs operationally, but at the same time repeatedly pointed to what he saw as a comparable weakness in the Hull-Spence $r_g - s_g$ construct.

Although the concept of cognition, however phrased, is the key one in Tolman's system, he considered other types of concepts and other kinds of learning. In his effort (1949b) to cover the major types of learning processes, he pointed to the following six "types of connections": *cathexes,* which represent the affective properties acquired by objects (similar to Lewin's *valence); equivalence beliefs,* which are the cognitive representations of subgoals, secondary reinforcers, or impending disturbances; *field expectancies* (earlier called *sign-Gestalt-expectations),* which are representations of the environment that make possible latent learning, shortcuts, etc.; *field-cognition modes,* which are the higher-order functions that produce field expectancies through perceptual, memorial, or inferential processes; *dive discriminations,* which are the demonstrated abilities of animals to behave differentially under different deprivation conditions; and *motor patterns,* which are the responses and combinations of responses (skills) themselves.

Tolman made only the sketchiest effort to indicate the kinds of laws, or empirical relationships between variables, that might relate to these various kinds of learning. No laws were seriously suggested, for example, for the important field-cognition modes or for drive discriminations. A simple contiguity principle, following Guthrie, was accepted for motor patterns. Hullian need reduction was considered to be at least partially responsible for cathexes and equivalence beliefs. And no definitive interpretations were offered for the key concept of field expectancies, although the reinforcement principle here was specifically denied more than an incidental role.

Tolman's (1951b) model contained three major constructs: the *need system,* closely related to orthodox drive notions; the behaviour *space,* closely related to Lewin's life space, described earlier in this chapter; and the *belief-value matrix,* which consists of hierarchies of learned expectations concerning environmental objects and their roles in relation to behaviour.

These brief sketches of Tolman's approach should indicate the essentially tentative and preliminary nature of his system. He seldom felt certain enough of his ground to suggest lawful relationships, or even logical relationships, between the variables of his system. Tolman was himself acutely aware of the questionable status of some aspects of his system (1959): ". . .I think the days of such grandiose, all-covering systems in psychology as mine attempted to be are, at least for the present, pretty much passe... I have an inveterate tendency to make my ideas too complicated and too high-flown so that they become less and less susceptible to empirical test" (pp. 93-94).

Tolman did not produce the kind of system he did because of his metatheoretical principles or his methodological ignorance, but because he was the kind of person he was. In his early works (1936, 1938), he had specified in some detail the particular variables which he felt were significant ones in behaviour and had indicated the kind of "standard" experimental situation in which their values might be determined. He was also early concerned with a prototype of experimental design intended to identify the functional interrelationships of independent, intervening, and dependent variables. Thus Tolman espoused a strict empirical methodology designed to uncover lawful relationships between variables, but he never carried his beliefs over into practice. The amount of tedium involved may well make such a programme impractical for anyone to carry out, and certainly it was not Tolman's kind of fun.

## Tolman's Experimentation

The kind of experimental research performed by Tolman is well illustrated by an early study on insight learning in the rat (Tolman & Honzik, 1930). An elevated maze with three alternative paths to the goal box was used, as shown in Figure 16.4. The three paths varied in length. In preliminary training path I, the shortest, was blocked, and the animals then learned to use the next shortest, path 2. It will be noted that paths I and 2 share the final part of the direct runway to the goal box. During training trials the block had been placed close to the starting place, well before the common segment of paths 1 and 2. For the test trials the block was moved to position B, toward the end of the common segment and close to the goal box. According to the insight prediction the animal would now turn to path 3, rather than to previously preferred path 2, since this was also blocked. A noninsight type of simple S-R

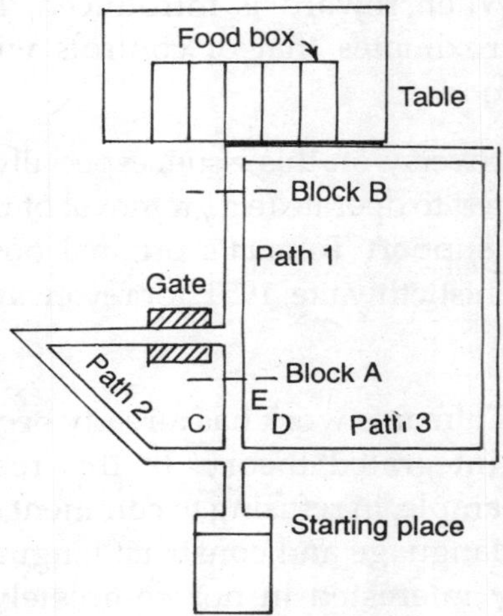


**Fig. 16.4.** Maze Used to test insight in rats. The paths become established as a hierarchy according to length, path 1 preferred to path 2, and path 2 Preferred to path 3 if path I is closed by block A, the rats run by path 2. If path I is closed by block '3, the rats run by path 3 if they have insight that the barrier closes path 2 as well as path I (From Tolman & Honzik,. 1930, p. 223.)

view would presumably predict the mechanical running off of the next strongest response in the hierarchy established in training, that of running down path 2. Most of the animals arrested in the study chose path 3, thus supporting Tolman's cognitive or expectancy position.

This experiment has been followed by several replications and modifications —not all of which have given clearly confirmatory results (cf. Hilgard, 1956, p. 195). It nevertheless stands as an important early research which not only supported Tolman's general cognitive theory but also served to stimulate further, more analytic researches. In these respects it is representative of much of Tolman's experimentation.

Even more characteristic of Tolman's research is the latent-learning experiment, originated by Blodgett (1929) in the California laboratory. The fundamental problem here is whether reward (or reinforcement) is essential for learning to occur. As a cognitive theorist, defining learning in terms of perceptual rather than response factors, Tolman insisted that learning will occur in the absence of reward but simply will not be demonstrated until the appropriate motivational conditions obtain.

In a typical latent-learning experiment, designed to test Tolman's cognitive position, a hungry animal is permitted access to a learning device, such as a maze, without being rewarded by food in the goal box. After a certain number of such trials, on which numerous errors are made and limited overt learning evidenced, the animal finds food in the goal box for the first time. The subsequent test trials generally show a remarkably improved performance, indicating that the animal had been learning something about the maze on the earlier trials but had not been motivated to perform appropriately (i.e., to take the true path to the goal box and avoid the blind alleys). When reward is introduced, the performance of such experimental animals quickly approximates that of controls which have had the same number of trials, all reinforced by food.

Although there is still some controversy on this issue, especially about the various subtle sources of reinforcement now suspected to operate (e.g., removal of the animal from the maze), the majority of the results seem to support Tolman's original position. (See Kimble, 1961; MacCorquodale & Meehl, 1951; and Thistlethwaite, 1951, for reviews of the pertinent literature.)

### Criticisms of Tolman

The most persistent criticism of Tolman's work has already been indicated: his failure to develop anything like a logically integrated theory. In this respect certain of his own comments may be instructive. For example, in refusing to comment on a requested distinction between his use of immediate data language and construct language, Tolman noted (1959) that "I myself can neither get very interested in nor completely understand such more refined logical distinctions" (p. 149). Apparently his lack of interest in problems of logical relationships at least partly accounts for the programmaticity of his systematizing.

One particular and important criticism which Tolman has shared with Lewin is that he has paid insufficient attention to the problem of relating overt behaviour to cognition and similar central states. Guthrie, for instance, has commented (1935) that Tolman leaves the rat "buried in thought" (p. 172). This weakness in Tolman's system may be seen as part of the overall inadequacy of specification, discussed above.

Finally, as a representative of a kind of commonsense approach to behaviour, Tolman has come in for a variety of criticisms from the more tough-minded type of psychologist. An obvious point of attack has involved his alleged mentalism largely as a result of the kind of language Tolman has used and the centralist nature of his constructs. In answer to such attacks, he has stoutly and persistently defended his basic behaviourism. Even the more Sympathetic of Tolman' critics, however, have entertained some doubt on this score Thus MacCorquodale and Meehl have noted (1954) "a certain affinity for the dualistic" even while not meaning "even to suggest that he is anything else [than a behaviourist] consciously or unconsciously" p. 185). In considering this criticism Tolman had at least a partial explanation, if not justification, to offer in terms of his initial exposure to objectivism. He has stated (1959) that "...although I was sold on objectivism and behaviourism as *the* method in psychology, the only categorizing rubrics which I had at hand were mentalistic ones. So when I began to try to develop a behaviouristic System of my own, what I really was doing was trying to rewrite a commonsense mentalistic psychology... in operational behaviouristic terms" (p. 94).

**Tolman's Contributions**

In spite of the undeniable programmaticity of his systematizing, Tolman has had a great influence upon the course of psychology over the past four decades. We shall describe several general forms of this influence and then mention some more specific contributions.

Tolman's role in leavening the behaviouristic loaf in its early, formative period was a most significant one. Although his emphasis on a molar point of view and an acceptance of purposiveness was never quite accepted by some behaviourists, nevertheless this kind of interpretation served to make the system more readily under. standable and acceptable to many others. Tolman thus saved for the consideration of the science of psychology concepts which might otherwise have been discarded completely because they were not easy to define operationally. The verdict of history has clearly favoured Tolman, particularly in the case of "purpose"; the science of cybernetics has objectified and precisely defined what it is for a machine to have a purpose, so that there are few left in or out of psychology who would now maintain that the concept cannot be objectified.

The influence of his cognitive learning system has also been very great. For two decades Tolman's cognitive position offered the major alternative to the Hullian need-reduction theory. As a matter of fact, much of the learning experimentation and literature was directly concerned with one attempt or another to pit cognitive theory against reinforcement theory. Thus in reviewing the learning literature for the first issue of the *Annual Review of Psychology*, Melton (1950) could say that "...these past twenty years of experimental-theoretical development have been increasingly under the influence of the opposed theoretical systems of Tolman and Hull" (p. 9).

A different kind of general influence may be noted in Tolman's long-standing support of the rat as a laboratory animal and appropriate subject for even the field-theoretical and centralist thinking which he espoused. Such use of this favoured laboratory animal by Tolman was undoubtedly responsible for a large amount of the acceptance generally accorded "rat psychology" in spite of the strong opposition of many psychologists. His position on this issue was very clearly and forcefully stated in his delightful (1945) essay. Here Tolman, always humorous and self-effacing, is at his best. The concluding sentences are especially noteworthy (1945, p. 166):

> What, by way of summary, can we now say as to the contributions of us rodent psychologist to human behaviour? What is it that we rat runners still have to contribute to the understanding of the deeds and the misdeeds, the absurdities and the tragedies of our friend, and our enemy—*homo sapiens?* The answer is that, whereas man's successes, persistences, and socially unacceptable divagations—that is, his intelligences, his motivations, and his instabilities—are all ultimately shaped and materialised by specific cultures, it is still true that most of the formal underlying laws of intelligence, motivation, and instability can still be studied in rats as well as, and more easily than, in men.
>
> And, as a final peroration, let it be noted that rats live in cages; they do not go on binges the night before one has planned an experiment; they do not kill each other off in wars; they do not invent engines of destruction, and, if they did, they would not be so inept about controlling such engines; they do not go in for either class conflicts or race conflicts; they avoid politics, economics, and papers in psychology. They are marvelous, pure, and delightful. And, as soon as I possibly can, I am going to climb back again out on that good old phylogenetic limb and sit there, this time right side up and unashamed, wiggling my whiskers at all the silly, yet at the same time far too complicated, specimens of *homo sapiens,* whom I shall see strutting and fighting and messing things up, down there on the ground below me.

Of many particular contributions that Tolman made, two early ones need to be mentioned. One is his invention (1936) of the intervening-variable paradigm, later adopted and much more thoroughly implemented by Hull (see Chapter 10). An intervening variable is an intraorganismic function (e.g., hunger) that is postulated to account for a particular kind of behaviour (e.g., eating) in a certain stimulus situation (e.g., presentation of food object after one day of food deprivation). Although Tolman apparently intended a purely abstractive usage of the intervening variable, he eventually renounced such a usage for the less operationally valid "hypothetical construct" (cf. Marx, 1963, Chs. 1, 5). He later stated (1959): "My intervening variables are generally speaking mere temporarily believed-in, inductive, more or less qualitative generalisations which categorise and sum up for me various empirically found relationships" (p. 97). He further observed (1959) that they are not "primarily neurophysiological . . but are derived rather from intuition, common experience, a little sophomoric neurology, and my own phenomenology" (pp. 98ff.).

Tolman is generally credited with having made the first effective distinction in the psychological literature between learning and performance. He early pointed out that learning alone is not sufficient to produce the learned behaviour, that the motivational conditions must also be appropriate. The distinction between learning and performance has been a most important one in the development of learning theory and research. Tolman credited Blodgett, who performed the first latent-learning experiment, for having forced this distinction on him and also noted (1959, p. 149) that Lashley had anticipated him.

Finally, Tolman must be credited with having played a in major role in the opening up of many significant areas of research. Of these, the most important are probably the latent-leaming problem, which deals with the necessity of the reinforcement principle in learning; the transposition problem, which Concerns the dependence of learning upon relative as contrasted with absolute cues; and the continuity-noncontinuity issue, which involves the question of whether each single reinforcement or non-reinforcement has an effect in learning (the continuity position). Each of these problem areas relates directly to the theoretical opposition between Hull and Tolman. While the large-scale systematic issues posed by these two views are no longer of prime concern to learning theorists, many of the particular problem areas developed in the theoretical controversy not only have produced much valuable research but also are still themselves of first importance in learning research. In this way Tolman, like Hull, has had a great and continuing influence on experimental-theoretical psychology.

## FIELD THEORY OF ACHIEVEMENT : BRUNSWIK'S PROBABILISTIC FUNCTIONALISM

The probabilistic functionalism developed and propounded by Egon Brunswik (1903-1955) is difficult to categorise within the simplified theoretical framework which we have utilised for expository purposes in the present volume. Certainly Brunswik was not an S-R theorist, although under the influence of Tolman and others' he very definitely moved in the direction of behaviourism after he came to this country. It is equally certain that he was in no obvious way a field theorist of the sort that Lewin represented. Although his research on the perceptual constancies was often related to orthodox Gestalt psychology, Brunswik himself (1949, p. 57) explicitly denied any such historical or conceptual relationship.

We have categorised Brunswik as a field theorist primarily because he so persistently and successfully considered the totality of interacting factors in his attempt to establish a meaningful systematic framework within which to evaluate psychological systems and behavioural problems. In this respect he outdid even Lewin, especially with his explicit emphasis upon distal, as compared with proximal, antecedent and consequent conditions. Furthermore, his insistence upon a representative, rather than merely a systematic, design for experimentation likewise indicates a deep concern for all the interacting factors involved in the determination of behaviour. These statements should be clearer after the reader has grasped some of the basic points that Brunswik attempted to make and to implement in his own research.

## Brunswik's Career

Egon Brunswik was born in Hungary, where he received an unusually varied education. After being trained in engineering and passing the first state examination, he shifted to the study of psychology at the University of Vienna. There he was much influenced by contacts with the 10- positivists, in the Vienna Circle. He studied psychology under Karl Buhler, taking his doctorate in 1927. In the meantime he passed the state examination for teaching mathematics and physics.

Following several years of various academic appointments, a critical turning point Brunswik's career occurred during the 1933-1934 academic year. E. C. Tolman, visiting in Vienna, met and was quite impressed with Brunswik. Two years later Brunswik received a Rockefeller Fellowship and, largely at Tolman's instigation, was invited to serve as visiting lecturer and research fellow in psychology at the Berkeley campus of the University of California. In 1937, he returned to Berkeley as assistant professor. He spent the remainder of his life there.

## Brunswik's Research

Brunswik is best known in psychology for the breadth and intensity of his research on visual constancy factors, usually referred to as *thing constancy.* This research programme was well begun in Europe and was a major factor in attracting Tolman to Brunswik. The heart of Brunswik's thing-constancy research is the dichotomy between the physical nature of an object and its sensory representation. The extent to which the perceptual effect tends to approximate the more remote physical (distal) or the more immediate sensory (proximal) value is the fundamental problem of this kind of research. For example, consider a wooden table. As a distal object', the table has a certain determinate physical length; as a proximate object, in perception, it also has a certain length, equivalent to the physical distance delimited on the appropriate receptor surface of the subject. It is the physical, or distal, dimension that remains relatively stable while a wide variety of other conditions, such as distance or angle of view, directly affect the proximal dimension.

The major finding of Brunswik's thing-constancy research was that there is almost inevitably a compromise in experience, or-more operationally in the subject's reported judgment, between the distal and the proximal dimensions. Normally the subject tends to approximate more closely the distal, or real, characteristics of the object in spite of the various distorting conditions: hence the term *thing constancy*. Appropriate instructions, however can markedly reduce the influence of the distal factor so that the proximal dimension is more closely approximated. The index of this influence (Thouless's 'regression to the real") is called the *Brunswik ratio.* This ratio is unity when constancy is perfect—that is, when perceived factors such as size, shape, and brightness are independent of distance, angle of tilt, luminous flux, etc. When the proximal (retinal) stimulus completely determines visual perception, the Brunswik ratio is zero. Thus the ratio indicates, on a scale ranging from zero to unity, the degree to which the constant aspects of the stimulus situation determine perception.

In subsequent research Brunswik extended this basic methodology to new problems of a somewhat wider interest. First, within the area of perception, he brought into his experiments such variables as monetary value. For example, in one experiment (Brunswik, 1934, pp. 147-150; see also Brunswik, 1956, p. 78) the experimenter asked subjects to make comparisons between cards containing varying numbers of coins of varying sizes and monetary value. In accordance with the basic principle repeatedly demonstrated in the simpler research, judgments of equality between stimuli were compromised to some extent by each of the three variables. Later, under the influence of Tolman and American neobehaviourism Brunswik came to concern himself with instrumental behaviour as well as perception (cf. the early collaborative paper, Tolman & Brunswik, 1935). In one important study (Brunswik, 1939b), he attacked the problem of what is now called *partial* or *intermittent reinforcement*. The all-or-one reward situation almost invariably 'used in American learning experimentation up to that time Brunswik felt to be quite unrepresentative of normal situations. Accordingly he varied the proportion of reward to total trials in the two ends of a standard T maze. The rat subjects cooperated and expressed preferences that were roughly correlated with degree of probability of reward in the two ends. This research is related, conceptually, to the earlier work in perception in that the primary concern, is again with the degree to which the subject normally achieves a kind of constancy relationship.

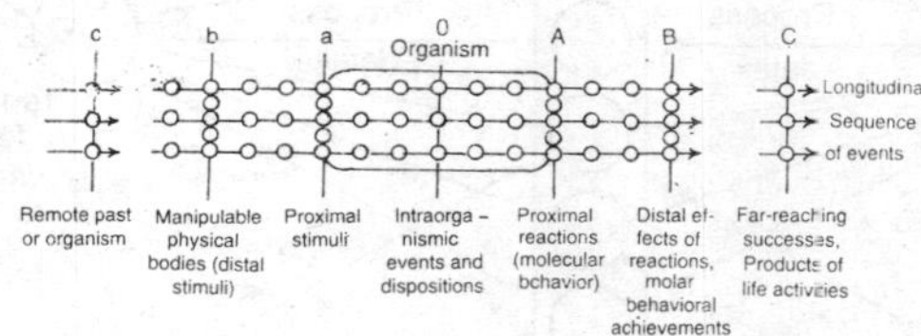


**Fig. 16.5.** Scheme of the organism in its surroundings. (From Brunswik, 1939a, p. 37.)

## Brunswik's System

The probabilistic functionalism which Brunswik came to feel most adequately systematises psychological problems was a fairly direct and logical outgrowth of the research programme outlined above. Brunswik's system is *probabilistic* since it holds that the perceptual and behavioural goals in the natural environment are related usually in an equivocal and rarely in a univocal manner to cues and responses. The system is a *functionalism* since it is concerned primarily with the degree of success, or achievement, in perception and instrumental behaviour.

An illustration of Brunswik's systematic thinking is his conceptual framework (1939a) in which a succession of temporally and spatially ordered "levels" or "layers" of variables is envisioned. These range from the temporally most remote (those furthest back in the past of the individual) through manipulable physical objects (distal stimuli) to the outer physical areas of the organism (proximal stimuli) and thence to intraorganismic functions and states; on the response side, a comparable array is conceptualised, from proximal reactions through distal effects (achievements in regard to environmental objects) to long-range successes and ultimate products of the individual's life-span. These relations are represented in Figure

16.5. Brunswik used his conceptual framework in the analysis, or characterisation, of psychological systems. For example, both structural and Gestalt psychologists, according to Brunswik's analysis of the situation, confined themselves primarily to the study of the relationships between proximal stimuli (level a in the scheme) and intraorganismic events and dispositions (level O). Classical behaviourism studied *a-A* relationships for the most part. Psychoanalysis, viewed in a simplified manner, would be described as concentrating on *e*-O relationships. The concentration of a functionalism or a molar behaviourism would tend to be on *b-B* relationships (the O level may enter into nearly any systematic position, depending on whether or not the particular investigator is interested in physiology or in introspective analysis).

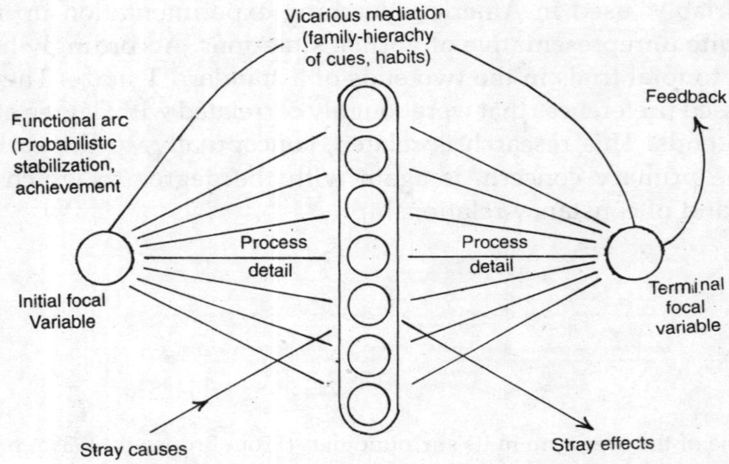


**Fig. 16.6.** The lens model: composite picture of the functional unit of behaviour. (From Brunswik, 1952. p. 20.)

Brunswik's lens model (1952), shown in Figure 16.6, illustrates the way in which a great variety of different but interacting processes can be initiated from a single focal factor (such as an object in the stimulus situation in perception research or some aspect of a learning problem in instrumental behaviour research) and also the way in which a similarly differentiated array of response processes mediated within the organism may focalise into a single perceptual or instrumental achievement. For an illustrative commonplace application of the lens model, consider the behaviour of a baseball player who is attempting to catch a high fly ball (the "initial focal variable"). A number of different perceptual cues emanate from the ball in flight-its speed, height, etc.-and must be quickly taken into account by the fielder as he estimates its trajectory and ultimate destination. Such "stray causes" as the direction and force of the wind and position of the sun may also need to be taken into account. On the response side, the fielder needs to mobilise his energies so as to time his movement toward the ball properly without interference from other stray causes such as teammates, fences, and the like. "Stray effects" would then be exemplified by collisions with other fielders, bumping into fences, etc. An ultimate instrumental achievement such as catching a difficult fly ball (the "terminal focal variable") is thus seen as dependent upon the successful coordination of a variety of process details" on both the perceptual and the response sides.

Brunswik felt that the double-convex model represents the manner in which an organism is able to mobilise its functions so as to maximise its utilisation of cues emanating from distal stimuli and achieve a reasonable amount of success in its control of the environments. He felt that problems of distal relationships need to be studied first, before problems of mediation by intraorganismic detail processes are investigated. His own research presents as good an example of this kind of experimentation as any.

Hursch, Hammond, and Hursch (1964) followed up Brunswik's suggestion that the relationships represented in the lens model could be more precisely studied by using multiple correlation methods. Their techniques make it possible to determine how well a subject can do on the basis of various ecological cues and how well he actually is using the available cues They show how their analysis can be applied to a case of probability learning and to a case of clinical inference. Although some additional experiments have used this type of analysis (for example, C. R. Peterson, Hammond, & Summers, 1965; Summers & Hammond, 1966), it is probable that the use of this particular derivation of Brunswik's thought has by no means reached its peak of popularity. With the increased respectability of naturalistic studies and the tremendous interest in ecology in general, it seems inevitable that applicable statistical techniques will be much in demand.

A major reason why Brunswik felt that problems involving particular mechanisms should wait until the fundamental achievement principles are worked out is the high degree of substitutability among such mechanisms. On the instrumental side, this may be simply illustrated by the variety of particular responses (habits) which a rat can use to depress a bar, or which a cat can use to tip a pole, and thereby open a restraining door, as in the Guthrie and Horton (1946) experiment. In these cases, the terminal-focal-effect is the same regardless of the particular mechanism used.

The same relationship of interchangeability among mechanisms may be illustrated, on the perceptual side, by the variety of cues that mediate visual depth perception (cf. Postman & Tolman, 1959, pp. 511ff.). The distal stimulus here is represented as a focal point, shown on the left in the double-convex lens model of Figure 16.6. A variety of different kinds of physical energies, represented by the diverging lines of the lens model, serve to produce the proximal distance cues (retinal disparity, accommodation, convergence, linear perspective, and the like), which are represented by circles in the center of the model. Intraorganismic mediating processes relate each proximal cue to the terminal perceptual event, in this case the distance judgment.

A number of interesting points are suggested by this kind of analysis. The *ecological validity* of cues (or habits) is defined as the degree of correlation between each such proximal condition and the value of the distal stimulus. For example, the ecological validity of retinal disparity is generally higher than that of accommodation or convergence as a cue to distance. This means simply that retinal disparity is a more effective cue, correlating more highly with physical distance. But it is not essential; other cues can substitute for it and mediate depth perception. In its normal adjustment to the flux of events in the environment the organism needs to have considerable flexibility with regard to which cues (or habits) are most often given the greatest weight. The necessarily probabilistic nature of the terminal focal events (perceptual and instrumental) is clearly indicated by this analysis. As Brunswik has put it (1955a, p. 207):

> The general pattern of the mediational strategy of the organism is predicated upon the limited ecological validity or trustworthiness of cue.... This forces a probabilistic strategy upon the organism. To improve its bet, it must accumulate and combine cues. . . . No matter how much the attainment is improved, however, distal function remains inherently probabilistic.

### Brunswik's Emphasis on Representative Design

Perhaps the most far-reaching aspect of Brunswik's conceptual formulation was his increasing emphasis on the necessity for psychology to use what he called *representative*, rather than systematic, design in its experimentation (Brunswik, 1956). This emphasis follows directly out of the probabilistic functionalism which he developed. As long as rigorous control of variables is practiced, in the orthodox systematic design used by most psychologists, there will be serious limitations on the degree to which experimental results are representative of the natural behaviour of the subject. In order to permit a more adequate analysis of the organism's achievements in relation to the environment—seen by Brunswik from his functionalistic position as the primary problem for psychology—a wider sampling of effective variables must be utilised, even if this means less rigorous control in the usual sense.

As a corollary of this position, the highly general laws aimed at in orthodox systematic research would need to be replaced by statistical statements in which only probabilistic values can be expressed. Such statistical expressions concern the probabilities with which the various conditions sampled are found to correlate with the achievements of the organism in dealing with the environment. In representative designs correlational techniques thus replace the statistical tests of differences that are usual in systematic designs.

Although the positive side of these methodological proposals seems reasonably clear, since they follow directly from Brunswik's own research programme, his criticisms of the orthodox type of systematic design may require further specification. Brunswik felt that any experiment which deals with only one variable at a time, in the classic manner, is hopelessly inadequate to present a realistic picture of the organism's behaviour. Although the recent trend toward multi-variate design was considered to be a step in the right direction, it has been nonetheless a small and seriously limited one. Furthermore, the variables ordinarily manipulated are proximal rather than distal ones, in the conceptual framework described above; from Brunswik's point of view, this places the emphasis on the wrong kind of investigation.

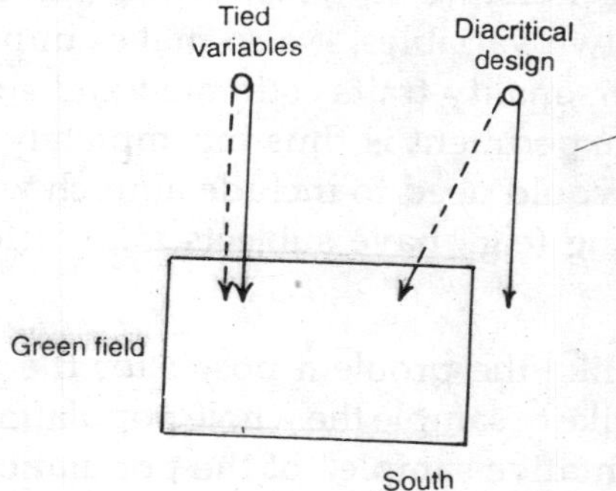


**Fig. 16.7.** Systematic design in the study of behaviour constancy. See text for explanation. (From Brunswik, 1955a, p. 194.)

Brunswik was also highly critical of the way in which variables are artificially "tied" and "untied," as well as "interlocked," in orthodox systematic design. Although a detailed specification of these problems is beyond the scope of the present book, the general point here is that a truly representative design should permit a freer kind of covariation among factors (see Postman & Tolman, 1959, pp. 516ff., for an especially clear presentation of this argument). This point may be illustrated by a relatively simple example which Brunswik (1955a, pp. 194ff.) developed on the basis of a problem earlier suggested by E. B. Holt (1915). Imagine a flock of birds flying (I) over a green field (dashed line) and (2) southward (solid line). As shown in Figure 16.7, these two variables are confounded, or tied. Merely returning the birds to point O does not resolve the confounding, nor does adding new subjects from the same population. The typical technique used to untie these two variables in systematically designed experimentation is called *diacritical* by Brunswik. It is indicated in Figure 16.7 by the movement of the birds to a new position, so that the two alternative interpretations may be clearly separated, that is, have different consequences (birds either fly to the green field and not directly south or fly south and thereby miss the green field). But, Brunswik pointed out (1955a, p. 195):

> We soon discover that southwardness is still tied to such factors as the general area of start, temperature and other climatic conditions, topographic landmarks, magnetic cues, and so forth; and so is the greenness of the field to its squareness or size. What we have accomplished in diacritical design is to separate or "split" an original encompassing cluster into two subclusters of tied variables; but we have not really "isolated" our variable as it may have seemed at first glance, and therefore are not yet entitled to speak of its attainment as a constant function.

For Brunswik the only satisfactory solution to this kind of problem would be a truly representative design in which a more adequate sampling of situational variables is possible. A partial solution would not be enough. A simple example of the inadequacy of such artificial untying of variables, in systematic design, has been provided by Brunswik (1956, p. 27). In an experiment on judgment of personality traits, subjects are placed in identical bodily positions and given identical clothes to wear. While this experimental procedure controls for the influence of these two variables, it also makes impossible the assay of any normal interaction between the personality traits estimated and such factors as body tone and dressing habits. This typical experiment is thus incompletely designed, according to Brunswik. For completeness, one would need to include a much wider range of important variables in the behaviour sampling (e.g., have subjects take different positions or wear different clothes).

The problem posed is indeed like the problem posed for the pollster asked to assess public opinion. The pollster would like to sample the whole population, but that is impractical. He therefore settles for a "representative sample" of the population. In the same way, the experimenter might like to sample all the variables, and all the interrelationships between variables, in order to arrive at psychological laws. Then he could use a systematic design, and the design would give him all the interrelationships between variables. Such a procedure is far more difficult even than sampling a complete population. Thus the experimenter, too, must take a sample, and the most useful sample to take is not one that is arbitrarily chosen, but one that characterises the variables and their values and interactions *as they occur in the actual environment*. Even if we could do a complete systematic experiment, we would not know what organisms would do until we studied the situations to which they would be exposed. Thus representative designs are necessary in principle as well as in practice.

**Brunswik's Contribution to Psychology**

Brunswik's logical analysis of design problems is almost certain to have more influence upon the future course of psychological science than is typical of such logical endeavors. Already there is evidence that his position is being implemented far outside the experimental study of perception in which it started. An outstanding example of this is K. R. Hammond's (1954, 1955) demonstration of the importance of considering representative design in clinical psychology. Research on the diagnostic use of test scores is criticised for not sampling adequately the personality characteristics of the examiners themselves and the situational variables involved in the test administration. As a matter of fact, frequently the range of examiners is severely limited, such as to a single person, for the express purpose of eliminating variability in results. Such application of the typical systematic design unfortunately has not prevented investigators from generalizing their results, at least implicitly, to a presumably wide range of examiners and situations, as well as to a population of tested individuals (the representativeness of whose selection in sampling is generally explicitly considered). Some extension of the principles of more fully representative design to other experimental and clinical situations would seem to be indicated, regardless of the extent to which one accepts Brunswik's strictures of orthodox systematic design.

Most of the criticisms of Brunswik's methodological points have centered around his apparent opposition to research on mediational mechanisms and his apparent assumption of a basic nonuniformity or nonuniversality in behavioural laws (cf. Hilgard, 1955; Postman, 1955). On the former point, Postman and Tolman (1959, p. 558) have attempted a clarification. They say that Brunswik was not so much opposed to the experimental analysis of mediational mechanisms as he was opposed to their being given priority over research on distal correlations involving perceptual and instrumental achievements. He was, of course, entitled to his opinion on this point, but, as we have pointed out before, it is difficult to say in advance which of several alternative procedures will be most effective; the safest position is simply to let each researcher follow his own inclinations on this issue, provided he is conversant with the alternatives. Brunswik's views must be admitted as among the most carefully reasoned and persuasive of those formulated by psychologists interested in general methodological problems. On the second point, Brunswik has taken pains to say that he did not think that behavioural laws are fundamentally probabilistic but only that their establishment is necessarily limited to statistical or probabilistic expression because of the limitations imposed by the great variety of interacting factors in behaviour. As he has put it (1955b): 'The crucial point is that while God may not gamble, animals and humans do, and that they cannot help but to gamble in an ecology that is of essence only partly accessible to their foresight" (p. 236).

Apart from the ultimate significance of his methodological position, Brunswik has contributed substantially to the advancement of our understanding of the perceptual constancies. Secondarily, he has helped to free research on instrumental learning from certain of its early limitations, as described above. These achievements, added to his insightful analyses of design problems, are more than sufficient to ensure a prominent place for him in the history of systematic psychology.

## MISCELLANEOUS RELATED THEORIES

### Barker's Ecological Psychology

Roger G. Barker (1903- ) received all his college degrees from Stanford University (Ph.D., 1934) When Kurt Lewin came to Stanford as a visiting professor in 1932, he and Barker began an association which led to the publication of the classic laboratory study of frustration and regression in children (Barker, Dembo, & Lewin, 1941), of which we shall have more to say later. After serving as an instructor at Harvard from 1937 to 1938, an assistant professor at the University of Illinois from 1938 to 1942, an associate professor at Stanford from 1942 to 1945, and a professor at Clark University from 1945 to 1947, Barker settled down as a professor at the University of Kansas. Barker and his colleague, Herbert F. Wright, established the Midwest Psychological Field Station in Oskaloosa, Kansas, in 1947. Barker's place in this volume is based largely on his first twenty years of work at the Midwest Station and at a station established in 1954, operated on a periodic basis, in Leyburn, Yorkshire, England. Comparisons between the findings at the two stations contribute to the fascination of the findings of Barker and his coworkers.

A cynic might claim that our inclusion of Barker as a field theorist can be based only on the rather bad pun between *field theory* and *fieldwork*, of which Barker has done a great deal. But we have already seen the meaning of *field* in physics and Its meaning in psychology are so distant that the application of the same word to theories in the two disciplines is already almost a pun. In addition, there is a distant relationship between the metatheory of field theory and the encouragement of naturalistic-field-observations. Finally, there is the historical connection between Barker and Lewin, who was the paradigmatic field theorist in psychology.

Barker's work is a natural combination and extension of the interests of Brunswik and Lewin. Brunswik's most persistent interest was in perception, where he insisted on the importance of naturalistic studies of perceptual achievements in a representative sample of ecological situations. Lewin became interested in what one might call "social ecology" when he was forced to examine the mechanisms via which food finds its way to the table, in connection with his wartime research on the manipulation of attitudes toward particular foods. Although Brunswik at times overemphasised the disordered and probabilistic nature of the environment, at other times his intuitive evaluations were prophetic of the empirical findings of Barker (Brunswik, 1956, p. 39):

Ecological generality of experimental or statistical results may thus be established along with populational generality. In fact, proper sampling of situations and problems may in the end be more important than proper sampling of subjects, considering the fact that individuals are probably on the whole much more alike than are situations among one another.

The following statement by Barker, who was *not* guessing, is very closely related (1968, p. 4):

> The environment is seen to consist of highly structured, improbable arrangements of objects and events which coerce behaviour in accordance with their own dynamic patterning. When, early in our work at the Field Station, we made long records of children's behaviour in real-life settings in accordance with a traditional person-centered approach, we found that some attributes of behaviour varied less across children within settings than across settings within the days of children. We found, in short, that we could predict some aspects of children's behaviour more adequately from knowledge of the behaviour characteristics of the drugstores, arithmetic classes, and basketball games they inhabited than from knowledge of the behaviour tendencies of particular children (Ashton, 1964; Barker & Gump, 1964; Raush et al., 1959, 1960). It was this experience that led us to look at the real-life environment in which behaviour occurs, with the methodological and theoretical consequences that are reported in this book.

One can only be grateful that Barker and his workers were led to look closely at this real-life environment in which behaviour occurs," for the results of that work have the kind of sturdy, unselfconscious beauty seen in the well-fed Hereford cows admired around Oskaloosa, Kansas. The data presented by Barker to illustrate molar units of individual behaviour exemplify the general sturdy empiricism of the approach. Five year-old Maud Pintner is in Clifford's Drugstore (1968, p. 146):

> Maud sat at the fountain waiting to order the treat her mother had promised her. On the stool next to Maud was her two-year-old brother, Fred; her mother sat beside Fred.
>
> 2:48 P.M. From her jeans pocket Maud now took an orange crayon. She brushed it across her lips as if it were a lipstick.
>
> Maud then leaned over, sliding her arms along the counter, as she watched a man serve a strawberry soda to his blond, curly-headed, three-year-old girl.
>
> Maud seemed fascinated by the procedure; she took in every detail of the situation.

From this, two molar units of behaviour, called *behaviour episodes,* were abstracted: *pretending to use lipstick* and *watching girl eat soda.* The isolation of these units, which might at first appear to be a simple task, is both difficult and of critical importance if effective fieldwork is to be done. Barker (1968) says of behaviour episodes. "Like crystals and cells that also have distinguishing attributes and limited size, ranges, behaviour episodes have as clear a position in the hierarchy of behaviour units as the former have in the hierarchies of physical and organic units" (p. 146).

Barker favours the gathering of data uncontaminated by the operation of the psychologist on the situation; the psychologist in the field can act simply as a transducer (and hence gathers T data, rather than the O data gathered by the psychologist who also operates in the situation). Barker illustrates the possible misleading conclusions that may be drawn from O data. His strictures are made doubly impressive by the fact that he uses his own classic study as the horrible example! Barker says (1968, pp. 144-145):

Experiments have provided basic information about the consequences for children of frustration, as defined and contrived in the experiments, e.g., Barker et al. (1941). But Fawl, who did *not* contrive frustration for his subjects, but studied it in transducer records of children's everyday behaviour, reported (Fawl, 1963, p. 99):

> The results. . . were surprising in two respects. First, even with a liberal interpretation of frustration fewer incidents were detected than we expected . . . Second . . . meaningful relationships could not be found between frustration . . . and consequent behaviour such as . . . regression . . . and other theoretically meaningful behavioural manifestations.
>
> In other words, frustration was rare in children's days, and when it did occur it did not have the behavioural consequences observed in the laboratory. It appears that the earlier experiments simulated frustration very well as defined and prescribed in theories, but the experiments did not simulate frustration as life prescribes it for children.

This constitutes an indirect plea for a thorough study of the ecology in which man grows and behaves, a plea which Barker has certainly not hesitated to make directly in other places. He points out that it is ironic that we know the percentage of each element to be found in the earth's crust, but do not have similar knowledge about man's *behavioural* surroundings. Barker makes his contribution to this effort by cataloging the "behaviour settings" of Oskaloosa, Kansas (the Midwest Psychological Field Station). His appendix lists 220 behaviour settings, from abstract and title company offices to X-ray laboratories. These are all public behaviour settings; one misses, for example, Maud Pintner's living room and awaits the Masters and Johnson of Oskaloosa, Kansas, to fill in the ecological picture.

In order to survey behaviour settings, Barker had first to define a behaviour setting—to discover or invent its identifying attributes. We shall list only the first three of seven attributes. First, a behaviour setting consists of one or more standing patterns of behaviour. Barker says that such patterns are clearly located in time and space, and he gives basketball games, worship services, and piano lessons as examples. Second, a behaviour setting consists of standing patterns of behaviour and milieu. That is, the setting includes the surroundings as well as the behaviour, and the surroundings may be man-made (such as buildings) or natural (such as trees). Third, the milieu is circumjacent to the behaviour—that is, the milieu surrounds the behaviour, rather than vice versa. The interested reader is invited to consult Barker (1968) for the remaining defining characteristics, as well as for the details of other aspects of his data and theory.

Finally, Barker considers the interactions between behaviour settings and the behaviours of the people who inhabit them. We might expect him to see the behaviour setting as a field, and the persons in it as particles, on the basis of an analogy with physics. Instead he borrows an almost opposite analogy from Heider and likens the behaviour setting to a "thing" and the people who inhabit it to a "medium." An example of a thing is a stone, which can be thrown into a pond, the medium. The medium, although it has characteristics of its own, is more flexible than the thing and so adapts itself to it. People in general adapt themselves to behaviour settings, partially because of the intervention of "environmental force units." But those are another part of the story, and we cannot tell it all. We shall conclude with the comment that Barker's 'work combines in a rare way the imaginative approach of the field theorist with the persistent empiricism which seems to have become connected more often with the image of the associationistic psychologist. Both his descriptive schemes and his theory of behaviour settings show great promise for stimulating further work in ecological psychology. The availability of usable descriptive categories makes Barker one of the few psychologists rich enough to throw away the following tidbits, among others, on a single page (1968, p. 41): Disturbances occur in a child's experience at a median rate of 5.4 per hour, half of the disturbances being occasioned by adults; the units of the Midwest children are shorter on the average than those of comparable "Yoredale" children; the Yoredale children receive four times as frequent devaluative input from adults as do the Midwest children.

### Lashley's Netropsychology

Karl S. Lashley (1890-1958) cannot be easily assigned to any single, simple category. He belongs in this chapter also, however, since as his career developed, he moved more and more in the direction of a kind of field theory and could be found increasingly on the Gestalt or field-theory side of particular theoretical issues.

Lashley did his graduate work at the University of Pittsburgh and Johns Hopkins University, receiving his Ph.D. in psychology in 1914 at the latter school. His major teaching appointments were at the Universities of Minnesota and Chicago and at Harvard. He then became director, in 1942, of the Yerkes laboratory of Primate Biology, the world-renowned chimpanzee-research station at Orange Park, Florida. In this capacity he retained his professorship at Harvard because the two institutions were then administratively related.

Lashley's earliest research was performed in collaboration with the biologist H. S. Jennings and the behaviourist John B. Watson at Johns Hopkins. His research interests ranged quite widely, from problems concerning the inheritance of size in paramecia to cerebral factors in migraine headaches in humans (see Beach, Hebb, Morgan, & Nissen, 1960 for these and many of his other papers). However, the problem of brain function related to behaviour was his most important and most persistent interest and the one for which he is best known.

Lashley's interest in brain function was formed early in his training, but it was only in 1917, when he became associated with the eminent neurophysiologist Franz, that he embarked upon the line of research utilizing ablation of the rat brain as a technique to determine localisation of function.

It is unfortunate that those who do not know Lashley's work well almost inevitably remember him for two vague principles with catchy names—*mass action* and *equipotentiality*. Even these names are not remembered precisely, for here is Lashley's statement of his famous principles (1929, p. 25):

> *Equipotentiality of parts.* The term "equipotentiality" I have used to designate the apparent capacity of any intact part of a functional area to carry out, with or without reduction in efficiency, the functions which are lost by destruction of the whole. This capacity varies from one area to another and with the character of the functions involved. It probably holds only for the association areas and for functions more complex than simple sensitivity or motor co-ordination.
>
> *Mass function.* I have already given evidence.... that the equipotentiality is not absolute but is subject to a law of mass action whereby the efficiency of performance of an entire complex function may be reduced in proportion to the extent of brain injury within an area whose parts are not more specialised for one component of the function than for another.

A careful reading of these principles makes any comment on their vagueness (and even some possible circularity) unnecessary. Krech (1962), in his excellent review of the problem of cortical localisation, credits Lashley with being aware of his own vagueness in stating these principles; Lashley stated the principles vaguely because the state of knowledge about brain mechanisms was 'ague!

Why, then, should Lashley be remembered? Pierre Flourens had reached similar conclusions on the basis of the results of similar ablations about one hundred years earlier. Lashley's unique contribution was that he brought far better, more analytic *behavioural* techniques into cooperation with the available physiological techniques. Lashley was not limited to the study of the effects of operations on naturally occurring behaviours; he experimentally created behaviours in mazes and discrimination problems, and he studied their retention and reacquisition after carefully planned ablations. His methodology was brilliant for his time, and his techniques excellent. He had been anticipated to some extent by his teacher, Franz, much as Isaac Newton was anticipated in the development of calculus by his teacher, Isaac Barrow; both pupils went far beyond their teachers.

There is no doubt, despite the vagueness of his statements, that Lashley strongly opposed the common belief in localisation of function. The problem is by no means settled, but the "final" decision on this problem will probably favour more localisation than Lashley believed likely. We still understand too little of the structure of behaviour to know what a unitary "function" is; until we know, it is difficult to attack the localisation problem. Lashley made a tremendous contribution to the beginning of the attack on the critical behavioural side of the question.

The extent to which Lashley was recognised by the physiologist as well as the psychologist is suggested by the tribute paid him by the neurologist Stanley Cobb, who said (Beach *et al.*, 1960) that in the early days at Hopkins, Lashley "fascinated us by the breadth of his interest and by his flair for ingenious and adventurous experimentation" (p. xvii). Cobb added (Beach et al., 1960): "During the next forty years, Lashley was to be the psychologist most frequently chosen by neurologists and psychiatrists to come to their meetings to give a paper or to discuss the papers of others" (p. xviii). He concluded by saying (Beach et al., 1960): "And so, in paying Karl Lashley our homage, we claim at least a tithe of his work for neurology!" (p. xx).

But it is, of course, not only for his neurological contributions that Lashley is honored in psychology. In a twin introduction to the memorial volume of Lashley's selected papers (Beach et al., 1960), E.G. Boring reviewed his systematic contributions to psychological theory. The field-theoretical flavor of Lashley's interpretations is illustrated in certain quotations selected by Boring. For example, Lashley wrote that "...it is the pattern and not the localisation of energy on the sense organ that determines the functional effect" (p. 492); and referring to brain action, that... all of the cells of the brain are constantly active and are participating, by a sort of algebraic summation, in every activity" (p. 500).

Leshley's field-theoretical orientation is illustrated also by his position in support of a pattern, or relational, interpretation of transposition learning rather than the S-R, or connectionistic, position. In his presidential address to the American Psychological Association in 1930, he attacked the simple connectionistic view. He later presented a novel alternative to the orthodox S-R interpretation of generalisation and discrimination learning. The [Lashley-Wade hypothesis is that differential training on several values of a stimulus dimension is necessary for generalisation to occur, denying the fundamental S-R assumption that reinforcement of a single stimulus value produces a generalisation gradient whereby similar values of the stimulus automatically gain similar but reduced potency to elicit the conditioned response. The controversy thus created has stimulated a good deal of research. Kimble (1961, pp. 369ff.) presents one review of the issue. Terrace (1966) more recently reached a conclusion which favours Lashley and Wade: "A differential reinforcement procedure is necessary for the typical generalisation gradient to emerge" (p. 339). Finally, Kalish (1969) reached something of a compromise position after a through and thoughtful review of the evidence.

Lashley made still other experimental and methodological contributions. For the former, his long series of researches on visual discrimination and the analysis of the visual cortex (see Beach et al., 1960) are perhaps the best examples; for the latter, his invention of the jumping stand, which forces an animal such as a rat to step or leap from a platform to one of two discriminable doors, is probably the most important contribution. This new experimental device enormously facilitated discrimination learning in the rat, presumably by forcing the animal to attend more directly to the relevant visual cues. Among the many subsequent users of the device, Norman R. F. Maier should be mentioned in the present context. Not only was he responsible for the most controversial utilisation of the jumping stand (1938, 1949; see also Chapter 1), but he also has been a strong supporter of the field-theoretical position (e.g., Maier & Schneirla, 1935).

In conclusion, it is fitting to quote Boring's final tribute to Lashley's scientific perspicacity (Beach et al., 1960): "The impressive thing about the papers in this volume is the way in which discovery leads speculation, not speculation discovery" (p. xvi).

### Kantor's Interbehaviourism

Jacob Robert Kantor (1888) was born in Pennsylvania and educated at the University of Chicago, receiving his Ph.D. in 1917. He was an instructor in philosophy and psychology for two years at the University of Minnesota and then for three years at the University of Chicago following his obtaining the doctoral degree. In 1920, he went to teach at Indiana University and served as professor of psychology there from 1923 until his retirement. Kantor has been a consistent and prolific writer; his bibliography includes eighty-eight items, seven of which are books, some multivolume works. Kantor's scholarship is further attested by his publication of eighty-three book reviews. In fact, Kantor probably became the grand old man of American psychology with the death of E.G. Boring in 1968. Like Boring, he has remained active even though formally retired; the second volume of his historical study, *The Scientific Evolution of Psychology,* appeared in 1969.

Kantor has been first and foremost a logical analyst and critic of the general scientific scene, with special reference to psychology. His major concern for over half a century has been, as he put it, "smoothing the path of psychology toward its goal of natural science" (1958, p. 223). Two favourite targets have been (1) "mental fictions" as represented in theoretical constructions within psychology and (2) major tenets of physiological psychology. These and related "errors" he attributed to the widespread acceptance in our culture of the dualistic heritage and the resultant failure of many scientists to look closely at their data. He has felt that the problems produced by the dualistic heritage are especially aggravated in psychology. Skinner, at least, appreciated Kantor's criticism of the surviving mentalism in psychology (1967): "Another behaviourist whose friendship I have valued is J. R. Kantor. In many discussions with him at Indiana I profited from his extraordinary scholarship. He convinced me that I had not wholly exorcised all the 'spooks' in my thinking" (p. 411).

Kantor does not have a system in the sense that Hull, or even Tolman or Lewin, had. Kantor has been above all else a metatheoretician, emphasizing a broad philosophical approach to behaviour problems rather than specific solutions to such problems. He has written on physiological psychology (1947), language (1936), logic (1945, 1950, 1953), and history (1963, 1969), but has not concentrated his efforts in any one field in a way that might have made him preeminent in a particular area. He has offered what he calls a "formal logical system" (1958, p. ix). This last-mentioned book was prepared, as he noted, in order to present his ideas more efficiently and to avoid an excess of duplication from earlier works.

The heart of Kantor's logical system is the notion of the interbehavioural field, which is an interaction between the "response functions" of the organism and the "stimulus functions" of the environment. These two basic factors must always be considered together, in Kantor's view. The properties of the interaction between organism and stimulus are built up largely in the history of the interbehavioural relation. Both biological and cultural factors need to be considered.

Except perhaps for a lessened enthusiasm for S-R psychology, Kantor's critical views have changed little throughout the course of his long career, beginning with the publication of his *Principles of psychology* in 1924. He has continued to stress the psychological field and its constantly changing interactions, and he is included in this chapter for that reason. This aspect of his views is related to Dewey's views as expressed in the famous paper on the reflex arc, and even to the Gestalt doctrine of emergence. Kantor, however, would be anxious to distinguish his views from those of the Gestalt psychologists and most other field theorists, since he saw remnants of mentalistic fictions in their views.

Kantor's stress on holism led him to criticise the doctrine of localisation of function (1947, pp. 80ff.) and to see language and logic as instances of the many products of, and participant: in, interbehavioural relation. He also saw clearly that environmental objects importantly in social relationships (1929); his views in this respect are consistent with those of Barker, whom we have just discussed.

Many papers by Kantor and by sympathetic students (on whom he has had a remarkably strong and lasting influence) can be found in the journal *Psychological Record,* which Kantor founded. There is some evidence that Kantor's influence may be increasing, despite his failure to found an active experimental school; N. W. Smith (personal communication) has found that Kantor's work was cited about twice as often in the ten-year period ending in 1966 as it had been in the preceding ten-year period. Perhaps psychology, at last, is ready to acknowledge this tough old critic.

**Wheeler's Organismic System**

Raymond Holder Wheeler (1892-1961) was born in Massachusetts and educated at Clark University (Ph.D., 1915). He then taught at the University of Oregon (1915 to 1925). The most important part of his academic career was spent at the University of Kansas (1925 to 1947), which under his influence became a kind of Gestalt oasis in the otherwise generally behaviouristic or at least functionalistic climate of the Middle West. This influence has persisted long after Wheeler's own departure from Kansas..

Wheeler developed a kind of Americanised Gestalt system. His formalisation, on a programmatic level at least, of basic Gestalt principles was of a much greater scope than the comparable efforts made by the major German proponents, whose work tended to stay closer to the original visual-perceptual demonstrations (cf. Chapter 8). Kohler had related Gestalt psychological principles to physics; Wheeler attempted to relate them to biology. His particular reference was to the rapidly developing discipline of experimental embryology, where field principles found their greatest biological utility. (See Hilgard, 1948, Ch. 9, for a simplified review of these relationships as well as a thorough description of Wheeler's system and its applicability to learning and education especially.)

The dynamic laws that Wheeler laid down for his organismic, or holistic, system were centered largely around the basic concept of the whole. They were most simply presented in his early version (Wheeler & Perkins, 1932) and were only slightly modified later (e.g., Wheeler, 1940). These principles dealt directly with the functions of wholes and may be summarised as follows: Wholes are more than the sum of their parts; wholes determine the properties and activities of their parts; wholes evolve and function (adjusting to disturbances and responding to energy transactions) as wholes; and parts emerge from wholes rather than vice versa. One additional principle involves the law of least action: Minimal energy will be expended when alternative behaviours are available to the organism.

An interesting sideline in Wheeler's career was his research and speculation concerning the manifold ways in which climate affects behaviour. In a literal sense, this application of a field approach to behavioural problems may be regarded as of the broadest possible scope. As a consequence of his historical research on the topic, Wheeler (1946) concluded that ". . . a culture pattern representing all important phases of human activity was fluctuating back and forth in rhythmic fashion as a vast, complex, but integrated whole or gestalt, each detail of which was related logically with the others in so intimate and clear a manner that, knowing one of them, the others could be predicted" (p. 81). In addition to his exhaustive historical and climatological research on the problem, Wheeler supervised laboratory investigations on the behaviour of white-rat colonies maintained under hot, cold, and normal temperature conditions. The data from these studies are interpreted as supporting his general position (Wheeler, 1946, pp. 84-85).

Although Wheeler's organismic formulations were influential for a time, that influence has within the past decade greatly declined. A major reason for this decline is probably the strongly polemic character of their presentation and the failure of effective empirical research to follow from them. Like Tolman, Wheeler presented a large number of provocative and suggestive notions without definitive theoretical statements of the sort Hull attempted; but unlike Tolman, he was not successful in translating these into equally provocative experimental designs and empirical demonstrations. As one indication of Wheeler's declining influence, one might cite Hilgard's comment (1956): "Because Wheeler's theory is no longer influential, the chapter has been dropped from this edition, despite some provocative ideas contained in the theory" (p. 225).

## SUMMARY AND CONCLUSIONS

The views of three theorists of "field" persuasion, and the work of several theorists with related attitudes, have been surveyed in this chapter. These theorists generally emphasise patterns of organisation at the expense of discrete connections. Following from this general attitude are a general tendency to study molar variables and a tendency to resort to field observations in order to get the overall view of behaviour and behaviour laws.

The field-theoretical view has a tendency to drive people away from simple cause-and-effect thinking because of the large number of potential variables in fields or wholes. Further, the insistence on completeness and a tinge of subjectivism which often accompany field theory lead to the inclusion of central, cognitive variables which are often difficult to measure. The number of possible variables and interactions between variables, plus the vague, non-operational character of some of them, tends to lose the potential experimenter in a maze of complexity and may paralyze experimental investigations. Yet the metatheoretical points made by theorists like Lewin and Brunswik are extremely persuasive.

The way out of the impasse seems to be shown by people like Kantor, who retains a general field orientation while providing a strong antidote for subjectivity and the dualism that may be associated with it. Even Skinner, who as far as we know has never been accused of being a field theorist, shows at least one attitude typical of field theorists when he attempts to let the experimental organism—rather than the experimenter—decide what the basic unit of analysis, the operant, shall be. A rapprochement with field-theoretical concerns with cognitive events is also represented by an increasing interest in the so-called S-R mediation theories. From the other side, we see people like Barker, who start from a more field-theoretical background, taking on some of the coloration of S-R theorists by making extremely careful and persistent empirical observations. Willems (1969) describes research activities in terms of a two-dimensional space, in which there is a place for the kinds of activities typical of the S-R psychologist and a place for the kinds of activities typical of the field theorist; his space forces the recognition that there is a continuity between the two kinds of activities, both of which contribute to the total scientific advance. Willems's two dimensions are degree of manipulation of antecedent conditions and degree of imposition of units. Field theorists have tended to be low on both dimensions, and S-R theorists high on both dimensions. Contemporary investigators tend to be spreading to many interesting intermediate positions, as well as occupying the old territories.

Still further rapprochement is represented by the increasing popularity of multivariate analysis, which combines the rigor typical of the S-R psychologist with the attempt to deal with complex interrelationships, which is demanded by the field theorist.

Brunswik was the field theorist most particularly insistent on the value of naturalistic, ecological study of the organism in its environment. Certainly such studies provide unique opportunities for discovering naturally occurring systems of interrelated variables, and they prevent the investigator from "wasting" time studying variables that do not have relevance to the world as it exists. However, an *exclusive* concern with naturalistic studies might prevent investigators from studying potential but nonexistent systems which could be artificially created with great benefit to mankind. As man determines more and more of his own environment, the charge of "artificiality" of psychological studies may become less and less significant.

The first of the three field theories considered was that presented by Kurt Lewin. Lewin's contributions have included a brilliant series of experimental attacks upon motivation and personality factors and the initiation of the group-dynamics movement; theoretically, however, he is best known for his conceptualisation of life space. The second field theory considered was that of E. C. Tolman, who early espoused a molar, purposive behaviourism. His experimental and conceptual innovations leavened the behaviouristic doctrine and gave cognitive psychology an experimental basis; for a time Tolman offered what seemed to be a clear contrast to Hullian, S-R doctrines. The third theory was Egon Brunswik's probabilistic functionalism, which offered alternatives to many otherwise unquestioned methodological assumption in perception and learning.

Briefer consideration was given to Barker's ecological psychology, Lashley's neurophysiological theory, Kantor's interbehaviourism, and Wheeler's organismic theory.

The major strength of field theory comes from the tact that it has unhesitatingly concerned itself with some critical problems which orthodox S-R theory has tended to avoid. These are in general problems concerning central functions (cf. Hebb, 1949; G. A. Miller, Galanter, & Pribram, 1960) rather than peripheralistic ones, the latter having been the typical concern of the S-R theorist.

At the present time, the kind of approach to behaviour problems represented by the field theorist is being increasingly supplemented by newer conceptual (e.g., the computer model of thinking) as well as experimental techniques. The major need in this kind of approach is to spell out more adequately the empirical referents for the central functions posited. To take one example from the present chapter, the concept of purpose, as conceived by Lewin and Tolman, is an obviously significant one in behaviour, but little seems to have been done to develop anything like an adequate *experimental* attack upon it. Unfortunately, the stimulating lead initiated by Lewin, particularly in his tension-system research and conceptualisation, has not as yet been fruitfully followed. When this kind of research is thoroughly developed, perhaps as a result of the amalgamation of field-theoretical and other more empirically oriented approaches, the promise implicit in the earlier field theories may well be fulfilled.

**Further Readings**

Volumes intended to illuminate cognitive, or field-theoretical, methodology are Kuenzli's *The Phenomenological Problem* (1959) and Bruner et al., *Contemporary approaches to cognition* (1957).

The best introduction to Lewin is provided by his four slender books published in English. *A Dynamic Theory of Personality* (1935) and *Principles of Topological Psychology* (1936) summarise the earlier, European phase of his career. *Resolving Social Conflicts* (1948) and *Field Theory in Social Science* (1951) are concerned with his later work in this country. His monograph, *The Conceptual Representation and Measurement of Psychological Forces* (1938), is a more elaborate but difficult exposition of his metatheoretical position. An early critique by Leeper (1943), Estes' very critical evaluation (1954b), and two more sympathetic reviews by Deutsch (1954) and by Cartwright (1959) are among the more useful of the secondary sources on Lewin and His psychology. A recent addition to the literature on Lewin is Marrow's *Practical Theorist* (1969). Tolman is well represented by his early book, *Purposive Behaviour in Animals and Men* (1932); his collected works, *Collected Papers in Psychology* (1951a) and his final systematic statement (1959). *In* addition, MacCorquodale and Meehl (1954) have provided an interesting and helpful formalisation of Tolman's system. Although there is no easy road to Brunswik's thinking, the reader may be referred to his much-cited paper, "The conceptual focus of some psychological systems" (1939a); his more difficult methodological monograph, *Perception and the representative design of psychological experiments* (1956); and his two papers (l955a, 1955b) in the symposium on probability theory. The latter, in the May, 1955, issue of *Psychological Review*, contains several other important papers on the topic and should be consulted by any interested student. Brunswik's system is also intensively treated by Postman and Tolman (1959). Barker puts his own best foot forward in his interesting and readable *Ecological Psychology* (1968). Lashley is well represented by *The Neuro-psychology of Lashley*, edited by F.A. Beach et al. (1960). Kantor's *Interbehavioural Psychology* (1958) is the best introduction to his systematic thinking. Wheeler's *Science of Psychology* (1940) is probably the most useful single source for his work.

# 17

# Varieties of Personality Theory

Personality theory is a kind of behaviour theory. We have already considered two of the most important theories of personality: psychoanalytic theory and Lewinian theory. However, classic personality theory does have some general characteristics that set it apart as a sub variety of behaviour theory. The very word *personality* tells us that, at least in the beginning, personality theory was based on the study of persons. In most personality theories, individual differences between persons are regarded as a very significant source of variance in behaviour; information about the unique characteristics of persons is therefore expected to be very useful in making predictions about behaviour.

There is great diversity of opinion and of emphasis on several issues connected with the study of the person. The first is the very basic set of opinions concerning the amount of variance which is attributed to persons, as compared with the amount attributed to situations. In the other chapter, we saw that Brunswik and Barker agreed that behaviour could be predicted to a great extent from knowledge of the situation, regardless of the person in the situation. Rogers, who emphasises the tendency of the person to develop his capacities "from within" (he calls this *self-actualisation*), probably best represents the opposite extreme—he is the greatest optimist about the extent of an individual's ability to determine his own fate. In this respect Rogers is close to the existentialists, who believe that each individual has irrevocable responsibility for his own choices. S-R theorists generally emphasise the influence of the situation, or stimulus, and show less interest in the unique characteristics of the individual person. These theorists have a related tendency toward denying the generality and permanence of "traits" of personality; for example, it would be characteristic of S-R theorists to deny that honesty is a general trait or that it is likely to be a permanent characteristic of a particular person. This is consistent with the so-called empty-organism approach, which places little reliance either on assumed physiological functions or on assumed personality structures such as traits or attitudes. In this sense, S-R theories are general behaviour theories, *not* personality theories in any restricted sense. However, we shall discuss one S-R theory below, partly to emphasise the continuity between behaviour theories and theories which are now representative of theories of personality.

Still another question concerns the extent to which personality structure whatever form it takes—is determined by nativistic factors and the extent to which it is determined by learning. The so-called self theorists are more likely to make a place in their scheme for nativistic factors than the S-R theorists, who quite naturally insist on the importance of learning. Later we shall see that there are still other questions related to the general question of the relative importance of individual differences, but, for the present, we shall turn to another set of distinguishing characteristics of personality theories.

Theories of personality attempt completeness. This may be an increasingly distinctive characteristic because theorists in other areas of psychology are *less* enamored of attempts to develop "grand theories" than they used to be. Increasingly they limit themselves to partial or hill explanations of things like one-trial framing by the method of paired associates in lists of nonsense syllables, auditory threshold effects, or some other closely circumscribed area. Not so the personality theorist. He has self-consciously chosen to explain the complex behaviour of the total human organism. To some extent this has led to discouragement and diffusion of effort on the part of the personality theorist. Adelson (1969, pp. 136-137) says in this connection:

> The impulse for synthesis, for finding unities, has for the moment been set aside. So, for example, the controversies we have—and there are surprisingly few—rarely center upon either large or substantive issues and usually involve internecine squabbling about this or that measure, method, or technique within a specific domain of research.
>
> The sprawl and diversity in personality can be seen as both a cause and a consequence of the virtual abandonment of large theoretical ambitions.

The other distinguishing characteristics of personality theory are related to its usual attempt at comprehensiveness. First, the functional nature of personality theory should be noted. Theories of personality focus upon an understanding of the development, survival, and general adjustment of the organism. Second, an emphasis on motivational ("dynamic") processes is characteristic of such theories. Third, the object of study is the whole person in his natural habitat. On this point, the study of personality clearly separates itself from the experimental tradition in psychology, which has typically advocated the study of more limited aspects of behaviour. Fourth, personality theories are characteristically integrative, whereas much of psychology has moved in the direction of more specialised explanatory attempts. Fifth, personality theories frequently have rebelled against the prevailing psychological thought of the times. Certainly Freud's psychoanalytic theory offered dissenting explanatory principles at the time of its inception. More recently, Gordon Allport has persisted in advocating the basic principles he felt necessary for an adequate theory of personality even when he seemed to stand alone. The fact that much of personality theory has developed outside the mainstream of academic psychology—frequently as a result of clinical observation—may account, in part, for its taking the highroad while the rest of psychology proceeded along the low road.

Thus we find in personality theories concern with variables typically left out of more limited theories. Psychoanalysts opened up the study of the unconscious determinants of behaviour and offered a model of the structure of personality; contains a more complete discussion of the empirical areas whose study was initiated by psychoanalysis. This personality theory and others have pointed to the need for detailed study of dynamic (motivational) variables, individual differences, heredity, biological factors, child and developmental psychology, abnormal and social psychology, and all the interrelationships between these and other fields. Every one of this formidable array of fields plays an important role in any attempt at a complete theory of personality.

Implied in the preceding discussion of the characteristics of personality theory are both its weaknesses and its strengths. The personality theorist is faced with a dilemma composed of, on the one hand, mounting needs to predict and control human behaviour and, on the other hand, a distressing scarcity of knowledge about the basic laws needed for the task. Consequently, the structure of personality theory tends to be loosely cemented for lack of sufficient cohesive material in the form of empirical observables. The major weakness of such theory, and the shortcoming at which criticism is continually leveled, is its disproportion of explanatory principles in relation to the amount of empirical data at hand. Similarly, personality theories frequently fail to distinguish clearly between that which they assume and that which is empirically testable. Consequently, the derivation of predictions and empirical hypotheses from these theories is severely hampered.

In spite of these problems, however, there has been a good amount of research in the area of personality. Adelson (1969), in the review of a year's literature which he published in 1969, says that an extremely modest estimate of the year's volume is 500 citations; he references 210 of them in his paper. Dahlstrom, in his 1970 review, refers to 366 articles from some presumably larger set. The problem is not a lack of data, but a lack of a tight relationship between the data and a general theoretical frame work. Even in this respect, one should not be altogether pessimistic; C.S. Hall and Lindzey, after examining seventeen theories of personality, conclude that twelve of them have been responsible for generating a considerable amount of research. Their comment on this finding is (1970, p. 595):

> It is reassuring that, in spite of the limitations of theories of personality as generators of research, the large majority of such theories has been accompanied by a considerable quantity of research. Whatever procedural limitations may inhere in these investigations, the fact remains that they document the interest of the theorists in examining the effectiveness of their theories in the face of empirical data. It is hard to believe that in the long run this attitude will not lead to progressive changes that will result in more effective theories.

It is, indeed, comforting to encounter optimism about the future of personality theory, for even more weaknesses exist at present than we have yet mentioned. For example, personality theory may be criticised even on the basis of its self-stated criterion-completeness—when it is noted that few theories, to date, have attempted to handle adequately all the areas considered essential to a comprehensive theory. Table 17.1, adapted from C.S. Hall and Lindzey (1970, p. 592), indicates these authors evaluation of the degree of attention paid to various factors by the theorists they review in their book. Freud, Sullivan, and Murray seem to deserve the highest "comprehensiveness" scores, and even they pay little attention to some issues.

**TABLE 17.1**

**Dimensional Comparison of Theories of Personality**

Interdisciplinary Emphasis

| | *Purpose* | *Unconscious Determinants* | *Reward* | *Contiguity* | *Learning Process* | *Formal Analysis* | *Personality Structure* | *Heredity* | *Early Development Experience* | *Continuity of Development* | *Organismic Emphasis* | *Field Emphasis* | *Uniqueness* | *Molar Units* | *Homeostatic Mechanisms* | *Psychological Environment* | *Self-Concept* | *Group Membership Determinants* | *Biology* | *Social Science* | *Multiplicity of Motives* | *Multiple Mechanisms* |
|---|---|---|---|---|---|---|---|---|---|---|---|---|---|---|---|---|---|---|---|---|---|---|
| Freud | H | H | H | M | M | M | H | H | H | H | M | L | M | M | H | H | H | M | H | H | L | H |
| Jung | H | H | M | L | L | M | H | H | M | L | H | L | M | M | H | H | H | L | H | L | M | H |
| Adler | H | M | L | L | L | M | M | H | H | H | M | H | H | M | H | M | H | H | M | H | L | L |
| Horney | H | H | M | L | M | L | M | L | M | M | M | M | M | M | H | M | H | H | L | H | L | L |
| Fromm | H | M | M | L | M | M | M | L | M | M | M | M | M | M | H | M | M | H | L | H | L | M |
| Sullivan | H | M | M | H | M | M | M | L | M | H | M | H | M | M | L | H | M | H | M | H | M | M |
| Lewin | M | L | M | L | M | H | M | L | L | L | L | H | H | L | H | H | M | H | L | M | H | M |
| Allport | H | L | L | M | M | M | H | M | L | L | H | M | H | H | H | M | H | L | H | L | H | M |
| Murray | H | H | M | L | L | M | H | M | H | H | H | H | H | M | H | H | M | M | H | H | H | H |
| Angyal | H | M | L | L | M | H | M | M | L | H | H | H | M | M | H | H | H | L | M | L | L | M |
| Goldstein | H | L | L | L | M | M | L | M | L | L | H | M | M | M | H | H | M | L | H | L | L | L |
| Sheldon | L | M | L | L | L | L | H | H | L | H | H | L | H | L | L | L | L | L | H | L | L | M |
| Cattell | M | M | M | M | M | L | H | H | M | M | L | M | M | M | L | L | H | M | M | L | H | H |
| Dollard and Miller | L | M | H | M | H | H | L | L | H | H | L | L | L | L | L | L | L | M | M | H | M | M |
| Skinner | L | L | H | M | H | H | L | M | M | H | L | L | L | L | L | L | L | L | L | L | L | L |
| Rogers | H | L | L | L | L | M | L | L | L | L | H | M | M | H | H | H | H | M | L | M | L | L |
| Binswanger and Boss | H | L | L | L | L | L | L | M | L | L | M | H | H | H | M | H | M | L | M | L | L | L |

Key: H, high (emphasised); M, moderate; L, low (deemphasised).
Source: C.S. Hall and G. Lindzey, *Theories of Personality* (2nd ed.), New York, Wiley, 1970, p. 592.

As to other limitations, we can save a great deal of time by saying that Freud's psychoanalytic theory is in many ways the most influential theory of personality and that most of the criticisms leveled against the form of, and evidence for, his theory also hold for the other theories of personality. However, this judgment will be modified somewhat as the individual theories are discussed.

And what of the positive functions of personality theory? Curiously, its strengths often derive from the same characteristics which harbor its weaknesses. Through its rebelliousness and its attempts at integration and completeness, it has drawn attention to previously neglected problem areas. Motivation, which only recently has received widespread attention from psychologists, has long been heralded by personality theorists as basic to the understanding of behaviour. In addition, personality theories have generated empirical investigation both directly and indirectly; directly, by providing a framework for research and parameters and dimensions suitable to the investigation of questions ratted by theory; indirectly, by engendering either curiosity or conviction in those who encounter the personality theorists efforts to describe the complex nature of human behaviour.

## S-R THEORIES

C.S. Hall and Lindzey (1970) list two S-R positions among their theories of personality: the theory of Dollard and Miller and that of Skinner and his followers. A look at Table 17.1 shows that Skinner pays little attention to fifteen of the twenty-two areas considered important by Hall and Lindzey and that Dollard and Miller ignore ten areas. We think this fact indicates that S-R theories are really *not* personality theories, but the hardheaded temper of our times has led many psychologists to ask whether personality theories are any more helpful to us in understanding personality than S-R theories, which can be at least partially applied to personality. The success of behaviour modifiers in working with clinical problems has lent some credence to this view and has helped to justify the inclusion of Skinner, especially, among the personality theorists. However, we have treated Skinner and his views rather fully, and his views on personality are wry dose to his views on behaviour in general. We shall therefore simply refer the leader to our earlier discussion for Skinner's "theory of personality," just as we do for Lewin, Freud, and to some extent others among the early psychoanalysts.

The work of Dollard and Miller in personality theory differs from that of Skinner in that the former authors did their work in personality as an effort somewhat distinct from what they did before and after that time. We shall therefore take them as our example of personality theorists whose theory is closest to traditional behaviour theory. They, like Skinner, have tried to develop a personality theory based on experimental data, and with a minimum of concepts added to Its basic principles of learning and behaving.

### Dollard and Miller's S-R Theory

John Dollard (1900—) and Neal Miner (1909—) began their collaboration at Yale's newly formed Institute of Human Relations in the 1930's. The institute—an innovation in cooperation among the behavioural sciences of psychology, psychiatry, sociology, and anthropology—provided an environment both receptive to psychoanalytic investigation and strongly influenced by Hull. We have already mentioned, that Hull was himself interested in exploring the relationship between his concepts and those of Freud, and he conducted a seminar on the topic in the academic year 1936-1937. Dullard and Miller conducted research at the institute and soon started a series of joint publications. The first effort (with other coauthors) was *Frustration and Aggression* (Dullard et al., 1939), in which S-R concepts were applied to the problem of frustration. Shortly thereafter Miller and Dollard (1941) published a volume on social learning that provided a basic S-R framework in which complex behaviour problems could be conceptualised. They subsequently explicated their joint theorising further in *Personality and Psychotherapy* (Dullard and Miller, 1950). Dullard remained at Yale, where he became a professor emeritus in 1969. Miner moved from Yale to Rockefeller University in 1966.

Aside from their joint theoretical effort, Dullard and Miller have contributed to different areas of psychology. Both received laboratory and clinical training. However, Dullard's work has been less centered on experimental problems than Miller's. Dullard received his Ph.D. in sociology at the University of Chicago and has taught both anthropology and sociology at Yale. Further training at the Berlin Psychoanalytic Institute crystallised his interest in psychoanalysis. Dullard has consistently dedicated himself to the unification of the social sciences and has published in the areas of anthropology and sociology (e.g., 1937). During World War II he conducted a psychological analysis of military behavior, published as *Fear in battle* (1943).

Miller took his Ph.D. at Yale and, shortly thereafter, became a Social Science Research Council traveling fellow. During his stay in Europe, he underwent training analysis at the Vienna Institute of Psychoanalysis. Miller directed psychological research for the Army Air Force during the war years and then returned to Yale. He is characteristically a careful experimentalist and theorist, having conducted numerous studies on drive acquisition, reinforcement, conflict, and, most recently, the effects of drugs and physiological variables on behaviour.

In their collaborative work Dullard and Miller have come closer to a complete theory of personality than any other S-R theorists, though Guthrie (1938) and Skinner (1953a) have generalised their findings freely to the human case. Lundin (1969) provides a full explanation of the Skinnerian approach to personality. Mowrer (1950) has also been interested in personality as well as in learning; however, none of these men have developed an integrated S-R personality theory as theory as Dullard and Miller have.

Dollard and Miller (1950; N.E. Miller, 1959) have not found the Hullian system, upon which their personality theory is ultimately based, adequate to the task without considerable interpretation. Both authors are interested in psychoanalytic theory as well as in S-R theory, and their interpretation takes the line of a reduction of many psychoanalytic concepts to S-R terms (e.g., N.E. Miller, 1948). Their aim is to combine the assets of the two systems; they need the scope of psychoanalytic theory in order to have anything like the desired coverage of dependent and independent variables. Where in Hull does one find a discussion of neurotic guilt or anxiety? At the same time, they prefer the greater precision of statement and degree of empirical confirmation found within the confines of Hullian theory. The drawing of precise parallels between theories as different as psychoanalysis and Hullian theory is always difficult, perhaps sometimes impossible. Yet Dullard and Miller have made an attempt at integration that is stimulating and worthwhile, though in their system it is possible to see the outlines of two distinct subsystems.

There are systematic similarities between psychoanalysis and Hullian theory which make a, partial amalgamation easier than might at first appear. A version of the law of effect is found in both. Freud speaks of maintaining a fixed tension level or reducing the tension level as a goal of the organism. Hull speaks of drive reduction, or a reduction in the intensity of a drive stimulus, as a condition which strengthens behaviour. Both formulations seem essentially the same on this point. There are also similarities in the attitude toward learning. Hull's basic learning construct, ${}_{S}H_{R}$, is conceived of as building up through repeated practice and staying at a high level; once ${}_{S}H_{R}$ builds up, it is not destroyed. If the behaviour which reflected ${}_{S}H_{R}$ stops, this happens because there is opposition to it by inhibitory factors or because there is no motivation left for the behaviour. This account of learning, with its assumption of the permanence of the effects of experience, is in this way much like Freud's; he also seemed to believe that early experiences leave ineradicable effects, though the effects might not be easily seen because of repression, a concept which here plays the same role as Hullian inhibition.

The heart of the Dullard-Miller account is learning, or habit formation. They point out four significant features of the learning process: drive, cue, response, and reward. They give as an example a child looking for concealed candy in a room containing bookshelves. The initial *drive* is the hunger for candy; the *cues* are the instructions for playing the game plus the stimuli from the room; varied *responses* are made until the candy is found behind a book; and the response of moving the appropriate book is reinforced by finding and eating the candy *reward*. If the game continues with the candy in the same place each time, the drive gradually decreases; the significant, discriminative cues become only those helpful in making the correct response; and the response is now made more quickly and strongly. In this way *habits are* reinforced and become the basic and enduring elements of personality.

Dollard and Miller have not borrowed only the simplest concepts from Hull's (1943) theory; they have found a use for the hierarchy of responses, secondary reinforcement, the generalisation gradient, and other more complex theoretical notions. They have also shown great ingenuity in relating complex concepts to simpler ones, thereby "explaining" what is involved. Their attempt to handle the problems of symbolic behaviour is particularly valuable.

One of the contributions which Dullard and Miller have made, then, is the integration of two originally separate—if not opposed—theories in such a way that it becomes reasonable to apply the results of laboratory investigations with animals to practical human problems. Though Hull intended his theory to have such applications, he never personally took time to show how they could be made. Two such human problems which Dullard and Miller have treated are fear and conflict.

Fear in the neurotic human being may seem an irrational thing. Dollard and Miller, however, believe that this irrationality is a matter of appearance only; we as observers of irrational human behaviour arrive upon the scene too late to observe the development of the fear, and we often do not know enough of the laws that determine the learning and spread of fear. Consider, in an analogous situation, a rat that is placed in a white box and shocked. If he is allowed to escape through a door to a black box, he will quickly learn to fear the white one. Furthermore, he will continue to respond in order to escape the white box even when there is no longer any shock present. The fear may even spread (generalise) to similar boxes. If we had not observed the learning process but only the fearful animal in a harmless white box, we should consider his fear irrational. Similarly, if we did not understand the process of generalisation, we should consider fear of a *light gray* box irrational even if we had observed the process.

Dullard and Miller have given an equally stimulating account of the nature of conflict. Their analytic approach involves at least five assumptions derived from theory or from empirical observations. They assume that (1) the tendency to approach a goal increases as the distance to the goal decreases, (2) the tendency to avoid a negative stimulus (punishment) increases as the distance to it decreases, (3) the gradient for negative stimuli is steeper than the gradient for positive stimuli, (4) changes in drive increase or decrease the *level* (not the slope) of the appropriate gradients, (5) if two responses (say, approach and avoidance) compete at any point, the one associated with the stronger tendency will occur. Empirical studies of this model have typically involved white rats, shock, food, and a spatial scale, but the model has been freely applied to quite different situations, such as bachelors contemplating marriage. Summaries of experimental research on this problem have been provided by Miller (1944, 1958b). He has also reviewed the relationship between the experimental results on conflict and the conduct of psychotherapy in a short chapter (1964) which also examines other implications of modern behaviour theory for psychotherapy. Finally, his work on the operant conditioning of autonomic responses (1969) has exciting implications for the acquisition and treatment of psychosomatic symptom, and will need to be incorporated into the conceptual schemes of all personality theories.

This short sketch should be enough to indicate that the original Contribution of Dullard and Miller shares the strengths and weaknesses of S-R theory more than it does those of psychoanalytic theory. Their approach tends more toward analysis and the application of laboratory principles to human behaviour. They take Hullian theory as the methodological model; psychoanalytic theory is used because it is based on the content, the observations, they wish to explain. Dollard and Miller seem to be molding psychoanalytic *content* into S-R *form*. Indoing so, it may be argued, they incorporate the elementaristic weakness of S-R theory. Their "personalities" become bundles of habits without the consistency and

purposefulness which most other personality theorists see as guiding human behaviour. In choosing a theory which treats learning much more thoroughly than other determinants of behaviour, Dullard and Miller take a more environmentalistic position than many theorists think is justifiable.

In spite of these criticisms, the Dullard-Miller theory seems to have earned an important place in the history of the development of personality theory. Skinner has followed them through the door they opened into the club of personality theorists as a member—not necessarily in good standing. It is now respectable to apply concepts and procedures modeled after the outcomes of laboratory experiments in clinical situations; in fact, it is scarcely respectable to do anything else. Dollard and Miller in effect claimed that anything the psychoanalyst could talk about, they could talk about; and they made the claim by example, in detail. Their case was convincing to many, especially those who preferred the language of S-R reinforcement learning theory to the language of psychoanalysis. Much of the interest in the details of the Dollard-Miller theory has probably waned, for both the component theories on which the effort was based have fallen into some disrepute. Hull's theory no longer dominates the field of learning, and Freud's is under strong attack in the field of personality. Nevertheless, Dullard and Miller deserve a tremendous amount of credit for indicating the character, the scope, and the feasibility of synthesising laboratory-derived and clinic-derived concepts in a theory of personality. *Personality and Psychotherapy* was a milestone, as yet perhaps too little appreciated, in the history of psychology.

## TRAIT AND FACTOR THEORIES

In addition to comprehensiveness, personality theories have another characteristic which generally sets them apart from other theories of behaviour: Nearly all personality theories have within them a concept which serves to explain and emphasise the *consistency* of behaviour per se. Nonpersonality theories typically predict such consistency only insofar as there is consistency of circumstances; that is, the same response should be observed only if the external stimuli are the same, if they are equivalent because experiences with each were the same, or if they are related closely enough via generalisation to produce the same response. Obviously, the *ifs* in the preceding sentence give the S-R theorist enough latitude to predict some consistency of behaviour, but most personality theorists have not been content with this. They insist that the behaviour is the same, or is consistent, because the behaving individual is the same. We pointed out at the beginning of this chapter that classic personality theorists generally maintain that much of the variance in behaviour is attributable to individual differences; the corollary to this is that much of the consistency in behaviour is attributable to *individual sameness*—that is, the same individual is behaving at different times or in different situations.

Two general classes of personality theory, not ordinarily categorised together, are alike in that they both give primary attention to the problem of consistency in behaviour, albeit in markedly different ways. These are the trait theories best exemplified by the views of G.W. Allport, and the factor theories, represented by the work of Eysenck and R.B. Cattell.

The trait theorist believes that the job of the personality theorist is to isolate and describe certain properties of the individual which underlie and determine overt behaviour, thereby giving the individual's behaviour a consistent, integrated direction. These properties are called *traits,* and the traits may be very general, influencing all or nearly all the individual's behaviour, or very specific, in which case only behaviour in certain kinds of situations is influenced by the trait.

The factor theorist derives concepts (factors) from a statistical analysis of consistency observed in test performance. Like traits, factors may be general or specific, though the nature of their derivation makes them usually less all-encompassing than a general trait.

**Allport's Trait Theory**

Gordon Willard Allport (1897-1967) was educated in a variety of fields and continued his interest in many of them. He received his A.B. at Harvard in economics, taught Sociology and English in Istanbul, returned to Harvard for his Ph.D., and subsequently studied at three European universities—Berlin, Hamburg, and Cambridge. While in Europe Allport developed his persisting interest in international affairs. As a by-product of his stay abroad, he became one of the major interpreters of German psychology in the United States.

Allport taught in the Department of Social Ethics at Harvard upon returning to the United States and then moved for a short time to Dartmouth. In 1930 he returned to Harvard, where he remained until his death in 1967. At Harvard he helped to form the Department of Social Relations, in which psychologists, sociologists, and anthropologists combined their talents. Allport received high professional honours in 1963, when he received the gold medal of the American Psychological Foundation, and in 1964, when he received the American Psychological Association's award for distinguished scientific contributions.

Allport's publications reflect his diversity of interests and his recognition of the complexity and uniqueness of human behaviour. A former editor of the *Journal of Abnormal and Social Psychology,* Allport wrote on subjects ranging from *The individual and his religion* (1950a) to *The psychology of radio* (G.W. Allport and Cantril, 1935). His major works in the area of personality theory are *Personality: A psychological interpretation* (1937), *The nature of personality: Selected papers* (1950b), *Becoming: Basic considerations for a psychology of personality* (1955), *Personality and social encounter: Selective essays* (1960), and *Pattern and growth in personality* (1961). Many of his important papers have been collected in *The person in psychology: Selected essays* (1968). Finally, in the area of test construction, Allport collaborated with his brother Floyd in the development of the *A-S reaction study* (G.W. Allport and Allport, 1928), and with P.E. Vernon to produce *A study of values* (1931).

Allport recognised that there are many factors which determine behaviour. These form a hierarchy from most specific to most general, as follows: conditioned reflex, habit, attitude, trait, self, and personality. The more general factors generally dominate the more specific ones. The most general factor, personality, was defined by Allport as follows (1937): "Personality is the dynamic organisation within the individual of those psychophysical systems that determine his unique adjustments to his environment (p. 48)."

Despite the dominating position of personality in the hierarchy of factors, Allport believed that the most profitable level for the personality theorist to study is the trait. He gave it its best-known definition (1937): "A generalised and focalised neuropsychic system (peculiar to the individual), with the capacity to render many stimuli, functionally equivalent, and to initiate and guide consistent (equivalent) forms of adaptive and expressive behaviour (p. 295)."

The comprehensive definition, though vague, points out clearly the role of a determiner of consistency in behaviour and reveals Allport's emphasis on individuality as well as his interest in adaptive and expressive behaviour. His studies of expressive behaviour (G.W. Allport and Vernon, 1933) have afforded evidence for consistency; they also indicate his interest in idiographic rather than nomothetic investigation. Idiographic studies lead to intensive study of individuals. Nomothetic investigation is concerned with lawful regularities in the "typical" individual, and Allport believed that such studies tend to overlook significant features of behaviour. Expressive behaviour is that aspect of behaviour which is related to an individual's own style of behaving rather than to the function of the behaviour in adaptation; for example, two individuals writing or saying the same words in response to a question may do so in quite different ways, their individual ways expressing their own personalities.

Allport and Vernon studied the expressive aspects of several types of behaviour, obtaining thirty-eight measures. They determined that there was satisfactory reliability for the measures when the behaviour was repeated and when the same behaviour was measured from different muscle groups. Then they examined the intercorrelations of their thirty-eight measures to see whether a few general traits or factors might account for the observed intercorrelations. They concluded that three general factors were indicated by the data: one was a kind of motor expansiveness indicated chiefly by the extensiveness of responses such as writing; a second was called the *centrifugal* group *factor,* related to distance from the individual's center and having to do with outward tendency and extroversion; and the third had to do with emphasis, as indicated by gestures made while speaking, writing pressure, and so on.

Typically, Allport did not rest content with the group aspect of the study. He and Vernon then proceeded to an intensive study of four individuals and conducted that the expressive measures were quite congruent with the subjective estimates of personality study. This part of the study is typical of both the strength and the weakness of Allport's approach; the results are suggestive and provocative and yet somewhat unconvincing because of their subjectivity and the lack of specific predictions.

There are several aspects of Allport's psychology which deserve comment, aside from his definition and study of traits. Allport emphasised the complexity and individuality of behaviour, together with the multiplicity of its determinants. Accordingly, he was not attracted by the aseptic laboratory studies which some others have used in the construction of their theories of personality. He felt very strongly that studies of group tendencies in a search for universal laws were overemphasised in American psychology; such studies he called *nomathetic*. Allport wished to foster intensive studies of the individual via methods which would reveal the uniqueness of that individual and thereby make it possible to predict his behaviour; this approach he called *idiographic*. When Allport (1937) imported into personality discussions this nomothetic-idiographic distinction (originally made by Windelband [1921], a philosopher), he stirred up controversy (Skaggs, 1945) and further discussions of the issues (see Beck, 1953; Eysenck, 1954; Falk, 1956). Allport had struck a nerve.

The nomothetic-idiographic distinction is complex, and we cannot stop to discuss all the issues here. Allport's point has been made in the very limited sense that intensive study of individuals is now regarded as necessary. We have seen that even Skinner and his followers have arrived at this conclusion, but their reasons for doing so are diametrically opposed to those advanced by Allport. The operant conditioner studies the individual case intensively to make sure that every individual follows the same behavioural laws; that is, he studies individual differences to make sure they do not interfere with the functional relationships revealed by *every* individual in the experiment. The operant conditioner studies individuals so that he can eliminate them from his laws; Allport would have us study individuals so that we can understand them in their uniqueness. In his detailed study of "Jenny" (1965), for example, Allport defends his idiographic approach by claiming to be able to predict her future behaviour because of its consistency with what she had done in the past. Such limited generality over time would seem to be all the truly idiographic scientist can aspire to. Traditional science has generally sought laws with the widest possible range of generality; although every condition studied has some unique features, the scientist has attempted to abstract from unique situations those features which are general. Few psychologists have been willing to abandon this view for Allport's more idiosyncratic perspective.

R.R. Holt (1962), who did one of the later and more thorough analyses of the issue raised by Allport, tries to lay the whole issue to rest. First he shows how the idiographic opposition to natural science (characterised at that as nomothetic) arose within the romantic movement. Holt then examines each idiographic assumption systematically and concludes that the phase *idiographic science* is self-contradictory. However, he does *not* embrace the conclusion that science is therefore nomothetic (1962, pp. 399-400):

> The nomothetic conception of science must be rejected as a caricature of what any contemporary scientist does. The only way to justify the application of the term nomothetic to the natural science of the present is to change the definition of the term so much that it no longer resembles its original meaning, and becomes an unnecessary redundancy... the nomothetic is as dead a duck today as the idiographic, and neither term adds anything to contemporary philosophy of science.

Allport's thinking in another area was more widely accepted. Psychoanalytic theory made it fashionable to emphasise past experiences and unconscious influences in the determination of behaviour. Allport provided a needed antidote by pointing out the necessity for determination of present behaviour by present influences and by insisting that, in normal people at least, conscious influences on behaviour are far more powerful than unconscious ones. It follows that the verbal report of an individual on the reasons for his behaviour is likely to be the best single source of information about those reasons. In addition, the conscious *intentions* of an individual provide a better indication of how he will behave than any searching into the past (see especially G.W. Allport, 1955).

Allport's ideas on the functional *autonomy* of motives (Allport, 1937) have inspired more criticism (see Bertocci, 1940, for an early example) than any other single one of his ideas. Behaviour, according to this view, may persist independently of the motive originally responsible for its occurrence. No other biological or primary motive need replace the original one; the behaviour, once it has become functionally autonomous, may be engaged in for its own sake only. The old track star who in college ran for adulation or for pay may continue to run years afterward when there is no motive, external to the behaviour itself, for continuing.

It is easy to see that such a concept invites critical attack. Allport cannot be saying that all behaviour becomes functionally autonomous, or extinction could never be observed. He should then give an account of why some behaviours or motives become autonomous and some do not. This Allport attempted to do (1961). His account of the reasons for functional autonomy seems to constitute a moderation of his original position. For one class of autonomous behaviours, he accepts an account in terms of fairly traditional mechanisms, like unusual resistance to extinction. For the second class, he maintains that the behaviours continue because they are consistent with the acquired structure of the person. It seems that Allport's later position is more congruent with the views of learning theorists. Allport has again succeeded in drawing attention to a serious problem by somewhat overstating his case. Most psychologists would now at least agree that one should attention to the contemporary dynamics of any given behaviour; one cannot rely exclusively on an account of the motives active when the behaviour was originally acquired.

We have pointed out ways in which Allport sometimes opposed prevailing opinion. Yet in many ways Allport's theory is a prototype of most personality theory. He emphasises structure and hierarchical arrangement of personality. He stresses the complexity and individuality of personality and the multiple determination of behaviour. He opposes laboratory methods and nomothetic studies, preferring some looseness of conceptualisation to oversimplification. For the tough-minded, these are serious defects; for the more tender-minded, the same attitudes are sources of inspiration and wisdom.

**Factor Theories**

Factor theories are conceptually related to Allport's trait theory though historically more closely related to a statistical technique called *factor analysis* (Spearman, 1931). The search of the factor analyst leads to something which accounts for an observed consistency of behaviour, that is, a something much like Allport's traits. The rigor of the method of search, however, tends to set factor theory apart from trait theory and give it a kinship in spirit with S-R theories, though the two proceed toward the goal of precision via very different paths (Cattell, 1959).

Factor theories are more closely related to a particular method of study than other personality theories are. To understand them we must know something of the reasoning behind factor analysis as a statistical technique. In order to make the discussion concrete, we shall relate factor analysis to the study of intelligence, the context in which it actually developed.

We may look at the problem in this way. Say that we have observed, in a gross way, that some people consistently stand higher than others on some loosely defined dimension which we shall call *intelligence.* We understand little about either the dimension or the reasons for individual variations in amount of intelligence. Assume now that we are able to agree on a large number of measures of behaviour which are related to this gross intelligence dimension. We can then find out how each of a large number of people scores on each of the measures. If there is a tendency for people who score high on one test also to score high on every other test, it is clear that these high-scoring people must possess a higher-than-usual amount of some general factor which plays a role in determining all the test scores. If smaller subgroups of the tests have a larger relationship than can be accounted for by the general factor, then there is a group factor present which underlies performance on just these groups of related tests. Any remaining variation in test scores must be attributable to factors useful only on the single test or to "errors" or unique circumstances surrounding the administration of the test. Burt (1941) has given a full description of these various types of factors.

There are generally several ways in which the tests can be associated so that mathematically reasonable factors can be isolated. In selecting a single one from the several available factor accounts of the observed correlations, a decision must be based upon some variety of psychological acumen.

Once the factors have been determined, the measures, or tests, can be looked at again. For an individual measure, we can ask how much its value has been determined by the general factor, how much by each of the group factors involved, and how much by specific and error factors. The pattern of determination for the measure is called the *factor loading*, or *saturation*, of the measure.

Finally, we can reexamine the gross concept, intelligence, and answer questions about its composition, its nature, and its usefulness as a concept. The outcome of the factor analysis will have suggested new ways to test intelligence and to conceive of intelligence; it may at this stage appear that intelligence is not what we thought it was or that our measures were not good measures of that which we wish to continue to call *intelligence.*

Although our discussion has been concerned with the more orthodox type of factor analysis in which scores from many individuals are analysed, it is also possible to apply factor analysis to the correlations between different tests taken repeatedly by a single individual. Stephenson (1953, 1961) has combined factor analysis with his Q sort to obtain information about the unique attitudinal organisation of individual persons. His subjects are required to make judgments concerning both themselves and others in a wide variety of situations, in order to provide data for the factor analysis. In this application of factor analysis to an individual, successive scores by a single individual can be treated as though they were made by different persons.

At this point it should be clear that factor analysis is a complex, sophisticated, and fascinating method for the study of multiple variables. As such, it is clearly applicable to the study of personality. But it, like any other method in any science, is no substitute for ingenuity and insight. It will not produce hypotheses or interpretations. Furthermore, it is important to remember that the results of a factor analysis can be no better than the data that are fed into it (see Anastasi, 1958, pp. 335ff., for a simple, well-reasoned discussion of this problem).

**Eysenck's Factor Theory.** Hans Jurgen Eysenck (1916), a German by birth, left his homeland during the rise of the Nazis and has spent most of his life in England. After taking his Ph.D. at the University of London, Eysenck served as a hospital psychologist during World War II. He then returned to the University of London and became director of the psychological department at the Institute of Psychiatry, where he conducted research in institute hospitals. Eysenck is presently associated with the University of London and serves as senior psychologist at two hospitals. During visits to the United States, he has taught briefly at the Universities of Pennsylvania and California.

Eysenck's contributions to personality theory are exemplified by *Dimensions of personality* (1947), *The scientific study of personality* (1952b), *The structure of* human *personality* (1953a), *The dynamics of anxiety and hysteria: An experimental application of modem learning theory to psychiatry* (1957), his editorship of the comprehensive *Handbook of abnormal psychology* (1961), and *The causes and cues of neurosis* 1965); of which Rachman is author. In addition to research in the areas of clinical psychology and personality, Eysenck has studied aesthetics, attitudes, and humor. Eysenck's publication:, too, have strayed from his major field of interest into *The psychology of politics* (1954) and the *Uses and abuses of psychology* (1953b).

As an outstanding contemporary factor theorist, Eysenck tends to be tough-minded and operational in approach. He puts little credence in the dimensions of personality which have been initiated from outside the framework of quantitative method. His general attitude, with which most of those in the "behaviour modification movement" enthusiastically agree, is well expressed in the following quotation (Eysenck and Rachman, 1965): "Learning theory does not postulate... 'unconscious' causes, but regards neurotic symptoms as simply learned habits; there is no neurosis underlying the symptom, but merely the symptom itself. *Get rid of the symptom (skeletal and autonomic) and you have eliminated the neurosis* (p. 10)."

The basic structure of Eysenck's theory is not unlike Allport's. He too recognises a hierarchical arrangement of consistencies from least to most: the specific response, the habitual response, the trait, and the type. The trait is an observed consistency of action tendencies, while the type is a constellation of traits. Most of Eysenck's interest is directed to the types, though much of his research is necessarily concerned with traits; one cannot constellate regularities in behaviour without first discovering them. Eysenck, with his operational orientation, does not accept traits unless they have been operationally validated.

In his early research on 700 neurotic soldiers, Eysenck (1947) uncovered two fundamental underlying variables, or typal polarities: introversion-extraversion and neuroticism. The first of these is recognised by Eysenck as almost exactly the introversion-extraversion earlier proposed by Jung as a basic personality dimension. It is different chiefly because it was extracted by Eysenck from the intercorrelations of a large number of ratings and classifications available on a large number of people. A major result of this study was that the neurotic type was found to be inferior in nearly every respect: intellectually, physically, emotionally, and especially with respect to the ability to sustain motivation.

Personality for Eysenck is divided, in the classic British tradition, into areas or sectors: the cognitive or intellectual, the conative, the affective, and the somatic. For the first three of these areas Eysenck is willing to suggest underlying general factors. For the first, of course, it is intelligence. Neuroticism is, in a sense, a conative or character defect, since it represents an inability to persist in the face of obstacles. Introversion-extraversion is a general factor in the affective area.

More recently (1952b) in a study of normal subjects and hospitalised mental patients, Eysenck discovered a third type, psychoticism. Somehow this does not seem surprising. Psychotics, like neurotics, tended to do more poorly than normals, though by no means on all tests. They were distinguished from normals and neurotics by a number of specific behavioural deficiencies.

Eysenck has made a methodological contribution which promises to be important. It is called the *method of criterion analysis* (1950). The method is simply a stipulation that the factor analyst should begin with two groups which are known to differ on some hypothesised underlying factor. Eysenck's normal and psychotic subjects would provide an example. When the measures are obtained from the two groups, only those which discriminate between the groups can justifiably be assumed to relate to the hypothesised factor. If Eysenck's criterion analysis is used, it ensures that the investigator will plan the investigation carefully in advance; he cannot simply administer a haphazard truckload of tests to a randomly selected flock of subjects and let the factors fail where they may.

Eysenck has been an extremely controversial figure. He is the kind of man who, if he were in India, might try to live on raw hamburger. He is a clinical psychologist who has characterised psychotherapy as a loose art form and has seriously questioned whether it does any good (1952a). Eysenck's forthright behaviour has not endeared him to all his colleagues, who have not hesitated to apply the same high standards to his work that he has applied to theirs. Serious questions have been raised about both the empirical and the theoretical aspects of his research. It has been frequently noted that the evidence for his assertions is typically meager; he has also been criticised for overlooking alternative interpretations of his data in the absence of adequate controls to eliminate such factors (e.g., cf. Jensen, 1958, p. 300).

Nevertheless, Eysenck's influence on personality theory has been substantial, and his research looks very promising. He has tended to toughen thinking without eliminating valuable methods of observation. He has applied quantitative methods to the data of the clinic; this has been one of the crying needs of personality research. He has been quite as willing to eliminate a concept as to accept it; yet he is not at all antitheoretical. If these techniques result in further integration of the relatively fragmentary factors thus far isolated and tested, they will have made a most significant contribution to personality theory.

**Cattell's Factor Theory.** Raymond Bernard Cattell (1905) was born and educated in England, where he was recognised as a leader in the field of personality research before coming to the United States. Cattell took his Ph.D. at the University of London and held both academic and clinical positions at that institution in close succession. His later career has been characterised by broad interests, encompassing both of these areas of psychology.

In the United States, Cattell has taught at Columbia Teachers College, Clark University, Harvard, and the University of Illinois, where he is now a research professor. His major works include *Personality and motivation structure and measurement* (1957) and two handbooks which he edited and to which he contributed chapters: *Handbook of multivariate experimental psychology* (1966) and *Handbook of modern personality theory* (1970). Besides other, older or less important work in personality theory, Cattell has to his credit work in the areas of measurement (1936, 1946) and experimental and social psychology (1952). Cattell has authored three widely used tests: The Culture Free Test of Intelligence (1944), The O-A Personality Test Battery (1954), and The 16 Personality Factor Questionnaire (1950). These are only a few of the tests with which Cattell has been involved; Cattell and Warburton (1967) list over 400 tests devised by Cattell and his students!

Like Eysenck, Cattell is intellectually indebted to the factor analysts; this is not surprising, since he studied under Spearman, who developed the essential ideas for factor analysis, which he applied to the study of intelligence. Cattell's general personality theory shows similarities to McDougall's in its tendency to look for underlying dimensions of behaviour; more directly, Cattell borrows McDougall's notion of the self-regarding sentiment. Cattell's developmental theory is markedly Freudian.

Cattell combines the qualities of tough-minded factor theorists like Eysenck with the qualities of more traditional personality theorists who stress comprehensiveness. His theory is therefore at once extensive and, in part, quantitative in emphasis and content. Eysenck has a far stronger tendency to limit himself to concepts derived from factor studies; Cattell sometimes allows himself more range in order to make his theory inclusive and to avoid ignoring data from other sources.

Cattell (1950) has defined personality as "that which permits a prediction of what a person will do in a given situation" (p. 2). This definition is consistent with our contention that a theory of personality is really identical with a general theory of behaviour, for Cattell's definition would fit theories of behaviour.

Traits are Cattell's basic elements of personality. He explicitly recognises that traits are concepts used to explain observed consistencies of behaviour, and he agrees with Allport and Eysenck that there are many levels of generality of traits, some applying only to particular individuals or circumstances, and others applying to very large groups. He has been concerned mainly, however, with the intraindividual organisation of traits.

The chief distinction made by Cattell is between *surface traits* and *source traits.* The former are based simply on observed behaviours that occur together, while the latter underlie the surface traits, determining observed behaviour consistencies through particular combinations. There is a rough correspondence between Eysenck's trait and Cattell's surface trait, and Eysenck's type and Cattell's source trait. The latter pair is in both cases more stable and more general, and both investigators have concentrated their interest more intensively upon such general factors.

Cattell also recognises two kinds of traits according to their origins: constitutional and environmental-mold traits. He has performed some ingenious research in an attempt to discover to what extent traits are determined via these two influences. For example, in one study (Cattell, Blewett, and Beloff, 1955) a personality test was administered to identical twins, to fraternal twins, to siblings reared together and apart, and to unrelated subjects. The test measured traits established as significant personality factors in earlier factor studies. Study of the results obtained with subjects who thus differed to varying degrees in both hereditary and environmental similarity allowed the investigators partially to evaluate the relative contributions of heredity and environment to the factors studied. Such research is noteworthy within the personality area for its logical consistency and coordination with earlier research as well as for its ingenuity.

Cattell differentiates between source traits on the basis of their origins. The is a dynamic source trait with a constitutional origin; the *metaerg* is identical except for its environmental origin; Both determine patterns of behaviour because they consist of motivational predispositions toward environmental objects. Metaerg: are further subdivided into attitudes, interests, and sentiments. Sentiments are the most stable class.

The most powerful sentiment of all is the self sentiment. Cattell, like other personality theorists, introduces the self to explain the consistency that seems to suffuse all the behaviour of an individual. Thus the self sentiment acts on all other sentiments and may strengthen or inhibit the tendency to action aroused by other sentiments. There are two selves, the real and the ideal. These have their obvious meaning, the former being the most realistic estimate an individual could make of himself, and the latter the individual as he would ideally like to be.

The development of personality depends upon the evolution of ergs and metaergs and the organisation of the self through the process of learning. Cattell accepts both contiguity and reinforcement as principles of learning. Learning is conceived of as occurring via a series of stages, each involving alternative outcomes called *crossroads* by Cattell.

The framework within which personality development takes place is the social context. Cattell has turned his talents to the description of this context as well as to the description of personality. The dimensions of social institutions combine to form an analog to individual personality, the *syntality* of the institution. In several studies (e.g., Cattell, 1949; Cattell and Wispe, 1948) he has found factors which he believes are useful for the description of families and nations. The use of a variety of measures to derive social factors is still another example of Cattell's originality and enterprise.

Cattell has made greater efforts to synthesise his concepts explicitly than most personality theorists have. One example of this is his dynamic lattice (1950), which diagrammatically interrelates the ergs, sentiments, and attitudes which constitute the most important elements of a personality structure. This lattice portrays the connections between ergs (e.g., sex, protection, and security) and sentiments (e.g., toward a wife), which are in turn related to attitudes (e.g., toward a wife's hairstyle). In addition, elements at the same level may be interrelated (e.g., sentiments regarding one's wife and one's bank account).

Finally, Cattell suggests an explicit way to combine information about an individual in order to predict what he will do in a specific situation. This is done through the *specification equation:*

$$R = s_1T_1 + s_2T_2 + s_3T_3 + \ldots + s_nT_n$$

Here $s_1$ represents the "weighting" of trait number 1 ($T_1$) in the situation in question, etc., The form of the equation is a simple linear sum. Cattell recognises both that the form of the equation might need to be complicated to represent more complex interactions between traits and that a more elaborate type of model might eventually be needed. However, he also notes that one must walk before one can run and that his equation *can be* applied to prediction of things like academic performance (Cattell and Butcher, 1968); that is more than the opposition can say.

Allport, Eysenck, and Cattell have developed theories which have considerable logical similarity. All three men are alike in their vigor and iconoclastic tendencies—traits which psychology presently needs, especially in personality theory. Allport is very different from the other two in attitude and in method of study, having little sympathy for factor analysis or for the massive experiment. Eysenck and Cattell have shown unusual aptitude for originating experimental designs that wed quantitative methods to the study of personality. Their theories promise a long and happy marriage.

## ORGANISMIC THEORIES

Many personality theorists start from a point of view systematically close to that of the

Gestalt psychologists. Murphy, Rogers, Goldstein, Angyal, Maslow, Lecky, Murray, and Sheldon are members of this class. Any or all of these men might be included as organismic theorists. The decision must be based on the extent to which a holistic, Gestalt orientation toward the individual is a *central* feature of their personality theories. Quite arbitrarily, we are choosing Goldstein and Sheldon as organismic theorists and omitting the rest or treating them in a separate section. The choice of Goldstein needs no justification; Sheldon would often be put in another class because the really central feature of his theory is his preoccupation with constitutional influences on personality; he does, however, espouse a general organismic point of view, and his interest in organic effects qualifies him as an organismic theorist in the popular meaning of the term.

**Goldstein's Holistic Theory**

Kurt Goldstein (1878-1965) established his reputation as a neuropsychiatrist in Europe before coming to this country in 1935. Having received his medical degree from the University of Breslau, he associated himself with the Psychiatric Hospital at Koningsberg. At an early age, Goldstein became a professor of neurology and psychiatry and director of the Neurological Institute at the University of Frankfurt. He later held a similar position at the University of Berlin.

During World War I, Goldstein conducted the fundamental studies of brain-injured soldiers which laid the groundwork for his organismic theory (1942) and his most significant publication, *The organism* (1939).

In the United States, Goldstein held academic and clinical positions in a variety of institutions, in addition to maintaining a private neuropsychiatry and psychotherapy practice in New York City for many years. He delivered the William James Lectures at Harvard, discussing human nature in the light of psychopathology (1940), and was associated with the New York Psychiatric Institute, Tufts Medical School in Boston, Columbia University, Brandeis University, City College of New York, and the New School for Social Research. Goldstein died in 1965, and his posthumously published autobiography (1967) gummed up the history of his intellectual development literally from beginning to end.

Aside from his theoretical and clinical work, Goldstein published works on language disturbances (1948) and, with Gelb (1920), on the Gestalt problem of figure-ground relationships (although Goldstein disclaimed any ties with Gestalt psychology).

To Goldstein, a primary feature of organisms is their organisation. In behaviour as in perception, processes are organised into figure and ground. The figure is the principal and outstanding feature of the ongoing activity, just as a perceptual figure stands out from its ground. In an organism's behaviour, those features which are related to the strongest drives stand out.

The normal organism is structured but flexible, capable of tailoring its behaviour to fit the needs of the ongoing stimulus situation. Its behaviour can be understood only as part of an organic unity; the significance of its behaviour can be assessed only as a contribution to the ongoing goal of the organism.

For Goldstein, the goal of the organism is unitary. It is self-actualisation. Self-actualisation sums up all the needs of the organism. A sexually driven organism actualises itself in coitus, and a hungry one in eating; but the self-actualisation of the complex human adult is expressed in many less organically driven acts. It is clear that on this point Goldstein is close to Carl Rogers, for whom self-actualisation is also a crucial concept. Indeed, there is inevitably a close kinship at the core between all self theories and all organismic theories, for both emphasise the basic unity of the personality. The two types of theories differ, when they do, in that the self theorist has a greater tendency to analyse out subsidiary structures which have some degree of independent existence.

Goldstein believed that the strongly organised organism is capable of choosing a favorable environment or manipulating an unfavorable one to some extent. It is thus not the victim of blind forces or the pawn of fortuitous stimulus situations. But no organism is insulated from environmental effects; it must thus come to terms with its environment. Only through accepting those terms of the environment which cannot be avoided or changed can the organism continue in its attempt to actualise itself. This aspect of Goldstein's thinking puts him close to the phenomenologists and existentialists—a similarity which Goldstein himself did not fail to note when, in his eighties, he wrote about his life (1967, pp. 161-164).

Organismic theorists tend to avoid analysis; Goldstein was no exception. If it is necessary to study every behaviour event within the context of the whole organism, it is tempting to stay on the level of generality without coming to terms with the problem of specificity of prediction. In this Goldstein was again no exception. His central concept, self-actualisation, leaves one uncertain of the defining characteristics of such behaviour and wondering whether there is much behaviour which is not in some sense self-actualising. Does this concept say very much more than that an organism will do what it will do, and that, if it does it, we assume that it needed to do it in order to actualise itself?

It is interesting that brain-injured patients and their symptoms led Goldstein to his holistic point of view. He found that the behaviour manifested by a patient with a brain injury could be understood only in terms of an examination of the whole matrix of the patient's behaviour. What at first appears to be a direct result of injury might, upon closer examination, turn out to be a quite indirect reaction stemming from an attempt to fit the results of injury into the mosaic of life. The same physical injury might lead to a variety of behaviour syndromes, depending upon the patient's circumstances and personality structure. In general, a specific deterioration in some ability would lead a patient to be generally more sensitive less self-confident, and more withdrawn; if one did not know this, he might uncritically attribute various performance decrements to direct results of injury rather than to these indirect manifestations.

With his background of clinical experience, it is natural that Goldstein should have preferred the intensive study of the individual to the group approach. Through his approach, Goldstein made his best-known discovery: The most characteristic difference between patients with extensive brain injury and normal individuals is that the former have lost the abstract attitude. Their ability to do concrete things and to react to concrete situations may be relatively unimpaired, but their ability to abstract is likely to be extremely limited. For example, the brain-injured patient may be unable to make statements that are obviously contrary to fact, such as "the moon is green." He cannot abstract common properties of dissimilar objects, such as a radio and a newspaper. This lack of abstract ability permeates his behaviour. Goldstein and Scheerer (1941, 1953) developed tests to determine the extent to which abstract behaviour is impaired; these tests therefore help to diagnose brain damage.

Goldstein was an example of an organismic theorist at his observational, clinical best. He was self-consciously antiexperimental, sharing the organismic belief that by thus restricting conditions and controlling behaviour, we lose the significance which the activity might have in its natural context. But Goldstein was shrewd and industrious in taking advantage of the wealth of material which paraded before him in his psychiatric practice. Methodologically, he added few innovations to the organismic view, which has said in essence: "Take Gestalt principles from the study of perception and apply them to the study of the whole individual."

**Sheldon's Typology**

William H. Sheldon (1899) is a trained physician, as his theoretical efforts to relate behavioural and body components might indicate. After receiving both his Ph.D. and his M.D. from the University of Chicago, he interned at a children's hospital. Sheldon taught at the University of Chicago, Northwestern University, and the University of Wisconsin before continuing his studies with two years of psychiatric training abroad. His visits with Jung, Freud, and Kretschmer contributed directly to his later theorising, which owes most to constitutional theorists such as Kretschmer and Viola, but which also shows resemblances to Freudian, and particularly Jungian, theory.

At Harvard, Sheldon entered into a collaborative relationship with experimentalist S.S. Stevens, who brought to Sheldon's work a new sophistication in procedure measurement. Together they published the basic works in constitutional psychology: *The varieties of temperament: A psychology of constitutional differences* (1942) and *The varieties of human physique: An introduction to constitutional psychology* (1940).

Sheldon's writing has been characterised by concern for the identification of, and relationships between, structural and temperamental factors, particularly as applied to the problem of delinquency (1949b). He has written a somatotyping guide, *Atlas of men: A guide for somatotyping the adult male at all ages* (1954). Always the taxonomist, Sheldon ventured away from personality theory temporarily, only to produce *Early American cents* (1949a)—a classification of coins!

Sheldon's road has not been an easy one. American psychology generally has been unfriendly to the idea that constitutional factors are important influences on behaviour. Our democratic ideals and, more specifically, the extreme environmentalism of John B. Watson have made us unwilling to believe that innate predispositions really have a directive influence on our personality.

Despite this resistance, it has remained obvious to the man in the street that there are associations between constitutional factors and personality. To him, the fat man appears jolly; the skinny kid with glasses remains a withdrawn bookworm. It is not surprising, then, that the man who reinforced these long-held popular beliefs is one of the better-known theorists.

Sheldon is also well known to the beginning psychology student, perhaps because he stands out among the personality theorists as a man who has said something comprehensible to the beginning student. Regrettably, Sheldon has sometimes been presented as having made ludicrous or incautious statements. He may have advocated something unpopular or capable of misinterpretation, but not something ludicrous.

Sheldon's system is a modern version of statements running back at least as far as Hippocrates, who believed that there were associations between body fluids and temperaments and that there were two basic types of physique: short and fat or long and thin. Ernst Kretschmer, many years later, added a third body type-the muscular-between the two extremes and designated them as follows: pykrtic, short and squatty; athletic, broad and muscular; and asthenic, tall and thin. He studied the relationship between these three types and the varieties of psychoses. Sheldon's continuity with his typological forebears has probably also contributed to his difficulty in getting a completely open-minded hearing from American psychologists. Hippocrates and his bilious temperaments are all too easy to laugh at, and some of this attitude toward humors has generalised to Sheldon. Psychology has been suspicious of typology as too easy a solution; even the description of personality in terms of patterns of traits is not above suspicion. Those familiar with the sad history of phrenology recognise both its similarity to trait psychology and its similarity to constitutional typology, for do not both phrenology and constitutional typology assess personality from physical measurements? It is easy to understand the rockiness of Sheldon's professional path. Fortunately, Sheldon seems well equipped to dish out punishment as well as to take it. He has written pungent criticisms of others, in addition to defending his own position.

Sheldon's contributions have been primarily an elaboration and tightening of Kretschmer's basic physical types and further empirical work in relating these types to behavioural variables. An important difference exists between his work and earlier theorising, such as Kretschmer's. Sheldon has recognised that any given individual is marked by some *degree* of each type and thus is in this sense always a blend of types rather than a pure type.

Sheldon's attempt to establish a constitutional interrelationship between behaviour and body build is anchored in the belief that the outward physical appearance (phenotype) is determined and guided by a hypothetical biological process (morphogenotype). Measurement of the physique is utilised by Sheldon in an attempt to evaluate indirectly the function of the morphogenotype. The obtained data fall into three categories of body types: endomorphy, mesomorphy, and ectomorphy.

This trichotomy was determined by evaluating 4,000 standardised photographs taken from three angles—front, back and side. These were sectioned into seventeen parts (Sheldon, 1940, p. 55), from which anthropometric measurements could be obtained. Sheldon is thus unique among personality theorists in being able to work with variables that can be, and have been, measured with a ruler. After analysing the data, Sheldon concluded that all the physical characteristics could be grouped into three components according to the presumed embryonic origin of most of the individual's tissue in the outer (ectomorphic), middle (mesomorphic), or inner (endomorphic) layer.

The endomorph tends to be soft, fleshy, and round; the mesomorph is square, tough; muscular, dense, and athletic; the ectomorph is tall, thin, fragile, and small-boned. The endomorph is massive in relation to his surface area; the mesomorph, intermediate; and the ectomorph, more exposed to the world because of his high proportion of surface area to mass.

Besides the primary components of body type there are several which are classified as secondary. These are dysplasia (disharmony between the body parts), gynandromorphy (bisexuality denoted by the physique), and texture (as of hairiness of the body) (1940, p. 7).

Three components of temperament correspond, according to Sheldon, to the three components of the physique: visceratonia, somatotonia, and cerebrotonia. The visceratonic individual loves comfort, food, and affection, and is good-natured. The somatotonic person is active, vigorous, and aggressive. The cerebrotonic individual is a bookish, sensitive, shy individual who withdraws from social contacts.

If we assume that there are such identifiable components of constitution and of personality, are the two related or not? Sheldon (1942, p. 400) found a remarkably high correlation between the components that one would expect to find associated: endomorphy-visceratonia; mesomorphy-somatotonia; and ectomorphy-cerebrotonia. These correlations are all about .80! Personality theorists seldom find their expectations so gratifyingly corroborated.

It is easy to be dubious about Sheldon's components of personality, since they seem so close to the layman's stereotypes, until one discovers that the clusters of-traits were derived from careful correlational studies using a large number of original traits rather than from the depths of the armchair (Sheldon, 1944, pp. 526-549). Sheldon's components of personality ate each defined by twenty related traits (Sheldon, 1942, p. 26).

Sheldon seems to be on safe ground when he maintains that, descriptively, the postulated correlations exist. However, other experimenters generally find that the correlations are lower than those obtained by Sheldon (Child, 1950; Lindzey, 1967; Sanford, 1953; Seltzer, Wells, and McTernan, 1948). The inflated correlations between temperament and physique could be attributed to a "halo effect" since both sets of ratings were done by the same person; that is, there was no attempt at blind analysis. Although in *The Varieties of Temperament* (1942, pp. 411-425) Sheldon made an effort to justify his position, his attempt in no way negates the possibility that a subjective bias may have contaminated the results. The procedure, despite the possibility of subjectivism, remained unaltered.

An additional criticism has been made by Lubin (1950), who discovered that some of the coefficients found in the tables of intercorrelation among the temperamental traits (Sheldon, 1942, pp. 506-511) are not mathematically possible.

Sheldon has also been attacked on the grounds that he assumes that genetic, strictly biological factors account for the observed correlations. If Sheldon really maintained that these direct biological influences were *the* reason for the correlations, he would be open to attack. He does not; he recognises, as do his detractors, that different cultural expectations or differential rewards related to different body builds might account for the observed personality differences. For example, a boy who is muscular by nature probably finds more reward in athletics than an endomorphic type. The rewards of Sport would then increase both active competitive behaviour and the accumulation of muscle tissue. Sheldon admits that, although the morphogenotype is invariant, the phenotype (from which measurements are taken) does fluctuate because of cultural and other influences. This admission forces him to relinquish partially his grasp on his basic theoretical relationship between the constitution and temperament. He says that the crucial relationship is between the morphogenotype and the temperament. The phenotype is only an attempt to measure the morphogenotype; this measurement is the best we have to date, despite its inexactness. It seems to us that operational criteria are highly applicable to this issue. Operationally, the morphogenotype has no meaning not exhausted by the measures of phenotype. The notion of morphogenotype may be lent credibility by analogy with other genetic characteristics, but no genetic observations directly justify the theoretical use of the morphogenotype. Therefore, we suggest, on grounds of parsimony, that the stated relationships be restricted to those holding between observed properties.

Sheldon is less willing to recognise the possibility that exclusively environmental factors, such as diet, might explain the observed relationships. However, Anastasi (1958) has pointed out that "Habitual overeating does lead to the accumulation of fat tissue. It is interesting to note in this connection that recent literature in abnormal Psychology as well as in psychosomatic medicine contains many references to 'psychological overeating' resulting from frustration and other emotional problems" (p. 182).

Anastasi has also stated (1958) that "The original identification of the three temperamental components...can likewise be questioned because of inadequacy of data" (p. 177). That is, in the original study there were only thirty-three male college subjects, and although further attempts were made to revise the original twenty-two traits, the procedure for doing so was clearly dependent upon the original study and its results.

A major asset of Sheldon's theory is that it has kept public the fact that there is some type of relationship between physique and temperament; at the present time, however, we cannot ascertain its direction. Does the physique direct the temperament, or does the temperament determine the physique; or, more logically, is it a two-way process whose exact interrelations have not yet been ferreted out?

## NEOANALYTIC PERSONALITY THEORIES

There are several closely related theories of personality that owe a great deal to psychoanalytic theory. Though they are by no means identical, their similarity of background and emphasis justifies their treatment under a single heading. The term *neoanalytic* is used to reflect their basic psychoanalytic framework as well as their modification of such principles in one way or another.

Karen Horney, Erich Fromm, Harry Stack Sullivan, and Henry Murray all developed their own personality theories as improvisations on the primary Freudian, Adlerian, and Jungian themes. In these newer theories social factors are emphasised. In playing up social factors, there has been a concomitant tendency to deemphasise biological factors. It is the relative neglect of the instinctive which sets these theories apart from Freudian analytic theory and which keeps at least the first three from having any basic commonality with Jungian theory.

All four of these theorists, and Sullivan especially, have contributed to the theory of ego functioning. This emphasis on ego functioning has been regarded as a strong point by sympathisers with the same point of view; on the other hand, some Freudians have regarded it as evidence that the theories represent an elaboration of Freudian theory rather than any really original contribution. Regardless of basic originality, each of these theorists has said unique things about the relationship of the individual to his society.

### Horney's Social Theory

The training and contributions of Karen Horney (1885-1952) were entirely within the field of psychoanalysis, although she represented an important outbranching from orthodox psychoanalytic theory. German by birth, Horney studied medicine at the University of Berlin and received her psychoanalytic training at the Berlin Psychoanalytic Institute, where she was analysed by Karl Abraham and Hans Sachs.

In the United States, Horney served as associate director of the Chicago Psychoanalytic Institute, taught at the New York Psychoanalytic Institute, and conducted a private practice in psychotherapy. Her efforts to break away from orthodox psychoanalysis led to the formation of the Association for the Advancement of Psychoanalysis and the American Institute of Psychoanalysis, of which she was dean.

Horney's theoretical emphasis is reflected in the titles of three of her works on personality theory. *Neurotic personality of our times* (1937), *Our inner conflicts* (1945), and *Neurosis and human growth* (1950). Her theory is further explicated in *New ways in psychoanalysis* (1939) and *Self-analysis* (1942).

Horney's social theory flies the banner of *basic anxiety.* This essential factor in personality development (Horney, 1937) is "the feeling a child has of being isolated and helpless in a potentially hostile world" (p. 79). Horney's concept of helplessness as experienced by the infant does not have the universal flavor that Adler assigned to it. It provides a predisposition for the future development of pathological conditions; it does not lead to a striving for superiority, but merely accentuates a predilection for security.

The home environment and the social structure within the family receive by far the most emphasis in Horney's theory. In this structure and the child's reaction to it Horney believed she had the key to the development of an individual's personality structure. The predominant reason that basic anxiety develops from parent-child relationships is the absence of genuine love and affection, and this can almost invariably be traced to neurotic parents. It should be noted, however, that Horney defines neurosis as any deviation from normal, efficient behaviour; the term is not used in a pathological context unless so indicated.

The child responds to his basic anxiety by developing some strategy of behaviour, *neurotic trends,* in an attempt to overcome it. It is this character structure arising from the reaction to basic anxiety which accounts for neurotic symptoms; it is not, as Freud said, a frustration of the sexual instinct. Horney maintained that sexual difficulty is the result and not the cause of conflicts. Furthermore, it is not a compulsion to repeat experiences based on unchanged, repressed childhood experiences (Horney, 1939): "There is no such thing as an isolated repetition of isolated experiences; but the entirety of, infantile experiences combines to form a certain character structure, and it is this structure from which later difficulties emanate" (p. 9).

The child also develops an idealised self-concept by internalising the aspirational levels and ethics of others in his culture. This concept develops without regard for his own potentialities or limitations. Consequently, when he attempts to realise these ideational concepts, he is curtailed both by his own limitations and by those which are imposed upon him by the existing culture. In other words, a person's basic conflict is between self-realisation and self-idealisation. The idealised self becomes a crutch for the neurotic person. He comes to believe that he is his idealised picture. This solution brings a temporary reduction of anxiety, but in the long run increases it. The attempts of the neurotic to live up to his idealised, unrealistic picture of himself result in new conflicts and consequently greater tension. The only real conflict which Horney recognised is that of the present situation and the demands it makes upon the individual.

The devices the individual uses to face his conflicts (neurotic trends) are generally unrealistic and lead to some degree of neurotic behaviour. These may be classified into two categories: (1) those which have their roots in the early developmental period of the child and which demonstrate a discernible etiology and (2) those which are a reaction to some situational stress and are usually transitory (Munroe, 1955). A vicious circle develops once these neurotic trends are initiated. Anxiety causes the original behaviour, which in turn, because of its inadequacy, leads to further anxiety that initiates another cycle.

In a person's attempt to find security, he utilises three types of behavioural patterns. He may move toward people, against them, or away from them (Horney, 1945). Fundamental to these three types of behaviour are the need for affection, the need for self-sufficiency, and the need to exploit people. In respect to the type of behaviour he selects there are corresponding personality types: compliant, aggressive, and detached. Again one must be cautioned not to assume that an individual utilises only a single type. As the person vacillates from one situation to another, he utilises the one most efficient for the specific situation. However, if one pattern is used exclusively, regardless of the situation, that is an index of neurosis.

The compliant individual relies upon other people; is ostensibly loving, kind, and loyal; and finds personal criticism devastating. Cynicism, a philosophy of the survival of the fittest, and extreme independence characterise the aggressive personality. The detached individual is perfectionistic, uncreative, and has a paucity of interpersonal relationships.

Horney emphasised only two of the many unconscious defense mechanisms: rationalisation and externalisation. Rationalisation is used in the Freudian sense except that it is explained in the context of the social theory of Horney; that is, it is concerned with the whole organism and is not related to Freud's instinctual personality components. Externalisation is merely a more general term for projection. The whole organism participates in an attempt to explain *every* motive and action externally, not just the undesirable ones.

Horney was optimistic about the possibility of avoiding neurotic reactions, as one tends to be when he believes that social factors are of preponderant importance. A secure and loving home would be insurance against the development of a neurotic character structure. Those, like Freud, who emphasise biological factors find it harder to be optimistic; if conflict is based on hereditary factors, change can come but slowly. Horney's more hopeful views have been welcomed by many as a relief from the oppressive pessimism of the orthodox Freudian assumptions. She has attempted to point the way to better families, to better societies, and, through them, to better people. Despite her long-term association with the training of analysts, Horney never formed a cohesive school of followers, nor did her theoretical views inspire research directly. As time passes, Horney's important contributions will probably become less associated with her name and more a part of the general *Zeitgeist* of psychology.

**Fromm's Escape-from-freedom Theory**

Erich Fromm (1900) was born and trained in Germany. He studied sociology and psychology at the Universities of Munich, Frankfurt, and Heidelberg, where he took his Ph.D. His psychoanalytic training was conducted mainly at the Berlin Psychoanalytic Institute.

Fromm cannot be clearly identified by his affiliation with any one institution, although he has lectured at the Chicago Psychoanalytic Institute and has taught at numerous universities and institutes in this country since he emigrated here in 1933. Since 1951 he has been a professor at the University of Mexico, where he now lives. He is also director of the Mexican Psychoanalytic Institute.

*Escape from Freedom* (1941), *Man for Himself* (1947), and *The Sane Society* (1955)—Fromm's major contributions to personality theory—probably have drawn more cross-scientific and public attention than the works of any other neo-Freudian.

Fromm's primary interests lie in the larger segments of society as they affect the individual (Fromm, 1955, 1961b). As a matter of fact, Fromm is a greater admirer of Marx (Fromm, 1961a) than of Freud (Fromm, 1959) and might as accurately be labeled a Marxist personality theorist as a Freudian personality theorist (see C.S. Hall and Lindzey, 1970, p. 130). Such a labeling, however, does not fit well into the categorisation system of American psychology!

However he is classified, Fromm believes that our political organisations no longer provide the firm direction and secure framework which they did when the units of political organisation were smaller and man had less freedom to determine his own fate. Today, man suffers from a feeling of insecure aloneness engendered by his lack of a framework; that is, man desires to actualise his self-potential and develop a feeling of belongingness.

Fromm's basic premise that an individual attempts to escape from freedom and return to a more secure existence first gained public notice through his *Escape from freedom*. A child's physical condition at birth and shortly thereafter makes his survival dependent upon his environment in general and upon his mother in particular. The child is soon weaned from his early postnatal surroundings and gradually achieves more and more independence. However, the accompanying amount of strength necessary to augment his Independence and to cope with the elements of society is conspicuously lacking. Moreover, man alone has the power to reason and imagine, and with the acquisition of this power he has lost the animal's ability to react instinctively, intimately, and directly to nature. Thus man finds himself in a unique position of being separated from his fellowman by political conditions and from the rest of nature by being a man. His first reaction to this situation is to try to recapture his earlier form of security. Upon finding this physically impossible and socially inefficient, he attempts other means. The two most common solution: are *authoritarianism* and *humanism.*

Broadly defined, authoritarianism is that which externally imposes a set of principles on society. It may be exemplified by a totalitarian state, or dictatorship, or belief in a supreme being. This solution is inadequate because it does not permit the individual an opportunity to realise his potentialities. Frustration and hostility against the imposed conditions are then mobilised.

Fromm believes that humanism is a better solution. All the actualities of human life have a chance to develop through love of fellowman and mutual cooperation. In a humanistic society, each man would be a brother to every man, and no man would be alone.

Fromm identified four ways of escaping the isolation and insecurity prevalent in modern society. He referred to them as types of orientation, or relatedness. They are receptive, exploitative, hoarding, and marketing. In addition, there is the healthy, or productive, orientation. No person exhibits a pure orientation. However it is possible to manifest one type so that it subordinates all others.

The receptive orientation (Fromm, 1947) "is often to be found in societies in which the right of one group to exploit another is firmly established" (p. 79). Individuals with this type of orientation sacrifice everything in order to maintain their identification with the group or the leader. They expect to receive something gratis, and when adversity occurs they are extremely rebellious and aggressive, exhibiting behaviour not unlike that of a spoiled child.

The philosophy of "might makes right" characterises exploitative individuals. The value which they place upon an object is directly proportional to the value which others place on it. They would feel no compunction about taking some object for no other reason than that it is highly prized by another.

The hoarding orientation is what one might expect it to be: frugal, impecunious, and miserly. Security is evaluated in terms of tangible physical wealth.

The last orientation, marketing, is relatively new and is associated with the advent of modern capitalism. Here the emphasis is centered upon such superficial objectives as keeping up with the Joneses and social climbing.

Fromm (1964) later added the biophilous type, who is in love with life. If love of life is frustrated, the person may become necrophilous (attracted to death).

As society now stands, it is absolutely necessary to warp the individual to fit the needs of society. Though man will always have to fit into human society, Fromm see hope in a society which would give each man a chance to develop into a fully human creature. Fromm has named his ideal society a *humanistic communitarian socialism*. His desperate concern for the development of such a society, born at least partly out of his own flight from Nazism, has put him in the forefront of the science of psychology, which is only now undergoing its social awakening. If Fromm were thirty, instead of seventy, he would probably be a folk hero of youth in the United States. There can be little doubt that his thinking has influenced our recent social upheavals, although, as usual, it is impossible for us to assess the extent of that influence. It seems clear that Fromm is an important intellectual father of some extremely important events.

**Murray's Need-Press Theory**

Henry Murray (1893) was a rigorously trained, productive biological scientist before turning to psychology. His academic degrees include an A.B. from Harvard in history, an MD. from Columbia's College of Physicians and Surgeons, and an M.S. in biology from Columbia. Murray subsequently completed a surgical internship at Columbia's Presbyterian Hospital, taught physiology at Harvard, conducted embryological research at the Rockefeller Institute for Medical Research, and then journeyed to England to take his Ph.D. in biochemistry at Cambridge University.

While in Europe, a visit with Jung dramatically Shifted Murray's interest to depth psychology. Shortly thereafter he took a position in academic psychology at Harvard and directed the Psychological Clinic there. He was on leave with the Office of Strategic Services during World War II, after which he returned to Harvard as a professor at the Psychological Clinic annex, where he remained until his retirement as professor emeritus in 1962. Murray's psychoanalytic training came under the direction of Franz Alexander and Hans Sachs; Murray paid his debt to psychoanalysis by helping found the Boston Psychoanalytic Society and by stimulating widespread interest in psychoanalytic research among his students. C.S. Hall and Lindzey (1970, p. 166) regret that Murray's conversations have not been preserved, since the richness of his thought and contribution is not fully represented in his published work. We shall see, however, that his published contributions are considerable! Murray, like another maverick, Gordon Allport, received the two highest awards his profession has to offer: the Distinguished Scientific Contribution Award of the APA and the Gold Medal Award of the American Psychological Foundation.

The Thematic Apperception Test (1943), which Murray developed has become one of the most widely used empirical tools of clinicians and personality theorists. His major theoretical work is *Explorations in personality* (1938). However, his *Assessment of men* (Office of Strategic Services, 1948), written as a result of his work in the Office of Strategic Services during World War II, is also considered a significant contribution to the area of personality assessment. As an intellectual sideline, Murray has engaged in a twenty-five-year study of Herman Melville and has published an analysis (1951) of the psychological meaning of the novel *Moby Dick*

One cannot read Murray (e.g., 1959) without receiving the impression that he is deeply preoccupied with the notions of process and field. Yet Murray is too well rounded to deny the importance of a controlled and reductive approach to psychology. The reductive approach is certainly foreign to Murray's own nature, for he sees too vividly the interactions that occur among all the processes that constitute a system. The system, to Murray as to the Gestaltist, is the unit to be studied. Only systems maintain their boundaries and provide the hope for that stability which is so rare in nature but so necessary to scientific study. Murray sees science as operating not primarily with stable structures but with processes which may, with some probability, be predictable.

Murray has said of himself (1959): "But at no time, to the annoyance of my friends, was a good Jungian, a good Freudian, a good Adlerian, or a good schoolman of any breed" (p. 13). Despite this independence of thought, Murray is close to Freud in many basic attitudes as well as in some of the details of his theory. Two of these attitudes are a belief in the great importance of the early history of the organism and an emphasis on the physiological processes accompanying the behavioural events in which the psychologist is interested. Murray allows for more changes of the personality by later events than Freud did. However, Murray still recognises the possibility that the effects of infantile experiences may be so great that they lead to various complexes in adulthood. On the physiological issue, Murray is one with Freud in recognising the independence of the science of psychology from that of physiology, while at the same time pointing out that there is a necessary relationship of dependence between the two types of events: without physiological processes, there can be no psychological processes. Some particular dominant configuration of processes in the brain always accompanies a particular conscious process.

Another theme in Murray's theorising is his recurrent clear statement that the concepts of his theory are constructions, hypothetical entities, not reality. Murray is not the kind of man who believes that nailing a name onto the flow of process can make it hold still or behave like a convenient structure that the scientist can then deal with complacently. Murray is more like a man who builds a transparent map with rough lines and shadings, through which he can view reality more conveniently; he builds and rebuilds Systems of classification, analyses and reanalyses processes as his understanding is enriched. His theory could be called a tool as much as a description.

Murray has presented one of the most elaborate taxonomies of needs (1938). He does not attempt to talk about needs as things isolated from the context of behaviour. Although needs are related to internal states, they are also related to the presence of valued external stimuli which impel to action (presses). The need directs behaviour to objects which can lead to a desired state; though this state may often involve the reduction of tension, it may sometimes involve an increase in tension. Murray does not believe that the normal person always seeks the numbness of no tension. Most needs have as accompaniments certain emotions and feelings.

Murray has redefined Freud's term *cathexis* to describe need-related objects; an object may have a positive or negative cathexis according to its ability to press the individual into responses of approach or avoidance. The individual's feeling for the object is called a *sentiment*. Cathexis and sentiment therefore refer to the same relationship between person and object; one is applicable when we are concerned with the properties of the object, the other when we are concerned with the properties of the person. Thus Murray has subdivided Freud's concept of cathexis into two parts.

Needs are interrelated as well as embedded in ongoing processes. Some needs are subsidiary to more global, superordinate needs, and the satisfaction of the subsidiary need is not an end in itself but only a step toward the greater satisfaction. Different needs may occur in the individual at the same time, in which case a conflict is engendered; one of the needs will be or become the strongest, in which case it is called *prepotent;* and will demand satisfaction before the concurrent needs can be attended to.

Closely related to Murray's acceptance of possible needs for tension increase is his description of two types of needs which do not involve a Thorndikian type of effect. He adds to the Thorndikian type of need *process needs* and *modal needs* Process needs are need: to do; for example, the adult may need to exercise, or the infant may need to babble. Modal needs are needs to perfect some behaviour and differ from process needs only in that the need to improve is involved.

Murray's thoroughness in his treatment of needs is also reflected in his full discussion of significant unit of behaviour. He has relatively little use for a formulation as molecular a: S-R. His most analytic unit is the *proceeding*, which is an interaction involving a person and an object or a person and a person; the interaction must be long enough to be of dynamic significance. The proceeding need not be overt; it may be a daydream or plan.

Proceedings may follow one another in a coherent fashion, in which case they may constitute another unit, a *serial*. The serial involves planning and organisation, and its nature imposes direction upon the proceeding: which constitute it. A marriage is an example of a serial. Proceedings, and therefore serials, may overlap and intertwine; all of us are involved in many endeavors in a single day or even hour.

A *thema* is another of Murray's behavioural units. It lays more emphasis upon the press and need which determine the behaviour in question and therefore is a more analytic and theoretical unit than the more descriptive proceeding. The thema, like the proceeding, may be serially organised. The thema is less fixed in scope than the proceeding and may persist over a longer period of time.

A serial programme may also be considered a unit of behaviour, but it lays emphasis upon the plans of the individual. He may plan a life goal, for example, college graduation, which involves a very large number of subgoals before it can be accomplished. A subgoal might be passing a course or completing a major.

We can see that Murray puts realism before precision, and creativity before compulsion, in his theory of personality. Though many of his ideas are basically psychoanalytic, there can be no doubt whatever that he is a thinker who is not afraid to modify or innovate whenever he feels that the evidence is in his favor. He has also devised new methods for getting evidence, as we know from his Thematic Apperception Test (TAT) (1943) and from the ingenuity of his wartime work in assessing men for special assignments (Office of Strategic Services, 1948).

C.S. Hall and Lindzey (1970) evaluate Murray's theory and his research as being out of tune with the times: "There is too much of the poet and too little of the positivist in his make-up" (p. 205). Murray has never shown a great desire to be in tune with the times and has had enough independent resources so that he has not had to be. His espousal of unpopular viewpoints may, as he thought, have been responsible for keeping him from getting tenure until he was fifty-five. At any rate, he was recently concerned that he might have achieved too much respectability (1967): "In due course the practice of introspection and the concept of motive force, in altered forms and disguised by fresh labels, surreptitiously regained their lost respectability; and after World War II, Freudian theory *in toto* overran large areas of American psychology as Napoleon overran Europe.... Murr found himself occupying a position of discomforting respectability" (p. 295).

As we have indicated in Chapter 9, we think that Freudian theory has met its Waterloo and is exiled to a quiet Island in the ocean of academic psychology. Thus Murr (the name Murray uses for himself in his autobiography) can rest easy in at least a partial unorthodoxy, a condition that he has always found comfortable and productive.

**Sullivan's Interpersonal Theory**

Harry Stack Sullivan (1892-1949) was first and foremost a psychiatrist, although his contribution to psychology through his personality theory is undeniable and he was also influential as a scientific statesman and educator. After receiving his M.D. from the Chicago College of Medicine and Surgery, Sullivan became a medical officer for the Federal Board for Vocational Education. He was later affiliated with the U.S. Public Health Service; with Saint Elizabeth's Hospital in Washington, D.C.; and with the University of Maryland medical school, where he conducted investigations of schizophrenia.

As a scientific statesman, Sullivan served as consultant for the Selective Service System and the UNESCO Tensions Project. He helped plan the International Congress of Mental Health. He also edited *Psychiatry*, a journal whose publication was stimulated mainly by the need to publicise Sullivan's theory.

Neuropsychiatrist William Alanson White exerted a permanent influence upon Sullivan, who later was president of the William Alanson White Foundation and founded and directed its training institution, the Washington School of Psychiatry. The influences of Sigmund Freud and Adolph Meyer are also discernible in Sullivan's theory. Sullivan published only one book in the area of personality theory, *Conceptions of Modem Psychiatry* (1947). After his death, he became much more influential; that is, five books based on his notes and recorded lectures have been published (1953, 1954, 1956, 1962, 1964).

The interpersonal theory of Sullivan is less exclusively analytic than that of Horney or Fromm. Although Sullivan acknowledged intellectual indebtedness to Freud, his theory bears a closer resemblance to Adler's. Much of Sullivan's thinking is related to men who have a nonanalytic approach, for example, William Alanson White, Adolph Meyer, and George Herbert Mead. Moreover, Sullivan's closer relationship to psychiatry and to academicians (particularly social scientists) has resulted in a greater acceptance of his theory and may have something to do with its fuller statement (Sullivan, 1953); these features of his theory have, in turn, led to greater acceptance among clinicians.

Personality as defined by Sullivan (1953) is "the relatively enduring pattern of recurrent interpersonal situations which characterise human life" (p. 111). That is, it is regarded as an intervening variable inferred from an individual's behaviour in relation to other people and objects. Personality exists only in interpersonal relationships. It follows that personality cannot be studied unless more than one person is interacting, although one of the persons need not be physically present; a persons interactions may be with an image, dream fictional character, and the like. Sullivan has not entirely rejected the influences of heredity and biological factors; in fact, he has acknowledged their importance during infancy and at puberty. He proposed a hierarchy of physiological needs from which tension arises, which must be dissipated by satisfying the needs. However, he held that man's distinctively human characteristics are interpersonally developed and may directly affect the physiological needs.

Sullivan stated that three processes are evidenced in the development of the personality: dynamism, personifications, and cognitive processes. A dynamism is a prolonged behaviour pattern which is revealed in characteristic interpersonal relationships. Dynamisms may also be described as classes of habits or personality traits which characterise an individual;

toward certain people an individual may display a dynamism of hostility or of friendliness, depending upon his habitual behaviour toward them. The self dynamism is the individual's picture of himself as he perceives it through his social interactions.

Personifications are images that an individual holds of other people or of himself. They are often products of his infancy. If they remain intact so that they influence his future opinion toward people, they are called *eidetic personification*. An example of this might be a child's attitude toward a domineering father; this personification could influence responses toward other authority figures. However, when an image occurs solely in connection with a particular situation, only the word *personification* is used. A stereotype is any personification which is held by a group of people. It is interesting to note that these are in some ways a socialised and conscious version of Jung's archetypes.

Cognitive processes are subdivided into three classes: *prototaxic, parataxic,* and *syntaxic*. In the prototaxic mode, the individual simply experiences directly, without connecting the raw feelings or attaching meaning to them. It is not unlike what has been called a "stream of consciousness": all the thoughts, visions, ideas, sensations, and perceptions occurring at any given moment. This is followed by the parataxic mode, in which the individual connects his experiences as they occur and regardless of their logical relations: casual relationships between nonrelated events and experiences. Logical connections are accomplished in the syntaxic mode by the use of *consensually validated* symbols. Consensual validation is a Sullivanian concept which refers to any symbol to which a particular meaning has become attached and agreed upon by a number of people. It is used chiefly for communication, and words are the most common example of such symbols.

Sullivan proposed six stages in the development of the individual. These are roughly delineated into age groups corresponding to maturational levels. However, the importance of maturation is limited in the degree to which it enables the individual to achieve a new and higher level of interpersonal relationships.

Sullivan noted that in the development of the individual, it is often apparent that certain entities are outside his realm of awareness. Three major reasons may be posited for this: selective inattention, disassociation, and parataxic distortion. Selective inattention is merely the unwillingness on the part of the individual to perceive in the immediate environment that which contradicts his beliefs. Disassociation is approximately what the Freudians refer to as *repression*. Parataxic distoration occurs when an individual's personal and autistic meanings, rather than the socially validated meanings, accrue to a symbol and influence his thinking.

In sum, Sullivan held that the individual functions because he needs to secure satisfaction; his basic needs are not instinctual or biological, as Freud would have us believe, but are based on interactions with people.

It is indeed curious that so little criticism has been directed at Sullivan's position. Scrutiny of several very recent volumes (e.g., C.S. Hall and Lindzey, 1970; Levy, 1970;

Maddi, 1968) failed to uncover any such criticism. Sullivan's system is an all-encompassing one that does not contain the outlandishly salient features (e.g., penis envy) that invite criticism in alternative positions such as Freud's. Also, he attempted to blunt criticism by incorporating many originally antagonistic views into his own system. Nevertheless, some critical comments can be made.

One immediately apparent omission is Sullivan's lack of direct attention to emotional factors in behaviour. This omission is incongruous in such an otherwise comprehensive system, and especially in view of the fact that Sullivan depicts the adult personality as developing from a physiological base. Although he does speak of anxiety, this concept is not sharply defined.

Along with the other specially oriented personality theorists, Sullivan must be credited for having helped to add a most valuable, much-needed dimension to the basically biological theory of Freud. Like the others, however, Sullivan did not attempt to detail the manner in which the process of socialisation occurs or the manner in which psychopathology is acquired.

Sullivan may also be credited with being the only social psychological theorist of his day who attempted to extend the Freudian developmental stages beyond puberty. Here again, however, he was programmatic. He failed to delineate the transition from one stage to another, the factors operating to produce smooth or difficult transitions, the role of the family setting (which is central in his theory, as it is in Horney's and Adler's), the role of the social order (which is focal in Fromm's theory), and how the latter two conditions interact.

Finally, Sullivan may be criticised for having failed to stimulate empirical research. This failure may be related to the somewhat vague and almost offhand manner in which he used most of his concepts (fruitful as these may have been in his clinical work). For example, it is often quite difficult for the reader to distinguish between two of his most crucial concepts, dynamisms and personifications.

Thus we have in Sullivan an enormously influential and comprehensive theorist whose strength is that he can accommodate what Freud on the one hand and the other socially oriented theorists on the other hand have been saying but whose weakness is that he has not provided the kind of precision in definition and theoretical specification of key concepts that is needed for the stimulation of important empirical research.

## SELF THEORIES

Habits, traits and factors of varying degrees of generality, the organism, social interaction—we have already run quite a gamut of concepts that are used either to explain or to describe the consistency of an individual's behaviour. The last organiser is the self. There are nearly as many definitions of self as there are self psychologists, and the definitions often seem to lack operational meaning; however, the common element in all definitions of self is the character of self as an organiser that imposes consistency on behaviour.

There are three general ways in which self has been postulated to operate in achieving a harmony of diverse activities. The time-honoured way was to use self as though it were a little man-inside-the-man who ordered all activities so that they pretty well suited his imperial selfship. Such a self, having his own sources of energy and will, is inaccessible to scientific investigation and is discredited in all scientific psychologies, including modern self theories.

A second way in which the self might organise behaviour is as a kind of template or picture into which all ongoing behaviour must fit. If the self is an objective, existing set of representations of an individual's past behaviours and experiences, these representations may somehow resist changes that would result from the impact of divergent new experiences on the old structure called *self.* We may think of this self as though it were a picture against which a contemplated new behaviour is projected; if the discrepancy between the picture as it presently exists and the picture as it would have to be modified to accommodate the new behaviour is too great, the behaviour does not occur.

The third view of self is as a summary name for a set of psychological processes. The exact processes that are subsumed vary from theorist to theorist, but generally include evaluative and attitudinal functions. These processes, acting upon the materials that govern behaviour, can thus themselves play a role in directing behaviour.

A danger in self theories is that a regression from meanings 2 and 3 to meaning 1 may occur. Certainly no theorist will intend such a regression and will, when defining self for theoretical purposes, carefully exclude meaning 1. The reason for a push back toward meaning 1 may be that it is clearer than the other two. In the second case, one might still be curious as to how the discrepancies between the self and experience or behaviour are resolved. Is it by a little man? If so, the regression is immediate. If not, then the structure which resolves discrepancies simply replaces the little man. In the case of meaning 3, the self-as-process shares the usual vagueness of such process concepts, and in addition it leaves one wondering why the concept is needed-at least it does if one has positivistic leanings. Self theorists, then, would seem to need logically to value fidelity of representation of complex human processes over strict positivism. In fact, they do.

**Rogers's Self Theory**

The career of Carl Ransom Rogers (1902—) has been marked by an interest in divergent fields, the first of which was scientific agriculture, which he encountered during his boyhood days on a farm (see Rogers, 1959, 1967a, for autobiographical information). Rogers subsequently attended the University of Wisconsin and Union Theological Seminary before terminating his education at Columbia Teachers College, where he took his Ph.D. and fell under the philosophical influence of John Dewey. Columbia also provided Rogers's first introduction to clinical psychology; he grew better acquainted with the field during his internship at the psychoanalytically oriented Institute for Child Guidance. While there he felt a definite conflict between psychoanalytic theory and the Thorndikian statistical influence which had prevailed at Columbia.

Rogers served as director of the Rochester Guidance Clinic, finding stimulation in the eclectic staff there. Their constant search for effective treatment was a problem Rogers turned to in *The clinical treatment of the problem child* (1939). He then shifted to academic psychology, teaching at Ohio State University, the University of Chicago, and the University of Wisconsin, but remained active in clinical activities. Rogers received the American Psychological Association's Distinguished Contribution Award in 1956. At Wisconsin, Rogers became progressively more disillusioned with what he thought were unduly stultifying rules imposed in the name of high standards by the psychology department. In 1963, he resigned from the department; in January, 1964, he joined the staff of the Western Behavioural Sciences Institute in San Diego, California, as a resident fellow; in 1968, he became a resident fellow at the Center for Studies of the Person in the same city.

The major stimulus for Rogers's personality theory came from his clinical therapeutic work, although he was strongly influenced by psychoanalyst Otto Ink. Rogers first advanced his views on personality in *Counseling and psychotherapy: Newer concepts in practice* (1942). That book was followed by his major theoretical work, *Client-centered therapy* (1951). He further explained his position in his chapter in Koch's *Psychology: A study of a science* (1 959). Several of his more important papers were edited and collected in his *On becoming a person* (1961), and his most extensive research effort was published later (1967b).

The central concept of Rogers's theory is the self. The therapy which Rogers developed over a period of time is consistent with the belief that the patient has a self structure which he himself must change if improvement is to occur. Rogers believes that his observations demand both this kind of therapy and a concept of self like the one he evolved.

To Rogers, the self is a structure compounded out of the experiences which the individual is able to attribute to his own body or to the results of his own behaviour; the self, then, is a self-picture, or self-awareness. The experiences come with value tags attached; that is, some aspects of the self-picture are positive, while others are negative. The self regulates behaviour, for behaviour that is not consistent with the self-picture either does not occur or is not fitted into the self-picture.

Though Rogers was at times subjected to psychoanalytic influences, he tends to reject the analytic emphasis on unconscious processes. He does recognise the possibility that self-inconsistent behaviours will occur as a result of unconscious influences, but he still feels that understanding of an individual can occur most easily if the therapist can enter the phenomenal field that appears to the patient. For Rogers, the consciousness of the individual contains most of what is needed for understanding his personality.

The self-picture is not supposed to be a static thing; although its structure has some stability, it can at times assimilate new experiences in such a way that the structure changes and the particular type of experience is subsequently experienced more easily. The threatened self is rigid and rejecting, but the secure self is fluid and tolerant. This single statement is the conceptual basis for Rogers's nondirective therapy.

Nondirective therapy sets a situation in which the patient can accept experiences into the self structure because the self is at no time threatened and reports of experiences are at no time rejected or devalued by the therapist. Studies have shown that, in therapeutic circumstances, the patients' conceptions of themselves and their ideal selves came into closer agreement (Butler and Haigh, 1954; Rudikoff, 1954, pp. 85-98). Whether the change occurs in the self-picture as such or in the ideal self, the observed changes in therapy should be helpful. The individual's experiences would be more easily assimilated as long as the real self was accepted as a satisfactory structure in relation to the ideal. The self would be less threatened and more subject tc adjustment as necessitated by life experiences.

Rogers, like Goldstein, believes that the organism has a single goal. It strives to actualise, enhance', and maintain itself. The possible lines of actualisation are laid down by heredity, and the organism has, as a part of its native equipment, a creative urge.( Human beings, however, cannot actualise themselves effectively unless they can symbolise their experiences and choose the path that leads to self-enhancement.

It is the failure to symbolise all experience which makes Rogers's distinction between the objective world and the world as perceived by the individual so important. The individual responds to his perceived world rather than directly to the objective world; thus it is essential for his adjustment that the two worlds be as similar as possible.

Carl Rogers is a clinician's clinician. He has spent much of his professional life in his role as therapist, and his theory could hardly be other than closely related to his therapy. We should not expect the theory to be simple, static, dogmatic, or complete. It is the opposite of all these. His theory is, and will be, inductive.

A surprising and often-criticised aspect of Rogers's theory is its strong emphasis upon conscious processes; one might expect that he would follow more behaviouristic or psychoanalytic lines, since he studied both at Columbia, where Thorndikian views were strong, and with Otto Rank. Though Thorndike was not a behaviourist, anyone familiar with his writing knows that he believed in the unconscious automaticity of the operation of the law of effect. Nevertheless, Rogers his preferred an attitude like that of Snygg and Combs (1949) and holds that the experienced world as available to the consciousness of the individual plays the preponderant role in the determination of his behaviour. Rogers thus stands with Allport and many others in stemming the psychoanalytic tide, which seems today to run less strongly toward the depths of the unconscious. That Rogers's own view the current status of psychoanalysis do not differ widely from ours is apparent from one of his statements describing a stay at the Center for Advanced Study in the Behavioural Sciences at Stanford (1967a, p. 372):

Another important influence was my contact with Erik Erikson, a splendid person whose very appearance is therapeutic, and several other psychoanalysts, foreign as well as American. From them I learned what I had strongly suspected—that psychoanalysis as a school of thought is dead-but that out of loyalty and other motives, none but the very brave analysts mention this fact as they go on to develop theories and ways of working very remote from, or entirely opposed to, the Freudian views.

Rogers differs from the psychoanalysts not only in that he assigns a small role to unconscious processes but also in that Rogers's self is a less differentiated entity than the psychoanalyst's mental apparatus. In fact, Rogers has been more concerned with personality *change* than with personality. It seems to us that he has contributed far more to therapeutic theory than to personality theory. Even when he discusses personality, his attention focuses on personality *development, breakdown,* or *functioning* (see Rogers, 1959, pp. 221-235), rather than on personality *structure.*

It is interesting to compare Rogers with Skinner, as we have compared him with Freud. Rogers and Skinner are usually regarded as being at opposite poles. American psychologists seem to regard getting Rogers and Skinner on the same symposium as better sport than baiting bears, and anyone who can succeed in setting up the game is assured of a huge audience and a lively time (see Rogers, 1956; Wann, 1964). Nevertheless, the contrast is in some respects overdrawn. Skinner himself says (quoted in Evans, 1968, pp. 67-68):

> The whole thing is a question of method. That's the crux of my argument with Carl Rogers; I'd like people to be approximately as Rogers wants them to be. I want independent people, and by that I mean people who don't have to be told when to act or who don't do things just because they've been told they're the right things to do... We agree on our goals; we each want people to be free of the control exercised by others-free of the education they have had, so that they profit by it but are not bound by it, and so on.

Skinner and Rogers, despite many disagreements on method, probably have some common attitudes even in this respect. Neither seeks to find out the details of the unconscious mental apparatus. Neither is greatly concerned to uncover the origins of the patient's symptoms in the past. Both would pay attention to current verbalisations, although the attitude toward the verbalisations would be different. Even some of Rogers's prescriptions can be translated into operant language, and the translation approved by Skinner. For example, Rogers, in outlining the necessary conditions for therapy, says a requirement is "That two persons are in *contact.*" Skinner could agree that only if the patient behaves in the presence of the therapist can the therapist effectively change his behaviour. Rogers: "The therapist is *experiencing unconditional positive regard* toward the client" Skinnerian translation: "An organism which is showing a behaviour deficit may be encouraged to behave if free reinforcement follows every identifiable behaviour emitted." Finally, both skinner and Rogers are optimistic about the possibilities for improving the lot of mankind.

We have no desire to gloss over the divisions between Rogers and Skinner (and thereby to ruin psychology's favorite spectator sport), and we have no illusions that Skinner and Rogers will suddenly experience unconditional positive professional regard for each other. However, it is worth noting that they have some fundamental agreements-such as shying away from complex inner structures-as well as some fundamental disagreements on other aspects of philosophy and method.

The fact that Rogers has shied away from the postulation of complex inner structures has made his ideas more amenable to empirical attack than the ideas of some other personality theorists. C.S. Hall and Lindzey (1970, p. 538) report a rather amusing finding from Rogers's (1967b) extensive study of therapy with schizophrenics. Several rating scales were being applied to the therapeutic interaction, and their reliability was being evaluated. One scale was to measure "unconditional positive regard," one of Rogers's key constructs (see, for example, 1959): "Putting this in simpler terms, to feel unconditional positive regard toward another is to 'prize' him (to use Dewey's term, recently used in this sense by Butler)" (p. 208).

Unfortunately, there was a *negative* correlation between the therapists'. evaluation of the therapeutic interaction and the evaluations by patients or by independent raters. This is embarrassing enough in its implications concerning a therapist's ability to judge whether a therapeutic relationship is worth saving, but it becomes even more embarrassing if the finding is attributed to unconscious defenses on the part of the therapists!

It is to the credit of Rogers and his theory that they can be embarrassed. Few theories of personality are explicit enough to be tested, and the exponents of those which are that explicit seldom test them. Rogers has tried.

Rogers has recently turned his attention largely to intensive group experiences with normal individuals, thus starting to explore yet another field. He is using the same phenomenological, existential approach that he was using before those labels came into American psychology. His concern with groups, like his earlier work, fits perfectly into the "third force"-the humanistic alternative to behaviourism and psychoanalysis-which has emerged in psychology. Rogers is either *a* leader or *the* leader in this movement. Near the end of his autobiography, Rogers says (1967a): "I want to have *impact*. I am not a person who is ambitious in the ordinary seense.... But it is important to me to have influence. I want what I do to *count*, to make a difference somewhere" (p. 380). Rogers has his wish. He counts. How high history will carry him now depends on the fate of our third force. It could be high indeed.

Gardner Murphy (1895—) has brought to psychology a wide range of and has made professional contributions in each of his seemingly divergent fields of endeavor. Educated at Yale, Harvard, and Columbia, Murphy turned first to academic psychology. While teaching at Columbia, he collaborated with Likert to publish to *Opinion and the individual* (1938) on the subject of polling and attitude measurement. Murphy later became department chairman at City College of New York. For fifteen years, from 1952 to 1967, he was director of research at the Menninger Foundation. In 1967, he went to George Washington University as a visiting professor, and he is still visiting.

Long interested in parapsychology, Murphy has served as president of the London

Society for Psychical Research and has been a strong and persistent exponent of the need for expansion of such research.

In the area of world peace and international relations, Murphy has studied social tensions in India as a UNESCO consultant and published *Human nature and enduring peace* (1945). He is also the author of two introductory psychology texts (1933, 1951) and has written on the history of psychology (1949), social psychology (Murphy and Murphy, 1931), perception (Solley and Murphy, 1960), and the effect of scientific choices today upon the world's tomorrows (1958). Murphy made his major contribution to personality theory in *Personality: A biosocial approach to origin and structure* (1947). Murphy has remained very productive, but his recent interests have been more in historical topics and in parapsychology than in, personality.

It would seem that Murphy's personality theory could be treated under any, heading. Murphy includes concepts from all important predecessors in his theory. His scholarship and literacy are highly esteemed. He exemplifies the fact that in personality theory, the eclectic needs to deal with the whole of psychology. It has been our contention that the final form of personality theory will be just a synthesis of all psychology; Murphy has come closer to this goal of selective synthesis than they other personality theorist. He has also introduced a number of key concepts which have been of wide influence.

Thumbnailing Murphy, then, is like thumbnailing a large part of the psychology of personality and does Murphy an even greater injustice than it does most other personality theorists. Murphy calls his approach *biosocial* and one can say that he emphasises everything: the biological organism, the individual personality the society, the physical environment, the field nature of events wherein inter changes between organism and environment take place, the stages of personality development—all are treated by Murphy.

Murphy displays more critical selectivity than unique originality, His strength lies in synthesis. Still, there are Striking aspects of Murphy's theory; for example, his definition of self is unexcelled for brevity and simplicity: "The individual as known to the individual" (1947). This definition stands as an island in an otherwise turgid sea.

One of Murphy's best-known concepts is called *canalisation*. There is some similarity between canalisation and Allport's functional autonomy. Murphy's word refers to the tendency individuals may develop to satisfy their drives in quite particular ways; for example, the hunger drive may always be satisfied by eating German food, or a particular kind of German food, when any food would satisfy the biological need as well. Murphy's canalisation does not require that the activity be engaged in for its own sake, but it is as if something like Allport's functional autonomy tipped the motivational scales in favor of the preferred mode of need reduction.

Murphy's research cuts across the boundaries of psychology. It is often used by him to demonstrate the unity of the individual, whose functioning can be understood only by viewing his part processes as they are embedded in the whole. One of Murphy's best-known studies (Levine, Chein, and Murphy, 1942) has been widely cited as demonstrating that the tendency for hungry subjects to report more food objects in ambiguous pictures is a function of food deprivation. This, according to Murphy, demonstrates the general point that no aspect of behaviour (such as perception) can be considered apart from other aspects (such as needs). Postman and Murphy (1943) similarly demonstrated that the degree to which pairs to be associated in memory fit into a subject's attitudinal framework has an important effect on his ability to learn and remember the associated pairs. Murphy later became involved at the Menninger Foundation in an extended programme, of studies in perceptual learning (Murphy, Santos, and Solley, 1968; Santos and Murphy, 1960).

There are numerous pitfalls in trying to be all things to all people, as Murphy in a sense has done. In his case, there are many benefits too. His theory, more than any other, tries to deal with all the facts in all their stubbornness, preferring to treat and relate all the features of personality theory rather than ignore factors which might not fit into any preconceived theory. In 1957, C.S. Hall and Lindzey p. 548) credited Murphy and Sullivan, alone among seventeen personality theorists, with having given a medium or high degree of attention to each of the eighteen dimensions of personality considered (which illustrates the advantages of eclecticism). In 1970, Hall and Lindzey did not treat Murphy's theory of personality either in their table or in the rest of their book (which illustrates the pitfalls of eclecticism). Scholarly eclecticism tends to be unexciting. Iconoclasts, which many personality theorists have been, are exciting, but it is hard for a scholar—and Murphy is a scholar—to be iconoclastic.

We think honest eclectics deserve a better fate, especially when they combine enough iconoclasm to make a long-term, serious study of ESP. If extrasensory abilities eventually become some of the traits to be considered in descriptions of personality, as Murphy thinks they may, he will be the man of the hour. Meanwhile, we might remember Murphy's own cautious credo (1947, p. 927):

Despite all these lessons of the past we write and speak today as if the full concept and stature of man were known. But like our predecessors, we shall rectify mistakes rot primarily by the minor readjustment of the lines of the argument but by the recognition of the fundamental limitations of the whole present system of conceptions. It is preparation for this destruction and rebirth of knowledge to which serious research should be directed.

## Summary and Conclusions

The present chapter has attempted to give a broad overview of the major theoretical approaches to personality. We have classified these theories into five major categories: S-R (Dollard and Miller); *trait and factor* (Allport, Eysenck, Cattell); *organismic* (Goldstein, Sheldon); *neoanalytic* (Horney, Fromm, Murray, Sullivan); and *self* (Rogers, Murphy). Salient characteristics of each of these types of theory have been examined.

It is necessary to make some final comment concerning the contemporary status and future prospects of the type of theory generally labeled "personality." In doing so, we shall distinguish between two groups of personality theory; the S-R and factor theories will be considered in the first group, and all other types of theory in the second.

We have already indicated our belief that psychoanalysis is no longer a viable theory of personality. As to organismic and self theories, it seems that these theorists have the right point of view. Then the next comment is, "So what?" A point of view is not a theory, and we know of no real organismic or self theory with enough structure to quality as a real theory. Trait theories are all right, but unless they are also factor theories, they do not seem to rest on a secure-enough empirical foundation to qualify as theories. Our guess is that in another twenty years, interest in all the preceding theories will be minimal in psychology as a scientific discipline. Humanistic psychology, which endeavors to stress human values in behaviour study, is not now a full-fledged science. These theories may have a place—even, perhaps, a more important place than they now have-in humanistic psychology.

We have also indicated that S-R theories are not really theories of personality. S-R types of theories will, of course, continue to develop. Perhaps, as S-R psychologists work increasingly with clinical problems, someone of that persuasion will work out a theory of personality. It may be more likely, however, that some personality theorist of the future will simply incorporate S-R concepts in an independently developed theory of personality. S-R technology almost certainly will be used increasingly in therapy.

This leaves us with factor theories. Cattell's factor theory is the best worked out and is buttressed with the greatest amount of empirical data. It is comprehensive enough to qualify as a bona fide theory of personality. It takes account of both constitutional and environmental variables. The theory is flexible. Its present form is far from the final word, and the theory may not yet have had enough input from the clinic and from the therapy situation. Nevertheless, if any of the "grand theories" is to survive, it may well be Cattell's. It is fortunate that he has based his work on the methodology of factor analysis; that seems to provide a systematic approach and a discipline that are especially needed in the free-wheeling atmosphere of the field and clinic.

Meanwhile, much research goes on related to specific problems, as we pointed out early in this chapter. It may be that an entirely new theory, or even a new type of theory, will arise out of the dust of this empiricism. We are confident that future theories of personality will incorporate more fully the work of the laboratory with the work of the clink. Such rapprochement would mark the real maturing of a scientific theory of personality.

# 18

# Psychology in Europe, Australia, and Canada

## EUROPE

In reviewing European psychology it is tempting to lay claim to all those trends with European origins. However, even restricting the task to current work inside Europe, it is impossible in a short survey of this kind to do justice to the variety of research going on in any one country, let alone Europe as a whole. Nor would it be particularly helpful, even if it were possible, to produce an annotated bibliography which had any claim to completeness. Moreover, the publication by the APA of *International opportunities for advanced training and research in psychology* (1966) gives a coverage of European institutions and the psychological courses they offer which could not be matched here. Instead, we have picked out a few key figures. The theoretical position of each of them is briefly indicated, and in a number of cases an example is given of the kind of data upon which the position rests.

Although World War II interrupted the theoretical development of psychology in Europe, the major trends were conserved and reconstituted under psychologists whose reputations were firmly established before the war. The death or retirement of giants of this generation, like Pieron, Michotte, and Von Frisch, together with an expansion in the subject, has brought many younger psychologists into senior positions. It is probably true that none of these has yet achieved "giant" status, but for many, like Broadbent, Ekman, and Fraisse, it is a considerable time since they could be regarded as psychological striplings.

In describing European psychology it is convenient to use linguistic rather than national boundaries. A common tongue means a common research literature, and other kinds of affinities soon develop. For our purposes German, French, and English are the most important languages. Psychologists belonging to the smaller linguistic groups, such as those of Scandinavia or the low Countries, try to publish in one or another of the three major languages. For example, the *Scandinavian Journal of Psychology* is published in English. The most notable exception continues to be the Italian research literature, which is considerable.

### Germany

Psychological work in Germany may be given first place if only on historical grounds.

World War II had a particularly crippling effect on research in Germany and Austria as a result of the great losses suffered through exile in the previous decade. Partly, too, this was due to the fact that German psychologists had for so long been accustomed to influence others and had thought of the outside world as a sort of academic colony. Under these conditions isolation was not felt to be a hardship, however serious its effects. The impact on American psychology of the flow of German immigrant psychologists has been described by Wellek (1964) and Buhler (1965). The full effect upon German psychology is difficult to assess, but intensification of certain rather characteristic kinds of German work followed—in particular, verbal, descriptive studies of personality—that nowadays seem to belong to literature rather than science. In its earlier manifestation this approach was important, and it continues to have an influence, especially in its typological forms. Spranger's *Types of Men* (1928) led to *The Study of Values* (1951), by Allport and Vernon. Jung's *Psychological types* (1924) gave our language *extravert* and *introvert*. Kretschmer's *Physique* and *Character* (1925) is the early formulation of a classification which has influenced, among others, Eysenck. Finally, the typological elements in Rorschach's *Psychodiagnostics* (1942), though much less prominent, are sufficiently definite to make it clear that he too belonged to this important German-speaking movement. His work has given rise to a whole research literature of its own.

It is easy to see how arbitrary and intuitive typologies could become under unfavorable circumstances, such as those provided by national socialism. Some good work continued, however, and since the later 1940s it has steadily become more empirical. A useful survey of the whole area, with comparisons between the German and other approaches, is to be found in *Perspectives in Personality Theory* (David and von Bracken, 1957).

There are, fortunately, clear signs that German psychology is breaking away from its former Insularity. For example, the Deutsche Forschungemeinschaft has commissioned a review of the redevelopment of German psychology since the war (Hoyos, 1961). More recently, direct comparisons between psychology in Germany and psychology in America have been made (Merz, 1960; Murch and Wesley, 1966; Russell and Roth, 1958; Wesley, 1966), and textbooks written in German which present some of the recent work outside Germany are appearing (Foppa, 1965).

It is clear from Hoyos's review that German psychologists still approach personality with a split-level treatment, which is nomothetic when typological and idiographic in the study of character. A recent text in the study of character is Wellek's book (1966). The German typological approach has perhaps been most clearly continued by Eysenck In Britain, with his recent attempts to find a genetic and physiological basis for introversion-extraversion (1963; 1963-1964).

Another field in which German psychology has held a distinctive position is perception. The Gestalt psychologists, first in Frankfurt-am-Main and then in Berlin, exercised a far-reaching influence from 1920 until 1934. The senior members of the group—Wertheimer, Kohler, Koffka, and Lewin—went into exile, but one or two good experimentalists among the younger generation stayed on. Of these, Metzger has been the most productive. His book *Gesetze des Sehens* appeared in a second edition in 1953 with many new data. In general, Metzger's work resembles most closely that of Koffka (1936), but increases the degree of stimulus complexity. In particular, there are some very interesting data on the kinds of perceptual organisation which occur when we are presented with visual stimuli in motion.

The extent of current work on perception in Germany which is cast in the Gestaltist mold may surprise anyone who believes that information theory has swallowed up Gestalttheorie. Whether it ever could is a question raised by Green and Courtis (1966). Their argument is that attempt to apply information theory to figure perception have concentrated on the properties of a figure, rather than on the perceptual process, and that in so doing, they have failed to define the ensembles of signs and their associated probabilities of occurrence, which are essential for any measure of association such as our measures of information.

Fairly typical of the bulk of recent perceptual studies in Germany are the papers by Farne *(1965)* on figural aftereffects, Graefe (1964) on the effect of inner contours on form discrimination, and Schmitt (1966), who lays claim to a new perceptual illusion. Kiekheben's (1966) paper, in which he presents work on a "motivating effect of non-pragnanz," although couched in Gestaltist terms, has affinities with Berlyne's work on perceptual novelty and inspection.

A record of the work of the much smaller "Ganzheit" school of psychology at Leipzig—Ganzheiten are distinguished from Gestalten by including in the "whole" the effects of previous experiences—has been published (Volkelt, 1963).

More original, and at present more influential in the field of perception, has been the work going on at Innsbruck Ivo Kohler has made a number of visits to the United States, and some of his experiments are well known. What Kohler does, as he puts it, is to place his laboratory on the bridge of his subject's nose—that is, he uses prisms and filters in a spectacle frame which allows an experiment to run for several weeks.

In such a frame, 10-degree prisms may be inserted with the same orientation, so as to produce a horizontal displacement of visual objects. The prisms are not corrected spherically or chromatically. At first the subject bumps into obstacles, sees vertical straight lines as curved, and finds that the world has become curiously elastic when he moves his head. In addition, all sharp vertical gradients of illumination show a marked fringe of blue or orange. Over a period of three days of continuous wear, these effects largely disappear. Some of the changes had already been described by Gibson (1933). The chromatic adaptation is unusual, however, since complementary aftersensations are obtained when the prisms are removed. These are not retinal, but may remain anchored to the vertical gradients of illumination, although the eyes may move. The theory which Kohler puts forward to account for these, and many other phenomena like them, which he has demonstrated, is not unlike Helson's adaptation level (1959). The organism establishes over time a null point for any constant feature of the stimulus milieu (Kohler, 1963). Kohler's work, originally published In two parts in 1951 and 1953, has more recently appeared in monograph form in English (1964). A useful discussion of Kohler's and other work on displaced vision is that by Harris (1965).

Further work along the same lines (Hajos and Ritter, 1965) has shown that some negative aftereffects are observed in both eyes even though one eye has been covered while the other has been seeing the world through a prism. Using prisms in opposed directions on the two eyes, the same workers have also demonstrated that each eye can develop its own adaptation independently of the other. Using a rather more conservative estimate, Ebenholtz (1966) found rather less interocular transfer.

Another feature of Kohler's work is his demonstration of "gaze-contingent" effects which are adapted to, and aftereffects which are produced by, prismatic transformation. Light falling on a subject's eye through a prism enters the prism at different angles, depending on the direction of the subject's gaze. Hence, if adaptation occurs, the subject must adapt to variations in the characteristics in the transformation which occurs when the eyes are moved, or even when the gaze direction is held constant and the subject moves his head. One recent study, has, however, failed to find gaze-contingent color aftereffects (Harrington, 1965).

Kohler's cybernetic interests are indicated, in an elementary fashion, in his outline of a simple electromechanical analog for classical conditioning (1962).

The third, and during the postwar decades the best-known, area of German research has been that of animal behavior. While American psychologists were coming more and more to depend upon the maze and the Skinner box, German biologists, protected against methodological insecurity by a great tradition, went on observing animals in their natural surroundings. Their observations were systematic, and nowadays a good deal of controlled experimentation goes on; however, the emphasis has always been upon the reactions of a particular species to the various characteristics of its natural environment.

The literature is a big one, and one or two striking studies must represent it. Von Frisch, whose work on bees had long been famous, made some observations during World War II that aroused a good deal of skepticism. He claimed that workers returning to the hive after discovering a new source of honey can indicate both the direction and the distance to their fellows. They do this by dancing. There are two dances—the "round" dance and the "waggle" dance. Round dances consistently indicate food 50 meters or less from the hive, and waggle dances are used for longer distances, but there is a range between 50 and 100 meters when either may occur. Over 100 meters, Increasing distance is coded into changes of pace and emphasis. The direction of the food is indicated simply by the direction of the straight part of the waggle dance if the bee is on a horizontal surface; if the bee is on a vertical surface, it indicates direction by quite a complicated code, using the position of the sun. If the waggle part of the dance moves upward, the food is toward the sun; if it moves downward, the food is away from the sun. A dance to the right means that the food is to the fight of the sun and at the angle by which the dance deviates from the vertical. The same holds true for all other directions. These remarkable observations have since been confirmed. A description of the dances and the table of observations may be found translated in "The dances of the honey bee" (Von Frisch, 1947) and in *The dancing bees* (Von Frisch, 1954).

For psychology, the most important of the German students of animal behavior is probably Lorenz. In particular, his work on the stimuli required to "release" certain characteristic behavior patterns has given rise to a new kind of psychophysics. One of lorenz's many contributions is the concept of "imprinting," the process by which the young of a species become attached normally to their mothers. At first this was described as sudden and irreversible. Perhaps it is not quite so dramatic as all that, but it still happens quite quickly and the species on which any individual imprints may determine its choice of a mate at sexual maturity. Schutz has recently shown, for example; that male mallards can be made homosexual if reared only with males throughout the time during which their species bond is formed (1965a).

Exploration of the stimulus parameters involved in imprinting shows that these vary from species to species. Ducklings will attach themselves to a box on wheels with a buzzer in it. Greylag goslings will convince themselves that they are human if a human being is the first large moving object they see, and so on. However, work on the formation of social bonds has shown that the species bonds are formed rather later than the initial imprinting (Shutz, 1965b). The literature on imprinting is a growing one and has been reviewed by Sluckin (1964).

Lorenz himself is perhaps at his best in English in the delightful and popular *King Solomon's ring* (1956). A more technical account of this kind of work is to be found in *A Study of Instinct* (1951), by Lorenz's disciple Tinbergen. Thorpe's *Learning and Instinct in Animals* (1963) makes an attempt to relate this biological field to studies of animal learning.

Lorenz has recently (1965) undertaken a typically vigorous defense of the importance of phylogenetic development for the understanding of animal behavior and an equally scathing attack on the Sort of operationist's view advanced by D.D. Jensen (1961).

Briefly stated, Lorenz's view is that for the study of adaptive behavior, the biologist is committed to study not only learning by the organism but also genetically coded and stored Information. The latter, Lorenz is at pains to point out, evolves from *successful* interaction with a species' environment and must be contained in all learning processes.

The biologist's approach to phylogenetically stored information is the deprivation experiment, in which the opportunity to respond to some environmental situation is withheld from the animal prior to testing. Such experimentation is dependent upon the successful isolation of the situation under test, which is often difficult and always requires thorough familiarity with the species' behavior. Deprivation experiments are valuable, however, in showing up the points in a species' behavior where learning processes are programmed to occur and in demonstrating what reinforcements are effective. Without this intrinsically interesting knowledge, our understanding of learning must remain incomplete.

Lorenz's book on aggression (1966), which was first published in German in 1963, deals with aggressivity as distinguished from predation, pointing out the social functions of aggression, as in the displays which are part of territorial defense behavior. In the final chapter of this book Lorenz discusses aggressive behavior in man.

One last development in German psychology is worthy of note. Since the 1950s there has been a great deal of psychological traffic in both directions across the Atlantic. As a result, a new generation of German psychologists is beginning to make its presence felt. Its work shows the rigor and methodological sophistication which was so lacking in the years Immediately before World War II, allied to a breadth and solidity which derives from the German academic tradition. Some idea of the growing community of interests between Anglo-Saxon and German psychology may be gained by looking at the volume *Psychologie* (Hoffstatter, 1965), in the Fischer Lexikon series. This book, first written in 1957, was revised in 1964 and reached a ninth edition in 1965. It is incidentally quite the best text for a student of psychology who wishes to improve his German (or even, in its Italian translation, his Italian). It is clear and well illustrated with enough familiar material to serve as a guide through linguistic novelties.

Another text which is worthy of mention is *Gesamtverzeichnis der deutschsprachigen psychologischen Literatur der Jahre 1942 bis 1960* (Wellek, 1965). It is to be hoped that this book, giving the titles of German psychological articles from 1942 to 1960, will quickly be translated into English for the benefit of the non-German-speaking psychological world.

**France**

For many years the French psychological scene has been dominated by the influence of three individuals: Pieron, Michotte, and Piaget. Each has been influential in his own distinctive way. It is interesting, but probably not significant, that only Pieron is a Frenchman; Michotte is Belgian, and Piaget is Swiss. Some work by each has been published in English; Piaget is particularly accessible in this respect. Of the three, Pieron is least easy to identify through his theoretical affiliation; above all lie is an empiricist and an experimentalist. He himself would perhaps have been prepared to trace his descent from Helmholtz. They share an interest in sensory processes and a conviction that psychology and philosophy should not be allowed to drift too far apart. Some impression of Pieron's enormous contribution to psychology may be gained from the pages of *L'Annee Psychologique* (founded in 1898) over the last forty years. As editor, research Worker, and reviewer, he has played a unique part. A comparison between *L'Annee Psychologique* and *Annual Review of Psychology* (founded in 1949) shows that the amount of material from the experimental, and especially the physiological, fields *is* greater in the French publication, though the difference *has* not been quite soo marked in the last few years. The chapter on brain functions by Hernandez-Peon and Sterman in the *Annual Review* (1966) provides proof of the continuing contribution of French workers in the field of physiological psychology. It is still true that the stereotype which represents European psychology as verbal and Philosophical finds no support at the Sorbonne. *L'Annee Psychologique* is of course not merely a review of the research publications in any given year; it is itself an Important source of new material.

Pieron is rather Inadequately represented in English; his *Thought and the brain* (1927) has been overtaken by events. *The Sensations* (1952) is perhaps a better sample of his work, but someone who reads no French or who fails to realise the dominating position of the Sorbonne in the academic life of France cannot hope to appreciate the extent of Pieron's influence. Some idea of Pieron's standpoint on psychophysics is available in *Traite de psychologie experimentale* (1963), Vol. 2, where he discusses critically "la psychophysique subjective," by which he means procedures not deriving from threshold and just-noticeable-difference determination, e.g., magnitude estimation and category scaling.

Michotte by contrast, seems to belong to quite a different tradition. He is a phenomenalist, interested in the characteristics of immediate experience. At the same time he illustrates the important fact that one can be a phenomenalist and an experimentalist of the first rank as well. Probably Wertheimer is the psychologist with whom Michotte has most in common, and so one can think of him as having worked out along highly original lines certain ideas put forward by the Gestalt psychologists. *The perception of causality* (1963) was first published in French in 1946 and is likely to remain a classic. It exemplifies admirably Michotte's approach. What Michotte does here is to study the conditions under which the apparent movements of two visual objects seem to be causally related to one another. The impression of causal relationship is stated to be immediate and not dependent upon inference or previous experience. Though he later used a pair of synchronised projectors, his first apparatus was very simple and ingenious. Two strips of different colors are drawn on a disk so that they approach and recede from each other. When this disk is rotated at various speeds behind a slit equal in width to either strip, two square objects appear to move toward each other and away again. The spatiotemporal characteristics of this movement determine whether it is seen as involving a causal relationship or not. If it is so seen, the causal relationship may be one of two kinds: *L'effet lancement*, or the launching effect, occurs when one square appears to push or propel the other in much the same way as a billiard ball might do when it strikes a second during the course of a game. *L'effet entrainement*, or the carrying effect, is quite easily distinguished. Here one square seems to drag or *bear* the other along with it. All the physical conditions for these two phenomena have been very carefully worked out, and quite confident predictions can now be made. More recently, Michotte had worked on the phenomenal characteristics which seem to distinguish mechanical causality from purposiveness or intentionality. His findings had much in common with those reported by Heider and Simmel (1944). Michotte's Causalite; *permanence et realite phenomenales* (1962) brings together his important publications plus some of those by his colleagues and his pupils.

Piaget is still very active, and his influence is spreading not merely across the Atlantic but across that much more formidable barrier, the English Channel. So original a thinker is hard to place in any historical sequence. Claparede provided the opportunity by founding the J. J. Rousseau Institute at Geneva, and Binet made an important early attempt to solve problems relating to the intellectual development of young children, but Piaget's mixture of logic and biology is his own and may well turn out to be the most important contemporary contribution to psychology in Europe. There are those who feel that his disregard for the nicer points of methodology makes his results suspect. Perhaps he does generalise too readily. It is important, however, to realise just what Piaget is doing. He is no hypothetico-deductive formalist trying to convince himself and his colleagues that he can operate in the manner of the more advanced physical sciences. Rather, he is a natural historian in the descriptive, data-collecting phase, and small errors of timing and identification are of little consequence when weighed against the wealth of insights and observations he has produced. A classificatory framework is not like a deductive theory, which can be invalidated by one wrong prediction. Its value depends on the simplifications it enables us to make and the controlled experiments it stimulates us to perform. In Montreal a group of Canadian psychologists—Therese Decarie, Monique Laurendeau, and Adrien Pinard—are in the vanguard of the attempt to assess Piaget's concepts of development with the methodological rigor which his own studies sometimes lack (e.g., Decarie, 1966).

Piaget's own work shows something of the developmental characteristics which it expounds. The ideas in his early work, such as on language and thought in children (Piaget, 1926) and on children's judgment and reasoning (Piaget, 1928), have been elaborated and specified by later studies on the conception of number (Piaget, 1952) and space (Piaget and Inhelder, 1956) in children. This latter work is of particular interest because of its relevance to the psychology of perception. Using such materials as drawings and simple performance tests, the development of spatial thinking is traced from its early beginning in notions like proximity, separation, and enclosure to fully developed geometrical operations. Piaget's treatment of linear and circular order may be used to illustrate his methods. Colored wooden beads or pieces of paper are arranged in order along a piece of string which, to begin with, is held straight and horizontal. The child is given a second piece of string and is asked to reproduce the order of colors on the first. Before the age of 3½ years, on the average, children, though they may enumerate all the required colors, seem to have no ability to arrange them in order. By four years, most children begin to copy with the notion of an ordered sequence as long a: they are allowed to lay their test string alongside the model and check the items one by one against each other. It is clear from the types of errors made that the second stage is reached because the child has become able to maintain a constant order of progression. At first, however, it is very easy to disrupt the ordered sequence by moving the model to one side or by having the child reproduce a vertical order on a horizontal string. The perceptual pattern is necessary to maintain the constant direction. Between five and six years new possibilities begin to emerge. The child can maintain the sequence and even reverse it without a point-to-point comparison. He is then given the model with the items arranged in a circle and is asked to produce the order on a straight line. Here he must work at a more abstract level, and the perceptual separation of the two ends of the line causes trouble. It is not until be is six or seven years old that the child is able to handle spatial order as such and to reproduce or reverse models presented to him vertically, circularly, or even twisted Into a figure eight.

One can see how this patient, rather Informal exploration could be used as the basis for test construction or a more rigorous experimental design, but Piaget's own interests seem to be moving in the direction of a theoretical analysis of thinking as such. *The growth of logical thinking from childhood to adolescence* (1958) and, more recently, his work on classification and seriation (Piaget and Inhelder, *1964)* give some indication of Piaget's activity in the field of thinking. *L 'image mentale chez l'enfant* (1966) is one of Piaget's most recent works on thinking and symbolic processes in children. Piaget's work up to about 1960 is discussed in Flavell's useful book *The Developmental Psychology of Jean Piaget* (1963).

The extent of Piaget's Influence is clearly seen in *Psychologie et epistemologie genetiques: themes Piagetiens* (Bresson and Montmollin, 1966). The contributors to this volume, published in Piaget's honor, include Berlyne (Canada), Smedslund (Norway), and Fraisse (France). Piaget's latest writings are *Biologie et connaissance: Essai sur les relations entre les regulations organiques et les processus cognitifs* (1967a) and, in translation, *Six psychological studies* (1967b).

Despite Piaget's stature as an innovator, it would be wrong to think of the work at Geneva as in any way isolated from French psychology as a whole. There are many links with Michotte's work through studies of causality, movement, and speed as understood by children, while Fraisse at the Sorbonne in *Les structures rhythmiques* (1957) shares with Piaget an interest in the development of the perception of time. An introduction to the work of Piaget and Fraisse which could be useful to someone who has no previous knowledge of Piaget's work on cognitive schematizlng and perception or of Fraisse's work on time perception is given in Vol. 6 of *Traite de psychologie experimentale* (Fraisse and Piaget, 1963).

The history of psychology in Belgium, and an assessment of recent trends there, is available in Nuttin's monograph (1961a). Nuttin's own experimentally based attack upon the Thorndikian view of the law of effect (1961b) has been largely neglected in the United States. His work on the spread of effect demonstrates this attack. Here, Nuttin sets out to demolish Thorudike's connectionist interpretation of spread-of-effect phenomenon, which accepted that S-R bonds are strengthened by reward and weakened by punishment

Nuttin (1949) suggests that more than one factor acts to produce the spread-of-effect result, and he demonstrates a similar phenomenon which is attributable to "spread of recall." What Nuttiri demonstrates is that *if one rearranges the order* of a list which has been presented once to a subject, items are now recalled as having been rewarded if, on the second (test) presentation, they are close to items which were rewarded. That is, recalling item: as having been rewarded, occurs significantly more frequently for those item: now nearest rewarded items than for items which were nearest on the first presentation of the list.

Marx (1956), who at the time seems to have been alone among American psychologists in considering Nuttin's work, found it difficult to distinguish Nuttin's interpretation of the phenomenon from Thorndike's. Greenwald (1966) points out clearly that Nuttin is trying to disentangle the effects of rewards as strengthening associations on the acquisition trial and, alternatively, producing mistaken recalls of having been rewarded—as a function of nearness to rewarded items, even when the list order is rearranged—on the test trial.

Nuttin's spread of recall is certainly not how Thorndike saw the spread of effect operating and can be viewed as complementing rather than supplementing Thorndike's view. But Marx is right to wonder how Nuttin would define the strength of a response, rejecting, as Nuttin explicity does, increase in the frequency of response repetition in the course of a learning experiment. Perhaps the issue here is that, for Thorndike, reward acts on the connection between stimulus and response items; for Nuttin the effect of reward generalises from the rewarded item to other nearby items.

Nuttin might have postulated a gradual decay of reward effect to explain why, in his experiments, there is still some tendency in the test trial for items nearest rewarded ones in the acquisition trial to be wrongly recalled as having been rewarded even though they are now furthest from a rewarded item. However, Nuttin appears to prefer the alternative that both spread of effect and spread of recall may underlie the phenomenon.

Nuttin's work is damaging to Thorndikian connectionism, but the connectionist standpoint keeps cropping up in psychology. Fairly recently, for example, Broadbent (1958, p.298) states that for the long term, the organism stores the conditional probabilities of past events. These, it can be argued, are precisely what Thorndike was manipulating through reinforcement in his "selecting and connecting."

This somewhat unlikely line of descent for Broadbent's idea of what is learned—which, in fact, probably derives from information-theory approaches—might also have included Skinner's response probability in the family tree. Technically, the main difference between Thorndike and Skinner is simply that, accepting the possibility of rewarding smaller segments of behavior, Skinner achieves a faster and more precise control of his subject's behavior than Thorndike did.

**Great Britain**

British psychology tends to look across the Atlantic just now, but it still retains a few distinctive features. Oddly enough in the country of the "English" empiricists and associationists, one of these features is a lack of interest in associationism (Drever, 1965). This is probably the result of historical accidents. Empirical psychology as formulated at the beginning of the present century by the philosophers Ward (1918) and Stout (1913) had been transformed by post-Kantian German thought. Bartlett, who more than anyone else determined the present nature of British psychology, was a pupil of Ward. This did not make him a philosopher—he has always been impatient of armchair theorising—but it did make him suspicious of a simple S-R approach. It is important for psychologists in the United States, or in Russia for that matter, to realise that the rather general European indifference to associationism springs from the fact that it is an "old-fashioned" point of view and can be found quite fully developed in the eighteenth century. While the Kantian reformation of Hume's position did not deal with associationism as such, it did imply the existence of cognitive structures other than those based upon contiguity and frequency. Since that time, all variants of the simple S-R theme have appeared too easy. This prejudice is held to have been justified by events, and there is a strong suspicion that the amount of information generated per rat-mile during the last fifty years has not been great.

*Bartlett's Remembering* (1932) is a study of perception and thinking as well as memory, and his more recent *Thinking* (1958) develops some of the themes in the earlier work. But Bartlett has been much more influential through his teaching than through his writings. The Cambridge laboratory was for many years a leading nursery for experimental psychologists. At one time more than two-thirds of the chairs in Great Britain were held by Bartlett's pupils. They may not all have been docile, but most of them show identifiable characteristics. Prominent among these are a preference for human rather than animal subjects and a tendency to use cognitive types of explanation. The latter are more often stated nowadays in neurological or electronic than in logical terms.

A key figure in the development of British psychology in the fields of perception and thinking was Craik, who died, still a young man, as the result of a road accident in 1945. He was a philosopher by training, an experimentalist by inclination, and a genius at inventing apparatus. Some of the basic ideas of cybernetics owe their origin to him. A short statement of his theoretical position is to be found in *The nature of explanation* (1943), and selected papers by Craik have recently been published (Craik, 1966).

Broadbent (1958) has described important experimental work which follows up some of Craik's ideas. According to Broadbent, two of the basic problems in perception as related to skilled performance are channel capacity and selectivity. How much information can the human operator handle, and how can he protect himself against overloading or from unwanted signals? In vision many of the necessary adjustments are carried out peripherally, but in hearing they must be done centrally. Thus Broadbent uses auditory stimuli in experiments where the subject has to listen selectively to one of two simultaneous messages or to a message accompanied by irrelevant noise; the filtering process which takes place is central rather than sensory. It depends upon the amount of information, as one might expect, but it also depends to a marked extent upon the sequential probability values within the two messages. It is this that makes the word *stimulus* about as specific and psychologically useful as the word *thing*. The theoretical position which emerges from Broadbent's work resembles that advocated by Bruner (1957) and others in the United States.

Broadhurst (1966), who is himself largely responsible for the recent redevelopment of interest in experimental psychogenetics in Britain, has seen in Broadbent's interest in introversion-extraversion "a hint of the merging interests of... Broadbent and Eysenck which, should it come to collaborative effort, might result in British psychology developing an impact born of coherent thought, the like of which it has not previously exerted." This, however, appears to ignore the fact that Broadbent (1958) relates introversion-extraversion to the length of "sample" of incoming data used by the individual. It also disregards the fact that predictions from Broadbent's model of introversion-extraversion have sometimes conflicted with predictions from the Eysenckian model (e.g., Broadbent, 1958; Griew and Lynn, 1960).

The work of the Applied Psychology Research Unit at Cambridge under Broadbent's direction is very much in the mainstream of Bartlettian influence. Some of the aspects of the unit's work are described by Poulton (1966) in his chapters on engineering psychology in the *Annual Review of Psychology* and on tracking in Bilodeau's *Acquisition of skill* (1966). This latter book betrays the fact that skilled performance in the United States is still, to a large extent, studied as a subdivision of learning. This is also true of the Soviet approach to skill, and it is not irrelevant that in both these countries monolithic theories of learning, which accept the conditioned response as a fixed behavioral unit, have held sway for long periods. In the United States the full extent of Watson's and Hull's influence may be seen in the fact that even authors who have rejected the conditioned response (for example, Tolman and Skinner) still discuss the (fixed) behavioral unit (Skinner, 1959; Tolman, 1932). Berlyne (1965) goes to some trouble to deny these fixed units....contemporary S-R psychology concerns itself with associations not between single stimuli and single responses (whatever those would be!) but between classes of stimulus situations and classes of behaviour (p. 8)." The temptation is to add "whatever those would be" again, but the main difference is that we retain freedom to *define* and, if necessary, *redefine* classes empirically rather than trying to force our behavioral analysis into inappropriate classes.

The Cambridge tradition in the study of skilled performance contrasts with this, asking the question: "How is complex purposive behavior organised?" and working by induction from finding to model, rather than deductively from theory' to prediction. The barrenness, for Hullians, of the prediction which is unconfirmed *is no more* admitted by them than the precariousness of Skinner's theoretical approach is admitted by Skinnerians.

The Cambridge tradition in the study of skilled performance is seen in Vol. 27 of *Acta Psychologica*, which is a special volume on attention and performance dedicated to the remembrance of Paul Fitts.

Other important work which lies outside the mainstream of Bartlett's influence is also being carried out at Cambridge. Two sets of studies are noteworthy: first, the work by Gregory on perception (Gregory, 1966a, 1966b; Gregory and Wallace, 1963). Gregory's size-constancy theory of the illusions, in particular, has produced great interest among, and a good deal of criticism from, other European workers (Virsu, 1967; Zanforlin, 1967). Second, the work at Cambridge on the effects of cortical ablation in primates (Cowey., 1967; Cowey and Weiskrantz, 1967; Humphrey and Weiskrantz, 1967) derived its initial impetus from Zangwill's active interest in the effects of specific lesions on behavior. How far the recent Cambridge interest in creativity (Hudson, 1966) derives from Bartlett is not clear, but he has certainly advocated a change in the usual form of intelligence test (1954) by suggesting that intelligence is at least as much a matter of the ways by which an issue, or an answer to a problem is reached, as of whether the issue, or the answer, can be called 'correct.'

Hudson's work is on convergent and divergent thinking following Guilford (1950). He has shown that the tendency is for divergers to seek arts specialisms and for convergers to choose the physical sciences. Hudson rejects the facile identification of creativity with divergent thinking, pointing out that in the physical sciences which attract convergers, the creative people still tend to be convergers, although they may be rather more like divergers than their less creative counterparts. The roots of convergent and divergent thinking Hudson suggests are to be found in the child's upbringing. Convergers may be made by parents who are unable to show affection easily. These parents, it is suggested, may typically find it easier to offer an academic sort of approval of more impersonal skills, thus leading the child to acquire these and find his security in them. The diverger's parents, on the other hand, tend to disregard the importance of practical achievements and to reserve their approval and affection for personal relationships. Such parents, Hudson argues, produce children who are "addicted to people," seeing them as the source of their security.

A second strand in British psychology can be traced back to Galton through Spearman, Thomson, and Burt. It was to the study of individual differences and the development of appropriate statistical techniques that Britain made its most distinctive psychological contribution during the first quarter of the present century. Spearman stated his hierarchical theory of intelligence in *The nature of "intelligence" and principles of cognition* (1923), followed by *The abilities of man* (1927). Thomson waited until 1939 to publish *The factorial analysis of human ability*, but the two had long been engaged in a lively academic duel. Thomson's attitude toward Spearman, and later toward Thurstone, was on the whole one of skepticism. In particular he doubted Spearman's claim that factor analysis could be used to prove the necessity of one particular solution. Burt is still active in statistical psychology, and his book *The factors of the mind* (1940) is an objective summing-up of the earlier controversies and the Statement of the still distinctive British position in the factor-analysis field. Burt was also the first psychologist who applied Mendelian genetics to the study of mental inheritance, and it is from him that the current interest in psychogenetics in Britain stems (Broadhurst, 1959).

The application of mental testing in British education has been surprisingly wide for a country with such a reputation for conservatism. Until the present government indicated their intention to alter the educational system, most children in the state school system were given the so-called 11-plus examination, which is an intelligence and achievement test. What happens educationally thereafter is determined, perhaps too much, by the results. As a consequence, much present-day British research in this area has a marked practical and educational bias, and theoretical issues are no longer being raised. Of the workers whose main contribution belongs to the period since World War II, P. E. Vernon has been most influential. He is a pupil of Bartlett who belongs to the school of Burt. In The *structure of human abilities* (1950) he shows an empirical and cautious approach with the marked practical bias that has just been mentioned. A book published in 1964 is a critical survey of personality assessment. The main theoretical conclusions of this book are summarised in an article (Vernon, 1965) appearing in a volume of essays by Burt's former pupils and others, compiled in recognition of his formidable contribution to psychology.

The British view of the nature of intelligence differs from the American in being hierarchical. Thorndike (1914) thought of intelligence as a multitude of specific skills. Thurstone (1938) later worked with a relatively large democratically, ordered collection of abilities. British workers in the field, though differing among themselves, have moved toward analysis of intelligence which starts with a general factor. Once the general factor has been removed from the matrix of test inter-correlation, it is found that two large group factors tend to show up—one of them verbal-numerical-educational in nature, and the other spatial-practical-mechanical. Below these again are smaller group factors corresponding roughly to the primary mental abilities of Thurstone, with specific factors deriving from particular skills and circumstances at the bottom. The differences between the British and the American views are not basic, but depend to some extent upon method. For example, Thurstone has a second-order general factor which in some respects resembles Spearman's original "g" factor.

To the outside observer, Eysenck might seem to belong here too, but impression is misleading. It is true that his early work was based on the factor analysis of personality tests, and at one stage he was influenced by Burt, but his statistical procedures are only part of a wider strategy. More recently Hullian learning theory has been utilised in the same way. As has been suggested, Eysenck has much in common with the German typologists, though his methods are much more rigorous than theirs tend to be. Even so, there are those who feel that sometimes uses his data in a forensic rather than a scientific way. At all event, his output is much greater than that of any other British psychologist just now and ranges all the way from highly technical to popular works. Perhaps *The scientific study of personality* (1952) gives the best general statement of his theoretical position. He is concerned, on the basis of objective test data, to rate his subjects on a number of dimensions of which introvert-extravert and normal-neurotic are the most important. Having done this, he hope: to identify the underlying neurological variables for these dimensions. Much of his work has been done in a clinical setting, and he has edited a handbook of abnormal psychology (1960) in which most of the contributors are present or former colleagues.

It is a strength of Eysenck's that his attempts to relate together the numerous and diverse results on introversion-extraversion appear receptive to new trends in psychology. That the *Zeilgeist* stalks the corridors of the Maudsley is used equally often as a criticism by Eysenck's antagonists, who point to his rather loose interrelating of Hullian reactive inhibition, Pavlovian cortical inhibition, Pavlovian "strength" of the nervous system, and, more recently, the tonic activity of the reticular formation of the brainstem.

It has been suggested by Eysenck (1963), with a hesitancy which many might judge uncharacteristic, that the ascending reticular formation has affinities with psychological concepts of excitatory and inhibitory potential. Certainly', experiments with stimulant and depressant drugs which work through the reticular formation have shown that more introverted behavior follows administration of the former and that more extraverted behavior follows administration of the latter.

This is a suggested basis for the apparently genetically constituted tendency toward introversion or extraversion shown by Shields (1962). Shields compared the personalities of monozygotic and fraternal twins reared separately or together. The correlation on extraversion scores for identical twins brought up apart was +.61 (forty-two pairs), and for identical twins brought up together it was +.42 (forty-three pairs), whereas for fraternal twins brought up together it was —.17. While twin studies are always hedged about with difficulties, these data seem to point to a genetic basis for introversion-extraversion.

It is unnecessary to do more than note in passing that the naturalistic study of animal behavior, which was a feature of British biology at the end of the nineteenth century, is again becoming more prevalent as a result of influences from the Continent. Reference has already been made to works by Tinbergen, now at Oxford, and by Thorpe, of Cambridge. Recent work by Tinbergen has appeared on the evolution of signaling devices (1964), and both Tingergen (behavior and natural selection) and Thorpe (development of behavior) have contributed chapters to *Ideas* at *modern biology* (Moore, 1965). Another contribution has been made by Thorpe and Davenport (1964) to the study of learning in invertebrates. Other publications in this field include *Brain and Behaviour in Cephalopods*, by Wells (1962), whose work has more in common with that of J.Z. Young than with that of Tinbergen. This kind of approach seems more congenial to British psychologists than the use of mazes and Skinner boxes but a good deal of animal research on quantitative lines is going on as well.

**Scandinavia**

Scandinavia, which is seemingly geographically remote, is often associated with scientific and cultural developments of an advanced kind. Psychology as a profession has obtained more official recognition here than elsewhere in Europe, and in Norway particularly an admirable scheme of training and certification has been worked out.

On the research side there is widespread activity in most fields of psychology. Piaget's influence is apparent in Scandinavia, as elsewhere in Europe (see Smedslund, 1964), and some interest in human learning is evident. Bjorgen's book on rote learning (1964) is an attempt to relate both meaningfulness and learning speed to some mediator which allows the item to be learned to be integrated into the subject's store of experiences. But perception continues to be by far the most active field of Scandinavian psychological research. Katz, though he came late to Stockholm, was very influential. The phenomenological point of view, which he shared with Rubin, is well stated by von Fieandt, of Helsinki (1958). Johansson, at Uppsala, is more an experimentalist than a theoretician (e.g., Johansson and Ottander, 1964), but both his work (1958, 1964) and that of von Fieandt (von Fieandt and Gibson, 1959) show affinities with that of Gibson at Cornell. The importance of psychophysics in Scandinavian psychology may be seen in the fact that a major link between Scandinavian and American psychology occurs through the work of the latter-day psychophysicists—Gibson, Helson, and Stevens. This is not to say that there is always agreement between the two sets of workers; Ross's book on psychological measurement and its underlying logic (1964) claims that in his direct scaling' methods, Stevens (in whose laboratory Ross had worked for a year) develops a subjective psychology. Ross's argument is not supported by the earlier work of Goude (1962), and the question is fully discussed by Eisler (1965), Helson's influence may be seen in the work of von Wright and Mikkonen (1963).

Much of the current work on psychophysics in Scandinavia has its direct origin in the laboratories at Stockholm, where Ekman is a figure of international reputation in the fields of psychophysics and scaling. Ekman's chapter, written with Sjoberg, on scaling (Ekman and Sibberg, 1965) gives some idea of the contribution he and his co-workers made in this field. On the physiological side, excretion rates of adrenaline and noradrenaline in cognitive tasks under stress have been the subject of a series of experiments by Frankenhaeuser and her colleagues (Frankenhaeuser, 1966a, 1966b).

There also appears to have developed a Scandinavian school with a common approach to problem solving which lays emphasis on the restructuring of experience (J. Jensen, 1960a, 1960b; Raaheim, 1960, 1961, 1962; Szekely, 1958, 1959).

**Holland**

Holland nowadays has much in common with Scandinavia. Applied psychology is quite advanced, particularly in the industrial and cultural fields, but there is no distinctive theoretical position. Social psychology is highly developed in Holland, as it is in Belgium and France, but as yet there is no sign of any European challenge to Michigan. Although the universities contribute a proportion of the current research on perception, as Amsterdam does under Duijker (e.g., Moed, 1964, 1965, 1966), the Institute for Perception R.V.O.-T.N.O. at Soesterberg is claiming a growing share of the output (e.g., Michon, 1965; Sanders, 1963, 1966), and already one good monograph (Levelt, 1965), on binocular rivalry, has emerged from the institute. Some of the institute's work is presented in the special volume of *Acta Psychologica* mentioned above (Vol. 27).

**Italy**

Italian psychology retained its Philosophical characteristics longer than the psychologies of the more northerly European countries. A notable early development of experimental work occurred at the Catholic University at Milan. Here Gemelli rivaled Pieron in the extent of his output and excelled him in diversity. In recent years there have been many signs of direct American influence upon Italian psychology, but earlier Gemelli played a twofold role. Not only was he a productive research worker and policy maker, but he also maintained a closer contact with the psychological world as a whole than any of his colleagues did.

Applied work in Italy, as at the National Institute of Psychology at Rome, derives mainly from Gemelli but also to a lesser degree from Ponzo's contributions to aptitude testing and selection and the recognition his efforts obtained for applied psychology in education, industry, and vocational guidance (see Misiak and Staudt, 1953).

Much of the psychological research in Italy either has an applied orientation-there is, for example, widespread interest in areas like accident prevention (Cesa-Bianchi and Di Naro, 1966; Iacono, 1966; Migliorino, 1965)—or is performed in areas where applied and theoretical issues come close to each other, for example, Tretini's (1966) formulation of a culturalisation rate, expressed as culture-free intelligence over culturalised intelligence, for use with socially deprived children; the work on risk-taking behavior by Spaltro (1965), comparing group and individual decisions; and that of Chiari (1966), who studied attitudes and risk perception in adolescents in everyday and occupational activities.

Some theoretically orientated research is, however, carried on, and even now, as in Battachi and Montanini's (1965) work on syntactic structures, it is possible to detect echoes of Gemelli's earlier original research, in this case his work on the acoustic analysis of language. In the north, in Trieste under Kanizsa and in Padua under Metelli, pure research flourishes in the field of perception (e.g., Flores d'Arcais, 1965). These perceptual studies show the influence which German psychology, and particularly Gestaltists like Kohler, has exerted in Italy.

**Australia**

Historically, psychology in Australia had its beginnings in education. Once psychology was under way in its own right, the bias of Australian psychologists, like A.H. Martin and H.T. Lovell, was toward applied and, specifically, vocational psychology. There are now vocational guidance divisions in each state run by the Commonwealth (Federal) labour Department, but Australian psychology has developed so rapidly that there is no disproportionate trend in current work to indicate its origins.

There are three main streams of current development in Australian psychology. The first, stemming perhaps from the influence of Champion and his colleagues at Sydney, is a widespread behavioristic approach to animal learning.

The second, deriving originally from the influence of A.J. Marshall at Western Australia and O'Neill at Sydney, is the present activity in perception. Here, as in Scandinavia, there is some identification with Gibson's approach. The Strongest research line is undoubtedly the study of aftereffects led by Day at Monash and his collaborator Singer at Macquarie. Two particularly interesting examples of this work are Day's work with Power and the explanation of sensory adaptation and aftereffect advanced by Day and Singer. Day and Power (1965) bring together under one interpretation rotary movement reversals, shown, for example, by Ames's window; apparent reversals in orientation of static figures, of which the ambiguous windmill is an example; and the kinetic depth effect. All these effects are explained in terms of "an identity of retinal projections for two or more motions or orientations of an object in space." Day and Singer, following Barlow and Hill (1963), suggest that the neural coding of stimulation is represented by the difference in firing levels between groups of neurons which are specific to a particular form of stimulation, e.g., clockwise or anticlockwise movement and blue or yellow light. What is suggested is that with prolonged stimulation, the activity of the stimulated neuron group diminishes—producing adaptation—so that on cessation of the stimulation, there is relatively greater activity by the nonstimulated neuron group, thus giving rise to an aftereffect or negative afterimage until the firing levels of both neural groups again balance.

There are some problems with this approach, particularly where intersensory effects on aftereffects have been observed (e.g., Day and Singer, 1964a, b), but it seems not at all impossible that eventually a common processor group of neural units will be identified which accepts and integrates similar information from different modalities (e.g., Morrell, 1967). Certainly the existence of cross-modal effects on aftereffects makes this seem entirely likely.

The third stream of psychological research has its roots in an environment where social influences on personality not only were considered to be an important area of academic interest but also were conceived of as a field of applied social engineering. Most of this sort of work centered on Melbourne (e.g., Oeser and Emery, 1954; Oeser and Hammond, 1954; Oeser and Harary, 1964; Oeser and O'Brien, 1967).

It is possible to discern that there may soon be a fourth major trend in Australian psychology, relating to physiological psychology and particularly to perceptual processes. The origins of this work probably go back to Eccles himself, but currently the work includes Bishop's interest in vertebrate vision and, more: lately, but also at Canberra, Horridge's work on invertebrates. What is presently lacking is a sufficient number of psychologists interested in attempting to relate this work to perception.

Outside the major trends, the main impression one gets of psychology at most Australian institutions is that it has a high degree of eclecticism. Hence, Sydney is a center not only of behaviorism in Champion's work but also of psychometrics (Sutcliffe, 1964, 1965; Sutcliffe and Bristow, 1966), and Canberra combines social psychology and an active Piagetian group with an essentially British approach to human performance. Adelaide's two universities are complementary in their coverage. The older university of Adelaide had its initial impetus from M.A. Jeeves's interest in cognitive psychology and shows strength in physiological and comparative psychology (e.g., Glow, Richardson, and Rose, 1967; Glow and Rose, 1966; Munn, 1964) and operant studies, together with a growing involvement with the cultural and social problems of Australia's Aboriginal population. More recently, however, under A.T. Welford, there has been an increasing emphasis on a Bartlettian approach to both theoretical and practical issues in the organisation of human skilled performance. The newer Flinders University, on the other hand, is geared to work in personality and social psychology; e.g., Feather's studies on persistence and achievement motivation extend the original work of McClelland and Atkinson. Feather's contribution is seen in his book, written jointly with Atkinson, entitled *A Theory of Achievement Motivation* (Atkinson and Feather, 1966).

Clinical and personality psychology is probably best represented outside the older universities at New South Wales (e.g., Hammer and Johnson, 1965) and Western Australia (e.g., Sarbin, Taft, and Bailey, 1960; Taft, 1959, 1966; Yates, 1962, 1966). Australian work goes beyond the particular biases mentioned, of course (e.g., Lafitte, 1957; O'Neil, 1962), but no major psychological innovation has yet originated in Australia.

**Canada**

There is currently a great volume of psychological research in Canada, with widespread interest in two fields. The first is verbal learning and memory research (Earhard and Earhard, 1967; Earhard and Mandler, 1965a, 1965b; Jung, 1967; Marshall, 1967; Murdock, 1967; Murray, 1967). The second field is motivation. Appley, who with Cofer wrote *Motivation: Theory and research* (Cofer and Appley, 1967), and Bindra, the author of *Motivation: A systematic reinterpretation* (1959), were both at Canadian universities Malmo's work on motivation at McGill relates the notion of a generalised nondirected drive and physiological arousal (Malmo, 1958), and lie tends to try to use physiological indicators of drive and emotion rather than more traditional behavioristic measures (1957, 1965). Berlyne's work on "novelty" or "surprisingness" (1954, 1960, 1961, 1963) relates the internal state of the animal, which may be called *attentional* and which includes level of arousal, and learning. He may be loosely grouped among the Canadian motivational workers, although his interests seem to have swung toward giving the neoassociationists a firm foothold in the field of thinking. Berlyne's book *Structure and direction in thinking* (1965) is an attempt to understand the "implicit responses" of intellectual processes in terms of the behaviorist's principles of overt behavior.

What is most distinctively Canadian in psychology, however, still derives from Hebb (1949). There appear to be two main lines of descent in Canadian psychology. The first involves work on sensory isolation (Bexton, Heron, and Scott, 1954) which is being carried on by Zubek and his co-workers, (Schutte and Zubek, 1967; Zubek and MacNeill, 1967). Work on perceptual isolation is not confined to Canada (see Fuller and Clark, 1966a, 1966b; Mason and Sponholz, 1963; Schultz, 1965), but Zubek's project is a systematic analysis of the separate effects of factors present in the original studies.

The second involves studies which are perhaps not immediately recognizable as being closely related to one another but which nevertheless have a link in their descent from Hebb's work. Hebb (1949, pp. 49-50) quoted the (then) unpublished work of Mishkin and Forgays (1952), showing that when words are tachistoscopically exposed in either left or right visual fields, they are more readily recognised in the right visual field. Hebb used these data in his attack upon Lashley's work on equipotentiality. Heron (1957) found results which went against Mishkin and Forgay's hypothesis that "a more efficient neural organisation" is established in the left cerebral hemisphere for verbal material. Heron preferred to explain the data in terms of a post exposure attentional process, involving learned eye movements, which is developed in learning to read. This work has sparked off a large number of other studies, mainly using tachistoscopic techniques on the effects of retinal location, cerebral dominance, and directional reading habits (Bryden, 1965, 1967; Bryden and Rainey, 1963; Hirata and Osaka, 1967; Kimura, 1961).

## Conclusion

Stepping back to look at psychology in these three parts of the world as a whole allows a few impressionistic comments. As a result of the use of computer techniques, information theory, and statistical decision theory, the discovery of a common language among experimental psychologists, and between psychologists and mathematicians and communications engineers, exemplified in Cherry's *On Human Communication* (1961), continues. Cherry himself (1957) gave a salutary reminder of the limitations of communication theory as a tool of experimental psychology, but the gains for theoretical development, which derive from this approach, are not yet exhausted. Other cognitive systems are being used in other contexts. Piaget's analysis of children's thinking is logical as well as descriptive.

What is conspicuously absent from the European scene is systematic learning theory of the Hullian type. This was largely an American phenomenon, just as a rigid conditioned reflex theory had to be characteristic of Russia. The East-West political division apart, the biggest gulf in the psychological world is still that between America and Europe. For reasons which are probably linguistic, an exception can be made in the cases of Britain and Scandinavia. For other European countries, however, what traffic these is in research and ideas seems to be largely one-way, with Europe following America's lead. This trend tends to reduce further the influence of European psychology, even inside Europe itself, and delays the assimilation of European discoveries within American psychology.

Nevertheless, the geographical peculiarities of psychology are slowly giving way before the current American move toward mediation types of formulation and the growing Russian interest in symbolic processes, shown, for example, by Luria (1959).

Skinner's influence, never very great in European research, is increasing slightly in applied fields, as in the use of autoeducational devices or in clinical work. But research into operant conditioning as a therapeutic procedure is still uncommon in much of Europe, where most clinicians pin their faith firmly to the advance of physical methods, particularly for the treatment of schizophrenia and the depressive illnesses.

Skinner's particular legacy to psychology will be a few valid and important generalisations and several useful techniques. In Europe at least, these may be incorporated into psychology without producing the research effort which usually surrounds a largely untested and complex theory such as Hull, for example, bequeathed to us.

Finally, it seems true that the major new trends in psychology are international. The move toward computer simulation as the new tool of psychology, toward psycholinguistics as a rapidly expanding field, and toward Piaget's thinking as, possibly, the main growing source of influence may be seen throughout most of the psychological world. This process is another important step in the maturation of Psychology as an experimental science.

## REFERENCES

Allport, G.W., and Vernon, P. E. *The Study of values: A scale for measuring the dominant interests in personality.* (Rev. ed.) Boston: Houghton Mifflin, 1951.

American Psychological Association. *International Opportunities for Advanced Training and Research in Psychology.* Washington, D.C.: A.P.A., 1966.

*Annual Review of Psychology,* 1949, 1.

Atkinson, J.W., and Feather, N.T. *A Theory of Achievement Motivation.* New York: Wiley, 1966.

Barlow, H.B., and Hill, R. M. Evidence of a physiological explanation of the waterfall phenomenon and figural aftereffects. *Nature,* 1963, 200, 1345-1347.

Bartlett, F.C. *Remembering.* London: Cambridge University Press, 1932.

Bartlett, Sir F.C. Intelligence tests. *Times Science Review,* Summer, *1954.*

Bartlett, F.C. *Thinking.* London: Methuen, 1958.

Battachi, M.W., and Montanini, M. M. Structure sintattiche e modelli di ordinamento seriale. *Rivista de Psicologia Sociale,* 1965, 32,193-205.

Berlyne, D.E. A theory of human curiosity. *British Journal of Psychology,* 1954, 45,180-191.

Berlyne, D.E. *Conflict, Arousal, and Curiosity.* New York: McGraw-Hill, 1960.

Berlyne, D.E. Conflict and the orientation reaction. *Journal of Experimental Psycholcgy,* 1961,62,8-13.

Berlyne, D.E. Motivational problems raised by exploratory and epistemic behaviour. In S. Koch (Ed.), *Psychology: A study of a science.* Vol. 5. *The Process Areas, the Person, and Some Applied Fields: Their place in psychology and in science.* New York: McGraw-Hill, 1963. pp: 284-364.

Berlyne, D.E. *Structure and Direction in Thinking.* New York: Wiley, 1965.

Bexton, W.H., Heron, W., and Scott, T.H. Effects of decreased variation in the sensory environment. *Canadian Journal of Psychology,* 1954, 8, 70-76.

Bilodeau, E.A. (Ed.) *Acquisition of skill.* New York: Academic Press, 1966.

Bindra, D. *Motivation: A systematic reinterpretation.* New York: Ronald Press, 1959.

Bjorgen, I.A. *A re-evaluation of rote learning.* Oslo: Oslo University Press, 1964.

Bresson, F. and de Montmollin, M. (Eds.) *Psychologie et epistemologie genetiques: Themes Piagetiens.* Paris, Dunod, 1966.

Broadbent, D. D. *Perception and Communication.* London: Pergamon Press, 1958.

Broadhurst, P.L. Application of biometrical genetics to behaviour in rats. *Nature,* 1959, 148, 1517-1518.

Broadhurst, P. L., and Broadhurst, A. Psychology in Britain today. *Indian Psychological Review,* 1966,3,1-12.

Bruner, J. S. On perceptual readiness. *Psychological Review,* 1957,64, 123-152.

Bryden, M. P. Tachistoscopic recognition, handedness, and cerebral dominance. *Neuropsychologia,* 1965, 3, 1-8.

Bryden, M. P. A model for the sequential organisation of behaviour. *Canadian Journal of Psychology,* 1967, 21, 37-56.

Bryden, M. P., and Rainey, C. A. Left-right differences in tachistoscopic recognition. *Journal of Experimental Psychology,* 1963,66, 568.571.

Buhler, C. Die Wiener Psychologische Schule in der Emigration. *Psychological Rundschau,* 1965, 16, 187-196.

Burt, C. *The factors of the mind.* London: University of London Press, 1940.

Cesa-Bianchi, M., and Di Naro, C. Ricerga sugli atteggiamenti verso i mezzi di protezione individuali. *Securitas,* 1966, 51, 89-126.

Champion, R.A. The latency of the conditioned fear-response. *American Journal of Psychology,* 1964,77, 75-83.

Champion, R.A. Reduced stimulus intensity as a CS in GSR conditoning. Journal *of Experimental Psychology,* 1967, 73, 503-508.

Champion, R.A., and Allen, G. An acquired drive based on conflict. *American Journal of Psychology,* 1966, 79, 111-115.

Champion, R.A., and Leung, S. Amount of reinforcement in human learning. *Australian Journal of Psychology.* 1964, 16, 185-189.

Champion, R.A., and Smith, L. R. Predicting discrimination learning from differential conditioning with amount of reinforcement as a variable. *Journal of Experimental Psychology,* 1966, 71, 529-534.

Cherry, E.C. On the validity of applying communication theory to experimental psychology. *British, Journal of Psychology,* 1957,48, 136-188.

Cherry, E.C. *On human communication.* (3rd ed.) New York: Science Editions, 1961.

Chiari, S. Concetto di pericolo e percezione del rischio nell'eta evolutiva: Un sondaggio preliminare. *Securitas*, 1966, 51, 127-141.

Cofer, C.N., and Appley, M.H. *Motivation: Theory and Research.* (2nd ed.) New York: Wiley, 1967.

Cowey, A. Perimetric study of field defects in monkeys after cortical and retinal ablations. *Quarterly Journal of Experimental Psychology*, 1967, 19, 232-245.

Cowey, A., and Weiskrantz, L. A comparison of the effects of inferotemporal and striate cortex lesions on the visual behaviour of rhesus monkeys. *Quarterly Journal of Experimental Psychology*, 1967, 19, 246-253.

Craik, K.J.W. *The nature of explanation.* London: Cambridge University Press, 1943.

Craik, K.J.W. *The nature of psychology.* London: Cambridge University Press, 1966.

David, H. P., and von Bracken, H. *Perspectives in personality theory.* London: Tavistock Publications, 1957.

Day, R.H., and Power. R.P. Apparent reversal (oscillation) of rotary motion in depth. *Psychological Review*, 1965, 72, 117-127.

Day, R.H., and Singer, G. A. Spatial aftereffects within and between kinesthesis and vision. *Journal of Experimental psychology*, 1964,68, 337-343(a).

Day, R.H., and Singer, G. A. A tactile spatial aftereffect. *Australian Journal of Psychology*, 1964, 16,33-37. (b)

Day, R.H., and Singer, G. Sensory adaptation and behavioural compensation with spatially transformed vision and hearing. *Psychological Bulletin*, 1967, 67, 307-322.

Decarie, T. *Intelligence and Affectivity in Early Childhood: An experimental study of Jean Piaget's object concept and object relations.* New York: International Universities Press, 1966.

Drever, J. The historical background for national trends in psychology: On the non-existence of English associations. *Journal of Historical Behavior Science*, 1965, 1, 123-130.

Earhard, B., and Earhard, M. Role of interference factors in 3-stage mediation paradigms. Journal of Experimental Psychology, 1967, 73, 526-531.

Earhard, B., and Mandler, G. Mediated associations: Paradigms, controls and mechanisms. Canadian Journal of Psychology, 1965, 1'9, 346-378. (a)

Earhard, B., and Mandler, G. Pseudomediation: A reply and more data. *Psychonomic Science*, 1965, 3, 137-138. (b)

Ebenholtz, S. M. Adaptation to a rotated visual field as a function of degree of optical tilt and exposure time. Journal of Experimental Psychology, 1966, 72, 629-634:

Eisler, H. On psychophysics in general and the general psychophysical equation in' particular. Scandinavian Journal of Psychology, 1965, 6, 85-102.

Ekman, G., and Sjoberg, L. Scaling. *Annual Review of Psychology*, 1965, 16, 451-474.

Eysenck, H. J. *The scientific study of personality.* London: Routledge, 1952.

Eysenck, H. J. (Ed.) Handbook of abnormal psychology. London: Pitman, 1960.

Eysenck, H. J. Biological basis of personality. Nature, 1963, 199, 1031.

Eysenck, H. J. The biological basis of criminal behaviour. Advancing Science, 1963-1964, 20, 1-111.

Farne, M. Figural after-effects with short exposure time. Psychologische Forschung, 1965, 28, 519-534.

Flavell, J. H. *The Developmental Psychology of Jean Piaget*. Princeton. N.J.: Van Nostrand, 1963.

Flores d'Arcais, G. B. Uber die Wirkung figuraler Merkmale auf die enstehende "induzierte Bewegung." *Psychologische Forschung*, 1965,28, 153-178.

Foppa, K. *Lernen Gedichtnis, Verhalten.* Cologne and Berlin: Kiepenheuer und Witsch, 1965.

Fraisse, P. *Les structures rhythmiques*. Paris: Presses Universitaires de France, 1957.

Fraisse, P., and Piaget, J. (Eds.) Traite de psychologie experimentale. Paris: Presses Universitaires de France, 1963.

Frankenhaeuser, M. Experimental approaches to the study of psychological stress. Symposium on higher nervous functions and occupational health. Vienna: Viennese Academy of Medicine, 1966. (a)

Frankenhacuser, M. Physiological, behavioural and subjective reactions to stress.

*Proceedings of the Second International Symposium on Environmental Problems of Man in Space.* Vienna: Springer, 1966. (b)

Fuller, J. L., and Clark, L. D. Effects of rearing with specific stimuli upon postisolation behaviour in dogs. *Journal of Comparative Physiological Psychology,* 1966, 61, 258-263. (a)

Fuller, J.L. and Clark, L.D. Genetic and treatment factors modifying the postisolation syndrome in dogs. *Journal of Comparative Physiological Psychology,* 1966, 61, 251-257. (b)

Gibson, J.J. Adaptation, after-effect, and contrast in the perception of curved lines. *Journal of Experimental Psychology,* 1933, 16, 1-31.

Glow, P., Richardson, A., and Rose, S. The effect of reduced cholinesterase activity on the maintenance of an operant response. *Journal of Comparative Physiological Psychology,* 1967,63, 155-157.

Glow, P., and Rose, S. Some relationships between enzyme activity levels and behaviour. *Proceedings of the Eighteenth International Congress of Psychology.* Moscow, 1966.

Goude, G. *On fundamental measurement in psychology.* Stockholm: Almquist and Wirksell, 1962.

Graefe, O. Qualitative Unterseuchungen uber Kontur und Flache in der optischen Figurwahrnehmung. *Psychologische Forschung,* 1964, 27,260-306.

Green, R. T., and Courtis, M. C. Information theory and figure perception: The metaphor that failed. *Acta Psychologica,* 1966, 25, 12-35.

Greenwald, A. G. Nuttin's neglected critique of the law of effect. *Psychological Bulletin,* 1966, 65, 199-205.

Gregory, R. L. *Eye and brain.* New York: World University Library, 1966. (a)

Gregory, R. L. Visual illusions. In B.M. Foss (Ed.), *New horizons in psychology.* Baltimore: Penguin, 1966, pp. 68-96. (b)

Gregory, R. L., and Wallace, J. G. Recovery from early blindness. *Quarterly Review of Experimental Psychology,* Monogr. 2, 1963.

Griew, S., and Lynn, R. Constructive "reactive inhibition" in the interpretation of age changes in performance. *Nature,* 1960, 186, 182.

Guilford, J. P. Creativity. *American Psychology,* 1950, 5, 444-454.

Hajos, A., and Ritter, M. Experiments on the problem of interocular transfer. *Acta Psychologica,* 1965,24, 81-90.

Hammer, A. G., and Johnson, L. Overinclusiveness in schizophrenia and organic psychosis. *British Journal of Social Clinical Psychology,* 1965, 4, 47-51.

Harrington, T. L. Adaptation of humans to colored split-field glasses. *Psychonomic Science,* 1965, 3, 71-72.

Harris, C. S. Perceptual adaptation to inverted, reversed and displaced vision. *Psychological Review,* 1965, 72, 419-444.

Hebb, D. O. *Organisation of behavior.* New York: Wiley, 1949.

Heider, F., and Simmel, M. An experimental study of apparent behavior. *American Journal of Psychology,* 1944, 57, 243.

Helson, H. Adaptation-level theory. In S. Koch (Ed.), *Psychology: A study of a science.* Vol. 1. *Sensory, perceptual, and physiological formulations.* New York: McGraw-Hill, 1959, pp. 565-621.

Hernandez-Peon, R., and Sterman, M. B. Brain functions. *Annual Review of Psychology,* 1966, 17, 363-394.

Heron, W. Perception as a function of retinal locus and attention. *American Journal of Psychology*, 1957, 70, 38-48.

Hirata, K., and Osaka, R. Tachistoscopic recognition of Japanese letter materials in left and right visual fields. *Psychologia*, 1967, 10, 7-1 8.

Hoffstatter, P.R. (Ed.) *Psychologie*. Frankfurt am Main: S. Fischer Verlag GmbH, 1965.

Hoyos, C. *Denkschrift zur Lage der Psychologie*. Wiesbaden: Steiner, 1961.

Hudson, *L. Contrary Imaginations*. London: Methuen, 1966.

Humphrey, N.K., and Weiskrantz, L. Vision in monkeys after removal of the striate cortex. *Nature*. 1967, 215, 595-597.

Iacono, G. Osservazioni sulla prevenzione degli infortuni in aziende siderurgiche statunitenzi. *Securitas*, 1966,51, 119-126.

Jensen, D.D. Operationism and the question, "Is this behaviour learned or innate?" *Behaviour*, 1961, 17, 1-18.

Jensen, J. On functional fixedness: Some critical remarks. *Scandinavian Journal of Psychology*. 1960, 1, 157-162. (a)

Jensen, J. On the Einstellung effect in problem solving: Some critical remarks. *Scandinavian Journal of Psychology*, 1960,1, 163-168. (b)

Johansson, G. Rigidity, stability, and motion in perceptual space. *Acta Psychologica*, 1958, 14, 359-370.

Johansson, G. Perception of motion and changing form. *Scandinavian Journal of Psychology*, 1964, 5, 181-208.

Johansson, G., and Ottander, C. Recovery time after glare. *Scandinavian Journal of Psychology*, 1964, 5, 17-25.

Jung, C. G. *Psychological types*. London: Routledge, 1924.

Jung, J. Cued versus non-cued incidental recall of successive work associations. *Canadian Journal of Psychology*, 1967, 21, 196-203.

Kiekheben, F. Der einfluss eines kaleidoskopischen figurwandels auf das erkundengsverhalten. *Psychologische Forsehung*, 1966, 30, 105-150.

Kimura, D. Cerebral dominance and the perception of verbal stimuli. *Canadian Journal of Psychology*. 1961, 15, 166-171.

Koffka, K. *Principles of Gestalt psychology*. London: Kegan Paul, Trench, Trubner, 1936.

Kohler, I. Pavlov and his dog. *Journal of Genetic Psychology*, 1962, 100, 331-335.

Kohler, I. The concept of adaptation in perception. Paper presented at the Seventeenth International Congress of Psychologists, Washington, D.C.: August, 1963.

Kohler, I. The formation and transformation of the perceptual world. *Psychological Issues*, 1964,3,1-173.

Kretschmer, E. Physique and character. London: Kegan Paul, Trench, Trubner, 1925.

Lafitte, P. *The person in psychology: Reality or abstraction*. London: Routledge, 1957.

Levelt, W. J. M. *On binocular rivalry*. Soesterberg: Institute for Perception, R.V.O.-T.N.O., 1965.

Lorenz, K.Z. *King Solomon's ring*. London: Methuen, 1956.

Lorenz, K.Z. *Evolution and modification of behaviour*. Chicago: University of Chicago Press, 1965.

Lorenz, K. *On aggression*. New York: Harcourt, Brace, and World, 1966.

Luria, A.R., and Vinogradova, O.S. An objective investigation of the dynamics of semantic systems. *British Journal of Psychology*, 1959, 50, 89-105.

Malmo, R.B. Anxiety and behavioural arousal. *Psychological Review*, 1957, 64, 276-287.

Malmo, R.B. Measurement of drive: An unsolved problem. In M. R. Jones (Ed.), *Nebraska Symposium on Motivation.* Lincoln: University of Nebraska Press, 1958, pp. 229-265.

Malmo, R.B. Physiological gradients and behaviour. *Psychological Bulletin,* 1965, *64,* 225-234.

Marshall, G.R. Effect of total association and conceptual cohesiveness among words on recall, clustering, and recognition association. *Psychological Reports.* 1967, **20,** 39-44.

Marx, M.H. Spread of effect: A critical review. *Genetic Psychology Monographs,* 1956, 53, 119-186.

Mason, W.A., and Sponholz, R.R. Behaviour of rhesus monkeys raised in isolation. *Journal of Psychiatric Research,* 1963, 1, 299-306.

Meili, R., and Rohracher, H. (Eds.) *Lehrbuch der experimentellen Psychologie.* Berne: Hans Huber, 1963.

Merz, F. Amerikanische und deutsche Psychologie. *Psychologie und Praxis,* 1960,4, 78-91.

Metzger, W. *Gesetze des Sehens.* (2nd ed.) Frankfurt: Waldemar Kramer, 1953.

Michon, J. Studies on subjective duration. II. *Acta Psychologica,* 1965, 24, 205-219.

Michotte, A., et. al. *Causalite, permanence et rialite phenominales.* Louvain: Publications Universitaires, 1962.

Michotte, A. *The perception of causality.* [Translation by T.R. Miles and Elaine Miles] New York: Basic Books, 1963.

Migliorino, G. La percepcion visual en relacion a la conduccion de vehiculos rapidos. *Revista de Psicologia General y Applicada,* 1965,20, 15-28.

Mikkonen, V., and von Wright, J. M. Changes in reproduction as a function of adaptation level. II. *Report of the Psychological Institute. University of Turku,* 1963, No. 8.

Mishkin, M., and Forgays, D. G. Word recognition as a function of retinal locus. *Journal of Experimental Psychology.* 1952, 43, 43-48.

Misiak, H., and Staudt, V. M. Psychology in Italy. *Psychological Bulletin,* 1953,50, 347-361.

Moed, H. K. W. Constancy and contrast. I. *Acta Psychologica,* 1964, 22, 272-320.

Moed, H. K. W. Constancy and contrast. II. *Acta Psychologica,* 1965, 24, 91-166.

Moed, H. K. W. Constancy and contrast. III. *Acta Psychologica,* 1966,25,222-292.

Moore, J. A. (Ed.) *Ideas in Modern Biology.* New York: Natural History Press, 1965.

Morrell, F. Electrical signs of sensory coding. In G.C. Quarton, T. Melnechuk, F.O. Schimitt, and Associates and Staff of the Neurosciences Research Program (Eds.), *The Neurosciences: A Study Program.* New York: Rockefeller University Press, 1967, pp. 452-469.

Munn, N.L. Discrimination-reversal learning in kangaroos. *Australian Journal of Psychology,* 1964, 16,1-8.

Murch, G.M., and Wesley, F. German psychology and its journals. *Psychological Bulletin,* 1966,66, 10-15.

Murdock, B.B. Distractor and probe techniques in short-term memory. *Canadian Journal of Psychology,* 1967, 21, 25-36.

Murray, D. J. The role of speech responses in short-term memory. *Canadian Journal of Psychology,* 1967, 21,263-276.

Nuttin, J.R. "Spread" in recalling success and failure. *Journal of Experimental Psychology,* 1949, 39, 690-699.

Nuttin, J.R. *Psychology in Belgium. Louvain:* Publications Universitaires, 1961. (a)

Nuttin, J.R. *Tache reussite et echec: Theorie de la conduite humaine.* (2nd ed.) Louvain: Publications Universities, 1961, (b)

Oeser, O.A., and Emery, F. E. *Social Structure and Personality in a Rural Community.* London: Routledge, 1954.

Oeser, O.A., and Hammond, S. B. (Eds.) *Social structure and personality in a city.* London: Routledge, 1954.

Oeser, O.A., and Harary, F. A mathematical model for structural role theory. II. *Human Relations*, 1964, 17, 3-1 7.

Oeser, 0. A., and O'Brien, G. A mathematical model for structural role theory. Ill. *Human Relations*, 1967, 20,83-97.

O'Neil, W. M. *An Introduction to Method in Psychology.* (2nd ed.) Melbourne: Melbourne University Press, 1962.

Piaget, J. *The Language and Thought of the Child.* London: Routledge, 1926.

Piaget, J. *Judgment and Reasoning in the Child.* London: Routledge, 1928.

Piaget, J. *The Child's Conception of Number.* London: Routledge, 1952.

Piaget, J. *The Growth of Logical Thinking from Childhood to Adolescence.* London: Routledge, 1958.

Piaget, J. *L'image mentale chez l'enfant.* Paris: Presses Universitaires de France, 1966.

Piaget, J. *Biologie et connaissance: Essai sur les relations entre les regulations organiques et les processus cognitifs.* Paris: Editions Gallimard, 1967. (a)

Piaget, J. *Six Psychological Studies.* New York: Random House, 1967. (b)

Piaget, j.; and Inhelder, B. *The Child's Conception of space.* London: Routledge, 1956.

Piaget, J., and Inhelder, B. *The Early Growth of Logic in the Child: Classification and seriation.* New York: Harper and Row, 1964.

Pieron, H. (Ed.) *L 'annee psychologique.* Paris: Presses Universitaires de France, 1898.

Pieron, H. *Thought and the Brain.* New York: Harcourt, Brace, 1927.

**Pieron,** H. *Les Problemes fondamentaux de la psycholophysique dans 'a science Actuelle.* Paris: Herman and Cie, 1951.

**Pieron,** *H. The sensations.* New Haven, Conn.: Yale University Press, 1952.

Poulton, E.C. Engineering psychology. *Annual Review of Psychology,* 1966, 17, 177-200.

Raaheim, K. Problem solving and the ability to find replacements. *Scandinavian Journal of Psychology.* 1960, 1, 14-18.

Raaheim, K. Problem solving: A new approach. *Acta Universitaires de Bergensis,* Ser. Hum. Litt., No. 5, Bergen, Norway, 1961.

Raaheim, K. Problem solving and the awareness of the missing part. *Scandinavian Journal of Psychology,* 1962,3,129-131.

Rorschach, H. *Psychodiagnostics;* New York: Grune and Śtratton, 1942.

Ross, S. *Logical Foundations of Psychological Measurement.* Copenhagen: Scandinavian University Books 1964.

Russell, W.A., and Roth, E. Psychologie in Deutschland und in Amerika: Eine Stadie in Gegensatzen. *Psychologie und Praxis,* 1958,2,223-231.

Sanders, A.F. *The Selective Process in the Functional Visual Field.* Soesterberg: Institute for Perception R.V.O.-T.N.O., 1963.

Sanders A.F. Expectancy: Application and measurement. *Acta Psychologica,* 1966, 25, 293-313.

Sarbin, T.R. Taft, R., and Bailey, D.E. *Clinical Inference and Cognitive Theory.* New York: Holt, 1960.

*Scandinavian Journal of Psychology,* Stockholm: Almquist and Wiksell, 1960.

Schmitt G.F. Eine neue wahrnehmungstauschung, *Psychologische Forschung,* 1966, 30, 200-240.

Schultz, D.P *Sensory restriction: Effects on behaviour.* New York: Academic Press, 1965.

Schutte, W., and Zubek, J P. Changes in olfactory and gustatory sensitivity after prolonged visual deprivation. *Canadian Journal of Psychology, 1967,* 21, 337-345,

Schutz, F. Homosexualitat und Pragung. *Psychologische Forschung*, 1965, 28, 439-463. (a)

Schutz, F. Sexuelle Pragung bei Antiden. *Zeitschrift fur Tierpsychologie, 1965*, 22, 50-103. (b)

Shields, J. *Monozygotic twins.* London: Oxford University Press, 1962.

Singer, G., and Day, R.H. The effects of spatial judgements on the perceptual aftereffect resulting from prismatically transformed vision. *Australian Journal of Psychology*, 1966, 18, 63-70. (a)

Singer, G., and Day, R.H. Interlimb and interjoint transfer of a kinesthetic spatial aftereffect. *Journal of Experimental Psychology*, 1966, 71, 109-114. (b)

Singer, G., and Day, R.H. Spatial adaptation and aftereffect with optically transformed vision. *Journal of Experimental Psychology*, 1966, 71, 725-731. (c)

Skinner, B.F. *Cumulative Record.* New York: Appleton-Century-Crafts, 1959.

Sluckin, W *Imprinting and early learning.* London: Methuen, 1964.

Smedslund, J. "Educational Psychology." In P.R. Farnsworth, O. McNemar, and Q. McNemar (Eds.), *Annual Review of Psychology.* California: Annual Reviews, 1964.

Spaltro, E. An analysis of risk-taking behaviour. *Archivio di Psicologia, Neurologia e Psichiatria*, 1965, 26, 7-25.

Spearman, C. *The Nature of "Intelligence" and the Principles of Cognition*, London: Macmillan, 1923.

Spearman, C. *The Abilities of Man: Their nature and measurement.* London: Macmillan, 1927.

Spranger, E. *Types of Men.* Halle: Niemeyer, 1928.

Stout, J.F. *Manual of Psychology*, London: University Tutorial Press, 1913.

Sutcliffe, J.P. Some aspects of rank ordering and scaling with paired comparisons data. *Australian Journal of Psychology*, 1964, 16, 137-149.

Sutcliffe, J.P. A probability model for errors of classifications. I. General considerations. *Psychometrika*, 1965, 30, 73-76.

Sutcliffe, J P., and Bristow, R.A. Do rank order and scale properties remain in variant under changes in the set of scaled stimuli? *Australian Journal of Psychology*, 1966, 18, 26-40.

Szekely, L. Some comments on problem solving, availability and test magic. *Nordisk Psychologi*, 1958, 10, 108-113.

Szekely, L. The problem of experience in Gestalt psychology. *Theoria*, 1959, 25, 179-186.

Taft, R. Multiple methods of personality assessment, *Psychological Bulletin*, 1959, 56, 333-352.

Taft, R. Accuracy of empathic judgements of acquaintances and strangers. *Journal of Personality and Social Psychology*, 1966, 3, 600-604.

Thomson, G.H. *The Factorial Analysis of Human Ability.* London: University of London Press, 1939.

Thorndike, E.L. *Educational Psychology* Vol. 3. New York: Teachers College, 1914.

Thorpe, W.H. *Learning and instinct in animals.* London: Methuen, 1956.

Thorpe, W.H. *Learning and instinct in animals.* (2nd ed.) London: Methuen, 1963.

Thorpe, W.H. The ontogeny of behaviour. In J.A. Moore (Ed.), *Ideas in modern biology.* New York: Natural History Press, 1965, pp. 483-518.

Thorpe, W.H., and Davenport, D. (Eds.) Learning and associated phenomena in invertebrates. *Animal Behaviour*, Suppl, 1, 64.

Thurstone, L.L. Primary mental abilities. *Psychometric Monograph*, 1938, 1.

Tinbergen, N. *A Study of Instinct.* Oxford: Clarendon Press, 1951.

Tinbergen, N. The evolution of signalling devices. In W. Edkin (Ed.), *Social Behaviour and Organisation Among Vertebrates.* Chicago: University of Chicago Press, 1964.

Tinbergen, N. Behaviour and natural selection. In J.A. Moore (Ed.), *Ideas in Modern Biology*. New York: Natural History Press, 1965, pp 519-542.

Tolman, E.C. *Purposive Behaviour in Animals and Men*. Los Angeles: University of California Press, 1932.

Tretini, G. Quotient of acculturalisation and adjustment classes in the actual social-scholastic situation in Italy. *Archivio di Psicologia, Neurologia e Psichiatria*, 1966, 27, 243-310.

Vernon, P.E. *The Structure of Human Abilities*. London: Methuen, 1950.

Vernon, P.E. *Personality assessment: A Critical Study*. London: Methuen, 1964.

Vernon, P.E. The personality system. In C. Banks (Ed.), *Stephanos; Studies in Psychology Presented to Cyril Burt*. London: University of London Press, 1965.

Virsu, V. Contrast and confluxion as components in geometric illusions. *Quarterly Journal of Experimental Psychology*, 1967, 19, 198-207.

Volkelt, H. *Grundfragen der Psychologie*. Munich: Beck, 1963.

Von Fieandt, K. Towards a unitary theory of perception. *Psychological Review*, 1958, 65, 315-320.

Von Fieandt, K., and Gibson, J.J. The sensitivity of the eye to two kinds of continuous transformation of a shadow pattern. *Journal of Experimental Psychology*, 1959, 57, 344-347.

Von Frisch, K. The dances of the honey bee. *Bulletin of Animal Behaviour*, 1947, 5, 1-22.

Von Frisch, K, *The dancing bees*. London: Methuen, 1954.

Von Wright, J.M., and Mikkonen, V. Changes in reproduction as a function of adaptation level. I. *Report of the Psychological Institute, University of Turku*, 1963, No. 1.

Von Wright, J.M., and Mikkonen, V. Changes in reproduction as a function of adaptation level. III. *Report of the Psychological Institute, University of Turku*, 1964, No. 12.

Ward, J. *Psychological principles*. London: Cambridge University Press, 1918.

Wellek, A. Der Einfluss der Deutschen Emigration und die Entwickling der Americanischen Psychologie. *Psychologische Rundschau*, 1964, XV, 1-4.

Wellek, A. (Ed.) *Gesamtverzeichnis der deutschsprachigen psychologischen Literatur der Jahre 1942 bis 1960*. Gottingen: Verlag fur Psychologie, 1965.

Wellek, A. *Die Polaritat im Aufbau des Charakters: System der Konkreten Characterkunde*, Berlin: Franke, 1966.

Wells, M.J. *Brain and behaviour in cephalopods*. London: Heinemann, 1962.

Wesley, F. Assessing German psychology. *Journal of Genetic Psychology*, 1966, 75, 273-277.

Yates, A.J. *Frustration and conflict*. London: Methuen, 1962.

Yates, A.J. Psychological deficit. *Annual Review of Psychology*, 1966, 17, 111-144.

Zanforlin, M. Some observations on Gregory's theory of perceptual illusions. *Quarterly Journal of Experimental Psychology*, 1967, 19, 193-197.

Zubek, J.P., and MacNeill, M. Perceptual deprivation phenomena: Role of the recumbent position. *Journal of Abnormal Psychology*, 1967, 72, 147-150.

# 19

# Soviet Psychology

The aim of this chapter is to familiarise the readers with the contemporary Soviet scene in psychology. Soviet psychology is still largely a *terra incognita* in the West. At first contact, it is puzzling as well. Two recent American "explorers" (Cole & Maltzman, 1969, p. 37) have described their initial reactions in vivid terms:

> Coming upon Soviet psychology and physiological psychology [the authors' term for the Pavlovian physiology of higher nervous activity for the first time is a little like Darwin first visiting the Galapagos. Different forms of species have evolved, as a result of isolation and interbreeding, which are adaptable to their environment.

Cole and Maltzman also shatter the all too frequent American stereotype of psychology in the Soviet Union (1969, p. 37):

> All too often Soviet psychology has been characterised as a rigid adherence to Pavlovian conditioning. This is simply not the case; but Pavlovian conditioning research and theory is itself far more sophisticated and complicated than the stereotyped and grossly oversimplified picture presented in most American [introductory] textbooks.

Since the chapter on Soviet psychology for the first edition of this book was written, in 1962, much has changed. For one thing, many of the individuals whose work was discussed—K. M. Bykov, N.I. Krasnogorskii, N. N. Ladygina-Kots—have died. Profound alterations, for the better, have taken place in the status of psychology in the U.S.S.R. While party ideology and the rigidly standardised formulations of dialectical materialism continue to reign unchallenged in journal editorials and introductions to textbooks, psychological research and theory have moved forward vigorously.

For all these reasons, a few touch-ups of the earlier chapter simply would not done. This presentation is a "supplement," endeavouring to reflect the recent developments and the current scene, not a "revision." Special attention will be given to the publications translated into English.

## SOME METATHEORETICAL CONSIDERATIONS

The investigative work of the scientist is embedded in a network of concepts and concerns going beyond (*meta*, in Greek) specific facts and "miniature theories" relating the facts within a circumscribed area. The complexes of ideas lying outside the domain of concrete facts placed in short-range perspective have a variety of functions. They may serve as a source of inspiration ("new world, brave and free," socialism with a human face," "Communist society"); as a guide in the selection of research problems; as ethical and methodological norms; as a clarification of the philosophical foundations of science (be they concerned with ontological or epistemological questions, i.e., the nature of reality or the nature of scientific knowledge); and as an interpretative framework (theory of evolution, cybernetics).

These considerations—ideological, philosophical, and metatheoretical—are a matrix in which the collection of data and the building of microtheories are immersed.

The matrix is universal, in the sense of being present in both East and West. It is not identical either in its content or in the degree to which psychologists are concerned with these matters.

In America, concern with "metatheories" is less intensive and less widespread. The temper is (or has been) largely aphilosophical. Characteristically, the opinion has been widely held that the research scientist performs most effectively if he keeps his nose to the grindstone and operates strictly within the framework of empirical data and miniature theories. This does not mean that psychologists do not hold, in fact, although tacitly for the most part, certain metatheoretical assumptions. Watson (1967) labels them *prescriptions*.

In the Soviet Union the presence of the metatheoretical considerations is made more palpable by the fact that the country has been governed for over fifty years by a single political party, with a single-minded, vocal ideology, and an allegiance to the philosophical heritage of Marx, Engels, and lenin.

It may be useful to point out that Marxism-leninism (Anonymous, 1961) is many things: a theory of reality and knowledge (dialectical materialism); a philosophy of history (historical materialism); a socioeconomic theory of capitalism, socialism, and communism; and the theory and tactics of the international Communist movement.

In Nikita Khrushchev': words of 1959, "The ideas of Marxim-Lenism [arel the ideology which has a complete sway over the Soviet society" (Blakely, 1961, p. 147). Importantly, not only are these ideas binding for the Soviet philosophers', but they also "are the guiding stars for the consideration of all theoretical problems of science" (Blakely, 1961, p. 98). Consequently, they constitute "the philosophical basis of Soviet psychology" as well (Blakely, 1961, p 103). In time, I. P. Pavlov's work on "higher nervous activity" was added as an essential ingredient of Soviet psychology's metatheoretical base.

### Philosophico-Theoretical Views on the Nature of the Mind and Its Relation to Matter

The synthesis of the Marxist-Leninist philosophy and of Pavlov's "physiology of the highest nervous activity" was accomplished only after a long period of discussion and debate, at times acrimonious. Because of their fundamental importance for Soviet psychology, the principles of "dialectical" and "Pavlovian" psychology will be presented in some detail, with specific reference to Rubinshtein's formulation. In our presentation we shall depend heavily on Payne's (1968) well-documented monograph.

In the thirties Rubinshtein sought a reunification of psychology, then split into warring "schools." His special concern was the achievement of a synthesis between the points of view, apparently irreconcilable, of the introspectionists, who regarded the immediate data of consciousness as the only legitimate subject matter of psychology, and the behaviourists, who disregarded consciousness and limited psychology to the study of objectively recorded reactions of the organism, animal and human. Rubinshtein conceived a reunification of psychology based on the principle of a "dialectical unity" of consciousness and behaviour, embodied in Marx's concept of human activity (Payne, 1968, p. 50):

> Through activity the subject reveals itself, objectivising the inner world of its consciousness. . . . At the same time man, by his activity, forms and develops his subjective world. [This activity] is not merely individual but is above all social. Man's consciousness, which is the guide of his activity, evolved originally in the process of social activity, and the external world with which man enters into synthesis by his activity, is not only the world of nature but, at the same time, of society. In consequence, human activity always remains a socially conditioned phenomenon.

Consciousness and behaviour are not viewed as separate aspects of the human organism, the one entirely "internal" and subjective and the other entirely "external" and objective. On the contrary, they represent a two-way interaction with external reality, from object to subject and from subject to object. Consciousness is a form of activity of the organism required for its adaptation to the demands of the constantly changing environment. It directs man's actions through which he modifies and changes the environment.

In *Fundamental of General Psychology* (in Russian), Rubinshtein formulated three principles he regarded as basic

1. *The principle of psychophysical unity.* The mind forms a twofold dialectical unity: with its organic substrate, the brain (of which it is a function), and with the external world (of which it is a reflection).
2. *The principle of mental development.* The mind *(psyche)* develops along with the changes in the structure of the organisms and the mode of life.
3. *The principle of "historicity."* Human consciousness changes with man's social conditions.

The fourth principle, noted by Payne (1968, p. 52), the principle of the unity of theory and practice, is a general principle of Marxism-leninism applicable to all sciences and not specific to psychology.

In the early fifties Rubinshtein responded to the critique that the philosophico-theoretical foundations of psychology are inadequate and must be reconstructed by taking into account the implications of the Pavlovian heritage. In his 1952 paper, Rubinshtein acknowledged that the chief defect of the *Fundamentals of general psychology* was its failure to follow the path laid down by Pavlov, and its uncritical acceptance of certain principles of foreign psychology.

The factual scope of the Pavlovian "reconstruction" of psychology, in Rubinshtein's hands, was less than one might have expected. The. primary change was the replacement of the principle of psychophysical unity by the principle of *materialist monism*, emphasising the primacy of the material, including the physiological brain processes. Mental processes are now *identified* with the "higher nervous," "reflex" activity of the brain.

The principle of psychophysical unity apparently came to be viewed as too "dualistic," implying that mental activity is *based* on higher nervous activity, which in turn is a direct function of the brain. In other words, the principle seemed to (or did) imply that the mental activity and the higher nervous activity represent two closely related but distinct series of events. According to materialist monism, the mental activity and the higher nervous activity constitute a single process.

Yet Rubinshtein continues to insist that mental activity is characterised not only by its physiological mechanisms but also by its content, i.e., by the fact that it is a reflection, by the brain, of the (external) material world.

This gives specificity to the mental phenomena which cannot be reduced, "without a remainder," to the processes studied by the neurophysiologist. Physiology abstracts from certain aspects of the process of man's interaction with the outer world. It is these "subjective" aspects that form the specific object of psychology. Mental phenomena, such as perceptions, thoughts, and feelings, represent a new, original "form of manifestation" *(forma proyavleniya)* of physiological phenomena.

The "reflection" of the world by man is not a passive process, a passive reception of images, but involves cognitive activity of the subject; the four basic cognitive operations are analysis and synthesis, abstraction and generalisation. Second, knowledge of outer reality is conditioned by the personal characteristics personality) of the subject (Payne, 1968, p. 143). Personality is defined as "a totality *(sovokupnost')* of the inner conditions [of the human organism] through which all external influences are refracted."

In the current formulation (Leont'ev, 1967), psychology is defined as the study of mental phenomena (such as sensation, perception, thought, and emotion:), viewed as process of an active reflection of objective reality. Leont'ev states categorically that the philosophical prerequisites *(predposylki)* for the development of psychology as an objective science were provided by dialectical materialism. A "reconstruction" *(perestroika)* of psychology on this basis was initiated, in the U.S.S.R., only in the 1920s.

Mind (*psikhika*) is tied closely to the development of the "living matter." It serves to orient organisms in regard to their environment, and it regulates their behaviour. The development of the specifically human mind, in the course of the evolution of man, is viewed as a product of social activities connected with human work, requiring interpersonal communication (verbal designation), and facilitating the development of consciousness *(soznanie)* as a special form of "reflection" of reality. Language becomes the medium *(nositel')* of "social consciousness" and the "substrate" of the consciousness of individuals.

There is a two-way relation between external and internal activities: External operations (behaviour) are transformed into internal, mental operations (process of interiorisation), but also the internal, mental operations are expressed in external activities (process of exteriorisation).

While, so far, Leont'ev's presentation has been a good deal more "Marxist-Leninist" than "Pavlovian," he does not neglect to point out that the study of the mind is closely bound to the physiological study of the activities of the brain. Yet mind is not reducible to "higher nervous activity"; mental "reflection" of reality—the very subject of psychology—is brought about by an active interaction of the individual with his environment, fashioned in the course of mankind's socio-historical development. In this process man as a biological being is transformed into a biosocial being. The reflection of reality has a specific content.

## SOVIET PSYCHOLOGY IN THE WESTERN LOOKING GLASS

Soviet psychology is distinct as regards the "metatheory," although, in part, this is a difference of vocabulary, framework, manner of presentation, and insistence. On the other hand, there is no single theory which would characterise scientific psychology in the Soviet Union as a "school" or "system." The field is more diversified than is frequently realised.

The total of the then current Soviet psychology was surveyed on several occasions (Brozek, 1964; Brozek & Hoskovec, 1966). No attempt can be made to do so again here, especially since our concern is to familiarise the reader with selected, "significant" aspects.

Like beauty, the historical significance of men, events, and ideas is, in part, in the eyes of the beholder. In order that we may arrive at a more objective portrait, unencumbered by one man's idiosyncrasies, and so that the reader may pursue, firsthand, his interests beyond our summary and comment, this section is based on Soviet monographs translated into English and published commercially outside the Soviet Union. The selection of materials to be translated involves appraisal by many individuals. It provides the best available objective criterion of significance, although *significance* is defined pragmatically and from the "Western" point of view.

Admittedly, the resulting portrait is not representative. The bias emerges dearly when the topics are matched with the factual spectrum of current Soviet psychological research (Brozek, 1969). The dominance of the physiologically oriented research and a gross underrepresentation of such areas as educational psychology and the psychology of sports (like caviar, a Russian specialty) become patent.

### Historical Roots

I. M. Sechenov's multifaceted work included contributions to psychology as well as to neurophysiology, physiology of, work, and physiological chemistry (Koshtoyants, 1964, Chs. 11-15). *Sechenov's Autobiographical notes* (1965a) provides an informative, personal account of the life (1829-1905) of one of the moving spirits of Russian science in the second half of the nineteenth century. Sechenov's forward-looking work, entitled *Reflexes of the brain* and first published in 1863, was made effectively available to the English-speaking scientific public about one hundred years after it appeared in Russian (Sechenov, 1965b).

In his postscript (Sechenov, 1965b, pp. 143-145), W. A. Rosenblith stresses three aspects of Sechenov's work:

1. His pioneering reflexological approach to the study of behaviour, as a prelude to Pavlov's research.
2. His discovery of the phenomenon of central inhibition, antedating neurophysiological investigations on reticular formation-one of the central topics of modern brain research.
3. His anticipation of physiological cybernetics and his role as a "too little appreciated intellectual forebear of Norbert Wiener," the author of *Cybernetics, or Control and communication in the animal and the machine* (1948).

In his *Reflexes of the Brain* Sechenov views man's mental activity as a function of the brain, manifested externally by muscular movements, whether they involve muscle groups controlling physical activity or those controlling verbal behaviour.

Both types of external manifestations of cerebral activity, i.e., "actions" and "words," can be reduced, ultimately, to a single phenomenon-muscular movements. The scientist's task is to determine the ways in which these movements originate in the brain regarded as a very intricate machine.

It has been well known that simple ("pure") reflexes can be elicited by stimulation of appropriate sensory nerves. Sechenov demonstrated experimentally, in 1862, the existence of mechanisms in the frog's brain which *inhibit* spinal reflex movements initiated by skin stimulation.

The concept that reflex movements can be both inhibited and intensified by the stimulation of different parts of the brain has important consequences for Sechenov's theory of "mental" phenomena. Thus in fright the effects of sensory stimuli are intensified by processes taking place in the cerebral hemispheres.

In human behaviour an important part is played by responses (reflexes) acquired by learning: mental development is based on memory, which preserves, in the central nervous system, sounds and images in a latent state. These responses include speech, which involves formation of the associations of auditory sensations with kinesthetic, visual, and tactile sensations. Words are "conditional sounds."

In silent thinking, the motor response (the last member of a reflex initiated by sensory stimulation which evokes central processes and, at times, sensations) is inhibited. Put the other way, to Sechenov a thought is "the first two thirds of a mental reflex." Similarly, other mental phenomena, such as intentions or wishes, may be viewed as reflexes without external manifestation. In contrast to mental reflexes with an "inhibited end, emotions represent mental reflexes with an "intensified end."

In regard to what appears as a "voluntary" action, Sechenov's point of view is rigorously deterministic: Given the same internal and external conditions, man's action will be similar.

Sechenov was aware of the limitations and deficiencies of *Reflexes of the brain*, but felt that he did demonstrate the feasibility of what was indicated by the initial title of the essay: "An attempt to establish the physiological basis of psychological processes."

### Individual Differences

One of the few areas in which the call for the "Pavlovisation" of psychology, heard in the early 1950s, resulted in a large volume of innovative, empirical research is the study of individual differences carried out in Moscow in one of the laboratories of the Institute of Psychology, U.S.S.R. Academy of Pedagogical Sciences. The series of volumes, beginning in 1956 and edited by B. M. Teplov, in which the results were reported was initially called *Typological features of higher nervous activity in man.* A more Pavlovian title could hardly have been found. The change in the title of the series, as of the sixth volume, to *Problems of differential psychophysiology* is highly significant. The editor (Nebylitsyn, 1969) points out that in part, the change in the title reflects an endeavor to attune it to a more contemporary scientific terminology. More importantly, the change indicates a shift in emphasis toward the study of the relation between the "properties of the nervous system," emotional behaviour, and performance in prolonged work and under the impact of other stresses.

In the Pavlovian tradition the *type of the nervous system* refers to two different concepts:

1. A complex of specific characteristics of the two basic, opposed nervous processes (excitation and inhibition), i.e., the "strength" of the excitatory process, "equilibrium" between excitabory and inhibitory processes, and "mobility." The opposite poles of the three dimensions are weakness, disequilibrium and inertness.
2. Characteristic patterns of animal and human behaviour.

The type in the first sense (a complex of specific properties of the nerve processes) was viewed as genotype and was referred to, in Pavlov's terminology, also as *temperament*, *nervous constitution*, or *type of higher nervous activity*.

The type in the second sense (habitual pattern of behaviour) represents a *phenotype*, referred to also as *character*. In Pavlov's formulation of 1930, referring to man (Teplov, 1964, p. 36):

Human personality is determined both by biological inheritance and by the environment, i.e., the conditions of upbringing. The strength [i.e., the type] of the nervous system (temperament) is an innate property; character or the form of behaviour consists to a large extent of acquisitions, habits formed during the individual's lifetime.

In later statements Pavlov spoke of the properties of the nervous system as "innate" or "congenital" rather than "inherited," though still retaining the term *genotype*. In this Pavlov was affected by Kupalov's findings that the properties of the nervous system may be modified during intrauterine development.

Historically, the individual differences between dogs were first described in terms of the animals' general behaviour (i.e., the visually observed motor responses in the experimental stand and "at liberty"). Gradually, reliance came to be placed on strictly experimental indicators derived from the study of the salivary conditioned responses.

The *strength* of the nervous system refers to "the working capacity of the cerebral cells," defined as the ability of the nerve cells to withstand long, concentrated excitation or the action of an "ultrastrong" stimulus, without passing into inhibition.

*Mobility* is defined in terms of the speed with which a stimulus produces a response. An important aspect of mobility is the ability of the organisms to adapt their responses to a reversal of the sign-positive (excitatory) or negative (inhibitory)—of the conditioned stimuli.

The specific tests for the characterisation of the typological properties of the animal nervous system are described in detail (Teplov, 1964, pp. 59-112).

Teplov (1964, p. 127) regards it as futile, and perhaps even harmful, to attempt to find quick methods of determining the type of nervous system in man, i.e., methods which would require only a few days or even a few hours. This would amount to a "testological approach," for which he has no sympathy.

The five reports of experiments from Teplov's laboratory, selected by Gray (1964, pp. 367-464) deal with the dimension of strength of the nervous system in man.

Gray (1964, pp. 157-287) summarised the results of the then available research, carried out in Teplov's laboratory', On strength of the excitatory processes (strength of nervous activity, strength of the nervous system), including a 1960 factor analysis of intercorrelations between twenty-one measures. In addition, he provided a reinterpretation (pp. 289-364) of the empirical findings obtained in Teplov's laboratory. Gray's interpretation employs concepts more familiar to Western psychologists than those of Pavlov, and it places reliance on more recent neurophysiological findings. Specifically, he sees merit in substituting for the dimension of strength of the nervous system that of arousability (levels of arousal), and he expresses (1964, p. 289) the belief that by making such a substitution, we can link together two different areas of research and so suggest fruitful lines of new research.

**A Vast Memory**

While studies on preschool and school-age children abound in Soviet psychology (Cole & Maltzman, 1969, pp. 41-273), Luria's (1968) volume extends the segment of the life cycle under observation from adolescence to maturity, exploring the ways in which imbalance in mental functioning affects the formation of personality.

In several ways, the "little book about a vast memory" is a fascinating case study. First, it covers a period of thirty years. Second, it deals with a remarkable individual. Third, it examines the individual broadly, as a person, not just as a mnemonic virtuoso.

The subject's memory was, indeed, fabulous, as documented by his capacity to reproduce long tables of numbers, letters, and nonsense syllables as well as complex formulas. The mechanisms of memorisation varied. The subject was able to form and retain, for years, images of the tables, simply "reading off" the digits or letters. Words were converted into graphic images. Later, when he gave public performances as a memonist, he strengthened the accuracy of his performance by "enlarging" the dimensions of his images, making sure that the graphic images were clearly visible ("clearly illuminated") and suitably arranged spatially (e.g., along an imaginary street). Eventually, he developed a system of simplified images, a kind of visual shorthand.

The single most outstanding feature of his perceptual processes was their multisensory nature (synesthesia). Sounds produced immediately an experience of light and color, and frequently, of taste and touch as well. Words had not only their meanings but also "shapes" and colors. Thus *wine* was perceived as a "dark word." In putting his baby brother to sleep, he had to "sing in a *loud* voice, since it has to be *foggy* if one's going to fall asleep."

The synesthetic features of perception were important in his recall since they provided extra cues during remembering.

The duration of the subject's retention of what he memorised and the fact that traces left by one stimulus did not inhibit the recall of other, similar stimuli were amazing. At the same time, his memory was not equally excellent for all kinds of material. Specifically, he complained that he had a poor memory for faces, seen as ever-changing patterns of light and shadow.

His dominant sense was vision and his "thinking" was primarily a manipulation of his vivid visual images. Once he commented: "Other people *think* as they read, but I *see* it all." Or again: "I can understand only what I can visualise." Overwhelmed by the richness of visual imagery, he found abstract thought difficult or impossible. He had difficulty understanding poetry and metaphoric expressions in general. In conversation the steady stream of emerging images led him into endless digressions.

His vivid imagination enabled him to control some of his body's autonomic functions, such as heart rate and body temperature. His images were so vivid that they took on the feel of reality. This resulted in lifelong daydreaming, which became a substitute for action. His attitude toward life was characterised by the expectation that something wonderful would happen to him, leading him to view all factual events as "temporary," as a prelude—a prelude to something that never materialised.

## Thought Pathology in Mental Diseases

In the 1920s Blyuma V Zeigarnik, author of *The pathology of thinking* (1965). was a student of Kurt Lewin in Berlin. At the tender age of twenty-seven years (tender, that is, for psychology's hall of fame) she became an eponym, giving name to the *Zeigarnik phenomenon* (Zeigarnik, 1927), which refers to a better recall of tasks that have not been completed and, more loosely, to an individual's concern over unresolved problems. Upon her return to the Soviet Union, she worked in the field of abnormal psychology with the many-sided L. S. Vygotskii. Pathology of thought became her speciality.

Her work fits the pattern of the long-standing, though not uninterrupted, Russian tradition of close ties between scientific psychology and psychiatry, stressed by S. S. Korsakov, V. M. Bekhterev, and V. Kh. Kandinskii, the founders of modern Russian psychiatry. In the framework of Korsakov's neuropsychiatric clinic, A. A. Tokarskii established a laboratory of psychology in 1894. For many years Zeigarnik has been in charge of the laboratory of experimental psychology associated with the Moscow Research Institute of Psychiatry, Ministry of Health.

Zeigarnik refers to the application of psychological methods in the psychiatric context as *pathopsychology*. This is a narrower concept than *medical psychology*, which includes, importantly, psychotherapy. Pathopsychology is a branch of psychology. In Western terms, it may be regarded as a sector of clinical psychology concerned with the psychological characterisation of individuals who are mentally ill. Zeigarnik's book is focused on one aspect of mental functioning, the thought processes.

The task of pathopsychology is viewed as twofold:

1. To meet the needs of psychiatric practice by contributing to the establishment of diagnosis: other authors would include also patho-Psychology's contribution to the appraisal of the effectiveness of therapy and, specifically, the evaluation of drug therapy.
2. To utilise the information acquired in dealing with these practical problems for further development of psychological theory. It is the latter aspect that is of direct interest here.

Thinking is defined by Zeigarnik (1965), in a leninist framework and terminology, as "a generalised and indirect reflection of the outside world" (p. 67), manifested in practical life as acquisition and assimilation of facts and utilisation of knowledge. Thinking refers to the processes of analysis and synthesis in which sensory and rational cognition is combined into a single activity: Stressing the dialectical unity of these two stages of cognition (sensory and rational), the founders of Marxism-Leninism point out that it is the rational stage which makes it possible to probe into the essence of things and events in nature and society.

Only conceptual thinking provides a full reflection of reality, enabling us to understand the internal connections between phenomena.

The thesis concerning the two stages of cognition is seen as being in harmony with Pavlov's theory of the two signal systems, sensory and symbolic. Symbols, of which words are the most important category, are "signals of signals." Speech provides the means for the analysis and synthesis of the sensory impressions received by the human organism from the outside word and of images.

The core of Zeigarnik's (1965) volume is an account of a study on the disturbances of thought in psychiatric patients. The patients are grouped into nine disease categories, with the size of the groups varying from fifteen to well over one hundred.

Using a variety of testing procedures, Zeigarnik examined the disturbances in three aspects of thinking: (1) abstraction and generalisation, (2) logical trend of thought, and (3) the purposive and critical character of thought.

Zeigarnik's data indicate that specific forms of disordered thought are not strictly limited to particular nosological categories. The conclusion is drawn that the results of psychological examinations of thought disturbances can aid in the establishment of a diagnosis, but are not specific enough, in themselves, for diagnostic purposes.

Zeigarnik suggests that the presence of a given type of thought disturbance in a group of mental diseases indicates a common underlying mental dysfunction: asthenia, with fatigability and emotional lability (in patients with cerebrovascular diseases and post-traumatic pychosis) and inertia (in oligophrenics and epileptics, who lack capacity for generalisation and are absorbed by details).

While the study was focused on disturbances of the thought processes, Zeigarnik stresses that thinking cannot be regarded as an isolated "mental function," existing apart from man's needs and attitudes. What appears to be an impaired capacity for critical thought may reflect an attitude of indifference toward the tasks presented to the patient.

Zeigarnik disagrees with the view of adult mental dysfunction as a regression to an earlier stage of mental development and insists that, despite some external similarities, there exist qualitative differences between the thinking of a mentally effective adult and the thinking of a child (Zeigarnik, 1965): "The disintegration of mental activity is not the antithesis of its development" (p. 193). In the Pavlovian framework, such manifestations of adult mental dysfunction as fluctuation in the level of mental performance and hyperresponsiveness to extraneous stimuli are interpreted as consequences of impaired cortical inhibition. On the other hand, the distractibility of the child is viewed as a manifestation of a powerful orienting reflex, indicative of a high level of cortical activity.

## Brain and Viscera

In Pavlov's view, the function of the brain is to maintain the adaptation of the organism to the changing environment (principle of the unity of the organism with the environment). The environment is twofold: external and internal. Under the influence of the French physiologist Claude Bernard (1813-1878), the internal environment *(milieu interieur)* was viewed, narrowly, as the fluids bathing the tissue cells of multicellular organisms. Exploration of the function of receptors located in the viscera, their cortical representation, and viscerocerebral and cerebrovisceral interaction has been pursued vigorously by the Russian physiologists, as indicated by the numerous references cited in Chernigovskiy's monograph (1967). In the monograph the interoceptors are grouped into four classes (mechanoreceptors, chemoreceptors, thermoreceptors, and osmoreceptors), and the mechanisms of their functioning are analysed.

L. A. Bekkers and V. M. Shumovskii reported in 1862 that stretching the walls of the urinary bladder by filling it with liquid, introduced through a thin catheter, initiated contractions of the bladder. This response is an example of a "natural" (or systemic) reflex. Increased stimulus intensity gives rise to "conjugate" (con-comitant, intersystemic) reflexes involving the activity of a number of effectors and manifested, for example, in the changes of respiration and a rise in blood pressure. Interoceptive stimulation can affect also sensory functions, e.g., the light threshold of the dark-adapted eye.

While the afferent impulses generated by the stimulation of interoceptors have also been studied electrophysiologically, it is the method of conditioned reflexes that served as the principal research tool in the Russian studies designed to clarify the two-way connections, through afferent and efferent pathways, between the internal organs and the central nervous system. Both aspects are of relevance to psychology.

It should be noted that, in man, conditioned visceral responses can be produced by conditioned stimuli of the first signal system (e.g., acoustic or tactile stimuli) as well as by words, regarded by Pavlov as conditioned stimuli belonging to the second (symbolic) signal system. The afferent and efferent chains may include the participation of the subcortical centers as well as of the endocrine system.

In Bykov's formulation (1959, p. 335), reflecting Pavlov's views:

> The cortex is clearly a masterful organ dedicated to the performance of complicated tasks, not only as regards information reaching it over external receptors but also with the analysis, and organisation of, impulses from the internal organs. It is the prime system for channelising the host of divergent and insistent signals, and of integrating them into the complex of action called behaviour.

The interaction between the brain and the internal organs is a two-way process. Let us begin by considering the viscerocerebral relations.

In regard to the afferent impulses originating in the interoceptors of the viscera, psychologists are interested in the effects of the signals of the state of the internal organs on the function of the higher regions of the central nervous system and the activity of the organism as a whole (behaviour).

Bykov showed, in 1928, that wetting of the gastric mucosa, paired with the application of an electrical shock to the hind limb of a dog, eventually elicited, when presented alone (i.e., without the shock), a lifting of the limb. This demonstrated that an interoceptive stimulus could elicit external behavior (a conditioned motor response). The development of complex (behavioural) reaction patterns involves an interaction of exteroceptive and interoceptive signals.

While for the most part we are not conscious of the afferent nervous impulses initiated by the interoceptors or the resulting sensations are "vague," they do affect importantly our moods, our feeling of well-being, and our self-awareness ("consciousness of one's body," in Bykov's terminology) and are an important part of the biological drives (hunger, elimination).

It was the remarkable I. M. Sechenov who, in 1863, wrote that the "dark" (obscure) sensations which accompany events taking place in the cavities of the chest. stomach, etc., "form one of the most potent motivation forces" (cited in Bykov, 1959, p. 405).

In the closing chapter of his monograph Cherngovskiy (1967) reviews experiments indicating that interoceptive signaling plays a role in the feeding behaviour of animals, search for food, food selection (food consumption) and suggests that the study of the function of the interoceptors may contribute to an objective analysis of some forms of instinctive behaviour.

The study of cerebrovisceral interactions, concerned with cerebral (and, in particular, cortical) regulation of visceral activities under conditions of health and with the role of malfunction of this regulation in the etiology of certain diseases, represents the Russian analog of Western psychophysiology and psychosomatic medicine.

Cerebrovisceral impulses can initiate or modify the activity of visceral organs. We speak of activating and regulating mechanisms, respectively.

The first data on the formation of urinary conditioned reflexes (diuresis elicited by a sound) were reported by K. M. Bykov and I. A. Alekseev-Berkman in 1926 Bykov's monograph (1957, 1959) documents the extension of the technique of conditioned reflexes to many other internal organs, in addition to the kidney.

Bykov and Kurtsin (1966) showed the importance of the disturbances of the cerebral (especially the cortical) regulation of gastric and duodenal function secretion of gastric juice, trophic processes in the gastric and intestinal wail, resistance to digestion of the tissues by gastric juice) in the development of peptic ulcer.

**Varieties of Behaviour**

Fragments of the work of I. S. Beritashvili (Beritov, in Russian), the outstanding Georgian neurophysiologist and student of animal behaviour, are contained in the proceedings of scientific conferences (Beritashvili, 1963; cf. also Beritashvili, 1968a, 1968b). A systematic presentation of his physiological analysis of animal behaviour. published originally in 1961, is now available in English (Beritoff, 1965).

Beritashvili differentiates four varieties of behaviour: innate (instinctive), conditioned, image-controlled, and conscious. The first three varieties characterise higher vertebrates. The latter variety is present only in adult normal man who formulates goals and plans action. However, the lower levels of behaviour may also be in evidence. Furthermore, initially conscious behaviour, through repetition, may be automatised and may resemble a conditioned chain reflex. Under these conditions the conscious control is reduced but not entirely eliminated.

In animals, the basic varieties are the instinctive behaviour, dependent upon the inborn organisation of the central nervous system and serving specific organic needs, and the individually acquired behaviour. While the instinctive behaviour represents predetermined sequences of operations, it is susceptible, in a measure, to modification by experience (learning, conditioning). The individually acquired animal behaviour falls, in its turn, into two categories: conditioned and image-directed.

The concept of image-directed behaviour, as a separate category of individually acquired behaviour, basically different from conditioned behaviour, was a truly revolutionary departure from the Pavlovian interpretative framework.

A typical experiment demonstrating image-guided behaviour proceeds as follows: A dog is taken out of his cage, is led to a place in the experimental room where he sees food being placed behind a screen, and is brought back to the cage. When released from the cage, he runs to the place where he had seen the food. While interpreting this behaviour as the result of an integrated, multilevel activity of the nervous system. Beritashvili assigns the leading role to "psychoneural activity of the cortex. This involves activation of a neuronal complex which reproduces images of vitally important aspects of the environment (goal objects). The images guide the behaviour.

The morphological substrate of image-guided behaviour is identified with the stellate (star-shaped) neurons of the neocortex.

A high level of excitability of the stellate neurons is maintained by impulses arriving from the nonspecific reticular formation in the lower brainstem. In agreement with I. M. Sechenov (1829-1905), Beritashvili views images as the main regulator of behaviour of higher vertebrates. The images regulate animal behaviour in essentially the same way as the direct perceptions of the environment do. Thus in the illustrative experiment described earlier, the hungry dog runs to the place at which the food was located, behind a screen, as he would if he actually saw it there. The image *guides* the behaviour, while an inborn drive to get food *motivates* the behaviour.

Man exhibits conscious behaviour, characterised by awareness of goals and planning of action. The results of action are anticipated prior to the actual onset of the action. Conscious behaviour is characteristic only of adult man, not of animals or human infants, and represents the product of social interaction involving verbal communication. The young child's behaviour is image-driven. Under certain conditions the behaviour of adult man can revert to this lower level or even to the level of conditioned reflexes.

An extensive, updated account of Beritashvili's views on the structure and function of the cerebral cortex and the subcortical structures, with emphasis on the highest,. "psychoneural activity of the brain, appeared in Russian at a time when the author, eighty-four years young, was still busily engaged in research on memory (Beritov, 1969).

**Experiments on Monkeys**

The first of the three parts constituting the volume edited by Utkin (1960) is devoted to the study of conditioned reflexes ("the physiology and pathology of highest nervous activity," in the Russian parlance).

L. N. Norkina used lever pressing as the preferred method of studying conditioned motor reflexes in monkeys. She discussed the procedures, the formation of conditioned reflexes, their ready disturbance (external inhibition) by a variety of extraneous stimuli, and their "internal inhibition" (e.g., extinction through nonreinforcement of the conditioned positive stimuli). A stable differential inhibition (inhibition of responses to nonreinforced stimuli) could be established only with difficulty.

Norkina also reported studies on the "type of highest nervous activity," along Pavlov's line, but replacing the salivary method by the study of conditioned motor reflexes. One of the observations concerned the high "mobility" of the processes of excitation and inhibition in the monkeys, manifested in a ready adaptation to changes in the sign (meaning) of the conditioned stimuli (from positive or excitatory to negative or inhibitory, and vice versa).

D. I. Miminoshvili produced experimental neurosis in monkeys by overstraining the cortical excitatory processes. This was achieved by prolonging the conditioned stimulus (red light reinforced by electrical stimulation of the skin). The animals ceased to eat, exhibited persistent motor excitement, and failed to discriminate between positive and negative (inhibitory) feeding signals, responding with a prolonged pressure on the lever. The rate of respiration was increased dramatically (from twenty-eight to seventy-five respiratory movements per minute).

An additional form of stress was the collision between a conditioned stimulus, reinforced by electrical shock, presented simultaneously with, or shortly after, a conditioned stimulus reinforced by feeding. This resulted in a violent general motor excitement or, on the other hand, a general torpor (catalepsis) and drowsiness.

In some monkeys, stress was induced by exposure to "natural conditioned stimuli," as when a sexually mature rhesus monkey, first kept together with the females, was later placed in a solitary cage located next to a group of female monkeys headed by a male "rival."

**Development of Animal Behaviour**

Krushinskii's *Animal behaviour* (1962) is not a comprehensive textbook but an exploration, in depth, of selected themes, such as the integration of innate and individually acquired components of behaviour. His approach involves the combination of laboratory methods for investigation of the Pavlovian "physiology of highest nervous activity" with the observation of behaviour under natural conditions.

As regards heredity, Krushinskii views only unconditioned reflexes as inherited. Behavioural acts vary widely in regard to the role of the individually acquired components. Instincts are defined not simply as unconditioned reflex behaviour, but as behavioural acts with a high proportion of innate components. The animal's behaviour is adapted to the concrete conditions of its existence through the formation of conditioned reflexes. Habits represent a form of behaviour in which the individually acquired components predominate.

The "excitability" of the nervous system of dogs exhibits large interindividual differences, with the scores in the two-minute test used by Krushinskii varying from 10 to 360 movements. Positive correlations were established between excitability and effectiveness in forming motor conditioned reflexes.

The "strength" of the nervous system is defined as its working capacity (endurance). Again, in dogs the criterion of strength correlated positively with the capacity to learn, though the reported *rs* were very low, varying from .06 to .33.

Hyperthyroidism results in an increased excitability of the nervous system, while extirpation of the thyroid gland or chemical blocking of its function has an opposite effect. Male dogs tend to have somewhat "stronger" nervous systems than females and to exhibit slightly more marked "active defensive reactions."

The appearance of epileptiform fits in rodents ("reflex epilepsy," in Krushin-skii's terminology), elicited by sound stimuli, is interpreted in terms of the irradiation of excitation produced in the auditory projection area of the cortex and not effectively inhibited. By the method of selection Krushinskii developed a line of experimental animals (rats) with a low threshold of motor excitation and convulsive fits.

"Extrapolation reflexes" refer (Krushinskii, 1962, p. xv) to behaviour by means of which some species of animals are able to grasp elementary cause-and-effect relationships between phenomena in the outside world. A nonlaboratory example of such behaviour is as follows: A crow is crossing a road, at a given pace. Then, "extrapolating" the speed of movements. It hurries up and avoids being hit by an oncoming car, thereafter resuming its initial rate of movement. A variety of laboratory test situations were devised for studies with various species of birds and with rabbits. Krushinskii viewed this behaviour as one of those types of reflex activity of the brain which may be characterised as elementary rational activity.

**Varia**

Limitations of space make it necessary to refer *briefly* to several additional monographs. We shall consider, in turn, the following topics: eye movements and vision, neurophysiological mechanisms of voluntary human movements, orienting reaction, set, thought and language, the role of speech in the regulation of human behaviour, mental retardation, and disturbances in mental functions resulting from brain lesions.

### *Eye Movements and Vision*

A. L Yarbus (born in 1914) was trained as a physicist. For many years he was associated with the Institute of Biophysics, U.S.S.R. Academy of Sciences. His extensive investigations are summarised in a volume (Yarbus, 1967) edited by L. A. Riggs, a fellow student of eye movements in the United States.

In 1956 Yarbus developed a miniaturised optical system, attached by suction to the human eye, which facilitates the study of eye movements. Eye movements were studied in a wide variety of conditions, including fixation on stationary objects, perception of moving objects, and perception of complex objects (pictures, optical illusions, text to be read). From the records of the eye movements one can determine which features of an object, such as a portrait of a person, attract the observer's eye, in what order, how often, and for how long.

When we view a picture, the eyes fixate primarily on the components which contain or may contain information essential for the comprehension of the meaning of the picture (Yarbus, 1967)-. "Eye movements reflect the human thought processes (p. 190). In observing human scenes, the eye movements will be markedly affected by the questions the experimenter asks the observer. The patterns of eye movements during such a "directed scanning" help to clarify the significance of the eye-movement records obtained during a free examination of the same picture.

During prolonged viewing of a given object the observer's eyes repeatedly return to the features yielding the primary information about the object.

Yarbus confirmed and enriched the earlier observations made by Western authors who reported that visual impressions, unchanging and stationary relative to the retina, become rapidly (within one to three seconds) invisible. Yarbus speaks of the formation of an "empty field" and suggests, in accordance with the electrophysiological data obtained in animals, that in man the immobility of retinal images sharply reduces or abolishes impulses entering the optic nerve from the eye.

### *Mechanisms of Movements*

The study of the neurophysiological mechanisms of human bodily movements was for many years the speciality of Nicholas Bernstein (1896.1966). He contributed to the development of photographic methods of motion an-is (so-called cyclography), mathematical characterisation of movement, and their novel physiological interpretation. With P. K. Anokhin, he was Russians pioneering physiological cyberneticist and in 1935, thirteens before the publication (in 1948) of N. Wiener's *Cybernetic,* was concerned with the functioning of self-regulating systems and stressed the crucial role of "feed-back" for the control of man's voluntary movements. A "reflex circle" (or "ring"), not a reflex arc, represents the proper model of the fundamental unit of human activity. Bernstein (1967, pp. 115-116) speaks of "circular control" of human movements.

Bernstein's approach to the organisation of goal-directed behaviour incorporates the concepts of the factual (present) value of a situational parameter *Iw (Ist-wert,* in German), the required (future) value of the parameter *Sw (Soll-vert),* and the discrepancy $\Delta w = Iw - Sw$. Thus, in picking up an object seen on a table, the position of the object which must be reached by the hand corresponds to *Sw*, the actual position of the hand at a given moment corresponds to *Iw*, and the diminishing distance between the object and the hand corresponds to $\Delta w$.

## Orienting Reaction

The "orienting reaction" (or investigatory, "what is it?" reflex) is another phenomenon in which physiologists and psychologists share interest. The phenomenon was described by Pavlov as far back as 1910 and, in greater detail, in 1922, but psychologists became involved in research on orienting reactions only in the last twenty years. The materials available in translation inform the reader about the Status of the field in the late 1950s. The volume edited by L. G. Voronin et al. (1965) constitutes the proceedings of a conference held in February, 1957.

The orienting reaction is a phenomenon of broad biological and psychological significance. For one thing, there is a link between the orienting reflex, as a nonspecific generalised reaction, and arousal, as a function of the reticular activating system. Second, orienting reaction interacts, in complex ways, with other activities of the organism. It may inhibit ongoing acts; on the other hand, it may enhance the dominant activity of the organism, such as an unconditioned defensive reflex. Third, seen in a more "psychological" perspective, the study of orienting reactions opens the possibility for empirical investigations of cognitive processes.

Sokolov's (1963) monograph, first published in 1958, is focused on the role of conditioned reflexes in perception. Orienting reflexes are viewed as responses which bring about increased sensory sensitivity in animals during such activities as listening, sniffing, and watching. New stimuli give rise to peripheral vascoconstriction and cephalic vasodilation. Both responses decrease in intensity and eventually cease upon the repetition of a given stimulus. The weakening of an orienting reaction (*diminished reactivity*) is associated with a rise in threshold values (*diminished sensitivity*).

The orienting reaction can be brought about not only by a new stimulus but also by a change in the given stimulus, such as a change in the stimulus intensity in either direction. In this case the intensity of the reaction is proportional to the intensity of the *change* in stimulus intensity.

The vasomotor responses represent only one component of the orienting reaction. The galvanic skin reflex (a fall in the resistance to electrical current passing through the body), recorded from the skin of the palm of the hand, is another component of the orienting reflex that was studied by Sokolov (1963, pp. 53-64). Latent period, magnitude, and duration of the reaction were measured. The response was similar to the vascular component of the orienting reaction, with a gradual extinction upon repeated presentation of the stimulus. In addition to the autonomic components noted above, orienting reacticns involve somatic (movements of the body, head, eyes, ears), other autonomic (respiratory), and electro-encephalographic (changes in the alpha rhythm) components.

The orienting reaction is viewed as a system of responses promoting, directly (through effects on cortical activity) or indirectly (by affecting cerebral blood supply), conditions favourable to stimulus reception (Sokolov, 1963, p. 285).

Sokolov uses a "neuronal model of the stimulus" to interpret physiologically the generation and extinction of orienting reactions. He postulates that the nervous system stores the information concerning the stimulus that is being presented repeatedly (its intensity, duration, and interstimulus interval) and compares the forecasts of future stimuli with the stimuli actually present. An orienting reaction takes place when the stimulus presented at a given time differs from the "neuronal model" of the stimulus.

Sokolov's neuronal model of the stimulus is closely related to P. K. Anokhin's concept of the "acceptor of action."

### *Set*

In the South, in faraway Tbilist in Georgia, D. N. Uznadze (1886-1950) and his co-workers have been engaged for many years in experimental investigations of "set" (*Einstellung,* in German; *untanovka,* in Russian). Two of Uznadze's monographs were translated and published in a book entitled *The psychology of set* (Uznadze, 1966).

In contrast to the prevailing Russian point of view, to Uznadze the human mind is not identical with consciousness. It includes, importantly, the nonconscious factors to which he refers as "sets." Sets are defined as states of an organism, activated by the organism's needs, which give direction to the organism's activity in specific environmental a situations. Usually, lie (man) is not aware of these sets. But this does not stop them from being the active forces controlling his activity (Uznadze, 1966). p. 243).

The concept of set has important implications for all forms of behaviour, from perception through the functioning of the normal personality to abnormal behaviour.

### *Thought and Language*

L. S. Vygotskii's (1896-1934) monograph was first published, in Russian, in 1934. It was regarded as important enough to merit a translation almost thirty years after it was written (Vygotsky, 1962). In one sense, it may be viewed as an early contribution to psycholinguistics and, specifically, to that segment of psycholinguistics which deals with the interrelations between intellective and verbal activity. But Vygotskii's work has broader implications for psychology. In the author's formulation (1962, p. 153):

Thought and language, which reflect reality in a way different from that of perception, are the key to the nature of human consciousness. Words play a central part not only in the development of thought but in the historical growth of consciousness as a whole. A word is a microcosm of human consciousness.

Just as physical work is performed by means of tools, mental activities involve the use of symbols, primarily verbal symbols (words). In the child's mental-development a crucial role is played by internalisation of overt behaviour and, in particular, of the external dialogue transformed into inner speech and thought.

### *Regulation of Human Behaviour*

A. R. Luria, of the contemporary Russian psychologists the best known in the West, was a close associate of Vygotskii, many of whose interests he shares, including an interest in speech (cf. Luria, 1960b, p. 142).

In his study of the development of voluntary action in children, Luria (1960a) takes as a point of departure Vygotskii's theory that speech—first external, later internal—is the chief mechanism of voluntary behaviour.

One of Luria's first books published in English after the war is a report of a study on the development of speech in a pair of identical twins, undertaken in cooperation with F. Ia. Yudovich (Luria & Yudovich, 1959). Having placed the twins in separate, parallel groups in a kindergarten, the authors observed the changes from a primitive, "synpractic" speech, closely tied to specific activities, to speech used by the twins for communication with others and for formulating the aims of their own activities.

In the course of the development of the child, the regulatory function of speech is carried out less and less by words as direct impulses to action and more and more by words as carriers of meaning (Luria, 1961). There is in the child a simultaneous shift, around the age of five years, from the external to the internal speech. At this stage of development, Luria notes, the internal speech comes to constitute the essential component both of thought and of voluntary behaviour.

### *Mental Retardation*

The role of speech in the control of behaviour is also one of the topics explored in a volume edited by Luria (1963a) and dealing with various aspects of the functioning of mentally retarded children, such as electrical activity of the brain, orientation reflexes, formation of conditioned reflexes, and verbal associations. The book is introduced by a revealing chapter entitled "The problem of mental retardation and its study." Rejecting the concept of inheritance of mental abilities, the Soviets view *all* instances of mental retardation as a consequence of a serious brain disease during the intrauterine or early postnatal period of development (Luria, 1963a, p. vii). The reader will also find some choice bits of misinformation about the use of mental tests in the "capitalist countries" (Luria, 1963a, pp.1-3). Mental testing is one area in which ideological conflict continues to create barriers to comprehension and the possibility of a reasoned dialogue.

### *Brain and Behaviour*

Several of Luria's books are the outcome of his investigations on the impact of brain lesions on mental functions. They represent important contributions both to applied psychology and to the theoretical interpretation of brain-mind relationships.

Luria's views differ from the concepts of traditional "morphopsychology," whether they had postulated rigid localisation of complex mental functions in specific "centers" or regarded mental activities as products of the brain operating as a whole. According to Luria, complex activities (such as locomotion or writing), are executed by a group of integrated structural units, central and peripheral (1966a, p. 468):

> We adopted as our starting point the idea of a dynamic, systemic localisation of functions, originally proposed by Pavlov and subsequently developed and applied to the higher mental functions of man by Vygotskii. We regard the higher cortical processes as complex, dynamically localised, functional systems.

Another book by Luria, published in Russian in 1948 (Luria, 1963b), is concerned with recovery after localised injury to the brain. The material on which the book is based was collected during and following World War II. The basic fact is that while the damaged brain cells do not regenerate, there is a partial restoration of the impaired brain function. The functions specifically considered by Luria include movements, visual perception, speech, thinking, and motivation.

Luria differentiates three types of mechanisms for the restoration of brain function: (1) restoration of temporarily inhibited functions (spontaneous deinhibition, restoration of synaptic transmission by pharmacological means, deinhibition by a change of mental orientation); (2) substitution of the opposite hemisphere; and (3) formation of new, compensatory functional connections between different areas of the cortex. In this way a new "functional system" is created involving areas of the brain that previously did not participate in a given activity (such as multiplication of numbers), impaired by focal brain lesions. Impairment of such complex activities as writing, reading, memorisation, or spatial orientation can be compensated by the introduction of auxiliary visual, accustic, or kinesthetic processes.

Luria's two large recent works (Luria, 1966a, 1966b) deal with a variety of topics in the area of neuropsychology, which connotes, in Luria's hands, largely the study of disturbances of behaviour in the presence of brain lesions, whether they are due to gunshot wounds or to tumors.

The first volume (Luria, 1966a) is a collection of ten essays, most of which were revised in 1962, written over a period of some thirty years. Sequelae of lesions of the anterior parts of the human brain represent the dominant theme. In the opening chapters the author discusses the more general problem of the functional organisation of the human brain.

The second volume (Luria, 1966b) is similar in organisation and content, with the first part concerned with the problem of localisation of mental functions, and the second part dealing with the disturbances of "higher cortical functions" in the presence of focal brain lesions. The third part is new and describes a variety of methods used by Soviet clinical psychologists. Since in the Soviet journal publications the description of methods is frequently cursory, this detailed account is a welcome source of information.

Because of importance of Luria's point of view on brain and behaviour—one of the basic issues of physiological psychology—we shall close this section by quoting him directly (1966a, p. xvii):

> Human mental processes are to be understood *as* complex functional systems, having a social-historical origin.... These processes take place as a result of the combined activity of several cortical zones, each of which plays its own specific role, and supplies an essential factor for the normal working of the system as a whole. A local brain lesion, directly causing the loss of one of the factors concerned in the construction of mental processes, thus leads to a secondary disturbance of the functional system as a whole; however, every disturbance has its own individual character depending on which link of the functional system is affected by each particular local brain lesion.

## A LOOK INTO THE FUTURE

In our attempt to "look around the corner," we could hardly ask for a more competent guide than A. N. Leont'ev, dean of Moscow University's College of Psychology (Leont'ev, 1968).

Leont'ev points out that in the past, much of Soviet psychological research was associated with problems of education—the instruction and upbringing of children. There is need for broadening the scope of the research in this area, tied in the past too one-sidedly to methods of teaching specific school subjects. Educational psychology needs an atmosphere conducive to the exploration of *psychological* ideas from which genuine innovations in "educational technology"—such as programmed instruction—may emerge.

In view of the rapid and continuing advances in science and technology, it is essential not so much to impart to students ready-made knowledge and skills as to create in them the capacity to assimilate the new advances. This calls for a fundamental reexamination of the learning processes. First and foremost, the problem must be viewed, in Leont'ev's opinion, as a problem of psychology, not primarily or solely as a pedagogical problem.

Systematic attention must be given to the psychological aspects of the acceleration of child development, including the impact of the changes in the source of information transmitted to the child (direct contact with other persons versus speech transmitted by radio), the markedly increased amount of information entering the child's brain via the mass media, and the changes in the technological aspects of the child's environment.

In recent years the general scope of Soviet psychology has been substantially broadened, in several directions, including engineering psychology, medical psychology, research on personality, and social psychology. These are the areas in which important further growth of Soviet psychology may be expected to take place in the foreseeable future.

In a way, all these fields may be viewed as areas of "borderline research" in which psychology has been confronting the data, conceptual systems, and terminology of other sciences—biological, social, and technological. Soviet psychological papers are beginning to be replete with neurophysiological, technological, and cybernetic terms and mathematical formulas.

One of the problems that call for rethinking concerns the relations between psychology and neurophysiology. Such a rethinking must go beyond the general discussions of reducibility or the impossibility of reducing the mental to the physiological. Leont'ev is impressed by the fact that such processes as perception and memory represent multilevel phenomena. Thus subliminal sensory processes cannot be viewed legitimately as "purely physiological" since under certain conditions they may affect (regulate) complex human activity. Research on memory is being carried out at levels varying from molecular and cellular to that of the intact human organism. This approach reveals the lack of validity of the conception of the physiological and the mental as two separate "realms" (or entities). Leont'ev views as a task of prime importance the bringing about of a "vertical synthesis" of the different horizontal layers, i.e., the clarification of the relationships between the processes taking place at different levels of multilevel phenomena and the investigations of the interlevel transitions.

The study of the multilevel systems involved in behaviour facilitates the rapprochement between the conceptualisation of the function of organisms and adaptive (cybernetic) machines, and it enhances our intellectual and technological mastery of man-machine systems.

The steadily advancing automation of industrial operations has shifted the focus of the study of human factors from psychophysiological concern with movements and physical work environment to the more "psychological" level of perception, memory, and thought. Psychology is faced with the task of describing mental operations in terms which permit their modeling and their transfer to machines (and a more effective linkage between man and machine).

In the last ten years, engineering psychology and "psychological bionics" experienced rapid development in the U.S.S.R. and constitute, at present, an important segment of Soviet psychology. Furthermore, these fields exercise a profound effect on the development of Soviet psychology as a whole, interacting closely with other sectors of psychology, especially general experimental psychology.

The application of social psychology in the industrial setting is in its beginnings. Leont'ev cites problems of motivation of the workers and of interpersonal relations in industry as topics calling for research. He refers also to the problem of alienation of the workers.

The political and economic differences between the Soviet Union and the "capitalist West" lend potential interest and importance to research in the field of industrial social psychology. On the other hand, this is a sensitive area, and it remains to be demonstrated that significant, objective research in this area is, in fact, possible in the U.S.S.R. We wish to make clear that this comment is ours, not Leont'ev's.

The situation of social psychology as a whole is designated by Leont'ev as "complicated." In the past, social psychology was almost totally neglected in the U.S.S.R. as a special branch of psychology. One of the roots of this neglect was the ideologists' horror that the pursuit of social psychology might lead to a tendency to "psychologise social phenomena," "to implant subjectivist conceptions in sociology." This, again, is our interpretation, not Leont'ev's.

Leont'ev feels that there exists a legitimate complex of sociopsychological problems (such as the creation of the "sense of community") which can be properly singled out as the subject matter of social psychology. At the same time he admits that an adequately formulated program for sociopsychological research does not yet exist in the Soviet Union.

The field referred to in the West as *clinical psychology* does not have a true homolog in the Soviet Union. B. V. Zeigarnik refers to the psychological study of patients with neuropsychiatric disorders as *pathopsychology.* A segment of this field which received much attention in the Soviet Union is concerned with the psychological impact of focal brain injuries and the restoration of mental function impaired as a result of these injuries. A. R. Luria refers to this sector as *neuropsychology.* The concept of *medical psychology* is broader and less clearly defined. It includes psychotherapy (which was not cultivated systematically, intensively, or imaginatively by Soviet psychiatrists and seems to be "out of bounds" for psychologists] and such problems as the psychological response of patients to actions of a physician. Of greater importance for psychology is the fact that in this context, psychologists come face to face with problems of personality. It should be clear, notes Leont'ev (1968, p. 114) with refreshing frankness, that Soviet psychologists:

> ...cannot avoid such questions as the problem of conflict experiences, emotional trauma, the role of the unconscious, and mental compensation—i.e., precisely those questions that in the past years have been ignored in the USSR not only in pathopsychology and general psychology, but also in child psychology.

## REFERENCES

Anonymous. *Fundamentals of Marxism-Leninism.* Moscow, Foreign Languages Publishing House, 1961.

Beritashvili, I.S., the characteristics and origin of voluntary movements in higher vertebrates. In G. Moruzzi, A. Fessard, and H.H. Jasper (Eds.), *Brain Mechanisms.* Amsterdam, Elsevier, 1963, pp. 340-348.

Beritashvili (Beritov), I.S. Central inhibition according to I.M. Sechenov's experiments and concepts and its modern interpretation. In E.A. Asratyan (Ed.), *Brain Reflexes.* Amsterdam, elsevier, 1968, pp. 21-31. (a)

Beritashvili, I.S. A modern interpretation of the mechanisms of I.M. Sechenov's psychical reflex medium member. In E.A. Asratyan (Ed.), *Brain Reflexes.* Amsterdam, Elsevier, 1968, pp. 252-264. (b)

Beritoff (Beritashvili), J.S., *Neural Mechanisms of Higher Vertebrate Behaviour.* (Trans, from the 1961 Russian ed. and ed. by W.T. Liberson) Boston, Little, Brown, 1965.

Beritov, I.S., *Struktura i funktsiya kory bol'shogo mozga [Structure and function of the cerebral cortex]*. Moscow, Mauka, 1969.

Bernstein, N. *The Coordination and Regulation of Movements.* (Tans. from Russian and German). New York, Macmillan, 1967.

Blakely, T.J., *Soviet Scholasticism.* Dordrecht, Netherlands, D. Reidel, 1961.

Brozek, J. Recent developments in Soviet psychology. *Annual Review of Psychology*, 1964, 15, 493-594.

Brozek, J. Spectrum of Soviet psychology, 1968 model. *American Psychologist*, 1969, 24, 944-946.

Brozek, J., and Hoskovec, J. Current Soviet psychology, A systematic review. *Soviet Psychology and Psychiatry*, 1966, 4 (3-4), 16-44.

Bykov, K.M., *The Cerebral Cortex and the Internal Organs.* Trans. by W.H. Gantt) New York, Chemical Publishing, 1957.

Bykov, K.M., *The Cerebral Cortex and the Internal Organs.* (Trans. from the 1954 [3rd] Russian ed. by R. Hodes) Moscow, Foreign Languages Publishing House 1959.

Bykov, K.M., and Kurtsin, I.T. *The Corticovisceral Theory of the Pathogenesis of Peptic Ulcer.* (Trans. by S.A. Corson) Oxford, Pergamon Press, 1966.

Chernigovskiy, V.N., *Interoceptors.* (Trans. from the 1960 Russian ed. by G. Onischenko; ed. by D.B. Linndsley) Washington, American Psychological Association, 1967.

Cole, M., and Maltzman, I. (Eds.) *A Handbook of Contemporary Soviet Psychology.* New York, Basic Books, 1969.

Gray, J.A., (Ed. and Trans.) *Pavlov's Typology.* (Intro. by H.J. Eysenck) Oxford, Pergamon Press, 1964.

Koshtoyants, Kh. S *Essays on the History of Physiology in Russia.* (Trans. from the 1946 Russian ed. by D.P. Boder, K. Hanes, and N. O'Brien.) Washington: American Psychological Association, 1964.

Krushinskii, L.V., *Animal Behaviour, its Normal and Abnormal Development.* (Trans. by B. Haigh from the 1960 Russian ed.) New York, Consultants Bureau, 1962.

Leont'ev, A. Psikhologiya [Psychology]. In *Filosofskaya entsiklopediya [Philosophical encyclopedia].* Moscow, Sovetskaya Entsiklopediya, 1967, pp. 420-422.

Leont'ev, A.N., Some prospective problems of Soviet psychology, *Soviet Psychology*, 1968, 6 (3-4), 112-125.

Luria, A.R., Experimental analysis of the development of voluntary action n children. In H.P. David and J.C., Brengelmann (Eds.) *Perspectives in personality research.* New York, Springer, 1960, pp. 139-149. (a)

Luria, A.R., *The Nature of Human Conflicts.* (Trans. by W.H. Gantt). W.H. Gantt). New York, Grove Press, 1960. (1st ed. 1932. (b)

Luria, A.R., *The Role of Speech in the Regulation of Normal and Abnormal Behaviour.* (Ed. by J Tizard) New York, Pergamon Press, 1961.

Luria, A.R., (Ed.) *The Mentally Retarded Child.* (Trans. by W.P. Robinson from the 1960 Russian ed. English trans. ed. by B. Korman) New York, Macmillan, 1963. (a)

Luria, A.R., *Restoration of Function after Brain Injury.* (Trans. from the 1948 Russian ed. by B. Haigh) New York, Macmillan, 1963. (b)

Luria, A.R., *Higher Cortical Functions in Man.* (Trans. from the 1962 Russian ed. by B. Haigh) New York, Basic Books and Consultants Bureau, 1966. (a)

Luria, A.R., *Human Brain and Psychological Processes.* (Trans. from the 1963 Russian ed. by B. Haigh) New York, Harper and Row, 1966. (b)

Luria, A.R., *The Mind of Mnemonist.* (Tran. from the 1968 Russian ed. by L. Solotaroff) New York, Basic Books, 1968.

Luria, A.R., and Yudovich, F. Ia., *Speech and Development Processes in the Child, An Experimental Investigation.* (Trans. from the 1956 Russian ed. by O. Kovacs and J. Simon; intro. by O. Zangwill) London, Staples Press, 1959.

Nebylitsyn, V.D. (Ed.), *Probably Differentsial'noi psikhofiziologii [Differential psychophysiology].* Moscow Prosveshchenie, 1969.

Payne, T.R., *S.L. Rubinstejn and the Philosophical Foundations of Soviet Psychology.* Dordrecht, Netherlands, D. Reidel and New York, Humanities Press, 1968.

Rosenblith, W.A., Postscript, In I.M., Schenov, *Reflexes of the brain.* Cambridge, Mass., M.I.T. Press, 1965, pp. 143-145.

Rubinshtein, S.L.I.P. Pavlov's theories and some problems of the reconstruction of psychology. (In Russian) *Voprosy filosofii,* 1952, 5, 197-210.

Sechenov, I.M. *Autobiographical notes.* (Trans. from a text, completed around 1904, by K. hanes) Washington, American Psychological Association, 1965. (a)

Sechenov, I.M. *Reflexes of the brain.* (Reprint of a 1961 trans. by S. Belsky, printed in Moscow, of a work first published in Russian in 1963). Cambridge, Mass, M.I.T. Press, 1965. (b)

Sokolov, Ye. N., *Perception and the conditioned reflex.* (Trans. from the 1958 Russian ed. by S.W. Waydenfeld) New York, Macmillan, 1963.

Teplov, B.M., Problems in the study of general types of higher nervous activity in man and animals. In J.A. Gray (Ed.), *Pavlov's typology.* Oxford, Pergamon Press, 1964, pp. 3-153.

Utkin, I.A., (Ed.) *Theoretical and Practical Problems of Medicine and Biology in Experiments on Monkeys.* (Trans. by R. Schachter) New York, Pergamon Press, 1960.

Uznadze, D.N. *The psychology of set.* (Trans. by B. Haigh) New York, consultants Bureau, 1966.

Voronin, L.G., et al. (Eds.) *Orienting Reflex and Exploratory Behaviour.* (Trans. from the 1958 Russian ed. by V. Shmelev & K. Hanes) Washington: American Psychological Association, 1965.

Vygotsky, L.S. *Thought and Language.* (Intro. by J.S. Bruner; Trans. from the 1934 Russian ed. by E. Hanfmann and G. Vakar) Cambridge, Mass., M.I.T., Press, 1962.

Watson, R.I., Psychology, A prescriptive science. *American Psychologists,* 1967, 22, 435-443.

Wiener, N. *Cybernetics, or Control and Communication in the Animal and the Machine.* New York, Wiley, 1948.

Yarbus, A.L., *Eye Movements and Vision.* (Trans. from the 1965 Russian ed. by B. Haigh; English trans. ed. by L.A. Riggs) New York, Plenum Press, 1967.

Zeigarnik, B.V. Uber das Behalten von erledigten and unerledigten Handlungen. *Psychologische Forschung,* 1927, 9, 1-85.

Zeigarnik, B.V., *The Pathology of Thinking.* (Trans. from the 1962 Russian ed. by B Haigh), New York, Consultants Bureau, 1965.

## Further Readings

Anokhin, P.K. Ivan P. Pavlov and psychology. In B.B. Wolman (Ed.), *Historical Roots of Contemporary Psychology.* New York, Harper and Row, 1968, pp. 131-159.

Bowden, D. Primate behavioural research in the USSR, the Sukhumi medicobiological station. *Folia Primatologica,* 1966, 4, 346-360.

Brozek, J. (Ed.) *Selected Aspects of Contemporary Psychology in the USSR, A symposium. Medical Reports* (Fordham University Institute for Contemporary Russian Studies), 1964, 6(1), 1-21.

Brozek, J. Contemporary Soviet psychology. *Transactions of the New York Academy of Science,* Ser. II, 1965, 27, 422-438.

Brozek, J., and Herz, A.P. Recent Russian books in Psychology. *Contemporary Psychology*, 1971, 16, 726-729.

Brozek, J., and Slobin, D.I. (Eds.) *Psychology in the USSR, An historical perspective.* White Plains, N.Y., International Arts and Sciences Press, 1972.

Leont'ev, A.N., Luria, A.A., The psychological ideas of L.S. Vygotskii. In B.B. Wolman (Ed.), *Historical Roots of Contemporary Psychology.* New York, Harper and Row, 1968, pp. 338-367.

Leont'ev, A., Luria, A., and Smirnov, A (Eds.), *Psychological Research in the USSR.* Vol. 1, Moscow, Progress Publishers, 1966.

Misiak, H., and Sexton, V.S., Psychology in the Soviet Union. In *History of Psychclogy, An Overview.* New York, Grune and Stratton, 1966, pp. 258-280.

Molino, J.A., Is there a new Soviet psychology? In A. Simirenko (Ed.), *Social Thought in the Soviet Union.* Chicago, Quadrangle Books, 1969, pp. 300-327.

O'Connor, N. Report on Soviet science, Psychology. 2. Trends past and present. *Survey* (London) 1964, No. 52, 125-134.

O'Connor, N. (Ed.) *Present-day Russian Psychology, A Symposium by seven authors.* Oxford, Pergamon Press, 1966.

Pick, H.L., Jr. Perception in Soviet psychology. *Psychological Bulletin*, 1964, 62, 21-35.

Razran, G. Russian physiologists' psychology and American experimental psychology, A historical and systematic collation and a look into the future. *Psychological Bulletin*, 1965, 63, 42-64.

Razran, G. Mind in Evolution, *An East-West Synthesis of Learned Behaviour and Cognition.* Boston, Houghton Mifflin, 1971.

Slobin, D.I. (Ed.) Handbook of Soviet Psychology. Special issue of *Soviet Psycholcgy and Psychiatry*, 1966, 4(3-4), 1-146.

Slobin, D.I., (Ed.), Special issue on Soviet psycholinguistics. *Soviet Psychology*, 1969, 7(3), 1-56.

USSR Academy of Sciences. *Social Sciences in the USSR.* New York, Basic Books, 1965.

Woodworth, R.S., and Sheehan, M.H. Soviet Psychology as a "school." In *Contemporary Schools of Psychology.* New York, Ronald Press, 1964, pp. 90-110.

Yaroshevskii, M.G. I.M. Sechenov: The founder of objective psychology. In B.B., Wolman (Ed.), *Historical Roots of Contemporary Psychology.* New York, Harper and Row, 1968, pp. 77-110.

Zangwill, O.I., Report on Soviet Science, Psychology. 1. Current approaches, *Survey* (London), 1964, No. 52-119-125.

# 20

# Oriental Psychology

Psychology in the Orient has been little known to the West (Europe and America) largely because of the language barrier. However, the language problem is one sided; the Asian scientist is likely to know English, German, and French, but the scientist in the West is very unlikely to be familiar with Asian languages. India, Pakistan, and Ceylon are exceptions since their scientific output is written mostly in English.

According to the *International Directory of Psychologists* (1966), about 17 per cent of all the psychologists in the world, exclusive of the United States, continental China, and a few other countries, are from Asian nations; of these, 67 per cent are Japanese, and 12 per cent are Indian.

## CLASSIC PSYCHOLOGY IN INDIA AND CHINA

The ancient Hindu and Buddhist literature contains various systematic approaches to human nature and experience. An abundance of psychological information is contained in the most ancient Rig-Veda and especially in the Upanishads, which were composed around 800 B.C. "after the period of the exuberant Vedic hymns, as life became stabilised in the Indian peninsula and as a warrior caste gave itself more and more to contemplation and to cultivation of the inner life" (Murphy and Murphy, 1968, p. 51).

According to one of the Upanishads (literally "Secret teaching"), four states of the mental processes are differentiated: sleeping, dreaming, the waiting state, and the superconscious (Akhilananda, 1953). The first two states, which belong to the subconscious, are considered by Hindu philosophers to be Important aspects of human experience. This is in contrast with some of the classic Western psychological systems such as English associationism, Wundtian structuralism, and Brentano's act psychology. Although these Western systems are considerably different from one another, they all deal with the intellectual and cognitive aspects of human experience as the subject matter of psychology. In addition, it is interesting to notice that Hindu workers differentiated sleeping from dreaming, since recent neurophysiologists generally support the dual theory of sleep: classical "slow" sleep and "paradoxical" sleep with dreaming (Thompson, 1967).

The Hindu psychologist, like the psychoanalyst, places special importance upon the subconscious *(samskara)* because it is believed to be an integration of past experiences, impressions, and tendencies of the individual. However, unlike psycho- analysis, Hindu psychology does not assume sex and death urges as the basic human instincts; the basic urge is, according to the Hindu theory, directed to eternal happiness or complete freedom from bondage. Notice its similarity to the Rogerian theory which postulates a drive toward growth, health, and adjustment of the individual.

The superconscious *(samadhi)* has no exact correlate in Western culture. It is an experience of spiritual enlightenment in which the individual is neither conscious nor subconscious, and it is quite different from hallucination or pathological states, since in such states spiritual insight cannot be attained. It is a mystic experience only in the sense that it is not intellectual, but is a whole mind-body experience or a holistic integration of the self and the world. The study of the superconsciousness is not unscientific. It can be experienced by the normal person. It does not matter whether he is Hindu, Buddhist, Christian, or atheist.

The Hindu and Buddhist thinkers not only have performed a detailed analysis of our inner life but also have shown a number of methods for attaining spiritual insight or samadhi, among which yoga (literally union) and Zen (a Japanese word, derived from *dhyana* meaning *meditation* in Sanskrit) are well known. Yoga and Zen appear quite different, but their underlying principles are similar. Zen is often said to be a blending of Indian rationalism, Chinese realism, and Japanese sentiments. In addition to yoga and Zen, a Burmese method of attaining meditation founded on Satipatthana sutra is now practiced in Burma, Thailand, and Ceylon (Dumoulin, 1962; Pe, 1966).

In ancient China, the universe was believed to consist of heaven the earth, and man, where heaven and the earth obey natural law, while man observes moral law. According to Confucius (551-479 B.C.), morality is based on the three faculties of wisdom, benevolence, and valor. Later, Mencius (ca. 372-289 B.C.) divided morality into five elements: benevolence, righteousness, propriety, wisdom, and sincerity.

Like Aristotle, the ancient Chinese believed that mind lies in the center (heart) of the body. Besides mind and body, Mencius assumed *chi'i,* which corresponds roughly to spiritual energy or pneuma in classical Western psychology. Body is filled with *chi'i,* which is controlled by mind. Later scholars argued that li and *chi'i* make personality; *li* is innate and identical in all human beings, while *chi'i* can be modified by learning and environment and thus is the main source of individual differences and temperament.

Personality traits were systematically investigated by Liu-shao in about 220. His theory was based on the then current doctrine of the five elements of the universe (wood, fire, earth, metal, and water) and assumed that body, temperament, duty, and morality each have five different characteristics corresponding to the five elements and that when all these are mixed in proper proportion, an ideal personality is attained (Kuroda, 1948). The Chinese typology bears a remarkable resemblance to the Hippocratic theory of temperament.

## ZEN BUDDHISM AND PSYCHOLOGY

Among various Oriental philosophical positions, Zen Buddhism is probably one of the best known in the West. It was early introduced to the West by Dr. Y. Motora of Tokyo University. He presented a paper entitled "The concept of self in the Oriental philosophy" at the Seventh International Congress of Psychology at Rome in 1905. There he criticised English associationism as mechanical and devoid of an active self. The essential nature of mind, according to him, is a dynamic psychic potentiality into which the subject-object dichotomy is *melted—tathata* in Zen theory (Motora, 1905).

Otsuka (1960) uses Kuroda's (1931) definition of psychology as a science of consciousness and comprehension *(kaku)*. Our usual experience is that volitional acts are eventually automatised with practice and become unconscious or half-conscious unless special attention is paid to them. This mental state is an example of comprehension. Another illustration of it is the knack, hunch, or *kan,* which refers to the occasional experience which we know but cannot make clear. Although comprehension is a naive, preanalytic mental state, it evidently directs our behaviour and plays an important role in our life. The purest form of comprehension, according to Kuroda, is the Zen enlightenment. Kuroda conducted a number of experiments on the exact nature of comprehension. A similar position has been taken by Chiba (1960).

Morita therapy, developed by the Japanese psychiatrist Dr. S. Morita, is a unique psychotherapy in the Zen mode of thought (Kora and Sato, 1958). According to Morita therapy, neurasthenia (or *nervosis,* in its own terminology) is attributable to a hypochondriac disposition and a mechanism of psychic interaction. The hypochondriac individual is overconscious of himself and feels that he is unusual or maladjusted; consequently, he concentrates attention upon his physical condition, especially upon his sensations, and thus his sensations become keener and in turn attract his attention. The interaction between sensation and attention exaggerates the hypochondriac tendency and consumes a great deal of mental energy with consequent behaviour disorders.

In order to break up this vicious circle, the patient must accept the sufferings and worries as they are and must become carefree. Morita therapy starts with an absolute bed-rest period, during which the patient is prohibited from reading, writing, and even talking with others and is instructed to leave himself to the dynamics of his present situation. Through a light-work period to a hard-work period, the patient is gradually guided to lead a realistic daily life. Unlike psycho- analysis, Morita therapy involves no free association or interpretation (Kawai and Kondo, 1960). Another characteristic point of the Oriental therapy is the absence of labeling during treatment.

Evidently, Morita therapy is closely related to Zen philosophy in that both emphasise the present situation, "letting-be," spontaneity rather than etiology, and direct guidance and interpretation (Kora and Sato, 1958). Doi (1962) compared Morita therapy with psychoanalysis and argued that the difference may be attributed to the cultural difference between Japanese and Western societies, especially in terms of their attitudes toward dependency.

In spite of all these works, Zen has only recently been introduced to the West, mainly through English publications by the late D.T. Suzuki and Dr. Koji Sato. According to Suzuki (1956), Zen is "the art of seeing into the nature of one's being and it points the way from bondage to freedom...[and] liberates all the energies properly and naturally stored in each of us, which are in ordinary circumstances cramped and distorted so that they find no channel for activity" (p. 3). The final goal of Zen is the experience of spiritual enlightenment, or *satori*, which is a kind of trance having direct contact with reality.

Sato has written a number of introductory papers on Zen for Western readers in *Psychologia: An International Journal of Psychology in the Orient*, of which he is editor. One of his articles gives a brief description of *zazen*, or seated Zen, which is one of the commonest means of attaining satori. In zazen, the individual sits squarely on his seat with half-opened eyes and breathes quietly with his whole body, some times adjusting respiration by counting it. Then, applying a strain to the abdomen, he starts with a calm cry and gradually increases the voice level, ending with a vigorous shout, which results in high muscular tension in face, shoulders, and arms. In the meantime, he is able to meditate deeply into himself without diverting his attention. Meditation is characterised by a condition of no mind, nothingness, or "being one with the world." If the practice is successful, satori occurs rather suddenly with the release of tension. One of Sato's students described his own Zen experience as follows (Sato, 1959): "The mind became clear and serene, and a kind of joy was felt, with a force coming up from the bottom of the belly" (p. 112).

According to recent psychophysiological studies (e.g., Kasamatsu and Hirai, 1966), zazen produces dominant and continuous alpha waves which are not easily blocked, as in the normal waking state. The pulse is normal, or slightly faster, and there occurs no change in perception. The EEG changes during zazen are classified into four stages: appearance of alpha waves, increase of alpha amplitude, decrease of alpha frequency, and appearance of the rhythmic theta train. These stages are found to correlate with the degree of meditation. No such EEG changes are shown during hypnotic trance.

The Japanese Zen literature has appealed to some Western scientists, including psychologists, psychoanalysts, existential psychotherapists, and general semanticists. Erich Fromm, for example, has enumerated several similarities between Zen and psychoanalysis. According to him (1959), the "description of Zen's aim could be applied without change as a description of what psychoanalysis aspires to achieve" (p. 86), and "Zen can have a most fertile and clarifying influence on the theory of psychoanalysis" (p. 98), even though the two methods are quite different.

Hora (1959) has discussed the close kinship between Taoism, Zen, and existential psychotherapy in their common emphasis on nonteleological, nonintellectual, and existential aspects as well as on openness and "letting-be." Morris (1951) stated that Zen therapy, although it may appear mystic; can be legitimately accepted by current general semantics, and Holmes (1957) pointed out the transactional aspect of Zen.

The French psychotherapist Hubert Benoit has emphasised the thorough- going naturalism and realism of Zen in contrast with the idealistic position of Christianity. In Christianity, said Ando (1965), the basic idea is original sin, or the absolute difference between man and God, while in Zen doctrine man's essential self is identical in root and nature to the universe.

Recently, some American scientists profess to have experienced satori with the use of LSD (Rogers, 1964; Van Dusen, 1961). Van Dusen (1961), for example, argued that LSD acts as a new method of arriving at the Zen experience of sudden enlightenment. However, Suzuki clearly differentiated between Zen and psychedelic experience since the goal of Zen centers on the *person* himself and not on the objective situation that the person *sees* or *hears*. Sato and Suzuki (1967) stated that LSD and other psychotropic drugs may help develop the process of Zen training if properly used.

After his comprehensive review of the psychological literature on Zen Buddhism, Maupin (1962) concluded that Zen experience is an adaptive type of regression in the service of the ego and that although the true satori takes years of training, the Zen meditation or zazen can still be used as a unique and powerful psychotherapeutic method which can be applicable for those patients who are inaccessible to other types of psychotherapy.

## INTRODUCTION OF WESTERN SCIENTIFIC PSYCHOLOGY AND CURRENT PSYCHOLOGICAL ACTIVITIES IN THE ORIENT

### India

Psychology has been included in philosophical courses in the Indian universities from the very beginning, but it was not until 1916 that the first psychological department and laboratory were started by Dr. N.N. Sengupta at the University of Calcutta (Pareek, 1957). Presently most of the universities offer both under-graduate and graduate courses in psychology.

From 1950 to 1960, educational, industrial, social, and personality psychology seemed to attract the attention of Indian workers much more than the other fields of psychology (Krishnan, 1961). According to Jayasuriya (personal communication), the psychometric tradition in India has been geared to the practical problems of guidance and selection, and this is perhaps the strongest feature of Indian psychology.

Among more than a dozen psychological journals now published in this country, *Journal of Education and Psychology* (founded in 1942), *Journal of Vocational and Educational Guidance* (founded in 1954), and *Indian Journal of Psychology* (founded in 1926) contain valuable contributions in various fields of psychology. Content analysis of the issues of the *Indian Journal of Psychology* that appeared between 1964 and 1966 reveals that as much as 87 per cent of the total number of articles deal with educational, personality, social, or industrial problems. A great number of psychometric tests and inventories have been either originally devised or adapted from foreign sources for Indian populations. Hundal (1966), for example, has standardised a group test of general mental ability by means of which he found the invariant factorial organisation of mental abilities across different grade levels. Application of the Maudsley Personality Inventory showed some salient differences between various occupational groups as well as between students with different majors (Rao, 1966), and Krishnakanth and Prasad (1967) studied socioeconomic differences on a reasoning test.

Although experimental studies have appeared less often in Indian journals, this area was the most popular in terms of the number of papers presented to the Indian Science Congress between 1925 and 1963; 27 per cent of the total psychological papers were devoted to experimental studies. Of the rest, 14 per cent dealt with educational psychology, 12 per cent with general and theoretical psychology, 11 per cent with abnormal and clinical psychology, 10 per cent with psychometry, 9 per cent with vocational and industrial psychology, 6 per cent with social psychology, and 5 per cent with personality. The remaining papers were on Indian psychology, criminal psychology, religious psychology, and aesthetic psychology (Joshi, 1965).

The traditional Indian concern with depth psychology and mental hygiene gave birth to the Indian Psychoanalytic Association as early as 1922, and its official journal, *Samiksa,* started in 1947. The mental hospital at Calcutta and the All-India Institute of Mental Health, Bangalore, have a number of clinical psychologists working in collaboration with the medical staff.

India is probably the only country in Asia which attaches a special importance to the classical thought characteristic of the country. Adequate acquaintance with the traditional psychological systems is recommended at the graduate level (Sen, 1958). For many of the same reasons, there has been a long-standing interest in paranormal and psychic phenomena. This is well exemplified by a separate department of parapsychology at the University of Rajasthan. According to Dhairyan (1961), "...there is a wealth of applied clinical psychological concepts in the Yogi practices and philosophy which has yet to be explored and made to enrich modern science" (p. 159).

**Pakistan, Ceylon, Burma, and Thailand**

Pakistan psychologists are also oriented toward educational psychology, social psychology, personality, and other applied fields, as Indian psychologists are. Psychological research in this country is published mainly in *Pakistan Philosophical Journal, Journal of Psychology, Psychology Quarterly, and Pakistan Journal of Psychology.* The University of Dacca and the University of Punjab have the oldest and best-organised psychological laboratories, and the University of Karachi has just initiated a program in counseling psychology.

There are a number of complicated sociopsychological problems in this country which need the immediate attention of social scientists. Zaidi (1964) assumed that "...most of the social issues of Pakistan society can be explained in terms of the observed conditions in a transitional society undergoing a stressful experience" (p. 19), and then he proposed a model predicting a number of stages involved in the adjustment of a group to a stressful situation with frustration and conflict.

A similar psychological trend is observed in Ceylon. Racial stereotypes, family relationships, vocational guidance, and personality and' intelligence testing have been most intensively studied among Ceylonese psychologists. For example, both Ceylonese and foreign scientists have conducted a number of cross-cultural studies using the Rorschach and intelligence tests. However, Jayasuriya (1965) warned in evaluating their results that many so-called culture-free tests are actually culture-bound unless they are equally standardised and meaningful for all groups concerned.

In Burma, the current research interests cover vocational guidance, counselling, and sociopsychological problems. The Universities of Burma and of Mandalay are the centers of the psychological activities in this country (Thwin, 1962).

The Psychological Association in Thailand, with administrative offices at Chulalongkorn University, was started in 1961, and it has been publishing a journal called *Psychology* under the editorship of Professor B. Chareanying, of the Institute for Child Study. The major areas of research interest and activity are child-rearing practices, problem children, and the development of various intelligence, achievement, and personality tests, In addition, cross-cultural projects are now being discussed between Thailand and Japan (Gardiner, 1968).

**Indonesia, the Philippines, Hong Kong, and the Republic of Korea**

The orientation and approach in Indonesian psychology are mainly European, although American books are also used. Most Indonesian psychologists are associated with the Faculty of Psychology, University of Indonesia, and with the Armed Forces, and their interest lies mainly in sociocultural and anthropophilosophical problems (Hassan, 1963).

The Psychological Association of the Philippines was established in 1962 (Lagmay, 1963), and its activities are in such areas as intelligence, achievement, personality testing, clinical psychology, social perception, attitude, and guidance (Guthrie and Bulatao, 1968).

In Hong Kong, the University of Hong Kong is the center of research and teaching in psychology.

The Korean Psychological Association was founded in 1946 and has its central offices at Seoul National University. The research output appears in a number of periodicals, including *Studies of Psychology,* of Seoul National University, and *Psychological Studies,* of Ewha Women's University. The main interest of the Korean psychologists is oriented toward industrial, clinical, counseling, and social psychology, as well as toward experimental studies. The Korean Psychological Association, in cooperation with the Pedagogical Association, offers in-service seminars in counseling once a year for those who are planning to be counseling specialists (Takahashi, 1967).

**Continental China and Taiwan**

The most drastic change in psychological thought occurred on the Chinese continent soon after the last world war. Before the war, Chinese psychologists had been indebted to American functionalism because of their realistic nature. The Chinese Association of

Psychological Testing (ChAPT) was begun in 1930, seven years before the Chinese Psychological Association was first established. After the war, the ChAPT disappeared in continental China, but has survived in Taiwan.

The new continental psychologists have attempted to reconstruct a scientific psychology based on Pavlovian theory and Marxist principles (Shuh, 1959). To attain this objective, in 1956 they published the *Translation Journal of Psychology*, which contained articles selected from the Russian journal *Voprosy Psikhologii (Problems of Psychology)*, but this translation journal was discontinued in 1958.

*Acta Psychologica Sinica*, (established in 1956) has been an official journal of the newly reconstructed (1955) Chinese Psychological Society. About half of the total articles in the issues of the journal appearing between 1956 and 1959 were either theoretical or political, such as "Problems on the object of psychology" (C.S. Chu, 1956) and "How psychology can be of service to the socialistic reconstruction" (D.J. Chen, 1959). According to the new Chinese view, psychology is a science whose aim is to explore the material basis of psyche and the functional laws governing the activities of the brain, as well as the physiological mechanisms underlying them (Shuh, 1959).

Both classical behaviourism and neobehaviourism were criticised from the Chinese Communist viewpoint. According to Ni (1957) and Ching (1965), behaviourism is a product of American capitalism. In order to secure greater profits, the capitalist class, then flourishing in America, attempted to make the laborer like a machine or a man without consciousness. Thus, behaviourism is fundamentally reactionary. What is worse, the behaviourist pretended to be a scientist by borrowing Pavlov's conditioning theory for his system, and so he deceived people. Z.Y. Kuo, a widely known animal psychologist who introduced behaviourism to China, is criticised as being one of the most reactionary propagandists of American capitalism.

Although behaviourism and Communist psychology are both based on a kind of materialism, they are otherwise entirely different. First, behaviourism is mechanistic, while Communist theory is dialectic. Second, the behaviourist erroneously limits the subject matter of psychology to stimulus and response, neglecting the important functions of the higher nervous systems, which are the bases of the psychic activities. Consciousness is denied by Watson, but is accepted by the Communist psychologist as a reflection of the objective world. Third, Watson confuses human psychology with animal psychology. According to the Chinese psychologist, man and animal are different in quality rather than in quantity; human behaviour is developed with a social and historical background, which is lacking in animals. Fourth, thinking in behaviouristic terms is nothing but inner speech or muscular activity. On the contrary, Communist theory maintains that thinking and speech or language are basically different; language, according to Stalin, is simply an instrument of thinking.

A critical evaluation of Gestalt theory was attempted by H.L. Chu (1958). According to him, Gestalt theory was born when capitalism had turned to imperialism and subjective idealism had been dominant in Europe. First, Gestalt theory, which emphasises totality and the risk of analysis, fails to recognise the fact that the brain has both analysing and synthesising functions, as was proved by Pavlov. The Pavlovian theory is based on dialectic materialism, but psychological theories coloured by capitalistic idealism cannot understand it. On the one hand, associationistic psychology puts too much emphasis on analysis and thus deviates from our daily experience, while Gestalt psychology concerns itself only with synthesis and consequently regresses to transcendental idealism. Second, isomorphism, proposed by Kohler, has no relationship to the Pavlovian theory. It is merely a mystic speculation based on misunderstood neurophysiology. Third, the Gestalt Concept of insight in chimpanzees is criticised as being anthropomorphic Animal mentality must be differentiated from human mentality because only the latter develops the second signal system, making dialectic thinking possible. Lastly, such terms as *behavioural environment* (Koffka) and *psychological environment* (lewin) are criticised as being typical examples of subjective idealism. Incidentally, it is interesting to note that the same Gestalt theory is still supported by Eastern German psychologists (K. Gottschalt, for example) who are related by blood to the advocates of Gestalt theory (Lun, 1958; Razran, 1958).

In 1962, the Congress of Educational Psychology was held, and in the next year the first academic meetings of the Chinese Psychological Society took place for ten days in Peking. A total of 203 papers were collected, 75 per cent of which were educational in a broad sense, and 15 per cent of which were theoretical. In addition, a number of symposia were held at the meetings (C.K. Chen, 1964). Evidently, the interest in educational psychology has rapidly increased, while theoretical papers have decreased in number. For example, in the 1965 issues of *Acta Psychologica Sinica*, only 10 per cent of the total articles are theoretical or political, while 53 per cent deal with educational problems, and 23 per cent are purely experimental articles, mainly on perception.

Educational and child psychological studies are both practical and experimental rather than basic and theoretical, although the underlying principles must be based on Chinese communism (J.C. Tsao, 1965). For example, C. Y. Tsao and Shen (1965) conducted a series of experiments on the learning and recognition of Chinese characters in primary school children, and Chou (1965) experimentally analysed errors made in learning the resolution of factors in junior middle school algebra;

The basic experimental research covers such areas as visual perception of size and velocity, interference in memory, and the EEG. Lambda waves in the human EEG were investigated by Tsai and Liu (1965), who found that they appear more frequently in young subjects than in adults, that they occur more during visual perception than during visual imagination, and that the same waves are more easily recorded for those who manifest "on responses" or "driving responses.

Medical psychology and industrial psychology are also well investigated in Communist China. K. C. Lu (1957) has proposed a therapeutic method, similar to Japanese seated Zen, which aims to cure mental diseases, and J.C. Tsao, Li, Ching, Chang, Yu, Feng, and Chu

(1966) studied the man-machine system in the control room of an electric power station.

In the Republic of China in Taiwan, the National Psychological Association was established in 1963 (Su, 1963). Although the association has no official journal, the National Taiwan University has been publishing *Acta Psychologica Taiwanica* since 1958, and the Taiwan Normal University started *Psychology and Education* in 1967 (Iwahara, 1967). A content analysis of the 1966 and 1967 issues of the two journals reveals that about 50 per cent of the articles concern experimental studies in learning, perception, and physiological psychology, and that the rest are in the areas of personality and of clinical, educational, and social psychology. For example, Yen and Cheng (1966) studied binocular disparity and related parameters in depth perception, and Lu and his co-workers examined whether Weber's law can be applied to the perception of angles, circles, and cubes (I. M. Lu and Hu, 1967). The values of Taiwan college students, as measured by the Edwards Personal Preference Schedule (EPPS), showed higher scores in deference, order, succorance, abasement, nurturance, and endurance and lower scores in exhibition, intraception, dominance, change, and heterosexuality, as compared with the American standards (Hwang, 1967). Roughly correspondent results were reported between Japanese and American students (Berrien, 1964).

In addition to the Chinese Psychological Association and the Chinese Association of Psychological Testing, Taiwan has the Chinese Guidance Association, which aims to promote sound counselor education (Brammer, 1965).

**TABLE 20.1**

**Major Areas of Research Interest, based on Content-analyis of Papers Presented at the 1968 JPA Convention and Appearing in Two JPA Journals**

| *Research Area* | *JPA Convention 1968, per cent* | *Japanese Journal of Psychology and Japanese Psychological Research, 1967, per cent* |
|---|---|---|
| General and statistics | 4 | 9 |
| Physiological | 11 | 5 |
| Perceptual | 14 | 31 |
| Learning | 11 | 28 |
| Personality and clinical | 15 | 14 |
| Education and developmental | 18 | 7 |
| Social | 11 | 7 |
| Industrial | 9 | 0 |
| Criminal | 2 | 0 |
| Other | 5 | 0 |
| Total | 100 (*N*=524) | 101 (*N*=58) |

## Japan

The Japanese Psychological Association (JPA) held its first annual meeting in 1927 with sixty-one papers presented; in 1968 it had a membership of about three thousand and more than five hundred papers were read at the annual convention. The JPA has three official periodicals: the *Japanese Journal of Psychology* (1926, bimonthly), *Japanese Psychological Research* (1954, English, quarterly), and *Japanese Psychological Monographs* (1965, quarterly).

Table 20.1 indicates the distribution of major areas of research interest as indicated by the papers presented at the 1968 JPA convention and in two JPA journals. There are more experimental studies in the journals than were presented to the convention, partly because nonexperimental articles are published in other journals in specific fields of psychology, as shown in Table 20.2.

**TABLE 20.2**
**Current Psychological Periodicals in Japan**

| *Periodical* | *Publisher or Editor* |
|---|---|
| *Annual of Animal Psychology* (1943) | Japanese Association of Animal Psychology |
| *Annals Japanese Social Psychology* (1960) | Japanese Association or Social Psychology |
| *Japanese Journal of Clinical Psychology* (1960) | Japanese Association of Clinical Psychology |
| *Japanese Journal of Counseling Science* (1967) | Japanese Association of Counseling Science |
| *Japanese Journal of Criminal Psychology* (1963) | Japanese Association of Criminal Psychology |
| *Japanese Journal of Educational Psychology* (1952) | Japanese Association of Educational Psychology |
| *Japanese Journal of Educational and Social Psychology* (1960) | Japanese Association of Group Dynamics |
| *Japanese Journal of Psychology* (1926) | Japanese Psychological Association |
| Japanese Psychological Monographs (1965) | Japanese Psychological Association |
| *Japanese Psychological Research** (1954) | Japanese Psychological Association |
| *Japanese Psychological Review* (1957) | Psychological Review Publisher (Kyoto University) |
| *Psychologia** (1957) | Psychologia Society (Otemongakuin University) |
| *Tohoku Psychologica Folia** (1933) | Tohoku University |

*Published mostly in English.

Notes: In addition to the psychological associations listed above, there is the Japanese Association of Applied Psychology, which publishes only the proceedings of the annual meetings. There are also interdisciplinary associations such as the Japanese Medical and Psychological Association of Hypnosis, the Japanese Association of Ergonomics, the Japanese Medical and Psychological Association of Aerospace Science, the Japanese Association of Conditioned Reflex, the Japanese Association of Electroencephalography, the Japanese Association of Colour Studies, and a few others.

Among the experimental fields, perception has attracted the attention of Japanese psychologists for more than forty years, and it is still one of the major research areas at most

Japanese universities. Recently Yuki (1965) and Tanaka (1966) overviewed Japanese perceptual studies for American readers. Some of the most intensively studied areas are optical illusions (Morinaga, Noguchi, and Ohnishi, 1962), figural aftereffects (Sagara and Oyama, 1957), constancy phenomena (Akishige, 1968), visual induction (Obonai, 1957), colour vision (Kaneko, 1968), psychometry of odor (Yoshida, 1964) and of taste (Indow, 1966), and binocular vision (Kakizaki, 1960).

Japanese perceptual psychologists are proud of their original works, but unfortunately many of them have been buried unknown to foreign workers because of a language barrier and lack of international communication. For example, the converse of the tau effect was discovered independently by two Japanese psychologists, Abe (1935) and Abbe (1936), but the same effect was reported by Cohen, Hansel, and Sylvester (1953), about two decades later, as a new phenomenon.

As for theoretical aspects, Obonai (1957) has been criticising Gestalt theory as philosophical romanticism and as being devoid of sound empirical basis. Scientific psychology, according to him, should be studied analytically and elementalistically like physics and physiology. On the basis of his voluminous and energetic works on visual perception, Obonai has proposed a theory called psychophysiological induction. Its basic idea is that the' stimulation of a receptor will induce both excitation and inhibition around the stimulated area and that the resulting effect is an algebraic summation of these antagonistic functions, leading to actual perception. The induction occurs temporally and spatially. Obonai claims that some perceptual phenomena which are treated separately can be integrated by this theory. For example, the simultaneous contrast-confluence illusion and the figural aftereffect are only different aspects of the same phenomenon (Ikeda and Obonai, 1955).

The Japanese physiologist K. Motokawa and his co-workers, including a number of psychologists, have investigated many aspects of visual perception. Using his own ingenious techniques, Motokawa found that the electric excitability of the retina changes as a function of time after cessation of illumination and that the time function is characteristic of the wavelength of the light used for illumination. According to Motokawa (1953): "As...the retina is ontogenetically a part of the brain, and its structure resembles that of central nervous system...it is not surprising that psychological phenomena such as optical illusions should be interpreted in terms of retinal processes [p. 369]."

Yokose (1957) has proposed an electromagnetic model of visual perception. In his theory, the field potential of a visual figure, as measured by the stimulus threshold around it, is principally the same function of a number of variables as predicted by Bivot Savart's law in electromagnetism. His isomorphic field theory has been confirmed by a series of experimental findings concerning the change of threshold around a segmental line, a square, a triangle, and other geometric figures.

The second most popular research area in experimental psychology is learning and memory. Umemoto (1959), Motoyoshi and Iwahara (1960), and Iwahara and Fujita (1963) wrote English reviews of Japanese studies in human and animal learning. One of the original works on memory is concerned with the function of stimulus and response words in paired-associate learning. Kuraishi (1937) established the relative difficulty of recalling a foreign word from the corresponding Japanese word, compared with the difficulty of recall in the reverse order, and explained the phenomenon in terms of Gestalt theory. This study was followed by those of Umemoto (1959) and Morikawa (1959), who argued that the stimulus item is learned as a cue to the response item, while the response item is acquired as the goal to be responded to, and that backward recall is thus inferior to forward recall.

I. Ishihara and his co-workers have intensively studied paired-associate learning, especially in relation to word association. For example, they proposed a new kind of association value, defined in terms of frequency of appearance as associated items in a given free-association situation. A series of experiments on verbal learning has been conducted on the functions of the new association value and other related problems (I. Ishihara, 1960).

Other areas of main interest in human learning and behaviour are mediated association (Kitao, 1967), massed and spaced practice (Akita, 1966), discrimination reversal (Sugimura, 1967), spread of effect (Iwahara, 1958), information theory (Pakada, 1960), and mathematical models of motor learning (Ono, 1966).

In the field of animal behaviour, S. Ishihara (1966) has found, in a series of her experiments, a decrement of response variability and facilitation of running response following nonreinforced trials; she called the phenomenon *induction* after Pavlov. Sukemune (1963) found that resistance to extinction in rats is a positive function of number of trials when both total amount of reinforcement and total number of reinforced trials are kept constant. Imanishi and his colleagues have been conducting a large-scale project on the social behaviour of primates both in Japan and abroad (Imanishi, 1957). Other interesting data have been reported on spontaneous alternation (Fujita, 1961), conditioned avoidance response (Matsuyama and Tsukioka, 1964), successive versus simultaneous discrimination learning (Motoyoshi, 1956), and incentive motivation (Imada, 1964).

Another trend in experimental psychology is a marked increase of activities in physiological psychology. For example, Niki (1964) reported the inhibitory control of the hippocampus upon operant behaviour in the rat, and Hirano (1965) investigated the effect of functional disturbance of the limbic system on memory consolidation. In another study, facilitation of running response due to partial reinforcement in the runway situation was found to be inhibited by a tranquiliser (chlordiazepoxide), but resistance to extinction after the same partial reinforcement was not affected by the drug (Iwahara, Nagamura, and Iwasaki. 1967).

Recently, a number of workers have been engaged in psychophysiological studies of sleep and wakefulness. Fujisawa (1960) has attempted a detailed analysis of EEG sleep patterns. Iwahara, Takeuchi, and Nagamura (1967) were interested in a multivariate analysis of EEG in both man and animals, and Niimi and his coworkers (Niimi, Kubota, and Iwama, 1968) studied spontaneous variation of the skin potential and skin-potential reflex during natural sleep in the cat.

The Japanese Association of Educational Psychology is the second largest psychological association, with a membership of about 1,500. Some of the most active research areas in educational psychology are personality adjustment in pupils and students, school counseling, developmental studies, teaching machines, and tests and measurements.

Most members of the Japanese Association of Clinical Psychology (member- ship of 1,300) have clinical experience, and they are interested in school refusal, early infantile autism, therapeutic processes, hypnotic therapy, emotionally disturbed children, projective and personality tests, and the legal status of the clinical psychologist.

The Japanese Association of Applied Psychology (membership of 1000) has recently been discussing such problems as school curricula, traffic safety, public nuisance, industrialisation and labor, physical education, and world peace and welfare.

Members of the Japanese Association of Social Psychology (membership of 550) and of the Japanese Association of Group Dynamics (membership of 200) are generally interested in human relationships in family, school, and other social situations; mass communication; attitudes and values; and person perception. The Japanese Association of Criminal Psychology (membership of 550) has no very close parallel in the United States. Most members of the association belong to juvenile delinquency detection and classification homes located in all prefectures of Japan. The current activities of the criminal psychologists are in such areas as diagnosis and prognosis of delinquent behaviour, therapeutic treatments, mechanism of criminal behaviour, psychedelic and hypnotic drugs, personality studies of violators of traffic regulations, and minority groups.

There are a few other associations of psychological science (see Table 20.2), among which the Japanese Association of Animal Psychology (founded in 1933) has the longest history.

**Conclusion**

It is hard to summarise Oriental psychology in a few lines, but it may be stated that Asian countries as a whole have common interests in applied psychology, especially in educational and social fields. In addition, the theoretical-political aspects of psychology are discussed in continental China, and experimental psychology flourishes in Japan.

Although Oriental psychology still remains relatively unknown in the West, there is a growing tendency in the Orient to publish psychology journals in English, as well as to add English abstracts when the original articles are written in the native language.

The Twentieth International Congress of Psychology is scheduled to be held in Japan in 1972, which will be the first time this body has met in the Orient. This will offer excellent opportunities for Asian psychologists to meet with non-Asian psychologists and to discuss their common problems.

## REFERENCES

The author has tried to restrict the references to those written in English. Unavoidable, however, some references are in other languages, which are indicated immediately after the titles.

Abe, S. Experimental study of the interrelation between time and space. *Tohoku Psychological Folia*, 1935, 3, 53-68.

Abbe, M. Der raumliche Effekt auf die Zeitauffassung. *Japanese Journal of Experimental Psychology*, 1936, 3, 1-52.

Akhilananda, S. *Hindu Psychology*. London: Routledge, 1953.

Akishige, Y. Studies on constancy problem. IIA. *Psychologia*, 1968, 11, 43-55.

Akita, K. Effect of the gradual change of distribution of practice in motor learning. *Japanese Psychological Research*, 1966, 8, 18-29.

Ando, S. Zen and Christianity. *Psychologia*, 1965, 8, 123-134.

Berrien, F.K. Values of Japanese and American students. Technical Report No. 14, Department of Defense, Office of Naval Research, Group Psychology Branch, Washington, 1964.

Brammer, L.M. Counselor education in the Republic of China: An outsider's view. *Psychologia*, 1965, 8, 220-222.

Chen, C.K. The 1963 annual psychological society. (In Chinese) *Acta Psychologica Sinica*, 1964, 8, 109-112.

Chen, D.J. How psychology can be of service to the socialistic reconstruction. (In Chinese) *Acta Psychologica Sinica*, 1959, 3, 142-145.

Chiba, T. On proper consciousness (Koyu-ishiki). *Psychologia*, 1960, 3, 65-72.

Ching, C.C. The behaviourism of J.B. Watson. (In Chinese) *Acta Psychologica Sinica*, 1965, 9, 361-374.

Chou, H.S. Analysis of mistakes made in learning resolution of factors by first grade junior middle school pupils. (In Chinese) *Acta Psychologica Sinica*, 1965, 8, 223-229.

Chu, C.S. Problems on the object of psychology. (In Chinese) *Acta Psychologica Sinica*, 1956, 1, 11-19.

Chu, H.L. Critical comments on Gestalt psychology. (In Chinese) *Acta Psychologica Sinica*, 1958, 2, 85-98.

Cohen, J., Hansel, C.E.M., and Sylvester, J.D. A new phenomenon in time judgment. *Nature*, 1953, 172-901.

Dhairyan, D. Research needs for development of psychotherapy in India. In T.K.N. Menon (Ed.), *Recent trends in psychology*. Oriental Longmans, 1961, pp. 154-161.

Doi, L.T. Morita therapy and psychoanalysis. *Psychologia*, 1962, 3, 117-123.

Dumoulin, H. Methods and aims of Buddhist meditation: Satipatthana and Zen. *Psychologia*, 1962, 5, 175-180.

Fromm, E. Psychoanalysis and Zen Buddhism. *Psychologia*, 1959, 2, 79-99.

Fujisawa, F. The psycho-physiological studies of sleep. *Japanese Psychological Research*, 1960, 2, 120-134.

Fujita, O. Studies of spontaneous alternation in rats. VIII. The effect of food deprivation, reward and intertrial interval. (In Japanese) *Japanese Journal of Psychology*, 1961, 32, 303-310.

Gardiner, H.M. Psychology in Thailand. *Psychologia*, 1968, 11, 122-124.

Guthrie, G.M., and Bulatao, J., S.J. Psychology in the Philippines. *Psychologia*, 1968, 11, 201-206.

Hassan, F. Letter to Dr. Koji Sato. *Psychologia*, 1963, 6, 179-180.

Hirano, T. Effects of functional disturbances of the limbic system on the memory consolidation. *Japanese Psychological Research*, 1965, 7, 171-182.

Holmes, S.W. Zen Buddhism and transactional psychology. *Etc.*; 1957, 14, 243-349.

Hora, T. Tao, Zen, and existential psychotherapy. *Psychologia*, 1959, 2, 236-249.

Hundal, P.S. Organisation of mental abilities at successive grade levels. *Indian Journal of Psychology*, 1966, 41, 65-72.

Hwang, C.H. A study of the personal preference of Chinese university students by Edwards Personal Preference Schedule. *Psychology and Education*, 1967, 1, 52-68.

Ikeda, H. and Obonai, T. Studies in figural after-effects. IV. The contrast-confluence illusion of concentric circles and the figural after-effect. *Japanese Psychological Research*, 1955, 2, 17-23.

Imada, H. "Vigor" of water drinking behaviour of rats as a function of thirst drive. *Japanese Psychological Research*, 1964, 6, 108-114.

Imanishi, K. Social behaviour in Japanese monkeys, *Macaca fuscata. Psychologia*, 1957, 1, 47-54.

Indow, T.A. General equi-distance scale of the four qualities of tastes *Japanese Psychological Research*, 1966, 8, 136-150.

Ishihara, I. *Psychology of Verbal Behaviour* (In Japanese) Tokyo: Kobunkan, 1960.

Ishihara, S. Growth and decay of induction. IX. Several aspects of behaviour in the semicircular apparatus. (In Japanese) *Japanese Journal of Psychology*, 1966, 37, 1-11.

Iwahara, S. Studies of the "spread of effect." V. The spread of verbal punishment and the meaningfulness of cue stimuli. *Japanese Psychological Research*, 1958, 5, 38-50.

Iwahara, S. Psychological activities at the University of the Ryukyus, the National Taiwan University and Taiwan Normal University. *Psychologia*, 1967, 10, 223-225.

Iwahara, S., and Fujita, O. Behaviourism in Japan. *Psychologia*, 1963, 4, 59-64.

Iwahara, S., Nagamura, N., and Iwasaki, T. Effect of chlordiazepoxide upon experimental extinction in the straight runway as a function of partial reinforcement in the rat. *Japanese Psychological Research*, 1967, 9, 128-134.

Iwahara, S., Takeuchi, E., and Nagamura, N. EEG patterns during natural sleep in the rat and their multivariate analyses. (In Japanese) *Bulletin of Faculty Education, Tokyo University of Education*, 1967, 13, 41-57.

Jayasuriya, D.L. Recent psychological research in Ceylon. *Psychologia*, 1965, 8, 169-174.

Joshi, M.C. Psychological researches in India. *Jalota Commemoration Volume*, 1965, 25-34.

Kakizaki, S. Binocular rivarly and stimulus intensity. *Japanese Psychological Research*, 1960, 2, 94-105.

Kaneko, T. *Science of color: Its psychophysiology.* (In Japanese) Tokyo: Misuzu-Shobo, 1968.

Kasamatsu, A., and Hirai, T. An electroencephalographic study of the Zen meditation (Zazen). *Folia Psychiatrica et Neurologica Japonica*, 1966, 20, 315-336.

Kawai, H., and Kondo, K. Discussion on Morita therapy. *Psychologia*, 1960, 3, 92-99.

Kitao, N. Effects of mediated association on paired-associate learning. VIII. About the degree of prior learning and instruction. (In Japanese) *Japanese Journal of Physiology*, 1967, 38, 137-147.

Kora, T., and Sato, K. Morita therapy: A psychotherapy in the way of Zen. Psychologia, 1958, 1, 219-225.

Krishnakanth, A., and Prasad, J.N. Socio-economic differences on a reasoning test. *Indian Psychological Review*, 1967, 3, 119-122.

Krishnan, B.A. review of contributions of Indian psychologists (1950-1960). In T.K.N. Menon (Ed.), *Recent Trends in Psychology*. Orient Longmans, 1961.

Kuraishi, S. On the reproduction of simple thought-configuration by using the method of paired comparison. (In Japanese) *Japanese Journal of Psychology*, 1937, 12, 578-602.

Kuroda, R. Stereopsychology: Its scope and method. *Acta Psychologica Keijo*, 1931, 1, 69-82.

Kuroda, R. *A History of Chinese Psychological Thought*. (In Japanese) Tokyo: Koyama-shoten, 1948.

Lagmay, A.V. Letter to Dr. Koji Sato. *Psychologia*, 1963, 6, 179-180.

Liu, I.M., and Hu, W. The cube and Weber's Law. *Acta Psychologica Taiwanica*, 1967, 9, 87-89.

Liu, K.C. *Practice on the Breathing Therapy.* (In Chinese) Hopei People's Press, 1957.

Lun, S.H. Researches in perception in Democratic Germany. (In Chinese) *Acta Psychologica Sinica*, 1958, 2, 45-52.

Matsuyama, Y., and Tsukioka, S. The intertrial-interval response in relation to amount of warning signal, and restraint time. *Japanese Psychological Research*, 1964, 6, 1-9.

Maupin, E.W. Zen Buddhism: A psychological review. *Journal of Consulting Psychology*, 1962, 26, 362-278.

Morikawa, Y. Functions of stimulus and response in paired-associate verbal learning. *Psychologia*, 1959, 2, 41-56.

Morinaga, S., Noguchi, K., and Ohnishi, A. The horizontal vertical illusion and the relation to spatial and retinal orientation. *Japanese Psychological Research*, 1962, 4, 25-29.

Morris, C.W. Comments on mysticism and its language. *Etc.*, 1951, 9, 3-8.

Motokawa, K. Retinal traces and visual perception of movement. *Journal of Experimental Psychology*, 1953, 45, 369-377.

Motora, Y. *An essay on Eastern philosophy.* Leipzig: Voigtlander, 1905.

Motoyoshi, R. Simultaneous and successive discrimination under three types of jumping platform. *Japanese Psychological Research*, 1956, 4, 50-61.

Motoyoshi, R., and Iwahara, S. Japanese studies on animal behaviour in the last decade. *Psychologia*, 1960, 3, 135-148.

Murphy, G., and Murphy, L.B. (Eds.) *Asian Psychology.* New York: Basic Books, 1968.

Ni, C.F. A preliminary criticism on the behaviourism of J.B. Watson. (In Chinese) *Acta Psychologica Sinica*, 1957, 1, 194-200.

Niimi, Y., Kubota, K., and Iwama, Y. Spontaneous variations of the sin potentials and skin potential reflexes during natural sleep in the cat. *Japanese Journal of Physiology*, 1968, 18, 190-197.

Niki, H. Response perseveration following the hippocampal ablation in the rat. *Japanese Psychological Research*, 1964, 6, 108-114.

Obonai, T. The concept of psychophysiological induction: A review of experimental works. *Psychologia*, 1957, 1, 3-9.

Ono, S. A mathematical analysis of motór learning: A control system model. *Japanese Psychological Research*, 1966, 8, 72-89.

Otsuka, N. Stereopsychology and studies on k'an by Ryo Kuroda. *Psychologia*, 1960, 3, 73-39.

Pareek, U. Psychology in India. *Psychologia*, 1957, 1, 55-59.

Pe, W. Mindfulness of sensation. *Psychologia*, 1966, 9, 195-198.

Rao, S. Occupational role and personality: A comparative study of a few occupational groups in India. *Indian Journal of Psychology*, 1966, 41, 59-64.

Razran, G. Psychology in Communist countries other than the U.S.S.R. *American Psychologist*, 1958, 13, 177-178.

Rogers, A.H. Zen and LSD: An enlightening experience. *Psychologia*, 1964, 7, 150-151.

Sagara, M., and Oyama, T. Experimental studies on figural aftereffects in Japan. *Psychological Bulletin*, 1957, 54, 327-338.

Sato, K. How to get Zen enlightenment: On Master Ishiguro's five-days' intensive course for its attainment. *Psychologia*, 1959, 2, 107-113.

Sato, K., and Suzuki, D.T. Zen and LSD 25. *Psychologia*, 1967, 10, 129-132.

Sen, I. Teaching of personality in Indian universities. *Indian Journal of Psychology*, 1958, 33, 129-133.

Shuh, P. China's recent research work in psychology. *Psychologia*, 1959, 2, 193-202.

Su, H.Y. Letter to Dr. Koji Sato. *Psychologia*, 1963, 6, 176.

Sugimura, T. Intradimensional and extradimensional shifts as a function of stimulus change and overtraining. *Japanese Psychological Research*, 1967, 9, 78-84.

Sukemune, S. Effects of total number of acquisition trials under partial reinforcement schedules on running speeds. *Japanese Psychological Research*, 1963, 5, 183-187.,

Suzuki, D.T. *Zen Buddhism*. Garden City, N.Y.: Anchor Books, 1956.

Takada, Y. Reaction time and information in the discrimination of length of lines. *Japanese Psychological Research*, 1960, 2, 14-24.

Takahashi, S. The present status of psychological activities in Korea. *Psychologia*, 1967, 10, 225-226.

Tanaka, Y. Status of Japanese experimental psychology. *Annual Review of Psychology*, 1966, 17, 233-272.

Thompson, R.F. *Foundations of physiological psychology*. New York: Harper and Row, 1967.

Thwin, H. Department of Psychology, University of Rangoon, Burma. *Psychologia*, 1962, 5, 107-111.

Tsai, H.J., and Liu, S.Y. Lambda waves of human subjects of different age levels. (In Chinese) *Acta Psychologica Sinica*, 1965, 8, 343-352.

Tsao, C., and Shen, Y. Developmental studies on the recognition and generalisation of Chinese characters in primary school children. III. Development of the discrimination of detail. (In Chinese) *Acta Psychologica Sinica*, 1965, 8, 135-140.

Tsao, J.C. On the fundamental viewpoints of psychology. (In Chinese) *Acta Psychologica Sinica*, 1965, 9, 101-105.

Tsao, J.C., Li, C.C., Ching, C.C., Chang, T.H., Yu, C.S., Feng, K.C., and Chu, T.H. Human factors in signal design of control room of an electric power station. (In Chinese) *Acta Psychologica Sinica*, 1966, 9, 53-58.

Umemoto, T. Japanese studies in verbal learning and memory. *Psychologia*, 1959, 2, 1-9.

Van Dusen, W. LSD and enlightenment of Zen. *Psychologia*, 1961, 4, 11-16.

Yen, F., and Cheng, F.Y. Binocular disparity, stimulus intensity, and the way of light presentation have to do with necessary stimulus duration time to produce depth perception. *Acta Psychologica Taiwanica*, 1966, 8, 85-91.

Yokose, Z. Theoretical formula of vector-field and its experimental proof. *Psychologia*, 1957, 1, 17-21.

Yoshida, M. Studies of psychometric classification of odors (5). *Japanese Psychological Research*, 1964, 6, 145-154.

Yuki, K. Experimental psychology. In A. II. Livermore (Ed.), *Science in Japan*. Washington, D.C.: American Association for the advancement of Science, 1965, pp. 335-373.

Zaidi, S.M.H. Pakistan: A society in transition. *Psychologia*, 1964, 7, 15-21.

# 21

# Psychology in the Emerging Nations: Latin America, Africa, and the Middle East

Very few attempts have been made by psychologists in the nations of Latin America, Africa, and the Middle East to build formal theories or systems. What little research has been executed usually has been oriented toward solving practical problems, ranging from the licensing of motor-vehicle operators to the acculturation of traditional peoples into modern industrial societies. Isolated instances of research of more general interest do occur, however.

Rather than review the sparse theory-building efforts, which frequently have been published in readily available journals of the affluent nations, we feel that it may be more profitable to consider the factors affecting the development of psychology in the emerging nations. Special emphasis will be devoted to factors that affect the growth of a scientific psychology, such as the adequacy of communication, the growth of industrial technology, and domination from abroad. It is hoped that this approach will in turn promote insight into the reasons for the differential growth of scientific psychology in various parts of the world, to the mutual benefit of colleagues in both the rich and poor nations.

## GENERAL CONDITIONS THAT AFFECT PSYCHOLOGY

The per capita annual income in the wealthy countries of the world has been estimated to be about $1,700. In the poor nations it is only about $110 (Blacked, 1967). It is not surprising, then, that the most salient characteristic of psychology in the emerging nations is its lack of economic support. Although many of the countries discussed in this appendix have enjoyed a long history in scientific-psychology, only Israel and the Republic of South Africa have provided psychology with the funds necessary for vigorous and autonomous growth.

In addition to the general lack of affluence characteristic of the emerging nations, psychology's poverty is also due to the lack of acceptance of the social sciences in these countries. The reasons vary greatly. Problems studied by social scientists compete for funds with more urgent problems, such as water purification, sanitation, and food production

(Mahal, 1967). In totalitarian states, which abound among the emerging nations, the social sciences may be suppressed because it is suspected that some findings may contradict prevailing ideologies (Horowitz, 1967; Sanford, 1952). Professors may be dismissed for political views (Hall, 1946) or imprisoned for their research (Chirinos, 1967). Military "committees of inquiry" continue to take their toll, and major universities recently have been destroyed by them (Nessenzveig, 1969). Countries with small, powerful elites may study social problems that result from the concentration of power, but classify the results to prevent their distribution (see Holleman, Mann, & Van den Berghe, 1962, for example). Even in relatively advanced countries psychological explanations of behaviour compete with superstition (Hartocollis, 1966; Hes, 1964; Jahoda, 1968). Everywhere public and governmental apathy regarding science, especially social science, compounds the problem. For example, while many psychologists from the emerging nations publish papers showing how psychology might be used in nation building, Mundy-Castle (1968) has observed that a special issue of the Organisation for Economic Cooperation and Development's *OECD Observer* (September, 1966), devoted to developmental aid, contains only fifteen lines on "social transformation." Some fifty pages are devoted to trade, foreign investment, and other topics outside the focus of the social sciences.

In many countries the newer disciplines, such as psychology and sociology, are actively opposed by better-established disciplines. Treatment of behaviour disorders by psychologists, for example, is likely to be opposed by medical associations, as is the case in Argentina (Ardila, 1968); In a few countries, such as Lebanon, such treatment is even prohibited by law (Melikian, 1964). Opposition and lack of interest are also reflected in the absence of legal recognition in most countries. In only two of fifteen Latin-American countries covered in a recent report was any legal recognition accorded to psychologists (Ardila, 1968).

Understandably, then, psychologists in the emerging nations have not been able to establish a clear image for themselves in the public eye. Psychologists frequently are seen as poorly trained physicians (Ardila, 1968), and physicians with training in psychotherapy, or other non-psychologists, may refer to themselves as psychologists (Abt, 1964). Part of the image problem emanates from the university, where psychology classes are often taught by M.D.'s, education specialists, etc. The failure of psychology to evoke a clear image of an independent discipline also hampers its search for support.

Whatever the causes, the consequences of underfunding and lack of recognition are severe and probably are related to the following characteristics of psychology in the nations under consideration.

## LOW BUDGETS FOR TRAINING

Funds for education are generally quite limited, and the problem is greater for psychologists and other behavioural scientists than for those in the older disciplines. Reports of internationally known professors in the social sciences who earn as little as $80 or $100 per month continue (Janowitz, 1968: Nussenzveig, 1969). A more typical case might be that of an acquaintance of the author who fared only slightly better. His appointment received from one of the largest universities in Latin America paid about $2,000 (plus health and other benefits) for the nine-month term. It was considered a half-time appointment, but included duties of teaching twenty hours per week in classes or laboratories!

In many Latin-American universities, including those which are state- supported, the salary may be so small as to constitute a mere honorarium. In such cases, professional persons contribute a few hours of their time each week to teach a single course in the spirit of public service or for prestige. As might be expected, the adequacy of instruction in such a system is quite variable.

Most of the countries of Africa and the Middle East are just beginning to train their own psychologists. With the exception of Israel, the Republic of South Africa, the United Arab Republic, and a very few others, countries there are relying on expatriate Europeans or others for their training.

## POOR COMMUNICATION

Publications. "Prestige" publications from the technologically advanced nations predominate in the emerging nations. Since much of this material must be translated into Arabic, Hebrew, Spanish, or other languages for maximum utilisation, communication problems are even more dependent upon money for solution in the emerging nations than in the affluent nations.

Good texts for advanced courses in scientific psychology are still rare, and the communication value even for good translated texts is limited by the long translation lag. For material translated from English into Spanish, for example, the lag is about 8.5 years (Campos, 1964). This lag, added to the estimated six-year publication lag for most data that eventually will be so translated (Diaz-Guerreo, 1968), makes such information old indeed when it first appears in Spanish. Because of the infrequency of translation, it can become much older still before newer information appears, as the author learned from a Latin American who studied general psychology a few years ago in a large Mexican university. That course's text was a translation of Max Meyer's *Psychology of the other one*, first published in 1921.

### *Conventions and Associations*

Poor written communication is paralleled by poor communication via conventions held by national or regional associations. Several Latin-American states have yet to found an association or hold a convention. In the Middle East and Africa, only Israel, the United Arab Republic, and the Republic of South Africa have national associations. Plans for national associations are nearing completion in Ghana, Nigeria, Iran, and Sierra Leone.

The only regional association of consequence is the Inter-American Society of Psychology, founded in 1951. Psychologists from virtually every country in both North and South America belong to this organisation. It has sponsored an almost yearly congress since the first in 1953. In recent years, the proceedings of the congress have been published, and since 1967 the *Revista Inter-Americana de Psicologia* has been published quarterly by this organisation. Both have greatly facilitated communication in the Americas.

No corresponding regional association is currently active in Africa or the Middle East, although a West African Psychological Association is being organised.

Other communication depends mainly upon the technologically advanced countries. The international Union of Psychological Science, for example, provides a variety of communication services for psychologists in any country, in addition to providing special recognition and aid to member associations. Five of its thirty-five member associations are found in Latin America. Only South Africa in Africa and Israel in the Middle East have member associations. Among its publications are the *International Journal of Psychology*, the *International Directory of Psychologists*, and, with the APA, *International Opportunities for Advanced Training and Research in Psychology*. It also sponsors meetings.

The United Nations Educational, Scientific, and Cultural Organisation publishes bibliographies and other materials, including the *International Social Science Journal*. Other communication resources for the emerging nations include the *Latin American Research Review*, published by the University of Texas; the *Newsletter*, from the University of Illinois; and *FAR Horizons*, from the Foreign Area Research Coordination Group of the United States government.

A little-known service is provided by the Science Information Exchange of the National Science Foundation. Created to provide information concerning research in progress, its abstracts are provided on demand to scientists in any country without charge. Its coverage of United States government-sponsored projects is moderately complete, and it also includes some projects sponsored by private foundations. Projects sponsored by Canada or other foreign nations are occasionally included.

## LACK OF RESEARCH

Psychology in the least developed countries may be described as predominantly academic—a classroom enterprise. In the more advanced of the emerging nations may be found at least some form of applied psychology, such as selection testing or psychological treatment of behavioural disorders, but seldom is there much emphasis upon research or training in research methodology.

The major impediment to research is, predictably, lack of funds. The funding problem is especially acute for cross-cultural and other research offering no obvious contribution to national development (Odbert, 1964; Santos, 1964).

### Research in Latin America

Research-oriented movements, such as behaviourism, are just beginning to make themselves felt in Latin America. Despite very early recognition of the possibility of scientific psychology by early Spaniards such as Juan Huarte, who in 1575 suggested the use of tests for academic selection, the general absence of science in Spain and Portugal has hampered the scientific movement in Latin America (Basalla, 1967). This absence was due, at least in part, to an aversion for manual labor. In Latin America this aversion is manifested in avoidance of such tedious activities as data collection. It is exemplified by early Brazilian naturalists who assigned their Negroes the task of collecting and preparing specimens (Kidder, 1845). Even Latin-American psychologists trained abroad have traditionally preferred a nonquantitative approach (Abt, 1964). This distaste for the manual labor of data collection is probably the result of many class-conscious members of Latin America's educated elite viewing it as a lower-class activity.

Coupled with a disdain for data collection and analysis is a glorification of philosophical approaches (Chavez, Lozada, & Arestegui, 1966; Hall, 1946). One reviewer of ten Latin-American introductory psychology texts found that nine devoted whole chapters to philosophical psychology. Other common topics were philosophical treatments of instincts, association of ideas, character, consciousness, passion, will, etc. (Campos, 1964). A typical author (Celaya, 1961) has asserted that he reduced the physiological basis of his text to a minimum and instead emphasised the cultural and spiritual. The affirmation by the first Congreso Argentino de Psicologia of the goal of valuable action, the truth, the core of human knowledge, and God, the meaning of everything that is, is not unusual in its alliance with the philosophical approach rather than with the scientific (Ruiz, 1963).

Another source of resistance to behavioural research can be traced to the arrival of French philosophical thought. The French viewpoint achieved dominance among Latin Americans during the last century, largely because French intellectuals espoused political freedom and independence cherished by nations newly independent of Spain. It was also esteemed because it was a Latin movement of some prestige among the nations of the world.

French positivism of the Comte school became especially influential. Unfortunately for scientific psychology, its emphasis upon strict operationalism quickly drove difficult psychological problems out of the laboratories and into philosophy departments, thus strengthening the affinity between psychology and philosophy (Beebe-Centre & McFarland, 1941). The early interpreters of positivism (such as Levy-Bruhl, 1900) also urged the division of empirical psychology into sociology and physiology. Acceptance of this doctrine, together with the founding of two of the first active psychological laboratories in Latin America around the turn of the century by a physiologist (Horacio Pinero), further fractionated psychology.

One might not expect the fraction of psychology belonging to the philosophers to develop an empirical tradition. It would seem, however, that the physiologists and physicians might have established an empirical psychology within their own discipline. The failure of this expectation to be fully realised as the educational and technological capability of these nations grew can be traced largely to the introduction of Freudian thought. The association of psychoanalysis with medicine led to its early acceptance by prestigious university faculties of medicine. Freud's philosophical style of thinking and writing seems to have been more attractive to Latin-American academicians than to those in non-Latin countries.

Philosophical psychoanalytical psychology now dominates psychology in almost all Latin-American universities. In keeping with this domination, Latin- American students studying in the United States are heard to complain that their classes should be more philosophical and clinical (Campos, 1964). One may predict that the resulting skepticism regarding the value of scientific research into clinical or other problems (for example, see Nunez, 1964) will continue to inhibit Latin-American empirical research on psychological topics.

**Research in Africa and the Middle East**

In Africa south of the Sahara, psychological research is well established only in South Africa. A beginning has been made in Zambia, Ghana, Senegal, Nigeria, Uganda, and a few other places. In most of these nations research is still guided by whites. It has been asserted that traditional African social values, while attractive for other reasons, modulate the tough-minded assertiveness that may be necessary for a rigorous science (Mundy-Castle, 1968). What research is performed seems to be found more frequently where the British academic tradition prevails than in the twenty French-speaking states, where psychology is often identified with philosophy (Prothro & Melikian, 1955). Accordingly, a reviewer of French-language psychological studies from Africa remarked that he found few relevant bibliographies (Wickert, 1967). It is tempting to speculate that the Latin turn of mind that seems to adore the philosophical approach when found among Latin Americans is also at work in French-speaking Africa. It should be noted, however, that other observers have reported a vigorous empirical psychology current in France itself (see Appendix A, for example), thus casting doubt on such a hypothesis.

In the Middle East, Israel clearly leads in research. Almost none seems to be executed in the Arab states outside of the United Arab Republic and, to a lesser degree, Lebanon. Competence in the latter nation is growing, but until recently only a few Lebanese publications appear to have had direct scientific value (Melikian, 1964).

In all the nations under consideration, the little research that is executed is focused on "applied" problems. "Basic" research is neglected. In Africa, this imbalance characterises research executed in the French as well as the English tradition (Wickert, 1967). In many nations applied research has preceded by many years any type or basic or academic research.

The pressure from governmental or other social institutions to solve practical problems has deflected all types of research away from the universities and into special institutes. Usually these institutes are concerned with specific objectives, such as rehabilitating juvenile delinquents, reducing alcoholism, aiding governmental licensing bodies, etc. The APA's *International Opportunities for Advanced Training and Research in Psychology* lists several dozen such institutes in Latin America, and observers have commented on their importance

(Beebe-Center & McFarland, 1941; Hall, 1946). Almost as many may be found in Africa and the Middle East.

The current growth of these institutions suggests that what resources are allotted to psychological research in the emerging nations will continue to be devoted to applied rather than basic problems. This trend is probably a healthy one in view of the current needs of these countries. One may hope, however, that eventually the emerging nations will elaborate their own viewpoints to complement the ethnocentric biases of the affluent nations—a problem to be treated at length in the following section.

## FOREIGN DOMINATION

This domination assumes several forms. The dominating position of foreign literature in the emerging nations was mentioned earlier in this appendix. An equally influential force involves the exchange of people. In the early 1960s about 270,000 students were abroad. About half of them were from the developing nations and were studying in the affluent nations (Ajmal, 1967; Angell, 1967). Many of the students, as well as more mature scholars who seek research or other experience in the affluent nations, fail to return. Such loss stunts the growth of the donor and, because of acculturation and training in the affluent culture, seldom makes psychology in the latter more universal. If the scholar does return home, he may not be easily reintegrated into his home culture because of "culture shock" or because he is viewed as a threat by older but less well-trained scholars (Gollin, 1964; Price-Williams, 1968; Whyte, 1969). Nor does sending teaching personnel from the affluent nations to the emerging nations reduce feelings of domination, for this procedure perpetuates the dependent role of the latter. Such teaching personnel are also finding themselves subject to increasing political attacks in the emerging nations. Distrust for United States personnel is especially great, for their activities are frequently seen to differ only in method from the intervention of the United States military or the CIA, which is almost, universally disapproved of in the countries under consideration (Whyte, 1969).

Neither the dominant position of foreign publications nor the migration of personnel, however, stirs international controversies among psychologists as much as research executed by the affluent nations in and on the emerging nations. One observer has noted that the resentment is understandable when one realises that the intellectual harvests from such projects inevitably are reaped mainly in the United States or other affluent nations that can afford to sponsor projects executed abroad (Smith, 1968b). Elsewhere he observed that no special empathy is required to understand why members of a modernised elite resent having their less sophisticated compatriots studied as "natives," specimens in a human museum (Smith, 1968a).

Aside from the above implications of research executed abroad, much of it may be described as "tourist research," executed by investigators who are unfamiliar with the host culture and who may spend no more than a few weeks during the summer in the host country. Research conducted in this manner is usually of doubtful validity (Mundy-Castle,

1967). An increasing number of areas are also being viewed as "overresearched" or "saturated" (Hughes, 1966; Walsh, 1966). A member of the US. Department of State reviewed a number of government documents and found 191 foreign-area research centers in United States universities alone (Platig, 1968).

For several years, citizens of the emerging nations have held the suspicion that United States psychological research might be an instrument of Western imperialism (Prothro & Melikian, 1955). The fact that currently more than 50 per cept of government-sponsored foreign-area research in the United States is supported by the Department of Defense (Platig, 1968) augments this suspicion.

The most startling evidence that psychology and other behavioural sciences could indeed serve Western imperialism is project Camelot (see Horowitz, 1965; Vallance, 1966; Walsh, 1966). This counterinsurgency project was expected to cost 4 to 6 million dollars over its anticipated life of three to four years. The American University in Washington, D.C., accustomed to executing research for the government, was chosen by the Army sponsors to administer the funds. It has been suggested that university identification was desired as camouflage for the militaristic implications of the project (Horowitz, 1965). That the project was hardly a disinterested search for understanding may be concluded from a recruiting letter sent to scholars throughout the world (but excluding the Communist nations, it is safe to assume). The goals, as stated in the letter, were to make it possible to predict and influence politically significant aspects of social change in the developing nations of the world. Needless to say, any increase in ability to influence politically significant aspects of social change would serve mainly the interests of the affluent nations and, perhaps, their wealthy friends in the developing nations.

Counter to the spirit of free inquiry, certain unquestioned assumptions seem to have been implicit in the project. Among them was the desirability of political stability. Studies of Paraguay, where; repressive dictatorship prevailed, were recommended, apparently because of that country's stability. The desirability of successful revolution appears never to have been considered by Camelot personnel, a point criticised by Senator Fulbright, chairman of the Senate Foreign Relations Committee. Knowledge of these assumptions and purposes disseminated in Chile caused such a furor that the project was aborted in mid-1965, before any data were collected, by then Secretary of Defense McNamara, after consultation with the President.

The project has been defended. Some have argued that its successful completion would have increased the behavioural scientists' ability to modify some of the unattractive aspects of militarism in our foreign policy. The fact that the Army even considered such a mammoth project was offered as evidence that the behavioural sciences could play a guiding role in certain military activities. More likely, however, the military viewed the project as quite minor, having committed to it less than 1/30,000th of its total budget anticipated for the three- or four-year period under consideration.

Perhaps extensive changes in attitudes may be required before the problems of foreign domination of the behavioural sciences in the developing nations can be significantly reduced. The nature of those changes may be inferred from questions posed by a United States sociologist (Moskos, 1968). He asks: "Why should it be so difficult to conceive of a group of Latin American sociologists studying the American military-industrial complex? Or to conceive of African economists looking at patterns of American investments overseas? Or to conceive of Asian political scientists examining the decision-making process in the growth of U.S. military commitments overseas?" (p. 2).

## STAGES OF DEVELOPMENT

The nations under consideration in this appendix might profitably be classified into three stages of development in regard to their achievements in scientific psychology. The following classification is made primarily on the basis of the education in psychology that is available within each country and the psychological research published by the country's scholars. Much of the information used for the classification (especially the information regarding education in psychology) comes from the APA's *International Opportunities for Advanced Training and Research in Psychology* (1966). Most of that information was submitted during 1964 and 1965 and therefore is somewhat dated. Newer information is available for some of the countries, but it was felt that mixing new with old information would reduce the comparability of the information upon which the classification rests. Table 21.1 presents the resulting classification. (Case studies for stage 2 and stage 3 are given at the end of this appendix.)

**TABLE 21.1**

**Stages of development in scientific psychology of nations in Latin America, Africa, and the Middle East**

| | |
|---|---|
| Stage I: | Aden, Afghanistan, Cameroon, Central African Republic, Chad, Congo (Brazzaville), Dahomey, Gabon, Federation of South Arabia, Ivory Coast, Jordan, Kuwait, Liberia, Libya, Morocco, Rhodesia, Saudi Arabia, Sierra Leone, Sudan, Syria, Tunisia<br>*Costa Rica, Ghana. Malagasy, Nigeria, Senegal, Uganda, Zambia* |
| Stage 2: | Algeria, Chile, Colombia, Congo (Leopoldville), Ecuador, El Salvador, Guatemala, Iran, Iraq, Lebanon, Panama, Paraguay, Peru, Uruguay<br>*Argentina, Brazil, Cuba, Mexico, United Arab Republic, Venezuela* |
| Stage 3: | Israel<br>*Republic of South Africa* |

NOTE: The italicised nations are considered to be somewhat advanced over others in the same stage of development.

### *Stage 1*

Countries at this stage of development do not have degree-granting psychology departments. However, a few of the nations italicised in the table, such as Senegal and Malagasy, offer certificates in psychological studies that are roughly equivalent to B-A-degrees in psychology. Little or no research is conducted by the nonitalicised countries. Most of the italicised nations have established at least one permanent center for psychological research that is relatively independent of the guidance of a foreign institution. These centers are usually staffed by expatriate psychologists from Europe or elsewhere.

***Stage 2***

Countries at this stage of development do have one or more universities that offer degrees in psychology. Frequently their universities are several centuries old and may have promoted psychological studies for as long as the average university in Europe or the United States. Generally they are wealthier than the countries in stage I. For one reason or another, however, psychology- especially rigorous, scientific psychology-has not prospered in most of these countries, where high-quality psychological education is rare. The nonitalicised countries conduct only sporadic research, except in connection with student theses. The italicised countries usually support at least a handful of researchers in psychology, but have achieved excellence in only a few areas of research.

***Stage 3***

Only the Republic of South Africa and Israel have achieved the breadth and rigor in psychology required for classification at stage 3. They also differ in that they are relatively affluent, with perhaps only Kuwait, Venezuela, and Argentina comparable to them on this dimension. South Africa is remarkably wealthy if the poverty of that nation's blacks is ignored. It should also be noted that both nations, but especially Israel, devote a large proportion of their wealth to education and welfare rather than to consumer goods. The number of TV sets per 1,000 population, for example, was recorded by the UN's *Statistical yearbook* (1965) as only six for Israel. This compares with three for Zambia, five for Iran, twelve for Syria, eighteen for Peru, and forty-two for Mexico, all countries that are poorer than Israel. Argentina and Venezuela, which are comparable to Israel in wealth, are reported to have had seventy-two and seventy-five, respectively. Israel's support of welfare is evidenced by the fact that it has perhaps the best doctor-population ratio of any country in the world.

## GROWTH AND PROSPECTS FOR THE FUTURE

It has been asserted that scientific research doubled in Africa during the period 1950 to 1964, when most nations there were enjoying their first years of independence (Adiseshiah, 1964). Psychological research there also exhibited some growth in quantity during that period. Greater advances were achieved in terms of the quality of psychological research. Research conducted prior to independence has frequently been charged with reflecting colonial bias (Doob, 1965; Wickert, 1967). Certainly the problems studied now are more relevant to the needs of the Africans than was the case during the colonial period.

Nevertheless, there are some factors operating on both continents that must lead one to modify the general prediction of continuing growth.

In Latin America, education definitely has lagged behind industrialisation and other trends toward modernisation. The literacy rate in some Latin-American nations actually may have fallen during the last two decades. In the mid 1960s, no major city in Latin America had classrooms for more than 70 per cent of its school-age population. Opportunities for education were much poorer still in rural areas. The quality of education was also marginal, with teaching usually considered to be an underpaid, low-status profession. There is no indication that education in Latin America will greatly improve in the foreseeable future.

Profound commitment to formal education has been said to distinguish the new African nations from other emerging nations (Foster, 1964). Several years ago some African nations were already enrolling up to 80 per cent of all primary-age children in school (Hunter, 1962). Unfortunately, fewer than 10 per cent or so of primary school graduates can be accommodated into secondary schools (McQueen, 1968). It is also true that, in spite of government commitment to education, the African populace remains uninspired by education. University education is still very rare in Africa, but the gains being reported in this area of education permit some degree of optimism.

Education in the Middle East varies from good in Israel and in tiny, wealthy Kuwait to inadequate almost everywhere else. In most places only a minority of school-age children attend school. Even Egypt entered the second half of this century with about two-thirds of its population illiterate, and Egypt is generally considered to be more advanced than most other countries in the Middle East in regard to education. The illiteracy rate there is probably still about 50 per cent.

Consideration of economic factors leads one to be no more optimistic regarding psychology's future than consideration of educational factors does. During the last decades of the colonial period, which ended in most places after World War II, the economies of the poor countries grew only about 1 per cent per year. Since then the increase has been about 4 per cent per year, but the population has increased at the rate of about 2.5 per cent per year. The net gain of about 1.5 per cent, although about 1 per cent lower than that in the wealthy countries nevertheless would permit a small rise in wealth (Blackett, 1967). Unfortunately there is reason to fear that the growth rate of the emerging nations may actually decline from its present low level. Past growth in many of the emerging nations has been purchased, at lent in part, at the expense of agricultural productivity and consumption. At least one analysis in fact shows a decline in animal-protein consumption in the emerging nations generally of about 10 per cent from the late thirties to the late fifties. At the end of that period, the emerging nations were consuming, per person, only about one-fifth the animal protein being consumed in the rich nations (Keyfitz, 1967). Total per capita food availability is also decreasing (Hoelscher, 1969). Surely the emerging nations must increase, or at least hold constant, their food consumption, even if this means some slowing of advancement in the fields of education and science.

It also appears that much of the past growth in the emerging nations has resulted from the rich nations' foreign-aid programs. Because of the tremendous wealth of the affluent nations, their contribution of only 1 per cent of their annual product would boost the income of the poor nations by about 6 per cent (Blackett 1967). At one time the United States; one of the biggest contributors of foreign aid, met the 1 per cent figure. But in recent years actual dollars-and-cents figures have declined, despite a booming economy and inflation that alone would have reduced the percentage contributed even if the dollars contributed had remained constant.

The recurrent financial problems of some of the nations that continue to commit a larger percentage to foreign aid, such as France, lead one to fear that they, too, may reduce their contributions. These decreases come at a time when many exports of the emerging nations are being driven from the markets by synthetic goods produced in the affluent nations. All these problems, compounded by religious and other opposition to birth-control attempts, paint a forbidding picture of the economic future of the emerging nations. To the extent that psychology's future is tied to educational and economic growth in these nations, slow growth would appear to be the most that realistically can be hoped for.

## CONCLUSION

In none of the emerging nations can one find a tradition of scientific psychology that is perceptibly autonomous from scientific psychology found in the industrialised nations. An autonomous psychology in Africa and in Israel is precluded by the dominating role of expatriates from the industrialised nations. Scientific psychology in the Arab Middle East is still too poorly supported to be able to elaborate own viewpoints.. The Moslem psychology found there clearly does offer alternative viewpoints. However, its tradition is much older than upstart scientific psychology's tradition, and it appears not yet to have felt the need to offer empirical data to support its hypotheses.

Latin-American psychologists generally remain skeptical regarding the value of scientific psychology. The few Latin Americans who have engaged in empirical psychological research usually have been those who have been most influenced by the viewpoints found in the industrialised nations. As might be expected, their contributions frequently reflect non-Latin thinking.

A strong case can be presented in support of the argument that the wealthy nations should help pay the costs of nurturing psychology's growth in the emerging nations. Apart from the moral issue involved in disregarding their perpetual poverty and dependency upon the industrialised nations, support for the emerging nations' intellectual as well as political independence could produce identifiable benefits for the rich nations too. The pinpointing of generalisation failures in our theories would be only the most obvious benefit. In addition, wholly unforeseen avenues of research might be fostered by psychologists who come from cultures that, for one reason or another, have not grown industrially as the rich nations have. If this turned out to be the case, then the sum sophistication of scientific explanations for behaviour probably would advance more than if the same amount of support were confined to research executed by the rich. And, to the extent that such explanations became integrated into the decision-making processes of the rich countries, perhaps even some of their socioeconomic problems might become more amenable to solution than hitherto has been the case.

An integrated psychology derived from the experiences of both the emerging and the developed nations appears difficult to achieve. Admittedly, the pattern of the fifties and the sixties that centered mostly upon counterinsurgency and the design and implementation of large-scale technical development projects has probably passed its zenith. But we need not mourn its decline. The counterinsurgency business probably was never wholesome for either the rich or the poor nations, and increasing evidence suggests that many of the development projects were not viable because of economic and technical factors that were overlooked by the experts (see Hoelscher, 1969, for recent examples of failures of expertise). Such projects did not warrant the social engineering that often was provided for them by scientific psychology. If scientific psychology has nothing more to offer, then perhaps it merits its infirmity in the emerging nations.

There is reason to hope, however, that a more salubrious role may be arising for social scientists. It was described well by George A. Miller (1969) in his presidential address to the APA. Miller claims that our responsibility is less to assume the role of experts than to give away scientific psychology to the people who really need it-everyone. Space limitations prohibit a delineation of his vision here, but it seems to the present author that it does not differ greatly from that which is forming in the United States "counterculture," with its distinctive life-style (see Roszak, 1969). Significantly, Miller draws some of his inspiration from a Latin American (Varela, 1970) and is echoed by an increasing number of scientists from the emerging nations who, despairing of political revolutions, are calling for profound social revolutions (e.g., see Chirinos, 1967; Nussenzveig, 1969). Feeble though this hope may be, it appears to be providing new vigor to many of our best minds and, if for no other reason, deserves further consideration.

**Course Studies**

***Mexico, Stage 2***

With a population of about 50 million, Mexico is the world's largest Spanish-speaking nation. Lees wealthy than several other stage 2 nations, its per capita gross national product is only about one-tenth that of the United States, and it is not well distributed. Labor's portion of the income is less than half of labor's portion in the United States, and it has steadily decreased for several decades, while the profit portion has greatly increased. Nevertheless, the expanding economy plus adequate control of inflation has provided improved living conditions for most Mexicans in recent years. Urbanisation is advancing at a fast pace, and a slight majority of Mexicans now live in cities with 5,000 or more inhabitants. Education has advanced much less rapidly than industrial growth or urbanisation. Probably fewer than half the nation's children between the ages of six and twelve attend school. Illiteracy estimates range from 30 to about 50 per cent.

Psychology courses in Mexico have been offered since 1918 (Nunez, 1961), and degrees have been offered since 1936 (Ribes-Inesta, 1968). Growth in psychology has accelerated in recent years. In 1964 only five universities offered degrees in psychology, whereas in 1968 more than twenty-five hundred psychology majors studied in ten universities (Ribes-Inesta, 1968). As elsewhere in Latin America, most were women—a consequence of psychology's low status there. The National University was the first in Latin America to grant the Ph.D. in psychology (Abt, 1964), but its graduate program still is not well developed.

At most Mexican universities, as elsewhere in Latin America, courses last both semesters rather than one, and they tend to be organised in lock-step sequence. Until the 1960s, full-time teachers of psychology were almost nonexistent in Mexico (Abt, 1964). Most courses have been taught by part-time professors trained in medicine, education, engineering, law or philosophy.

No legal recognition has been achieved for psychologists except for occasional local laws regarding the use of the title *psychologist*. Several psychological journals have appeared in Mexico, but now are defunct. The Mexican Psychological Society, organised in 1967, plans to publish a journal of psychological research in the near future (Ribes-Inesta, 1968).

Psychological research of sorts began in Mexico in 1925, when examination of juvenile delinquents prior to sentencing was instituted. The Psycho-pedagogical Institute, a branch of the Department of Public Education, then was founded for studying and resolving the problems of school-age children (Nunez, 1961). Probably no more than a dozen or so Mexican psychologists currently are engaged in research as a regular part of their professional activities. What research is executed is funded by the universities or by occasional grants from the United States government or philanthropic organisations. There is no regular source of support for research outside the universities.

At least three scholars in Mexico may be said to have achieved international recognition for their work on topics of interest to psychologists. Raul Hernandez-Peon, who received his training in medicine at the National University in Mexico City, was well known for his work in physiological psychology. A review of his and other investigation' studies of brain functions, especially those related to sleep, may be found in a paper in the *Annual Review of Phychology* (Hernandez-Peon & Sterman, 1966). A review of his work on the role of reticular mechanisms in sensory control may be found in an earlier paper (Hernandez-Peon, 1961).

Perhaps the most significant single study covered in the latter review is one that examines neural mechanisms involved in the direction of attention (Hernandez-Peon, Scherrer, & Jouvet 1956). In this study, it was shown that the neural activity in the auditory nerve of cats practically disappeared when a jar of mice was placed in front of the subject. Other attention-getting stimuli, such as fish odors or a shock to the forepaw, produced similar results. It would appear that the auditory response is suppressed or tuned out when attention is directed elsewhere. Other sensory modes, such as vision, presumably are affected similarly by shifting attention.

Recently Hernandez-Peon and his students undertook an extensive series of studies into the implications for brain functioning of Freud's speculations on dreams. For a review of the preliminary findings of this research, see Hernandez-Peon (1967). His untimely death in 1968 represents a costly loss not only to Mexico but also to physiological psychology generally.

Rogelio Diaz-Guerrero received both his M.A. and his Ph.D. during the years spent at the State University of Iowa. He also holds an M.D. from the National University. As the third president of the Mexican Psychological Society, a past president of the Interamerican Society of Psychology, and a member of other organisations, he has been active in professional affairs as well as in research and teaching. Several of his cross-cultural comparisons and other social-psychological studies may be found in his book (Diaz-Guerrero, 1967). He has held several positions in the National University.

Erich Fromm is in charge of training in psychotherapy at the medical school of the National University. His speculations have furnished personality theorists with hypotheses during many years of work in Mexico and elsewhere.

A review of research in Mexico would not be complete without mention of the Instituto Interuniversitario para Investigations Fundamentales en Ciencias Sociales en Yucatan, A.C. More than five hundred scholars from psychology and at least fourteen other disciplines visited the institute during the first five years after its activation in 1964. Funded by grants obtained by Fred L. Strodtbeck, of the University of Chicago, and others, it has worked in close collaboration with Mexican scholars. Victor Castillo Vales, chairman of the University of Yucatan's psychology department, has provided especially valuable guidance for many non-Mexican social scientists who have conducted research there, including the present author.

### *Israel, Stage 3*

Israel was created in 1948 by the United Nations. At that time it was a poor nation with a population of about 700,000. The total population in 1965 was about 2.6 million, of which about 300,000 were non-Jews. Much of the population growth since 1948 is attributable to the immigration of about 1.1 million Jews between 1948 and 1965, of which about 400,000 were from Europe or the United States (Weinberg, 1967).

Primary education is excellent and enrolls most of the children. However, only a minority attend secondary schools. As of 1965, psychology was offered as a major subject at three universities. The M.A. in psychology was offered at Bar-Ilan University, and the Ph.D. at the Hebrew University of Jerusalem. New advanced degree programs are being organised at other universities. The quality of instruction is excellent. Nevertheless, a substantial proportion of students still seek training abroad. Psychology in Israel continues to be dominated by those who have studied in the United States, Europe, and the U.S.S.R.

Until 1948, Israeli psychology was oriented toward the psychoanalytic approach. Then the only department was at the Hebrew University. When the head of the department was killed in an ambush, the department became inactive until 1956. In that year both Hebrew University and Bar-Ilan University opened new departments. In contrast to the previous emphasis upon psychoanalytical clinical psychology, these new departments both were experimentally oriented (Greenbaum, 1967).

Research is currently conducted in at least a dozen special institutes, hospitals, and governmental agencies, as well as in the universities. It is predominantly centered upon problems of social or national interest. Often it is experimental in method. Basic research is by no means neglected, and it is supported both by Israeli governmental and other Israeli organisations and by foreign groups. Research is frequently conducted in collaboration with investigators in the United States or another foreign country.

The influence of the United States is especially notable in Israeli research. This influence is attributable to the United States psychologists who have accepted permanent positions in Israel, and it is maintained by a steady stream of visiting psychologists from the United States and by research funds supplied by United States organisations.

One institute of special interest that is partly supported by United States organisations (The American Committee for Social Research in Israel, Inc., and others) is the Israel Institute of Applied Social Research. First formed as a volunteer research group by the underground defense army in 1947, the institute was officially established in 1949 by Louis Guttman (known in the United States for his work in the measurement of attitudes) and Uriel G. Foa with the aid of a grant by the Israeli government. After operating under the auspices of the Defense Ministry, and later under the Prime Minister's Office, the institute now functions as an independent, nonprofit organisation. Its permanent professional staff of about twenty performs under the leadership of Guttman, who stayed on after the founding to become its scientific director. A part-time field staff working throughout the country facilitates large-scale studies in opinion polling, economics, mass communications, community planning, social problems of medicine and health, etc. To date, several hundred projects have been completed in the above fields, plus others in the general areas of social psychology, sociology, and psychology.

## REFERENCES


Abt, L.E. Clinical psychology in Latin America. In L.E. Abt and B.F. Riess (Eds.), *Progress in Clinical Psychology*. Vol. 6. New York: Grune and Stratton, 1964, pp. 235-241.

Adiseshiah, M.S. The planned development of scientific research. *Impact of Science on Society*, 1964, 14(3), 137-144.

Ajmal, M. Academic freedom. *Psychological Quarterly*, 1967, 2, 14-18.

Angell, R.C. The growth of transnational participation. *Journal of Social Issues*, 1967, 23, 108-129.

Ardila, R. La psicologia en Colombia. *Revista Inter-Americana de Psicologia*, 1967, 1, 239-249.

Ardila, R. Psychology in Latin America. *American Psychologist*, 1968, 23, 567-574. Basalla, G. The spread of Western science. *Science*, 1967, 156, 611-621.

Beebe-Center, J.G., and McFraland, R. Psychology in South America. *Psychological Bulletin*, 1941, 38, 627-667.

Blackett, P.M.S., The ever widening gap. *Science,* 1967, 155, 959-964.

Campos, L.P., Some problems in the teaching of psychology in Spanish at the Covell College, U.S.A. Paper presented at the Ninth Interamerican Congress of Psychology, Miami, December, 1964.

Celaya, M. *Psicologia.* (Primera edic.) Buenos Aires: Luis Lassere and Cia, S.A., Editores, 1961.

Chavez, E.U., Lozada, N.B., and Arestegui, A.A. Estudio comparativo de la formacion academica del psicologo. Paper presented at the Tenth Inteamerican Congress of Psychology, Lima, April, 1966.

Congress of Psychology, Lima, April, 1966.

Chirinos, E. Limitaciones y perspectivas de la psicologia y de las ciencias del comportamiento en los paises de subdesarrollo economico. *Proceedings of the Eleventh Interamerican Congress of Psychology,* Universidad Nacional Autonomo de Mexico, 1967.

Diaz-Guerrero, R. Estudios de priscolgia del Mexicano. Mexico: Editorial F. Trillas, S.A., 1967.

Diaz-Guerrero, R. Problems of scientific communication. *Journal of Social Issues,* 1968, 24, 217-226.

Doob, L., Psychology. In R.A., Lystad (ed.), *The African World: A Survey of Social Research.* London, Pall Mall Press for African Studies Association, 1965.

Foster, P.J. Status, power, and education in a traditional community. *School Review,* 1964, 72, 158-182.

# 22

# Science of Psychology

There is hardly any science about which there are as many misconceptions in the minds of the people as there are about psychology. Many of these misconceptions originate in the historical background of psychology and many in the efforts of some cunning persons to exploit the credulity of others in the fair and prestigious name of psychology. It is necessary, therefore, to begin our discussion by clearing some of these misconceptions at the very outset.

The word, 'psychology', literally means a science of the *mind* or *soul* (*psyche*—soul or mind, *logos*—reasoned discourse or science). This etymological or literal meaning of psychology has been very much in the minds of both laymen and scholars ever since the dawn of civilisation and its expression in the teachings and writings of both ancient and medieval thinkers and philosophers of Greece, India, China and Europe. Actually, psychology had no separate existence as a science until the turn of the last century and was always regarded as part of philosophy. It is no wonder, therefore, that, even today, both laymen and educated people attach the traditional meaning to the word 'psychology.'

For psychologists, however, the meaning of the word has undergone a lot of change and today we have hardly any psychologists who think of it as a science of the soul or mind. There are reasons for this. First, today, psychology is looked upon as a science, like physics, chemistry or biology. Secondly, because of the tremendous progress in our knowledge in the last two centuries, we are today in a better position to think of psychology in more precise terms than was ever possible earlier. Many people are unaware of these facts and keep attaching the same meaning to psychology as was attached traditionally.

A great number of misconceptions about psychology age, however, spread by many self-styled psychologists, who are to be found almost in every society under different names. Some call themselves mind-readers, thought-readers, crystal-gazers, phrenologists, palmists ana so on. Many of these are shrewd observers of human behaviour, particularly human weaknesses. They use their skill to gain the confidence of, and exploit the credulous and the gullible for some private ends of their own. They are not psychologists but *psycho-quacks* and belong to that underworld which flourishes almost in the name of all the great sciences.

Apart from the misconceptions and psychological racketeering, the term psychology or psychological is often used very loosely in everyday life. In fact, it is very often used when we are in great difficulty to explain something about somebody. It comes very often as a very handy phrase to shield our ignorance or lack of understanding.

What we must remember is that psychology is a *science,* and a person who calls himself a psychologist is a man who is well-trained not only in the knowledge of psychological principles that explain various complexities of psychological life of man but also in its methods of acquiring such knowledge, just as a doctor who is well-trained in the methods and principles of medical science is able to explain disease and treat it, or a physicist who is trained in the science of physics, is able to explain the laws governing the physical bodies, their movement etc.

Keeping these things in our mind, we may now take up the question: "What is Psychology?"

## WHAT PSYCHOLOGY IS?: HOW IT VIEWS MAN AND HIS BEHAVIOUR?

We may broadly say that the roots of psychology lie deep in our curiosity to know ourselves as well as our fellowmen, to reach deeper and fuller understanding of the psychological principles that govern human and animal behaviour. But this curiosity has both advantages as well as disadvantages. The advantages are that our curiosity to know ourselves and others may stimulate our interest in ourselves and in others, but very often it may lead only to some superficial understanding of human nature or behaviour. In fact, many of the psycho-quacks we mention earlier may have only a very superficial understanding of human behaviour, but that is hardly enough Psychology, on the other hand, aims at a fuller, truer and deeper understanding of the principles that govern human behaviour, and this it achieves by utilising proven and almost infallible methods of science. For understanding how psychology approaches the study of man to understand his psychological processes we must glance briefly at the history of psychology. This will also help us to know how modern psychology has developed out of the efforts of many great psychologists of bygone days.

### *Approaches to the Study of Man*

Psychology emerged as a science less than a century ago. In fact, it may be said without any reservation that certain discoveries of sciences like physics and physiology during the last century had a deep impact on the thinking of psychologists of those days. For instance, the discovery of the physicists that the sound sensations we experience are dependent upon the frequencies of the sound waves had a great impact on the thinking of early psychologists. Similarly, the physiologists in those days had shown that an artificial stimulation of certain structures of the sense organs and brain gives rise not only to *sensations* of various sorts, but also to *reflexes* and various other aspects of behaviour. These and various other discoveries led psychologists in those days to think that psychology, like other sciences, could forge ahead by utilising the scientific methods. Many *schools* or *isms* developed in those days. They differed in their views of man, objectives of psychology, and their approaches to study man. Often, these schools clashed, with each other, and many lively psychological controversies arose. Some of these schools have no doubt enriched our understanding of man and his behaviour by their unique contributions and, as we shall see, influenced the development of psychology to some extent. It is necessary, therefore, to know these views for a better understanding of modern psychology. The important among them are reviewed briefly below as different approaches to the study of man.

***Structuralism***

Structuralism was one of the earliest schools to propose its own view of man. It owes its ideas to the scientific climate of those days and influenced the thinking of early experimental psychologists. The central thought of the school was borrowed from physics and chemistry known as the *atomic theory* of matter. The theory stated that all complex substances (or matter) are composed of fine elements and these could be analysed into their elements, or *atoms*. Even modern physics and chemistry subscribe to this view.

Taking inspiration from the atomic theory, some psychologists started searching for *mental elements* from which, they thought, they could describe the various mental functions. According to them, *sensations* (resulting from a stimulation of sense organs) like blue, green, sweet, putrid, etc., were such elements. They also tried to discover the laws or principles by which such elements could be combined and gave rise to various mental functions.

**Fig. 22.1.** Wilhelm Wundt, who established his first psychology laboratory in Leipzig in 1879, was a structurialst.

For discovering the elements, the structuralists used a special experimental method known as *introspection*, by which the subjects were trained to look into themselves, observe their simple experiences and describe them as accurately as possible. For instance, some visual, auditory, tactile or smell stimuli were presented to the subject, and he was asked to describe his experience as precisely as possible according to some set instructions.

Structuralism contributed a great deal to our understanding of sensory processes: but soon its own studies revealed that the mind, which they were trying to investigate, was not a composite thing made up of elements (known as sensations), but something much more complex. Structuralism has disappeared from the psychological scene, in the sense that now no one subscribes to this view; but the *mind,* which the structuralists tried to probe by their own methods, is still very much a live issue in modern psychology.

Weber (1795-1898), Fechner (1801-1887), Wundt (1832-1920) and Titchner (1867-1927) were leading structuralists of the time.

***Functionalism***

In the latter half of the 19th century and the early years of the present century, the theory of evolution pro-pounded by Sir Gharles Darwin (1809-1882) exercised a great influence on the minds of thinkers all over the world. Even the psychologists of that era were no exception to this. In brief, Darwin's theory is of natural selection, which emphasises that it is the struggle for existence which leads to the survival of the few that are the fittest. The fittest are those who *adapt* themselves most adequately to their environment, those who cannot adapt, perish and leave no offsprings. The survivors transmit their desirable characteristics to their offsprings through the process of heredity. The theory further states that the process of natural selection, carried over millions of years, leads to such distinctly different organisms as cats, monkeys and man.

**Fig. 22.2.** William James, Founder of Functionalism

Darwin further pointed out that man's structural as well as psychological characteristics have evolved from those of prehuman organisms like the monkeys. Under the influence of Darwin's theory, psychologists as well as biologists became interested in the investigation of animal behaviour. These studies were mainly aimed at answering such questions as: How do the sensory processes of animals work? What are their learning abilities? At what level of evolution does *consciousness* appear in animals? Does it in any way resemble human consciousness? Can animals think or reason?

Physiologists and biologists have found out the answers to many of these questions, but they have miserably railed to get inside the animals and study their consciousness. We can tell whether or not an animal can respond to various aspects of its environment, but we do not know what an animal consciousness is like, or even whether it exists.

An American school of psychology that arose under the influence of Darwin is known as *functionalism.* Its two eminent proponents were William James (1842-1910) and John Dewey (1859-1952). The functionalist's point of view is contained in James's book, *The Principles of Psychology.* Like Darwin, the functionalists believe that behaviour and mental processes are *adaptive* in their nature and help an organism to *adjust* itself with its ever-changing environment. While Wundt and his followers had been trying to describe human consciousness and experience in terms of basic elements, the functionalists thought that consciousness should be studied from the standpoint of how it *helps in adjustment.* However, the functionalists, who believed that psychology should deal primarily with human capacities and abilities, did not know when consciousness appeared in animal life. They also could not devise adequate method: of investigating consciousness. They made use of introspection (a method used by the structuralists) and experimental observation to study the adaptive characteristics of behaviour.

Functionalists, thus, emphasised the *functions* rather than the *contents* or *composition* of consciousness. Unlike the structuralists, they were more interested in determining what consciousness *does* than what it *is.* It was a psychology of adaptation or adjustment, or the application of Darwin's theory to the psychological field. They used the introspection method, and *behaviour,* as a means of *adjustment,* came under their very close scrutiny.

Present-day psychology may be broadly called functional in its nature because it studies the adjustment of an organism to its environment. But, as we shall see, under the influence of some new views, it has driven out of its field, all such concepts as the consciousness and the mind.

### *Behaviourism*

The school of psychology, which has influenced modern psychological thought very deeply and holds its firm sway even today, is known as *behaviourism.* The leader of this school was John B. Watson (1878-1958) of the Johns Hopkins University in the United States. Watson grew up in the traditions of functionalism and his 'ism' may be more appropriately called "objective functionalism." The main point of difference between functionalism and Watson's behaviourism is that he was strongly opposed to the use of mental concepts like mind or consciousness. Watson contended that psychology should give up studying consciousness (conscious experience), whether in terms of its content or its functions. He also felt that the introspective method, which was used by many functionalists, (and also the structuralists) was an entirely *subjective* method and that no science worth its name could use it for collecting data for the science of psychology. He argued that in order to make psychology a full-fledged objective science, its data must be open to public inspection like the data of any other science. As long as you study what an organism *does* or *accomplishes*, you have an *objective* science, distinct from a *subjective* science to which introspection confines you. Behaviour is public, consciousness is private (because nobody except the introspecting individual can perceive it), and science should deal with public facts rather than subjective ones. Watson Wanted psychologists to look *outward* to obtain facts, like such other natural scientists like the physicists and the biologists, and not *inward* as the functionalists or the structuralists did.

**Fig. 22.3.** John B. Watson, founder of behaviourism, who did pioneer research on animal and child psychology.

Watson's thinking was deeply influenced by the investigations in contemporary biology and physiology which studied such physiological mechanisms as the brain, nerves, glands and muscles, underlying oven (observable) responses to stimuli. He based his psychology on *Stimulus-Response* connections (S-R connection) which, he believed, were established through a process very much like the process of the *association of ideas*, first proposed by Aristotle and later developed by many British philosophers.

The basic concept of the behaviourists is that behaviour grows more and more complex through the process of forming new connections (associations) between the stimuli and responses which were originally unrelated. Thus, the behaviourists viewed man's behaviour as composed of discrete and independent *stimulus-response units* tied together by some connection or bond of association. Behaviourism is also a sort of atomism like structuralism. The basic behaviour element, according to behaviourists, is the S-R connection. Watson was influenced considerably by the work of such Russian physiologists as I. P. Pavlov and Bechterev.

**Fig. 22.4.** Ivan Pavlov, Nobel Prize-winning Russian Physiologist, whose work on conditioned reflexes influenced Behaviorism.

Because of the inherent weaknesses of functionalism, behaviourism caught on very rapidly in America in the twenties, but the initial excitement created by Behaviourism has now subsided considerably. One important remnant of Behaviourism in the contemporary psychology is known as S-R Psychologists (Stimulus-Response psycologists). These psychologists maintain that psychological phenomena can be best investigated by determining causal connections *between stimulating* conditions and *responses* of a wide variety. According to them, all behaviour is response to stimuli, whether the behaviour is *overt* (like running, shouting crying) or *covert* (like thinking, feeling or dreaming). One advantage of the S-R psychology is that it is easily amenable to objective scientific investigation. Presently, many psychologists have enlarged upon original S-R theory by inserting an '0' between S and R, that is S-O-R, which stands for such aspects of responding *organism* as its typical characteristics, motivation, previous experience and other such things which may also influence the R (response), besides the S (stimulating conditions). The present status of behaviourism is that of a methodology, that is, a means of discovering information about behaviour and not so much as that of a school with its own philosophy materialism.

Many of the contemporary psychologists agree with Watson that psychology should be a natural science like physics or chemistry, with emphasis on its objective methodology.

They, however, refuse to accept his materialistic philosophy because they feel that behaviourism is an elective scientific methodology for discovering facts about behaviour and in no sense a philosophy or ism laying down the nature of the ultimate reality. That is why contemporary behaviour psychologists may use behaviouristic methodology' without necessarily subscribing to Watson's materialistic thought.

### *Gestalt Psychology*

When Behaviourism was gaining ground in America in the early years of this century, another new school of psychology was appearing in Germany under the name of *Gestalt Psychology*. This school was founded by Max Wertheimer (1880-1943) and was best known in America by the works of Wolfgang Kohler (1887-1937), Kurt Koffka (1886-1941) and Kurt Lewin (1890-1947)—all exiles from Germany. In many respects, Gestalt psychology was a protest against certain aspects of both Structuralism and Behaviourism. It indicated that both Structuralism and Behaviourism had given a wrong lead to psychology by subscribing to the atomistic view and searching in vain for such elements of behaviour as sensations or conditioned reflexes. The word Gestalt may be translated as *form* or *configuration*. Sometimes, these Gestalt psychologists are also called *configurationalists* or *holists* because of their emphasis on the "whole person" or the "whole situation".

**Fig. 22.5.** Wolfgang Kohler, one of the founders of the Gestalt School of Psychology.

According to them, our experiences and behaviour are not compounded of simple elements for which the structuralists and behaviourists searched. Rather they are the patterns, or organisations, similar to those in the *magnetic field* in which events in one part of the field (organisation) may be influenced by the events in any other part of the field. Just as a house is much more than a mere pile of bricks (having qualities like architectural style proportion which are not *reducible* to the bricks), an act is more than a group of reflexes; and a conscious experience is more than a group of sensations, feelings and images, usually organised in some pattern or configuration. Thus, according to the Gestalists, our experience depends upon the *pattern* that the stimuli form or on the *organisation* of our experience. What we see or perceive is always relative to the background and other aspects of the whole.

These psychologists used a method known as *phenomenology*, which is very similar to the method of introspection outlined earlier except that in this method, the introspecting subject is not trained to analyse his experience, but to convey his impressions about the experience without making any attempt at *analysis* or *dissection* of the experience.

Gestalt psychologists derived psychological principles on the basis of their study of perception, and then they applied them systematically to various aspects of life like memory, problem-solving and learning.

### *Psychoanalysis*

At about the same time functionalism began to thrive in America, the school of psychoanalysis came into existence in Europe. The schools of psychology discussed above developed within the *sphere* of psychology, but psychoanalysis was an exception to this. It developed out of the psychiatric practice of Dr. Sigmund Freud (1856-1939), a Viennese physician who became interested in the treatment of various forms of neurosis. The major contribution of psychoanalysis is that it has suggested a new approach to the study of human behaviour; its emphasis is on unconscious mental processes. Freud and his followers held that the great driving forces of humanity are unconscious systems of ideas or cravings of a sexual nature. Freud used the term *"sex"* broadly to include any craving for pleasure. According to him, these wishes or urges were usually not felt directly in the consciousness, yet they influenced behaviour in numerous indirect ways unknown to the individual.

Psychoanalysis started as a means of discovering the causes and cure of the personality defects which arise from unconscious urges. Its therapy mainly consists in bringing the unconscious drives into the consciousness and learning to control their working. This is done by a technique known as Free Association, in which the patient freely speaks about whatever that comes to his mind.

There are many traditional problems in psychology about which psychoanalysis has very little to say: for instance, problems such as the nature of learning and the organisation of human abilities. Moreover, it relies entirely on the clinical method, neglecting experimental verification of its theories. However, in recent years, a lot of experimental verification of psychoanalytic concepts has been undertaken.

The major contribution of this approach is to the study of abnormal behaviour and personality developrnent, and its theories have very profoundly influenced modern Child Psychology, Abronmal Psychology and Personality Theory.

The classical psychoanalysis of Dr. Sigmund Freud has undergone a sea-change in the last fifty years, though its contribution to psychological thought has been unique. The other isms or schools of thought which arose from the influence of psychoanalysis are *Analytical Psychology* founded by Carl Jung (1875-1961) and *Individual Psychology* of Alfred Adler (1870-1937). Freud occupies an unique place in psychology and he is often compared with such great scientists as Newton or Einstein.

**Fig. 22.6.** Dr. Sigmund Feud, founder of Psychoanalysis

### *Humanistic Psychology*

As the Gestalt School of Psychology arose as a protest against atomistic interpretation of the structuralists and behaviourists to understand man, *the Humanistic School* of psychology has come up as a reaction to the over-emphasis of modern psychology on the use of scientific and analytic methods in understanding man. One important aspect of the modern scientific method is its craze for breaking down behaviour into its constituent parts (known as *reductionism)* with a view to understanding behaviour by utilising controlled experimental procedures. But in recent times, many psychologists have rebelled against this because they feel that such an approach will never give them an understanding of the *whole* individual and his *true* nature. "How can we," they ask, "construct a picture of the total man, first by reducing him into innumerable fragments and then by trying to know what he is, by piecing together these fragments? In doing so, are we not destroying those integrative elements which hold him together?"

Humanistic psychology is relatively a latest development, and much of its inspiration comes from a school of modern European philosophy known as existentialism developed by such eminent philosophers as Kierkegaard, Nietzsche, Heidegger, and Sartre, and many American psychologists such as Tillich, Rollo May, Eric Formm, Maslow, Allport and Rogers. Existentialism is not a clear and complete personality theory; but it emphasises the uniqueness of the individual, the consciousness of his own self, his freedom or choice, his quest for the values of life, and his responsibility for determining the meaning of his existence.

**Fig. 22.7.** Charlotte Buhler, leading spokesman of the Humanistic School of Psychology

Charlotte Buhler is a leading spokesman of the Humanistic School of Psychology. 'This school attempts to understand a human being as a whole. This is possible only if an intimate knowledge of the individual's experiential history is taken into account. Such knowledge alone can give some clue to an individual's present behaviour. Humanistic psychology also lays emphasis on understanding an individual's motives and intentions because they are the basis of meaning and values in an individual's life. It also believes that each individual is unique in his motives, intentions, and the values and meaning he attaches to his life. It is, therefore, meaningless to generalise from one individual's experiences to another, as psychologists usually do. Because of their great emphasis on understanding the innermost self of the individual, the humanist psychologists do not have any faith in the extreme objective methods like experimentation used by the behaviourists and other psychologists. They feel that any attempt to analyse the individual's behaviour inevitably results in our overlooking the integrative constituents of the human personality, and thus makes the total understanding of an individual impossible.

### *Neurobiological Approach*

The human brain is supposed to be the greatest marvel that Nature has produced. Its twelve billion cells and their infinitely complex interconnections control almost every aspect of our behaviour. Neurobiology tries to reduce our overt behaviour and mental events to various events taking place in our *brain* and *nervous system*. In short, it tries to relate various human responses, including memory, learning and thinking, to the neural activities in the brain and the nervous system.

Advances in electronic technology and other branches of science have made it possible for us today to investigate the functions of the various parts of our brain with considerable ease, With the new knowledge obtained by these methods, of the functioning of the brain and the nervous system, many psychologists are thinking now of specifying; every human action in terms of the neurobiological mechanisms underlying them. These psychologists feel that it would be possible to build up a comprehensive neurobiological theory of man in the very near future. The main difficulty in such efforts, however, is the non-availability of live human subjects, who could serve as the guinea pigs for such experimentations, Again the task seems to be extremely complex because even if these processes are understood they may not explain all the varieties of human experience. But no one can tell what possible developments the present research will lead to in future.

***Eclectic Approach***

We have only broadly outlined some of the major approaches to the study of man, and it is quite likely that you will get at times dismayed and confused by their conflicting positions. It is, therefore, necessary that we specify our own approach to the study of man so that such confusion may be avoided. As we are going to study Psychology as a science, we shall obviously place greater emphasis on the understanding of behaviour on the basis of the scientific and experimental work already done rather than on rigidly following any particular ism or school of psychology. The obvious intention in doing this is, of course, to be as objective in our understanding of behaviour as possible. By and large, such an approach has always been fruitful and has led to a greater understanding of behaviour. It is known as *eclectic* approach or an approach which chooses the best things out of the various views or isms which we considered so far.

Each of the principle schools we have discussed above has made an important contribution to the development of psychology and has left its mark on it. Few contemporary psychologists adhere whole-heartedly to one or another of these isms. Psychology, today, is characterised by a broadened viewpoint, which accepts each school for what it has to offer in achieving the fundamental aim of psychology-understanding of man and his behaviour or experience. Although controversies and even hostilities have often raged among diverse schools, there has now come about a compromise towards a more constructive approach to the theories which are essential for the study of man.

Besides, the theoretical orientation of a psychologist depends largely upon the field of study in which he is engaged. For instance, a clinical psychologist would find psychoanalysis more valuable than behaviourism or structuaralism, while the animal psychologist will be influenced by behaviourism, and an educational psychologist may subscribe to the tenets of Gestalt and the functional school. Thus, isms in psychology today have restricted spheres of influence. As we are going to be scientific in our discussions, we shall obviously place more emphasis on scientific facts and describe other viewpoints on specific topics wherever possible.

## DEFINITION AND NATURE OF PSYCHOLOGY

Psychology may be defined as the science of human and animal behaviour. For this definition to be more meaningful to you, it is necessary to specify clearly what psychologists mean by *behaviour* and *science.*

### *Behaviour*

The worn behaviour is used in a very broad sense in psychology, and it includes all the activities of an organism which can be observed by another person or by means of an experimenter's instruments.

Most of the verbs like eating, sleeping, drinking, blushing, running, cycling, crying, weeping, yawning actually describe behaviour of some sort or the other which can be observed by the naked eye; but there can be other activities of an organism, which may be observed with the aid of some instruments; for example, changes in blood pressure, breathing, electrical potentials of the muscles or brain waves, electrical resistance of the skin and various reflexes, which can be recorded with the help of instruments; and on the basis of such records, some activities of an organism can be inferred. Thus, in psychology, not all behaviour is observed by our senses; some can be better observed by utilising certain techniques or instruments, and can he thus inferred from such records.

Besides these, organisms often show a number of goal-directed activities like seeking food, sex, avoiding pain, etc. These are also grouped under behaviour.

Again, a number of internal processes like thinking, remembering, learning, and emotional responses are regarded as behaviour of an organism. Many of these, like thinking, for example, cannot be directly observed; but something about it can be inferred from the behaviour of an organism, when it faces a problematic situation.

Because of its close relationship with the biological sciences, psychology is not only interested in human behaviour but also in animal behaviour. In a majority of studies on animal behaviour, however, the objective is often to see how such studies can give us a better understanding of human behaviour. On the whole, the experience of psychologists shows that a study of the behaviour of the lower animals is often very useful in understanding human beings because of the great similarities in human and animal behaviour. This, however, does not mean that there are no striking differences between animal and human behaviour. In fact, there are many. Nevertheless, with proper precautions in interpretation, studies in animal behaviour very often throw an interesting light on human behaviour.

One important reason why animal studies occupy such an important place in modern psychology is that we can control the lives of the lower animals in the laboratory right from the time of their birth, which is very often useful for us in understanding such powerful influences on behaviour a heredity and environment. Similarly, many laboratory experiments, which we can perform on animals, can never be done on human beings for various ethical and other reasons. For example, in many animal studies, brain surgery is undertaken with a view to observing its effects on animal behaviour, or in some studies the sex behaviour of the animal is controlled according to the experimenter's convenience to study certain effects. Who can think of subjecting a human being to such experimental conditions without violating many ethical and other considerations? In any case, studies of animal behaviour are of great help in understanding man and his behaviour.

### *Conscious Processes and Behaviour*

Initially, many psychology students often fail to appreciate how psychologists can understand man without taking into account certain inner processes which are often termed as *consciousness* or conscious experience. We must, therefore, be explicit here about certain things in order to clear up such confusions.

Each one knows the feelings one has experienced when one is hungry or angry, or when one is praised or rebuked, or when one is undergoing some conflict or anxiety in one's life. Each one has his own world of memories, flights of imagination, pleasures, pains, fears, dreams, ambitions, values, etc. This is the private world of one's own *consciousness* or *conscious experience.* By conscious experience we mean *those aspects of the human personality of which only the person himself is aware.*

Psychologists are also interested in this world of consciousness even though they have no method of observing it directly except by using *inference* as the only tool. It is common knowledge that we can know about a person's inner world—at least to a certain extent—by observing some external signs. For example, we can know whether a man is in pain or joy by carefully observing his facial and other expressions. Yet the actual experience of pleasure or pain he is experiencing may be of his own, belonging entirely to his own conscious experience.

There is a great controversy among psychologists about the place of conscious experience (conscious processes) in psychology (to which we have already referred indirectly while discussing the various approaches to the study of man). Some psychologists, belonging to the School of Behaviourism, believe the private experiences have no place in psychology, because psychology is an outright objective science. The best way for psychology to achieve cent per cent objectivity in its observations is to study human beings just as we study animals. In the study of animal behaviour, we never ask them questions about their feeling and experience because they cannot speak; yet we can study animal behaviour. Why should we not follow the same objective techniques in the study of man? This is how these psychologists argue.

There are many others however, who do not subscribe to the above view. Their argument is that the private experiences of man are just as much a part of his world as are the activities which are readily observable. It is true, they argue, that science should be objective; but this does not mean that verbal reports (about a person's conscious experiences collected by using the method of introspection, in which the scientist describes his feelings or experience in relation to a stimulating situation) of a person's experiences are not objective data—because what you report about your inner experience is also a part of your observable behaviour, for it can be recorded and even replayed for an understanding of its significance in the light of the other aspects of a person's behaviour. It is true that such reports may not give full access to a person's inner world of consciousness; yet many valuable inferences can be drawn and have been drawn from such reports. Thus, these psychologists believe that even introspective reports of an individual's conscious experiences are very useful because we can infer from them things that would be valuable not only to the person concerned but also to psychology.

### *Unconscious Processes and Behaviour*

Conscious processes are those private and personal experiences of an individual of which he may be aware himself, so that he can express them in his own words. But *man is not always aware of all his wishes, thoughts, feelings and urges and yet they may influence his behaviour in various ways—these are called unconscious processes.* These, no doubt, exist and influence our behaviour is known to psychologists beyond any shadow of doubt. The question that arises is: "Can we classify such processes as behaviour?" Here, again, psychologists are divided. Obviously, those who restrict the meaning of behaviour only to the observable activities (including those that can be recorded by instruments) of an, organism and are of the view that conscious processes should not be taken into consideration in any study of psychology, are opposed to the inclusion of unconscious processes as a form of behaviour. But there are many psychologists who feel that these processes should also be included in behaviour. These psychologists feel that from speech, gestures and various other signs of behaviour, it is not difficult to infer some unconscious processes in man. For example, a man who wears excessively gaudy and loud clothes or who talks boastingly about his imaginary or real exploits may be unknowingly or unconsciously trying to seek attention from others or hide his own feeling of inferiority. In fact, it is difficult to draw a sharp distinguishing line between conscious and unconscious processes. Many psychologists feel that there are degrees of awareness or consciousness, So, we may be *clearly* aware of some of our conscious experiences, only *dimly* aware of some, and *not at all* aware of a few. But by observing behaviour, including answers given to probing questions, it is not difficult to draw correct inferences about these processes. This is the reason why many psychologists are inclined to include them in the definition of the term behaviour.

The above discussion should make clear the meaning of the word *behaviour* as it is used in the definition of psychology. Thus, we may define behaviour as those activities of an organism which can be observed by another person or by an experimenter's instruments and such activities may include verbal reports of the subjective experiences of varying degrees of consciousness.

### *Science*

Science is another key word in the definition of psychology, which we often use in written and spoken language. It is a fact, however, that many of us do not understand its real meaning. It is necessary, therefore, to know precisely what we mean by science and what are the true characteristics of science.

*General Nature of Science:* Science begins with observation, the importance of which is very well illustrated by a humorous story from a famous thinker and founder of modern science, Francis Bacon (1905), which is summarised in the following paragraph:

"In the year 1432, there arose a grievious quarrel among the brethren over the number of teeth in the mouth of a horse. For thirteen days the dispute was raised. All the ancient books and chronicles were consulted, weighty arguments and counter arguments were put forth, but the end of the dispute did not come in sight. On the fourteenth day, a young friar arose and suggested the quarrelling men to look into the open mouth of a horse and find the answer to their question. But the men were greatly humiliated by the suggestion; they felt that Satan must have possessed the young man to suggest such an unholy and unheard of way of finding the truth, contrary to all the teachings of their forefathers. Their anger was so great that after pelting the young man sufficiently, they bodily threw him out of their assembly."

Actually, the youthful friar had stated a fundamental principle of science, namely, *to find the facts* rather than *depend upon authority* or *sheer speculation.* It is in this sense that all the sciences, including psychology, are *empirical,* that is, they collect their facts by direct observation and/or by experiment Authority, opinion, intention, speculation and guess work have no place in any science including psychology.

A scientist's observation or experiment begins with some question or problem; then he looks for relevant information to find the answer to the problem. If such information is not available from other sources or scientists, he carries out his own observations or experiments in such a way that other persons could do similar observations or experiments and can *verify* the data or the information obtained by him.

*Verifiability* is, thus, another most distinguishing characteristic of science; it adds to the reliability and accuracy of a scientist's information because the observations on which the information is based can be checked by repeating them by any one who is doubtful about them.

A scientist also uses *reasoning* as a main tool in order to arrive at the principles and generalisations of the science. For this purpose, he makes use of both the *inductive* and *deductive* methods of reasoning. The most distinguishing feature of scientific reasoning is that it is based upon most reliable and valid facts obtained by scientific methods of observation (which we shall discuss in some detail in the next section). This is the reason why scientific knowledge is always more *secure* than any other knowledge, for it is always based on repeatedly verified, rechecked and proven facts. This is also the reason why science proceeds, at times, with painfully slow speed, obtaining only small bits of information after a painstaking research for the facts that have to be checked and rechecked before they are finally admitted to the body of knowledge known as science. *Science may be, thus, defined as a systematized body of knowledge, obtained by carefully observing and measuring events, or of proven facts.*

As the scientific process proceeds, more and more facts are collected and a stage is reached when a scientist begins to realise that seemingly *disparate* facts are *interrelated.* He realises that *this plus this* leads to *this.* Such interrelated facts are then woven into systems of thoughts known as *theories,* which are attempts at explaining groups of facts in a most consistent and meaningful way. Theories are essential in science because mere facts, by themselves, have hardly any meaning. It is the theories which make them meaningful. Theories are formulated when there are sufficient facts from which it is possible to *reason* and to *go beyond* the facts. They are essential for science because they always mean a step further in the progress of science. Huxley says: "Those who refuse to go beyond facts rarely get as far as facts." Science would stagnate in the absence of theories.

When there are a sufficient number of theories to explain the various interrelated facts, science reaches a stage where seemingly *disparate* theories may begin to show some *interrelationship* and pave the way for building more and more *comprehensive theories.* It is a stage in which the scientist may argue: "If *this* leads to *this* and *that,* then *they* must lead to such and such. . . ."

A theory, whether it is more comprehensive or less comprehensive, always leads to more observations to test its adequacy or remove its defects, if it is inadequate. Science is a continual process in which new theories are *constructed,* inadequate theories are *rejected* and effective theories are *assimilated* to the main body of science, depending upon their adequacy in explaining old and newly discovered facts. There are no final answers in science. New facts may dislodge old theories; sometimes scientists may have to modify them or-enlarge upon them or construct new theories which, in the course of time, may undergo the same fate. This is why science is an *ever-widening process,* bringing under its purview the dark and unilluminated regions of the unknown.

Because of their penchant for precision and accuracy, all modem sciences dense their own techniques of measuring phenomena and thus unambiguously describing them under their own particular field of investigation. *Measurement* automatically implies the use of quantitative measures or numbers, and reaches its utmost perfection in mathematics and certain natural sciences like physics and chemistry. But in many others, like zoology, botany or psychology, it may not be always possible to achieve that precision or accuracy because of the very nature of these sciences. Under such circumstances, the scientists may devise methods of measuring phenomena in some less precise manner, such as by methods of classification and categories, or by some accurate verbal descriptions to serve the same objective which is often achieved by numbers or numerical measurement. We shall come across many such measures in the course of our study. This is the reason why, despite the earnest attempts of psychologists, many psychological concepts like intelligence, learning, memorising, and motivation do not have the same meaning for all the psychologists, mainly because of the enormous complexity of psychological processes and also their dynamic nature. Sciences like physics are not beset with this problem because their subject is inanimate matter and can he measured very precisely.

We must accept the fact that psychology is a science because it possesses all the basic characteristics of a systematised body of knowledge called "science". Psychology is governed by the same rules of scientific enquiry which we discussed in some detail so far, and applies them to its own objective of *understanding man, animals and their behaviour*.

## PSYCHOLOGY AND OTHER SCIENCES

Psychology has a close affinity with many sciences, although it belongs to a group of sciences known as *behavioural sciences*. Other sciences belonging to this group are anthropology, sociology, economics, history and political science. Among these, psychology has a closer affinity with anthropology and sociology because many of their interests overlap.

*Anthropology* is the study of the *physical evolution of mankind*. It *studies* the origins of racial groups and the development of civilisations and various preliterate cultures. Anthropological studies have helped psychology in understanding the role of cultural factors in shaping human behaviour and personality.

*Sociology* studies the laws underlying the development and functioning of groups of all kind—social, political, economic, religious, etc. It studies both formal and informal groups, with special emphasis on the observable characteristics of groups, their structure and functioning. Sociology has helped psychology not only in understanding group behaviour but also the social factors that influence individual behaviour.

### *Psychology and Physical Sciences*

Besides the behavioural sciences described above, psychology also has a close affinity with many physical sciences, from which it has borrowed not only ideas but also instruments and equipment for psychological laboratories. For example, physics has supplied psychology with instruments like Galvanometers, amplifiers, time-measuring devices, electric computers, and so on. Many methods of chemical analysis are also used by psychological laboratories for such diverse purposes as determination of blood composition under varying psychological conditions, or determination of the effects of drugs and hormones, etc., on behaviour.

### *Psychology and Biological Sciences*

*Biology* and *physiology* are two other sciences which have contributed immensely to an understanding of behaviour. Many of the early experiments in psychology were concerned with sensory processes and hence with sense organs and the nervous structures, which are mainly studied by *physiologists* and *anatomists*. Similarly, studies on brain lesions and their correlation with behaviour were made possible only because of the advances in *neurology* and related sciences. *Genetics* has contributed to the psychologist's understanding of the role of such factors as heredity. *Embryology* has contributed to an understanding of the development of animal and human behaviour, while *Ecology* has contributed to an understanding of the adaptation of an organism to its environment.

### *Psychology and Medicine*

Among the medical sciences, psychology has a very close affinity with *psychiatry*, often called *medical psychology.* It has contributed largely to our understanding of abnormal behaviour. *Pharmacology* has contributed to the study of effects of drugs and hormones on behaviour, while a special branch, known as *psycholo-pharmacology,* has been growing rapidly to study the effects of drugs on beahviour. Another branch of medicine, known as *psycho-somatic medicine,* is more interested in how psychological tensions, anxieties, anger, worries may produce various organic ailments like ulcers, asthma, and so on.

In short, we may say that psychology is being constantly influenced by a host of other sciences. It has also many overlapping interests with many sciences. And, of course, psychology itself has influenced other sciences in many ways because there is not a single sphere of human activity in which psychology does not enter, directly or indirectly.

## SUBFIELDS OF PSYCHOLOGY

The science of psychology was launched when the German psychologist Wundt founded his first psychological laboratory in Leipzig in 1879. Last year, i.e., in 1979, psychology celebrated its first centenary with great pride because what started as a small seedling has now sprouted into a giant tree with many prosperous branches bearing veritable fruit:. Today there is hardly any field of human endeavour which is not affected by psychology in some way or the other. Its influence has become almost all-pervasive and has affected human thoughts and ideas in a wide variety of ways. It will be our endeavour in this section to survey the entire field of psychology so that you can understand how it has contributed, and continues to contribute to our understanding of man and his behaviour, and what the psychologists are doing in various fields of life.

It must be stated, however, that our review will be very brief because each major branch of psychology has amassed a wealth of information which is not easy to summarise within a small compass. We have, therefore, outlined only the main activities of the psychologists working in each branch. If the number of the active psychological researchers in each subfield is used as a criterion, the order in which we have outlined the subfields below should serve as an indication of their importance, usefulness and popularity.

### *Clinical Psychology*

About 30 per cent of the total number of American psychologists are clinical psychologists, their main preoccupation being with abnormal or deviant behaviour. In India also clinical psychology is the largest subfield of Indian psychology. A clinical psychologist is basically one who has received specialised training in the *causation of* abnormal behaviour, its *diagnosis* and often its *treatment* by the psychotherapeutic methods used in the correction of abnormal behaviour.

A clinical psychologist is well trained in the *aetiology* (causation) of the various forms of abnormal behaviour such as psychoneurosis, psychosis, mental retardation, psychopathic personality and many other forms of abnormal behaviour. He is also trained in the various methods of *diagnosing* abnormal behaviour through psychological testing, interview, case study and similar other techniques of diagnosis. Besides, he often specialises in *psychotherapy* or psychological methods of treating abnormal behaviour. Psychotherapy, in its simpler forms, consists in giving support to the patient at the time of crises. In its highly complex forms, however, it requires a deep understanding of the patient's motives, emotions, thoughts, and gives him an *insight* into his own problems to restore him to a state of sanity.

Clinical psychologists are usually attached to mental hospitals, but they may also be engaged in private practice. Some may be attached to community health centres, while others may be engaged in related research.

Many people often mistake clinical psychologists for *psychiatrists*. A psychiatrist is usually a person with a degree in medicine and specialised medical training in the diagnosis and treatment of mental disorders by *medical* rather than by psychotherapeutic methods. His treatment may often consist of drugs, electric or some other type of shock therapy. A psychiatrist's knowledge of psychology may not always be as extensive as that of a clinical psychologist. This is the reason why, very often, we find clinical psychologists and psychiatrists working in close co-operation. To such a team, yet another specialist in abnormal behaviour, known as a *psychoanalyst*, may often be attached. Psychoanalysts are trained in medicine but they have also specialised in the theory and treatment of abnormal behaviour known as *psychoanalysis*. This school of psychology was established by Dr. Signund Freud and has contributed greatly to our understanding of the causes and treatment of abnormal behaviour. The basic teachings of this school have already been outlined briefly (see, Approaches to the study of man). We shall have further opportunity to know about psychoanalysis in the Chapter 11, on personality.

### *Counselling Psychology*

Psychologists often make a distinction between *major* and *minor* problems of *adjustment*. The major ones, like psychoses and neuroses, fall within the scope of clinical psychology and psychiatry and often need specialised techniques of diagnosis as well as treatment. However, there are a host of other psychological problems which are less serious and which often require different skills and techniques of treatment. Psychologists who *are well versed in the diagnosis and treatment of such minor behavioural problems are known as psychological counsellors.* Very often, these counsellors have specialised in dealing with certain types of human problems. Hence there are marriage counsellors, who are skilled in treating problems in marital adjustment, child counsellors, who are skilled in dealing with the various problems of children; school or college counsellors, who deal with the problems of school and college students. We always encounter a number of problems in the various areas of life, and often don't know how to cope up with them. Counsellors are the best help in such matters. Their skill lies not only in making you understand your problem objectively but also in developing your insight into your problems so that you may gradually learn to make healthier adjustments with life.

In India, counsellors are not to be round everywhere as in the U.S.A. or many other advanced countries. A few schools and colleges in our country have started employing them in recent years. But it must be admitted that counsellors are the custodians of the mental health of the people, for they are often responsible for saving a lot of trouble, difficulties and unhappiness. Counsellors can spot out cases of persons who are likely to suffer from major mental disorders in the long run and by helping them on the path of sanity before it is too late. Counsellors can actually do a lot of worthwhile preventive work.

### *Experimental Psychology*

Experimental psychology is one of the fundamental subfields of psychology—fundamental in the sense that it carries on research and experimental work in many basic aspects of behaviour. Actually, as we have noted earlier, psychology started as a venture in which men like Weber, Fechner and Wundt tried to apply the experimental methodology of natural sciences to certain psychological problems like sensation, perception, memory, and so on. This is possibly the reason why the experimental psychology of today is also more confined to certain traditional topics of investigation like perception, learning, memorising and problem-solving. To these topics some new topic: like motivation have been added in recent years. The distinguishing characteristic of experimental psychology is that it uses the *experimental method* as the main tool of investigation and all its experiments are carried out under the rigorous control of variables (see discussion on the experimental method). Experimenters usually try to establish *causal* relationships between various stimulating conditions and behaviour. Obviously the S-R model, to which we referred while discussing behaviourism, is best suited for their purpose. Experimental psychologists also make greater use of animal subjects because of the case with which experiments can be performed on them. Most of modern psychology is actually the systematisation and application of the various psychological laws and principles discovered by experimental psychologists. It is in this sense that the experimental psychology is engaged in the fundamental research in behaviour. It should be, however, noted that today the use of experimental method is extended to social psychology, abnormal psychology and many other subfields of psychology.

### *Industrial Psychology*

The fourth largest subfield of modern psychology is *industrial psychology*. About 10 per cent of the American psychologists are directly or indirectly working in this field. In India also it is the fourth largest subfield of psychology. Its use in large industries, military, and government administration is on the increase, particularly in the post-independence era. This is because of the great strides in our country. The application of psychology in industrial and business fields, started with the use of psychological tests for the selection of the right workers for the right job; but currently the scope of industrial psychology has broadened so much that it has already its two separate subdivisions known as *personnel psychology* and *engineering psychology*. Personnel psychology is more concerned with ***selection*** and *placement* problems. The work of the industrial psychologist usually consists in the administration or psychological tests for the selection of applicants for various jobs in large industrial and business establishments. He knows the techniques of test construction so that he can construct new tests for the recruiting of personnel for various types of jobs as well as use available tests. The objective of using readymade or newly-constructed tests is two-fold: proper selection increases the efficiency of the company and it also makes the employee more efficient and happy if he is placed in a job of his own liking and interest. An industrial psychologist is also responsible for *devising* and *carrying out* effective *training programmes* of the organisation because he is well-versed in the psychology of learning and training. Moreover, an industrial psychologist acts as a *counsellor* for the employees of the company with a view to ensuring that they adjust themselves to their jobs and family life in a more satisfactory manner. An industrial psychologist is also called upon to solve a number of *inter-personal* and *human relations problems* of the establishment because of his excellent knowledge of group dynamics and human relations. Such problems often involve keeping the channels of communication open between the management and the employees so that the relations between them may run smoothly and harmoniously. To achieve these ends, an industrial psychologist may carry on opinion- and-attitude surveys and recommend various measures to the employer for an efficient, smooth and tension-free running of the establishment.

The World War II has brought to the fore many problems concerning the *relationship* between the *employee* and the *equipment* or machines which he operates. By making a judicious use of the principles of the psychology of learning, perception and human performance, *engineering psychologists* have suggested several changes in the designs and operations or the machines so that employees may have greater ease in operating them with the minimum possible expenditure of energy. The work of *human engineers* has brought about radical changes in the designs of the most commonly used equipment in various industries and many home appliances, such as stoves and refrigerators. Today, human engineering or engineering psychology is a regular branch of industrial psychology.

### *Educational Psychology*

Educational and school psychology are the two inter-related subfields of psychology ; but their objectives and aims are not the same. About 19 per cent of the total number of American psychologists work either as educational psychologists or as school psychologists. In India also there are many educational psychologists, though not many school psychologists. In Indian psychology, it is the fifth largest subfield of psychology with considerably long history—probably because we have too many people to educate.

Educational psychologists are more concerned with general psychological principles underlying the entire process of education. The main questions which educational psychology tries to answer are *When to teach? What* to *teach?* and *How* to *teach?* The first question refers to the developmental processes that gradually mature as the child grows up. It is an important problem because we should have fine judgements regarding the things to be taught at different stages of the growth of a person. Educational psychology tries to answer this question in the light of studies based on the development of the psychological processes in human beings.

Similarly, the problem of *what to teach* is important because of its close relationship with the process of maturation. Certain types of learning can be useful to the child only when he has matured sufficiently in certain faculties. Whatever is taught must also be such as to bring about an all-round development of a student's personality. We cannot think of teaching mathematics to a three-year old child, though he may be taught to count simple things.

The problem of *'how to teach'* is equally important because there are ways and means of teaching which can make education more effective, meaningful and useful, whether it is at school, high school or college level.

Psychological processes—such as maturation, learning, effective methods of teaching and training and motivating the students in the process of education-acquire great importance in the eyes of educational psychologists. Thus, broadly, we may say that the major task of educational psychology is to discover the principles upon which a sound and effective educational system may be based.

### School Psychology

Even though school (and also college) psychology has many things common with educational psychology, the school psychologists (also often known as school counsellors) are more concerned with the *problems of individual students* than with the general principles of education. Their main task is to *help* students with *various problems* to reach full *adjustment* to the school and/or college situation. These psychologists make use of psychological tests and interviews to locate the various difficulties a student is likely to face in a school or a college situation. They are well-versed in problems peculiar to the youth and are in a position to give them good guidance to reach an effective adjustment. Such a guidance usually relates to intellectual and emotional problems, difficulties in concentration on study; slow speed of reading, low motivation, vocational guidance, etc., which are very commonly encountered in school and college life. In our country, however, the school or college counselling is still in infancy and has a long way to go.

### Social Psychology

Man is primarily a social animal. He grows in the company of other people almost from the moment of his birth. Parents, members of the family, peers, neighbourhood, school, society, clubs and social institutions provide an increasingly larger social context in which he grows, being constantly influenced by other people in his environment. Man's social environment makes an indelible imprint on his behaviour. It shapes his attitudes, goals, ways of thinking, feelings, his motives, ambitions, his entire personality. Social psychology is mainly concerned with the influence of various social forces on the behaviour of an individual. Or, put in simple words, *it is concerned* with *the behaviour of man as a member of social groups.* Social psychology has a close affinity with sociology, which studies group structure and the formal characteristics of various groups. Social psychology, on the other hand, studies the impact of group life on various aspects of individual behaviour. Because of the peculiarity of its subject matter, social psychology uses its own methods of investigation and has contributed greatly to our understanding of the social behaviour of individuals. Some of the major topics which social psychology studies are: basis of interpersonal attraction;

socialisation of an individual; and group phenomena such as group structure, group dynamics, leadership, social communication, social prejudice, group tensions, social cognition, group attitudes, public opinion, national and international tension, and so on. In India, social psychology is the third largest subfield of psychology and a large number of Indian psychologists are working in this field.

### *Developmental Psychology*

The main objective of *developmental psychology* is to investigate the *changes in human behaviour that accompany changes in age.* It is an ontogenetic (relating to origin and development) study of the human organism from the time of conception to death. The individual's growth in his environment and culture forms its major concern, so that man may know himself better as well as those around him. In its effort to obtain a meaningful picture of human development through its various stages of growth, such as infancy, childhood, adolescence, youth, adulthood and old age, developmental psychology seeks to discover sequential changes in the human personality by utilising specialised scientific techniques. *Child psychology* is only a part of developmental psychology, though an important part, because behaviour and abilities grow very rapidly during this stage and early influences on behaviour leave their lasting marks on the human personality. This is, of course, not to deny the importance of other stages in human development, with peculiar problems of each age Developmental psychology has made a rich contribution to psychology by its systematic studies of intellectual and cognitive development in the early years and also by investigating a wide variety problems of adolescents, adults and aged people. Knowledge of human growth and development forms the very basis of many subfields of psychology, such as educational and school psychology.

### *Personality Psychology*

The main objective of psychological science is not only to understand the behaviour of man, but, through his understanding, construct a meaningful picture of the human personality, which is a major concern of the *personality psychologists.* This is no doubt a difficult task because individual behaviour, in view of its infinite variety, cannot be easily fitted into ready-made moulds. Yet many psychologists have tried to construct a consistent picture of the human personality on the basis of the available data obtained by using such devices as psychological tests, interviews, naturalistic observation and even experimentation. Many such models of the human personality are available today. We shall have occasion to study some of these models when we discuss the human personality in the next chapter.

It is important to note here that many of the present-day personality theories are strongly biased by the isms or the systems of psychology to which they subscribe. Such a divergence in views makes the complex task before the personality psychologists all the more difficult.

Strangely, in India the subfield, personality psychology, is the second largest, only next to clinical psychology. In America it ranks ninth, with about two per cent American psychologists working in it. It is difficult to explain why so many Indian psychologists are attracted to this field.

### *Psychometric Psychology*

Measurement of the various characteristics of human personality—such as intelligence, aptitudes, interests, attitudes and traits—has occupied the attention of psychologists almost since its inception as a science in 1879. The instruments used for such measurement are known as psychological tests and the psychologists who construct them are usually called *psychometricians.* In the last eighty years, the science of psychological testing and measurement has made stupendous progress, and many highly complex statistical and analytical techniques are used today in psychological measurement and test construction. All such measuring techniques form the major province of psychometric psychology. To establish the reliability and validity of the test constructed for measuring various aspect of the human personality is a highly sophisticated job requiring training in statistical techniques. The psychometricians are well-versed in such techniques. Sometimes a distinction is made between the *psychometricians* and the *psychometrists.* The former art fully trained in the technical aspects of test construction, while the latter are more concerned with administering and interpreting test scores.

### *Psychology in Other Fields*

The above outline of various subfields of psychology should give us a clear idea about its present scope. Psychology, however, is not restricted merely to these spheres. In fact, it would not be an exaggeration if we say that applications of the principles of psychology are to be found in almost all the spheres of human life.

Take for instance, the field of law. In a number of legal problems psychology has become useful. For instance, the lie detector technique, which is essentially a psychological technique, has been used in criminal investigations for detecting the guilty from innocents. Again, a lot of psychological research has shown the possible pitfalls in the examination of witnesses in the courts of law. Psychologists have also contributed considerably to the understanding of criminal behaviour and delinquency. Many of the methods suggested by psychologists for reformation of these people have been accepted and widely practised in prisons and remand homes.

Similarly, in the field of medical research. psychologists have made their own contributions of finding out the effects of various drugs on behaviour. Some investigations have shown how mental worries and tensions can cause physical diseases.

The military psychology also has a long history. In the development of military psychology, psychological testing, social psychology, clinical psychology and industrial psychology have made significant contributions.

Psychology also has its applications in the fields of politics and government administration. The knowledge or certain psychological principles has proved to be of immense use in the theory and practice of government.

These are only some important applications of psychological principles in various spheres of life.

## METHOD OF PSYCHOLOGY

Science is invariably characterised by its methodology or its methods of collecting facts. These methods must be such that every new information discovered by them must be verifiable if another scientist wants to repeat the same observations under similar conditions. We have seen already that it is this quality of verifiability of facts which gives scientific knowledge the validity that is rarely to be found in other branches or kinds of knowledge. Psychology uses many scientific methods which attain or approximate to this ideal of verifiability. Some of them are briefly outlined below.

### Experimental Method

The most highly developed and accurate of all the scientific methods is the experimental method. It provides a procedure for testing the validity of a tentative *hypothesis* or explanations that have been formulated or advanced on the basis of previously observed facts. This is the *most preferred* method of psychology, and has uncovered most of the basic facts of psychology. The experimental method, as applied to the subject matter of psychology, is mainly aimed at finding out the underlying causes (which are some internal or external stimulating conditions) of behaviours (responses of the organism) of various sorts. The following steps are usually to be found in psychological experimentation.

### Problem

Experimentation usually begins when there is a *problem* for which there is no satisfactory answer. Why do we forget? Why do we dream? How do we learn? How can we perceive the world in three dimensions? What happens when a man is frustrated? Why some marriages break? These are a few examples of simple psychological problems. Before beginning his observations, the Experimenter (E) carefully defines and analyses the problem under investigation. Such an analysis is very essential for framing a tentative explanation or answer to the problem on hand. It is the tentative answer that is known as *hypothesis*.

### Experimental Design

Then comes the formal statement under which observations have to be made. This is called *experimental design* and it states (i) the conditions under which the observation is to be made, (ii) describes the apparatus or instruments, if any, to be used by the experimenter for making the observations as accurate as possible and (iii) outlines the procedures to be followed and the interpretation of results. The greatest advantage of formal design is that it allows the same experimenter or other experimenters to repeat the observations with a view to check lug and rechecking the results, so that he can be reasonably sure of their truth.

### Type of Experiment

The experiments may be designed to answer two type: or problems. The first, the less sophisticated one, may be called *I wonder what would happen if I do this* design. For example, let us say a psychologist has come across some new drug X which he feels, if taken in sufficient quantities, may result in improving the memory. To find out if this is really so, he may undertake the "I wonder" type of experiment, that is he may ask himself "I wonder whether memory will really improve if the drug X is administered in sufficient quantities to human beings?" For this he will use some memorising task and also an accurate method of measuring improvement in memory. Then he may form two groups, one of which will be given a daily dose of the drug while the other group will not be given the dose. After a predetermined period, both the groups will be tested to determine the improvement in memory. If the comparisons demonstrate that the group which bad taken the drug shows considerable improvement in memory, the experimenter may conclude that the drug X is really effective.

A more evolved and sophisticated approach of forming and testing a hypothesis is known as *I bet this will happen if I do this* design. Let us take an example to illustrate this approach. Suppose that the drug X (in the previous illustration) has shown very promising results in improving memory. Then the psychologist may go a step further and reason to himself: "If the drug X improves the memory of human beings, I bet it will also improve the memory of chimpanzees because there is a great similarity in the brain and body structure of both." An experiment of this type may be performed in more or less the same manner, but the experimenter will have to devise new methods for testing the memory of the chimpanzees and also solve many other problems that may arise.

The earlier experiments in most of the sciences are of *I wonder what will happen...* type, mostly arising out of the curiosity to know and explain. But as more and more facts are accumulated by such experiments, the experimenter begins to *reason out* the possibilities by putting the relevant facts together, and performs the *I bet this will happen....* type of experiments. In such experiments, he is more certain about the outcome because he has already many facts from which he can reason out new possibilities. This type of experimentation is often known as *hypothesis testing* experimentation and is very commonly found in the advanced stages of the development of sciences. It involves deducing new relationships from the already available facts and theories and then actually testing them by performing new experiments; or deducing from well established theories, new relationships and testing them to see whether the theory is sound and adequate.

### *Experimental Variables*

The crux of the experimental method lies in the typical procedure used in testing a hypothesis, which is usually a statement concerning the *cause and-effect relationship* between the factors involved (in our example, the drug X = cause, improvement in memory-effect) in the hypothesis. In experimental terminology, these factors are called *variables.* Most of the experiments involve three kinds of variables known as (*i*) the Independent Variable (IV), (*ii*) the Dependent Variable (DV), (*iii*) the Relevant Variable (RV).

*An independent variable* is usually the cause whose effects are being studied (the drug X in our example which is supposed to cause improvement in memory). The experimenter changes or varies IV (by giving it to some *Ss* and not to other *Ss*) to find out what effects such changes produce on DV. The *dependent variable* is a factor which, according to the experimenter, is related to the independent variable as an effect, so that when the experimenter varies the independent variable, certain changes will be brought about in the dependent variable.

The effects of variation in the IV on the DV can be determined only when the possible effects of other factors in the experiment (which might also produce some changes) on the DV are fully known. The factors or variables which are likely to affect the DV, besides the IV, are known as *relevant variables* (RV). In any experiment, these relevant variables have to be *controlled* or *held constant* during the experiment: otherwise we can never reach any definite conclusion concerning the relationship between the IV and the DV because if a third factor can also influence the DV, we will never know whether it is the DV or the third factor that has brought about the changes in the DV. This requires some techniques or methods of regulating the various variables in an experiment. This process of regulating all the variables in the experiment is known as *experimental control.*

### *Control*

The main objective of experimental control is to ensure that the influence of all the relevant variables is the same for all the *Ss* and does not change during the experiment. If the experimental variables are not properly controlled, we shall never know whether it is the IV or some other uncontrolled relevant variable in the experiment which is producing these changes in the IV. That is why control is regarded as the very breath of an experiment. If it is perfect, the experiment findings are sound.

### *Experimental and Control Group*

To study the effects of the independent variable on the dependent variable, the experimenter must manipulate the variables very systematically. One commonly used technique to achieve this objective is illustrated by the use of two groups known as the (i) *experimental group* and the (ii) *control group.* As far as possible, both the groups must be exactly of the same characteristics, the only difference between them being that the IV *is introduced* to the *experimental group,* whereas it is *not introduced* to the *control group.* In such a double-group design of the experiment, the relevant variables in the experiment are held at a constant level for both the groups. This enables the experimenter to reach unambiguous conclusions regarding the relationship between the IV and the DV. The reason is that both the groups are almost identical in all respects except that the experimental group is introduced with the IV, whereas the control group is not. Thus, if the DV of the experimental group shows changes whereas that of the control group does not, the experimenter is in a position to ascribe the changes in the DV to the IV without any doubt in his mind.

Sometimes, another experimental design is used to manipulate the IV. In this, the experimenter uses the same experimental group on two different occasions. For example, in our illustration, a group may be first tested on their memory power without the IV (drug X) and then again on the second occasion after administering the IV (the drug X). Such a design is known as a *before and after test design.* However, in such an experiment, the experimenter will have to be very careful in controlling some of the relevant variables. Taking our illustration again, we can very easily see that the earlier practice in remembering the task may show some improvement in the Ss memory on the second occasion. If the experimenter has some method by which he can compute such an improvement, he can make allowance for it while interpreting his results. This can often be achieved by using another group of a similar sort, but without introducing the IV.

There are some more sophisticated experimental designs in which the effects of more than one single independent variable can also be measured simultaneously; but all such experiments are usually mere combinations of several experiments in *cne.*

### *Apparatus*

Psychological experiments are usually performed in psychological laboratories, which are the places best equipped with many facilities, instruments and apparatus of a wide variety. The main function of the laboratory equipment or apparatus is usually to aid the *control* of the conditions under which observations are made. Today, the psychological laboratories are equipped with such standard instruments as timers, mazes, memory drums, electroencephalographs, polygraphs, etc., which are useful in psychological research. But very often new apparatus have to be constructed to facilitate the recording and control of experimental conditions, depending upon the specific requirements of experiments. Recent developments in electronics have made it possible for us to record faithfully many unseen responses of the body to a wide variety of stimulating conditions, such as brain waves, blood pressure, electrical changes in the skin. However, it must be remembered that apparatus are only a means that can be helpful in experimental research and they can never take the place of the scientific reasoning that goes in making an experiment a success. Many worthwhile experiments in psychology have been actually performed without the aid of any apparatus, or very simple apparatus.

We have discussed above some outstanding features of the experimental method. It is no doubt a most preferred method of science; but it is not without its own shortcomings. First, the method can be used only where rigid control of experimental variables is feasible. Unfortunately, however, this is not always possible. Secondly. bringing something under investigation to the laboratory gets it often stripped off its realistic context and gives it an air of artificiality which is often not conducive to good scientific work. Thirdly, it has often been observed that the Ss participating in experiments do not always behave in a normal fashion and sometimes react to an experimental situation with a heightened motivation or nervousness. An expert experimenter, however, always knows how to minimise these disadvantages of the method. Again, the advantages of the method are so great that one may say, without the slightest exaggeration, that a large measure of the progress of psychological science or for that matter any other science, is mainly due to this wonderful method of science.

### *Field Study Method*

The field study method, also known as the method of *naturalistic observation* or *systematic observation,* is one of the oldest research methods which was used by astronomers, geologists; physicists and biologists of the olden days. But even today it is one of the most commonly used methods by many disciplines in science. Careful observation of animal and human behaviour is very often the starting point in psychology. Many facts of human as well as animal behaviour are learned in this fashion. The use of this method becomes all the more essential in science because it is often difficult to perform experiments on all the problems we come across. It is definitely not a substitute for an experimental method but is often applicable where experimentation is impossible.

The field study method may be described as making *direct observation of a phenomenon under investigation by going to the very palce in which it occurs.* The observer simply goes to the place with a definite question or set of questions in his mind to find out their answers by *a* careful observation of the prevalent conditions. He has, obviously, little or no control over the happenings and cannot get any cooperation from his subject. In fact, some field studies are most successful when the subjects are not aware that they are being observed. One of the greatest advantages of this method is that once the possible causes of a phenomenon are ascertained by direct and systematic observation, it often becomes easier to study the same conditions in a laboratory by introducing appropriate controls of conditions. It is in this sense that the field study method may be required as sort of a preliminary preparation for experimentation. Actually, many of the experiments in psychology are suggested by field observations.

One can very easily see the similarities and differences in this method and the experimental method. The observer, when using this method, may have some hypothesis regarding the independent variable and the dependent variable when he sets out on observation. His observations gradually reveal to him whether his hypothesis is correct or not. The difference in the two methods is mainly in the control or the phenomenon under investigation. The experimenter has full control over the conditions of observation, while the naturalistic observer has very little or almost no control. This is the reason why the results of this method are not always as reliable as those of the experimental method.

The method of field study is often very useful in psychology and can be applied with great ease in studies of public opinion, the effects of advertisements and other mass communication systems on consumer preferences and a host of social problems, and even in determining the role of such factors as heredity and environment. Anthropologists, ethologists, sociologists, social psychologists, animal psychologists, industrial psychologists and child psychologists often make use of this method for investigations in their respective areas of study because in these areas the scope for experimentation is very limited. It has been found that if proper are is taken, this method can produce results comparable to those of the method of experimentation. The value of this method is limited by the fact that anecdotes (stories, tales, etc.) may sometime usurp the place of genuine observation, and very often the observer's own interpretation of the phenomenon may mar its objective description. However, it must be pointed out here that many schools in psychology which are averse to experimental method because of its excessively analytic nature favour this method and feel that its results are much more wholesome ana better.

### *Clinical Methods*

We have already seen that clinical psychology is one of the major fields of psychology and is concerned mainly with the diagnosis, treatment and prevention of mental disorders at the individual level. A clinical psychologist wants to know what is wrong with Mr. X when the latter goes to him with some serious problem of adjustment. The question "what is wrong?" Can be answered with the help of psychological tests and clinical interviews. But when the clinician wants to treat the patient so that he may be restored to normality, he has to probe deeper into the genesis of his problem to find out the *causes* of the disorder. A clinical psychologist usually does this by constructing a detailed case history of his patient. Such a case history may often begin with the birth of the patient and may contain detailed information about the ways in which he was brought up, his relationship to his parents, friends, relatives; his likes, dislikes, worries, fears, conflicts the incidents which led to his present symptoms; his behaviour in various situations in life, and many other related things. By utilising this information, a clinician may get some insight into his patient's problem. Such information is also useful in suggesting the treatment for the patient.

Clinical psychologists probe deeper into an individual's life because his experiential background often determines his peculiar symptoms which provides for the clinical psychologist, an insight into the causation of the disorder. By utilising this method, clinical psychologists are often able to construct their own theories of mental disorders and also the methods or techniques of treatment. A classic example of this is to be found in the system of diagnosis and treatment of neurosis developed by Dr. Sigmund Freud. His knowledge of hundreds of cases of neurosis and its treatment led to the formulation of the theory of psychoanalysis.

Information obtained by the clinical method is, however, not always conducive to an understanding of abnormal behaviour. Some clinicians like Dr. Freud, however, do develop insight into the problems of mental disorder and enrich our understanding of human behaviour.

As a method of psychology, the clinical method is much inferior to the method of experimentation and even of systematic observation because it is usually too subjective, casual, uncontrolled and lacking in precise measurement.

## MEASUREMENT IN PSYCHOLOGY

Our discussion on the nature of the psychological sciences cannot be complete unless we take into account the problem of measurement in psychology. From its inception, psychology has been fashioned on the lines of natural sciences, most of which are mainly concerned with the measurement of various physical phenomena in precise, numerical terms. This is but natural because nothing can be described accurately and precisely without the use of a reliable system of measurement. Another advantage that follows from the use of measurement is that it makes the task of deduction and induction, involved in every scientific effort, easier.

However, when we talk of measurement in psychology, we are at once faced with difficulties which are not easy to overcome. First, it is difficult to define a standard unit of psychological measurement (like inches, kilos, seconds, minutes, etc.). For example, we do not have standard units for measuring such characteristics as introversion, courage and love so that we can measure them as reliably as we can measure height. Under such circumstances, a psychologist has often to utilise *relative* or *comparative* measures. For example, he implies something about introversion when he says: "A is having greater introversion than B "or" that which is possessed averagely by his age group". The problem of measurement in psychology can be best understood if we know the four basic types of measuring scales, namely, (i) Nominal Scales, (ii) Ordinal Scales, (iii) Interval Scales, and (iv) Ratio Scales.

*Nominal scales* represent the lowest level of measurement and impart the least information. The best example of such measures is provided by the large numbers printed on the shirts of the football team. They do not tell us anything, nor even about the great importance of large numbers or the low importance of small numbers.

*Ordinal scales* are slightly better, for they do not only distinguish one person from another but also tell us whether a person has more or less of the trait that is being measured. The best example of these scales is the runners in a race. The one who finishes first is faster than the second, and the second is faster than the third, and so on. By noting the order of winners, we can say who is faster or less fast; yet the order does not tell us how much the first one is faster than the second and so on, nor do we know the differences in their speeds.

The *Interval scales* have properties of nominal and ordinal scales as well as the property of equal units—that is, equal differences in scores represent equal differences in what is being measured. For example, a difference in temperature of 50° and 60° as indicated on a thermometer at a time is the same as between 20° and 30° shown at any other time. This is what we mean by equal interval units. However, from interval scales, like the one just mentioned, we cannot argue that a temperature of 60° is exactly twice as hot as that of 30°. This would have been true only if the object having 0° temperature did not have any warmth at all. But we know that a zero temperature occurs—at—273 degrees Centigrade. This means that an object with a temperature of 25° is really 298 degrees warmer than an object with zero degree temperature. Many psychological scales are of this type, that is they often have equal units but no zero value, which we find in the finest type of measuring scales known as ratio scales.

The *Ratio scales* are the highest and most ideal scales because in addition to all the qualities of the scales we have described so far, they have an additional property of an *absolute zero* at the point of origin. Thus, inches, miles, seconds, minutes, weights and measures of all sorts have an absolute zero and also equal units ; that is why the measures made in them are most reliable and can be added, divided or subtracted without any difficulty. It is also possible to think of zero length, zero time, zero weight.

**In short, the higher the level of measurement, the more accurate it is, and more information**

is obtained about the attribute that is measured. In psychology, it is often difficult to think of measures in terms of ratio scales and we have often to fall back on ordinal or equal interval scales. But we cannot help this because of the difficulties involved in the measurement of psychological characteristics.

### *Use of Statistics*

The information obtained from psychological experimentation or observation is usually in the form of one or the other measure or measures described above. But the measures, in scale units, do not by themselves give any meaning to data. They need to be treated in a certain fashion before they acquire any meaning. This is the purpose of statistics in psychology. There are a number of statistics used in psychological research. However, the statistics to be used would depend upon the measurement scale used and the information desired by the user.

Psychological statistics is of two types (1) *Descriptive* and (2) *Inferential*. The first one gives us three types of information which is very commonly used in psychological research for describing the various trends in research data, and therefore every student of psychology must know these measures.

The three types of measures used in descriptive statistics are: (1) *the measures of central tendency*, such as (i) mean, (ii) median and (iii) mode. The second type of statistics is known as *measures of variability* and its four measures are (i) range, (ii) standard deviation, (iii) partiles and (iv) standard score. The third type of statistics is known as *measures of correlation*. We have introduced here only the descriptive statistics, which is essential for understanding this book. No one should however think that statistics ends there. No, it can be highly complex.

The various measures of descriptive statistics briefly outlined below are in their simplest forms. When the data treated are very small, these measures are generally used.

## Measures of Central Tendency

### *Mode*

Mode is the easiest measure of central tendency. It is defined as the most *recurring score* or number in a group of measures. In general, the mode tells us just where in the distribution (group of measures) the concentration of measures exists. It is not a very reliable measure, but often serves as a quick, easy measure of central tendency. In A, B, and C in Table 22.1, the modes of each distribution are shown. Distribution C shows that a distribution can have more than one mode. Such distributions are called *multi-modal distributions*.

### *Median*

A median is a better measure than a mode. It is defined as the *midpoint of series of numbers*. To find out the median of a distribution, one places the numbers in a distribution in a rank order from the lowest to the highest, or vice versa, and then finds the midpoint of the distribution. This is the median. When the number of the measures in a distribution is odd, the *central number* is the median. When it is even, the two central scores are added and divided by 2 to obtain the median. The following examples illustrate these points:

**TABLE 22.1**

**Detemining the Modes of Simple Distributions**

| | DISTRIBUTIONS | |
|---|---|---|
| *A* | *B* | C |
| 3 | 0 | 1 |
| 5 | 5 | 3 |
| 7 | 2 | 3 |
| 7 | 4 | 2 |
| 7 | 3 | 4 |
| 10 | 5 | 6 |
| 11 | 7 | 6 |
| 14 | 9 | 6 |
| 16 | 5 | 7 |
| 17 | 6 | 3 |
| MODE 7 | 5 | 3 and 6 |

**TABLE 23.2**

**Determining the medians of various distributions**

| | | DISTRIBUTIONS | | |
|---|---|---|---|---|
| | *A* | *B* | C | *D* |
| | 1 | 1 | 6 | 4 |
| | 2 | 2 | 7 | 5 |
| | 3 | 3 | 4 | 7 |
| | 4 | 4 | 3 | 7 |
| | (5) median | (5) | 9 | 6 |
| | | (6) | | |
| | 6 | 7 | 8 | 5 |
| | 7 | 8 | 2 | 4 |
| | 8 | 9 | 10 | 4 |
| | 9 | 10 | 18 | 3 |
| **Median** | 5 | 5+6÷2=5.5 | 7 | 5 |

## Mean

Mean is the most frequently used and most reliable measure of central tendency. It is defined as the *average* or the *"arithmetic mean"* of a distribution. To obtain the value of the mean of distributions, first add all the measures in the distribution and then divide them by the number of the measures in the distribution. A computation of the mean, when the measures are ungrouped, is expressed by the following formula:

$$M = \frac{\Sigma X}{N}$$

When M=mean, Σ means=sum of, X=the scores, and N=the number of the scores in the distribution.

The following is an example:

Scores: 4, 7, 5, 3, 9, 2, 6, 8, 1, 7.

$$N = 10$$

$$EX = 52$$

$$M = \frac{\Sigma X}{N} = \frac{52}{10} = 5.2$$

## Measures of Variability or Spread

Two sets of scores or two distributions are rarely identical that is, they not only differ in the measures of central tendency like mode, mean and median, but also differ in terms of their *variability* or *spread* (also called *scatter*). The following distributions in the table show this:

**TABLE 23.3**

**Showing Computation of Range of 4 distributions.**

DISTRIBUTIONS

| | A | B | C | D |
|---|---|---|---|---|
| | 4 | 2 | 1 | 1 |
| | 5 | 2 | 1 | 1 |
| | 6 | 16 | 1 | 2 |
| | 7 | 19 | 2 | 2 |
| | 9 | 38 | 3 | 2 |
| | 13 | 72 | 3 | 3 |
| | 14 | 104 | 4 | 3 |
| | 20 | 119 | 4 | 3 |
| | 21 | 120 | 5 | 3 |
| | 32 | 133 | 6 | 10 |
| Mean | 13.1 | 61.5 | 3.0 | 3.0 |
| Range | 4–32=29 | 2–133=132 | 1–6=6 | 1–10=10 |

In the distributions A and B, we see that B has a greater spread than A. In the distributions C and D, we see that although the mean is the same, the variability or spread in C is less than that of D.

### *Range*

The simplest way of knowing the variability or spread of a distribution is to determine the *range* of the distribution, which can be determined by using the following equation:

$$R = H - L + 1$$

where R is the Range, H is the highest number in the distribution and L is the lowest number in the distribution.

Thus, for distribution A,

$$\begin{aligned} R &= 32 - 4 + 1 \\ &= 29 \end{aligned}$$

A range is, however, a crude measure of variability and should be used only when one has to obtain a rough measure of variability of different distributions. This point is well brought out by the distribution D in the table, in which we find that almost nine-tenths of the scores are not higher than 3 and only one of the scores is 10. In such cases the range cannot give us the real picture of a spread : rather, it conceal, it because the presence of large gaps in the score alters the size of the range. A range is therefore a useless measure when the distribution is made up of extreme scores.

### *Standard Deviation*

The words Standard Deviation are often abbreviated as SD or σ. Standard Deviation is one of the best measures of variability, and that is why it is most frequently used in psychological statistics as a sound measure of variability. When the data are ungrouped, the following procedure may be followed for determining the Standard Deviation.

(1) Find the mean of the distribution.

(2) Make a column d, and record in it the deviation of each score from the man, symbolically, X–M.

(3) Make another column $d^2$, and record in it the square of each deviation in the d column.

(4) Find the sum of $D^2$ column.

(5) Apply the following formula:

$$\text{SD or } \sigma = \sqrt{\frac{Ed^2}{N}}$$

where SD or σ is the standard deviation, $d^2$ is the sum of the deviation squared, and N is the number of the measures in the distribution. See table 23.4, which illustrates the method of computing SD.

**TABLE 23.4**

**Showing the method of determining SD when data are ungrouped**

| *Measure* | *d* | $d^2$ |
|---|---|---|
| 1 | –4 | 16 |
| 2 | –3 | 9 |
| 2 | –3 | 9 |
| 3 | –2 | 4 |
| 4 | –1 | 1 |
| 5 | –0 | 0 |
| 6 | 1 | 1 |
| 8 | 3 | 9 |
| 9 | 4 | 16 |
| 10 | 5 | 25 |
| Mean 5 | $d^2$ 90 | |

$$SD = \sqrt{\frac{d^2}{N}} = = \sqrt{\frac{90}{10}}$$

$$SD = \sqrt{9}$$

$$SD = 3$$

### *Partiles*

Partiles are the points which divide a distribution of scores into some number of *equal parts.* For example, a median may be called a partile because it divides the distribution into exactly two parts. Another very commonly used partile is known as a *quartile* or measure which divides a distribution into four equal parts or quarters. There are three quartiles in a distribution. Three-fourths of the scores are below quartile 3 or Q3, one half of the scores are below quartile 2 or Q2. The median of a distribution and Q2 are usually the same measures because they divide the distribution in two exact halves. One-fourth of the scores are below quartile 1 or Q1.

Another most commonly used partile is known as a *centile.* There are 99 centiles in a distribution, dividing it into 100 equal parts. Ninety-nine per cent of the scores are below the 99th centile, or 50 per cent of the scores are below the 50th centile.

Yet another measure is known as a *decile,* which divides the distribution into 10 equal parts, as a centile divides it into 100 equal parts. Fixing quartiles, centiles or deciles in a distribution requires transformation of the given data by statistical procedures which are too elaborate to be discussed here. These measures are very useful in psychological testing where comparisons of an individual's characteristics are to the made in relation to a group. They have many other uses too.

### *Standard Score*

Measures of variability are useful in summarising individual differences in a group. They can also serve to establish a standard unit of measurement. Suppose you want to know from Mr. X's test results, given below, whether he is fond of arithmetic or of geometry in relation to his class.

| *Test* | *Class mean* | *Mr. X's Scores* |
|---|---|---|
| Arithmetic | 13 | 20 |
| Geometry | 44 | 48 |

From the class averages and X's scores, it is obvious that the score of X is above average in both the tests: but we do not know exactly how much above average. We cannot compare these two test scores because we do not know whether one point in one test is equal to one point in the other test.

Under such circumstances, in order to relate the units in one test to another, we may make use of the measures of variability we have discussed earlier. Suppose we computed the standard deviation of the geometry and arithmetic score distributions, and they are respectively 3.57 and 4.00. This would mean X was *one* standard deviation above the mean in geometry and *two* standard deviations above the mean in arithmetic. This would mean that X did better in arithmetic than in geometry. It is possible to express any individual's deviation in similar standard deviation units. Scores expressed in this way are called standard scores or Z scores. The simple formula for expressing Z scores is:

$$\text{Z Score} = \frac{(X - \overline{X})}{SD}$$

Where Z = Standard Score

X = Ss' score

$\overline{X}$ = group mean

For example, X's score in arithmetic is 20. The mean of the group is 13, and the Sd of the distribution is 3.8. Thus:

$$\text{Z Score of X in arithmatic} = \frac{(20-13)}{3.7} = 1.8$$

An individual's standard scores in two tests may be compared directly because standard scores are expressed in equivalent standard deviation units. It must be noted, however, that what a standard score gives us is a person's position in relation to his group. It is like answering a question like: "Is X's relative performance in geometry better (or worse) than his relative performance in arithmetic, when the performance of the entire group is taken into account?" There are various other ways of determining standard scores, and they are very useful measures in descriptive statistics.

## Measures of Correlation

In psychological research, it often becomes necessary to determine the degree of relationship between two sets of scores measuring different characteristics of behaviour or between various sets of scores obtained for a number of reasons. In determining such relationships, the psychologist uses a statistical method known as *correlation*.

Correlation refers to the degree to which the paired scores on two or more variables (characteristics) tend to *vary* together. The degree of variation being always mentioned in terms of the *co-efficient of correlation*. The co-efficient of correlation indicates how much one variable *changes* with the other variable. For example, as temperature changes (that is increases), the height of mercury in the barometer changes (that is, increases). This is a perfectly close relationship. We also know that as a person's height increases, his weight also increases; but there are often exceptions to such relationship. This is not such a perfectly close relationship. Sometimes there may be no relationship at all. For example, can we say that as the weight of a person increases, his capacity to solve mathematical problems increases? In some cases, we may obtain, what is known as a negative or inverse relationship. For example, there is always a negative correlation between the IQ of an individual and the number of his failures in his school career, that is, the greater the number of failures, the lower is the IQ.

When one variable increases with the other, the relationship between them is called *positive*. All the co-efficients of correlation (computed by employing the methods described in the next section), ranging from +. 1 to + 1, indicate positive correlationships between variables. Others ranging from –.1 to –1 indicate *negative correlation-ships;* when there is no relationship at all, the co-efficient of correlation is *zero* or near *zero*. The most important advantage of correlation is that it can tell us instantly the exact degree of correlationship between two variables on the basis of the scores obtained on them by the same group of individuals. You will see later that such relationships are extremely important for psychologists in a wide variety of research and experimentation.

### *Methods of Determining Correlation*

There are several methods of determining the co-efficient of correlation, of which the Product Moment Method and the Rank Order Method are very frequently used. The Rank Order Method of determining correlation is also known as the Spearman's Rank Difference Method. The co-efficient determined by this method is indicated by ρ, pronounced as *rho*. The method is usually used when the scores are in terms of ranks. The Steps in Finding Rank Order Correlation are outlined below:

*Step 1:* Record paired raw scores in column XY (as shown in table 22.5.)

*Step 2:* Assign ranks to each score in the X column, then do the same for the Y column. Assign rank 1 to the lowest score in the column, then 2,3,4 and so on to the higher scores. In case two or more subjects receive the same rank, first average the ranks their scores would occupy and then assign the mean rank value to each. (For example, subjects G and I secure a score of 4 on distribution Y. Ordinarily, they should have been assigned ranks 2 and 3. Since one should not get higher rank than the other, the two ranks are averaged and the rank 2.5 is assigned to each. We treat the other duplicate scores in the same manner.)

**TABLE 23.5**

**Method of computing rank difference correlation of ungrouped data.**

| | *Score* | | *Ranks* | | | |
|---|---|---|---|---|---|---|
| *Subjects* | *X* | *Y* | *X*¹ | *Y*¹ | *D* | *D2* |
| A | 4 | 6 | 4 | 6.0 | 2.0 | 4.00 |
| B | 5 | 5 | 5 | 4.5 | 0.5 | 0.25 |
| C | 6 | 7 | 6 | 7.0 | 1.0 | 1.00 |
| D | 9 | 8 | 9 | 8.5 | 0.5 | 0.25 |
| E | 11 | 9 | 10 | 10.0 | 0.0 | 0.00 |
| F | 7 | 8 | 7 | 8.5 | 1.5 | 20.25 |
| G | 8 | 4 | 8 | 2.5 | 5.5 | 30.25 |
| H | 1 | 2 | 2 | 1.0 | 1.0 | 1.00 |
| I | 0 | 4 | 1 | 2.5 | 1.5 | 2.26 |
| J | 2 | 5 | 3 | 4.5 | 1.5 | 2.25 |

$$N = 10.\ \Sigma D^2 = 43.50$$

$$\rho = 1-\frac{6\Sigma D^2}{N(N^2-1)}$$

$$= 1-\frac{6(43.50)}{10(100-1)}$$

$$= 1-\frac{261}{990}$$

$$= 1-.263$$

$$= .74$$

*Step 3 :* Make a D Column which is filled in by subtracting the two ranks in columns $X_1$

$Y_1$ for each corresponding pair of scores.

*Step 4* : Make $D^2$ column, which is filled in by squaring each D value in column D.

*Step 5* : Find $ED^2$ by adding $D^2$ column.

*Step 6* : Now substitute the values in the following formula:

$$\rho = 1 - \frac{16\Sigma D^2}{N(N^2-1)}$$

***Steps in finding product Moment Correlation***

Another way of determining the co-efficient of correlation is usually called the *Produce Moment Method* or, sometimes, *Pearson's product Moment Method*. This co-efficient of correlation is designated by letter *r* and is more accurate and more convenient when the number of cases is very large. The itemised procedure given below may be used only when the data are ungrouped.

*Step 1:* Find the means of X and Y columns of the raw scores.

*Step 2* : make a *dx* column which records the deviations of each raw score in column X from the *mean* of the column X, that is, (X–M). Similarly, make a column *dy* and record in it the deviations of each raw score in column Y, that is, (Y–M). In both the cases, make sure that the minus sign precedes the deviation if the mean is larger than the score from which it is subtracted.

*Step 3:* Multiply each number in the *dx* column by a corresponding number in the *dy* column and record the product in the *dxdy* column. Make certain that a correct sign is affixed to the products in the *dxdy* column. Sum up the *dxdy* column and record the sum as $\Sigma\, dxdy$.

*Step 4:* Square each number in the *dx* column and record it in the $dx^2$ column. Square each number in the *dy* column and record in the $dy^2$ column. Find the mean of each of these columns and record as:

$$\frac{\Sigma dx^2}{N} \text{ and } \frac{\Sigma dy^2}{N}$$

*Step 5:* Find out the standard deviation (σ) of *x by* taking the square root of $\frac{\Sigma dx^2}{N}$. Do the same with *y* and find out the standard deviation (σ) of *y* by taking out the square root of $\frac{\Sigma dy^2}{N}$.

*Step 6* : Substitute the above mentioned values in the following formulas to obtain the co-efficient of correlation between X and Y:

$$\gamma\, xy = \frac{\Sigma\ dxdy}{N(\sigma x)\ (\sigma y)}$$

All the above steps are illustrated in the following table with the help of a concrete example:

**TABLE 23.6**

**Method of computing the Product Moment Correlation of undrgrouped data**

| *Subject* | X | Y | *dx* | *dy* | *dxdy* | *dx2* | *dy2* |
|---|---|---|---|---|---|---|---|
| A | 4 | 6 | −1.3 | .2 | −.26 | 1.69 | .04 |
| B | 5 | 5 | −.3 | −.8 | .24 | .09 | .64 |
| C | 6 | 7 | .7 | 1.2 | .84 | .49 | 1.44 |
| D | 9 | 8 | 3.1 | 2.2 | 8.14 | 13.69 | 4.84 |
| E | 11 | 9 | 5.7 | 3.2 | 18.24 | 32.49 | 10.24 |
| F | 7 | 8 | 1.7 | 2.2 | 3.74 | 2.89 | 4.84 |
| G | 8 | 4 | 2.7 | −1.8 | −4.86 | 1.29 | 3.24 |
| H | 1 | 2 | −4.3 | −3.8 | 16.34 | 18.49 | 14.44 |
| I | 0 | 4 | −5.3 | −1.8 | 9.54 | 28.09 | 3.24 |
| J | 2 | 5 | −3.3 | .8 | 2.64 | 10.89 | .64 |
| N | 10 | 10 | | | Sums 54.60 | 116.10 | 43.60 |

N = 10. Mx = 5.3 My = 5.8 $\Sigma dxdy = 54.60$ $\Sigma dx^2 = 16.10$

$\Sigma = 43.60$ $\Sigma dx^2 = 43.60$

$$\gamma\, xy = \frac{\Sigma\ dxdy}{N(\sigma x)\ (\sigma y)} \qquad \frac{\Sigma dx^2}{N} = 11.61 \qquad \frac{\Sigma dy^2}{N} = 4.36$$

$$= \frac{54.60}{10(3.4)(2.1)}$$

$$= .765 \qquad \sigma x = \sqrt{\frac{\Sigma dx^2}{N}} = 3.4$$

$$\sigma y = \sqrt{\frac{\Sigma dy^2}{N}} = 2.1$$

## PSYCHOLOGY IN INDIA

Our students mostly read books written by foreign authors, which rarely make any reference to the psychologists in India or their work. This need not lead us to believe that there is no psychological research work done in our country—and for that matter many other countries in the west and east. It is true that the word psychology is used today synonymously to mean American psychology, because, of all the nations, it has made tremendous progress in psychological research. There is no wonder, therefore, our psychology has been deeply influenced by American and to a smaller extent by the works of British psychologists; yet, it must be admitted that we have a tradition in psychological research which dates back to 1912. The present section is written with the intention of giving you an overview of psychology in India.

## *Psychology in Ancient India*

The origin of Indian Psychology goes back to the period of the Rigveda and the Upanishads. The Upanishads, particularly, have a wealth of material that is of great psychological interest. There are statements and intricate discussions on the nature of the self (*atman*), mind (*manas*), senses (*indriyas*), and *buddhi* (intellect) and their inter-relationships. They give us a deep insight into the psychological thoughts of our ancestors. What is mot amazing about them is that many of them lay down the techniques of the control of the mind and discuss in detail how such a control can lead ultimately to an understanding of the *self*. The understanding of the true nature of self, according to Indian-philosophers, is the highest ideal a man can attain. Many modern critics are of the Opinion that the Upanishads are more concerned with the Psychological nature of man than with building a metaphysics or a theory of the creation of the world. The culmination of 2 the psychological thought of the Upanishads is to be found in the philosophy of Yoga, which is actually a System of normal and para psychology. The Yoga system applies the philosophy of the Upanishads to an individual's salvation through the eradication of psychological error and the cultivation of knowledge of self. The eight-fold path prescribed by the Yoga for the Attainment of the self, forms the very core of Indian psychology. Only those who have read carefully through the *Yoga sutras* of Patanjali, which is actually a practice guide to self-realisation, can understand how carefully Indian thinkers had laid down their own theory of knowledge based on subtle observations of our sensory and perceptual processes and their control through the techniques of concentration, meditation and the autonomic functions of the body.

Following the revival of interest in Yoga all over the world, the day is not very far off when it will acquire a place of honour in the psychological systems of the world, because many of its claims are substantiated by scientific research.

Though the Scientific verification of the various claims of the yogic psychology is relatively a new development in modern psychology, some promising work done in this country and abroad shows that the psychological thoughts of our ancestors were far advanced even though they were based on simple observations and reasoning. However, it will be several years before we are able to see through the many riddles of the yoga and the authenticity of many of its astounding claims.

### *Modern Developments*

Scientific or empirical psychology in India, however, is of recent origin. Though We are far behind some countries notably Japan, America, Soviet Russia and Great Britain — in psychological research, we have already made many hopeful and promising beginnings. In the following Paragraphs, an attempt is made to present a thumb-nail picture of psychology in India by reviewing the progress it has made in the last sixty years.

The first Indian psychological laboratory was established in Calcutta in 1915, about thirty-five years after Wundt had established his first ever psychological laboratory in Leipzig in Germany. This was followed by the formation of the *psycho-analytic society* in India by Dr. Bose in 1922 and the *Indian Psychological Association* in 1925. Departments of psychology were established in Mysore University in 1924 ana in Lucknow in 1926. During the Second World War, psychological activity in India had come to a temporary standstill. In 1946, however, Patna University started two full-fledged departments of experimental and applied psychology. Most of these departments offered instruction in psychology at graduate and post-graduate levels. At the same time some stray research work was carried out at Calcutta, Lucknow and Mysore.

In the post-independence period, there has been a rapid development of psychology. At present, there are as many as thirty-seven university departments of psychology in India; and the number seems to be increasing every year. It is also heartening to note that about 90 per cent of the total research and publication work in psychology reported so far was done mainly in the period following 1950. Today, as many as 17 psychological research journals are published in India compared to only three in the pre-independence period. Inportant among them are: Indian Journal of Applied Psychology, Indian Journal of Experimental Psychology, Indian Journal of Psychology, Indian Psychological Reivew, Journal of Applied Psycliology, Journal of Psychological Researches, Manas, Psychological Studies, Indian Psychology, Transactions of Mental Health and Bombay Psychologist, a journal published from Bombay.

Some research articles written by the Indian psychologists have appeared in foreign journals and also in journals published by the universities and by independent centres of psychological research. At present, an average of 150 papers in the various sub-fields of psychology are published every year. The main reason for this small output appears to be general apathy towards research even among educated and fairly well-qualified people. The general atmosphere in the country is also not very conducive to research in psychology because the psychological problems that beset the highly affluent and industrially and technologically advanced societies are not to be found in India on a large scale; and even if they exist, there is very little awareness among people that they can be tackled by psychological research. However, with rapid developments in industrialisation, psychology seems to be picking up in India. There are also very hopeful signs that research in all the social sciences, including psychology, will get a further boost because of the concentrated efforts of the Government of India and its organs like the Indian Council of Social Science Research (ICSSR). The new pattern of education that has been introduced in the country is also likely to drovide more and better opportunities to college and university students and teachers for research and make them more research conscious. The impact of these measures, however, will be felt only after ten or fifteen years.

Psychology in India is, however, not confined to the small departments in various universities and some colleges affected to them. In fact, psychological research is more vigorously pursued in many para-educational and psychological research centres scattered all over India. Among these, mention must be made of those institutions which have already contributed substantially to psychological research, and most of which have come up during the post-Independence period. They are: the Directorate of Psychological Research attached to the Defence Sciences Organisation of the Ministry of Defence the Indian Institute of Technology, the Indian Agricultural Research Institute, the Indian Institute of Mass Communication, the National Council of Educational Research and Training (NCERT), National Institute of Community Development, the National Institute of Family Planning, the National Institute of Health Administration and Education, Shri Ram Centre for Industrial Relations, A. N. Sinha Institute of Social Studies, the Tata Institute of Social Sciences, and the All India Institute of Public Health and Hygiene. The very names of these institutions indicate the varied areas in which Indian psychologists are working today. Some psychologists have been trained abroad, but a number of them have received their training only in India. Research carried out in some of these institutions has won recognition abroad and often thrown an interesting light on certain Indian psychological problems.

A recent survey of psychological research, published by the Indian Council of Social Science Research, shows that, till 1969, there were approximately 250 persons who had received their doctorate (Ph.D.) in psychology from various Indian Universities, and about 300 were enrolled for the doctoral degree in psychology. The number of graduate and post-graduate students in psychology has shown a sudden spurt in the last eight years. Research work, however, has not proportionately increased. According to the latest estimates, there are nearly 3500 psychologists working as teachers, researchers, consultants, and government employees.

### Research in Sub-Fields

If we take into account the research activity in the various sub-fields of psychology in India, we find that about 73 per cent of the 2,981 research papers published between 1950 and 1970 related to only six major areas in psychology, *viz*., (I) Clinical Psychology (19%), Personality Psychology (17%), Social Psychology (16%), Industrial Psychology (10%) and Experimental Psychology (10%). Percentage-wise, the work in the remaining areas is as follows:

Militaty Psychology (6%), Educational Psychology (6%), Methodology (6%), Developmental Psychology (4%), and Physiological and Comparative Psychology (2%). These figures should give us some idea about the present stale of research in various sub-fields. The following is a brief review of the work that is being done in some major sub-fields.

### *Clinical Psychology*

The study of clinical psychology is gradually expanding in our country, but the rate of its progress is very slow, considering the large numbers of people who have been afflicted by mental disorders and problems of various sorts. However, in the post-independence period, rapid technological and industrial development and the growing influence or Western ideas have created a greater awareness of the mental health today than we had 20 years ago. This awareness, however, has not resulted in any spectacular research activity in this area. There are reasons enough for this fact. In the first place, the graduates coming out of Indian Universities every year are ill-equipped to carry out any meaningful research. Even those who are working in mental asylums and hospitals have been provided with very little or no research facilities.

Judged in this light, the work done so far is no doubt encouraging. Of the 2,981 papers published in psychology between 1950 and 1970, 577 are on various topics related to clinical psychology. Some of the areas in which Indian clinical psychologists have been working are psychotheraphy, psychodiagnosis, psychoanalytic interpretations of the Indian personality, physical handicaps, neurological disorders like brain damage and epilepsy; behavioural disorders like drug addiction, crime, alcoholism, delinquency, suicide, neurosis and emotional disturbances; psychosis, mental health rehabilitation, and counselling. With a few exceptions, the work done so far is, however, based on Western models.

### *Personality Psychology*

This is the second largest sub-field of Indian psychology. Of the total 2,981 research papers published between 1950 and 1970, 525 papers were on personality psychology — a sure enough indication or the popularity of this field among Indian psychologists. The major topics on which research has been done since 1950 are: personality assessment techniques (like interview, psychological tests, case studies), motivation, the concept of self, learning, perception, psychopharmacology, delinquency, criminality and abnormal personality. Some work has been done on the Hindu concept of personality and also on the parapsychological aspects of personality like ESP and its related personality variables. It is heartening to note that, over the years, the quality of the work has considerably improved. Yet, with the exception of a few, the majority of studies are based on Western models. Even the tests used in many personality studies have not been standardised in accordance with Indian conditions. Their uncritical application has undoubtedly lowered the quality of research. Theory-building activity is also at its lowest ebb, and most of the work, with a few exceptions, is inspired by Western theories of personality.

### *Social Psychology*

Since 1950, about 402 studies have been published on various topics related to social psychology, most of them in the last ten to fifteen years. Though several areas of social psychology have been covered, some appear to be the favourites of Indian researchers. The largest number of papers (277) have been written on topics related to social and cultural processes. The other topics are: attitude and opinion research (93 papers) and group and interpersonal processes (71 papers each). Most of the research is more problem-oriented than theoretical. Theory and methodology have been mostly neglected in the studies. The other areas which have received some scanty attention are communication, sexual behaviour, smoking, drugs and alcohol.

On the whole, the work done so far is quite extensive but it is very discrete and unrelated. Some subjects have only been touched and then abandoned without any further or deeper probing. This has made it extremely difficult for others to inter-relate the work that has been done so far.

### *Experimental Psychology*

Experimental psychology may be regarded as the third largest sub-field of Indian psychology. Since *1950*, over the period of about twenty five-years nearly 288 papers have been published on various topics in Experimental Psychology.

Most of the earliest work was in the area of psychophysics and was inspired by the experimental work of Wundt, Fechner, and Weber and some British psychologists, particularly Bartlett and Burt. A quick survey of the work in this branch shows that Indian psychologists have been active in almost all the traditional areas of experimental psychology—sensory processes, perception, attention, reaction time, work, fatigue, conditioned response, learning, verbal learning, memory, transfer, retroactive inhibition, motivation, probability learning, thinking and problem solving.

Again, we find that most of the work is replicative or corroborative and, with a few exceptions, shows no sign of inventiveness or creativity of any sort. It is also scattered and, except in a few cases, does not show any continuity and consistency of purpose. Because of its sporadic nature, theory building activity has been negligible. The only redeeming feature is that our experimental psychologists have considerably improved upon their methodology, though here also the inspiration does not seem to be native. Another heartening thing is that, quantitatively speaking, there has been some improvement in research output in the last ten years.

Experimental psychology is an area which is not easy to cultivate. In the last two decades, advances in technology, electronics, and expansion in the knowledge of fields related to experimental psychology have reached the level of such great sophistication that, without sufficient financial backing, team-work and the utmost devotion, it is all but impossible to carry on any worthwhile research in this branch.

### *Industrial Psychology*

Most of the published research bearing on industrial psychology belongs to the post-independence period. Industrial psychology was only a subject of academic interest in India for quite a long time but with rapid strides in industrialisation in the post-independence period, there has been a spurt in research in this sub-field.

Nearly 380 papers have been published on the subject between *1950* and 1970. In the pre-independence period greater stress was laid on topics like selection and placement procedures, and very little work was done in other areas. In the post-independence period, however, most of the areas in industrial psychology have been researched. Among them are: (i) vocational choice, guidance and selection, with special reference to such selection procedures as tests, questionnaires and interviews; (ii) job satisfaction and related problems like labour turnover and absenteeism; (iii) accidents; (iv) industrial efficiency and environmental improvement; (v) consumer psychology, including advertisements; (vi) job analysis; (vii) management and organisation ; and (viii) engineering psychology.

Many of the published papers in this sub-field have been written by persons working in industry and industrial research institutions. However, though they show a great diversity of interest, it must be admitted that they are replicative and corroborative rather than inventive or creative. The research has probably been hampered by the lukewarm attitude of the Indian industry towards new and progressive concepts and its emphasis on traditional methods of management. However, during the last decade, there has been a growing understanding of the role of industrial psychology at least among the highly organised mass- scale industries. It is not so rare now to meet a psychologist in industry, as it was some twenty years ago. If the pattern of the growth of psychology in various countries is taken into account, industrial psychology seems to be one of the few sub-fields which has a very bright future in India.

# 23

# Social Influences on Human Behaviour

Up to till now, we were deeply involved with the psychology of the individual, and with such basic psychological processes as motivation, perception, learning, memory and thinking which constitute the psychological make-up of a man. We were also concerned with the ways in which they operate and influence his behaviour. But an individual rarely lives alone; he is surrounded by other people—his social world or social environment which also exerts a most powerful and all-pervasive influence on him. In fact, it is difficult to think of an individual on whom these social influences do not operate. It is in this sense, that almost all of psychology is social psychology because, right from the time of his birth, an individual comes in constant contact with other people and his personality as well as his behaviour is profoundly affected by their interactions with him.

It should be noted here that the study of an individual in society is mainly undertaken by social psychologists and sociologists though there is some difference in their perspectives and approaches. Social psychology studies the behaviour of an individual in society as it is influenced by the presence of other people and their beliefs, actions, sub-groups, culture and such other social forces as are all-pervasive and ever present. Sociology, on the other hand, is concerned with the behaviour of a group taken as a whole. Obviously, there are many overlapping interests among sociologists and social psychologists.

In order to understand the various social influences on human behaviour, we should first take into account some of the basic concepts in social psychology which enable us to understand the various social influences on human behaviour. They are discussed under the following heads:

(i) Socialisation
(ii) Culture
(iii) Social structure
(iv) Positions, roles and status
(v) Social Class system ; and (vi) Social Groups.

## Socialisation

Every individual, belonging to any society, is exposed to several social influences from the time he is born and while he grows within his social environment. As a result of this, he learns many ways of understanding and reacting to his social reality. *Socialisation* is the name given to the social learning of the individual as he begins to grow as a member of his society. It is these social influences which mould him in various ways and leave a deep mark on his personality and behaviour. For instance, an infant is trained in attitudes and beliefs and behaviours that are regarded as appropriate in his own social environment. By the time he begins to talk and is able to take part in the activities of his group, his habits, beliefs and activities of his own social group have influenced him so much that he carries almost a permanent brand of his social group and culture which easily distinguish him from the members of other groups or cultures. The process of socialisation helps a growing child to learn how to get along in the world and with other people in his environment. It is also through the process of socialisation that he learns his culture or what we call his *social heritage*.

## Culture

The term 'culture' may be defined as the *man made* part of environment. When individuals living together in society *interact* with each other and participate in varying group activities, they produce new cultural stimuli besides those that are handed down to them by the previous generations. Culture is a highly complex concept ; and it is only the human species which has the capacity to build culture. Culture has mainly two aspects—*material* and *non-material*. Material culture consists of those products of human interactions and labour which can be perceived, handled or manipulated. Buildings, playgrounds, technological products like trains, buses, planes, means of communication like T.V., radio, films, etc., furniture, gadgets of various sorts used in day-to-day life—these are the examples of material culture in most modern societies. Many of these products may not be found in primitive societies, for their culture is simple or underdeveloped and unsophisticated. In short, the material aspects of culture consist of the things created by man in a particular society for the satisfaction of his various needs and solution of his numerous problems.

When an individual repeatedly faces and uses the various items in his material culture, he develops *typical ways* of reacting to them. These reactions are usually in the form of judgements and may be broadly referred to as his *attitudes*. Attitudes may be formed as a result of an individual's experiences with such material cultural products or as a result of his knowledge of them from other people. Since the material aspects of the culture are very closely related to an individual's style of living, the items of material culture may exert great influence on his viewpoints about them or his attitudes towards them. Thus, material products like cars, television, clothes may become status symbols (in some cultures) and an individual's behaviour may be guided by his desire to acquire them.

### *Non-Material Aspects of Culture*

All the products of human interactions are not tangible, as are the material aspects of the culture mentioned earlier. Man's language, his various social institutions—the family, religious, political and several other affiliations, his art forms, music, norms concerning vital activities, his views concerning himself and his universe—all these may be a part of his non-material culture. Among these, the system of social values and the norms of social behaviour (the behaviours which are regarded as desirable or undesirable in a given society) are the most important for social psychologists because they exert a profound influence on an individual's behaviour. In the process of socialisation, these norms of behaviour and social value systems are learned by an individual and then they become his guiding principles in his behaviour or in all that he does. Often, the value system of a society is expressed in a condensed language in such forms as proverbs or commandments; for example, "Thou shall not lie," "Thou shall not kill," "*You* will earn your bread by the sweat of your brow." Each culture, of course, has its own set of values, which may be entirely different from those of another society or culture. But whatever they are, they are always transmitted to successive generations in such a way that they become the internalised guiding principles of an individual's behaviour as he progresses through the process of socialisation or, what we may call, social learning.

**Social Structure**

As each social culture has its distinctive pattern of norms and values, so it has its own distinctive *social structure.* By structure we mean that each culture assigns *ranks* to its people, some important some less important, some performing certain functions, others performing functions of a different type. It also expects its families to be constituted in certain ways and its members to have certain attitudes and beliefs (see the discussion on Beliefs and Attitudes in the next Chapter). Different cultures vary in these matters and individuals show some peculiarities in their social behaviour which are not to be found in other cultures. Sociologists believe that the social structure of a culture mainly determines the type of work people do in a given society to satisfy their tangible and intangible needs. It makes distinctions between people performing certain types of jobs, and rates them as high or low. On the basis of their work or acquisitions. In short, it creates a *hierarchical* system of status. By *status* we mean the rank or position of an individual in the hierarchy of the group or community. An example of social structure is to be found in the hierarchical system of the castes in Hindu society, which was probably stratified on the basis of the work performed by an individual in early Aryan society, giving the *sudras* the lowest status in society because they performed menial work and higher levels of status to others on the basis of the value attached to their work.

Society, not only assigns general value labels to the broad groups of people working in it, but also to the individuals in its various sub- groups. There are hierarchical ranks in each sub-group, indicating its own peculiar structure. Again, among the *sudras* or in the Harijan community, we may come across a hierarchy of status, the more successful among them occupying top positions, while others occupy subsidiary positions in the hierarchy, each according to his contribution to their group's stability and well being. Similar structure patterns are found in a family, the father occupying the key position, the mother the second important position, with each child occupying a particular position according to his age or importance in the family or his contribution to its wealth.

## Positions, Roles and Status

### *Positions*

When, to understand the functioning of a society, we study communities, the first thing that strikes us is that each community or social group develops a system of well-defined psychological niches or positions, for which its individuals are trained and into which they are fitted. Sociologists and social psychologists, who study social groups and organisations, feel that the functioning of any social organisation depends upon the presence of patterned behaviour which become institutionalised in an organised group of society, so that each position within the structure of the group is associated with a common body of beliefs and expectations which are shared by all its members. Psychologists, therefore, refer to *position* as a sort of a slot or a niche within the structure of a social organisation which is occupied by a particular individual; and with each slot, position or niche, certain beliefs and expectations are associated. These become the guiding factors for an individual's behaviour. Mother, father, child, youth, manager, director, professor, teacher—these are some examples of such positions which are invariably found in all societies.

### *Role*

Closely associated with the concept of *position* is the concept of *role*, which may be defined as a set of expectations held by other members (than the one occupying a position) of the behaviour to be displayed by an individual occupying a specific position in a group. It is through such expectations that the group exerts its regulative influence on an individual's behaviour.

We may further elaborate the concept of position by taking into account the five ways of classifying people that give any group a structure. They are:

(i) Kinship (family) groupings;
(ii) Age and sex groupings;
(iii) Friendship (interest) groupings;
(iv) Occupational groupings; and
(v) Status groupings.

Within each of these groupings, different categories are specified. These categories are called *positions*.

For instance, in the age-sex classification for males, there are specific categories or positions like those of infant, boy, adult male, old male. We find similar positions in the various groupings mentioned above.

Each individual in a society necessarily occupies a position. Some positions usually change. Some are natural in the sense that an individual occupies one of them automatically; the age positions—that of a baby, a boy or adult—or the sex positions—that of a man or a woman—are of this type. However, many are acquired through accomplishments. For instance, the positions of a teacher, a doctor, a businessman, are acquired positions. Each position is associated with certain expected functions; the mother's position, for example, carries with it the functions or behaviour associated with motherhood. But how an individual fulfills the expected functions of a position may vary within certain limits; some mothers may deviate from the behaviour expected of them. Undue deviation from the expected function may be looked upon by society as deviant behaviour and may be disapproved; it may even be punished.

What we call a *role* is actually a *function* related to a position as viewed by the members of a society. The role actually involves the duties and obligations of positions, as well as the rights that go with those positions. A doctor's role consists of his many duties towards his patient, his obligation to take care of the sick as well as his right to charge fees, prescribe what he thinks is suitable for his patient, and so on.

Each individual may occupy a number of different positions in his life and may play a number of different roles. The doctor may be a father, husband, friend, and in each of these positions, he plays a different role. Multiple positions and multiple roles are typical of individuals living in modern complex societies.

Though individuals occupying the same position do not behave identically, positions and roles do bring about a broad patterning of behaviour which is more or less uniform for any specific position and role. Society expects an individual occupying a position to behave in a certain manner, within certain limits; he would suffer some punishment or disapproval if there is a deviation from the expected behaviour associated with his position. This is how society exerts its influence on an individual's behaviour.

### *Status*

Besides their positions and the roles related to each position, people differ in status; some are perceived as being of a superior status, others of an inferior status. In most highly developed societies, there is a complex and elaborate status system. Within each of these status systems, persons are ranked in terms of the prestige or social worth they have. Generally speaking, members of an organised group behave differently in their interactions with others according to their status within that group.

Research on an individual's status in an organised group has shown that persons of a high status are more likely to be the focus of attention (of others) than individuals of a low status. Moreover they are generally better satisfied with their positions than those of a lower status. There is some evidence to indicate that individuals of a high status have a greater freedom for the expression in so far as their attitudes and behaviour are concerned; they may deviate with inpunity from these attitudes and behaviour. They are also more likely to enjoy leadership positions than persons of a lower status. The status of a person may, therefore, be viewed as the worth of a person as estimated by a group or a class of persons. Most often, but not always, the status accorded to a person is derived from the social position he occupies as a result of his occupation or his role as a leader of a group.

Many attributes may contribute to this status of an individual in modern society. The examples of the attributes that contribute to status, however, may vary from one group to another—the beauty of a women or the wealth of a person, are, for example, very common attributes of status in most groups. In a family setting, the father often enjoys a high status because of the key position he occupies in the family. Status may also come from personal accomplishments, a position of eminence, a prestigious occupation, noteworthy contribution, which are held in high esteem by the general members of a group. It is apparent from the foregoing discussion that an individual may hold a multiple status at one and the same time and may also pass on front one to another. This may again shape his behaviour in various ways because on each of the status situations the roles he plays may be different.

## SOCIAL CLASS SYSTEM

One of the most pervasive status systems in modern societies is that of the *social class.* The concept of the social class has been variously defined by social scientists, and each definition is often conditioned by their theoretical orientation. We should note that an individual's needs, motives, goals, interpersonal response traits, values and attitudes are heavily conditioned by his social environment which, in turn, is determined by the social class to which he belongs. This is the reason why *social class* assumes great importance for social psychologists as an explanatory concept. That *social class* plays a pivotal role in the developing of an individual and his behaviour is evident from the fact that it defines and systematises different learning environments in different classes and develops his personality with specific brand of his class culture, values, expectations and attitudes.

### Social Class Studies

Major American social class studies appeared in the forties; and they attracted a great deal of attention because, for the first time, they showed convincingly that America was not a classless society, as had been wishfully believed and made out by many. These studies on social class in America exploded this myth.

The first of these classic studies was conducted by two sociologists, W. Lloyd Warner and Paul S. Lunt who used their own method of investigation (known as the Reputational Method). The first study appeared in 1941 under the title of *Social Life of a Modern Community,* which related to a town in New England with a population of 17,000. The two other studies related to "Old City," a Southern town of about 10,000, and Elm Town, with a population of 6,000, in Illinois.

In all the three communities, a social class hierarchy was found to exist. For instance, the uppermost class, called the Upper Upper (UU) consisted of persons of aristocratic birth and wealth—old, historical families with inherited money. The Lower Upper Class (LU) is similar to the upper and is made up of wealthy families which have newly acquired riches. The Upper Middle Class (UMC) is the third of the three higher classes, which extend over the level of what is known as the *common man* or the pillars of society. The other classes belonging to this group are the Lower Middle Class (LMC), a class of small businessmen, clerical and other white collar employees, the Upper Lower Class (ULC) of skilled workers, semi-skilled workers and small trades people and the Lower Lower Class (LLC) is a group of non-respectable persons in a community consisting largely of semiskilled and unskilled workers. Its members live in slum areas and often on doles.

All the three studies discovered almost similar proportions of the distribution of these classes with slight variations in their percentages (see Fig. 23.1) Other researchers, using different methods of investigation, have arrived at similar distribution of social classes in American society, though they have used a different terminology for the various classes. Some such classifications are given in Figure 23.1, which indicates the names used by the different researchers and also the distribution of the classes in American Society.

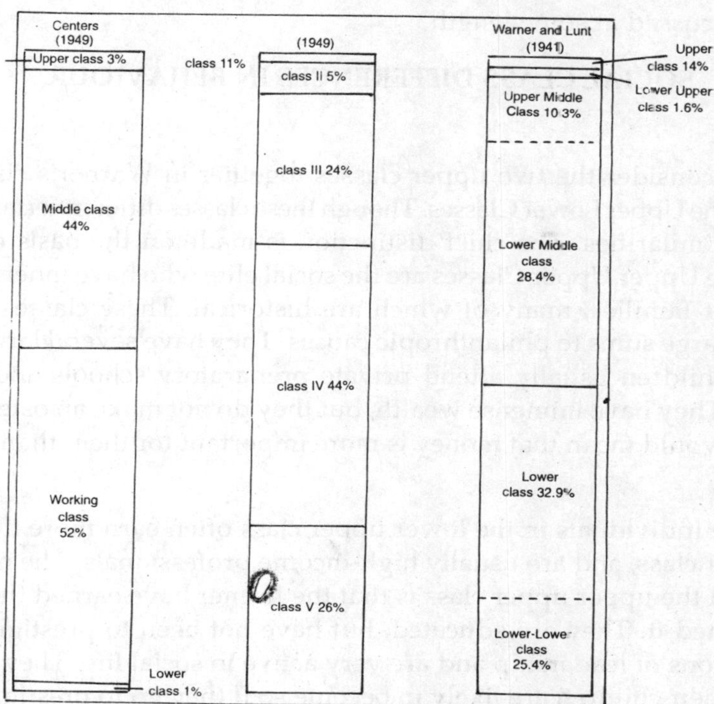


Fig. 23.1

Warner's method of determining social class membership is known as the reputational method. It defines the social class in terms of how the members of a community place each other in the status system of the community. The method is actually borrowed from anthropology. Generally, the investigators live in a community for an extended period of time, taking part in its social activities and interviewing social informants from different social levels. By such techniques information is obtained not only on the overall class but also on the class membership of individual persons.

In recent years, more objective methods of determining class membership have been developed. The wealth of a person, the source of this wealth, his occupation, education, type of his dwelling, the area in which he lives—these are taken as the criteria for determining class membership. These social class studies, have attracted the attention of social psychologists for a variety of reasons, some of which have already been mentioned.

Social class differences lie at the root of many behavioural differences among people. There are literally hundreds of studies which show that each class forms a sort of sub-culture of the general culture and that certain attitudes, values and life styles are associated with each sub-culture. These make the behaviour of the members of the class group much more homogeneous than, and distinct from, that of the members of the other class. The research on class differences has amply proved this point. In the following sections, these differences are discussed at some length.

## SOCIAL CLASS DIFFERENCES IN BEHAVIOUR

### Upper Class

Here we shall consider the two upper classes together in Warner's classification—the Upper Upper and the Upper Lower Classes. Though these classes differ in certain characteristics, they have many similarities. The chief distinction is made on the basis of inherited and earned wealth. The Upper Upper Classes are the social elite who have inherited wealth from socially prominent families, many of which are historical. These classes hold expensive bails, and donate large sums to philanthropic causes. They have several large apartments or mansions. Their children usually attend private preparatory schools and graduate from selected colleges. They have immense wealth, but they do not make an ostentatious display of it because that would mean that money is more important for them than their reputation and high status.

In contrast, the individuals in the lower upper class often earn more money than those in the upper upper class, and are usually high-income professionals. The major differences between these and the upper upper class is that the former have earned their own position rather than inherited it. They are educated, but have not been to prestigious institutions. They accept positions of leadership and are very active in social life. They are not a part of the elite, though their children are likely to become so if they go to prestigious schools and colleges, and marry into upper upper class families. They indulge in conspicuous consumption and often run after such status symbols as costly homes, automobiles, yachts, swimming pools, etc. Their women are most expensively dressed. They guard their status most zealously and carefully; acid this attitude blocks their contacts with the lower classes.

The most discouraging characteristics of these persons is that, with them, the reputation of their family counts for a great deal. They usually marry among their equals in reputation and prestige. The economic and social future of most upper upper class youth is almost guaranteed by their prestigious position in society. They, therefore, lack the combativeness and competitiveness of upper middle class youths.

A major difference between the upper upper class and the lower upper class persons lies in the extent of the influence they wield. Usually, the upper upper class persons are regarded as more influential than the lower upper class only because of the name and fame of their families. This is the reason why they often occupy positions as figureheads in nationally important social and political organisations. The upper class women usually play a very eminent role in family affairs, and are usually trend-setters in the activities of their own limited sub-culture.

### The Middle Class

The largest number of research studies in behavioural differences are on the middle class, which consists of the upper middle and the lower middle class. They are also, according to Warner, the most representative classes holding norms, attitudes, values and life styles which may be called typical of any society. The middle class, is mainly a class of white-collar workers—the professionals, and managerial and clerical cadres in most societies are drawn from this class. Education is the key value in middle class families, which are the most educated group in the society. The lower component of the middle class differs slightly from the upper middle class. It exemplifies the most typical average citizen of American culture. These persons have conscientious work habits, are respectable and adhere to cultural values, both religious and social. For the middle class people, the home is the most important place in life. They usually own their homes, and life around the home interests them a great deal. The typical middle class values are self-improvement, cleanliness, thrift, high regard for learning, adherence to the duties and responsibilities of family, and pride in one's own family possessions, including children. "A good man", according to the middle class concept, is a "good husband, a good father", "a man who builds a solid home life", and who is sensitive, serious and earnest about the future of his children. Because of their careerist outlook, the middle class people usually do not shirk hard work. They are largely future oriented and ready to postpone immediate pleasures for careers in the future. As a result, they are the most restrained people in so far as aggressive and negative impulses are concerned. In most middle class persons, impulsiveness is controlled and directed into a socially accepted behaviour. Middle class men rarely exhibit the toughness of the lower middle class men, in face, are regarded effiminate. Because of their limited income, most middle class people are thrifty. It is very common among them to save regularly to meet their various future neebs and objectives. Most middle class women are great hagglers and spend a lot of time moving about the home, inspecting things. They also demonstrate the highest price sensitivity, probably because the lower the income, the higher the aspirations. Reduction sales have an enormous attraction for them.

### Lower Class

The upper lower and lower lower class in Warner's classification may be collectively referred to as the lower class. These two classes constitute the largest section of the population, and have many similarities and differences as well. Warner calls these two classes as the upper lower and lower lower and not as the working class and the lower class, as Centers calls them, or Class V. as Holingshed refers to them, We shall use Warner's designation, as we have done in all our discussions so fan.

The distinguishing characteristic of the upper lower class is that it leads a routine life of unchanged activities and usually lives in dull and small houses. Most of the members of this class possess some moderate-to-better skills. This is actually a class of the upper range blue-collar workers. Their wives have a very crowded routine; and in many families children are the most prized possessions. These people have close family ties, and most of their personal contacts are limited to their neighbours, workmates and relatives. They are content with the routine of their lives and with their modest income, and are rarely social climbers. In many cities, the upper lower persons stay in middle class localities and imitate their life styles. Often, their income is higher than that of the lower middle class people. In both the lower classes, the women's status is typically inferior; man is usually the dominant member.

The lower lower class consists of the lowest class of persons who usually stay in slums and shanty housing colonies segregated from the middle and upper class localities. These people mostly engage in menial jobs In contrast to the upper lower class people, they do not believe in middle class values. They usually have little or no education, and have a low intelligence. Their family life is not as well-knit as that of the upper lower and middle class people.

**Social Class Structure in India**

When we consider the social class structure of Indian Society in the light of the above discussion, we find some similarities as well differences between it and the American class structure. The caste system which prevails in India is somewhat similar to the concept of the social class; but because it is traditional and based on religious distinctions, it is much more rigid. The social class of an individual is determined by birth in India and attaches to him like a stigma or decoration throughout his life. The mobility which we find in American society is a rare thing in India because Indian culture lays emphasis on the fact that man should do the duty that is expected of him by reason of his birth in a particular caste. The rigidity so acquired is further strengthened by emphasis on the rewards that may be expected in the life after death and not in this life. The stark rigidity of this caste ridden society is, however; experienced only in remote parts of India, where modernity has not yet arrived.

The rigid class structure of Indian society has, however, been rapidly crumbling after independence. The castes have lost their firm grip on individuals living in big cities; and a social class system has emerged which is comparable to the American system. Though structural changes in society do no occur as fast as one would expect, the fact remains that one still has glimpses of the society that will emerge tomorrow and which it is hoped, would be very much like the one found in other countries. The point to remember, however, is to understand how social class membership of an individual will influence his behaviour in various ways.

## ROLE CONFLICT

An individual occupies a number of positions and statuses in relation to other people in his group and plays various roles as he progresses in his life. When he simultaneously occupies two or more positions or statuses whose roles are incompatible with one another, we have what is known as *role conflict.* Students of psychology, who are familiar with the concept of the motivational conflict, should have no difficulty in understanding the nature of role conflict, which is not a conflict of motives within him but the result of the antagonistic demands made on his behaviour by the roles he has to play and the behavioural expectations of others he has to fulfil when occupying various positions and statuses.

A working woman, for example, who is also a mother, plays the role of an employee, and devotes her time to work. At the same time she experiences a severe guilty feeling for not appropriately performing her mother's role. In most such situations, an individual is unable to perform either role adequately, and therefore suffers from a feeling of discontent. There is a large body of research work on certain types of role conflict, especially on role conflict in women.

Role conflicts are often resolved in much the same way as motivational conflicts are resolved. A person caught in this conflict may resort to various defence mechanisms to alleviate the tensions and anxieties arising from it. Burchard, who studied the role conflicts among military personnel, found that the clergymen attached to military units as military officers (during the World War II) suffered from role conflict. They were more profoundly conscious of their officer rank than any other officers in the group, and tried hard to seem to belong as the officers belonging to the group. Enlisted men, on the other hand, had to maintain a certain distance from the officers, which these "priestly" officers found extremely difficult to maintain because that was something which went against their previous role as priests. To resolve this conflict between their officer role and their peaceful, non-violent role as clergymen, they used several defence mechanisms. They rationalised their role behaviour by saying that someone must carry the gospel to the rank ani file in the armed forces, even if they were military officers. Often, they tried to compartmentalise the two roles by saying that they had to do the things they had to as military officers and as priests as well. Sometimes, they repressed the conflict by saying: "I don't see any conflict at all." At others, they engaged in withdrawal by saying: "I would rather not talk about it (conflict)."

Many such role conflict situations are encountered in everyday life. Many studies have highlighted the conflicts between the expectations associated with the role of a profession and that of an employee in a bureaucratic set-up. In a highly commercialised educational institution, a sensitive teacher or professor. who is well aware of his duties and who knows that education can be uplifting and meaningful for students, may feel stifled by his commercial role as a wage- earner. Social workers in bureaucratically organised agencies, physicians and scientists in the government may experience similar strains arising from the conflict between the expectations of autonomy associated with their role as professionals and the expectation that, like any other employee, they would have to submit to bureaucratic control.

The severity of a role conflict may depend upon two factors:

(i) The relative incompatibility of the expectations involved, and

(ii) The rigour with which these expectations are defined in a given situation.

For example, an examination of the three roles of the modern woman—of wife, mother and employee—would disclose that the role of wife and mother would contain many more common expectations than either would have in common with the role of an employee. A woman who occupies the role of a wife and mother experiences a lesser conflict between the roles than if she occupies the roles of wife and employee. ra the latter case, she is under considerably greater strain because of the greater incompatibility of the roles. Moreover, the conflict would be further accentuated if the employer and the husband hold highly rigid traditional expectations of the roles of employee, wife and mother.

### *Role Conflicts in Women*

A lot of research work centres round the role conflicts in women, because newly emerging values often clash with their traditional role as wives and mothers. Psychiatrist Carl Binger, who had made a special study of this role conflict in women, says: "The educational system in America (and also in our own country) confronts college Women with a choice between marriage and a career. No matter how this choice is resolved, the women are likely to feel guilty because their people would expect them to marry and fulfil the woman's traditional role." She may also feel that she has missed something vital for herself by deciding to go in for a career without a marriage. Similarly, one who opts for marriage is likely to feel guilty because she knows that she could have made a life of her own, which is also a very tempting new role for a woman. One who combines marriage and career is also not likely to be happy because all the time she would feel that she is playing the two roles half-heartedly. Men are usually not beset with such problems for the simple reason that to be working and self- sufficient is one of the important obligations of the male role in most societies. In fact, idleness is regarded as something which is contrary to the role of the male.

Binger points out that such role conflicts in college-going women produce undue tensions and anxieties which often manifest themselves in depression, exhaustion and some psychosomatic ailments. It goes without saying that the severity of the conflict will depend largely upon the felt or perceived degree of incompatibility between the roles as well as the rigidity with which they are enforced on a person.

As we have pointed out earlier, role conflicts arise when an individual occupying various positions in life has to play incompatible roles. These conflicts lead to strain and anxiety, the degree of which would depend upon their severity and also upon the vigour and seriousness with which an individual plays his roles. But, whatever the nature and degree of the severity of a role conflict, an individual always tries to reduce them in various ways, some of which are inherent in his own efforts.

## SOCIAL GROUPS

Each society has, as we have seen so far, a culture; a social structure, a status system, and a system of positions and roles. Besides these, it contains social groups. A social group may be considered as any group of people, assembled or dispersed, who are related to each other by some common interest or attachment. We shall enlarge upon this concept of social group further, keeping in mind the fact that each society contains such groups.

### *Definition and Nature or Groups*

The word *group* is used in common parlance with considerable ambiguity, and usually denotes a congregation of individuals, whether these individuals &e in active interactions with one another or not. Social psychologists, however, use the phrase *psychological or functional group* to avoid any possible confusion in the meanings of what they imply. Functional or psychological groups are distinguished by the following characteristics:

(i) They are collections of two or more individuals who are inter- dependent in their relations or in some communication or interaction with each other.

(ii) The members share an ideology, that is, a set of beliefs, values, objectives, and norms, which regulates their mutual conduct. The ideology may develop when they work together on a common task. In the course of time, this ideology may become to some extent peculiar to them as members of a group, and set their group apart from other groups. There are many kinds of groups which meet these criteria—families, friendship circles, political and other types of clubs, religious, educational, recreational and other such groups.

When many such groups are functionally related to other groups taken together, they form what is technically known as a *social organisation.* A social organisation is thus a system of inter-related psychological groups formed to accomplish stated objectives. A political party, with its many political clubs, or leader cliques; labour unions with their several branches; or clubs of various types, or friendship groups—these are examples of social organisations.

The characteristics of groups may, to a smaller or greater extent, he present in even the smallest informal groups consisting of two individuals (dyads); but they are best found in those which have become stable and have acquired a definite structure. Yet groups may be formed accidentally as a result of some fonuitous circumstances—at bus stops, bazaars, in trains, etc., where strangers may enter into transitory communication with one another and exchange some information or talk about something. Such groups are referred to as *informal groups.* They may survive for two or three minutes, or they may continue for some time. Some other groups, which have acquired a definite structure, may continue for a longer time, maybe for generations, in the from of social organisations, societies and nations. These groups are the most complex and highly stable and often survive for centuries.

## Types of Groups

Psychological research has shown that there are different types of groups and that an individual's behaviour is influenced by the type of group to which he belongs. The following classification of groups is not exhaustive, though it is commonly used in most psychological literature; and the student should know his group terminology.

### *Primary and Secondary Groups*

On the basis of the nature of inter-personal relations among the members of a group, Cooley classified groups into primary and secondary groups. According to him, certain groups—the family, for example—exercise a considerable influence on an individual's personality, values, beliefs and attitudes because of frequent, intimate, and face-to-face contacts. He calls such groups primary groups. On the other hand, members of secondary groups do not show such frequency and intimacy in their interactions; they are formalised and contractual in their nature. An individual's membership of such a group is likely to come about as a result of some expectation—the acquisition of status, information, money, goods, services—rather than as a result of love and affection, which motivate members of such a primary group as the family. Family groups, friendship groups—these are some of the examples of primary groups, while professional and occupational groups, social organisations and clubs are examples of secondary groups. Because of the intimacy and close relationship which obtain in primary groups, individuals have greater freedom to express their emotional wants and needs than is possible among those is a secondary group.

### *Formal and Informal Groups*

It is possible to classify groups on the basis of their structure. An accidentally formed group, for example, has only some semblance of structure in comparison with the highly complex and stable structure of a social organisation, or what we referred to as a secondary group in an earlier paragraph. The first type of groups are known as *informal groups,* while the second type are referred to as *formal groups.* In most formal groups, the positions and roles of group members are fixed according to the expectations of the members and the objectives or the goals of a group. In fact, their positions and roles in secondary groups promote their stability and effectiveness. Because of this stability of the structure, the replacements of members in a formal group does not effect its objectives or stability in any way. Most social organisations, including nations, may be called formal groups in this sense.

### *Exclusive and Inclusive Groups*

The groups in which membership is restricted to persons having specified characteristics are called *exclusive groups.* Most of the professional and occupational groups, known as associations, may be called exclusive groups because of the restrictions they place on their membership. Any one cannot become a member of an Engineers' Association or a Medical Association or a Women's Association. Most exclusive groups are formal and are usually formed to exchange and communicate information and skills in their specialised fields, though some of them are recreational groups. The origin of such exclusive groups may lie in an ulterior motive, and may be sectarian, communal or religious in their objectives; they may even look down upon the principle of equality among human beings.

*Inclusive groups* are in sharp contrast to exclusive groups, for their membership is open to all without any distinction; that may be regional, national and even universal. Political parties and many social welfare and cultural organisations, such as the Red Cross or Amnesty International, are examples of exclusive groups which are international in their character.

### *Ingroup and Outgroup*

Exclusive groups often create barriers between those who are in and those who are out of them. There is a general tendency among people to be loyal to, proud of; sympathetic to and identified with the group to which they belong. This tendency often creates a strong *we* feeling among group members and leads to referring to others as *you* people. Most national, cultural, religious and communal groups have Ibis *we* or *ingroup* feeling, which is distinguished from what may be called the *they* feeling. Ingroups and outgroups are thus relative terms, which are often useful in describing certain group processes. Such ingroups exist at all levels and in every nation. Examples of these are some well known families which usually display their names, political power cliques, and economically influential people, who regard themselves as an ingroup because of their closely intermeshed vested interests. Such ingroups usually maintain their identity by drastically restricting their contacts with the members of an outgroup or by admitting others into their own ingroup in very small numbers. However, in many cases, the highly structured relationship among such groups and their exclusiveness weakens their effectiveness. History abounds in examples of such groups and also their invitable downfall. The Egyptian within the family marriage system may be cited as an historical example of this.

### *Membership and Reference Groups*

Whatever may be the type of group to which an individual belongs, it usually influences his behaviour in many ways. This is so because when one becomes a member of a group, one accepts its goals, beliefs, norms and values, and these obviously change one's behaviour in many ways. We may refer to all such groups to which individuals belong, by accident or by choice, as *membership groups.*

But it is not always necessary that a person should be a member of a group so that his behaviour may be influenced in some ways. *Reference groups* are groups of which an individual may not be an actual member; he may, however, identify himself with their goals, norms and values; and these may bring about changes in his behaviour. For example, a son of peasant, who aspires to middle class status, tends to accept middle class values and attitudes, and his behaviour is deeply influenced by this fact. He may dress like a middle class person, talk like him, hold political and other views like him. A reference group may thus be thought of as a group with which an individual *relates* himself *psychologically,* and of which he aspires to be a member. A reference group may serve an individual as a source of his attitudes and values, because he may imitate them as his model. An individual does not have to be a member of a reference group in order to be influenced by it. Singers, actors, actresses, or sportsmen are reference groups for all young people, who themselves may not be actors or singers. On the other hand, the group of which an individual is a member is also a reference group for him in the sense that he uses it as the basis of his learning, attitudes, and patterns of behaviour.

In modern times, young people imitate other reference groups in schools and colleges. Even films, radio, television and comic strip characters like cowboys, though they are fictitious, may serve as reference groups for young and old alike. How these groups may affect an individual's behaviour is best illustrated in a study by New comb and Behmann of the effect of reference groups on the values of college students. The study indicated that when students joined a university faculty, the liberal values of the faculty, which served as a reference group, were gradually accepted by them, and they became more receptive to new ideas and more rational and scientific in their outlook. There are many studies which indicate that references groups often deeply influence the behaviour of individuals.

## GROUP PROCESSES

Social groups may differ in many of their characteristics. A study of these characteristics is referred to by the well known American social psychologist, Curt Lewin, as Group Dynamics. The terms *group processes* is also synonymously used. Though the terms are loosely used, several important characteristics of groups, such as how groups develop, bow they function and also the various factors which emerge out of the interactions of group members and which influence the structure and functions of the group are usually covered by them. As many of these topics are beyond the scope of this book, we shall consider here only some of the important group processes under the following convenient headings:

(i) Patterns of Group Interactions;
(ii) Communication in a Group; and
(iii) Leader-Follower Patterns in Groups.

### Patterns of Group Interactions

Psychologists have devised several methods and techniques to study the patterns of social interactions and social communication and to analyse group processes and group behaviour.

#### *Methods of Studying Group Behaviour*

Since the end of World War II, there has been an increase in the studies on groups. Today, we have a number of well-developed methods of studying the various aspects of group processes. A substantial amount of work on group dynamics was initiated by Curt Lewin, which has attracted a great deal of attention of researchers in social psychology. Lewin has emphasised the value of group studies in a laboratory setting; but whether they are laboratory studies or field studies, most of such studies call for a careful description and a quantitative measurement of the relevant dimensions of group structure and group functioning. Let us consider some of the methods which are frequently used in such studies.

In the studies on groups in their natural settings, two principal methods of the recording of social behaviour are usually employed. They are: the rating scales and the category system method.

### *Rating Scales*

Most psychology students are familiar with the rating scales. Some of these were introduced in the earlier Chapters on Attitudes and Social Influence, in which we discussed at some length the nature of the rating scales. When using them in a study of groups, an observer usually rates specific dimensions of group behaviour periodically in the entire course of group activity, or he may make his rating after group activities have ended. Sometimes, it is convenient to obtain a complete permanent record of the behaviour of a group by transcribing. or filming its activities, and rating them later on. Such techniques are now very commonly used. One of the great advantages of these is that they bring considerable precision to rating because tapes and films can be repeatedly heard or seen.

### *Category System*

In using the category system, an observer classifies or codes the actions of the members of a group into separate categories. The types of categories and their number usually depends upon the requirements of the researcher. One of the best known and most frequently used category systems is known as Bales's *Interaction Process Analysis.* Bales has developed a standard set of categories which can be used to study any group. These categories are supposed to he independent of each other and non-overlapping. Table 23.1 illustrates Bales's categories.

**TABLE 23.1**

**Observation Categories Developed by Bales, known as Interaction Process Analysis**

A. EMOTIONALLY POSITIVE RESPONSES

1. Shows solidarity, raises another's status, gives help, reward;
2. Shows tension release, jokes, laughs, shows satisfaction;
3. Agrees, shows passive acceptance, understands, concurs, complies.

B. PROBLEM-SOLVING RESPONSES: ANSWERS

4. Gives suggestion, direction, implying autonomy for others;
5. Gives opinion, evaluation, analysis, expresses feeling, wish;
6. Gives orientation, information, repeats, clarifies, confirms.

C. PROBLEM-SOLVING RESPONSES: QUESTIONS

7. Asks for orientation, information, repetition, confirmation;
8. Asks for opinion, evaluation, analysis, expression of feeling;
9. Asks for suggestion, direction, possible ways of action.

D. EMOTIONALLY NEGATIVE RESPONSES

10. Disagrees, shows passive rejection, formality, withholds help;
11. Shows tension, asks for help, withdraws out of field;
12. Shows antagonism, deflates another's status, defends or asserts himself.

An observer's task is usually to classify each act of every member of a group into one of the twelve categories. The unit of observation is the smallest discriminable segment of behaviour, whether verbal or non-verbal, which an observer can classify. For verbal behaviour, each simple sentence is regarded as a unit. Complex sentences, however, may contain more than one unit. As non-verbal behaviour is continuous and not easy to break into units, the manner in which a subject behaves in a one-minute interval is recorded. The following example from Bales illustrates this method.

"The chairman brings the meeting up to date with a few remarks. He says: 'At the end of our last meeting, we decided that we would have to consider our budget before laying out plans in greater detail'."

"The interaction observer looks over the set of twelve categories and decides that this remark is most relevant to the *problems of orientation* and, specifically, that it takes the form of an *attempted answer* to this problem, and so he classifies it in Category B6. The observer has already decided that he will designate the chairman by the number 1 and each person around the table in turn by the numbers 2, 3, 4 and 5. The group as a whole will be designated by the chairman. The question was apparently addressed to the group as a whole, so the observer writes down the symbols 1-6 in one of the spaces following Category 6. The observer has thus isolated a unit of speech or process which he considers a proper *unit* for classification, has classified it according to its quality, identified the member who performed the act, and the person or persons to whom it was directed."

Bales's category system provides a number of scores which quantitatively describe the interactions and the structure of a group. The distribution of the total number of each type of category responses may be worked out and plotted on a graph.

It is possible to derive the various index scores from the interaction analysis. A simple example of this is a ratio of the number of acts in category 7 (asks for orientation), and the number of acts in this category, *plus* those in category 6 (gives orientation); thus provides a measure of the orientation difficulty. Bales's method may be used in experimental as well as open field studies; but it is more suitable when groups are small and work under controlled conditions.

When the Bales's system is used to investigate the interactions of small groups engaged in problem-solving tasks, it has been found that in the first phase of group interaction, the discussion in the group tends to emphasise orientation and clarification of interaction pertaining to the problem. The middle portion of the discussion emphasises the analysis and evaluation of the task; it is only in the final phase of the discussion that the emphasis is on the solution of the task. The frequency of the positive and negative reactions usually increases as the session proceeds, and are highest at the end of the discussion.

Studies with the Bales's analysis further show that two types of leadership emerge in most group problem solving situations; the first one is called the *conventional leader* or the person in the group who contributes most to the solution of the problem in hand, and the other one is the *emotional leader*, who is the best liked person in the group, who keeps the group members in good spirits, relieves tensions, makes them smile and laugh. It is only in rare cases that these two leadership qualities are combined in a single person. That is why there are usually two types of leaders in a group.

### *Participant Observation*

By this method, an observer participates with group members in their various activities. A continuous record of the frequency and kind of the interactions of a group is maintained, and from this a picture of the structure and functioning of a group is constructed. A classic study by this method is that of Whyte, who spent three and a half years in the slums of Boston as a *quasi*-member of various street-corne-groups, participating in a semidetatched role by joining in various group activities-playing ball, drinking and eating together. Whyte's observations revealed many interesting characteristics of groups—the various sub-groups in the slum's social and atheletic clubs, the status of men in the sub-groups, and their power to influence the members of their group. Very often, such observations were recorded on the maps which revealed the various aspects of group structure.

### *Self-Report Method*

Anthropologists often rely on a method of group analysis which is known as the self-report or *field-interview* method. This method is mainly used to study the culture of groups; but it can also be used to study various aspects of group behaviour. It is particularly useful in studying the norms, values and beliefs of a group. It uses the interview as the chief tool. The interviewer systematically frames and asks the respondent to answer questions which supply information on the beliefs, values and norms of the behaviour of a group.

### *Sociometric Method*

This method was developed by Moreno and is the most useful method for the study of group structure, its leadership, cohesiveness and morale. Essentially, it aims at obtaining qualitative data on the preferences of the members of a group. In a typical test situation, persons indicate their choice or rejection of other group members for association in some specific group activity. For instance, students may be asked who is best among them to lead a debating team to some contest; or whom from among their class-mates they would like to work with on a research project. Almost any criterion of choice can be indicated.

The responses may be summarised in a number of ways. But the best technique is to construct a sociogram. A sociogram consists of a number of circles, which usually represent each member in the group; the lines, indicating-choice, are then drawn from one circle (representing a group member) to another. For instance, the solid lines in the Fig. 23.2 with the directing arrows may indicate choices which dotted line drawn in a similar fashion may indicate rejection or dislike. The circles in the sociogram are usually drawn in such a manner that the distance between them may represent positive attraction among the persons in the group. For instance, persons who choose each other, may be placed closer (see 2 and 3 in the Figure) on the sociogram as against those only of whom chooses another (3 and 5 in the Figure). Similarly, the persons who reject one another are drawn at a longer distance than the one who rejects only one (3 and 9 in the Figure).

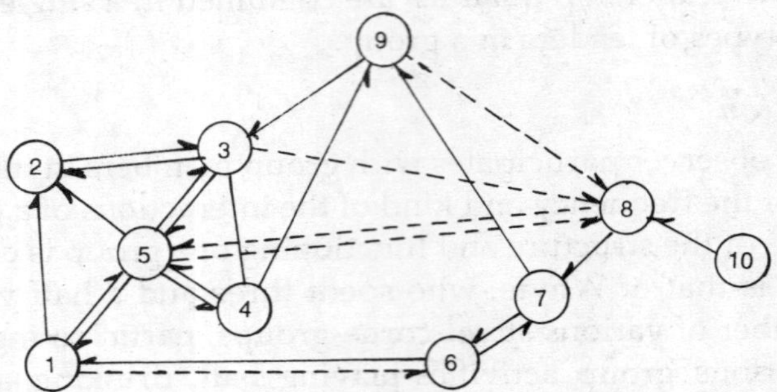


**Fig. 23.2.** A sociogram constructed on the basis of selection and rejection responses of 10 subjects.

## GROUP COMMUNICATION

By group communication we mean interchange of meaning among the members of a group which is primarily accomplised by the use of conventional symbols like language. Communication in a group is a highly complicated matter, and seems to be closely related with the pattern of group structure. It is not only affected by the persons in the group who wish to talk, but also by those who are permitted to do so. In most formal and even informal groups, free discussion is rarely allowed. In formal groups, the formal leaders, for example, the president or the chairman, usually control the communication among members by permitting some and not permitting others to speak. In such matters, status relationships also play an important part for high status persons generally communicate more than low status persons. Such factors always affect the flow of communication in specified directions.

Psychological research has shown that there are usually two broad patterns of communication. In the first, which may be called *free communicaiton,* the members of a group may he free to communicate with one another without any restriction. Ihis pattern of communication is usually known as circle or "free communication" pattern. The situation is symbolically stated in Fig. 23.3. In this Figure, the situation C symbolises another situation in which each member in the group can communicate only with the person in the centre. If the messages are to be sent from one person to another, they must be sent through the central person. This pattern is usually known as the *wheel communication pattern*. There are other patterns of communication known as the chain, Y etc. which state the basic patterns of communication occurring among groups with different structure. But we need not consider them here. The important point to note is that the pattern of communication that exists in a group often results in the effectiveness or otherwise of the group. Such information is particularly useful when we are concerned with the hundreds of thousands of persons who work in small and large groups in industry and business.

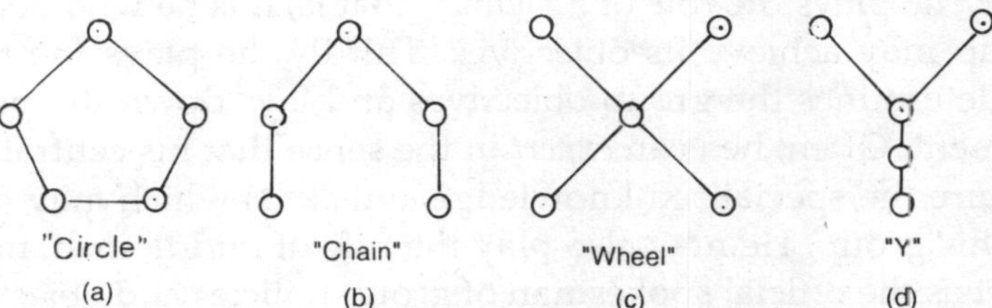


**Fig. 23.3.** A schematic representation of the four basic patterns of group communication.

Many psychological studies have pointed out that free communication networks are often much more satisfying for the members of a group and that such groups show a better morale and cohesiveness than the groups in which the star or other pattern of communication exists; but the former often lack the kind of working efficiency which we find in the group which uses the star pattern of communication. The reasons for this are not difficult to understand. In the free communication pattern, the group members feel more independent because they can talk and pass on or receive information from any member of the group. This does not happen in the star or wheel pattern, for the members depend upon the central person for all their information, and this is usually resented by them. All the same, the lack of Co-ordination of information and the wastage of it, which we find in free communication, is not to be found in the star pattern. The better co-ordination of information by the central person in the wheel pattern often makes a group a more efficient working group. We must, however, note that it is not generally easy to say that this or that type of Communication pattern is good or can make for greater group efficiency because, in the ultimate analysis, group effectiveness depends upon several factors and on leadership.

## LEADER-FOLLOWER PATTERNS IN GROUPS

Another distinguishing characteristic of a group is that it has leaders who influence its members and who, in their turn, are influenced by group members. The importance of a leader stems from the fact that he performs several functions for his group members which often serve as a binding force for the group. Psychological studies of leadership have given us many insights into the phenomenon of leadership, some of which are briefly outlined below.

### *Functions of a Leader*

A leader has manifold functions to perform in relation to his followers and his group; and these are often determined by the structure of the group itself. For example, the functions which a democratic leader performs may be considerably different from those of an autocratic leader. However, certain functions are common in most leaderships.

First of all, the leader has to play the role of an *executive* or a *co-ordinator* of the activities of the group; he is also responsible for the *objectives* and *policies* of his group and their execution. Secondly, he plays the role of a *planner,* that is, it is he who determines the ways by which the group may achieve its objectives. Thirdly, he plays the role of the policy-maker, that is he determines the group objectives and lays down the policies which may lead to their fulfilment. Often, he is an *expert* in the sense that his centralised position may enable him to acquire the specialised knowledge and skills which may not be available to other members of his group. He may also play the role of middleman, make contacts with other groups, or act as the official spokesman of group policies and objectives. He plays the role of *controlling* the relationships among the members of his group or of the various subgroups in his group. He is looked upon as an *example* or as a *model* of behaviour by his group members and thus determines the norms or standards of behaviour for his group members. Often, he is a creator of an *ideology,* that is, he may instill new values and beliefs in his group members. Marx, Lenin, Mao, Gandhi, Nehru are the best examples of ideologist leaders. Besides, a leader may be looked upon by his followers as a *father figure* and serve as a focus for positive emotional feelings (reverence, love, regard). But, in times of crises, particularly in failures, he may also serve as a scapegoat and become the target of the wrath of his followers.

In summing up the functions of a leader, we must note that some of them-such as those of an executive, planner, policy-maker. expert, group representative, giver of rewards and punishment are the primary functions of most leaders. Often, however, he has to take on himself several additional functions—like those of a father figure, arbitrator, exampler and so on. These functions are, therefore, regarded as *secondary.* Which of these functions a group leader will have to perform may depend upon group structure and the objective of the group. But in most stable groups a leader will have to possess these qualities in some measure.

### *Personality Traits of Leaders*

There are many misconceptions about the qualities of leadership because leadership in different spheres of life often calls for the exercise of many different qualities. A political leader may need qualities that may be different from those of a leader of an industrial organisation, or a democratic leader may exhibit qualities which are different from those of an authoritarian leader. All the same, there appear to be certain qualities which are common to all the types of leaders. Psychological studies of personality *trails* of leaders have revealed that the people who emerge as leaders in any group are the persons who are most active participants in group activities. Secondly, the persons who have greater capacity to mould the opinions and behaviour of others are more likely to become leaders. This inevitably leads us to the question: Who are the people who can influence others? It seems that a combination of physical and mental qualities is necessary for this purpose. A leader must be of more than average intelligence, he must have something of a domineering nature, should be well adjusted, active, extrovertive, progressive and have a capacity for keeping at a safe distance from and an impartial attitude towards his followers. Most successful leaders possess these qualities in a certain measure—and they probably help them to have a greater sway over their followers.

### *Formal and Informal Leaders*

It is essential to make a clear distinction between two broad categories of leaders—formal and informal—because the sources from which these two types of leaders acquire their influence over their followers are different. A formal leader, who is usually the head of a formal social organisation like a company, (president, chairman, director, etc.) or a state (a king, prime minister) gains the power of influencing his group members because of the authority that is vested in him. The followers accept his commands and dictates because he has the power of rewarding or punishing them by virtue of the position of authority he occupies. It is for these reasons that a formal leader may last as long as he wields authority and is capable of punishing or rewarding others.

In contrast to this, an informal leader's influence is not derived from his explicit position of authority, but because the members of his group have faith in his leadership, in his personal qualities to lead them and satisfy their own social or personal needs. Obviously, the emergence of an informal leader often depends upon the inability or failure of the members of his group to satisfy their needs and also upon the competence of one of their members to provide a way out by way of a solution. But competence is not the only thing which determines the emergence of the group leader; he must also enjoy popularity which depends upon his social skill and his ability to maintain good relations with his group members. Besides, his thinking should be acceptable to or in some way similar to that of the group members. Studies show that an assertive person or a person who has prolific ideas and a capacity to forge ahead is wore likely to emerge as a leader. At the same time too much assertiveness is likely to frustrate some other group members.

## Group Membership and Behaviour

### *Group Conformity*

The fact of belonging to a group has always a profound effect on the behaviour of group members because it moulds their beliefs, attitudes, actions, and decisions. To understand the influence of a group on its members, we must first take into account the concept of *conformity* or tendency of group members to *go along* with group beliefs, attitudes, actions and decisions because, knowingly or unknowingly, they believe in group goals, beliefs, attitudes, etc. Thus, when we speak of the conformity of group members, we are simply referring to their tendency to go along with the group without specifying whether their conformity is based on their tacit acceptance of group norms or whether they behave like the other members of the group because of group pressures. In the latter case, the term *compliance* is often used, which indicates the tendency to go along with the group even when one's beliefs and attitudes are not in conformity with those of the group as a whole.

### *Group Norms*

As we have pointed out earlier, every group has a structure and every person occupying a position in its structure has a role (prescribed by the group) to play. The phrase *group norms* usually refers to the *role behaviour* expected of a group member—in most cases, this behaviour is standardised in some way so that the group rewards those who conform to these expected standards of behaviour or punishes those who transgress or deviate from them beyond certain limits. We all know that, as members of a family or a college group, we have some expected roles to play; for example, to respect the elders in the family, to contribute to family welfare etc. As members of a college group, we are expected to study, obey the college authorities, listen to the teachers, without behaving wildly, and so on. Such expectations of behaviour are, of course, determined by the roles prescribed by the group, and any violation of them is likely to invite some punishment.

One important fact about group norms is that they emerge from the interactions of group members and are often highly formalised in the groups that have become stable. We know that as family members, certain beliefs and attitudes are shared by the family, as are the many peculiarities of behaviour—such as getting up in the morning at a particular time, or returning home at specified time or dining together. All these are almost formalised and when they are violated there is always the possibility of disapproval, by other members of the family. Similarly, as a member of a larger group like a community, one is supposed to marry Some one who has certain qualifications which are considered desirable by the members of the community—to wear a certain kind of dress or have a particular hair style, or that not to use a particular kind of language when talking to elders or to women folk. Each group has such norms, which evolve out of the interactions of group members and become unwritten rules and regulations of behaviour. A person who transgresses them is likely to be punished in some way, depending upon how serious is his deviation from the group norms. Society as a larger group—to which many small groups belong—also enforces conformity on its members by prescribing standards of desirable and undesirable behaviour which are laid down in written and unwritten laws any transgression of which is mildly or severely punished.

### *Experimental Work on Conformity*

Social psychologists, in their efforts to analyse and understand conformity behaviour, have performed several experiments which shed an interesting light on it. As early as *1935*, Sherif showed that when an individual in a group faced with two stationary specks of light in an entirely darkened room, was asked to report in loud voice how far each speck moved from the other (a speck of light in darkened place is likely to create an illusion of movement, known as the autokinetic effect, caused by the head movements of the perceiver). He found that, in the beginning the judgments of the subjects (concerning the movements of lights in inches) were considerably different. But when more trials were run, they tallied considerably. Sherif interpreted this close similarity of judgments as a result of the *effects* of judgments of *others* on the perceivers. In other words, when there are no objective cues to help us to judge a situation, we are most likely to look for help to others and accept their judgments as our own. Asch also performed similar experiments with different lengths of lines drawn on cards; and he asked the Ss to judge their length in a group and in a lone situation. Often, he planted his own accomplices in the groups and asked them to give certain faked judgments concerning the lengths. The interesting thing was that, in most cases, the naive subjects were highly influenced by the judgment of the experimenter's accomplices; but their judgments were much more objective when they were made in lone situations. It is not possible to go into many other interesting facts uncovered by these experiments. But one thing which is relevant to our discussion here is that an individual is likely to be guided by the norms established by others, particularly when he is not very sure of his own judgment. This is precisely what happens in many practical situations; we uncritically follow or accept the norms of behaviour or judgments set up by our group and thus show conformity to them. This fact has been verified in a number of experiments which involved similar but many more complex and contrived experimental situations.

## Factors in Conformity Behaviour

Conformity behaviour may be caused by a number of factors. Psychologists have put forward some interesting theories to explain why people show conformity behaviour, specially in the context of groups. Some of the important factors and theories are outlined in the section that follows.

### *Group as a Satisfier of Individual Needs*

As we have pointed out already, an individual joins a group because many of his psychological needs are satisfied when he becomes its member. The greater the satisfaction of his needs, the greater his attraction towards his group. The attraction or the feeling of belongingness to a group is however, governed by an individual member's conformity to the group,—his sharing of group norms, beliefs, attitudes. He is, however, well aware that any behaviour which is contrary to group norms would be frowned upon and may even lead to his expulsion from the group. Thus his desire to go along with the group (conformity) may result from his fear of losing group membership which is so very valuable to him because it satisfied many of his needs.

### *Need to be Accepted and Liked*

Among the various needs of an individual member which a group satisfies, the most important one seems to be his need to be accepted and liked by the group he values. This need may also lead to conformity or compliance behaviour. The best example of this kind of conformity comes from adolescent groups, in which a member may imitate his group members in hair styles, dress, in speech, and may participate in such of its activities as play, smoking, plotting, dancing and so on. At the root of this behaviour is their anxiety to be accepted and liked by the other group members. Often, we come across people who may be called *non-conformists* or those who refuse to dress or behave like the other members of a group; but even such people may show a great deal of conformity in the views, opinions and behaviour which are expected of them by the group.

Even in *ingratiation,* a behaviour in which we seek favours of other more powerful persons by subtly agreeing with their opinions or views, we actually make use of conformity (agreeing with their opinion) to seek approval and acceptance of our needs.

### *Perceived Unanimity in Views*

Another factor which has often been revealed as conforming behaviour is more likely to occur when there is unanimity of views or opinions in a group on the issues in hand. Such an unanimity is often referred to as *consensus* and wherever there is a consensus, the individual members of a group are more likely to agree with it. But when there is lack of unanimity in group opinion, there is every possibility that the individual may disagree with the opinion of the minority and go with the majority. This was clearly demonstrated in many of the experiments by Asch, who employed the techniques mentioned earlier. For instance, he demonstrated that when there was a dispute in a group in regard to judgments about the length of the lines shown to them, the individual members (in the group situation) usually gave judgments which were in conformity with those held by the majority of the participating subjects.

Another fact that has emerged clearly in experiments on conformity is that when an individual is reluctant to comply with something, he may be gradually forced to do so, if he is first pursuaded to comply with the minor requests. This is often known as the *foot-in-the-door technique,* which is best illustrated in some sales situations. For instance, a salesman knocks on the door and first pacifies the irate housewife when she opens the door and then begins his sales talk which in all probability, succeeds in pursuading the housewife to buy his product. Freedman and Fraser, replicating this type of situation, have demonstrated that this is exactly what happens in a majority of cases. The basic psychological processes involved in such situations are not difficult to explain. The grant of a small favour lowers the psychological resistance of the person and then he or she is less able to resist a request for a bigger favour (which he/she could have definitely rejected if it had been made initially). Many other explanations are also possible, one of which is in terms of the dissonance theory of Festinger outlined in the next section of this Chapter. According to him conforming behaviour persists, once it occurs because non-compliance may cause dissonance, or a feeling that a person's behaviour is *inconsistent* with his earlier behaviour (see congnitive dissonance in a later section).

## Theories of Conformity

Why do individuals exhibit conformity behaviour? A number of theories have been advanced by psychologists to account for this phenomenon, which partly supports the various factors which we outlined in the last section. The following are some:

### *Social Comparison Theory*

The social comparison theory holds that in ambiguous situations, an individual does not know what is expected of him (how he should behave or what judgment he should pass). In such circumstances, he seeks to compare his behaviour with that of others who are in the same predicament. If the situation is beyond the individual's comprehension, he feels it safer, therefore, to be guided by the judgment of others and accept their views rather than express his own.

### *Social Approval Theory*

The social approval theory states that the desire for approval is so strong in an individual that he may conform rather then take a dissident view of a situation. He probably fears that such a view might call forth the disapproval of others, which he tries to avoid by conforming to their views.

### *Dissonance Reduction Theory*

This explanation is based on Festinger's theory of *cognitive dissonance.* According to this view. when an individual is faced with a conflict between his own view and that of others—this type of conflict is similar to the one when two ideas (or cognitions of a situation) are in disagreement—there is a strong tendency on his part to reduce the inconsistency in the ideas by changing his own opinion in favour of the opinios of others. It is as if, he is saying to himself: "After all, what these good people are saying may be correct and if I go along with their opinion (by giving up my own opinion), my judgment cannot be very wrong." Thus, the positive group evaluation which may follow from his conformity, resolves the dissonance of ideas. A non-conformity, on the other hand, may resolve the conflict by devaluating the group judgement (idea) but not his own.

## SOCIAL BARGAINING

Another aspect of social interactions is to be found in the types of norms which emerge in the process of group living. There are a number of rules and regulations concerning who has to do what, in which particular way a thing is to be done, how the spoils of the joint efforts are to be shared, and so on. Such rules and regulations are actually norms and are based upon certain tacit agreements among, and expectations of, the interacting people. They arise because people bargain and interact with each other. Psychologists have investigated such behaviour by experimenting on small groups, mostly dyads, that is, two-person groups.

### *Exchange Theory*

One of the important conclusions of such studies is that people generally try to *maximise reward* and reduce costs when they are involved in social interactions. The word *reward* is used here in a broad sense; it refers to the feeling of gratification, satisfaction, material gain and enhancement of self-esteem that may result from social approval. *Cost*, on the other hand, means exactly the opposite of this; it is the feeling that may result from loss of material gain or which, in some way, leads to a state of reduced self-esteem. In, all social interactions, an individual is mostly guided in his behaviour in such a way as to ensure that the *costs* are kept at the minimum level and *rewards* are *enhanced* or maximised. A theory based on these assumptions has been put forward by Homan and is known as *exchange theory.* People try to maximise rewards and minimise costs in the present and plan actions to minimise costs and gain rewards in the future. What is cost or reward in the case of an individual, however, depends upon what Homan calls the *comparison level*, which is a sort of a *subjective* criterion (concerning whether the action is satisfying or not satisfying). If gratifying outcome exceeds the comparison level of an individual in a social interaction, such an interaction may be regarded as satisfactory by the individual; but if the outcomes are likely to fall below (the comparison level) the interaction may be regarded as unsatisfactory. Of course, the comparison level of each individual is determined by his past experience in similar interaction situations. Obviously, therefore, an individual will maintain contacts with another only if the outcomes are satisfactory or positive; or otherwise he may not continue to maintain the contacts. Extending this logic further, Homan says that the groups, in which its members draw satisfactory rewards from group interaction, are very stable and durable; and exactly the opposite may happen when the interactions are unsatisfactory.

These interactions, however, are more likely to occur when interacting people are of an equal status. But what will happen if one is of a high status or is more powerful than the other? Will a stable relationship emerge between them? The answer, according to Homan, is that a stable relationship emerges only if there is a strong interdependence between them; otherwise it will be guided by the same cost-and-reward outcomes which have peen mentioned before. Homan further states that persons who give more to others try to get more from others, and that the persons who get much from others are under pressure to give more to them. Such expectations concerning exchange produce a balance and stability in the relationships of the members of a group and most social interactions in any given society are guided by this principle of *reciprocity*.

## INTERPERSONAL ATTRACTION

The discussion of social interactions logically leads to many other equally important questions: "Why do people like (or dislike) one another?" "What brings them together in friendship?" "Is there any possibility of friendship between persons who are poles apart in their mental make-up?' These and many related questions are important for social psychologists because mutual attraction is the basis of all social groups, whether large or small. Fortunately, social research has uncovered a number of factors which are at the basis of inter- personal attraction. We may be well aware of some of these factors; but we know very little about how they work.

### *Physical Appearence*

It is everybody's experience that we like (or are attracted by) people who are physically attractive; at least that seems to be true at first sight. But research has revealed that appearence does not play such an important role in our liking of other people. Perrin, for instance, showed as early as 1921 that American college students played down good looks as a criterion for the purpose of dates and the selection of a mate, and generally attached greater importance to such qualities as character, personality and emotional stability. In a recent study (1971), Tesser and Brodie, too, founa that among the qualities on the basis of which students selected their marriage partners or friends, "good looks" ranked eleventh.

But observations based on the actual behaviour of the people have always shown different results; in fact, they have shown that, at dancing parties, the partner was generally selected on the basis of his/her looks and there was the possibility that a man would ask for date from an attractive woman far more often than from an unattractive woman. These results on heterosexual attraction have been substantially corroborated by many subsequent studies.

But many studies have also reported what is now known as a *matching phenomenon;* that is, in actually pairing off in situations like dancing and dating, people usually tend to select partners who come very close to their own physical attractiveness.

The fact of physical attractiveness is not confined merely to the heterosexual groups involved in dating, dancing and mating, but it is also evident among children in the 4-12 age group. In an interesting study, Dion has demonstrated that even children view attractive-looking children much more favourably than unattractive children, and that they ascribe to them better personal qualities even when the latter are projected in a favourable light by the researcher. Similarly, one study quotes that American graduates who were 6'.2" tall received on an average 12.4 per cent higher salary than those who were under 6 feet height. Even elected American presidents are generally taller than their contestants.

What seems to be a reasonable inference from these and other studies is that physical appearance does play an important role, though it is not always a very important factor in all the cases of attraction. This will be clear from what follows.

***Similarity***

Besides physical attraction, another and perhaps a more powerful factor in interpersonal attraction is *similarity;* that is, similarity of beliefs, attitudes, values, views, hobbies, likings, interests, sociological characteristics, physical characteristics—height, the colour of eyes, fatness—and psychological characteristics like intelligence. A very large number of statistical studies have proved beyond any doubt that liking is positively correlated with the *similarities* (among interacting persons) on these dimensions. Often, we come across friends or couples who seem to be strikingly different from each other; but when we go deeper into their personality qualities, we usually come across the fact that they are similar in many respects. For instance, we often come across cases of dominant husbands and submissive wives or vice versa. Many psychologists have suggested a theory of *complementarity* to explain such attractions between the opposites. But if we look deeper, we find that such a relationship works smoothly only if both are in *agreement* or on the *appropriateness* of their respective roles. In other words, successful complementarity presupposes similar attitudes to dissimilarity among them.

***Reciprocity in Liking and Hate***

The famous adage "Love begets love", seems to hold true for liking as well. We usually like people who like us and make no bones about disliking those who dislike us. This seems to be all the more relevant when we are very badly in need of being liked by others. Experimental evidence has very clearly demonstrated this truth. The reasons are not difficult to understand. When others express their liking for US, our self esteem is enhanced and we feel a liking for the person who does this because it is a most gratifying (rewarding) experience which we would like to repeat by maintaining and strengthening contacts with those who like us.

***Familiarity***

Many studies have very clearly shown that attraction is more likely to be developed among the people who are *familiar* with one another than among those who are strangers. In fact, familiarity may be cited as a precursor of attraction. There is sufficient animal as well as human evidence to corroborate this fact. Newcomb, for instance, has demonstrated that among the students living in a college dormitory, those who developed a close friendship at the end of one year's stay were generally room-mates.

### *Competence*

Competence is also a factor in interpersonal attraction. By competence we mean resourcefulness and efficiency, which is also sometimes the basis of attraction. But the relationship between competence and attraction is not really a straightforward relationship because those who are very highly competent are not necessarily those who are well-liked. Research evidence has shown that highly competent persons are often likely to be perceived by others as super- human and therefore not fit for friendship. However, when such persons are seen as fallible, as most human beings are, they may be liked by others. A dramatic illustration of this comes from the sudden spurt in President Kennedy's popularity after the fiasco of the Bay of the Pigs. After analysing this phenomenon, Oronson showed that Kennedy was looked upon by Americans as almost superhuman and infallible before the incident; but when he recorded this failure, he was perceived by the people as more human and therefore lovable. Oronson simulated this situation in many of his experiments, and concluded that a blunder makes a highly superior competent person more human, more like us, and therefore more likable. But if we ourselves are also highly competent (which is rarely the case), then a blundering competent person is likely to be pitied or ridiculed by us.

In summarising our discussion, we may say that attraction is rarely determined by any single factor; many may combine to produce it. But of all the factors, familiarity and similarity appear to be the moat potent factors, while appearance, competence, etc., may contribute to attraction to some extent.

## ALTRUISTLC BEHAVIOUR

Though modern society is solely based on selfish considerations, it cannot be proved that man has no other motivation because many human activities seem to have their basis in the *altruistic motive.* There are, for example, people who contribute to charities, donate blood, volunteer to participate in worthy causes, risk their lives to save someone. But psychologists have argued that even such activities very often imply *self-orientation* rather than true *other-orientation.* Whatever may be the truth, social psychologists try to answer, within the framework of social psychology, such questions as: "Why does helpfulness or *altruistic behaviour* occur at all?" and "Why do so many people help others even at some cost to themselves?" They think that the various forms of altruistic behaviour can be explained in terms of social influence in a better way than by arguing that it is an expression of some innate *altruistic* tendency in human beings. Social psychologists feel that there are many ways of explaining why people help others in difficulties, emergencies and in many similar situations. We shall first take into account some general explanations and then see how altruism can be explained in terms of social influence.

### *Altruism as a Learned Response*

One explanation comes in terms of *instrumental* learning or conditioning. People can be conditioned to help others by suitable rewards. In individuals, who have a tendency to help others or who are altruistic, there must be some such type of conditioning from their early life experiences, when help rendered to suffering persons may have resulted in most gratifying consequences; and this fact must have remained in the repertoire of that person's behaviour and been strengthened by occasional reinforcement. Altruism may then be viewed as a result of some reward.

### *Reciprocity Norm*

Another explanation comes in the form of reciprocity: "You help me and I shall help you," or "give" in order to "get". It is true that most transactions in life are of this type but it cannot be said to be true of all the transactions. Though it is difficult to pinpoint such motives, everyone has experience of this type in one's life. In these instances, the person involved recognises a social *ideal* or *norm* that he should pay the individual back for the benefits the latter has conferred on him. Sociologist Goulder points out that there is a very pervasive moral code to this effect in every society in the world, though the exact nature of this reciprocity norm varies. In Indian culture, for instance, a person who ill treats his benefactor is called a *namak haram* and is looked down upon.

### *Altruism as Conformity to Social Norms*

In 1960, a young girl, Kitty Genovese, was attacked in a residental area of New York, and was repeatedly stabbed. Her screams and singlehanded fight against the assailant did not bring out a single person (there were 38 neighbours) from the safety of their homes to help her. This crime received wide publicity; and there was much speculation about why people did not go to the rescue of their fellowmen in such situations. The incident also aroused great interest among psychologists, and they tried to discover the conditions under which individuals *do not* go to the rescue of people in distress.

That people should go to the help of a person in distress is actually a norm of social responsibility. It is a social expectation that people should help those who are defenceless, or who find them- selves in a dangerous situation, or who are generally in need of urgent assistance. This is a social responsibility norm. As a corollary to this is the social norm that people should not intentionally harm others. It is very likely that people go out of their way to help others because they almost compulsively stick to such social norms and also because, a violation of them may make them unhappy, or guilty, and not because necessarily they *feel* for the victim.

We shall examine how situational factors may play an important role in *conforming* or *not conforming* to the norms of social responsibility. These factors operate through their effect on the rewards and the costs of conformity, that is, through an individual's definition of a norm as relevant or irrelevant to the situation.

### *Altruism as a Personal Responsibility*

Shalome Schwartz in his comprehensive analysis of the situations in which altruistic choices rise, has demonstrated that an individual will be socially responsible and help those in distress, (i) when he recognises that those others are confronting a situation that has dangerous consequence for him; (ii) when he is aware of the moral norms that are pertinent to the occasion; and (iii) when he believes that he has a personal responsibility in such a situation. The neighbours in the Kitty Genovese case might have failed to act because they might have felt that it was not their job to rush to the rescue of the victim, that it was somebody else's duty to do so—may be a policeman's or some other strong and courageous person's. They had the *ideal* (that help should be given to a person in distress); but they did not think that they themselves had anything to do with the situation. They did not involve themselves in the situation because they did not feel that it was their *personal responsibility* to do so.

In another experiment, Schwartz investigated the effects of a person's habitual inclination to accept or deny personal responsibility for the welfare of others.

In this investigation, the female clerks working in Government offices, were first tapped by a questionnaire on what their attitude towards "bone marrow donations" was. They were also asked whether they would feel a *moral obligation* to donate if a stranger needed a bone marrow transplant, assuming that each one of them was a suitable donor. The questionnaire also aimed at ascertaining their tendency to ascribe responsibility to themselves in such circumstances.

Three months later, an appeal from a renowned transplant surgeon was sent to those women who had replied to the questionnaire (without any mention of their earlier response). The appeal asked them to join the pool of donors and was accompanied by a reply card on which the subject had to indicate her willingness to do so. The replies were then analysed in terms of *personal norms* and of acceptance of *personal responsibility*. The women who had accepted personal responsibility for others showed more inclination to live up to their own ideas than women who *only* held personal norms of helping others.

This and many other studies very clearly bring out the importance of an individual's sense of personal responsibility in matters which call for his help for others.

### *Altruism as a Diffusion of Responsibility*

This study by Schwartz indicates how the lowering or diffusion of personal responsibility may affect our willingness to help others. If our immediate concern for another person's welfare prompts us to aid that individual, we may be more inclined to do so if we are in sole charge of his fate. But when other persons are also involved, we can say to ourselves: "Let someone else help." Probably this was the reaction of the 38 neighbours in the Kitty Genovese case. As they listened to her screams, each one was well aware of the fact that the others, too, must have heard her cries for help. They could, therefore, easily pass the buck, or assume that someone else was responding to her appeal. As the situation was somewhat vague, they might have also thought: "Let someone else call the police and find out. I don't have to get involved in this situation."

Actually, this is what happens in most such cases; and this was demonstrated by Latane and Darley in an experiment. When the helper is alone with the victim, then he is most *likely* to go out to help under the compulsion of sticking to his latent norm (we must help distressed people). But when there are many potential helpers, the helper is confused because he does not know whether the norm applies to him or to another, a more qualified person.

A somewhat similar situation arises in real life. If a good many bystanders are around, the chances that someone will come forward to help will increase with an increasing number of such bystanders; but the possibility that the observer will go to the rescue of the victim increases only when the onlooker is *alone*.

### *Altruism and Conflict of Norms*

In the Kitty Genovese case, many neighbours, when interviewed, claimed that they did not want to meddle into a stranger's private business. Their claim seems to be convincing because though it is a social norm to go to the rescue of a distressed person, there is also an equally strong norm that one should not meddle in another's business. It is not unlikely that such a conflict in the onlooker's mind may have deterred many of them in Miss Kitty's case. Another social norm, which may influence an onlooker's behaviour, is that Americans (at least) are taught to be cool and not to get emotional or excited. A person who runs to the help of a victim in distress may thus be behaving against the social norm of remaining cool; he may not, therefore, go to the rescue of the victim and make himself conspicuous.

This suggests the possibility that the rules that restrain people from being altruistic may actually be learned. As a psychologist has pointed out, a child is inclined to aid another in distress from the time he is in the kindergarten up to the time he reaches the second grade; but by the time he is in the sixth grade, he becomes hesitant and cautious in such situations. It is not therefore difficult to conceive that when a person finds himself in an emergency situation, he is often faced with conflicting norms. He may feel reluctant to intervene, for he is not sure what is right. The possibility of such conflicts paralysing our actions cannot be easily denied. Hence, irrespective of whether altruism is innate or not, social learning seems to influence altruistic behaviour. It is also likely that it is in childhood that the relevant altruistic values and attitudes are learned. In one study, the effects of modelling on such behaviour were demonstrated by a researcher, who showed that, in kindergarten class, children learn altruistic behaviour in the presence of an appropriate model followed by a reward rather than from mere stories about, or talks on, altruistic behaviour.

# 24

# Psychology Around the World

In the contemporary world, American psychology has been one of the greatest sources of inspiration for psychologists around the world. In very few other countries has the development and growth of psychology been so vigorous, spectacular and promising. The credit of course, must go to the industry, affluence and resourcefulness of the American people. In the post-Second World War period, the influence of American psychology has spread all over the world. India is perhaps the best example of this. Almost ninety per cent of the books used as text books in our universities are written by American psychologists and the remaining are the pale copies of their by our authors. What goes in the name of Indian psychological research and publications is often a replication of the work done in American or British universities, with a few illustrious exceptions.

Most of us know very little about psychology outside the English speaking world where psychological research has attained a very high level of sophistication, and psychological concepts and theories of considerable importance have been developed. Most of this ignorance of psychological development in other countries, is, of course, due to language barriers.

In this context, it is interesting to see what the American psychologists themselves have to say about the development of psychology in other countries. In his article in *The American Psychologist*, L.W. Brandt writes: "American psychology disregards almost completely the research done in other countries and particularly in other languages—there is no English language market for foreign research that does not fit into the American way of life. Many foreign language psychological publications containing research that conflict with American psychology have never been translated into English though they are so widely accepted outside the English language psychology that several editions have already been published."

The curiosity to know *oneself*, know *man* is a universal attribute which has fascinated man for centuries. It is not the monopoly of any linguistic group or nation; but the barriers created by language are often formidable and not easy to overcome.

The following review of psychology in a few representative countries in the East and the West will enable our students of psychology to have some idea of the growth of psychology in England, France, Germany, Japan, China and Soviet Russia. It would have been possible to include many other countries; but for want of space we have chosen only a few representative countries. It is worth noting here that psychology has taken deep roots in as many as forty countries in the world. In Austria, Belgium, Denmark, Czechoslovakia, Ireland, Italy, Spain, Sweden, Switzerland and Soviet Russia, it has had a long and sustained history, even though there was some let-up of interest because of the catastrophic events that took place all over Europe during the Second World War. But in most of them it has since made a very rapid recovery and progress. Among Asian countries—India, China, Japan, Iran and Israel—there has been a sudden spurt in psychological activity during the last thirty years. Even in Black Africa—that is, in Africa, south of the Sahara, and in South Africa—psychology has made rapid progress during the last two decades. Besides these, Latin America, Mexico and Australia have many centres of psychological research which have made their own contribution to the development of the science of psychology.

## Psychology in England

One of the distinguishing characteristics of British psychology is that it is more empirical than theoretical. Its development has largely been influenced by Professor F.C. Bartlett (1881-1967) who taught are Cambridge; and most of today's British professors were his students. Another strong trend in British psychology is marked by the establishment of applied and industrial psychology. Bartlett himself thought that psychology might best develop through trying to solve applied problems. An important difference in British psychology and psychology in other European countries is that the former is still strongly influenced by a school of thought known as *Associationism* which was developed by such British philosophers as Bain, Brown and Mill. Another strong historical trend is that of physiological psychology, which arose in the last century and has been very much influenced by the thinking of Jackson, Henry Head, and Charles Sherington and not so much of Pavlov, the Russian psychologist, whose influence on American psychology is well known.

Among modern British psychologists, the most outstanding work is that of Hans Eysenck at the institute of Psychiatry in London. It encompasses almost all the branches of psychology, particularly of personality. Mention may also be made of N. O'Connor, Tizard, Mittler and Clark, who have done original work in mental deficiency. Bruner, a professor at Oxford University, has also contributed a great deal to the psychology of infancy and education. John Bowlby, the British psychoanalyst, who has been influenced by the ethological studies of Neco Tinbergen, has become famous for his theories of human development. Others using the ethological techniques are Blurton-Jones, Vowels and Schaffer. The work of T. Bower on the development of perception is, of course, well known.

Present work in British psychology does not reflect any definite national trend but rather international interest. In any case, British psychologists are more active in the fields of experimental psychology personality, physiological psychology, clinical psychology, developmental psychology and occupational psychology.

## Psychology in France

T. Rebot (1839-1916) is considered as the father of psychology and psychopathology in

France. During the last hundred years many French psychologists have left their mark on world psychological thinking. Among them mention may be made of F. Magendie, the neurophysiologist, Gall, the phrenologist, Esquirol, the psychopathologist, whose contribution enriched early French psychology. The contributions of notable French neurologists, such as P. Janet, J. Charscot, F. Mesmer and Brenheim on hypnosis and mental illness are also well known. Alfred Binet's contribution to psychological testing has been internationally acknowledged. Much of today's psychological testing is mere elaboration and application of Binet's principles to the various aspects of human behaviour. Frenchmen claim that it was Pieron, a Professor of Psychology at the Sorbonne University, who was the first to define psychology as the science of behaviour long before Watson came on the scene. His work on the physiology of sensation, memory, and human differences has found wide acceptance.

The most developed branch of French psychology today is physiological psychology. Fessard, Bonvallet, Dell and Hugelin are some of the well known workers in the field. The functioning of reticular activiction system, analysis of electric brain activity, genetic analysis of behaviour are some of the areas in which somesound work has been done, and is being done in France.

Besides physiological psychology, the other areas of psychology which have received considerable attention from French psychologists are animal behaviour, sensation, learning, conditioning, memory, perception and personality. French psychologists are also active in child psychology and psychopedagogy. The works of P. Gwillium and Wollon have become internationally known.

Since 1950, industrial psychology in France has received renewed attention following the studies of Faverge, Leplat and Montmollin on the analysis of work. Similarly, the problem of selection and training of workers has also attracted a great deal of attention of French psychologists.

Social psychology is relatively a recent development in France. The areas in which research in this field has been concentrated are sociometry, attitude and opinion measurement, interpersonal relations and group dynamics. Most of the work has been inspired by British and American influences.

An interesting development is known as Economic Psychology, which seeks to reach a synthesis between economics and psychology. This new field has many practical applications.

## Psychology in Germany

Modern psychology was born in Germany as an offspring of physics, and its foundations were laid by J.F. Herbert (1776-1841) with his publication entitled *Psychology as a Science, Newly-Founded as a experience, Metaphysics and Mathematics* in 1825. A few years later, the philosopher Beneke thought of psychology as the physics of inner experience. Lotze, Lange, Weber, Fechner and Wundt are some of the earlier German psychologists, who have left an indelible mark on modern psychology. In fact, many regard Wundt as the Father of Modern

Psychology because he was the first to set up a psychology laboratory in Leipzig in 1879.

Around 1990, some dissatisfaction in the Classical German Psychology School led to a fragmentation of German psychology and many new schools arose. Among them are the well known Woorzberg School established by Kulpe in 1896 and the Gestalt School founded by Wertheimer in Frankfurt in 1912. It is to this latter school that the great psychologists—Kohler, Koffka and Lewin—worked before they migrated to America. A second school, under the leadership of F. Kneger, was started in Leipzig in 1905 and is known as the Leipzig School of Totality Psychology. Durkheim, Klemn, Russel and Sanders were some of its leading lights.

The Nazi regime came as a great blow to German psychology, particularly to the Gestalt School. Most of its leading lights went into exile. An almost similar fate awaited the other schools.

The post-Second World War development of German psychology is marked by certain new trends. In the first place, the political division of Germany has affected psychology. The American and Russian influences permeate psychology in West and East Germany respectively. But, on the whole, the American influence is must stronger because American psychology did not suffer much, compared to Russian psychology, during the World War II.

On the whole, we may say that, at the present time, there is greater emphasis on refining methodology in Germany than on theory-building. Research in almost all the areas of psychology is growing, though German psychologists have been prominently occupied with cognitive development, thought and psycholinguistics, motivation, conflict, decision-making and aggression.

Among the various sub-fields of psychology, the most vigorous research activity is found in social psychology, though work in this field began as recently as in 1950. Clinical psychology is yet another field in which theories of Freud, Adler and Jung still exercise considerable influence on German psychologists, though many seem to be greatly interested in Behaviour Therapy as well. Personality psychology also has a very long history in Germany. Earlier German concepts of personality were over-laden with the problems of morale and character and were in the philosophical tradition. Since the 1950s, however, there has been a great change and research in this field has already started reflecting international trends.

Among the other areas of research, in which there is a great deal of interest among German psychologists, we have psychologists, we have psychodiagnostics, genetic psychology, educational psychology, forensic psychology and industrial psychology. It is also interesting to note that parapsychology has been gaining ground in Germany since 1956.

Psychological statistics show that the main body of German psychologists, known as the professional Association of German Psychologists, has about 2,600 members. There were nearly 48 psychological institutes in the Federal Republic with a membership of about 1,200 psychologists and having about 13,000 psychology students on the rolls in 1973. The number must have gone far beyond this in the last seven years.

**Psychology in Japan**

Psychology in Japan began with the publication of the *Experimental Record of the Mind* by the Zen priest, Tanzan Hara, in 1873. It was the first empirical study of the mind, about the same time. Western psychology was introduced in Japan by Nishi and Nishimara. In 1903, the first psychology laboratory came up in Tokyo University. Some of the early Japanese psychologists—Motora and Matsumoto—were trained in Germany and were responsible for the Gestalt influence on Japanese psychology. In 1920, Gestalt psychology in Japan was further strengthened by the work of Sakuma and Onoshima.

Before the World War II, most of the Japanese psychologists were professors, and the areas of their interest were perception, verbal learning, and developmental and educational psychology. The excellent work done in Japan, however, is more or less unknown to the outside world because of the language barrier.

The mainstream of Japanese psychology has been experimental psychology. Perception, especially perceptual constancies, is the most extensively and intensively researched field. Excellent experimental work is also to be found in traditional areas of experimental psychology like memory and learning. Animal psychology is another field in which the Japanese have made their own specific contributions to primate psychology an studies on the lower vertebrates, but very little is known about them in other parts of the world. In the field of physiological psychological psychology, some interesting work has been done on EEG correlates of learning and EEG changes during Zen meditation. One of the most interesting features of this research is that it has almost successfully verified certain claims of Zen psychology. Some interesting work is also being done on the part played by the various parts of the brain in behaviour.

Japanese psychologists are also very active in the field of child and developmental psychology, psychological testing and educational psychology.

Obviously influenced by their Zen Buddhistic traditions, some well known Japanese psychologists—Watanabe, Motara and Soto—have tried to project their own theory of personality based on Zen Buddhistic principles. However, the Western influence on personality studies in Japan is also very clearly discernible. Clinical and counselling psychology are relatively new developments in Japan, but the vigour and the activity in this field clearly show that they are soon going to be a most important area of research in Japan. Already a great deal of work has been done in psychodiagnostics and psychotherapy.

The other fields in which Japan has made good progress are social psychology, industrial and criminal psychology. Social psychologists are particularly interested in the study of the Japanese personality in the context of the present rapidly changing times. Work is also being done on group dynamics, group structure, cross-cultural studies and leadership behaviour. In industrial psychology, the emphasis now is on safety problems and human relations rather than on efficiency, job analysis and selection. In criminal psychology, work is being done in areas like diagnosis, causation, detection and the dynamics of criminal behaviour.

The Japanese Psychological Association as established in 1926. Today, it has a membership of 2,530. The Association holds annual meetings, at which almost 50 per cent of its members read their papers. Before 1939, there were only 15 colleges and universities offering psychology. This number has now gone upto 86, and must have further increased.

**Psychology in China**

In mainland of China, psychology as a branch of social sciences has been strongly influenced by the political philosophy of her rulers. Chinese psychologists use the naturalistic approach to the study of psychological problems and do not apply psychological testing and inferential statistics at all. The psychologists in Taiwan, on the other hand, are deeply influenced by American psychology.

In mainland China, Maoism is not only the most powerful political theory but it encompasses almost every aspect of life and even the philosophy of social sciences. To understand Chinese psychological thought, one must therefore have an adequate knowledge of Mao's theory of contradictions. Because of the stranglehold of Mao's theory on Chinese psychologists' thinking, it is difficult to assert that Chinese psychology is psychology in the traditional sense. Yet the Chinese are wrestling with many psychological problems in their own way, and have developed viewpoints which are highly coloured by Mao's teachings and entirely different from those found elsewhere.

The theory of pain, developed in the light of Chinese experience with the technique of acupuncture, may be cited as an example of the peculiarity in Chinese thinking on various psychological problems. The theory gives an altogether different version of brain functioning from the one that is accepted in the Western world. The Chinese approach to the problem of mental illness is also unique in that it combines Western and Chinese traditional methods—herbal medicines, breathing exercise, analysis of personal contradiction based on Mao's techniques, acupuncture to relieve tensions and a number of physical exercises. Mental illness is thought of by the Chinese as the outcome of fantasy reasoning.

The Chinese have devoted a great deal of thought to the problem of delinquency in China. Kuo, a leading Chinese psychologist, interprets juvenile delinquency as a crisis of identity. This theory is mostly accepted in China.

The study of social psychology is very rare in the Mainland because Communist thinkers have only recently started forming theories of the nature of social class and its influence on interest and attitudes. In Taiwan, however, Western techniques have been used in many studies. EEG and other techniques have been used in the Mainland in the areas of developmental psychology and mental retardation.

As some Chinese psychologists have pointed out, the Chinese people do not have any need of psychology as have the Americans and other highly industrialised nations suffering from a loss of identity arising out of automation and the pressures and anxiety created by competition and greed. The Chinese, these psychologists contend, are free from these courses of modernity.

**Psychology in Soviet Russia**

E.G. Boring in his *History of Experimental Psychology,* writes: "The most important self-conscious school of objectivism has been the Russian, which began with the work of I.M. Sechenov (1829-1905) and was continued with the researches of Bekhterev and Pavlov. Bekhterev used it and then called it *reflexology*". The great inspirer of Russian psychology was, of course, Sechenov, whose work on the psychological processes of body was carried a step further by Palvov and Bekhterev. Sechenov was a Professor of Physiology at the Military Academy at St. Petersberg. In a monograph published in 1863, he argued that all thinking and intelligence depends for their exercise on stimulation, and all acts of conscious or unconscious life are reflexes. But he was condemned for his materialistic views by his Czarist rulers, who, in 1866, banned the sale of his book. Sechenov, looked upon as the Father of Russian Reflexology, held that only physiologists are capable of investigating the problems of psychology by studying reflexes.

I.P. Pavlov was profoundly influenced by Sechenov's work Pavlov's work on gastro-intestinal processes in dogs led him first to talk about physical secretions in dogs, which in later years became the famous "conditioned reflex", making the formation of the Behaviourist psychology a reality.

Very little is known about the development of Russian psychology after the Russian Revolution, though determined efforts were made to create a truly Marxian psychology. In the 1920s, Russia had shown some interest in Behaviourism and the Gestalt psychology; but after 1931, behaviourism was denounced in Russia.

We know fairly well the developments that took place in Russian psychology in the last twenty years. Till his death in 1953, Stalin's dogmatism had inhibited the development of scientific psychology in the Soviet Union. After his death, however, great interest in new branches in psychology has developed—for example, in engineering psychology and social psychology. There was also a revival of interest in the traditional areas of psychology and in the works of such earlier Russian psychologists as Pavlov. Besides, Russian psychologists have been able to forge very close ties with the new disciplines of science, such as cybernetics (science of communication) and the theory of information. They have also utilised advanced statistical methods, and have shown great interest in the new technology and modelling of psychological functions. A good deal of research in Russia is concerned with the psychology of sports and physical education.

In 1955, a new journal of psychology was established in Russia. The Soviet Psychological Society held its All-Union meeting in Moscow in 1957, after a lapse of nearly twenty years. Thereafter, regular yearly meetings have been held in various places in Russia. At the Fourth Congress of Soviet Psychological Society held in 1971, 1,160 papers were read and discussed. The largest number of papers were on cognitive processes and communication

(229), followed, in order, by personality psychology (183), medical psychology (172), industrial and engineering psychology (150), educational and developmental psychology (133), differential psychology (90), social psychology (87), sports and physical education (48), and physiological psychology (30).

These statistics should give us some idea of Russian psychological research. Despite the period of slump during Stalin's regime, Russian psychological research has shown vigour, inventiveness and creativity which compare favourably with those associated with the developments in psychology in the United States. But the main body of the Russian psychological work remains unknown to the rest of the world because of the barrier of language.

## REFERENCES


1. Morgan, C.T. and King, R.A.: *Introduction to Psychology*, 5th TMH Editor, Delhi, 1975.
2. Hilgard E.R., Atkinson, R.C. and Atkinson, R.L.: *Introduction to Psychology*, 5th Edition, Harcourt-Brace, Ivanovic, 1974.
3. Munn, N.L.: *Introduction of Psychology*, 3rd Edition, Oxford and Amarind, 1975.
4. Brown, E. and Herrentin, R.J.: *Psychology*, Methuen, London, 1975.
5. Floyed, L. Ruch: *Psychology and Life*, D.B. Taraporevala and Company Ltd., Bombay, 1970.
6. James C. Coleman: *Abnormal Psychology and Modern Life*, D.B. Taraporevala and Co. Ltd.. Bombay, 1970.
7. Duglas, K. Kendland: *Psychology: An Experimental Approach*, McGraw Hill Book Company, New York, 1968.
8. Karlins, M. (Ed.), *Psychology in the Service of Man: A Book of Readings*, New York, Wiley, 1973 (Paperback).
9. Boring, E.G.: *A History of Experimental Psychology* (2nd Ed.), New York, Appleton-Century-Crofts, 1950.
10. Woodworth, R.S. and Sheehan, M.R.: *Contemporary Schools of Psychology* (3rd Ed.), New York, Ronald, 1964.
11. Edwards, A.L.: *Statistical Methods* (3rd Ed.), New York: Holt, Rinehart and Winston, 1973.
12. Guilford, J.P.: *Fundamental Statistics in Psychology and Education* (5th Ed.), New York: McGraw Hill, 1973.
13. Manning, A.: *An Introduction to Animal Behaviour* (2nd Ed.), Reading, Mass., Addison-Wesley, 1972 (Paperback).
14. Lorenz, K.: *On Aggression*, New York, Bantam Books, 1967 (paperback).
15. Mussen, P.H., Conger, J.J. and Kagan: *Child Development and Personality* (4th Ed.), New York, Harper and Row, 1974.
16. Beard, R.M.: *An Outline of Piaget's Developmental Psychology from Childhood to Adolescence*, New York, Basic Books, 1958.

# 25

# Psychology, Science and Man

Several years ago a professor teaching psychology at a large university had to ask his assistant, a young man of great intelligence but little experience, to take over the introductory psychology course for a short time. The assistant was challenged by the opportunity and planned an ambitious series of lectures. But he made a mistake. He decided to open with a short definition of his classroom two weeks later he found his conscientious assistant still struggling to define psychology.

An alternative approach is to assume at the very outset that every-body knows, more or less, what psychology is all about. 'Psychology', said William James in the first sentence of his classic text, 'is the science of mental life.' Although this definition on longer means what it did when James wrote *The Principles of Psychology* in 1890, it is relatively familiar and mercifully short. We can use it to launch our discussion of psychology without prolonged introductions.

*Psychology is the science of mental life.* The key words here are *science* and *mental.*

Our conception of what a science of mental life should be has changed considerably since James's time. In 1890 mantel life seemed to be a well-defined thing. No one doubted that a mind was there waiting for scientists to study it. But today, after seventy years of trying to study it scientifically, we are less certain. No longer is it self-evident what a psychologist means when he says that he studies mental life. The modern mind seems to be concealed form view, a mental iceberg floating nine-tenths hidden in a vague, unconscious sea; even its owner can do little more than guess which way it will drift next. At the time James wrote, scientific psychology was very young and the mental life that psychologists had been able to study was largely limited to the *conscious* mental life or *sane, well-educated, adult, western European, human* beings. Today, everyone of the restrictions implied by those adjectives has been removed. As the science of mental life developed, its base broadened to include children, animals, preliterate peoples, the mentally retarded, the insane. It is not obvious that all these new-comers share anything we could call a mental life, in the sense understood during the nineteenth century.

At the time James wrote, his claim that psychology was a science was little more than an expression of hope and enthusiasm. In 1890 scientific psychology was still a possible future development. A few men had begun to ask what they might do to make this branch of philosophy more empirical in its methods and conceptions. A few small laboratories had been founded, a few methods of measurement had been adopted, a few preliminary results had been reported. Whipped together with physiology, philosophy, and great common sense in the delightful Jamesian prose, the result was engaging and full of promise, but still a good deal less than a true science of the mind,

Scientific methods, however, are notoriously successful. Since James wrote his *Principles* there has been a remarkable growth in both the quantity and the quality of scientific research on psychological problems. Today when we say that psychology is a science we support the claim with several impressive accomplishments. Indeed, the rapid development of this young science has disrupted the daily pattern of our lives in scores of ways.

Scientific accomplishments usually affect us on at least two levels. On the one hand, scientific knowledge provides a foundation for technological advances, for the solution of practical problems that arise in the daily affairs of ordinary people. In this aspect, science is something that we exploit, just as we would exploit a natural resource. Many people think that this is all there is to science; they are confused by distinctions between scientists and engineers, between science and technology. But in its essence, science is something more than a useful art. Science has understanding, as well as control, as one of its aims. Thus science affects us at a deeper level by changing the way we understand the world we live in. Scientific advances mould our vision of reality, our fundamental and often unspoken set of assumptions about how the world *really* runs and what people are *really* like. Such effects of science are less tangible than the technological ones, but it is perilous to assume they are less important.

Like all sciences, psychology has influenced our lives on both levels. It has given us technical tricks and it has changed our conception of human nature.

When new fields of scientific activity first take form they begin, almost necessarily, with things and ideas that are part of the common experience of all men. During this early period of growth the science is widely intelligible, and the discoveries it makes can be understood, argued, resisted, supported, or ridiculed by millions of people. At a later stage the science may become more precise, may achieve deeper insight or soar to greater heights of intellectual virtuosity, but it will never again have quite the same impact on the average man's view of himself and the world around him. At this later stage the science may be supported for the technical miracles it mysteriously provides, but it is no longer a living reality to more than a handful of specialists. As its technological impact on society tends to increase, its impact on the common understanding often fades into the background.

Psychology is currently passing through its initial stage. It is still intelligible to most people. It is not unusual to hear a layman say, 'I amsomething of a psychologist myself, and I think...' What he thinks is often subtle and interesting and would not embarrass a more professional practitioner. In order to stay alive among our fellow men, we must all be psychologist. Of course, survival requires us to be mathematicians, physicists, chemists, and biologists, too, but there the distance has grown too great; no layman claims brotherhood without a prolonged initiation ritual conducted at some accredited university. It was not always so. There was a time when Everyman was a physicist, when Shakespeare would interrupt a play to argue against the heliocentric theory of the universe, just as a modern playwright may digress to illustrate or to oppose some new psychological theory today. It is in this initial stage of development that a science is most visible, most controversial, and most likely to change our vision of reality.

In spite of psychology's youth, however, the little knowledge it has painfully gained has fed a thousand different human needs. In some quarters demand has so far outrun supply that many psychologists fear their science has been oversold to an overwilling public. Yet even when we try to be conservative in our appraisal, it is plain that the new psychotechnology has already changed the way we live.

Consider American public schools. Everyone in the United States has felt the influence of modern psychology through its effects on our educational system. Indeed, there was a time when our schools seemed little more than a vast laboratory to test the psychological theories of John Dewey. The modern teacher has tried to use psychology — he has thumbed many a textbook ragged in search of the psychological principles underlying good teaching. Frequently the answer he seeks is not to be found, and the educator's pressing responsibilities to the young force him to extrapolate far beyond the established facts of scientific psychology; he hopes his guesses will be more intelligent if he tries to use psychology. Psychologists have tried to find answers for him. They have carefully explored a variety of conditions that affect how quickly a child can learn. They have painstakingly charted the stages of mental and social development. They have developed better techniques for measuring the progress of the child and the effectiveness of the teaching. They have provided counselling and guidance services outside the classroom. And they have given teachers that indispensable tool, the intelligence test. Yet all this is far too little, for the teacher's needs are great and vitally important.

The mention of intelligence tests is a reminder of another area of psychotechnology, the mental testing business. It is a sizeable business. It has been estimated that in 1960 there were 130 million psychological tests given to U.S. school children, or approximately three tests for every child from the first grade through college.

Mental tests, like the airplane, are part of our heritage from World War I. Before that time the tests were given individually to school children, and they tested nothing but intelligence. During the war, however, psychologists in the U.S. Army developed a pencil-and-paper test of adult intelligence that could be given to thousands of draftees — the famous Army Alpha Test — and so the large-scale testing procedures became firmly established in the public's consciousness. After that the testers began to branch out. They began to test aptitudes, to classify interests, to evaluate achievements. Now they can pigeonhole your personality, assess your emotional stability, your masculinity, your imagination, executive potential, chances of marital bliss, conformity to an employer's stereotype, or ability to operate a turret lathe. Whatever you plan to do, there seems to be a psychological test you should take first. Citizens who resent the many hours spent answering pointless questions are apparently in the minority, since enterprising newspapers and magazines have found that they can boost sales by providing daily or weekly questionnaires for their readers to answer. The flood of tests that has poured out across the nation has included many frauds — tests that are poorly conceived, confusingly phrased, completely unstandardised, and never validated. Psychologists have maintained reasonable professional standards among themselves, but it is not always easy to restrain the amateurs — it is as if everyone who bought a knife became a surgeon. Yet, in spite of these problems, the mental testing movement in the United States has managed to perform a needed service for both the individual and the community.

Once the army saw how useful psychologists could be in the assessment of men, it began to discover other problems of a similar nature. Soon the psychologist became a familiar member of the military team. For example, during World War II much highly technical military equipment was developed that had never existed before. In the developmental stages it often seemed that no one less gifted than Superman would be able to operate the equipment. The task of making the equipment fit the man was tackled by psychologists, who were able to contribute their knowledge of what a human eye could see or a human ear could hear, how far and how fast a human hand could move, how much interference and distraction a human mind could overcome. Psychologists can help to design trainers and simulators, to plan training programmes, to select men who are likely to succeed in each type of job. Moreover, in addition to man-machine problems, the military services have a vast range of psychological problems in the area known as mental health, where psychologists work together with psychiatrists to maintain morale and to heal the mentally wounded. A military branch is a small society unto itself — each application of psychology in our larger society has its parallel in this more limited world of warriors.

One large and active sector of psychotechnology goes under the trade name of industrial psychology. Many of industry's concerns are similar to the army's — how to select men who will be successful at different types of jobs, how to train workers to do their jobs better. Industrial psychologists have worked on the problem of fatigue: how should intervals of rest and work be alternated to give the greatest output with the least fatigue for the worker? The discovery that an employer often got less for his money from a labourer who worked a eight-hour day than from the one who worked an eight-hour day helped to change management's attitude toward many of labour's demands. Questions of fatigue lead quickly into questions of morale; industrial psychologists have worried mightily over this important factor. And morale, in turn, leads into questions of emotional adjustment. Clinical psychologists and psychiatrists have found their niche in the industrial wine, with a consequent reduction, so it is claimed, in illness, absenteeism, and accidents. Even the executives have succumbed to the psychologist's charms, and many a firm's management has been overhauled on the recommendation of a psychological consultant. There are people who feel that if the traditionally bard-headed American businessman is enough convinced of the usefulness of psychology to spend his own dollars on it, then there must be something to it after all!

A possible reason why some businessmen are willing to tolerate a psychologist underfoot is that they may have made a good profit by following his advice about advertising and selling the company's product. The psychologist has been keenly interested in techniques of persuasion, and his discoveries have coloured our advertising, propaganda, politics, and entertainment as these are distributed broadside through our mass media of communication. And by probing around in the consumer's unconscious, a psychologist may turn up some useful information for the advertising agency. Just how far one can go in shaping the public mind with a television screen is debatable. But it is apparent that there are both good and bad ways to advertise; psychologists can often help distinguish between them in advance.

Business is not the only place where careful attention is paid to surveys of public opinion. Government agencies have used polls for years to guide our public policies; politicians are particularly sensitive to fluctuations in their popularity with the voters. And feedback from the grass roots is just one of several ways that social psychology is involved in the processes of government. For example, in 1954 psychological evidence was used in the United States Supreme Court decisions against racial segregation in the public schools, where it was held that separate but equal facilities for both races were impossible because the psychological consequences of segregation were too great a handicap for the minority group. The court's decision rested as much on a point of psychology as on a point of law.

This recital could be extended for several pages. Psychological dogma influences the way we discipline our children, manage our businesses, and run our marriages. Studies of abnormal behaviour modify our conception and treatment of mental illness, incompetence, perversion, criminality, and delinquency. The priest and the rabbi agree in their use of psychological techniques to guide their flocks to salvation. Novels, plays, and movies now feature psychological themes as one of their standard formulas. Psychological drugs have already changed the situation in our mental hospitals, and more are yet to come. Wherever people are involved, psychology can be useful — and that is almost everywhere. Whether we like it or not, the practical application of psychology to our daily affairs is already in an advanced stage.

It must be admitted, however, that not every application of psychology is firmly grounded in scientific evidence. Those who apply psychology to the dynamic processes of an evolving society often jump to conclusions that make their laboratory colleagues tremble and turn pale. But when decisions must be made here and now, they must be made in the light of the evidence at hand, no matter how fragmentary and inconclusive that may be. In the past the same decisions had to be made with even less help; today the man who must take the responsibility can at least console himself that he tried to be intelligent, that his guess was informed by whatever evidence existed. The sun will not stand while he discovers and verifies every fact he needs to know. He works by guess and hunch scientific success have been more modest. And with man, the most complicated of all living systems, it was not immediately obvious to everyone that the methods could be applied at all.

The modern psychologist's faith that scientific methods can be applied to the mental life of human beings is inherited from the nineteenth century, a time when science looked bigger than the universe itself.

## WILHELM WUNDT, PSYCHOLOGIST

Psychology became an experimental science during the closing decades of the nineteenth century, at a time when European thought was dominated by *positivism* In its narrowest sense positivism was the philosophy of Auguste Comte, who invented the term as a name for his ambitious work, *The Positive Philosophy.* Comte's aim was to provide a systematic survey of all knowledge. In order to cope with so large an enterprise, he had to limit himself strictly to facts whose truth was unquestionable, whose validity was insured by the recognised methods of science. Some men would have regretted this limitation, but Comte considered it one of the great merits of his work. It was acceptance of these limitations to which he gave the name, positivism.

Once invented, however, the term soon came to be used rather loosely to describe any discussion of human beings phrased in the language of natural science. That is the broader sense intended here.

Positivism is positive in a polemical sense, meaning that it is not metaphysical. Any speculation about transcendental powers, hidden essences, or ultimate causes is dismissed as sophistry and illusion. The worst insult a positivist can give is to call one a metaphysician. A positive philosophy accepts as real only those things that can be known. Everything that is mere conjecture, unsupportable by argument or observation, must be rejected. Philosophy must be based squarely on knowledge. A theory that cannot be tested by an appeal to facts is mere humbug. In particular, if nothing recommends a hypothesis except the satisfaction and comfort it can provide, commit it to the flames! This attitude inevitably gives offence to those who cherish their religious beliefs.

The men who tried to maintain this hardheaded, no-nonsense philosophy in every situation discovered that certain other philosophical ideas were particularly appealing. On the one hand, the positivists were powerfully attracted to the *empiricists,* who believed that the only source of true knowledge about the universe is sensory experience — what can be seen, heard, felt, tasted, or, smelled, or what can be inferred about the relations between, or invariances among, such sensory facts. Thus when a positivist said that he based his philosophy on knowledge, what he usually meant was that he based it on the evidence of his senses, the kind of evidence that had proved so spectacularly successful in the natural sciences.

Positivists also found strong support — sometimes more than they wanted — from the *materialists,* who believed that everything in the universe can be understood in terms of the properties of matter and energy, and reduced to descriptions expressed in centimetres, grammes, and seconds. Materialists usually believe that all the phenomena of consciousness will eventually be explained by the laws of physics and chemistry. Thus in psychological arguments they tend to focus attention on the anatomy and physiology — the structure and function — of the brain.

And from still another direction, the positivists — especially Comtean positivists — had a very close tie with the *evolutionists.* It is a part of Comte's theory that civilisation evolves through three stages: the theological, the metaphysical, and the positive. These stages represent an evolutionary theory of society. It is not surprising, therefore, that Comte's followers were among the first to support Darwin's theory of biological evolution when it appeared in 1859. They, with Herbert Spencer and Thomas Huxley, grafted Darwin's theory on to the positive philosophy.

Thus positivism found strong allies. Empiricism, materialism, and evolutionism were the philosophical foundations of a scientific revolution that was rapidly changing the nineteenth-century man's conception of himself and his world. Because psychology became an experimental science during this period, all three of these great traditions contributed to it, nourished it, and helped to define its problems and its methods.

Of these three traditions, empiricism was probably the most important during the initial development of scientific psychology. Empiricism has played a dual role in the history of psychology, for it provides both a *method* to increase knowledge and a *theory* about the growth of the mind. As a method, empiricism means that we learn by making observations, by having new experiences, by conducting experiments. As a psychological theory, empiricism means that a child's mind at birth is a blank slate upon which experience will write. It is possible, of course, to apply the empirical method without subscribing to an empiricist theory of the mind — but the historical fact is that men who subscribed to one often believed the other as well. If you hold an empiricist theory about the growth of the mind, you are likely to see the empirical method as the only possible way for anyone to acquire knowledge — the scientist, philosopher, child, or plain man. An empiricist theory of the mind is particularly useful to support and explain the success of empirical methods in modern science.

Empirical methods are sometimes contrasted with rational methods of acquiring knowledge. In this context, the empirical method is said to be inductive, whereas the rational method is deductive. The empiricist theory, on the other hand, has generally been contrasted with a *nativist* theory of the mind; the empiricist says that a child must learn everything through experience; and the nativist replies that some things are inherited and must be present at birth.

Although it is possible to find clear anticipations of empiricism — it was Aristotle, after all, who coined the famous metaphor about the baby's mind being a blank slate—its greatest thrust was felt in the writings of the seventeenth-century British philosopher John Locke. Locke deeply admired Isaac Newton and tried to develop a philosophy based, like Newton's science, on observable things and events.

In his great *An Essay Concerning Human Understanding* (1690), Locke defended the premise that all ideas originate in experience:

Let us then suppose the mind to be, as we say, white paper void of all characters, without any ideas: How comes it to be furnished? Whence comes it by that vast store which the busy and boundless fancy of man has painted on it with an almost endless variety? Whence has it all the *materials* of reason and knowledge? To this I answer, in one word, from *experience.* In that all our knowledge is founded; and from that it ultimately derives itself. Our observation, employed either about external sensible objects, or about the internal operations of our minds, perceived and reflected on by ourselves, is that which supplies our understandings with all the *materials* of thinking. These two are the fountains of knowledge, from whence all the ideas we have, or can naturally have, do spring.

A newborn infant must acquire his ideas of this world by observing what goes on around him; the limits of his understanding are set by the limits of his senses and his reason.

Locke's argument was immediately successful, and empiricism rapidly became the dominant philosophy oft he eighteenth century. Its influence extended into every intellectual nook and cranny; into education, into social, political, and economic theory. Its effect on psychology was only one aspect of this broad and influential movement.

We can summarise briefly the major implications for psychology: First, of course, empiricism places enormous emphasis upon the processes or *sensation,* for the senses are the doors to the mind through which all knowledge of the world must pass. The British — always the most loyal adherents to an empiricist position — have forever baffled their Continental friends by their faith in perception as the cornerstone of all philosophical truth. Second, empiricism usually leads to analysis into *elements,* analysis of conscious experience into the simple ideas that are the basic building blocks of the mind. The simple ideas — blueness, loudness, saltiness, the odour of turpentine — are sensory elements into which the more complicated ideas can eventually be analysed. Third, empirical analysis into elements creates a need for a corresponding conception of empirical synthesis into compounds—a theory of *association* whereby simple elements can combine to form more complicated elements. As the empiricists developed their doctrine, the importance of associative processes became more and more obvious; there was much debate over rival sets of laws describing how associations are formed. Fourth, empiricism emphasises the importance of *conscious* processes in knowledge — of perceptions and images — and neglects the possibility that mental processes might not always be immediately apparent to their host. Fifth, it is a theory about the *individual* mind; social implications are not considered. All minds are created free and equal. An individual mind is a private, personal thing, completely independent of all other private, personal minds and free to enter into any contracts or agreements with others that suit its own purposes.

Even in its youth empiricism made easy alliances with materialism. A worthy precursor of positivistic thinking about the human mind was provided by a British physician, David Hartley, who in 1749 explained in his *Observations on Man* how our ideas become associated with one another. It is simply a matter of resonance. According to Hartley, an idea is a vibration in the nerves. By resonance, one vibration sets off another. Thus he explained how one idea can lead to another, and so proposed a material basis for the empiricist theory of the mind.

By the second half of the nineteenth century, of course, physiological theories had advanced well beyond Hartley's mechanical vibrations in the nerves; by then it was clear that chemical and electrical processes were involved. But the general purpose of the endeavour did not change. Materialists are never satisfied that they understand something until they can explain it in terms of the properties of material substances. Their task is to find a materialistic basis for everything, including thought, that takes place in the human body. This was the programme for physiology during the nineteenth century — and by 1870 the doctrine that all human acts can be explained by physico-chemical principles had completely captured the thinking of physiologists and physicians.

Sensory physiology developed quite rapidly during the nineteenth century. Physiologists who studied the nervous system scored some of their earliest successes with the receptor organs and with the sensory nerves leading from the receptors to the brain. The bulk of this work was done in Germany — G. T. Fechner, Hermann Ludwig von Helmholtz, Ewald Hering were among the leaders — but the work bore an interesting relation to the empiricist philosophy of England. The Germans knew how the receptors worked; the British knew why they were important. Given the positivistic spirit of the times it was inevitable that the two lines or thought should converge. When this happened, psychology became an experimental science.

Wilhelm Wundt, the son of a Lutheran pastor, was born in 1832 at Neckarau, a suburb of Mannheim, in the German state of Baden. His childhood was solemn and studious. When he was eight years old, his schooling became the responsibility of his father's assistant, a vicar whose room Wilhelm shared. The boy formed a deep attachment to his mentor, who received the affection normally reserved for parents, and, when the vicar was called to a neighbouring town, Wilhelm went with him. There is no record of any other boyhood friends, no foolish pranks or young adventures, no boisterous laughter or silly giggles — only study, reading, work, and more study. So far as one can tell, he was a humourless, indefatigable scholar from the day of his birth.

The Wundts were not a wealthy family, and Wilhelm had to consider how he would support himself. He decided to become a physician. It would enable him to earn a living and to study science simultaneously. At Heidelberg, therefore, he studied anatomy, physiology, physics, chemistry, and medicine, and slowly discovered that the medical profession was not for him. He had instead the luckiest of gifts, a calling, something he loved to do, and he determined to answer it by becoming an academician. The fact that his subject was physiology was accidental, and almost incidental. His real goal was to satisfy a lifelong lust for scholarship. He took his doctorate in medicine at Heidelberg in 1856 and was then habilitated as *Privatdozent* in physiology.

In 1858 Hermann Ludwig von Helmholtz, soon to become the greatest physiologist in the world, moved to Heidelberg. Young Wundt received an appointment as his assistant. But it was dreary work; Wundt was responsible for drilling the sudden influx of new students in their laboratory fundamentals. After a few years of this routine he resigned in order to resume his former position. The years spent in the same laboratory with Helmholtz did not inspire him to novel achievements in physiology. Indeed, it was during this period that he lost interest in pure physiology and began to question the positivistic philosophy. He was finding himself intellectually, deciding his position, and laying out the programme of work that would occupy him for the rest of his life. For six decades, long after he had left Heidelberg to become the famous professor at Leipzig, Wundt followed this programme with persistence and unremitting energy.

What Wundt did was to look at the psychological problems posed by the British philosophers with the eyes of a man trained in the traditions of German physiology. The notion that psychology could become a science of observation and experiment had been stated clearly and explicitly by the British philosopher John Stuart Mill in his *Logic* as early as 1843, but it required a person who really knew how observation and experiments are made to bring it off. Wundt was that person.

It would be wrong, however, to think of Wundtian psychology as a simple union of empiricist British philosophy and materialist German physiology. Wundt was not willing to reduce the mind to a physical process in the brain, nor was he willing to abandon metaphysics as empty nonsense. Thus, even though positivism had created an intellectual atmosphere in which it seemed reasonable to be scientific about everything, even consciousness, the founder of this new science thought of himself as in revolt against the positivistic spirit of his day. In this respect Wundt anticipated some aspects of the upheaval of the 1890s when a great flood or genius — Weber, Durkheim, Sorel, Pareto, Freud, James, Dewey, Croce, Bergson — broke free at last from the constrictions positivism had placed on social and psychological thought.

The programme to which Wundt devoted his life was first published in the introduction to his book, *Contributions to the Theory of Sensory Perception*, in 1862. The body of the book — a summary of the medical psychology of perception — is of little value a century later. But the introduction is interesting. It sets forth three projects that the young physiologist invented: to create an experimental psychology, to create a scientific metaphysics, and to create a social psychology. He then set to work with what may have been the most tireless pen in the whole history of German scholarship. By 1920, some fifty thousand pages later, his projects were complete and he could permit himself to die.

The sheer bulk of his writing made Wundt almost immune to criticism. A critic would be outwritten, evaded by qualifications, and buried under mountains of detail. Wundt's theories were more like classification schemes than like systems of functional relations; they tended to be loosely knit and almost impossible either to prove or to disprove. There was no vital centre to his thought where an opponent could slay him with a single blow. 'Cut him up like a worm,' said William James, 'and each fragment crawls.' The same quality makes it impossible to summarise his work or reduce it to a simple formula.

For Wundt, psychology involved the analysis of consciousness into elements, the determination of the manner in which these elements are connected, and the determination of the laws of connection. This conception he borrowed from the British empiricists. Just as chemists had analysed matter into atoms and anatomists had analysed living systems into cells, psychologists, he decided, must analyse mind into the elementary sensations and feelings that make it up. Wundt once summarised this thesis in a ponderous, German way:

> All the contents of psychical experience are of a composite character. It follows, therefore, that *psychical elements,* or the absolutely simple and irreducible components of psychical phenomena, are the products of analysis and abstraction.... As a result of psychical analysis, we find that them am *psychical elements of two kinds....* The elements of the objective contents we call *sensational elements,* or simply *sensations:* such are a tone, or a particular sensation of heat, cold, or light, if in each case we neglect for the moment all the connexions or these sensations with others, and also their spatial and temporal relations. The subjective elements, on the other hand, are designed as *affective elements,* or *simple feelings....* The actual contents of psychical experience always consist of various combinations of sensational and affective elements, so that the specific character of a given psychical process depends for the most part, not on the nature of its elements, so much as on the union of these elements into a composite psychical compound.

Since the contents of psychical experience at any given instant are likely to be rather complex, the variety of ways to analyse them into elements, to classify and relate those elements to one another provided material for almost endless subtleties and fine distinctions—a realm in which the patient, scholarly, encyclopedic Wundt was grand master.

Yet his purpose was as straightforward as his arguments were complicated. His first goal was to establish psychology as a science. By 1874, the year he moved to Leipzig as professor of philosophy, the hard-working Wundt was well along towards his goal. That year the first edition of his *Physiological Psychology* was published. In he preface he said: 'The work which I here present to the public is an attempt to mark out a new domain of science.' This book, which he rewrote and expanded five times, was Wundt's masterpiece. It firmly established psychology as a laboratory science with its own problems and its own experimental methods. This scientific version became known as 'the new psychology', in order to distinguish it from 'the old psychology' that had been produced in the philosopher's armchair.

When a living system is studied from the outside, it is physiology. According to Wundt, when we study a living system from the inside, it is psychology. The only way we can study a living system from within is by self-observation, or *introspection.* Of course, the most remarkable thing about introspection is that we can do it at all — but Wundt could shed no more light on that accomplishment than we can today. So he accepted it as given and went on to ask what could be learned from it.

We learn little about our minds from casual, haphazard self-observation, just as we learned little about mechanics from centuries of casual, uncontrolled observation of falling bodies. It is essential that observations be made by trained observers under carefully specified conditions for the purpose of answering well-defined questions. To Wundt, 'scientific' meant 'experimental'; if psychology was to become a science, it would have to use its introspective approach in an experimental situation in a laboratory where all conditions could be precisely controlled and repeated. Only in the special environment of a laboratory could the elusive elements of conscious experience be analysed accurately.

At Leipzig Wundt presented the odd spectacle of a professor of philosophy who gave scientific demonstrations during his lectures. How else could an ex-physiologist make his point? These demonstrations became such an important part of his thinking that in 1879 he started his own laboratory — the world's first formal laboratory of psychology. And as he began to train young philosophers to use the scientific method, it became necessary to find some place to publish their results. In 1881 he started a magazine called the *Philosophische Studien,* the first effective journal for experimental psychology. With a handbook, a laboratory, and a scholarly journal, the new psychology was well under way.

In his prime, *Herr Geheimrat* Professor Doctor Wilhelm Wundt was tall, thin, slightly stooped, with a large head, a pleasant face, and a full beard. He wore thick, dark glasses and could use only part of the vision of one eye during the last half of his life. In spite of this handicap, he worked with unflagging zeal. He seems to have had no capacity for boredom. In the morning he worked at home on the many books that remain his monument, read student theses, and edited his journal. In the afternoon he took a walk, and attended examinations or visited his laboratory. On his arrival at the laboratory, he went directly to his private room, where he held conferences. Some days he toured the laboratory and inspected the experiments. His lectures were given at four o'clock, well after dark during the winter months. As a professor he enjoyed a high social standing and easy financial circumstances, a position of privilege granted all German professors before World War I. His security and his family made life seem both cheerful and productive.

Wundt was the most popular lecturer at Leipzig," the largest lecture hall was never large enough to hold all those who wanted to hear him. One of his most famous students, E. B. Titchener — who later disseminated Wundtian psychology to America from his professorial chair at Cornell University — recalled vividly the great man's classroom manner Wundt would appear at exactly the correct minute — punctuality was essential — dressed all in black and carrying a small sheaf of lecture notes. He clattered up the side aisle to the platforrn with an awkward shuffle and a sound as if his soles were made of wood. On the platform was a long desk where demonstrations were performed. He made a few gestures — a forefinger across his forehead, a rearrangement of his chalk — then faced the audience and placed his elbows on the bookrest. His voice was weak at first, then gained in strength and emphasis. As he talked his arms and hands moved up and down, pointing and waving, in some mysterious way illustrative. His head and body were rigid, and only the hands played back and forth. He seldom referred to the few jotted notes. As the clock struck the end of the hour he stopped and, stooping a little, clattered out as he had clattered in.

The work done in his new laboratory and published in his new journal extended in several directions. Most of it, of course, concerned sensation and perception, particularly vision and hearing; perception was the problem considered fundamental in Wundt's empirical philosophy. In these experiments Wundt was able to exploit the methods of measurement devised by that eccentric genius, Gustav Theodor Fechner; and he had the famous Fechner Law to guide him. In every respect, the analysis of perceptual processes into their elements was the simplest and most profitable line to follow in the new psychology. Next most popular were the studies of reaction time, for these seemed to provide a way to measure the speed of thought.

Psychology cannot be constructed entirely in terms of elementary sensations and their modes and levels of integration. The field of consciousness, said Wundt, has a small, bright area at its centre; he directed some of his students into research on the problems of attention. Other students attempted to study association and memory. Still others introspected on their feelings and emotions. The six rooms of his little laboratory buzzed with the discoveries and arguments of the students as they applied analytic introspection to one problem after another.

One series of experiments on attention used a metronome, an instrument for marking exact time in music. As all music students know, a metronome produces clearly audible clicks at regular intervals; the rate of the clicks can be adjusted to suit the tempo of the music. Wundt's listeners were asked to form rhythmic groupings of the clicks and to report their conscious experiences. The introspective method used in such experiments is simple to describe, but it requires considerable training and self-discipline to use. Stimuli — in this case the sequence of clicks — are presented while the subject pays careful attention to all that he notices. When stimulation ends, the subject gives a full verbal report. In an experiment on attention, the subject may be interested in whether a particular pattern of clicks can be held in consciousness as a unitary whole. However, exactly the same source of stimulation can be used to investigate other aspects of conscious experience.

Consider how he worked: Wundt reported from his own introspections that at the end of a rhythmic row of beats he had the impression of an agreeable whole. That is, some rhythmic patterns are more pleasant, more agreeable than others. He concluded from this self-observation that part of the experience of any pattern of beats is a subjective feeling of pleasure or displeasure, a feeling that can be located somewhere along a continuum ranging from that agreeable to the disagreeable. While he listened to the clicks, however, he detected another kind of feeling about them. As he expectantly awaited each successive click he felt a slight tension; after the anticipated click occurred he felt relief. This alternation between tension and relief was clearest when the clicks came at a slow rate. In addition to a pleasure-displeasure continuum, therefore, his feelings seemed to have a tension-relief dimension. But that was not all. When the rate of the clicks was increased, he said, he felt mildly excited; when the rate slowed, he had a quieting feeling. In this way, by patiently varying the speed of the metrenome and carefully noting his subjective experience—his sensations and feelings — Wundt teased out three distinct and independent dimensions: agreeableness-disagreeableness, strain-relaxation, excitement-calm. Every conscious feeling, he said, can be located somewhere in three-dimensional space [Figure 25.1].

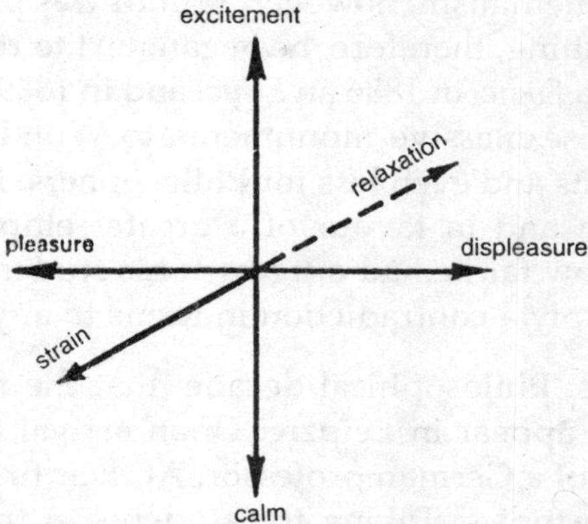


**Fig. 25.1.** Wundt's tri-dimensional theory of feeling. Every feeling is supposed to be located somewhere in this space.

This was the kind of introspective evidence on which he based his hotly disputed tri-dimensional theory of feeling. Emotions, he argued, are complex combinations or patterns of these elementary conscious feelings, and each elementary feeling can be completely described by stating its position along each one of three dimensions. History has dealt harshly with his effort to reduce emotions to conscious contents of the mind: emotions may involve feelings, people may be able to make judgements based on those feelings, but it is not possible to say that emotions are *nothing but* feelings. Wundt's analysis ignored the meaning of the situation in which the motion is experienced.

Nevertheless, Wundt's introspections held a great fascination or his students. Who would have guessed that anything as familiar is one's own mind could harbour all these shadowy and unexpected elements? Who could guess what other pumpkins might turn into coaches when examined with the marvellous inner eye? Wundt's talent for making the perfectly familiar seem completely novel and mysterious — by stripping off its meaning and cutting it up in pieces — was the source of both his strength and his weakness as a psychologist.

Note how hard it is to disprove his claims. If your own introspections give you a different result, how can you decide who is right? Perhaps you misunderstand his description of his experience; perhaps you paid attention to the wrong things; perhaps you do not know how to introspect properly; perhaps you and Wundt are not made the same way; and so on. His experiments, unlike experiments elsewhere in science, do not insure agreement among all hose who witness them. Introspective observation is essentially private, and disagreements cannot be settled by repeated observations.

But scientific psychology had to start somewhere. It was not obvious in advance that a direct attack on the mind would not be the best approach. And there was always the hope that introspective reports would parallel the physiological indicators.

In spite of his eccentric experimentalism, however, Wundt was professor of philosophy. With scientific psychology flourishing, therefore, he began next to record his philosophical convictions. In 1880 he produced a *Logic,* in 1886 an *Ethic,* and in 1889 the crown of his work, a *System of Philosophy.* Today these massive monuments to Wundt's tireless scholarship hold little interest for psychologists and even less for Philosophers. But that he could argue against the prevailing Positivism and in favour of a greater emphasis on metaphysical problems in Philosophy shows how far he had outgrown his student days. His conception of scientific metaphysics was simply a contradiction in terms to any good Positivist.

It was during this time — his 'Philosophical decade' that the first of a long string of students from America began to appear in Leipzig. Upon arrival they found themselves apprenticed to the perfect model of a German professor. At their first conference he would appear holding a list of research topics. Taking the students in the order in which they stood—there was no question of their being seated — he assigned one topic to each. He supervised their work on these topics most carefully; when the thesis was completed he held complete power of acceptance or rejection. If part of the work failed to support his theories, it might be instantly deleted. German scientific dogmatism was no myth, and it flourished undisguised in the little laboratory at Leipzig.

The last of Wundt's three lifetime projects was to create social psychology. This he did with characteristic industry in the ten volumes of his *Elements of Folk Psychology* which appeared during the last twenty years of his life. The concept of *Volk* which had gradually emerged during Germany's struggle for political unification now seemed ripe for psychological exploitation. Thus he moved even further away from positivism; in his view, the collective, social, folk mind transcended the individual minds that composed it. The folk mind manifested itself in languages, art, myths, social customs, law, and morals — cultural works that an individual never makes in isolation.

This opinion had an important implication, for it divided his science of psychology into two parts, the experimental and the social. According to Wundt, the simpler mental functions — sensation, perception, memory, simple feelings — can be studied by laboratory experiments on the minds of individuals. But the higher rental processes involved in human thinking are so strongly conditioned by linguistic habits, moral ideas, and ideological convictions that scientific experiments are impossible. Human thinking, he said, can be explored only by the nonexperimental methods of anthropology, sociology, and social psychology. Thinking cannot be understood through the analysis of logic, for it is too often illogical; and it is too complicated to be studied by simple introspection on the mental events that accompany it. Only by studying he *products* of thought as these have accumulated during man's history can we hope to understand thinking.

Wundt's observation that social products, especially language, play a central role in all of the more complicated mental processes of an educated, adult human being is both true and important. But the conclusion he based on this observation — that complicated mental processes cannot be studied experimentally — has not stood the test of time. Other psychologists have proved that experiments can be done on the so-called higher mental processes. The proofs is the experiments themselves. It was necessary to burst through the rigid, introspective limits that Wundt had set for his new science, to devise new methods and invent new theories; this was done. Almost before it was properly born, therefore, scientific psychology began to evolve and to expand.

Wundt's genius was the kind Thomas Edison described — one per cent inspiration and ninety-nine per cent perspiration. One cannot help marvelling at Wundt's energy and endurance over a period of sixty years. Yet it is his first achievement — the creation of a scientific, experimental psychology — that must command our greatest respect. His later work is now largely forgotten. His philosophy was undistinguished, and his social psychology came too late.

It was his experimental psychology, and his enormous scholarship, exhibited in three fat volumes, that made Wundt's influence felt. Where Mill only talked about doing psychological experiments, Wundt did them. He conducted them in a laboratory that he designed for the purpose, published them in his own journal, and tried to incorporate them into a systematic theory of the human mind. And he trained his students well; they founded more laboratories and continued to experiment. As a direct result of his labours, psychology was provided with all the trappings of a modern science. For that service, all psychologists, even those who bitterly opposed his theories, are permanently indebted to the indefatigable Wilhelm Wundt.

> The biologically, culturally, and socially influenced process of memory organisation [said Schachtel] results in the formation of categories (schemata) of memory which are not suitable vehicles to receive and reproduce experiences of the quality and intensity typical of early childhood. The world of modern Western civilisation has no use for this type of experience. In fact, it cannot permit itself to have any use for it, it cannot permit the memory of it, because such memory, if universal would explode the restrictive social order of this civilisation.

These intimate memories of childhood are obviously of great concern to students of personality, many of whom believe that the adult personality sets like plaster after the first few years of life. Freud particularly emphasised the social necessity of repressing childish memories of sexual pleasure, in order to enable the adult to function effectively in Western culture. But Freud's observation does not explain why all our childhood memories, sexual and asexual alike, are so thoroughly forgotten. In the course of growing up there are several cognitive revolutions that completely reorganise a child's intellectual life. As new and more efficient cognitive systems emerge, the peculiarly intense memories of a child find no place in them. The child is not forgotten; it is simply isolated from the day-to-day experience of the normal adult, because the child existed before the categories of the adult mind had been achieved.

An attentive reader will not have overlooked the metaphorical basis of this discussion — the assumption that memory is a place where information can be stored, just as a warehouse is a place where merchandise can be stored. This seems to make memory a substantial thing that a person possesses in the same way he possesses a head and two hands. Although the metaphor may help us to organise and understand many phenomena of memory that are psychologically significant, it is difficult to suppress a certain uneasiness about this reification of the memory process. To avoid this metaphor, many psychologists prefer to speak of memory as something a person does, rather than something he has. This attitude leads to another set of questions about the effects of past experience on present behaviour.

## IVAN PETROVICH PAVLOV, PHYSIOLOGIST

This is *materialism.* At the time Bernard wrote, materialism was generally considered a necessary assumption for any scientific inquiry into living systems. When you study Bernard's book carefully, however, you discover that the great French physiologist was less concerned to reduce all vital phenomena to matter and energy than to show that they are — potentially — as intelligible as the more familiar physico-chemical phenomena. No divine soul or free will capriciously altered his measurements, no supernatural or inexplicable forces intervened unpredictably to spoil his experiments. Bernard fully expected to see vital phenomena reduced to materialistic terms, but this meant less to him than the broader principle that scientific methods can be successfully applied to giving organisms. Vital phenomena are governed by laws — laws true always and everywhere.

The positivistic faith (that science can be applied to man and all his affairs) and the materialistic faith (that the results will be expressed as physico-chemical laws) are not always kept apart; they were never closer than when Bernard wrote. In Germany, for example, the science of physiology was controlled by four men: Hermann Ludwig von Helmholtz, Emil Du Bois-Reymond, Ernst Brucke, and Carl Ludwig. These four formed a private club in Berlin whose members were pledged to destroy vitalism, a pledge that one of them phrased so:

> No other forces than the common physical-chemical ones are active within the organism. In those cases which cannot at the time be explained by these forces one has either to find the specific way or form of their action by means of the physical-mathematical method or assume new forces equal in dignity to the chemical-physical forces inherent in matter, reducible to the force of attraction and repulsion.

This pledge expresses materialism in a pure form, flatly denying that life might involve vital forces transcending the force of attraction and repulsion'. It is curious to see how easily positivism, which began in violent opposition to any metaphysical dogma whatsoever, slips over into this kind of materialism — into the metaphysical dogma that true existence is reserved exclusively for physical and chemical objects. There is no way to know in advance what kinds or laws will prove necessary as science advances, yet a materialist feels comforted to think that the new laws will always look just like the old ones.

During the last half of the nineteenth century the Helmholtz school of medicine, brandishing its materialistic credo, completely dominated physiological and medical thinking. It was into this intellectual atmosphere that scientific psychology was born.

And it was in this intellectual atmosphere that the pioneer psychologists were educated. Freud was Brucke's student; Pavlov studied under Ludwig; Wundt was Du Bois-Reymond's student and Helmholtz's assistant. With physiology reduced to chemistry and physics, the next step was to reduce psychology to physiology. In that way the students were expected to carry on the work of their teachers. Freud to the end of his life talked about the mind in hydraulic, mechanical, electrical, and physical metaphors. Pavlov would never concede that his physiological interpretation of conditioning experiments was merely an elaborate figure of speech. And even Wundt, who tried to break with the positivistic tradition, founded his new psychology by writing a text, not on psychology, but on physiological psychology.

But the students were not always loyal to their teachers. Wundt deliberately defected. Freud tried to remain loyal, but supplied the revolt with powerful ammunition. Of all the pioneer psychologists the one most faithful to the materialistic standards of nineteenth century science was Pavlov, probably because he never realised that he had become a psychologist.

When materialists try to defend the idea that living systems are nothing but machines they generally begin with the most automatic and involuntary activities they can think of. Those are the reflexes and instincts. Exactly what an instinct is has been the focus of much argument. Some people use the term to mean all the driving desires and passions of the flesh; others mean any reactions in organism is born with and so does not need to learn: and still others take the position that an instinct is any highly automatic, involuntary, sequence of responses. The importance of instincts for a materialist conception of man has waxed and waned from me generation to the next. The reflex, however, has played a more constant role.

A reflex is an involuntary, unlearned, predictable response to a proven stimulus (or class of stimuli), a response that is not influenced by any conscious thought or resolution, but that can usually be ten to have some clear purpose in protecting the organism or helping it to adjust to its environment. The study of reflex action has a long history. Probably the first person to give a systematic discussion resembling our modern conception of the reflex was the French philosopher Rene Descarts. A mechanistic description of the body was a fundamental part of the Cartesian philosophy, which distinguished sharply between the mortal body — a machine and the immortal soul that transcended space and time yet was somehow capable of controlling the material body. The automatic actions that the soul was unable to control voluntarily were what Descartes called reflexes. The seventeenth century's ideas about physiology were rather crude, however; Descartes spoke of animal spirits being reflected (hence the term reflex) into the muscles by an image in the pineal gland.

In the years that followed, a brilliant array of men — philosophers, physicians, natural scientists — contributed to the growing knowledge about the structure and function of the nervous system. The most significant step forward was probably the discovery, early in the nineteenth century, that the nerves attached to the spinal cord had a clear division of function. Sir Charles Bell in England and Francois Magendie in France were able to show that he nerves entering the back side of the spinal cord were important for sensory processes, and nerves entering the front side were important for muscular movements. Thus some of the neural pathways involved in reflex action were first revealed.

One of the most attractive figures in this story was the enthusiastic Scottish physician Marshall Hall, who had a rare gift for thinking clearly and simply in his experiments, his theories, and his writings. Hall's major argument was that reflexes are unconscious, an argument that struck at the well-established myth that all nervous activity is, or could be, conscious. Hall won his point so thoroughly that half a century later Wundt took it for granted that his new psychology could have nothing to do with reflexes. If they were unconscious, they were not accessible to introspection and so must be relegated to physiology. This convenient distinction between unconscious physiology and conscious psychology exploded, however, when Freud showed how much of our mental life is unconscious and when Pavlov adopted the reflexes as the fundamental building blocks for all behaviour.

After Pavlov many psychologists especially some American behaviourists, went to the opposite extreme from Wundt and based all psychology on reflexes. Their theories would have been nonsense, of course, if all the reflexes had to be inborn. Reflexes could not possibly play such an important role unless they could somehow be modified as the result of experience. But how can experience modify a reflex? This was the crucial question Pavlov tried to answer.

Ivan Petrovich Pavlov was born in 1849 in Ryazan, a provincial town in central Russia. He was the first of many children, most of whom died in infancy. His grandfather was a peasant and his father a priest; in nineteenth-century Russia that had a rather special meaning.

The social structure of Russia prior to the middle of the nineteenth century was exceedingly simple. There were effectively two social classes: the gentry, or aristocracy, which held all wealth and privilege, and the peasantry, which made up about ninety per cent of the population. (The clergy served the peasantry and were close to them.) The Russian government was equally simple; it consisted of a military aristocracy that did little more than maintain order at home and wage war abroad. During the nineteenth century, however; a third, intermediate class, the intelligentsia, began to emerge from the educational system fostered by Alexander I. It consisted of members of the aristocracy who had fallen upon hard times and members of the peasantry whose talent and energy had lifted them above their class into an Intellectual life centred around the universities. The intelligentsia was a uniquely Russian institution, a social class united solely by bonds of education and moral passion. In so far as they filled a position intermediate between the gentry and the peasantry, the members of the intelligentsia might be compared with the middle-class *bourgeoisie* in the rest of Europe. But the comparison would be quite misleading. The Russian intelligentsia did not play any commercial role; its special dedication was to reform the Russian government.

As a son of a clergyman, Vanya was permitted to attend the local theological seminary, where his interest in science was encouraged, and in 1870 he was able to continue his studies at the University or St Petersburg (now Leningrad). In that way he joined the socially intermediate class, too well-educated and too intelligent for the peasantry from which he came, but too common and too poor for the aristocracy into which he could never rise. These social conditions often produced an especially dedicated intellectual, one whose entire life "as centred on the intellectual pursuits that justified his existence. And so it was with Pavlov, whose almost fanatic devotion to pure science and to experimental research was supported by the energy and simplicity of a Russian peasant. Those traits characterised the man and his work throughout his life.

In the theological seminary Pavlov was encouraged to follow his own intellectual inclinations, a freedom denied in most Russian schools at that time. His early reading included Herbert Spencer, who became one or his favourite authors, and Charles Darwin, whose teachings and personality he idolised to the end of his days. While still a boy of fifteen he read a Russian translation of George Henry Lewes's *Physiology of Common Life* and became intrigued with a complicated drawing of the digestive system that Lewes had reproduced from Claude Bernard. Pavlov's interest in the physiology of digestion, which culminated in a Nobel prize forty years later, began when he looked at Bernard's drawing and asked himself how such a complicated system could work.

At the University of St Petersburg the teacher who influenced him most was Ilya Cyon, the professor of physiology. Cyon was an artistic experimenter with exceptional skill in surgery; he wrote a first-rate text on experimental techniques in physiology; his lectures were both masterful and inspiring. 'Never can such a teacher be forgotten said Pavlov. It was Cyon who started Pavlov, then still an undergraduate, on his first physiological experiment. Upon graduation Pavlov was to have become a research assistant, but when Cyon was dismissed for political reasons, Pavlov resigned in protest.

Pavlov's determination to become an experimental physiologist seems never to have wavered. After one taste of research all the practical issues — his position, salary, living conditions, even the clothes he wore — became little more than unavoidable annoyances intruding upon the only part of life that really mattered. In the early years his single-mindedness protected him from the anxieties of poverty; later it protected him from the distractions of fame and administrative responsibility.

In 1881 he married Seraphima Karchevskaya, who devoted her life to protecting him from all mundane intrusions. She discovered her responsibilities rather suddenly when Ivan Petrovich turned up without the money to pay for their wedding or their return fares to St Petersburg. So she paid their expenses out of her own savings, and the two of them arrived penniless in St Petersburg. Pavlov's entire income was fifty rubles a month, but he refused to let Sara find a job. He borrowed two hundred rubles, and somehow they managed to exist. It was characteristic of him that Sara often had to remind him when it was time to go and collect his salary.

Only unwavering faith enabled his wife and friends to put up with him. His complete inability to manage his financial affairs was not his only peculiarity: he was equally difficult in other matters. For example, he liked to take long walks with his wife, but he set such a strenuous pace that she often had to run to keep up. During her first pregnancy this exertion caused Sara to miscarry. When he realised what had happened, of course, Pavlov was greatly dismayed. During her second pregnancy, therefore, he was determined to be more careful. So he swung over to the opposite extreme and even insisted on carrying her in his arms up their fourth-floor apartment. In every way he was the tender thoughtful husband. But when the child was born, he had no honey to support it.

He once accepted an invitation for Sara and himself to attend a party at a professor's home. She was to go alone; he would join her there as soon as he could get away from a scientific meeting. It was a rare treat for her. She had a new dress, she was in excellent spirits, witty, animated, talkative. When Pavlov arrived later the host jokingly reproached him for having hidden so lovely a person from them all. Pavlov frowned. He had a headache. He was going home at once. Sara could stay if she liked. She left with him, told him everything she had said at the party and promised never to go anywhere again without him, but he sulked for two days.

> This was so painful to me [she wrote later] that I told myself that I would not take so much interest in dresses and that I would make a vow of silence. This attitude on my part brought extremely good results. Ivan Petrovich was spared sleepless nights and saved from unpleasant and painful thoughts.

In the words of James Thurber, a woman's place is in the wrong.

The Russian peasant custom of swaddling their babies for long periods, alternating with joyous episodes of play and affection, has been blamed for generating personalities that alternate between stolid, patient, self-restraint and explosive, emotional release.' Whether or not swaddling has anything to do with these extreme fluctuations is debatable, but certainly Pavlov's behaviour often cli into this pattern. He would flare up at trivialities. If his surgery vent badly, he might blame his assistant, waving his arms and wearing profusely. Once he hot-headedly whipped a dog whose whining bothered him, then admonished the assistant never to whip a dog because it might spoil his experiment. During the revolution he scolded one of his assistants for arriving ten minutes ate for an experiment; shooting and fighting in the streets should not interfere when there was work to be done in the laboratory. Usually these outbursts were quickly forgotten. When a student discovered that no grudges were held, that no subtle meanings.

Eventually the dog would begin to salivate as soon as it saw the bread. But if bread was repeatedly shown and withheld, the dog would gradually stop responding to the visual stimulus. The reflex salivation when bread was placed in its mouth was a natural reflex of the digestive system — what Pavlov called an inborn or unconditional reflex. Salivation at the sight of the bread, however was not an inborn reflex, but was something the dog learned soda; Pavlov called the response at the sight of the food a conditional reflex because its occurrence was conditional upon a prior association between seeing the food and tasting it.

Pavlov thought of, and occasionally discussed, the difference between these two kinds of reflexes by analogy with a telephone system. For a reflex to occur when the appropriate stimulus is given, he believed, there must be a neural path connecting the receptor organ to the gland or muscle that makes the response. For the inborn reflex that path is already completed at birth and corresponds to a direct telephone line. The path of a conditional reflex, however, must be created by making a connexion through the central switchboard, by creating an engram in the central nervous system.

He soon discovered that conditional reflexes are affected by everything that goes on around the animal. In order to eliminate as many haphazard influences as he could, he put the dog and the experimenter in separate rooms. The dog was loosely strapped into a test frame where, like a swaddled Russian baby, he remained patiently immobile for hours at a time. Pavlov devised elaborate, systems of tubes for presenting the stimuli and observing the secretory response (usually salivation) from outside the animal's room. And he substituted arbitrary conditional stimuli — a bell or a light — in place of the sight of bread in his band. He discovered that any stimulus whatever could be made the occasion for conditional salivation.

In this way he arrived at the experimental procedure known as conditioning: a bell (conditional stimulus) is repeatedly sounded just before food (unconditional stimulus) is placed in the mouth to produce salivation (unconditional response), until eventually the sound of the bell causes salivation (conditional responsed before the food is presented. This was the weapon with which Pavlov attacked the terrible riddles of the central nervous system.

He took special pride in the fact that his method was completely objective. In 1903 in one of his first public descriptions of this research he emphatically rejected any of the subjective methods of psychology.

In hour 'psychical' experiments on the salivary glands, (he said] at first we honestly endeavoured to explain our results by fancying the subjective condition of the animal. But nothing came of it except unsuccessful controversies, and individual, personal, uncoordinated opinions. We had to alternative but to place the investigation on a purely objective basis. For Pavlov, a single line separated physiology from psychology, objective from subjective, and science from metaphysics. But his own work helped to destroy this simple distinction by giving psychologists another way to study their subjective problems objectively.

Around 1907 Pavlov came into public conflict with Bechterev. Vladimir M. Bechterev provides an interesting contrast to Pavlov in several respects. Bechterev, the son of a minor government official, was an idealist far more typical than Pavlov of the Russian intelligentsia of the time. Both men, like many young Russian scientists in those days, went abroad for advanced studies; Pavlov took it as just another step in a direction he was already offered to increase his food rations. When a commissar phoned to say he should send for the chicken and eggs that he was allowed Pavlov said, 'No, I refuse. As long as you do not give them to every one of my collaborators, I will not take them.'

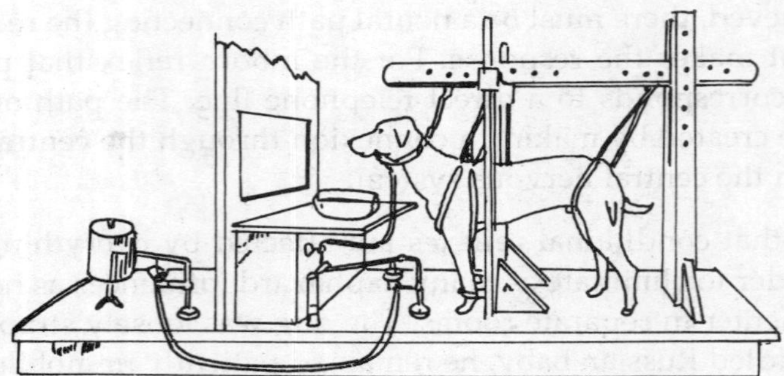

**Fig. 25.2.** Pavlov's arrangement for studying the conditional salivary reflex in dogs.

In 1927 when the sons of priests were expelled from the medical schools, he resigned from his chair as Professor of Physiology, saying, 'I am the son of a priest and if you expel the others, I will go too.' And when the so-called Red professors were forcibly admitted into the hitherto autonomous Academy of Science, Pavlov wrote strong letters of protest to Stalin and was the only Academician to vote against them. In order to demonstrate his disapproval of the Soviet regime he stayed away from Russian scientific meetings, even though the Congress of Physiologists regularly elected him honorary chairman in *absentia*. (In 1930, however, they passed him by and in his place elected the entire Polit Bureau of the Communist Party.)

In 1930 the central theme of a popular play, *Fear*, by Afinogenov, dealt with an eminent professor of physiology who had unconsciously played into the hands of the enemies of the Soviet state by working out a theory that fear was the essential motive in the behaviour of the Soviet people.' His theory was exposed in a public meeting by an old Bolshevik woman whose political experience compensated for her lack of formal education. She concluded her indictment of the professor with a cry to the audience to be merciless towards the real enemies of the state. The professor, converted, promised to give a public criticism of his malicious theory and to hand over all the keys to his research institute. Of course, nothing was said in the play about the Pavlov affair, but the parallel would have been hard to miss.

In 1933 apparently Pavlov had become convinced that the new government was going to survive, that it had in fact united the Russian people, and that the lavish support of science, which, in Pavlov's positivistic opinion, would in the long run resolve all social problems, meant that the government shared his own high regard for scientific truth and freedom. For the final three years of his life, therefore, Pavlov and Soviet Russia lived together in peace. Since his death in 1936 his research has been continued, his memory preserved, and his writings used to justify new scientific projects in physiology and psychology. When Russians talk about Pavlov today, the difficult interlude from 1917 to 1933 is no longer mentioned.

Why was the conditioning experiment so important? Because of its apparent simplicity, a tremendously important, voluminously discussed, little understood phenomenon, something that philosophers and psychologists had called association, was here captured in simple, objective, experimental terms.

Ordinary human behaviour is so enormously complicated that a scientist has great difficulty in knowing where to take hold of it. The first step is to find a satisfactory unit of analysis, a simple building block with which the complicated patterns of our daily conduct can be constructed. Presumably, complex behaviour could be analysed into unconditional and conditional reflexes. Pavlov's genius was to show how those simple elements could be isolated, analysed, and controlled in the laboratory.

But, if the conditional reflex is so simple, what was Pavlov doing between 1902 and 1936? The simplicity of this reflex unit has not prevented experimenters from finding many aspects of it worthy of careful study. Pavlov's experimental situation seems simple only by comparison with the overwhelming complexity of our uncontrolled behaviour. Consider a few of the dimensions that must be explored.

First, there is the time dimension: How long should the experimenter wait between successive trials? If he varies the time at which the conditional and unconditional stimuli are turned on (or turned off), what happens? Is it possible to use an empty interval of time itself as a conditional stimulus? Many experiments had to be done on these questions of timing alone.

But that was only a start. There are several aspects of the unconditional stimulus that had to be investigated: What inborn reflexes are available for an experimenter to work with? Can a well-established conditional stimulus serve as an unconditional stimulus for a higher-order reflex? What happens when the amount of the unconditional stimulus is increased? What is the effect of withholding it repeatedly, or according to some fixed or random schedule?

Similar questions can be posed about the conditional stimulus: What physical energies can be used as conditional stimuli? How sharp a distinction can an animal make between the conditional stimulus and all other stimuli?

The response also suggests several experimental questions: Is a conditional response exactly the same as an unconditional response? What aspects of a response — reaction time, probability magnitude, variability, duration — should be recorded? What other responses normally accompany the unconditional response?

And some of the most important questions concern the animals: Does conditioning depend upon its state of deprivation — hunger thirst, and the like? Or upon the time of day? Are some animals easier to condition than others? What are the effects of previous experience? Can conditional reflexes be abolished by destroying various parts of the nervous system? What would happen with a species of animal other than Pavlov's beloved dogs; with men, for example?

These questions suggest some of the variables that had to be studied. The simplicity of the conditioning situation is only relative. The important thing, however, is that all these questions can be answered-answered in objective terms. What is needed is patient experimentation, and that is exactly what Pavlov and his small army of students and assistants provided. After twenty years of research Pavlov was ready to report his preliminary answers to some of these questions, along with his theory as to why the answers came out as they did. In 1923 he published a collection of speeches, articles, and reports under the Russian title *Twenty Years of Objective Study of the Higher Nervous Activity (Behaviour) in Animals;* the anthology was ill-assorted, but Pavlov hoped it would to some extent foreshadow the book lie was planning to write later. His more systematic report appeared in 1926 under the Russian title *Lectures on Conditional Reflexes.* The delay between the time Pavlov began to study conditioning and the time he published these books was less the result of his advancing age—although he was near seventy-five — than of the great scope of the problem and his feelings of scientific responsibility for the validity of everything he published.

When a conditional salivary reflex is established by repeatedly pairing some arbitrary stimulus with food, there is characteristically a generalisation from that particular conditional stimulus to others that resemble it. For instance, if a tone of 1,000 cycles per second is established as a conditional stimulus, other tones spontaneously acquire similar properties. The ability of the other tones to evoke the conditional reflex diminishes in proportion to the intervals between these tones and 1,000 cycles. Similarly, if touching a definite circumscribed area of skin is made into a conditional stimulus, touching other skin areas will also elicit some conditional reaction, the effect diminishing with increasing distance of these areas from the one for which the conditional reflex was originally established. This phenomenon, called stimulus generalisation, is of great psychological significance; it illustrates how reactions acquired in one situation can be transferred to similar situations. If such transfer did not occur, animals, man included, would profit little from experience.

From an experimental point of view, the generalisation experiment provides a way to measure how similar two situations are for the animal; the greater the similarity, the greater will be the stimulus generalisation. Moreover, the experiment can be used to study how accurately the animal can perceive differences in its environment. Psychologists seized upon stimulus generalisation as an especially clear instance of a very important psychological process.

To Pavlov, however, stimulus generalisation was a direct indicator of physiological processes taking place in the brain. He believed that there are. two complementary processes, excitation and inhibition, perhaps corresponding to two different chemicals, that compete for control of the various parts of the brain. When a conditional reflex is formed, the conditional stimulus acquires excitatory powers; the differentiation of that particular stimulus from all others depends upon the development of inhibition for all non-reinforced stimuli.

Different stimuli affect different points on the surface of the brain. Stimulus similarity is, in Pavlovian theory, a matter of distance in the brain; the more alike two things are, the closer their neural representations will be and the greater the interaction between them. When a point is given excitatory (or inhibitory) properties by the conditioning procedure, stimulation of the point will produce a wave of excitation (or inhibition) radiating into the adjacent brain tissue, which thus lends its excitatory (or inhibitory) properties to similar stimuli. When a conditional discrimination is firmly established, only a small region of the brain corresponding to the conditional stimulus will produce a response. Inhibition lies over the rest of the brain like winter over the empty plains of central Russia, limiting all activity to the lonely stockades.

Just prior to the time Pavlov began his research on the higher nervous centres in the brain, interest in the activity of the lower nervous centres in the spinal cord had developed independently in England. C. S. Sherrington and his school carried out a brilliant analysis of the interactions among the various spinal reflexes; their results are today a generally accepted part of physiological knowledge. It is interesting historically that Pavlov's work, similar in purpose and equally brilliant, has had almost no influence upon other branches of physiology. Pavlov's principal impact has been felt in psychology. The fact is a bit ironic, considering his low opinion of psychology as a science, but the reason is not difficult to find. Pavlov did not make any direct observations of the processes going on in the brain. He based his opinion of them entirely upon inferences from what the animals did in his experiments. What he looked at directly was not the animal's brain, but the animal's behaviour. Consequently, all his statements about waves of excitation and inhibition that irradiate over the surface of the brain are little more than plausible fictions; if you opened up the skull you would not know how or where to look for them. His description of the animal's behaviour in the conditioning experiment, however, is wonderfully acute. Since experimental psychologists, inspired in no small measure by Pavlov's success, have pursued the objective description and analysis of behaviour, Pavlov's work has had its major effect on behaviouristic psychology, rather than on physiology.

From a psychological point of view one of his most interesting discoveries was experimental neurosis. If a dog is forced to learn a very difficult discrimination between two stimuli, it may become extremely disturbed. The first systematic observations of this emotional reaction were made in 1914. A dog was trained to salivate when it saw a circle. Then an ellipse was presented without any reinforcement by food; the discrimination was easily established. On subsequent days the difference between the ellipse and the circle was reduced progressively. Finally the two were so much alike that discrimination failed. After three weeks of unsuccessful training the whole behaviour of the dog changed abruptly:

> The hitherto quiet dog began to squeal in its stand, kept wriggling about, tore off with its teeth the apparatus for mechanical stimulation of the skin, and bit through the tubes connecting the animal's room with the observer, a behaviour which never happened before. On being taken into the experimental room the dog now barked violently, which was also contrary to its usual custom; in short it presented all the symptoms of a condition of acute neurosis.

Pavlov explained these symptoms as a conflict between the excitatory and inhibitory processes. Ordinarily the nervous system can establish an equilibrium between them, but, when the sources of excitation and inhibition get very close together, the equilibrium breaks down and a generally excited or inhibited state appears.

The explanation is ingenious but somewhat unreal. Considering the amount of frustration normally involved in a conditioning experiment — the restraint in the test frame, the monotonous repetition of particular stimuli — the addition of a difficult discrimination seems but a small part or the animal's discomfort. If Pavlov's excitation and inhibition had been less metaphorical, it would have been easier to test his theory directly. But it is not a physiological theory at all; it is a psychological theory disguised in physiological language.

Pavlov's interest in experimental neurosis increased as he grew older; he devoted the last decade of his life largely to psychiatric problems. When at last he began to think seriously about human behaviour Pavlov recognised that the enormous complexities introduced by language required new explanations. To his earlier distinction between inborn and conditional reflexes, therefore, he added verbal symbols. The conditional reflexes that he had so long studied in animals comprised a 'first signalling system', Men, he aid, have evolved another, a 'second signalling system' of verbal symbols. Although he was not able to develop this proposal himself, it has stimulated considerable speculation and research by subsequent generations of Russian psychologists.

Pavlov's contributions to science are everywhere known and admired, but their implications for social policy and their effects upon our conception of human nature are often deplored. Many people have been frightened by grim visions of a brave, new world where machines will condition every child into submissive uniformity. Such fears are fed by ignorance, but some fairly able spokesmen have given voice to them. George Bernard Shaw once called Pavlov a scoundrel and his teaching a crackle of blazing nonsense from beginning to end. Similar appreciations have been expressed by many other humanists.

Pavlov has often been classed with Freud as a major source of anti-intellectualism in the twentieth century. In their hands Sovereign Reason, benevolent ruler of the eighteenth-century mind, crumbled into unconscious reflexes and instincts, automatic processes that are the very antithesis of ratiocinative thought. Reason seemed to refute itself. Yet both men, Pavlov and Freud, were true children of the Enlightenment; both believed that the search for knowledge must never stop, that only knowledge allows reason to function, that only reason can make men free. Both were loyal to the highest values of their positivistic education. What they both attacked was not sovereign reason, but foolish optimism about the inevitability of human progress. To dismiss them as anti-intellectuals is a dangerous over-simplification.

No doubt Pavlov himself would prefer to be classed with his hero Darwin, with the famous biologist rather than the famous psychologist. And there is reason to respect his wish. Where Darwin showed how living organisms can adapt to their environments by hanging slowly from one generation to the next, Pavlov showed tow a living organism can adapt by changing rapidly during its own lifetime. And, like Darwin, Pavlov angered the non-scientists whose preconceived notions were threatened by his discoveries. But such anger is the way we pay our greatest men. It is a special tribute reserved for those whose work is truly significant.

# 26

# The Search for Behavioural Atoms

"If I attempt to analyse a man's entire mind [said Edward Lee Thorndike, a psychologist who for forty years was an intellectual leader on the faculty of Columbia University's famed Teachers College] I find connexions of varying strength between (a) situations, elements of situations, and compounds of situations and (b) responses, readinesses to respond, facilitations, inhibitions, and directions of responses. If all these could be completely inventoried, telling what the man would think and do and what would satisfy and annoy him, in every conceivable situation, it seems to me that nothing would be left out. . . . Learning is connecting. The mind is man's connexion-system."

Such was the associationist position in 1931. It was a linear descendant of an older associationism that began with John Locke and that inspired British empiricists for two centuries. But there was a crucial difference. Instead of connexions between ideas, Thorndike talked about connexions between situations and responses. In this way he accepted into his psychological theory a physiological frame of reference.

Thorndike stood in a proud tradition, and he spoke for a sizeable constituency among America's academic psychologists during the twenties and thirties. If the mind is man's connexion-system, then the programme of research that lay ahead was clear. Isolate the elementary connexion processes, and you will have under your control the very stuff that minds are made of. Pavlov had shown one way to study the formation of connexion in animals. Similar analysis should be possible for human behaviour, too.

Consider a person who deliberately and intentionally sets out to memorise certain verbal responses to a given set of verbal stimuli. To be definite, imagine an English-speaking student of the French language who undertakes to memorise a new section of French vocabulary. What he will try to do is to learn the meanings of unfamiliar nonsense. The kind that psychologists have standardised, following Ebbinghaus, is a three-letter, consonant-vowel Consonant (C.V.C.) 'syllable'. (C.V.C. sequences that spell familiar words are frequently considered ineligible.)

In a typical experiment on serial rote memorisation, for example, a subject may be presented with a list of ten or twelve nonsense syllables, one at a time. They appear at regular intervals, usually in the window of a mechanical device designed for this purpose.

(In one simple version a cylindrical drum papered with the syllable list slowly rotates behind a covering hood arranged to expose the syllables in a window one at a time—see Figure 26.1.) As each syllable appears in the window, the memoriser is supposed to pronounce (or spell, since some syllables may be unpronounceable) the *next* syllable on the list. The first time around, of course, he will not anticipate any of the syllables correctly, but gradually, after repeated trials, he will do better and better until eventually he will be able to anticipate each syllable before it appears.

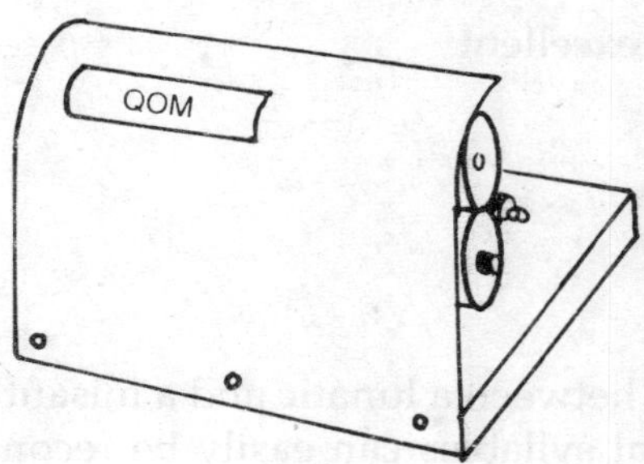


**Fig. 26.1.** A Teaching Machine That Presents Nonsense Syllables One At A Time

Psychologists soon discovered that some nonsense syllables are more nonsensical than others. For example, 'BAL', 'BIZ', 'DUL', 'JAN', 'TAL' have associations for almost everyone who speaks English, but 'CEF', 'GIW', 'MEQ', 'XAD', 'ZOJ' do not often stir our memories. In order to eliminate mnemonic tricks, therefore, it is generally assumed that nonsense syllables having low association values should be used. A sample task consisting of twelve units might be the following:

YIC
QOM
GEP
DUZ
RIJ
NAW
XOL
HUQ
TEF
ZIK
VOB
PAH

At first glance it would appear that all previous training in the use of words and sentences has been rendered worthless and inoperative. Now, surely, any learner must start afresh and form new associations for us. But never underestimate a subject's cleverness.

One person made up the following sentences in order to memorise the above list of syllables:

Why, I see qom
Qom
gets
duz,
right?
Nah!
You need excellent
hucksters
t' have
sick
vob.
Pah!

True, it sounds like an argument between a lunatic and a misanthrope, but it is not difficult to remember; from it the original syllables can easily be reconstructed. The first time he memorises such a list, a typical subject spends much of his time composing just such mnemonic crutches to guide his recitation. Syllables with low association values are more difficult to learn because it is harder, and takes longer, to construct the meaningful translation.

Even these Spartan measures, therefore, do not frustrate what has been called the learner's effort after meaning. A psychologist who is convinced that the real process of learning consists of lowering resistance to the flow of nerve impulses along certain pathways—leading from the receptor that senses the stimulus to the muscles that make the response—will look upon these verbal shenanigans as a pure nuisance. Of course, it is possible to ignore them, to deal only with an average number of correct responses on successive repetitions of the list. But if we want to examine a particular stimulus-response connexion, averages do not tell us much. Some other approach is needed. If nonsense syllables do not eliminate the use of mnemonic tricks, then they are too complicated and something still simpler should be learned. Perhaps nonsense syllables are still too much like meaningful words. To set something completely non-verbal, the task has to be simplified. Perhaps the study of motor skills can furnish what is required.

Such skills, it must be admitted, are seldom learned without any taint of verbal guidance. Even if one ignores as obviously too verbal two such carefully analysed skills as typewriting and radiotelegraphy, it remains that a verbal description of the general strategy a learner should pursue can be a tremendous aid. If you want to teach someone to hit targets that are under water, a verbal explanation of the principle of refraction can speed the learning considerably. Or if you tell a person who is learning to ride a bicycle that he should turn the front wheel in the same direction he is falling, you may shorten his learning time considerably. But verbal hints and helps are not easily discovered for every situation, and In any case it is always possible to withhold them, thus apparently forcing the learner to work without symbolic aids Here, it would seem, is a place where the elementary connexions can be studied. And, to a limited extent, this is true.

But the picture is still not as clean and neat as one might wish for the purposes of an analysis of stimuli and responses. A skilled motor performance usually runs on continuously in time, and it is not obvious where it should be dissected into discrete stimuli and responses. It is not only that both the stimulus and the response are continuous functions of time; the problem is further complicated by the fact that the consequences of the responses are fed back and modify the stimulus. Thus, one can no longer equate stimulus and response with antecedent and consequent, respectively.

The skill involved in steering a car along a winding road provides an obvious example. The road is a continuously varying stimulus that swerves left and right. The driver makes a continuously varying response as he moves the steering wheel left and right. But if he moves the wheel too far in one direction, the error shows up in the path of the car; the stimulus to turn back is correspondingly greater. The stimulus is not the road or the' direction of the car; the stimulus is the discrepancy between the two. And the driver's response is to keep that stimulus as small as he can. The complete stimulus-response-feedback loop is closely analogous to what is called a servo-mechanism, and it is a good deal more complicated than the simple S-R atom we started looking for. Apparently, the situation has still not been sufficiently simplified.

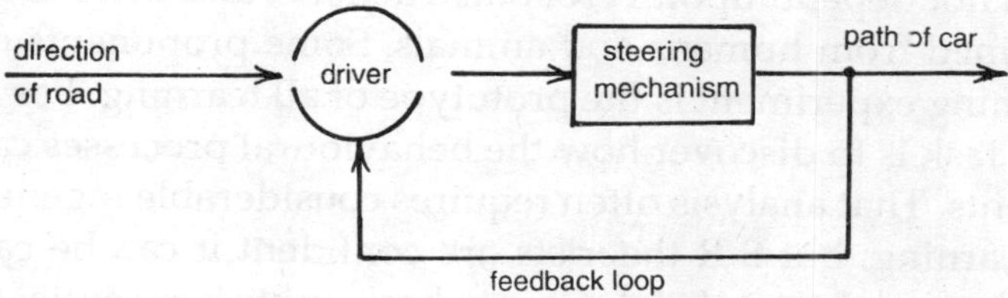


**Fig. 26.2.** Representation or an automobile and its driver as a servo-mechanism. The driver compares the direction of the road with the path of his car, and adjusts the steering mechanism to reduce the discrepancy between them.

What is necessary is to strip the learning situation to its bare essentials. It is a typical story in science. To study gravity, one must ignore the falling leaves and the drifting clouds and the winged birds that fly upward—one must get to the naked essentials that are retained when a body falls freely through a vacuum. What the S-R theorist is trying to do is to find an experimental situation that, like bodies falling in a vacuum, will provide simple, quantitative laws for the basic, underlying processes in learning. Once the laws governing (his fundamental S-R process are understood, complications can be added as they are required.

Consider the following simplification of the learning situation: A subject sits with one finger touching an electrode and a second electrode strapped to his wrist. When the experimenter closes a switch a painful electric shock results. The experimenter never closes the switch to deliver the shock, however, without first turning on a tone just a half second before. In the beginning the subject does not respond to the tone, but after a few trials in which the tone is followed by shock, he learns to straighten out his finger, thus lifting it from the electrode and avoiding the shock. So an association is established between the tonal stimulus and the response of straightening the finger.

This kind of learning is, of course, conditioning. It resembles the general pattern of experimentation used by Pavlov, but a human subject has replaced Pavlov's dog. The electric shock is an unconditional stimulus; the withdrawal by straightening and lifting the finger to escape the shock is an unconditional response; the tone that comes on a half-second before the shock is a conditional stimulus; and the withdrawal by straightening and lifting the finger when the tone sounds and before the shock occurs—the response that avoids the shock—is a conditional response.

The principal difference between this procedure and Pavlov's is that here the unconditional stimulus is not given if the conditional response occurs soon enough to avoid it. The difference is important. The procedure just described above is often called *instrumental* conditioning (the response is instrumental in avoiding the shock), to distinguish it from the classical form of Pavlovian conditioning, where the unconditional stimulus is always presented on every training trial.

Here we have reached something basic. The instrumental conditioning experiment is extremely simple, it does not depend upon verbal instructions, and there is a close parallel between the results obtained from humans and animals. Some proponents of S-R theories assume that the conditioning experiment is the prototype of all learning. For more complex situations the theoretical task is to discover how the behavioural processes can be analysed into these basic components. That analysis often requires considerable ingenuity, especially in the realm or verbal learning, but S-R theorists are confident it can be carried through successfully. 'After all', they might say, 'analysis into basic units is essential to all scientific progress: look at the analysis of matter into atoms, or the analysis of organisms into cells. Everywhere in science it is the same. We must find the proper elements and then discover the laws of their combination. That was, after all, what Wilhelm Wundt wanted to do; the trouble with Wundt was that he chose the idea instead of the S-R bond as his element.'

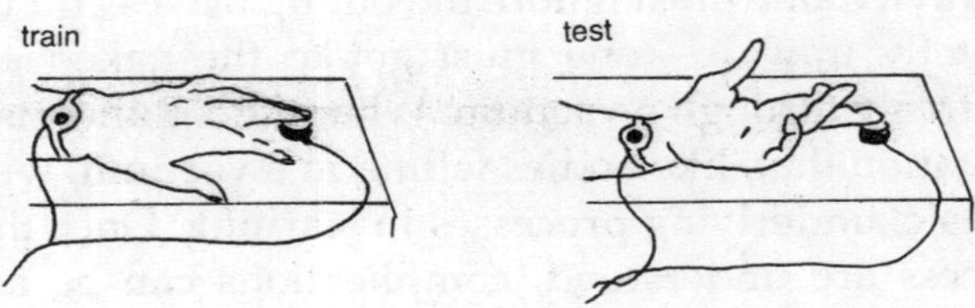


**Fig. 26.3.** Arrangement Used to Demonstrate Response Generalisation

But there are still problems that must be solved before one can accept this argument. For example, suppose in the finger-withdrawal experiment just described, one asks the subject after one or two hundred conditioning trials, to turn his hand over (as shown in Figure 26.3). Now, with his hand in this new position, if he straightens his finger it will still be touching the electrode and he will not avoid the shock. To avoid or escape the shock when his hand has been turned over the person must bend his finger, the exact opposite of the movement he had been conditioned to make. What will happen? Will he make the same *response* and extend his finger? Or will he perform the same *act* and flex his finger?

About seven out of every ten subjects flex the finger, even after many long trials in which they have been conditioned to extend it.' Twenty-five per cent do nothing at all, and about five per cent persist in making the extensor movement. The subjects themselves can provide no explanation; they report later that the finger acted in the way it did more or less of its own accord. Moreover, there is no satisfactory way to discriminate in advance between people who will flex the finger and people who will continue to extend it. But the gross statistical fact can scarcely be avoided: for most subjects, the result of the conditioning procedure has been to condition the *act* of withdrawal, not the *response of* finger extension. This Outcome can be called response generalisation—the S-R bond has generalised from the extensor response to the flexor response—but whatever one calls it, it makes a conditional reflex in a human subject appear somewhat more complicated than before.

When you stop to think about it, this conditioning experiment is an unusual way to get a person to lift his finger at the sound of a tone. As R.S. Woodworth pointed out, an occasional subject will misunderstand the experiment and assume that the experimenter wants him to keep his finger on the electrode and take the shock. If his finger does withdraw before the shock, he feels silly and ashamed and increases his effort to keep it in place; and he does not develop a conditional response even after many sessions. Why does the experimenter let this misunderstanding persist? He could simply say to the subject, 'I will give you strong shocks preceded by tones. I wish to discover how long it will take you to learn to avoid the shock by raising your finger when the tone comes on. 'But if he said that, his experiment would lose all points! Once again, verbal processes seem able to interfere with the basic process being studied. In an effort to escape the interfering effects of a human subject's symbolic habits the investigator has worked himself into the position of trying to fool the subject about what he is Supposed to do.

Lest one becomes discouraged about conditioning human beings, however, a word of warning is needed. The fact that this particular experiment is not as simple as it looks must not be interpreted to mean that human beings are invulnerable to Pavlov's procedures. All the evidence suggests that we can be conditioned, that we are being conditioned every day. We seem to be especially vulnerable when we are not actively aware of the conditional situation and when the response is made by our autonomic nervous system.

The autonomic nervous system controls the vegetative functions of our glands and smooth muscles, vital functions that involve few conscious decisions on our part. Pavlov, for example, worked with responses of the digestive glands; his Russian successors have extended his method to responses of other digestive glands, to stomach contractions and contractions of blood vessels, to heart rate and metabolic rate, and so on. It seems plausible that many of the emotional symptoms of psychoneurosis are created by the pervasive action of the reflexes encompassed by Pavlov's laws on these autonomic processes of the body.

The finger-withdrawal experiment, however, involves a voluntary response of the striped musculature, which is under the control of the central nervous system. In man, the enormous central nervous system—brain and spinal cord—supports symbolic processes that introduce a whole new level of complexity into the control of our behaviour. It is this very complexity that seems to thwart our efforts to find a pure example of an S-R connexion.

Where can one find learning that is mediated by the central nervous system and yet is not impossibly complicated by all the verbal, pictorial, and formal symbol-systems that are such characteristic ornaments of the human mind? An obvious answer is, in the study of other animals. And, in fact, that is where many psychologists have turned.

The consequences have been rather curious. Animals provide fascinating problems for a psychologist. However, many psychologists who study animals have no profound interest in them except insofar as their behaviour can be related to human psychology. Such psychologists would prefer to study the creation of new S-R connexions in man, but in order to demonstrate the learning process in its raw and primitive form they are forced to use inarticulate subjects. Admittedly it is a dangerous business to argue by analogy from one species to another, yet many distinguished psychologists are convinced that the fundamental laws of learning are so simple and universal that they can be studied anywhere in the animal kingdom, or, at least, anywhere among the vertebrates. So, in this excellent company, let us descend one more step in our effort to simplify the study of the learning process.

One of the first attempts to use animals in a psychological study of learning was Thorndike's early (1898) experiment with cats in a puzzle box. Thorndike put his cats into a rough wooden crate built or slats. The box had a door that was held shut by a button and a catch. If the cat could either turn the button or pull a loop that hung inside the box and that was connected directly to the catch, it could escape. The cats wanted to get out; they seemed to dislike the confinement. To reinforce this dislike, Thorndike 'deprived them of food prior to the tests and then fed them when they escaped.

On their first confinement in the box, the cats, particularly the young ones, scrambled around vigorously, attacked the bars, cracks, corners, and, eventually, the loop or the button until they accidentally worked the escape mechanism. There was no intelligent study of the situation, no insight, no plan: merely random, trial-and-error movements. But once the response that led to escape had been made, the cat could begin to strengthen the connexion between its response and the escape mechanism, and to eliminate the responses that did not lead to escape. As the successful association grew stronger on repeated trials, the time it took for the cat to escape grew shorter, but the irregular nature of the function (see Figure 26.4) is eloquent testimony to the haphazard, trial-and-error nature of the learning process.

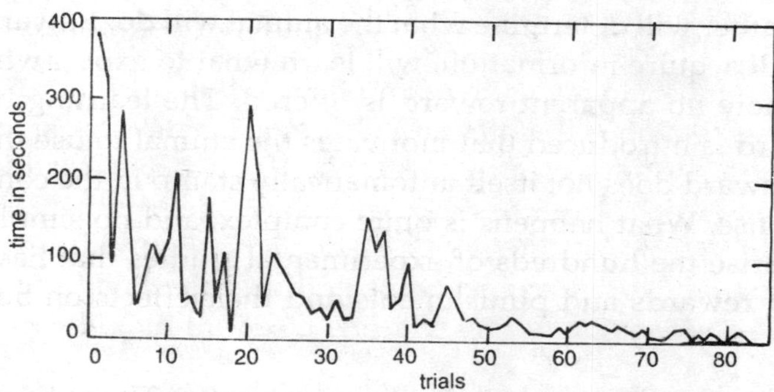


**Fig. 26.4.** There were large variations from trial to trial in the length of time it took this eat to escape from Thorndike's puzzle box.

Here is a good example of experimental evidence that encourages S-R theorists to believe that learning is nothing but the formation of connexions between stimuli and responses. Given that experimental paradigm, it is then possible to search for laws governing the rise and fall of associative strengths. Thorndike proposed two fundamental laws:

*The Law of Exercise.* The more often a given situation is followed by a particular response, the stronger will be the associative bond between them. Exercise—use, repetition, practice—makes perfect.

*The Law of Effect.* If a response produces a good effect and leads to a satisfying state of affairs, it will tend to be repeated when the situation arises again. It is a variant of this law that Hull later adopted as the foundation of his S-R theory of learning.

Both of Thorndike's laws are excellent descriptive statements. Animals, including men, tend to repeat activities that are profitable or rewarding, and the more often they repeat them, the better they perform. There are exceptions, but on the whole these phenomena characterise much of the behaviour we want to understand.

A large part of scientific psychology in America in the twentieth century has been based on, or directed at, these two laws. The conclusion seems to be that if they are interpreted literally as causal explanations, they are not true. Thorndike himself discredited the Law of Exercise by demonstrating that when a learner is denied information as to whether he succeeds or fails, all the exercise in the world cannot result in learning. On the other hand, the Law of Effect has had a more chequered career; it is not yet obvious that nothing will come of it. What is involved is a particular type of feedback loop; the satisfying effect of a response is fed back to strengthen it on future occasions. A major difficulty arises, however, in the attempt to define what is meant by a 'satisfying state' of a response. Hull defined it as a reduction of a biological drive, but this additional assumption raises as many questions as it answers.

A strong case can be made that the satisfying state of affairs does not determine what the animal will learn, but rather will determine what the animal will do. Edward C. Tolman has argued that animals will acquire information, will learn what to expect when certain signs occur, in situations where no apparent reward is offered. The learning becomes evident only later when a reward is introduced that motivates the animal to use the information it has acquired. But the reward does not itself automatically stamp in the connexion between a stimulus and a response. What happens is quite complex, and no simple generalisation can adequately summarise the hundreds of experimental studies that have been directed toward the problem of rewards and punishments and their effects on both learning and performance.

Let us return to the cats in the puzzle box. Many years after Thorndike's original study the work was repeated with better equipment. The box was arranged with a pole in the centre. If the cat pushed against the pole and tilted it, an electric contact was made that released the door. Moreover, a camera was set to take a photograph of the cat at the instant the successful response occurred.

The pictures revealed a surprising thing: the cat's movements at the instant of escape were highly stereotyped for many trials in a row. For example, one of the cats, cat T, on the first trial happened to activate the mechanism by lying down, pausing, then rolling over until it hit the pole. The cat then repeated almost exactly the same elaborate pattern or actions on succeeding trials. Tracings from the photographic record are shown for the first eight escape trials in Figure 26.5. Other animals regularly brushed against the pole, or always chewed it, or always hit it with their tails, or always stepped on the base. A particular movement pattern would be repeated until by accident it failed to hit the post (or occasionally, the release mechanism in the box failed to work), and then the cat might discover another way to get out and would persist in using those movements for the next five or ten trials.

The regularity of these stereotyped movements has led to the suggestion that what the cats learned initially was an association between the stimuli provided by the box and a very specific pattern of movements, not an association between the stimuli and a purposeful act. The association seemed to be formed after a single successful pairing of stimulus with response. According to Edwin R. Guthrie, in the course of many successive trials the animal built up several alternative movements that opened the door, and so appeared to be acquiring a specific skill. Thus, he argued, the act is slowly learned, yet the individual associations that comprise the act are each learned in a single trial.

Other psychologists have questioned Guthrie's conclusions, however. In maze learning, for example, one might suppose that an animal could learn a thoroughly stereotyped set of movements that would take it from the starting box through the maze to the goal box. But Karl Lash Icy showed that if rats which have acquired such a maze habit, are operated upon, and their motor coordination is so disturbed by surgery that they are no longer capable of making the same movements, they will still be able to run the maze correctly. They may have to roll or somersault or drag paralysed limbs, but they do not make mistakes. They have learned an act that takes them to a particular place; they have not learned a set of specific limb or muscle reactions.' The cats in the puzzle box are an exception to the general picture one gets from other research on this problem. Perhaps the cats cannot learn an act, but are forced to learn a response because the escape mechanism is so arbitrary, so impossible for them to understand. What alternative would they have but trial-and-error?

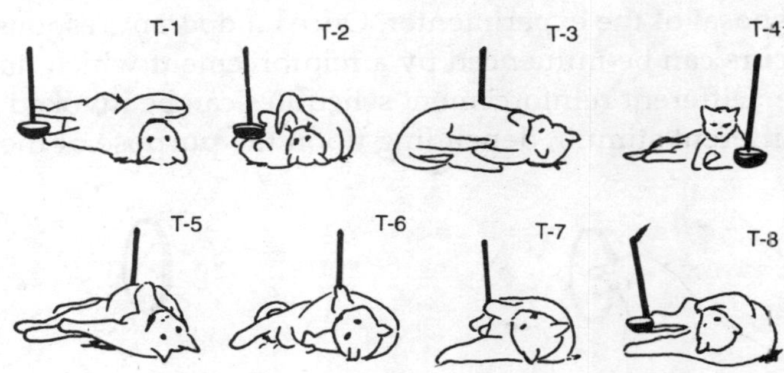


**Fig. 26.5.** Escape behaviour in cats is highly stereotyped Here are tracings to show the position of cat T at the instant he activated the release mechanism on the first eight trials. (From E.R. Guthrie and O.P. Horton, *Cais in a Puzzle Box,* New York: Rinehart, 1946.)

Many psychologists, even those who admire the hardheaded, quantitative posture of S-R theory, have come to a reluctant judgement that simple S-R connexions are often more plausible than real. The apparently simple connexion of a response to a stimulus situation has not been a convenient element to use in the general analysis of behaviour. Faced with this dilemma, one must either broaden the meaning of stimuli and responses so as to include perceptions and acts, which is to retreat from the hardheaded objectivity of true behaviourism, or propose an alternative element that will be easier to define and study. Many psychologists have broadened their definitions of stimulus and response to include unobservable events and processes that play much the same role in their theories as perceptions, images, ideas, and intentions played in the older psychologies. That is, they have adopted a contradictory Position which might be called subjective behaviourism.

Those who resist such contradictions have tried to find alternatives that will enable them to hold on to the ideal of a radically objective behaviourism. One of the most attractive alternative has been B. F. Skinner's formulation of openiu conditioning. Skinner points to the crushing difficulties encountered in finding a stimulus for every response. He proposes instead to distinguish two classes of response, elicited and emitted. Responses elicited by known stimuli are respondents; they can be studied by the traditional S-R approach. Operants are responses emitted without any known stimuli. Since there is no known stimulus for an operant response, it is logically impossible to talk about the strength of an S-R bond. As an alternative, therefore, Skinner proposes to measure the rate at which the operant is emitted and to explore all the variables that can be shown to affect the rate of responding.

In a typical experiment with operant conditioning, a hungry animal—usually a rat or pigeon—is placed inside a small, soundproofed compartment (known in laboratory jargon as a Skinner box) and taught to make a simple response, to press a bar or peck a key in order to obtain food. The grand convenience of this experimental situation derives from the fact that the relation between the animal's response and the presentation of food is completely arbitrary and at the disposal of the experimenter. Once an operant response is established, the rate at which it occurs can be influenced by a reinforcement which itself is contingent upon the response rate. Different reinforcement schedules can be invoked at various times or in the presence of different stimuli, depending upon the purpose of the experiment.

**Fig. 26.6.** A hungry pigeon learns to peck at a key, then is reinforced by presentation of grain in the food tray.

For example, when the key is illuminated by a red light, a pigeon may be reinforced, say, after every fifth peck, or haphazardly at a rate not faster than once a minute, and so on. But when the key turns green, perhaps, no reinforcements are given for pecking. In this example a the peeking-response would soon come under the control of the red and green lights, which are called discriminative stimuli. In this way Skinner can bring an operant response under the control of a discriminative stimulus, a stimulus such as the red or green light that indicates when the response may be reinforced. The S-R connexion is thus preserved, but in a broader and more flexible conception of the learning process.

These efforts to find a fundamental unit of behaviour are continuing vigorously into the second half of the twentieth century. The time to summarise them is not yet at hand. And even after the guide posts are agreed upon there will still be a long road to travel between operant response of a pigeon or a rodent and the discursive intelligence of a modern, civilised man.

Many learning experiments seem rather trivial, especially when isolated from their theoretical contexts. Indeed, it should probably be admitted that many of them would seem trivial in any context. But that must not mislead us. A most valuable strategy for the scientist is to take a plausible hypothesis and push it until it becomes ridiculous. Only in that way can he discover the range and power of his hypothesis, perhaps even find a better one. The ancient belief that learning is associative and that the mind is man's connexion-system is a plausible hypothesis. But until it has been pushed as hard as possible one cannot tell how much truth there is in it.

Eventually this tedious pushing and testing may produce a valid scientific law, one whose importance could be literally overwhelming. Our entire way of life is predicated upon our ability to learn. Not only do we rely on learning to give us the basic skills with which we earn our daily bread, but also to educate our children for citizenship in a free society. It is a solid axiom of the great liberal tradition in England and America that education is the best tool for social progress. We believe that people learn their system of values, learn to love themselves and others, learn to channel their biological drives, even learn to be mentally ill. When we begin to analyse the learning process, therefore, we are probing the ultimate sources of our humanity. No one can now foresee what benefits or dangers may someday come from these fumbling efforts with caged animals and nonsense syllables—but we had better be prepared for success.

# 27

# Sigmund Freud, Psychoanalyst

It comes as something of a surprise that Freud—sensitive prober of dreams, outspoken defender of sexuality, patient interpreter of the neurotic and the insane—should have regarded his life's work as an inevitable extension of the positivistic tradition in which he was trained as a medical student. No one revolted more effectively, or showed more clearly the narrowness of the mechanistic conceptions of man that dominated European thought in the nineteenth century. Yet throughout his life he considered himself faithful to the precepts of Helmholtz. He was a rebel, but he was a loyal one. In order to appreciate just how much of a rebel he was, it is necessary to resurrect an earlier conception of human nature.

Some historians say that modern intellectual history began sometime in the seventeenth century when—largely as a result of Descartes' teachings—mathematics replaced theology as the Queen of the Sciences. Men became convinced that natural laws are always true everywhere and that the human mind is capable of understanding them. Faith in the powers of human reason persisted without effective scientific criticism for about two hundred years and provided the moving spirit of that great, optimistic period of modern history called the Enlightenment. Anyone who might have questioned sovereign reason was refuted immediately by examples from the natural sciences.

But what about man's own affairs? Can men live together rationally? If reason can comprehend the cosmos, does that mean it can serve equally well as a guide in social and economic matters? Can a society, having no mind of its own, be rational? It was generally assumed that either a rational God would do the necessary thinking for society or, in more positivistic quarters, that if every individual member of society did the most intelligent thing he could possibly do, given his personal circumstances, the cumulative effect of so much rationality would itself be rational. In other words, if every individual would make his decisions in a reasonable way so as to advance his own best interests, he would simultaneously advance the interests of society generally.

The whole matter was reduced to its crudest fundamentals by Jeremy Bentham near the close of the eighteenth century. Although Bentham was somewhat extreme, his arguments were only exaggerated versions of views widely held in his time. 'Nature has placed mankind under the governance of two sovereign masters, pain and pleasure', said Bentham. 'It is for them alone to point out what we ought to do, as well as to determine what we shall do.' In England and France Bentham's philosophy, called utilitarianism, was a close partner of positivism. Along with materialism, empiricism, and evolutionism—the nineteenth century bristles with *isms*—Bentham's utilitarianism was especially attractive to those who wished to discuss man in the language of the natural sciences.

The utilitarian philosophy consists of four simple propositions:

1. All that anybody wants is to be as happy as possible, to maximise his own happiness.
2. It Is morally good for him to maximise his happiness as effectively, as intelligently, as he can.
3. Society must be organised so that maximising his own happiness is always the most beneficial thing for his fellow men.
4. It is possible to calculate the quantities of pleasure and pain (by Bentham's 'felicific calculus') expected from different kinds of behaviour, and to arrange society so as to produce the greatest happiness for the greatest number.

Bentham coupled these utilitarian propositions with a firm belief in empiricism and the laws of the association of ideas. It was central to his thinking that men should be simple machines whose choices and decisions could be anticipated perfectly and allowed for in a set of laws and social institutions that would automatically maximise the amount of happiness available for everyone.

It is not our task to criticise Bentham's ethical assumption that, because it is desired, happiness must be desirable. The fact remains that Bentham and his followers were remarkably influential in nineteenth-century England; utilitarianism was one of the intellectual foundations of British democratic thought and, by and large, its consequences were liberal and humanitarian. Each person was considered free to enter into any social contract that made II 'iii happy. Nevertheless, it was psychological nonsense; and it is remarkable that such an odd conception of man (as a felicity computer) captured the leading minds of the day. John Stuart Mill and Herbert Spencer both defended the 'maximum happiness principle' and made it a part of their social philosophy. There were critics; but the utilitarians were able to remain in the ascendancy. In the hands of Jevons, Walras, Menger, Marshall, and others, utilitarianism later became the foundation for much of modern economic theory. Even those who questioned the ethical assumption that it is good to pursue happiness were inclined to accept the psychological assumption that each man automatically and inevitably pursues his own pleasure.

Psychological objections centre around the fact that happiness depends far more upon what you expect than upon what you get. There is no absolute scale of happiness along which every possible event can be measured. The human ability to experience happiness is limited, it does not go on increasing indefinitely. There is no evidence that the rich are always happier than the poor. Indeed, there is not even any evidence that social progress promotes happiness, that Parisians are essentially happier than African Bushmen.

Not until the nineteenth century was drawing to a close did utilitarianism lose its iron grip on the scientific mind. One of the most effective attacks on it was initiated by a French sociologist, Emile Durkheim, who asked how such a theory could account for suicide. Obviously, suicide is not motivated by happiness; it seems reasonable to suppose that a person who takes his own life is unhappy. If this is so, and if Bentham was right that unhappiness results from a loss of valuable possessions, then one should expect to find that the suicide rate increases during periods of economic depression. And this is in fact the case. But Durkheim turned up another fact that was more puzzling, namely, that suicide is frequently caused by sudden success during periods of unusual prosperity. This is difficult for a utilitarian to explain. Why should a man who is just beginning to prosper consider killing himself? Prosperity should make him happy.

Durkheim argued that happiness has little to do with it. Unexpected wealth can disorient a person with respect to all the social values that had previously governed his life; sudden wealth can weaken or destroy his former ties with a social group. The resulting loss of his goals and values, the resulting state of social disequilibrium—Durkheim termed it *anomie*—might in severe cases lead to suicide. And for the same reason a sudden loss of wealth is also dangerous; it weakens a person's ties with his social group. It is a loss of love, of sympathetic acceptance into the lives of other people, not a loss of material possessions, that can make a man take his own life. To strengthen his argument, Durkheim demonstrated that suicide is relatively rare among the perpetually poor, who are necessarily well integrated into their own social groups.

Durkheim considered himself a thorough positivist, carrying on the scientific traditions of the nineteenth century. He used empirical data on suicide rates and he analysed then, statistically with scientific precision; certainly there was nothing metaphysical in his method or his results. Yet his explanation in terms of loosening the sympathetic ties of the individual with his group has an almost spiritual character. How does one measure anomie in centimetres, grammes, and seconds? If Durkheim was right—and his evidence was compelling—then somehow society has claims upon us far subtler and more complex than anyone in the eighteenth century would admit. To preserve a positivistic tradition, to make possible the continuation of the study of man and his affairs in scientific terms, the materialistic conception of science has to be enlarged.

Durkheim was one of several who, around the turn of the century, helped to expand our conception of science as it applies to human beings. Others included William James, Henri Bergson, Max Weber, Benedetto Croce, Vilfredo Pareto; beginning about 1890 a rebellious generation of genius completely reoriented European social thought. And the most important of these young rebels was the Austrian Jew, Sigmund Freud.

Freud was born at Freiberg, Moravia, in 1856. Except for the first three and the last two years of his life, however, he lived in, and was a part of, Vienna. His father, a tall, kindly man who was said to resemble Garibaldi, was an unsuccessful wool merchant; when his business failed in Moravia he moved his growing family to Leipzig, then to Vienna. Their life was not easy, for anti-Semitism was rampant in Imperial Austria. Nevertheless, Jews had been granted citizenship and one who was willing to step into the gutter to let a Christian pass could earn a meagre living.

At seventeen Sigmund entered the University of Vienna, a somewhat reluctant medical student in negligent pursuit of anatomy, botany, chemistry, physics, physiology, and zoology. We get glimpses of him studying Aristotle's logic, engaging in violent arguments with fellow students and obstinately refusing to apologise for his rudeness in philosophic debate. During this period he received a thorough grounding in the positivistic science of the nineteenth century. First he concentrated on biology, and as a research project dissected more than four hundred male eels in search of their testes. Next he moved on to physiology and the spinal cord of the fish; he spent countless hours hunched over a microscope in Ernest Brucke's laboratory. In 1881 he received his M.D. degree, but even that did not interrupt his devotions at the microscope. Finally Brucke explained to him that a penniless Jew could never become Professor of Neurology. It was a rude shock, but of course Brucke was right; the Vienna that was to give lessons to Adolf Hitler was a difficult place for a Jew, even one as brilliant as Freud.

Yet he must have known what was coming, for his decision to study medicine in the first place had been based on the assumption that he could, if necessary, practise for a living. So he left the scientific life of the university and hung out his shingle as a clinical neurologist. It was a difficult thing for him to do; even though he became famous for his neurological research, he was 'ever greatly attracted to the practice of clinical neurology. Fortunately for him, however, most of the patients who went to see a neurologist were actually psychoneurotic.

In June 1882 he became engaged to Martha Bernays, who was as penniless as he. Although he loved her passionately, it was necessary repeatedly to postpone their marriage until he could earn enough money to support her. For four intense, frustrated years he worked and saved and waited. There was hardly a moment in the long engagement when the first thought in his mind was that how soon he could convert it to marriage. Finally he could wait no longer; in September 1886 they were married. The young couple managed to exist through their first months together by borrowing, by pawning their watches, until finally the tide began to turn. But the terrible poverty of those early years left a lasting impression on him.

It was during that difficult time that he became friendly with Joseph Breuer, who loaned him money and discussed interesting cases with him. Breuer had discovered a new way to use hypnosis in the treatment of hysteria. Hysteria is a form of neurosis in which there are bodily symptoms, paralysis and abnormal sensations, that cannot be attributed to any obvious abnormality of the nervous system. Actually the discovery was made by one of Breuer's patients, a stubborn young woman known to history only as Fraulein Anna O., who insisted that talking about her problems while she was hypnotised would relieve her anxieties and temporarily cure her hysterical symptoms. Freud was very interested in Anna O. and tried to use Breuer's technique with other patients.

Although at this time Freud was publishing important work in neurology, his interests were steadily shifting toward his psychological studies with Breuer; in 1895 they published a book, *Studies on Hysteria*. By the time it appeared, however, Freud was already breaking off his personal friendship with Breuer and was well along toward replacing hypnosis by free association as a better method for treating hysteria. His adoption of free association was a critical step in the development of psychoanalysis.

In free association a person starts with some element of emotional significance and lets, or tries to let, his ideas flow spontaneously until, for one reason or another, they seem to break off He then takes another item and repeats the process. Speaking freely of whatever enters one's head is not easy. Even without intending to, a person protects himself in certain matters. These points of resistance became the focus of Freud's inquiry and his basis for psychotherapy. The great advantage of free association over hypnosis is that these areas of resistance can be located and explored; the patient himself is forced to recognise consciously the nature of his problem.

Freud also discovered that a rich source of emotionally significant ideas, suitable to start the process of free association, can be found in a patient's dreams, which often contain valuable clues to the psychological problems underlying his sickness.

As a positivist, committed to the belief that everything has a cause, he knew that events in a dream cannot be as senseless as they seem. They must be the result of something going on in the person's mind, if not consciously, then unconsciously. He decided that there must be truth in the ancient theory that dream images are symbolic. They do not symbolise future events, of course; they refer to personal matters, things that can arouse strong emotions. It seemed to him that the purpose of a dream is to preserve sleep. If the emotionally charged images were to appear undisguised in the dream, they would be so disturbing that they would interrupt the sleeping state. So they appear only indirectly in a harmless, symbolic form. Instead of dreaming about a penis, the dreamer may substitute the image of a gun, a snake, a fountain pen, the number three, and so on. For masturbation the dream symbol may be climbing a tree, or playing the piano. By recognising these substitutions, therefore, it is possible to recover the true meaning of the dream.

It is a little hard, of course, to believe that a sleeping mind can perform all these complicated substitutions in its state of reduced activation. To Freud this meant that the unconscious is much cleverer than we usually give it credit for. It is possible to argue, however, that the symbols are not disguises at all, but are more like slang, or figures of speech, C.S. Hall has pointed out that a dreamer may have a disguised dream of an incestuous relationship one night and a perfectly barefaced dream of incest the next night. If the symbol is hiding something obnoxious, why is it hidden one time and not another? But even though his hypothesis that symbols are protective disguises may be more imaginative than necessary, it remains that Freud discovered in dream analysis a very useful way to explore a person's emotional life.

Freud tried to get his neurotic patients to remember the events that had caused their symptoms; free association provided a method to probe their memories. The associations did not stop with a painful event, but often extended back into early childhood. Moreover, many of the most significant memories were of sexual experience. Freud gradually became convinced that sexual disturbances are the essential causes of neurosis. In particular, he observed that his hysterical patients always reported a premature sexual experience during their childhood. He was convinced of the validity of his method, and in all good faith he presented this observation publicly as his theory of hysteria. But then the truth dawned on him: most of the reported childhood seductions had never occurred. They were fantasies nourished by unconscious processes unrelated to ordinary reality. This realisation was a severe jolt to his pride, but when he had time to ponder its implications he was not ashamed of his blunder. It had forced him to recognise the fundamental nature of infantile sexuality and soled him to one of his major contributions to psychological theory.

In the summer of 1897 Freud decided to apply his technique to himself. Them were several reasons: his father's death had occurred a few months earlier and Freud wished to explore the emotions it had aroused; he was concerned by his increasing hostility towards an old friend; he wanted to be able to understand his patients better. He worked principally with his dreams, seeking to discover the unconscious processes that formed them. It was lonely work, but he slowly made progress. He recognised the truth about his father and separated it from ideas that he had projected into his image of his father. He remembered sexual feelings towards his mother and jealous rivalries with other children. And he rediscovered a nurse who had caused him most of his later troubles. The results were not magical, but he persisted and eventually mastered many of the problems that had disturbed him. For the rest of his life he spent the last half hour of each day in self-analysis.

In 1900 he published his major account of this work in *The Interpretation of Dreams*. It was written during the period of his self-analysis and is profusely illustrated with his own dreams. The book was received with thunderous indifference by both neurologists and psychologists; it took eight years to sell the first printing of 600 copies. Nevertheless, *The Interpretation of Dreams* is Freud's most important work. In particular, the seventh and last chapter contains the theory of mind that he was to amplify and develop in the period ahead.

For ten lonely but productive years he worked almost alone on his new ideas. In 1904 he wrote *The Psychopathology of Everyday Life* in which he described the now famous Freudian slip, and in the following year the *Three Essays on Sexuality*. But not until 1906 did he begin to attract colleagues and followers, and he did not gain international recognition until 1909, when he was invited to the United States, with Alfred Adler and C.G. Jung, to give a series of lectures at Clark University.

Those years were also filled with much bureaucratic activity centred around the founding of international societies and their journals. Freud tolerated no dissent from his emphasis on sexuality as the great motivating force behind all abnormal psychological processes; anyone who disagreed was excommunicated. In the second volume of his fine biography of Freud, Ernest Jones has sympathetically described these political struggles, with their attendant concern that psychoanalysis would be rejected by Gentiles.

The psychoanalytic movement was launched much as a political party would be launched, or as a new church might be founded. Thus when Freud broke with Adler in 1911 and with Jung in 1913 it was more than a scientific disagreement about the evidence and the conclusions that could be based on the evidence; it was also a personal quarrel, a political defection, and a religious heresy.

In 1914, pressed by fear that psychoanalysis would be discredited because its major proponents could not agree among themselves, Freud wrote a polemical *History of the Psychoanalytic Movement:*

'Psychoanalysis is my creation', he said. 'For ten years I was the only one occupied with it.... Nobody knows better than I what psychoanalysis is.' One can sympathise with his attitude towards quarrelsome disciples. But the important distinction between a political movement and a scientific theory should never be forgotten; the success of one does not test the truth of the other.

Freud continued to live in Vienna, practising as a psychoanalyst and writing many books of an increasingly speculative nature. In 1910 he wrote a psychoanalytic biography of Leonardo da Vinci. In 1913 he wrote *Totem and Taboo,* an imaginative anthropological adventure. He extended psychoanalysis further into the realm of social theory with *The Future of an Illusion* (1927) and *Civilisation and its Discontents* (1930). When the Nazis absorbed Austria in 1938, he escaped to London, carrying under his arm the manuscript of a book on *Moses and Monotheism.* The following year he died at the age of eighty-three.

It is sometimes said that anybody who had as much interest in sex as Freud, must have led a lusty and exciting life. As near as one can tell from published biographies this is simply not true; in his private life he appears to have been a complete puritan. He was so inhibited, in fact, that some writers have speculated that his sexual theories were rationalisations of his inability to love other people. No insatiable lust inspired him; his mission was to save civilisation. In his prime he dreamed of being a modern Leonardo, the creative genius; in his old age he saw himself as a modern Moses, the great lawgiver. He expected others to follow him and to sacrifice their independence and intellectual freedom for him. Certainly he must have been a difficult man to work with. He had his faults, for which his friends paid dearly, but lechery was not one of them. The sexual licence that has so often been justified in terms of his theories must have been hateful to him, a sad mockery of his life and ideals.

Freud introduced a number of new terms for the theoretical constructs he used to describe the human mind. He believed that the total personality is organised into three major systems: the *id,* which is concerned with the immediate discharge of energy or tension; the *ego,* which regulates the interactions of the person with his environment; and the *superego,* which represents the moral and judicial aspects of personality. These three systems are in constant interaction.

In his early work Freud used a simpler twofold distinction between the conscious and the unconscious mind. Later, the unconscious became the id, the conscious the ego; and the superego was added to his theory as a new concept. This remarkable and imaginative man never shirked the burden of self-criticism and revision, and his theories grew and evolved continually for almost half a century. In describing psychoanalytic doctrine, therefore, it is always necessary to specify whether the ideas come from the early or the late Freud.

Dynamic aspects of personality depend upon a supply of instinctual energy from the id; Freud made the same distinction between the mind and its source of energy that an engineer would make between an engine and its fuel. Although he modified his theories several times, towards the end of his life he recognised two great groups of instincts that provide energy for the id. One group serves the purposes of life: their energy is called *libido.* The life instincts are a constant source of emotional tension, whose conscious impact is painful and unpleasant. One of Freud's first and most fundamental assumptions was that all activities of the mind are driven by the need to reduce or eliminate this tension. Because a conscious experience of pleasure was supposed to accompany all tension reduction, Freud called this fundamental assumption the *pleasure principle.* The second group of instincts, introduced later and never so well described, are in the service of death. These destructive instincts represent Freud's attempt to explain the sources of energy for aggression, for sadism and masochism, for suicide. That he toyed with so odd a conception as an instinct for death and destruction indicates how deeply he was impressed by the irrational hatred and violence he saw everywhere around him.

In a very young infant the functions of the id are purely automatic. But when reflex action fails, as eventually it must, frustration causes emotional tension to build up. The baby must then learn to form an image of the object that reduces its tensions. At first, this image, which is generated by the *primary process,* is offered as a kind of substitute satisfaction whenever frustration occurs. This use of imagery is pure wish-fulfilment. Freud believed that wish-fulfilments, or attempted wish-fulfilments, persist into adulthood; dreams were his prime example.

The ego is the executive branch of the personality. It operates according to a *reality principle,* rather than the pleasure principle. When reflex action and wish-fulfilling imagery have both failed, the child begins to develop a secondary process; the thinking, knowing, problem-solving processes necessary to produce the desired object itself. As a consequence of the secondary process, a plan of action is created and tested. The testing is called *reality testing.* Most of the psychological functions that had been studied prior to Freud's work—sensation, perception, learning, thinking, memory, action, will, and so on—are pure ego functions in Freudian terminology.

The ego has no energy of its own, so it steals energy from the id by a process known as *identification.* The theft is perpetrated as follows: the id invests its instinctual energy in the images that its primary process creates, but the Id has no way to distinguish between its own wish-fulfilling imagination and the veridical images of perception. To achieve gratification the id's fomenting energy must be invested in an accurate image of a tension-reducing object; the imagination image that the id desires and the perceptual image of the goal object must be in good agreement. When the internal image corresponds closely to the perceptual object, the idea can be identified with the object, and the idea's psychic energy can be transferred to it. This identification process enables the energies of the id to be guided by an accurate representation of reality, and makes possible the further development of the ego.

The superego, which develops at a later age, is said to include two subsystems, an *ego-ideal* and a *conscience.* Both are assimilated by the child from examples and teachings provided by his parents. The ego-ideal is the child's conception of what his parents will approve; his conscience is the child's conception of what they will condemn as morally bad. The ego-ideal is learned through rewards, the conscience through punishments. The superego, in short, is the repository of social norms—Freud's way of dealing with the kinds of problems that Durkheim discovered in his studies of social action.

It should be noted that the superego was Freud's way of going beyond the felicity calculators that utilitarians had believed in. The id wants happiness and the ego does the calculating—that much of the older theory he preserved intact—but the superego is something more, something that holds the happiness-calculator within bounds set by society, something that introduces the social norms that are so necessary for our understanding of human society. Much that was most revolutionary in Freud's thinking had to do with how these social restraints become internalised to form the superego.

The process of investing instinctual energy is called *cathexis.* The id has only cathexes, but the ego and the superego can use the energy at their disposal in either of two ways, for cathexis or *anticathexis.* Anticathexis, which manifests itself in terms of self-frustration, is the way the ego and the superego keep the id in check. Perhaps the most important example of anticathexis has to do with memory. A person may fail to recall something, Freud would say, because the memory trace is not sufficiently charged with energy—it is too weakly cathected. But sometimes his memory may fail because the cathexis is opposed by an even stronger anticathexis; in that case a memory is said to be *repressed.* The repressive mechanism is one way—a very common way—the ego protects itself against painful memories and the discomfort or anxiety they would arouse.

Anxiety is a crucial concept in psychoanalytic theory, especially when the theory deals with neurosis and psychosis." Freud distinguished between objective, neurotic, and moral anxiety. Objective anxiety is a painful emotion aroused by the recognition of a real, objective danger. Neurotic anxiety is aroused by a recognition of danger from instinctual forces—by fear that the anticathexes of the ego will not be strong enough to prevent instinctual energy from being discharged in an impulsive action. When neurotic anxiety is focused upon a particular object or situation, it is called a *phobia;* when a person is unable to specify what is causing his discomfort, his anxiety is called *free-flooring.* Moral anxiety is aroused by the recognition of danger from the conscience, and appears as feelings of guilt or of shame at what one has done or, more often, what one is contemplating doing. A virtuous person with a well-developed conscience always experiences more shame, more moral anxiety, than a less virtuous person.

To protect itself from anxiety, the Freudian ego develops various defensive methods or mechanisms. We have already mentioned identification. When identification is used as a defence mechanism, the person identifies himself with someone who seems desirable or admirable, with someone who would not be vulnerable to the danger that is causing the subject anxiety. We have also mentioned repression, which simply prevents an anxiety-arousing situation from becoming conscious. Other mechanisms include *sublimation* (a socially more acceptable goal is substituted for one that cannot be directly satisfied), *projection* (attributing the source of the anxiety to someone or something else external to the person), *reaction formation* (concealing a disturbing impulse by converting it into its opposite), *fixation* (refusing to take the next step in normal development because of anxiety aroused by fear of the new and the unknown), *regression* (retreating to an earlier stage of development when there was greater security, when this anxiety did not arise). A large part of the theoretical machinery developed by Freud and his followers is concerned with the various strategies whereby a person tries—usually irrationally and unsuccessfully—to escape from the intolerably unpleasant emotional experience of anxiety.

J.S. Bruner has aptly called this a dramatic theory of personality:

Freud's is a theory or a proto-theory peopled with actors. The characters are from life: the blind, energetic, pleasure-seeking id; the priggish and punitive superego; the ego, battling for its being by diverting the energy or others to its own use. The drama has an economy and a terseness. The ego develops canny mechanisms for dealing with the threat or id impulses; denial, projection, and the rest. Balances are struck between the actors, and In the balance is character and neurosis. Freud was using the dramatic technique of decomposition, the play whose actors are parts of a single life.

Because neurotic patients taught him that their troubles began in childhood, Freud developed an elaborate theory of how children grow up, how their sexual instincts develop and mature. The evidence for his theory of development came largely from retrospective accounts by adults; at first it had little support from actual observations of children. Even so, by placing his usual heavy emphasis on sexuality he forced child psychologists to recognise something that it had always been easier to ignore: Sweet, innocent, little children are just as sexual as anybody else. Sex does not spring suddenly into existence at puberty; it is there all along. Many people found psychoanalytic theory most shocking at this very point. One distinguished critic complained that in the study of infantile sexuality, 'Freud went down deeper, stayed down longer, and came up dirtier than anyone else.' But such complaints miss the point of Freud's insight. He was not talking of dirty habits in nasty little brats; he was telling the story of a force of nature.

Freud was the first psychologist who took systematic account of he pleasures and problems every child has with the apertures of his body. He believed that a child's sexual gratifications come from different openings—different *erogenous zones*—at different ages. In unfortunate circumstances, a child can become fixated at an infantile stage and thus develop personality traits corresponding to that particular level. According to Freud, the first erogenous zone is the mouth, where a baby first gets pleasure from sucking, then from biting. If any psychic energy becomes fixated on the *oral zone* during the ingestive, sucking stage, it wilt produce a dependent personality in the adult. If trouble arises later during the oral biting phase, the person will become aggressive in an oral sense: verbal scorn, sarcasm, cynicism are typical expressions of oral aggression. These problems can appear first when a child is being weaned, so the weaning practices of mothers have assumed great theoretical interest.

In the normal course of development, however, sexual gratification shifts from the mouth to the other end of the alimentary tract; he child will begin to experience pleasure in the *anal zone*. Again here are two modes of functioning: holding back and giving up. If there is important conflict during the period of toilet training, a person may grow up with an anal expulsive character—messy, dirty, wasteful, extravagant—r with an anal retentive character—neat, clean, compulsive, fastidious.

The next Freudian stage occurs when erotic impulses migrate to the sexual zone and the child enters the *phallic singe*. Masturbation and incestuous longings for the parents, who area child's first love objects, must be brought under control; how that is achieved is one of the central features of Freudian theory and usually a central problem that has to be worked through and accepted by the patient during psychotherapy.

When a little boy begins to feel sexual impulses towards his mother, Freud said, he becomes jealous of his rival, the father. Since this family crisis was discussed in terms of the Greek legend about Oedipus, who killed his father and married his mother, the boy's dilemma is generally referred to as an *Oedipus complex*. According to Freud, a boy normally becomes afraid that his father will castrate him as punishment for his incestuous desires; this *castration anxiety* eventually forces him to repress both his desire for his mother and his hostility towards his father. When the repression is complete, the Oedipus complex finally disappears. At this point he may identify with either the rather or the mother, depending upon whether the masculine or the feminine components of his personality are dominant. In this process of identification the boy adopts the parental values and morality that will constitute his Superego as an adult.

The little girl is not so thoroughly explained. She is supposed to develop *penis envy*, a female counterpart of the boy's castration anxiety, and she too may resolve her conflict by identifying with either parent. But many clinicians feel that Freud's theory is weakest in dealing with feminine psychology.

It is interesting to note that here, as elsewhere, Freud had an attitude characteristic of the nineteenth-century middle class, which was more concerned with having than with being. His deepest fears were always of losing something one has, a love object, a feeling, or the genital organs. Thus castration anxiety and penis envy seemed to him the most powerful emotional forces that any child would have to cope with.

If, by a miracle, one manages to get through all these Freudian stages with some psychic energy left, one will, after a normal period of latency from about five to twelve years of age, pass into a final, adult phase of genital sexuality. People who negotiate the course successfully, however, seldom turn up in a psychoanalyst's office asking for help. Hence there is little psychoanalytic description of what the genital stage of adult sexuality is like.

Freud's theories often seem absurd, if not downright false, to readers who encounter them first in a brief summary such as this. It is an easy exercise for a detached outsider to be critical; Freud has little to say to someone who is not personally involved in psychoanalysis. Those who are involved, however, are usually less confident in their criticisms. Once the psychoanalytic expedition back into childhood begins, once the personal commitment to the therapeutic process is given, once one tries to look honestly at oneself, it is no longer so obvious what is reasonable and what is absurd. There is some merit to the claim that the criticism of psychoanalysis is best left to those who have experienced it. In this respect, at least, it is more like a way of life than like a scientific theory.

Freud's first and major contribution was his psychological theory of personality and neurosis, but he was also, particularly in the later years of his life, a social theorist of considerable importance. His first efforts in that direction were presented in *Totem and Taboo*, published in 1913. His point of departure was the family, the basic building block of all larger social groups, and a powerful influence on the psychosexual development of the child. His social argument—a modern version of the ancient doctrine of original sin—rested on a vast elaboration of the Oedipus complex, an elaboration that made the complex as important in the development of society as in the development of an individual personality. *Totem and Taboo* is an allegory about a 'primal horde' and the banding together of the sons to slay their father and eat of his flesh. But Freud did not intend to be allegorical; he insisted that he was describing actual events that must have been repeated thousands of times before civilisation could have been achieved.

It was Freud's idea that the uncivilised sons hated and feared their uncivilised father because he monopolised the women. After they killed him they felt remorse perhaps, but, more important, they recognised that they needed to replace him with a new moral authority or they would all perish in bloody strife of brother against brother. So they began to discipline themselves. Their first step was to impose a taboo on incest, outlawing the possibility of competition with the father for the mother and sisters. Only with an incest taboo is it possible for males to live together peacefully in a single family group. This first and most fundamental prohibition was later followed by others, which became equally binding. These socially necessary restraints have never been completely accepted, however, so the battle has to be fought all over again in the development of every male child.

It is curious how culture-bound Freud was when he ventured into anthropology. Bronislaw Malinowski, who tried to use psychoanalytic concepts in his anthropological studies of the family, once commented that Freud, in a most attractive but fantastic hypothesis, equipped his primal horde with all the bias, maladjustments, and ill-tempers of a middle-class European family let loose in a prehistoric jungle.

The implication or Freud's argument is that guilt (anxiety aroused by threats from the superego) is the motive force behind all social solidarity. Locke, Spencer, and the utilitarians explained social integration in terms of a social contract between individuals free to maximise their own happiness; Durkheim discussed the social facts that exist external to the actor yet somehow tie him to his group by providing norms and ideals; William James made habit the great flywheel of society that keeps us all within the bounds of ordinance; in place of these theories Freud proposed to substitute a vast burden of guilt shared by every civilised person. The is impulses spring up in all of us; we want to destroy authority and enjoy our sensual pleasures. But in a civilised person the thought arouses guilt; self-indulgence is repressed to protect the ego. Thus social restraints are imposed by a superego that holds over us the unbearable threat of guilt, of moral anxiety. The more a social group imposes constraints upon the sexuality of an individual, the more powerful his superego must become and the greater must be the guilt he experiences. His feelings of guilt may increase beyond all tolerable bounds, until they usurp all his psychic energy and leave him helpless.

Is there some way to prevent this? Could we organise a society around love and reason, rather than around fear and guilt? On this question Freud was basically pessimistic. He had seen too much persecution of his own people, and he had listened to too many neurotic patients describe their inner thoughts ever to be lulled into thinking that men are gentle, friendly creatures who fight only when they are attacked. The great optimist herbert Spencer could argue all he liked that the predatory habits of modern men were only vestigial survivals that would soon vanish in the upward sweep of evolution; Freud saw only the increasing burdens that modern society was placing on the ego, burdens that would create an ever-increasing measure of guilt and aggression.

When we compare his concept ion of man with the hopeful mood of the Enlightenment in the eighteenth century, it is obvious why he has so often been called the great anti-intellectual, the great destroyer of faith in rationality. Yet Freud never wavered in his faith that the search for truth must continue. He wrote:

> We may insist as much as we like that the human intellect is weak in comparison with human instincts, and be right in doing so. But nevertheless there is something peculiar about this weakness. The voice of the intellect is a soft one, but it does not rest until it has gained a hearing. Ultimately, after endlessly repeated rebuffs, it succeeds.

Freud struggled to see man as he is, not as he ought to be or as Freud would have liked to imagine him. As one trained in the Helmholtz school of medicine, he carried on this struggle in a positivistic spirit with what he felt were scientific methods of observation and analysis. He was convinced that all mental events are completely determined—even mistakes have a cause. And to the end of his life he used the mechanical, electrical, hydraulic terminology of his positivistic teachers. Thus we must classify him as loyal to the positivistic tradition. But in spite of his loyalty, he was a most powerful and damaging critic. After he had completed his demonstration of the importance of unconscious, instinctual forces in human conduct, the old faith in the inevitability of human progress through man's constant growth of knowledge and understanding sounded like an innocent myth concocted to amuse little children. Few men have influenced us so deeply.

# 28

# Alfred Binet, Psychologist

During the early years of the French Revolution a remarkable man named Philippe Pinel became chief physician at a Paris hospital filled with madmen. As a beginning Pinel proposed to take off their chains. When the President of the Commune heard this reckless proposal he came in person to reassure himself. The lunatics greeted him with shouts, curses, and the clanking of chains.

'Citizen', he shouted to Pinel above the din, 'are you mad yourself that you would unchain such beasts?'

'I am convinced', said Pinel, 'that these mentally ill are intractable only because they are deprived of fresh air and their liberty.'

It speaks volumes for Gallic intelligence that Pinel was allowed to conduct his experiment. For the first time the insane were treated, not as criminals, not as if they were possessed by demons, but with the restraint and kindness that sickness requires. Pinel's reforms turned a madhouse into a mental hospital and laid new foundations for the psychiatry of the future.

If insanity is a sickness, it would seem to be a sickness of the brain. In order to cure it, therefore, one must understand how the brain works. This line of reasoning, as old as Hippocrates, but especially appealing to positivistic thinkers in the nineteenth century, led to many important discoveries about the psychological effects or organic injuries and diseases in the nervous system. Psychiatrists who worked in this tradition found their major ally was the neurologist, and their favourite theories of insanity were theories of neural damage. In spite of noteworthy successes, however, not all mental disorders could be traced directly to organic causes. The difficulties with a purely organic theory first became obvious, not in the study of psychosis, but in the study of neurosis. (As a rough and ready rule: If cognitive disorders predominate, it is usually psychosis; if emotional disorders predominate, it is usually neurosis; if moral disorders predominate, it is usually psychopathy.)

Once again a Frenchman led the way. The particular kind of neurosis that was to prove so very instructive was called *hysteria.* A patient with hysterical symptoms seems to have a great and senseless variety of bodily ailments. Parts of his body may be paralysed so that he cannot move them or cannot feel anything in them, his vision and hearing may be impaired, his memory may be faulty, and the like. Hysteria was once considered a woman's disease, but this theory was discredited when the neurologist Jean Martin Charcot discovered male patients suffering from all the classical symptoms. For many years Charcot shared with his fellow neurologists the assumption that hysteria was a disease of the nervous system. There seemed little reason to doubt it—all the symptoms appeared to be organic in nature.

But then the neurologists learned about hypnosis. Some of charcot's assistants at the famous neurological clinic he had created at the Salpetriere in Paris became interested in hypnotism; they began to try it on one another and on the patients. They discovered that they could produce all the symptoms of hysteria in a normal person and then could cure him instantaneously, first by hypnotising him and telling him he could not move, or could not feel, or could not see, and so on, then by awakening him from the hypnotic state. Even the great Charcot was unable to tell the difference between simulated, hypnotic symptoms and true, hysterical symptoms.

The possibility of psychological involvement in these apparently organic ailments put the whole problem of hysteria in a new light. Charcot began to examine hysterical symptoms in great detail; he soon discovered convincing evidence that they are not due to peripheral organic injury. For example, a neurologist knows from his study of anatomy which parts of the body are served by which nerves. In particular, he knows which areas of the skin will become insensitive if a particular nerve branch is damaged. When a patient complains that he cannot feel anything in his hand, a neurologist can usually diagnose which nerve must have been damaged, by carefully mapping out the insensitive area. If the area of anaesthesia does not make anatomical sense—if it follows the pattern of a glove, say, rather than the true pattern of the nerve endings in the skin—the complaint cannot be attributed to organic damage to the peripheral nerves in the arm. Charcot discovered that hysterical symptoms usually made this kind of neurological nonsense, and that the same nonsense could be produced by hypnosis. In certain cases, apparently, it was even possible to relieve hysterical symptoms by hypnotising the patient and telling him his symptom would vanish. The older view that mental illness is caused by damage to the nervous system clearly needed to be revised to include psychological causes. How that revision was to be phrased, however remained obscure.

Pierre Janet, a student of Charcot, saw clearly that the emphasis should be shifted from the hysterical patient's symptoms to his state of mind. After observing many hysterical patients Janet concluded that they suffered from mental dissociation. An emotional system of ideas becomes isolated from the rest of his mental life and takes control of part of his body or part of his memory. These Insulated sub-systems cannot be controlled voluntarily by the patient. Today it seems obvious that Janet's descriptions of hysterical patients moved the problem of accounting for this neurosis from neurology into psychology. But Janet, paralysed by the positivistic spirit of nineteenth-century medicine, hesitated to give a frankly psychological explanation. Perhaps, he thought, hysterics have an hereditary inability to integrate their experience. He saw the emotional struggles and conflicts that his patients were going through and he described the dissociation that existed in their mental life, but he could not accept the conflicts as the *cause* of the dissociation. That step was left for another student of charcot—Sigmund Freud.

In spite of their reluctance to accept a purely psychological explanation of mental disorders, Charcot and Janet created in Paris an environment where psychogenic and somatogenic theories could compete, where the precise measurements of the laboratory and the rough-and-ready methods of the clinic could be used side by side. It was in this environment that Alfred Binet learned his psychology and adopted the catholic attitude that he carried into all of his later research. This proved to be perfect preparation for the work he was to perform.

Alfred Binet was born in Nice in 1857. His mother, a talented painter, took him to Paris while he was still a boy; there he received his education at the centre of French cultural and intellectual life. After taking his baccalaureate degree from the Lycee Saint-Louis he embarked upon the study of law. He enjoyed life as a law student and often talked about it in later years, but he discovered that his interest in law was only marginal. Instead of devoting himself single-mindedly to his law books, he found himself being pulled in several different directions at once. Paris was then as now an enormously stimulating place for a young intellectual, and Binet's energy could scarcely be contained by any single field of study. In particular, he could not suppress his interest in the natural sciences and especially in medicine. His fascination with medicine was a family affair—his father and his grandfather were physicians.

Binet was never socially ambitious, but he did form many friendships with fellow students and collaborators, and much of his later research was published with co-authors. Among his friends at the Lycee was Babinski, later to become a famous neurologist; it was probably Babinski who introduced Binet to Charles Fere, an enthusiastic disciple of Charcot. Fere and iii net began to collaborate actively in research on abnormal psychology and hypnotism at Charcot's clinic in the Salpetriere. And at the same time he was absorbing the medical psychology of Charcot's clinic. Binet was also studying under the direction of his father-in-law, the histologist Balbiani, for his degree in science from the Sorbonne. It is characteristic of Binet's omnivorous intellectual appetite that in 1878, the same year he received his licence as a lawyer, he published a scientific article on the psychic life of microorganisms.

During these years Binet's interests shifted more and more towards psychological problems. The shift was stimulated principally by his work with Fere in Charcot's clinic, but his newly awakened curiosity was not confined solely to the psychological problems of the clinical practitioner. He began to devour the British empiricist philosophers. His special interest was in the process of association and, like all of Binet's interests, it was quickly reflected in print. As early as 1880 he published a short paper on the fusion of images, a subject he was led to directly by reading about the association of ideas.

Although Binet is remembered today principally for his way of testing the intelligence of children, his contributions to psychology were much broader than that. It is the case of a mountain dwarfing some very respectable hills nearby. Binet's first book, *The Psychology of Reasoning* (1886), had as its subtitle, *Experimental Studies of Hypnotism;* it was the result of combining British associationism with French hypnotism. His knowledge of hypnotism derived from the work with Fore; his knowledge of associationism came from reading, not the German Wilhelm Wundt, but the British John Stuart Mill. Binet had no formal instructor in psychology, no one to teach him either the old, philosophical version or the new, experimental kind. What he knew of it he picked up by reading a few books: Ribot, Taine, Hamilton, and others, especially Mill. His training as an experimental investigator was obtained through his studies in biology and medicine, and through his experience in the neurological clinic. He admired British psychology and in later years was probably nearer to Galton than to Charcot in his sympathies. But most or his psychological ideas came from his own thinking and his own observations, a fact which gave his work a freshness and originality that were characteristically his own. Of all his work his first book was the most heavily dependent upon traditional views. As he grew older he came to rely more and more upon his own intuition and experience.

In 1887, with Fere as co-author, he published his second book, *Animal Magnetism. On Double Consciousness* appeared in an English edition in 1889; and *Personality Deviations,* his fourth book in six years, in 1892. All were written from a clinical, psychiatric view of psychology, but they indicate a period of transition in Binet's life, when his Interests were moving from the abnormal to the normal. In spite of the speed with which they appeared, these books were both original and readable. Binet had enormous energy for hard work and a capacity to write about it rapidly in clear and flowing prose. Work cost him no effort. 'I work quite naturally,' he once said, 'as a hen lays eggs.'

In the summer of 1892 Binet was on his way to a little beach at Saint-Valery, where he spent his vacations with his family, when he happened to meet the physiologist H. Beaunis on the platform or the railroad station at Rouen. Beaunis was director of the laboratory or physiological psychology that had been created at the Sorbonne in 1889. The two men fell into a friendly argument about hypnosis and in the course of it Binet asked if he might do some work in the laboratory. Beaunis was glad to have this energetic young man as a collaborator, so a decision was made that fixed the future direction of Binet's career. He joined the four-room laboratory first as Beaunis's assistant, then became associate director and finally director when Beaunis retired in 1894. The directorship carried no specific responsibilities and, since he had an independent income, it left him completely free to pursue his own research.

The year 1894 was eventful for Binet. Not only did he become director of a laboratory. He also completed his doctorate in science with a thesis on the nervous system of insects. He published two more books: *The Psychology of Great Calculators and Chess Players,* a minor work, with Henneguy, and *Introduction to Experimental Psychology,* which reviewed both the standard methods of measuring sensation, reaction time, and memory, and the newer methods that used questionnaires. This latter part of the *introduction* anticipated the methods which he was soon to use so effectively in his studies of children. It was in 1894 also that he founded his own journal, *L'Annee psychologique.*

Binet remained the editor and a major contributor to *L'Annee* through fourteen volumes until his death in 1911. During those years he wrote a large book on *Suggestibility* (1900) which summarised his work on hypnosis, contributed *The Soul and the Body* (1906) to a traditional philosophical debate, and averaged about ten articles a year in his own and other journals.

Binet worked frequently with collaborators—although his dominating energy frequently antagonised them—but he was not a professor and he did no teaching. Students would have got in his way. He seldom appeared in public, being too busy with research and writing. His only deviation from complete loyalty to psychology seems to have been his tendency to write plays that were successfully produced in Paris. But even his plays usually had a psychological theme.

Binet performed experiments on adult subjects, but he preferred to work with children. There is one advantage (along with many disadvantages) in using the schoolroom for psychological experiments: young subjects are available in large numbers and are accustomed to following instructions. A long series of studies of children during the 1890s provided the necessary background for Binet's most famous work—the Binet-Simon scale for measuring the intelligence of school children.

A mark of a good idea is that it makes one forget how confusing things were before it was invented. Today the Binet-Simon scale seems such a simple and obvious way to measure intelligence that it is hard to believe how many brilliant men were unable to think of it. Francis Galton, for example, wanted to measure intelligence. He developed a collection of tests, and he contributed the statistical tools necessary to analyse the results. But Galton's tests were aimed at psychological processes fashionable in his day. He measured visual and auditory acuity and observed that, 'The more perceptive the senses are of differences, the larger is the field upon which our judgement and intelligence can act'. It was a good idea, but it didn't work.

James McKeen Cattell was similarly hobbled by the empiricist tradition in the psychology of his day. Cattell, student of Wundt and friend of Galton, was one of the brightest lights in American psychology at the turn of the century. Yet look at the list of tests he proposed to measure intelligence:

1. *Dynamometer Pressure.* How tightly can the hand squeeze?

2. *Rate of Movement.* How quickly can the hand be moved through a distance of fifty cm.?

3. *Sensation-areas.* How far apart must two points be on the skin to be recognised as two rather than one?

4. *Pressure Causing Pain.* How much pressure on the forehead is necessary to cause pain?

5. *Least Noticeable Difference in Weight.* How large must the difference be between two weights before it is reliably detected?

6. *Reaction-time for Sound.* How quickly can the hand be moved at the onset of an auditory signal?

7. *Time for Naming Colours.* How long does it take to name a strip of ten coloured papers?

8. *Bisection of a fifty-cm. Line.* How accurately can one point to the centre of an ebony rule?

9. *Judgement often-sec. Time.* How accurately can an interval of ten seconds be judged?

10. *Number of Letters Remembered on Once Hearing.* How many letters, ordered at random, can be repeated exactly after one presentation?

Cattell described these tests as beginning with bodily measures, then proceeding through psychophysical to mental measures. If indeed there is any continuum of measurements running from bodily to mental, Galton and Cattell explored only the bodily end of it. Today we know that of all Cattell's tests only the last, measurement of memory span, provides any indication or a person's intelligence, and even this measurement is of limited value.

The Frenchmen Binet, Henri, and Simon took up where Galton, Cattell, and others had left off. They pushed boldly along the imaginary continuum towards the higher mental processes, into measures of memory, imagination, attention, comprehension; it was at that end of the continuum that they began to get results. But it took someone with clinical attitudes to attempt such measures; the laboratory scientists knew intuitively that the higher mental processes were too complicated to permit of valid measurement.

In a series of articles in *L'Annee psychologique* from 1894 to 1898 Binet and his assistant Victor Henri described their attempts to measure higher mental processes in children and adults. They were quite clear that sensory and motor measurements were easier to make and less variable when repeated, but, for all their virtues, such tests did not seem to distinguish sufficiently among different people. Binet wanted to measure mental functions that different people performed in different ways, with different degrees of skill. Since memory is an important component or intelligence, everyone agreed that it should be included. But Binet thought it might be possible to make similar measurements on many other psychological functions. For example, why not measure the vividness of imagery, or the kind of imagery that a person has? Why not test attention, both its scope and its duration? Why not test comprehension of sentences, or synonyms, or ask the person to find logical errors in a text? Many tests of suggestibility were available from the studies of hypnosis; could suggestibility be related to intelligence? Even aesthetic judgements could be obtained and scored against the aesthetic judgements of experts. Why not ask people to make moral judgements, or judge emotions from pictures of facial expression? Why not study their will by asking then' to withstand pain or fatigue? Why not measure the speed with which they could acquire a motor skill?

Why not, Indeed? Who could say that all those higher mental functions were not involved in intelligence? No one had ever measured those functions in a large number of different people in order to relate the results to intelligence. The reasons for this neglect were unclear except for the fact that the inquiry did not seem tidy. In the minds or such academic psychologists as Wundt, psychology should begin with the simplest measures of the simplest mental elements. Wundt flatly denied that psychology could study thinking. Even those who were more optimistic felt that psychology could build up toward these more complicated kinds of measures only slowly. Psychology wasn't ready to jump into the middle of the mind without any notion of what might be encountered.

Such a jump is what one might expect from a psychologist trained in the clinic. Because no two patients ever suffer from exactly the same complaints, a clinician is seldom able to repeat his observations precisely; if he is not to lose his way, he must inure himself to the complexities and variabilities that his patients exhibit, and learn to discover order in the most untidy and abnormal kinds of behaviour. But the complexities a clinician must learn to live with frequently serve only to convince experimentalists that clinical data are worse than useless.

In 1904 the Minister of Public Instruction in Paris assembled a commission to consider the problem of subnormal children in the public schools. If the children who were likely to fail could be placed in special schools, they might be helped; Binet, whose studies of child psychology were well known, was a member of the commission. As early as 1894 he had begun to try his tests on school children; in 1903 he had reported an intensive study of the intellectual development of his own two daughters.

Binet quickly became disturbed because the discussions of the commission were so vague that everything they tried to do seemed con fused and pointless. He took it upon himself, therefore, to provide clear definitions for the terms that were being used to describe subnormal children. He devoted his research thereafter to the problem of finding a scientific basis for a medical classification that would be more useful to educators. His principal collaborator in this attempt was Dr. Simon, a young physician in an asylum for backward children. From 1905 until Binet's death in 1911 at least twenty-eight articles and one book were written by Binet and Simon together.

In 1905, primarily to facilitate the work of the commission, Binet and Simon published their first results. They used a large battery of different mental tests, some hard, some easy. Binet collected tests from everywhere, and his own mind bubbled over with ideas for others. To discover which tests were useful, he and Simon spent endless hours in the schools with the children, watching, asking, testing, recording. Each proposed test had to be given to a large number of children. If a test did not distinguish the brighter from the duller, or the older from the younger, it was abandoned. Tests that worked were retained, even though they often failed to conform with the theoretical principles Binet and Henri had announced ten years earlier. The memory tests worked. And the tests of comprehension worked—comprehension of words, of statements, of concepts, of pictures. Binet did not retain the tests on the basis of a theory; he watched the children and let their behaviour decide which tests were good and which were irrelevant. The 1905 version of the 'Metrical Scale of Intelligence' simply arranged all the tests that Binet had selected in an order of increasing difficulty. Each child passed as many tests as he could until they became too difficult for him. How far the child got down the list of tests could then be compared with how far other children of the same age usually got.

In 1908 a revised version was published. The tests were grouped according to the age at which fifty to seventy-five per cent of a large sample of children passed them, from age three up to age thirteen. In 1911, the year of Binet's death, there was still another revision that extended the age up to fifteen years.

According to the 1911 scale an average three-year-old French child should pass half these tests: he should be able to point to his nose, eyes, and mouth; repeat two digits; enumerate objects in a picture; give his family name; and repeat a sentence of six syllables. By age seven the child should pass half of these tests: be able to show his right hand and left ear; describe a picture; execute three commands given simultaneously; count the value of six suns, three of which are double; and name four cardinal colours. By fifteen the youngster should be able to repeat seven digits; find three rhymes for a given word in one minute; repeat a sentence of twenty-six syllables; interpret pictures; and interpret given facts.

These should give the flavour of Binet's tests to anyone who (though it is hard to imagine how) might have been sheltered from them heretofore. The age group of tests that a child could pass half the time defined his mental age, regardless of what his chronological age might be.

Binet used as the measure of retardation simply the difference between the child's mental age and chronological age. Thus a child who was six years old but passed only the items on the four-year age group would have a mental age of four, and so would be retarded two years in mental development. Binet regarded two years as a serious deficiency. Other psychologists decided later that it was better to use the ratio, rather than the difference between the two ages. Mental age divided by chronological age gives a mental quotient. If the two ages are the same, then the child is average for his age and the quotient is unity. If the child is retarded, the mental is less than the chronological age, and the quotient is less than unity. If he is advanced, the quotient will be greater than unity. When this quotient is multiplied by 100, the result is usually referred to as the intelligence quotient, or I.Q. The various confusing arguments about whether the I.Q. is constant throughout life, or whether it can be raised or lowered with special circumstances, came later and cannot be blamed on Binet. His contribution was a simple, reliable method for determining a child's mental age.

One of Binet's advantages in solving this problem may have been that, although he read English fluently, he did not know a word of German. Some such insulation from Fechner, Helmholtz, and Wundt was probably necessary. If he had known more about what happened east of the Rhine, he might have been more willing to top short with the study of sensations and reaction times. Fortunately, he was not over-concerned with scientific purity; he had a practical problem he urgently wanted to solve, and he did whatever seemed necessary to solve it. The solution did not come through an elegant experiment conceived in an armchair and conducted in a laboratory. It came through tedious hours spent testing children in the schools of Paris.

Instead of experiments, Binet conducted interviews—in the best tradition of the clinical interview.

For the all-round clinical appraisal of a subject's intellectual level [wrote Lewis M. Terman many years later] the Binet type of scale has no serious rival. It is not merely an intelligence test; it is a method of standardised interview which is highly interesting to the subject and calls forth his natural responses to an extraordinary variety of situations.

Within ten years of Binet's death in 1911, translations and revisions of the Binet-Simon scale were in use all over the world. The immediate, international enthusiasm demonstrated how great the need for such a measuring device had been. Oddly enough, the scale gained little fame in France. In his old age Simon recalled that it was not until the early 1920s that a French social worker, having visited clinics in the United States, found the Binet-Simon scale frequently mentioned there. On her return to France the social worker was instrumental in reintroducing the test to the land of its birth. During World War II the test became very fashionable in France but under the names of Terman and Merrill, the Americans who revised it for use in the United States!

Binet was not a great man. He was a competent, hard-working psychologist whose career ended abruptly when he was still in his prime and still had much left to do. He trained no students, he wrote no immortal books, and his memory has been little honoured by his countrymen. But even though he was not great, he was important—made important by subsequent events.

Over the years the demand for mental tests has steadily grown. The individual differences explored by psychological testing now include innumerable varieties, and the statistical methods or analysing test data have grown in power and sophistication. The vein that Binet opened up is still being mined today —and still yields ore of the highest grade.

Imagine that you are given a number, somewhere between 0 and 1,000, and are told that it represents a person's age in months. How much would you know about the person?

If the number is somewhere in the middle of the range—between 200 and 800, say—it would not tell you very much. Since you do not know the person's sex, education, native ability, or even the society in which he (she) lives, you could not form any clear picture of him (her). If the number gets large enough, of course, you have some feeling for the kind of constraints old age imposes. But you will extract the greatest amount of information from the number when it is small, and the smaller it gets the more accurate you can be.

Small numbers place the person in the time of life called his growth period, when successive phases unfold themselves in regular order. The predictable succession of changes in bodily size and structure, in motor skills, in mental competence and achievement, in social and emotional adjustment is generally familiar to everyone. For those who wish to know more—parents, say, who wonder if their child is developing properly, or educators trying to plan a school curriculum—many detailed facts have been collected and tabulated for ready reference, both in popular guides and in technical handbooks.

A regular procession of structural changes is something we all take for granted. The emergence of motor skills is almost equally reliable. And cognitive development is only slightly more variable. Hundreds of studies—beginning even before Alfred Binet's experiments in the schools of Paris—have demonstrated convincingly that mental growth also pursues an orderly course, that measurable skills appear at predictable ages, that deviations above or below the average are not accidental. Binet calibrated a whole battery of tests, to which many subsequent workers have added, so that today we can sample quite different aspects of the unfolding process of mental growth. With those tests it has become possible to measure the growth of the mind.

But there are still many problems that remain unsettled.

Take, for example, that hotly debated subject, the constancy of the intelligence quotient. Adherents of hereditary theories of mental ability like to think of the I.Q. as if it were printed indelibly on (he chromosomes at the moment of conception. Empiricists, on the other hand, credit experience and education for all our mental accomplishments and recognise no other factors which might limit a child's I.Q. score. In the twentieth century this ancient argument has come to rest—or roost—on the question of whether or not an I.Q. score is indeed constant throughout life.

Consider what this constancy would imply. Suppose one thousand children of the same age are tested every year until they are adults. If the intelligence of every child is constant, their rank order from best to worst, from brightest to dullest, would never change—except, perhaps, for random errors inherent in the measuring instruments. The child who ranked 100 at the age of one year would still rank 100 at the age of twenty years.

When studies of this sort are actually done, however, it is found that the rank orderings can change markedly from year to year.'. One child shows a sudden spurt in skill A while a second is developing skill B and a third seems to be standing still. In the first years of life the scores change considerably; after six or seven years they begin to settle down and our predictions get better and better.

It may be suggested, therefore, that the I.Q. is variable at birth, but becomes more stable as we get older. It is not apparent whether this finding favours either side of the heredity-environment battle. Perhaps one inherits one's constant I.Q. the way a man Inherits his beard— it doesn't appear until the age is right. Or perhaps one needs time to decide what I.Q. will be necessary in one's social environment. Increasing stability of the I.Q. can be explained away by proponents of either theory. Nevertheless, it is fair to say that informed opinion in the United States is currently on the side of the environmentalist—if not completely, at least in spirit and emphasis. Within limits, Johnny can change his position in the rank ordering—although it becomes more and more difficult to do so as he grows older.

Psychologists who have puzzled over the instability of predictions based on the early years do not believe that it can be attributed to poor measurements—not entirely, anyhow. There is reason to think that even the most accurate tests during infancy have little power to predict adult intelligence.

Consider the following argument: Suppose that mental growth is cumulative, so that the level a child attains by the age of nine is simply the sum of all he has achieved in each of his preceding years. If this assumption were reasonable, it would mean that our prediction from age nine to age ten would be very good, since nine-tenths of the basis for the new measurement would be the same as for the old and only one-tenth would be attributable to new growth or experience during the tenth year. And by the same argument, the prediction of the child's I.Q. score at age two on the basis of his score at age one would be based half on old achievements and half on novel achievements—hence the prediction would be less accurate. On a relative basis, therefore, more could happen to change the relative standings early in life than later on. Every baseball fan who has watched batting averages vary wildly during the early part of the season and then settle down as the players accumulated more turns at bat will understand this explanation of why the test scores should become more reliable as the children grow older.

For older children, at least, mental tests can give a valuable measure of mental age, one that can be usefully compared with chronological age. But there are still other problems we should recognise when we try to understand what an intelligence score means.

By combining all the individual tests in order to obtain a single number that represents a child's status, psychologists have encouraged uncritical people to imagine that mental growth is an undifferentiated process, to think that a child's mind grows like a potato. Even psychologists who should know better have been tempted to plot smooth curves of mental growth, forgetting that they were actually dealing with a composite of many separate curves for Separate skills. The practical convenience of having a single number is, of course, too great to resist. But a scientist must look more closely.

As stated earlier, to measure a process is not necessarily to understand it. Mental tests may give a number — mental age — that is highly correlated with mental growth, but they do not contain within themselves any coherent explanation of that growth. One has to take the single number part to see what it consists of. Why do certain skills emerge before others? Why are sonic tasks easy and others so difficult? What does a child actually do in the process of finding an answer to a test item? What manner of thing is the mind of a child that his abilities should multiply in this particular fashion? Binet's achievement cried out for support from a more comprehensive theory of mental growth.

A common assumption, already mentioned, is that mental growth is a cumulative affair, that new skills can be added steadily without modifying old skills in any significant way. An alternative assumption is that childhood is a series of abrupt transitions from one fairly stable stage to another which is equally stable but more advanced and (presumably) more complex. According to this view of development, the reason that early measures do not predict later measures of intelligence is that very different psychological processes are involved at different stages; a child might excel at one stage, yet be mediocre at another. These transitions supposedly have the character of sudden and radical reorganisations; they are not a simple summation of new and old. Different kinds of observations are relevant and necessary at different times in a child's life. The cumulative hypothesis is simpler, perhaps, but the hypothesis of distinct stages with critical transitions between them also has much to recommend it.

Undoubtedly the most dramatic illustration of a sudden transition is birth Itself. The transition from the foetal stage to an independent and reactive stage of infancy may seem to be a sudden, mechanical process, but evidence indicates that the transition Is neither brief nor simple. For months afterwards constant stimulation and mothering are required in order to get an infant successfully through this transition.

The tragic effects of maternal neglect at this stage can be seen in very young babies who have lost their mothers. They commonly develop a regressive kind of reaction. In the first stages of this reaction the orphaned infant may fall into a light stupor when given his bottle, so that strong stimulation is needed to keep the infant active and sucking. His muscles become flaccid and his skin begins to turn pale. As the condition gets more serious there may be vomiting and diarrhoea, hiccups, and irregular breathing. Still later his skin may become grey and wrinkled. All the symptoms point to a regression by the baby to the prenatal mode of functioning, when breathing and circulation of the blood were the mother's responsibility. Poor breathing and poor circulation may interfere with the normal development of the nervous system, which in turn can have physiological and psychological consequences that persist throughout life. If nothing is done to prevent it, a baby may waste away and die, a fate that was once quite common in orphanages and hospitals. Today doctors know that the regression can be prevented by massage and stimulation, and by vigorously exciting the sucking reflex. The prescription they usually give is T.L.C.—a daily dose of Tender Loving Care.

The transition from foetus to infant is assumed to be merely the first of a long series of passages that the child must negotiate. Students of personality development generally concentrate on the important transitions involved in weaning, toilet training, sex training—on all the little tragedies and comedies that are required in order to develop competence in managing the orifices, of the body. Certainly these are the crises most apparent to a mother and probably to the child himself. The way they are handled is believed to have significant influences upon the way the child's personality develops, although opinions are easier to find than proof.

Cognitive transitions are less immediately apparent, but are equally important for the growth of a normal, intelligent, human being. By cognitive transitions are meant changes in the child's manner of knowing—knowing about himself and the world in which he lives.

Their subtle consequences often go unnoticed by the parent; the child does not notice them because his new way of knowing destroys the old. But the changes occur, nonetheless.

An adult deals with his world easily, almost automatically, in terms of certain concepts or systems of concepts involving space, time, number, quantity, causality, motion, velocity, and so on. These provide a frame of reference for all his other thoughts. Certain philosophers have assumed that, because these concepts are so important, they must be given immediately to all minds by a kind of *a priori* intuition. The fact is, however, that the concepts are acquired rather slowly during childhood and pass through several more-or-less predictable stages before attaining the obviously correct form familiar to all intelligent adults. The development of these fundamental concepts has been studied with particular care and ingenuity by Jean Piaget, Professor of Psychology at the Universities of Geneva and of Paris, and by his students and associates.

If Piaget's observations are correct, even so simple an idea as that of an object—a relatively permanent, enduring thing that continues to exist regardless of whether you are looking at it—is one that must be slowly and patiently learned during the first two years of life. An adult considers space and substance to be very different things, but to an infant who has no concept of an object, this difference between space and substance is literally inconceivable.

Consider some of the necessary steps along the path from birth to the final development of an object concept.

What does a baby do when the perceptual image of an object disappears from view? This question is relevant from the first week of life. What does the baby do when the mother's breast escapes his lips? At first his response is undirected, but after the second week a nursling is able to find the nipple and differentiate it from other objects. Now we ask the following question: can it be assumed that a baby recognises the nipple or has any conception that the nipple just recovered at this instant is identical with the nipple that escaped a few seconds ago?

Or, to choose other examples: when mother's face disappears from view and then reappears, does baby recognise it as the same face? Where does a baby think the face goes when it disappears?

At first, of course, the baby cannot think about such matters at all, for he does not have the concepts available to think with. Nevertheless, it is possible, as Piaget has demonstrated, to infer something of the nature of the child's world from his behaviour. As soon as the child is old enough to follow a moving image with his eyes, we can watch him search for vanished objects and thus learn at least a little about his conception of the things he is looking for.

Few objects are more interesting to a baby than his bottle. Piaget always had a cooperative collaborator when the object that appeared and disappeared in the various tests was a bottle of milk.

At six months and nineteen days [said Piaget of a child he had studied most carefully] Laurent immediately began to cry from hunger and impatience on seeing his bottle (he was already whimpering, as he does quite regularly at mealtime). But at the very moment when I make the bottle disappear behind my hand or under the table—he follows me with his eyes—he stops crying. As soon as the object reappears, a new outburst of desire; then flat calm after it disappears. I repeat the experiment four more times; the result is constant until poor Laurent, beginning to think the Joke had, becomes violently angry.

At this age—around six months—when the bottle disappears from view, it ceases to exist.

A very young child seems to behave as if an object were merely a visual image that enters and leaves the field of view capriciously, appearing for no particular reason and disappearing into the void just as unpredictably as it came. A toy that falls from the child's hand vanishes instantly from the universe. Hut before the same child is six months old he will begin to coordinate his visual and tactual worlds. He begins to reach towards and grasp things in his visual field. Then a series of skills are learned in quick succession. This learning does not seem to require any biological satisfactions to reinforce it; the child seems to regard competence as its own reward. He learns to move his eyes slightly in advance of an object; hence a rapidly moving object that vanishes briefly and reappears is correctly followed. He begins to practise at making images enter or leave his visual field at will. He learns to reconstruct the whole object when only a part is visible. He learns to pull or push aside things that block his view of an object he is searching for. Each step represents a separate triumph of infantile persistence. But even at this stage the child does not yet seem to dissociate his own actions from the objects themselves.

By the time a child is nine or ten months old he will ordinarily have achieved a rather stable concept of an object. Human beings provide the child with the best instances. But even at this late age it is possible to uncover surprising reactions if one looks carefully. For example, the child watches while a toy that he has often played with is put under a cloth. The situation is pictured at the top of Figure 28.1. After a little experience the child learns to pull the cloth aside and find the toy. But now the same toy is put under another coverlet at a slightly different place. The child is baffled, looks under the original cloth, then stops searching! As shown at the bottom of Figure 28.1, he does not look where he saw the object last, but where he found it before.

Piaget describes another example in the following passage:

Gerard, at thirteen months, knows how to walk, and is playing ball in a large room. He throws the ball, or rather lets it drop in front of him and, either on his feet or on all fours, hurries to pick it up. At a given moment the ball rolls under an armchair. Gerard sees it and, not without some difficulty, takes it out in order to resume the game. Then the ball rolls under a sofa at the other end of the room. Gerard has seen it pass under the fringe of the sofa; he bends down to recover it. But as the sora is deeper than the armchair and the fringe does prevent a clear view, Gerard gives up after a moment; he gets up, crosses the room,

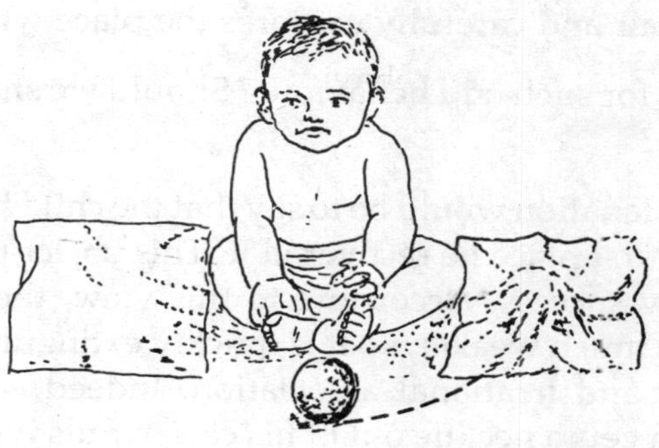

**Fig. 28.1.** A child sees a toy placed under a cloth and learn to find it there. When it placed under a second cloth, he looks again under the first. (J. Piaget, 'The Child's View of Reality', *Scientific American*, March, 1957.)

goes right under the armchair and carefully explores the place where the ball was before.

How should we account for such odd behaviour? Should we shrug and say that children are naturally unpredictable?

Perhaps the simplest explanation would be to say that the child has learned an association between the object and the first place he recovered it. This object-place connexion has been practised and reinforced by success. According to this view, the connexion between the object and a new location is much weaker, so it is quickly extinguished, and the child is left with the prior, but strong and irrational association. Indeed, such experiences are not confined to children. A man gets a necktie out of his closet, puts it where he can reach it; but when he is ready to put it on he goes back to the closet to look for it. We all do such foolish things every day. Perhaps the child has merely suffered a common lapse of memory. But no.

According to Piaget, the difference is that a man is capable of remembering but has momentarily forgotten, whereas the child is incapable of remembering—he does not know he is dealing with a single object. For the child, ball-under-the-armchair is one thing and ball-under-the-sofa is another. Having lost the ball-under-the-sofa, he decides to play with the other ball instead. The association between object and place that the child has established is complete; he does not yet have a clear enough conception of an object to realise that the same ball might be associated with two different places. The child has not forgotten anything. Instead, he is remembering something different from what an adult would remember. In an adult, object-place associations are much more flexible than they are for the child; the same object can be recalled as being in any of several different places. Thus the child's apparently poor memory, and his deficient conception of physical objects are simply two different aspects of the same psychological process. The child has established the various appearances of the ball as forming a class of equivalent objects, but he has not yet thoroughly mastered the concept of a single, identical object.

Recognition that a variety of sensory images can he generated by an identical, individual, physical object is learned so young that we cannot remember how we did it or what life was like without the concept. We can try to imagine a preobjective state of consciousness by observing carefully what happens when, for example, we enter a new visual world through a telescope or under a microscope. But comparisons of this experience with a child's perceptual world can be little more than a suggestive fantasy.

The first two years of life are devoted to the acquisition of many perceptual-motor coordinations. Out of them the child develops a concept of permanent objects—objects existing in a spatial framework defined by his own bodily orientation.

Next the child is ready to develop symbols associated with these sensory-motor objects. As his language begins to develop, he is launched into a new domain of learning, into completely flew ways of coping with his environment.

An average child is capable of imitating speech sounds and forming simple words during his second year of life, but not until he is about two years old does he seem capable of sustaining true symbolic processes. This ability can be observed in his play activities as well as in his vocalisations. For a very young child, play is merely a kind of exercise. But as he develops he becomes able to carry out actions that would be appropriate in a situation riot actually experienced—for example, pretending to sleep, or pretending that the teddy bear is asleep. Such activities are a form of symbolic play. Once the child has achieved the symbolic processes necessary for enjoying this kind of play, he has developed all that is needed to begin using spoken noises to signify an possibly but not necessarily) absent thing or situation.

It is at about this stage-when language is first beginning to play an important role—that most children develop a kind of wilfulness. They begin to assert their own opinions and to make some of their own decisions. The development of volition and of language must be closely related, since voluntary actions are so often responses to verbal commands generated internally and sub-vocally. But talking to yourself about what you must do is a very complicated skill, one that children develop only slowly over several years.

It is possible to study the way in which words come to control behaviour; Russian psychologists have found this especially interesting.

Imagine two different pictures. One shows a bright red circle on a pale yellow background, the other a bright green circle on a grey background. The child is told something like this: 'When I show you the picture with the pale-yellow background, I want you to 'else your *right* hand. When I show you the picture with the grey background, I want you to raise your *left* hand.' This is a simple task and young children have little trouble performing it correctly.

Now notice what has been done with the verbal instructions. The child's attention has been directed to the part of the picture that is the least impressive, that has the least attention value. We tell him to ignore the strong red and green colours and to pay attention instead to the pale background colours. He may not learn the task exactly the way we described it, however. It is more natural to look at the bright colours. For a child to be able to follow the instructions, he must control his attention by the use of words, by internal commands.

It is easy to test the child and to see which way he has solved the problem. One merely reverses the circles and their backgrounds. If the red circle was at first on a pale yellow background, one now puts a red circle on a grey background and shows this new picture to the child. Will he respond to the bright red circle (which is the natural thing to do) or will he respond to the pale background (which is what we told him to do)? IC the child raises his right hand, we know he was paying attention to the dominant red circle; If he raises his left hand, we know he was paying attention to the weaker background colour.

Russian psychologists have found that children three years old do not follow the verbal command; they pay attention to the impressive colour of the circle instead. At four years they seem confused, now doing one thing, now the other. Not until the child is five.will a verbal command produce a stable reorganisation of this perceptual field.

Experiments of this sort illustrate the fact that long after a child has mastered the basic skills needed for social communication there are still important changes going on in the way these linguistic skills modify and control other aspects of his cognitive life. The reorganisation of thought in terms of verbal symbols has a number of advantages in terms of easier communication, more abstract kinds of thinking, greater speed and efficiency in processing information, and soon. One of the most important advantages however, is that after the psychological processes have been brought under the control of verbal symbols it becomes possible for the child to control himself with his own words. Eventually, the child can give himself the orders that he has heard so often from his parents—parental control can be internalised. Then he can begin to explore the realm of self-control, the realm of independent, voluntary behaviour that is so important for psychological maturity.

By the time a child is four years old his skill with language will have progressed to a point where one can talk with him and ask indirect questions about his concepts. If the questions are artfully posed, surprising results may turn up. Consider the following example:

> Two small glasses A and $A_2$, or identical shape and size, are each filled with an equal number of beads, and this equality is acknowledged by the child, who has filled the glasses himself, e.g., by placing a bead in A with one hand every time he places a bead in $A_2$ with the other hand. Next, $A_2$ is emptied into a differently shaped glass B, while A is left as a standard. Children of four to five years then conclude that the quantity of beads has changed, even though they are sure none has been removed or added. If the glass B is tall and thin they will say that there are 'more beads than before' because 'it is higher', or that there are fewer because 'it is thinner', but they agree on the non-conservation of the whole."

Children who give this response are following the maxim that seeing is believing, that the world is the way it appears to be. When the beads are poured into B there appear to be more of them; therefore, there are more of them!

If the same experiment is tried with a child seven or older, the question will surprise him. He may look around on the floor to see if any beads were spilled. Or he may think the experimenter is joking. Of course, he says, the two are the same. Pouring them from one glass to another does not create or destroy beads. The seven-year-old responds as would an adult.

Suppose, however, that we question him. Our (imaginary) conversation might sound like this:

'How do you know that they are the same?' we ask.

'Because I put the same number of beads in both glasses,' he replies.

The four-year-old interrupts. 'I knew *that*,' he says.

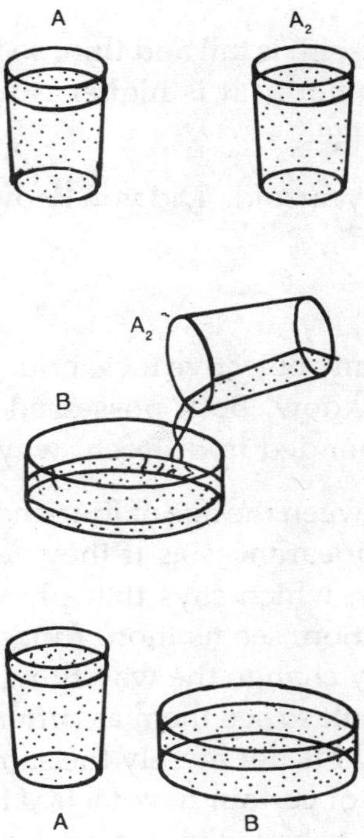


**Fig. 28.2.** A child of five years agrees that beaker A and beaker $A_2$ contain the same amount of juice. He then pours the contents of $A_2$ into another beaker B of a different shape. When asked, he judges that A and B do not contain the same amount of juice. At seven years, however, the child knows that A must equal B.

We ask the seven-year-old, 'Is that the only reason you said they were equal?'

'You didn't spill any, did you?'

'No,' we admit, 'we didn't spill any.'

We turn to the younger child. 'Did you know that we didn't spill any?' we ask him.

'Yes, I knew that.'

We press the seven-year-old again. 'Is that the only way you knew?'

He considers a moment. 'Well...if you pour them back into the first glass again, it will come to the same level.'

We turn again to the younger child. 'Did you know that?' we ask.

'Yes,' he replies, 'I knew that.'

What facts, what evidence, what new data does the older child have to guide him so easily to the correct answer? Surely there must be some crucial fact that the older child observed but the younger child missed. But what can it be? We insist, 'What other reasons do you have?'

'The new glass,' says the seven-year-old, is tall and thin, so the level is higher and maybe it looks as if there are more. But the amount it is higher is just equal to the amount it is narrower, so there really isn't any change.'

We turn back once more to the four-year-old. 'Did you know that the new glass made the beads look both taller and also thinner?'

'Yes,' he replies, 'I could see that.'

Try as we may, we cannot discover any objective fact about the beads that the older child knew and the younger child did not know. Both possessed the same information. Both understood the question. Yet they responded in different ways. Why?

According to Piaget, somewhere between the age of four and seven a cognitive revolution takes place. Instead of dealing with appearances as if they were the true reality, an older child believes in a theory. This theory, which says that physical quantities are invariant under simple changes in shape or location, seems more fundamental to him than the way the world looks. Indeed, it will actually change the way things look. When he knows they are the same, he may find it very difficult to see them as different. But the important point is that the universe of the seven-year-old is not merely the same old universe he lived in at the age of four with a simple addition of certain new facts. His world is organised—seen, remembered, imagined, thought about, behaved in—in a new and better way. Moreover, it is difficult for him to remember how the world appeared to him before he organised it in this new way. Memories stored in terms of the old concepts become almost inaccessible after such revolutions; therein lies the source of much of our childhood amnesia, our inability to recall our earliest experiences.

A seven-year-old child cannot state explicitly in so many words the nature of the theory he has adopted; that must come at a still later stage of intellectual development. And at first his theory may be somewhat limited in its range of applications; it must be discovered all over again in a new context.

For example, suppose he is given two balls or modelling clay which he recognises as equal. Then one of the two balls is mashed flat. Which contains the more clay? The young child takes this question seriously. If he is impressed by the density per unit area as he holds the ball in the palm of his hand, he may say the ball has more clay. If he is impressed by the visual extent of the clay pancake, he may nominate it as having more clay. As he grows older, however, the day will arrive when he says they must be equal. Yet, on that very day, if we ask him which one weighs the most, (which we can do in the course of playing with a balance), the same child will usually be surprised to find they weigh the same. Moreover, even after both quantity and weight are known to be conserved in spite of the mashing, he may expect the pancake to displace more water from a full glass than would the ball. Conservation of volume is the last to appear; that may not happen until the eleventh or twelfth year.

Boys and girls five years old have many curious ideas about their world. They are not clear about the difference between some and all. Their notions of contradiction, even of negation, are not the adult notions. Time, movement, and speed are mutually con founded in a world where the distance travelled is more important than the time elapsed. Space is plastic, bearing only a crude, topological resemblance to what an adult means by space. It is rather marvellous that such intuitive thinkers manage to survive long enough to grow up and join the ruling majority.

Of course, Piaget does not say that children are incapable of forming the more sophisticated concepts before they are seven years old. He says merely that in the normal Swiss environment they do not develop these concepts until about the age they start school. What they might be able to do, given appropriate coaching, is still unknown. But this exciting possibility has not yet been carefully explored.

Dependence upon the perceptual field, with little capacity for going beyond or behind it, characterises a young child's orientation towards space as well as towards quantity. Consider this example: Three cardboard mountains are constructed on top of a square table. A child is brought in and walked around the table, inspecting the mountains from every angle. Then he sits down and watches while a doll is moved around the table. His task is to select out of a set of pictures the one that corresponds to the way the mountains might look to the doll. Now, even though the child understands the task perfectly well, if he is under seven or eight he will select a picture that shows how the mountains look to him and he seems to believe that this is also how the mountains must look to the doll. His own perception is the only reality.

Another way to study a child's orientation in space is to ask which way is up. Under normal conditions this is an easy question to answer, but psychologists know how to make. it difficult. The child sits In a chair that can be tilted to the left or right. He looks at a visual display, a room with clear indications of vertical and horizontal. As shown in Figure 28.3, the room can also be tilted.

The child's problem is to adjust the tilt of his chair to zero, that is to say, to bring himself to a normal sitting position while he is looking at the room. When asked, 'Is this the way you sit when you eat your dinner?' The child who has adjusted his chair properly should say, 'Yes', without any hesitation.

In this situation some people align themselves fairly accurately with the true vertical, that is to say, with the vertical determined by gravitation. But many do not feel they are vertical until their bodies line up with the visual directions they see in the slanted room. When they are looking at a very tilted visual field they may have to tilt themselves as much as 35 degrees before they feel upright. The instant they shut their eyes, of course, they know they are tilted.

Children at the age of eight will be strongly dominated by the visual field. They will accept as up whatever *looks* up. But between the ages of eight and about thirteen there is marked learning, so that older children are better able to ignore the visual appearance and to judge on the basis of internal clues.

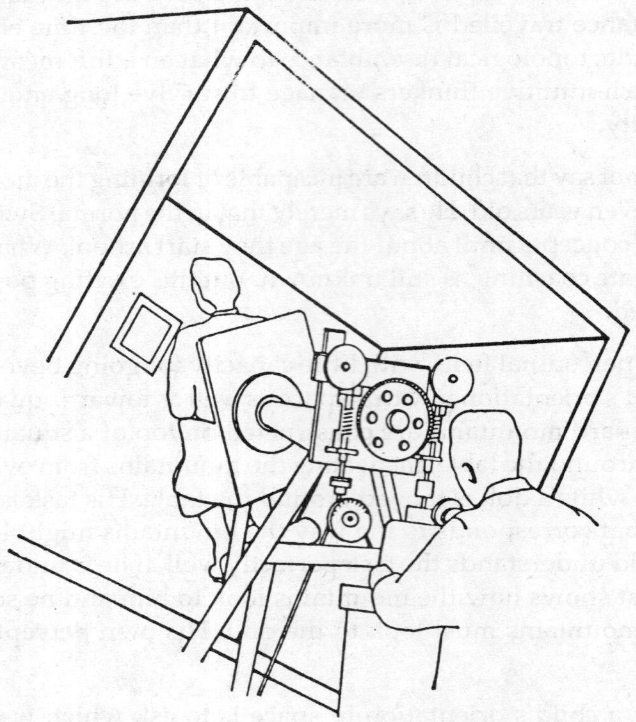

**Fig. 28.3.** The girl who is seated in a tilted chair, looking at a tilted room, has been challenged to adjust her chair to the upright. Younger children are more affected by visual cues, tend to adjust the chair off the true upright in the direction suggested visually by the tilted room.

The final phase of intellectual development begins when the child starts to describe or explain the principles and operations that he has previously learned in a tacit, unverbalised way. From about eight to twelve years the child's knowledge is largely organised in terms of concrete operations to be performed on concrete objects. In many situations the child obviously knows the rules for performing a task, since he can be consistently successful, yet at the same time he does not know them, since he cannot communicate them. A boy who is quite expert at catching a ball will be completely unable to explain anything about its trajectory; a girl who rides her bicycle with great skill will have nothing, to say about balance or the centre of gravity. Their situation can be rudely described by saying that they know a great deal more than they understand. Adolescence, famous for its social crises and its emotional tempests, is also the period during which the tacit becomes explicit, when what is known becomes understood.

The process of converting tacit into explicit knowledge may continue throughout life as a part of the never-ending education of those who try to stay intellectually alive. Probably there will never come a time when everything will be explicit, when everything that can be known can be written down on paper. But the adolescent is beginning to move in this direction; he is beginning to codify his knowledge, to extend it in ways that only formal, abstract thought can support.

What advantages are there in making tacit knowledge explicit? An obvious advantage is that the knowledge thereby becomes communicable. Science is a prime example of the enormous benefits that can result.

But there are personal consequences as well. When facts are well expressed in terms of a symbol system, it becomes clear that certain relations between propositions are necessary. When this symbol system is imposed upon reality a similar kind of necessity is attached to the physical events. Where, before, a relation may have seemed arbitrary or accidental, it now inherits requiredness from its symbolic representation.

Still another important advantage of symbolic knowledge is that it can be broadly generalised. Quite different situations can, when summarised symbolically, be seen as variations on a single theme. Behind apparent diversity one discovers a formal core, a single scheme, that can be expressed and manipulated symbolically. Once this is seen, knowledge gained in one situation can be transferred immediately to all other situations fitting the same schema. As in the child's earlier intellectual revolutions, this one also extends his ability to see behind and beyond the surface of things. Whereas at first he went beyond sensations to discover perceptual objects, and then went beyond perception to discover physical objects and operations, now he goes beyond physical things to discover the conceptual symbols and transformations of language and logic. Each stage of development carries with it new rewards in terms of greater power, subtlety, and economy of thought.

An example may make these claims more intelligible. A group of children are asked to play a kind of billiard game. Balls are launched with a tubular spring device that can be pivoted around a fixed point and aimed in various directions. The ball is shot against one wall of the billiard table. The wall, like all billiard tables, has a rubber cushion. The ball rebounds out on to the table. The nature of this game should be clear from Figure 28.4. A target is placed at successively different points on the table and the children are asked to make the ball hit it. Afterwards, they report what they observed.

The psychological question is not how accurately they manage to aim the ball at the target, but how they cope with a simple principle, namely, that the angles of incidence and reflection are equal.

Young children are concerned only with success or failure. They often manage to hit the target, but when asked about it they will usually describe the path of the ball as a smooth curve. They may ignore the angle of rebound entirely. They may realise that moving the plunger changes the direction the ball will go, but they do not explore the matter in a systematic way.

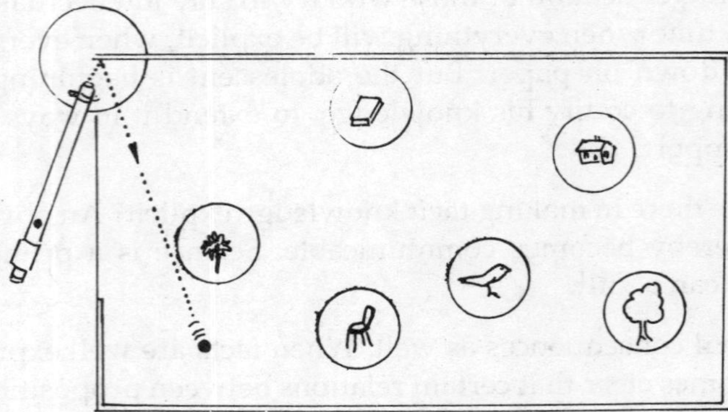

**Fig. 28.4.** The equality or the angles of incidence and reflection is demonstrated for children on this billiard table. (The dotted line shows the path of the ball.) Targets are placed on the circles and balls are shot out of the plunger, which can he pivoted and aimed by the child. (After B. Inhelder and J. Piaget, *The Growth of Logical Thinking*, New York: Basic Books, 1958.)

At age eight or so, however, most children attain complete mastery of the concrete operations involved in hitting the target. They clearly recognise the rectilinear trajectory and rebound, and will even make such spontaneous comments as, 'The more I move the plunger this way, the more the ball will go that way.' These children see the relation between plunger position and trajectory quite clearly. But they do not attempt to go beyond this *observation*, which is sufficient for hitting the targets consistently.

Boys and girls do not discover that the angles are equal until they are somewhere between eleven and fourteen. At first the equality seems to them a curious fact, interesting perhaps, but little more. Finally, there is a recognition that the equality of the angles is necessary. The recognition usually follows a comment about lines that are perpendicular to the wall of the table at the point of impact. Suddenly they are convinced that the equality is not accidental. The angles *must* be equal. The necessity of the principle becomes clear to them once they recognise that the ball returns to its starting point when the plunger is perpendicular to the wall. With this insight, they can break up the total angle into component parts and recognise the symmetry around an imaginary perpendicular line. At this point the children have achieved a formal principle that is not restricted to this particular game of billiards. Their new comprehension can now be transferred easily to any new situation that involves reflection.

It is a long and tenuous path that leads from the cradle to symbolic knowledge. The wonderful thing is how often the path is pursued successfully to its conclusion, how seldom any one of a thousand components fails to make its contribution in the right place at the right time. The growth of human understanding in a young child is one of the most intricate, amazing, and beautiful phenomena in nature.

# 29

# The Scope of Psychology

'Psychology is the Science of Mental Life,' both of its phenomena and of their conditions. The phenomena are such things as we call feelings, desires, cognitions reasonings, decisions, and the like; and, superficially considered, their variety and complexity is such as to leave a chaotic impression on the observer. The most natural and consequently the earliest way of unifying the material was, first, to classify it as well as might be, and, secondly, to affiliate the diverse mental modes thus found, upon a simple entity, the personal Soul, of which they are taken to be so many facultative manifestations. Now, for instance, the Soul manifests its faculty of Memory, now of Reasoning, now of Volition, or again its Imagination or its Appetite. This is the orthodox 'spiritualistic' theory of scholasticism and of common-sense. Another and a less obvious way of unifying the chaos is to seek common elements *in* the divers mental facts rather than a common agent behind them, and to explain them constructively by the various forms of arrangement of these elements, as one explains houses by stones and bricks. The 'associationist' schools of Herbart in Germany, and of Hume, the Mills and Bain in Britain, have thus constructed a *psychology without a soul* by taking discrete 'ideas,' faint or vivid, and showing how, by their cohesions, repulsions, and forms of succession, such things as reminiscences, perceptions, emotions, volitions, passions, theories, and all the other furnishings of an individual's mind may be engendered. The very Self or *ego* of the individual comes in this way to be viewed no longer as the pre-existing source of the representations, but rather as their last and most complicated fruit.

Now, if we strive rigorously to simplify the phenomena in either of these ways, we soon become aware of inadequacies in our method. Any particular cognition, for example, or recollection, is accounted for on the soul-theory by being referred to the spiritual faculties of Cognition or of Memory. These faculties themselves are thought of as absolute properties of the soul; that is, to take the case of memory, no reason is given why we should remember a fact as it happened, except that so to remember it constitutes the essence of our Recollective Power. We may, as spiritualists, try to explain our memory's failures and blunders by secondary causes. But its *successes* can invoke no factors save the existence of certain objective things to be remembered on the one hand, and of our faculty of memory on the other. When, for instance, I recall my graduation-day, and drag all its incidents and emotions up from death's dateless night, no mechanical cause can explain this process, nor can any analysis reduce it to lower terms or make its nature seem other than an ultimate *datum,* which, whether we rebel or not at its mysteriousness, must simply be taken for granted if we are to psychologise at all. However the associationist may represent the present ideas as thronging and arranging themselves, still, the spiritualist insists, he has in the end to admit that *something,* be it brain, be it 'ideas,' be it 'association,' *knows* past time as past, and fills it out with this or that event. And when the spiritualist calls memory an 'irreducible faculty,' he says no more than this admission of the associationist already grants.

And yet the admission is far from being a satisfactory simplification of the concrete facts. For why should this absolute god-given Faculty retain so much better the events of yesterday than those of last year, and, best of all, those of an hour ago? Why, again, in old age should its grasp of childhood's events seem firmest? Why should illness and exhaustion enfeeble it? Why should repeating an experience strengthen our recollection of it? Why should drugs, fevers, asphyxia, and excitement resuscitate things long since forgotten? If we content ourselves with merely affirming that the faculty of memory is so peculiarly constituted by nature as to exhibit just these oddities, we seem little the better for having invoked it, for our explanation becomes as complicated as that of the crude facts with which we started. Moreover there is something grotesque and irrational in the supposition that the sour is equipped with elementary powers of such an ingeniously intricate sort. Why *should* our memory cling more easily to the near than the remote? Why should it lose' its grasp of proper sooner than of abstract names? Such peculiarities seem quite fantastic; and might, for aught we can see a *priori,* be the precise opposites of what they are. Evidently, then, *the faculty does not exist absolutely, but works under conditions;* and *the quest of the conditions* becomes the psychologist's most interesting task.

However firmly he may hold to the soul and her remembering faculty, he must acknowledge that she never exerts the latter without a *cue,* and that something must always precede and *remind* us of whatever we are to recollect. "An *idea!*" says the associationist, "an idea associated with the remembered thing; and this explains also why things repeatedly met with are more easily recollected, for their associates on the various occasions furnish so many distinct avenues of recall." But this does not explain the effects of fever, exhaustion, hypnotism, old age, and the like. And in general, the pure associationist's account of our mental life is almost as bewildering as that of the pure spiritualist. This multitude of ideas, existing absolutely, yet clinging together, and weaving an endless carpet of themselves, like dominoes in ceaseless change, or the bits of glass in a kaleidoscope,—whence do they get their fantastic laws of clinging, and why do they cling in just the shapes they do?

For this the associationist must introduce the order of experience in the outer world. The dance of the ideas is a copy, somewhat mutilated and altered, of the order of phenomena. But the slightest reflection shows that phenomena have absolutely no power to influence our ideas until they have first impressed our senses and our brain. The bare existence of a past fact is no ground for our remembering it. Unless we have seen it, or somehow *undergone* it, we shall never know of its having been. The experiences of the body are thus one of the conditions of the faculty of memory being what it is. And a very small amount of reflection on facts shows that one part of the body, namely, the brain, is the part whose experiences are directly concerned. If the nervous communication be cut off between the brain and other parts, the experiences of those other parts are non-existent for the mind. The eye is blind, the ear deaf, the hand insensible and motionless. And conversely, if the brain be injured, consciousness is abolished or altered, even although every other organ in the body be ready to play its normal part. A blow on the head, a sudden subtraction of blood, the pressure of an apoplectic hemorrhage, may have the first effect; whilst a very few ounces of alcohol or grains of opium or hasheesh, or a whiff of chloroform or nitrous oxide gas, are sure to have the second. The delirium of fever, the altered self of insanity, are all due to foreign matters circulating through the brain, or to pathological changes in that organ's substance. The fact that the brain is the one immediate bodily condition of the mental operations is indeed so universally admitted nowadays that I need spend no more time in illustrating it, but will simply postulate it and pass on. The whole remainder of the book will be more or less of a proof that the postulate was correct.

Bodily experiences, therefore, and more particularly brain-experiences, must take a place amongst those conditions of the mental life of which Psychology need take account. *The spiritualist and the associationist must both be 'cerebralists,'* to the extent at least of admitting that certain peculiarities in the way of working of their own favorite principles are explicable only by the fact that the brain laws are a codeterminant of the result.

Our first conclusion, then, is that a certain amount of brain-physiology must be presupposed or included in Psychology.[1]

In still another way the psychologist is forced to be something of a nerve-physiologist. Mental phenomena are not only conditioned *a parte ante* by bodily processes; but they lead to them *a parte post*. That they lead to *acts* is of course the most familiar of truths, but I do not merely mean acts in the sense of voluntary and deliberate muscular performances. Mental states occasion also changes in the calibre of blood-vessels, or alteration in the heartbeats, or processes more subtle still, in glands and viscera. If these are taken into account, as well as acts which follow at some *remote period* because the mental state was once there, it will be safe to lay down the general law that *no mental modification ever occurs which is not accompanied or followed by a bodily change.* The ideas and feelings, e.g., which these present printed characters excite in the reader's mind not only occasion movements of his eyes and nascent movements of articulation in him, but will some day make him speak, or take sides in a discussion, or give advice, or choose a book to read, differently from what would have been the case had they never impressed his retina. Our psychology must therefore take account not only of the conditions antecedent to mental states, but of their resultant consequences as well.

But actions originally prompted by conscious intelligence may grow so automatic by dint of habit as to be apparently unconsciously performed. Standing, walking, buttoning and unbuttoning piano-playing, talking, even saying one's prayers, may be done when the mind is absorbed in other things. The performances of animal *instinct* seem semi-automatic, and the *reflex acts* of self preservation certainly are so. Yet they resemble intelligent acts in bringing about the *same ends* at which the animals' consciousness, on other occasions, deliberately aims. Shall the study of such machine-like yet purposive acts as these he included in Psychology?

The boundary-line of the mental is certainly vague. It is better not to be pedantic, but to let the science be as vague as its subject, and include such phenomena as these if by so doing we can throw any light on the main business in hand. It will ere long be seen. I trust, that we can; and that we gain much more by a broad than by a narrow conception of our subject. At a certain stage in the development of every science a degree of vagueness is what best consists with fertility. On the whole, few recent formulas have done more real service of a rough sort in psychology than the Spencerian one that the essence of mental life and of bodily life are one, namely, 'the adjustment of inner to outer relations.' Such a formula is vagueness incarnate; but because it takes into account the fact that minds inhabit environments which act on them and on which they in turn react; because, in short, it takes mind in the midst of all its concrete relations, it is immensely more fertile than the old-fashioned 'rational psychology,' which treated the soul as a detached existent, sufficient unto itself, and assumed to consider only its nature and properties. I shall therefore feel free to make any sallies into zoology or into pure nerve-physiology which may seem instructive for our purposes, but otherwise shall leave those sciences to the physiologists.

Can we state more distinctly still the manner in which the mental life seems to intervene between impressions made from without upon the body, and reactions of the body upon the outer world again? Let us look at a few facts.

If some iron filings be sprinkled oh a table and a magnet brought near them, they will fly through the air for a certain distance and stick to its surface. A savage seeing the phenomenon explains it as the result of an attraction or love between the magnet and the filings. But let a card cover the poles of the magnet, and the filings will press forever against its surface without its ever occurring to them to pass around its sides and thus come into more direct contact with the object of their love. Blow bubbles through a tube into the bottom of a pail of water, they will rise to the surface and mingle with the air. Their action may again be poetically interpreted as due to a longing to recombine with the mother-atmosphere above the surface. But if you invert a jar full of water over the pail, they will rise and remain lodged beneath its bottom, shut in from the outer air, although a slight deflection from their course at the outset or a re-descent towards the rim of the jar when they found their upward course impeded, would easily have set them free.

If now we pass from such actions as these to those of living things, we notice a striking difference. Romeo wants Juliet as the filings want the magnet; and if no obstacles intervene he moves towards her by as straight a line as they. But Romeo and Juliet, if a wall be built between them, do not remain idiotically pressing their faces against its opposite sides like the magnet and the filings with the card. Romeo soon finds a circuitous way, by scaling the wall or otherwise, of touching Juliet's lips directly. With the filings the path is fixed;

whether it reaches the end depends on accidents. With the lover it is the end which is fixed, the path may be modified indefinitely.

Suppose a living frog in the position in which we placed our bubbles of air, namely, at the bottom of a jar of water. The want of breath will soon make him also long to rejoin the mother-atmosphere, and he will take the shortest path to his end by swimming straight upwards. But if a jar full of water be inverted over him, he will not, like the bubbles, perpetually press his nose against its unyielding roof, but will restlessly explore the neighborhood until by re-descending again he has discovered a path round its brim to the goal of his desires. Again the fixed end, the varying means!

Such contrasts between living and inanimate performances end by leading men to deny that in the physical world final purposes exist at all. Loves and desires are to-day no longer imputed to particles of iron or of air. No one supposes now that the end of any activity which they may display is an ideal purpose presiding over the activity from its outset and soliciting or drawing it into being by a sort of *visa fronte.* The end, on the contrary, is deemed a mere passive result, pushed into being *a tergo,* having had, so to speak, no voice in its own production. Alter the pre-existing conditions, and with inorganic materials you bring forth each time a different apparent end. But with intelligent agents, altering the conditions changes the activity displayed, but not the end reached; for here the idea of the yet unrealised end co-operates with the conditions to determine what the activities shall be.

*The pursuance of future ends and the choice of means for their attainment are thus the mark and criterion of the presence of mentality* in a phenomenon. We all use this test to discriminate between an intelligent and a mechanical performance. We impute no mentality to sticks and stones, because they never seem to move for *the sake of* anything, but always when pushed, and then indifferently and with no sign of choice. So we unhesitatingly call them senseless.

Just so we form our decision upon the deepest of all philosophic problems: Is the Kosmos an expression of intelligence rational in its inward nature, or a brute external fact pure and simple? If we find ourselves, in contemplating it, unable to banish the impression that it is a realm of final purposes, that it exists for the sake of something, we place intelligence at the heart of it and have a religion. If, on the contrary, in surveying its irremediable flux, we can think of the present only as so much mere mechanical sprouting from the past, occurring with no reference to the future, we are atheists and materialists.

In the lengthy discussions which psychologists have carried on about the amount of intelligence displayed by lower mammals, or the amount of consciousness involved in the functions of the nerve-centres of reptiles, the same test has always been applied: Is the character of the actions such that we must believe them to be performed *for the sake* of their result? The result in question, as we shall hereafter abundantly see, is as a rule a useful one,—the animal is, on the whole, safer under the circumstances for bringing it forth. So far the action has a teleological character; but such mere outward teleology as this might still be the blind result of *vis a tergo.* The growth and movements of plants, the processes of development, digestion, secretion, etc., in animals, supply innumerable instances of performances useful to the individual which may nevertheless be, and by most of us are supposed to be, produced by automatic mechanism. The physiologist does not confidently assert conscious intelligence in the frog's spinal cord until he has shown that the useful result which the nervous machinery brings forth under a given irritation *remains the same when the machinery is altered*. If, to take the stock-instance, the right knee of a headless frog be irritated with acid, the right foot will wipe it off. When, however, this foot is amputated, the animal will often raise the *left* foot to the spot and wipe the offending material away.

Pfluger and Lewes reason from such facts in the following way: If the first reaction were the result of mere machinery, they say; if that irritated portion of the skin discharged the right leg as a trigger discharges its own barrel of a shotgun; then amputating the right foot would indeed frustrate the wiping, but would not make the *left* leg move. It would simply result in the right stump moving through the empty air (which is in fact the phenomenon sometimes observed). The right trigger makes no effort to discharge the left barrel if the right one be unloaded; nor does an electrical machine ever get restless because it can only emit sparks, and not hem pillow-cases like a sewing-machine.

If, on the contrary, the right leg originally moved for the *purpose* of wiping the acid, then nothing is more natural than that, when the easiest means of effecting that purpose prove fruitless, other means should be tried. Every failure must keep the animal in a state of disappointment which will lead to all sorts of new trials and devices; and tranquillity will not ensue till one of these, by a happy stroke, achieves the wished-for end.

In a similar way Goltz ascribes intelligence to the frog's optic lobes and cerebellum. We alluded above to the manner in which a sound frog imprisoned in water will discover an outlet to the atmosphere. Goltz found that frogs deprived of their cerebral hemispheres would often exhibit a like ingenuity. Such a frog, after rising from the bottom and finding his farther upward progress checked by the glass bell which has been inverted over him, will not persist in butting his nose against the obstacle until dead of suffocation, but will often re-descend and emerge from under its rim as if, not a definite mechanical propulsion upwards, but rather a conscious desire to reach the air by hook or crook were the mainspring of his activity. Goltz concluded from this that the hemispheres are not the seat of intellectual power in frogs. He made the same inference from observing that a brainless frog will turn over from his back to his belly when one of his legs is sewed up, although the movements required are then very different from those excited under normal circumstances by the same annoying position. They seem determined, consequently, not merely by the antecedent irritant, but by the final end,—though the irritant of course is what makes the end desired.

Another brilliant German author, Liebmann,[2] argues against the brain's mechanism accounting for mental action, by very similar considerations. A machine as such, he says, will bring forth right results when it is in good order, and wrong results if out of repair. But both kinds of result flow with equally fatal necessity from their conditions. We cannot suppose the clock-work whose structure fatally determines it to a certain rate of speed, noticing that this speed is too slow or too fast and vainly trying to correct it. Its conscience, if it have any, should be as good as that of the best chronometer, for both alike obey equally well the same eternal mechanical laws—laws from behind. But if the *brain* be out of order and the man says "Twice four are two," instead of "Twice four are eight," or else "I must go to the coal to buy the wharf," instead of "I must go to the wharf to buy the coal," instantly there arises a consciousness of error. The wrong performance, though it obey the same mechanical law as the right, is nevertheless condemned,—condemned as contradicting the inner law—the law from in front, the purpose or ideal for which the brain *should* act, whether it do so or not.

We need not discuss here whether these writers in drawing their conclusion have done justice to all the premises involved in the cases they treat of. We quote their arguments only to show how they appeal to the principle that *no actions but such as are done for an end, and show a choice of means, can be called indubitable expressions of Mind.*

I shall then adopt this as the criterion by which to circumscribe the subject-matter of this work so far as action enters into it. Many nervous performances will therefore be unmentioned, as being purely physiological. Nor will the anatomy of the nervous system and organs of sense be described anew. The reader will find in H.N. Martin's *Human Body*, in G.T. Ladd's *Physiological Psychology* and in all the other standard Anatomies and Physiologies, a mass of information which we must regard as preliminary and take for granted in the present work.[3] Of the functions of the cerebral hemispheres, however, since they directly subserve consciousness, it will be well to give some little account.

## NOTES

1. Cf. George T. Ladd, *Elements of Physiological Psychology* (1887), pt. III, chap. III, §§ 9, 12.
2. *Zur Analysis der Wirklichkeit*, p. 489.
3. Nothing is easier than to familiarise one's self with the mammalian brain. Get a sheep's head, a small saw, chisel, scalpel and forceps (all three can best be had from a surgical-instrument maker), and unravel its parts either by the aid of a human dissecting book, such as Holden's *Manual* of *Anatomy*, or by the specific directions *ad hoc* given in such books as Foster and Langley's *Practical Physiology* (Macmillan) or Morrell's *Comparative Anatomy, and Guide to Dissection* (Longman and Co.).

# 30

# The Automaton Theory

In describing the functions of the hemispheres a short way back, we used language derived from both the bodily and the mental life, saying now that the animal made indeterminate and unforeseeable reactions, and anon that he was swayed by considerations of future good and evil; treating his hemispheres sometimes as the seat of memory and ideas in the psychic sense, and sometimes talking of them as simply a complicated addition to his reflex machinery. This sort of vacillation in the point of view is a fatal incident of all ordinary talk about these questions; but I must now settle my scores with those readers to whom I already dropped a word in passing and who have probably been dissatisfied with my conduct ever since.

Suppose we restrict our view to facts of one and the same plane, and let that be the bodily plane: cannot all the outward phenomena of intelligence still be exhaustively described? Those mental images, those 'considerations,' whereof we spoke,—presumably they do not arise without neural processes arising simultaneously with them, and presumably each consideration corresponds to a process *sui generis*, and unlike all the rest. In other words, however numerous and delicately differentiated the train of ideas may be, the train of brain-events that runs alongside of it must in both respects be exactly its match, and we must postulate a neural machinery that offers a living counterpart for every shading, however fine, of the history of its owner's mind. whatever degree of complication the latter may reach, the complication of the machinery must be quite as extreme, otherwise we should have to admit that there may be mental events to which no brain-events correspond. But such an admission as this the physiologist is reluctant to make. It would violate all his beliefs. 'No psychosis without neurosis,' is one form which the principle of continuity takes in his mind.

But this principle forces the physiologist to make still another step. If neural action is as complicated as mind; and if in the sympathetic system and lower spinal cord we see what, so far as we know, is unconscious neural action executing deeds that to all outward intent may be called intelligent; what is there to hinder us from supposing that even where we know consciousness to be there, the still more complicated neural action which we believe to be its inseparable companion is alone and of itself the real agent of whatever intelligent deeds may appear? "As actions of a certain degree of complexity are brought about by mere mechanism, why may not actions of a still greater degree of complexity be the result of a more refined mechanism?" The conception of reflex action is surely one of the best conquests of physiological theory; why not be radical with it? Why not say that just as the spinal cord is a machine with few reflexes, so the hemispheres are a machine with many, and that is all the difference? The principle of continuity would press us to accept this view.

But what on this view could he the function of the consciousness itself? *Mechanical* function it would have none. The sense-organs would awaken the brain-cells; these would awaken each other in rational and orderly sequence, until the time for action came; and then the last brain-vibration would discharge downwards into the motor tracts. But this would be a quite autonomous chain of occurrences, and whatever mind went with it would be there only as an 'epiphenomenon,' an inert spectator, a sort of 'foam, aura, or melody' as Mr. Hodgson says, whose opposition or whose furtherance would be alike powerless over the occurrences themselves. When talking, some time ago, we ought not, accordingly, *as physiologists,* to have said anything about 'considerations' as guiding the animal. We ought to have said 'paths left in the hemispherical cortex by former currents,' and nothing more.

Now so simple and attractive is this conception from the consistently physiological point of view, that it is quite wonderful to see how late it was stumbled on in philosophy, and how few people, even when it has been explained to them, fully and easily realize its import. Much of the polemic writing against it is by men who have as yet failed to take it into their imaginations. Since this has been the case, it seems worth while to devote a few more words to making it plausible, before criticising it ourselves.

To Descartes belongs the credit of having first been bold enough to conceive of a completely self-sufficing nervous mechanism which should be able to perform complicated and apparently intelligent acts. By a singularly arbitrary restriction, however, Descartes stopped short at man, and while contending that in beasts the nervous machinery was all, he held that the higher acts of man were the result of the agency of his rational soul. The opinion that beasts have no consciousness at all was of course too paradoxical to maintain itself long as anything more than a curious item in the history of philosophy. And with its abandonment the very notion that the nervous system *per se* might work the work of intelligence, which was an integral, though detachable part of the whole theory, seemed also to slip out of men's conception, until, in this century, the elaboration of the doctrine of reflex action made it possible and natural that it should again arise. But it was not till 1870, 1 believe, that Mr. Hodgson made the decisive step, by saying that feelings, no matter how intensely they may be present, can have no causal efficacy whatever, and comparing them to the colors laid on the surface of a mosaic, of which the events in the nervous system are represented by the stones.[1] Obviously the stones are held in place by each other and not by the several colors which they support.

About the same time Mr. Spalding, and a little later Messrs. Huxley and Clifford, gave great publicity to an identical doctrine, though in their case it was backed by less refined metaphysical considerations.[2]

A few sentences from Huxley and Clifford may be subjoined to make the matter entirely clear. Professor Huxley says:

"The consciousness of brutes would appear to be related to the mechanism of their body simply as a collateral product of its working, and to be as completely without any power of modifying that working, as the steam-whistle which accompanies the work of a locomotive engine is without influence upon its machinery. Their volition, if they have any, is an emotion *indicative* of physical changes, not a *cause* of such changes. . . . The soul stands related to the body as the bell of a clock to the works, and consciousness answers to the sound which the bell gives out when it is struck. Thus far I have strictly confined myself to. . . the automatism of brutes. . . . It is quite true that, to the best of my judgment, the argumentation which applies to brutes holds equally good of men; and, therefore, that all states of consciousness in us, as in them, are immediately caused by molecular changes of the brain-substance. It seems to me that in men, as in brutes, there is no proof that any state of consciousness is the cause of change in the motion of the matter of the organism. If these positions are well based, it follows that our mental conditions are simply the symbols in consciousness of the changes which take place automatically in the organism; and that, to take an extreme illustration, the feeling we call volition is not the cause of a voluntary act, but the symbol of that state of the brain which is the immediate cause of that act. We are conscious automata."

Professor Clifford writes:

> "All the evidence that we have goes to show that the physical world gets along entirely by itself, according to practically universal rules. . . . The train of physical facts between the stimulus sent into the eye, or to any one of our senses, and the exertion which follows it, and the train of physical facts which goes on in the brain, even when there is no stimulus and no exertion,—these are perfectly complete physical trains, and every step is fully accounted for by mechanical conditions. ... The two things are on utterly different platforms—the physical facts go along by themselves, and the mental facts go along by themselves. There is a parallelism between them, but there is no interference of one with the other. Again, if anybody says that the will influences matter, the statement is not untrue, but it is nonsense. . . . Such an assertion belongs to the crude materialism of the savage. The only thing which influences matter is the position of surrounding matter or the motion of surrounding matter.... The assertion that another man's volition, a feeling in his consciousness which I cannot perceive, is part of the train of physical facts which I may perceive,—this is neither true nor untrue, but nonsense; it is a combination of words whose corresponding ideas will not go together. . . . Sometimes one series is known better, and. . . . sometimes the other; so that in telling a story we speak sometimes of mental and sometimes of material facts. A feeling of chill made a man run; strictly speaking, the nervous disturbance which coexisted with that feeling of chill made him run, if we want to talk about material facts; or the feeling of chill produced the form of sub-consciousness which coexists with the motion of legs, if we want to talk about mental

> facts. . . . When, therefore, we ask, 'What is the physical link between the ongoing message from chilled skin and the outgoing message which moves the leg?' and the answer is, 'A man's Will,' we have as much right to be amused as if we had asked our friend with the picture what pigment was used in painting the cannon in the foreground, and received the answer, 'Wrought iron.' It will be found excellent practice in the mental operations required by this doctrine to imagine a train, the fore part of which is an engine and three carriages linked with iron couplings, and the hind part three other carriages linked with iron couplings; the bond between the two parts being made out of the sentiments of amity subsisting between the stoker and the guard."

To comprehend completely the consequences of the dogma so confidently enunciated, one should unflinchingly apply it to the most complicated examples. The movements of our tongues and pens, the flashings of our eyes in conversation, are of course events of a material order, and as such their causal antecedents must be exclusively material. If we knew thoroughly the nervous system of Shakespeare, and as thoroughly all his environing conditions, we should be able to show why at a certain period of his life his hand came to trace on certain sheets of paper those crabbed little black marks which we for shortness' sake call the manuscript of *Hamlet.* We should understand the rationale of every erasure and alteration therein, and we should understand all this without in the slightest degree acknowledging the existence of the thoughts in Shakespeare's mind. The words and sentences would be taken, not as signs of anything beyond themselves, but as little outward facts, pure and simple. In like manner we might exhaustively write the biography of those two hundred pounds, more or less, of warmish albuminoid matter called Martin Luther, without ever implying that it felt.

But, on the other hand, nothing in all this could prevent us from giving an equally complete account of either Luther's or Shakespeare's spiritual history, an account in which every gleam of thought and emotion should find its place. The mind-history would run alongside of the body-history of each man, and each point in the one would correspond to, but not react upon, a point in the other.! So the melody floats from the harp-string, but neither checks nor quickens its vibrations; so the shadow runs alongside the pedestrian, but in no way influences his steps.

Another inference, apparently more paradoxical still, needs to be made, though, as far as I am aware, Dr. Hodgson is the only writer who has explicitly drawn it. That inference is that feelings, not causing nerve-actions, cannot even cause each other. To ordinary common-sense, felt pain is, as such, not only the cause of outward tears and cries, but also the cause of such inward events as sorrow, compunction, desire, or inventive thought. So the consciousness of good news is the direct producer of the feeling of joy, the awareness of premises that of the belief in conclusions. But according to the automaton-theory, each of the feelings mentioned is only the correlate of some nerve-movement whose *cause* lay wholly in a previous nerve-movement. The first nerve-movement called up the second; whatever feeling was attached to the second consequently found itself following upon the feeling that was attached to the first. If, for example, good news was the consciousness correlated with the first movement, then joy turned out to be the correlate in consciousness of the second. But all the while the items of the nerve series were the only ones in causal continuity; the items of the conscious series, however inwardly rational their sequence, were simply juxtaposed.

**Reasons for the Theory**

The 'conscious automaton-theory,' as this conception is generally called, is thus a radical and simple conception of the manner in which certain facts may possibly occur. But between conception and belief, proof ought to lie. And when we ask, 'What proves that all this is more than a mere conception of the possible?' It is not easy to get a sufficient reply. If we start from the frog's spinal cord and reason by continuity, saying, as that acts so intelligently, *though unconscious,* so the higher centres, *though conscious,* may have the intelligence they show quite as mechanically based; we are immediately met by the exact counter-argument from continuity, an argument actually urged by such writers as Pfluger and Lewes, which starts from the acts of the hemispheres, and says: "As *these* owe *their* intelligence to the consciousness which we know to be there, so the intelligence of the spinal cord's acts must really be due to the invision presence or a consciousness. All arguments from continuity work in two ways: you can either level up or level down by their means. And it is clear that such arguments as these can eat each other up to all eternity.

There remains a sort of philosophic faith, bred like most faiths from an asthetic demand. Mental and physical events are, on all hands, admitted to present the strongest contrast in the entire field of being. The chasm which yawns between them is less easily bridged over by the mind than any interval we know. Why, then, not call it an absolute chasm, and say not only that the two worlds are different, but that they are independent? This gives us the comfort of all simple and absolute formulas, and it makes each chain homogeneous to our consideration. When talking of nervous tremors and bodily actions, we may feel secure against intrusion from an irrelevant mental world. When, on the other hand, we speak of feelings, we may with equal consistency use terms always of one denomination, and never be annoyed by what Aristotle calls 'slipping into another kind.' The desire on the part of men educated in laboratories not to have their physical reasonings mixed up with such incommensurable factors as feelings is certainly very strong. I have heard a most intelligent biologist say: "It is high time for scientific men to protest against the recognition of any such thing as consciousness in a scientific investigation." In a word, feeling constitutes the 'unscientific' half of existence, and anyone who enjoys calling himself a 'scientist' will be too happy to purchase an untrammelled homogeneity of terms in the studies of his predilection, at the slight cost of admitting a dualism which, in the same breath that it allows to mind an independent status of being, banishes it to a limbo of causal inertness, front whence no intrusion or interruption on its part need ever be feared.

Over and above this great postulate that matters must be kept simple, there is, it must be confessed, still another highly abstract reason for denying causal efficacity to our feelings. We can form no positive image of the *modus operandi* of a volition or other thought affecting the cerebral molecules.

"Let us try to imagine an idea—say of food, producing a movement, say of tarrying food to the mouth.... What is the method of its action? Does it assist the decomposition of the molecules of the gray matter, or does it retard the process, or does it alter the direction in which the shocks are distributed? Let us imagine the molecules of the gray matter on the impact of an incident force. Now, suppose the incident force, in the shape of a: shock from some ocher centre, to impinge upon these molecules. By hypothesis, it will decompose them, and they will fall into the simpler combination. How is the idea of food to prevent this decomposition? Manifestly it can do so only by increasing the force which binds the molecules together. Good! Try to imagine the idea of a beefsteak binding two molecules together. It is impossible. Equally impossible is it to imagine a similar idea loosening the attractive force between two molecules."[3]

This passage from an exceedingly clever writer expresses admirably the difficulty to which I allude. Combined with a strong sense of the 'chasm' between the two worlds, and with a lively faith in reflex machinery, the sense of this difficulty can hardly fail to make one turn consciousness out of the door as a superfluity so far as one's explanations go. One may bow her out politely, allow her to remain as an 'epiphenomenon' (invaluable word!), but one insists that matter shall hold all the power.

"Having thoroughly recognised the fathomless abyss that separates mind from matter, and having so blended the notion into his very nature, that there is no chance of his ever forgetting it, or failing to saturate with it all his meditations, the student of psychology has next to appreciate the association between these two orders of phenomena. . . . They are associated in a manner so intimate that some of the greatest thinkers consider them different aspects of the same process. . . . When the rearrangement of molecules takes place in the higher regions of the brain, a change of consciousness simultaneously occurs. . . . The change of consciousness never takes place without the change in the brain; the change in the brain never . . . without the change in consciousness. But *why* the two occur together, or what the link is which connects them, we do not know, and most authorities believe that we never shall and never can know. Having firmly and tenaciously grasped these two notions, of the absolute separateness of mind and matter, and of the invariable concomitance of a mental change with a bodily change, the student will enter oil the study of psychology with half his difficulties surmounted."[4]

Half his difficulties ignored, I should prefer to say. For this 'concomitance' in the midst of 'absolute separateness' is an utterly irrational notion. It is to my mind quite inconceivable that consciousness should have *nothing to do* with a business which it so faithfully attends. And the question, 'What has it to do?' Is one which psychology has no right to 'surmount,' for it is her plain duty to consider it. The fact is that the whole question of interaction and influence between things is a metaphysical question, and cannot be discussed at all by those who are unwilling to go into matters thoroughly. It is truly enough hard to imagine the 'idea of a beef-steak binding two molecules together'; but since Hume's time it has been equally hard to imagine *anything* binding them together. The whole notion of 'binding' is a mystery, the first step towards the solution of which is to clear scholastic rubbish out of the way. Popular science talks of 'forces,' 'attractions' or 'affinities' as binding the molecules; but clear science, though she may use such words to abbreviate discourse, has no use for the conceptions, and is satisfied when she can express in simple 'laws' the bare space-relations of the molecules as functions of each other and of time. To the more curiously inquiring mind, however, this simplified expression of the bare facts is not enough; there must be a 'reason' for them, and something must 'determine' the laws. And when one seriously sits down to consider what sort of a thing one *means* when one asks for a 'reason,' one is led so far afield, so far away from popular science and its scholasticism, as to see that even such a fact as the existence or non-existence in the universe of 'the idea of a beef-steak' may not be wholly indifferent to other facts in the same universe, and in particular may have something to do with determining the distance at which two molecules in that universe shall lie apart. If this is so, then common-sense, though the intimate nature of causality and of the connection of things in the universe lies beyond her pitifully bounded horizon, has the root and gist of the truth in her hands when she obstinately holds to it that feelings and ideas are causes. However inadequate our ideas of causal efficacy may be, we are less wide of the mark when we say that our ideas and feelings have it, than the Automatists are when they say they haven't it. As in the night all cats are gray, so in the darkness of metaphysical criticism all causes are obscure. But one has no right to pull the pall over the psychic half of the subject only, as the automatists do, and to say that *that* causation is unintelligible, whilst in the same breath one dogmatizes about *material* causation as if Hume, Kant, and Lotze had never been born. One cannot thus blow hot and cold. One must be impartially *naif* or impartially critical. If the latter, the reconstruction must be thorough-going or 'metaphysical,' and will probably preserve the common-sense view that ideas are forces, in some translated form. But Psychology is a mere natural science, accepting certain terms uncritically as her data, and stopping short of metaphysical reconstruction. Like physics, she must he *naive;* and if she finds that in her very peculiar field of study ideas *seem* to be causes, she had better continue to talk of them as such. She gains absolutely nothing by a breach with common-sense in this matter, and she loses, to say the least, all naturalness of speech. If feelings are causes, of course their effects must be furtherances and checkings of internal cerebral motions, of which in themselves we are entirely without knowledge. It is probable that for years to come we shall have to infer what happens in the brain either from our feelings or from motor effects which we observe. The organ will be for us a sort of vat in which feelings and motions somehow go on stewing together, and in which innumerable things happen of which we catch but the statistical result. Why, under these circumstances, we should be asked to forswear the language of our childhood I cannot well imagine, especially as it is perfectly compatible with the language of physiology. The feelings can produce nothing absolutely new, they can only reinforce and inhibit reflex currents which already exist, and the original organization of these by physiological forces must always be the ground-work of the psychological scheme.

My conclusion is that to urge the automaton-theory upon us, as it is now urged, on purely a *priori* and *quasi*-metaphysical grounds, is an *unwarrantable impertinence in the present state of psychology.*[5]

**Reasons Against the Theory**

But there are much more positive reasons than this why we ought to continue to talk in psychology as if consciousness had causal efficacy. The *particulars of the distribution of consciousness,* so far as we know them, *point to its being efficacious.* Let us trace some of them.

It is very generally admitted, though the point would be hard to prove, that consciousness grows the more complex and intense the higher we rise in the animal kingdom. That of a man must exceed that of an oyster. From this point of view it seems an organ super-added to the other organs which maintain the animal in the struggle for existence; and the presumption of course is that it helps him in some way in the struggle, just as they do. But it cannot help him without being in some way efficacious and influencing the course of his bodily history. If now it could be shown in what way consciousness *might* help him, and if, moreover, the defects of his other organs (where consciousness is most developed) are such as to make them need just the kind of help that consciousness would bring provided it *were* efficacious; why, then the plausible inference would be that it came just *because* of its efficacy—in other words, its efficacy would be inductively proved.

Now the study of the phenomena of consciousness which we shall make throughout the rest of this book will show us that consciousness is at all times primarily a *selecting agency.*[6] Whether we take it in the lowest sphere of sense, or in the highest of intellection, we find it always doing one thing, choosing one out of several of the materials so presented to its notice, emphasizing and accentuating that and suppressing as far as possible all the rest. The item emphasized is always in close connection with some *interest* felt by consciousness to be paramount at the time.

But what are now the defects of the nervous system in those animals whose consciousness seems most highly developed? Chief among them must be *instability.* The cerebral hemispheres are the characteristically 'high' nerve-centres, and we saw how indeterminate and unforeseeable their performances were in comparison with those of the basal ganglia and the cord. But this very vagueness constitutes their advantage. They allow their possessor to adapt his conduct to the minutest alterations in the environing circumstances, any one of which may be for him a sign, suggesting distant motives more powerful than any present solicitations of sense. It seems as if certain mechanical conclusions should be drawn from this state of things. An organ swayed by slight impressions is an organ whose natural state is one of unstable equilibrium. We may imagine the various lines of discharge in the cerebrum to be almost on a par in point of permeability—what discharge a given small impression will produce may be called *accidental,* in the sense in which we say it is a matter of accident whether a rain-drop falling on a mountain ridge descend the eastern or the western slope. It is be a boy or a girl. The ovum is so unstable a body that certain causes too minute for our apprehension may at a certain moment tip it one way or the other. The natural law of an organ constituted after this fashion can be nothing but a law of caprice. I do not see how one could reasonably expect from it any certain pursuance of useful lines of reaction, such as the few and fatally determined performances of the lower centres constitute within their narrow sphere. The dilemma in regard to the nervous system seems, in short, to be of the following kind. We may construct one which will react infallibly and certainly, but it will then be capable of reacting to very few changes in the environment—it will fail to be adapted to all the rest. We may, on the other hand, construct a nervous system potentially adapted to respond to an infinite variety of minute features in the situation; but its fallibility will then be as great as its elaboration. We can never be sure that its equilibrium will be upset in the appropriate direction. In short, a high brain may do many things, and may do each of them at a very slight hint. But its hair-trigger organization makes of it a happy-go-lucky, hit-or-miss affair. It is as likely to do the crazy as the sane thing at any given moment. A low brain does few things, and in doing them perfectly forfeits all other use. The performances of a high brain are like dice thrown forever on a table. Unless they be loaded, what chance is there that the highest number will turn up oftener than the lowest?

All this is said of the brain as a physical machine pure and simple. *Can consciousness increase its efficiency by loading its dice?* Such is the problem.

Loading its dice would mean bringing a more or less constant pressure to bear in favor of *those* of its performances which make for the most permanent interests of the brain's owner; it would mean a constant inhibition of the tendencies to stray aside.

Well, just such pressure and such inhibition are what consciousness *seems* to be exerting all the while. And the interests in whose favor it seems to exert them are *its* interests and its alone, interests which it *creates*, and which, but for it, would have no status in the realm of being whatever.

There is yet another set of facts which seem explicable on the supposition that consciousness has causal efficacy. *It is a well-known fact that pleasures are generally associated with beneficial, pains with detrimental, experiences.* All the fundamental vital processes illustrate this law. Starvation, suffocation, privation of food, drink and sleep, work when exhausted, burns, wounds, inflammation, the effects of poison, are as disagreeable as filling the hungry stomach, enjoying rest and sleep after fatigue, exercise after rest, and a sound skin and unbroken bones at all times, are pleasant. Mr. Spencer and others have suggested that these coincidences are due, not to any pre-established harmony, but to the mere action of natural selection which would certainly kill off in the long-run any breed of creatures to whom the fundamentally noxious experience seemed enjoyable. An animal that should take pleasure in a feeling of suffocation would, if that pleasure were efficacious enough to make him immerse his head in water, enjoy a longevity of four or five minutes. But if pleasures and pains have no efficacy, one does not see (without some such a *priori* rational harmony as would be scouted by the 'scientific' champions of the automaton-theory) why the most noxious acts, such as burning, might not give thrills of delight, and the most necessary' ones, such as breathing, cause agony. The exceptions to the law are, it is true, numerous, but relate to experiences that are either not vital or not universal. Drunkenness, for instance, which though noxious, is to many persons delightful, is a very exceptional experience. But, as the excellent physiologist Fick remarks, if all rivers and springs ran alcohol instead of water, either all men would now be born to hate it or our nerves would have been selected so as to drink it with impunity. The only considerable attempt, in fact, that has been made to explain the *distribution* of our feelings is that of Mr. Grant Allen in his suggestive little work *Physiological 'Esthetics;* and his reasoning is based exclusively on that causal efficacy of pleasures and pains which the 'double-aspect' partisans so strenuously deny.

Thus, then, from every point of view the circumstantial evidence against that theory is strong. *A priori* analysis of both brain-action and conscious action shows us that if the latter were efficacious it would, by its selective emphasis, make amends for the indeterminateness of the former; whilst the study *a posteriori* of the *distribution* of consciousness shows it to be exactly such as we might expect in an organ added for the sake of steering a nervous system grown too complex to regulate itself. The conclusion that it is useful is, after all this, quite justifiable. But, if it is useful, it must be so through its causal efficaciousness, and the automaton-theory must succumb to the theory of common-sense.

## REFERENCES

1. The *Theory of Practice*, vol. I, p. 416 ff.
2. "The present writer recalls bow in 1869, when still a medial student, he began to write an essay showing how almost everyone who speculated about brain-processes illicitly interpolated into his account of them links derived from the entirely heterogeneous universe of Feeling. Spencer, Hodgson (in his *Time and Space)*, Maudsley, Lockhart Clarke, Bain, Dr. Carpenter, and other authors were cited as having been guilty of the confusion. The writing was soon stopped because he perceived that the view which he was upholding against these authors was a pure conception. with no proofs to be adduced of its reality. Later it seemed to him that whatever *proofs* existed really told in favor of their view.
3. Charles Mercier, *The Nervous System and the Mind* (1888), p. 8.
4. *Op. cit.*, p. 10.
5. Cf. *infra* vol. II, 1185-1186.
6. See in particular the end of Chapter IX.

# 31

# The Mind-Stuff Theory

The reader who found himself swamped with too much metaphysics in the next chapter will have a still worse time of it in this one, which is exclusively metaphysical. Metaphysics means nothing but an unusually obstinate effort to think clearly. The fundamental conceptions of psychology are practically very clear to us, but theoretically they are very confused, and one easily makes the obscurest assumptions in this science without realizing, until challenged, what internal difficulties they involve. When these assumptions have once established themselves (as they have a way of doing in our very descriptions of the phenomenal facts) it is almost impossible to get rid of them afterwards or to make anyone see that they are not essential features of the subject. The only way to prevent this disaster is to scrutinize them beforehand and make them give an articulate account of themselves before letting them pass. One of the obscurest of the assumptions of which I speak is *the assumption that our mental states are composite in structure, made rip of smaller slates conjoined*. This hypothesis has outward advantages which make it almost irresistibly attractive to the intellect, and yet it is inwardly quite unintelligible. Of its unintelligibility, however, half the writers on psychology seem unaware. As our own aim is *to understand* if possible, I make no apology for singling out this particular notion for very explicit treatment before taking up the descriptive part of our work. *The theory of 'mind-stuff' is the theory that our mental states are compounds*, expressed in its most radical form.

In a general theory of evolution the inorganic comes first, then the lowest forms of animal and vegetable life, then forms of life that possess mentality, and finally those like ourselves that possess it in a high degree. As long as we keep to the consideration of purely outward facts, even the most complicated facts of biology, our task as evolutionists is comparatively easy. We are dealing all the time with matter and its aggregations and separations; and although our treatment must perforce be hypothetical, this does not prevent it from being *continuous*. The point which as evolutionists we are bound to hold fast to is that all the new forms of being that make their appearance are really nothing more than results of the redistribution of the original and unchanging materials. The self-same atoms which, chaotically dispersed, made the nebula, now, jammed and temporarily caught in peculiar positions, form our brains; and the 'evolution' of the brains, if understood, would be simply the account of how the atoms came to be so caught and jammed. In this story no new *natures*, no factors not present at the beginning, are introduced at any later stage.

But with the dawn of consciousness an entirely new nature seems to slip in, something whereof the potency was *not* given in the mere outward atoms of the original chaos.

The enemies of evolution have been quick to pounce upon this undeniable discontinuity in the data of the world, and many of them, from the failure of evolutionary explanations at this point, have inferred their general incapacity all along the line. Everyone admits the entire incommensurability of feeling as such with material motion as such. "A motion became a feeling! "—no phrase that our lips can frame is so devoid of apprehensible meaning. Accordingly, even the vaguest of evolutionary enthusiasts, when deliberately comparing material with mental facts, have been as forward as anyone else to emphasize the 'chasm' between the inner and the outer worlds.

"Can the oscillation of a molecule," says Mr. Spencer, "be represented side by side with a nervous shock [he means a mental shock], and the two be recognized as one? No effort enables us to assimilate them. That a unit of feeling has nothing in common with a unit of motion, becomes more than ever manifest when we bring the two into juxtaposition."[1]

And again:

"Suppose it to have become quite clear that a shock in consciousness and a molecular motion, are the subjective and objective faces of the same thing; we continue utterly incapable of uniting the two, so as to conceive that reality of which they are the opposite faces."[2]

In other words, incapable of perceiving in them any common character. So Tyndall, in that lucky paragraph which has been quoted so often that everyone knows it by heart:

"The passage from the physics of the brain to the corresponding facts of consciousness is unthinkable. Granted that a definite thought, and a definite molecular action in the brain, occur simultaneously; we do not possess the intellectual organ, nor apparently any rudiment of the organ, which would enable us to pass, by a process of reasoning. from the one to the other."[3]

Or in this other passage:

"We can trace the development of a nervous system, and correlate with it the parallel phenomena of sensation and thought. We see with undoubting certainty that they go hand in hand. But we try to soar in a vacuum the moment we seek to comprehend the connection between them here is no fusion possible between the two classes of facts—no motor energy in the intellect of man to carry it without logical rupture from the one to the other."[4]

None the less easily, however, when the evolutionary afflatus is upon them, do the very same writers leap over the breach whose flagrancy they are the foremost to announce, and talk as if mind grew out of body in a continuous way. Mr. Spencer, looking back on his review of mental evolution, tells us how "in tracing up the increase we found ourselves passing *without break* from the phenomena of bodily life to the phenomena of mental life."[5]

And Mr. Tyndall, in the same Belfast Address from which we just quoted, delivers his other famous passage:

"Abandoning all disguise, the confession that I feel bound to make before you is that I prolong the vision backward across the boundary of the experimental evidence, and discern in that matter, which we in our ignorance, and notwithstanding our professed reverence for its Creator, have hitherto covered with opprobrium, the promise and potency of every form and quality of life."[6]

—mental life included, as a matter of course.

So strong a postulate is continuity! Now this book will tend to show that mental postulates are on the whole to be respected. The demand for continuity has, over large tracts of science, proved itself to possess true prophetic power. We ought therefore ourselves sincerely to try every possible mode of conceiving the dawn of consciousness so that it may *not* appear equivalent to the irruption into the universe of a new nature, non-existent until then.

Merely to call the consciousness 'nascent' will not serve our turn.[7] It is true that the word signifies not yet *quite* born, and so seems to from a sort of bridge between existence and nonentity. But that is a verbal quibble. The fact is that discontinuity comes in if a new nature comes in at all. The *quantity* of the latter is quite immaterial. The girl in *Midshipman Easy* could not excuse the illegitimacy of her child by saying, 'it was a very little one.' And Consciousness, however little, is an illegitimate birth in any philosophy that starts without it, and yet professes to explain all facts by continuous evolution.

*If evolution is to work smoothly, consciousness in some shape must have been present at the very origin of things.* Accordingly we find that the more clear-sighted evolutionary philosophers are beginning to posit it there. Each atom of the nebula, they suppose, must have had an aboriginal atom of consciousness linked with it; and, just as the material atoms have formed bodies and brains by massing themselves together, so the mental atoms, by an analogous process of aggregation, have fused into those larger consciousnesses which we know in ourselves and suppose to exist in our fellow- animals. Some such doctrine of *atomistic hylozoism* as this is an indispensable part of a thorough-going philosophy of evolution. According to it there must be an infinite number of degrees of consciousness, following the degrees of complication and aggregation of the primordial mind-dust. To prove the separate existence of these degrees of consciousness by indirect evidence, since direct intuition of them is not to be had, becomes therefore the first duty of psychological evolutionism.

Some of this duty we find already performed by a number of philosophers who, though not interested at all in evolution, have nevertheless on independent grounds convinced themselves of the existence of a vast amount of sub-conscious mental life. The criticism of this general opinion and its grounds will have to be postponed for a while, At present let us merely deal with the arguments assumed to prove aggregation of bits of mind-stuff into distinctly sensible feelings. They are clear and admit of a clear reply.

The German physiologist A. Fick, in 1864, was, so far as I know, the first to use them. He made experiments on the discrimination of the feelings of warmth and of touch, when only a very small portion of the skin was excited through a hole in a card, the surrounding parts being protected by the card. He found that under these circumstances mistakes were frequently made by the patient,[8] and concluded that this must be because the number of sensations from the elementary nerve-tips affected was too small to sum itself distinctly into either of the qualities of feeling in question. He tried to show how a different manner of the summation might give rise in one case to the heat and in another to the touch.

"A feeling of temperature," he says, "arises when the intensities of the units of feeling are evenly gradated, so that between two elements *a* and *b* no other unit can spatially intervene whose intensity is not also *between* that of a and *b*. A feeling of contact perhaps arises when this condition is not fulfilled. Both kinds of feeling, however, are composed of the same units."

But it is obviously far clearer to interpret such a gradation of intensities as a brain-fact than as a mind-fact. If in the brain a tract were first excited in one of the ways suggested by Prof. Fick, and then again in the other, it might very well happen, for aught we can say to the contrary, that the psychic accompaniment in the one case would be heat, and in the other pain. The pain and the heat would, however, not be composed of psychic units, but would each be the direct result of one total brain-process. So long as this latter interpretation remains open, Fick cannot be held to have proved psychic summation.

Later, both Spencer and Tame, independently of each other, took up the same line of thought. Mr. Spencer's reasoning is worth quoting *in extenso*. He writes:

"Although the individual sensations and emotions, real or ideal, of which consciousness is built up, appear to be severally simple, homogeneous, unanalysable, or of inscrutable natures, yet they are not so. There is at least one kind of feeling which, as ordinarily experienced, seems elementary, that is demonstrably not elementary. And after resolving it into its proximate components, we can scarcely help suspecting that other apparently-elementary feelings are also compound, and may have proximate components like those which we can in this one instance identify.

"Musical sound is the name we give to this seemingly-simple feeling which is clearly resolvable into simpler feelings. Well-known experiments prove that when equal blows or taps are made one after another at a rate not exceeding some sixteen per second, the effect of each is perceived as a separate noise: but when the rapidity with which the blows follow one another exceeds this, the noises are no longer identified in separate states of consciousness, and there arises in place of them a continuous state of consciousness, called a tone. On further increasing the rapidity of the blows, the tone undergoes the change of quality distinguished as a rise in pitch; and it continues to rise in pitch as the blows continue to increase in rapidity, until it reaches an acuteness beyond which it is no longer appreciable as a tone. So that out of units of feeling of the same kind, many feelings distinguishable from one another in quality result, according as the units are more or less integrated.

"This is not all. The inquiries of Professor Helmholtz have shown that when, along with one series of these rapidly-recurring noises, there is generated another series in which the noises are more rapid though not so loud, the effect is a change in that quality of the tone known as its *timbre.* As various musical instruments show us, tones which are alike in pitch and strength are distinguishable by their harshness or sweetness, their ringing or their liquid characters; and all their specific peculiarities are proved to arise from the combination of one, two, three, or more, supplementary series of recurrent noises with the chief series of recurrent noises. So that while the unlikenesses of feeling known as differences of pitch in tones, are due to differences of integration among the recurrent noises of one series, the unlikenesses of feeling known as differences of *timbre,* are due to the simultaneous integration with this series of other series having other degrees of integration. And thus an enormous number of qualitatively-contrasted kinds of consciousness that seem severally elementary, prove to be composed of one simple kind of consciousness, combined and re-combined with itself in multitudinous ways.

"Can we stop short here? If the different sensations known as sounds are built out of a common unit, is it riot to be rationally inferred that so likewise are the different sensations known as tastes, and the different sensations known as tastes, and the different sensations known as colours? Nay, shall we not regard it as probable that there is a unit common to all these strongly-contrasted classes of sensations? If the unlikenesses among the sensations of each class may be due to unlikenesses among the modes of aggregation of a unit of consciousness common to them all: so, too, may the much greater unlikenesses between the sensations of each class and those of other classes. There may be a single primordial element of consciousness, and the countless kinds of consciousness may be produced by the compounding of this element with itself and the re-compounding of its compounds with one another in higher and higher degrees: so producing increased multiplicity, variety, and complexity.

"Have we any clue to this primordial element? I think we have. That simple mental impression which proves to be the unit of composition of the sensation of musical tone, is allied to certain other simple mental impressions differently originated. The subjective effect produced by a crack or noise that has no appreciable duration, is little else than a nervous shock. Though we distinguish such a nervous shock as belonging to what we call sounds, yet it does not differ very much from nervous shocks of other kinds. An electric discharge sent through the body, causes a feeling akin to that which a sudden loud report causes. A strong unexpected impression made through the eyes, as by a flash of lightning, similarly gives rise to a start or shock; and though the feeling so named seems, like the electric shock, to have the body at large for its seat, and may therefore be regarded as the correlative rather of the efferent than of the afferent disturbance, yet on remembering the mental change that results from the instantaneous transit of an object across the field of vision, I think it may be perceived that the feeling accompanying the efferent disturbance is itself reduced very nearly to the same form. The state of " consciousness so generated is, in fact, comparable in quality to the initial state of consciousness caused by a blow (distinguishing it from the pain or other feeling that commences the instant after); which state of consciousness caused by a blow, may be taken as the primitive and typical form of the nervous shock. The fact that sudden brief disturbances thus set up by different stimuli through different sets of nerves, cause feelings scarcely distinguishable in quality, will not appear strange when we recollect that distinguishableness of feeling implies appreciable duration; and that when the duration is greatly abridged, nothing more is known than that some mental change has occurred and ceased. To have a sensation of redness, to know a tone as acute or grave, to be conscious of a taste as sweet, implies in each case a considerable continuity of state. If the state does not last long enough to admit of its being contemplated, it cannot be classed as of this or that kind; and becomes a momentary modification very similar to momentary modifications otherwise caused.

"It is possible, then—may we not even say probable—that something of the same order as that which we call a nervous shock is the ultimate unit of consciousness; and that all the unlikenesses among our feelings result from unlike modes of integration of this ultimate unit. I say of the same order, because there are discernible differences among nervous shocks that are differently caused; and the primitive nervous shock probably differs somewhat from each of them. And I say of the same order for the further reason, that while we may ascribe to them a general likeness in nature we must suppose a great unlikeness in degree. The nervous shocks recognized as such, are violent—must be violent before they can be perceived amid the procession of multitudinous vivid feelings suddenly interrupted by them. But the rapidly—recurring nervous shocks of which the different forms of feeling consist, we must assume to be of comparatively moderate, or even of very slight, intensity. Were our various sensations and emotions composed of rapidly-recurring shocks as strong as those ordinarily called shocks, they' would be unbearable: indeed life would cease at once. We must think of them rather as successive faint pulses of subjective change, each having the same quality as the strong pulse of subjective change distinguished as a nervous shock."[9]

### Insufficiency of These Proofs

Convincing as this argument of Mr. Spencer's may appear on a first reading, it is singular how weak it really is.[10] We do, it is true, when we study the connection between a musical note and its outward cause, find the note simple and continuous while the cause is multiple and discrete. Somewhere, then, there is a transformation, reduction, or fusion. The question is, Where?—in the nerve-world or in the mind-world? Really we have no experimental proof by which to decide; and if decide we must, analogy and a *priori* probability can alone guide us. Mr. Spencer assumes that the fusion must come to pass in the mental world, and that the physical processes get through air and ear, auditory nerve and medulla, lower brain and hemispheres, without their number being reduced. Figure 31.1 will make the point clear.

Let the line *a-b* represent the threshold of consciousness: then everything drawn below that line will symbolize a physical process, everything above it will mean a fact of mind. Let the crosses stand for the physical blows, the circles for the events in successively higher orders of nerve-cells, and the horizontal marks for the facts of feeling. Spencer's argument implies that each order of cells transmits just as many impulses as it receives to the cells above it; so that if the blows come at the rate of 20,000 in a second the cortical cells discharge at the same rate, and one unit of feeling corresponds to each one of the 20,000 discharges. Then, and only then, does 'integration' occur, by the 20,000 units of feeling 'compounding with themselves' into the 'continuous state of consciousness' represented by the short line at the top of the figure.

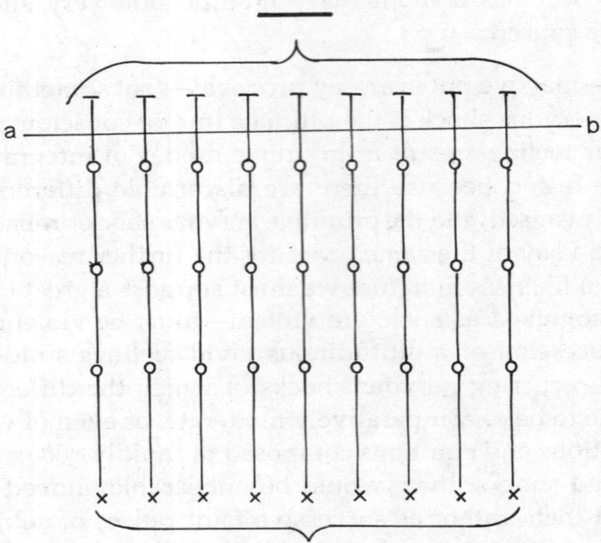


**Fig. 31.1.** One second of time.

Now such an interpretation as this flies in the face of physical analogy, no less than of logical intelligibility. Consider physical analogy first.

A pendulum may be deflected by a single blow, and swing back. Will it swing back the more often the more we multiply the blows? No; for if they rain upon the pendulum too fast, it will not swing at all but remain deflected in a sensibly stationary state. In other words, increasing the cause numerically need not equally increase numerically the effect. Blow through a tube: you get a certain musical note; and increasing the blowing increases for a certain time the loudness of the note. Will this be true indefinitely? No; for when a certain force is reached, the note, instead of growing louder, suddenly disappears and is replaced by its higher octave. Turn on the gas slightly and light it: you get a tiny flame. Turn on more gas, and the breadth of the flame increases. Will this relation increase indefinitely? No, again; for at a certain moment up shoots the flame into a ragged streamer and begins to hiss. Send slowly through the nerve of a frog's gastrocnemius muscle a succession of galvanic shocks: you get a succession of twitches. Increasing the number of shocks does not increase the twitching; on the contrary, it stops it, and we have the muscle in the apparently stationary state of contraction called tetanus. This last fact is the true analogue of what must happen between the nerve-cell and the sensory fibre. It is certain that cells are more inert than fibres, and that rapid vibrations in the latter can only arouse relatively simple processes or states in the former. The higher cells may have even a slower rate of explosion than the lower, and so the twenty thousand supposed blows of the outer air may be 'integrated' in the cortex into a very small number of cell-discharges in a second. This other diagram will serve to contrast this supposition with Spencer's. In Fig. 31.2 all 'integration' occurs below the threshold of consciousness. The frequency of cell-events becomes more and more reduced as we approach the cells to which feeling is most directly attached, until at last we come to a condition of things symbolized by the larger ellipse, which may be taken to stand for some rather massive and slow process of tension and discharge in the cortical centres, to which, *as a whole*, the feeling of musical tone symbolized by the line at the top of the diagram *simply and totally* corresponds. It is as if a long file of men were to start one after the other to reach a distant point. The road at first is good and they keep their original distance apart. Presently it is intersected by bogs each worse than the last, so that the front men get so retarded that the hinder ones catch up with them before the journey is done, and all arrive together at the goal.[11]

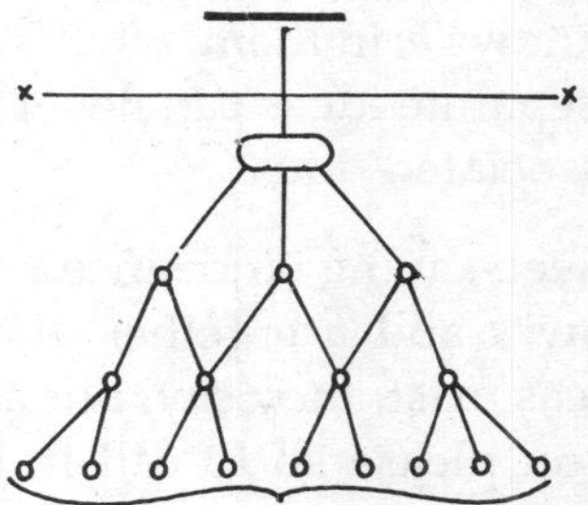

**Fig. 31.2.** One second of time

On this supposition there *are* no unperceived units of mind-stuff preceding and composing the full consciousness. The latter is itself an immediate psychic fact and bears an immediate relation to the neural state which is its unconditional accompaniment.

Just so, in the parallelogram of forces, the 'forces' themselves do not combine into the diagonal resultant; a *body* is needed on which they may impinge, to exhibit their resultant effect. No more do musical sounds combine *per se* into concords or discords. Concord and discord are names for their combined effects on that external medium, the *ear*.

Where the elemental units are supposed to be feelings, the case is in no wise altered. Take a hundred of them, shuffle them and pack them as close together as you can (whatever that may mean); still each remains the same feeling it always was, shut in its own skin, windowless, ignorant of what the other feelings are and mean. There would be a hundred-and-first feeling there, if, when a group or series of such feelings were set up, a consciousness *belonging to the group as such* should emerge. And this 101st feeling would be a totally new fact; the 100 original feelings might, by a curious physical law, be' a signal for its *creation*, when they came together; but they would have no substantial identity with it, nor it with them, and one could never deduce the one from the others, or (in any intelligible sense) say that they *evolved* it.

Take a sentence of a dozen words, and take twelve men and tell to each one word. Then stand the men in a row or jam them in a bunch, and let each think of his word as intently as he will; nowhere will there be a consciousness of the whole sentence.[12] We talk of the 'spirit of the age,' and the 'sentiment of the people,' and in various ways we hypostatize 'public opinion.' But we know this to be symbolic speech, and never dream that the spirit, opinion, sentiment, etc., constitute a consciousness other than, and additional to, that of the several individuals whom the words 'age,' 'people,' or 'public' denote. The private minds do not agglomerate into a higher compound mind. This has always been the invincible contention of the spiritualists against the associationists in Psychology,—a contention which we shall take up at greater length in previous chapters. The associationists say the mind is constituted by a multiplicity of distinct 'ideas' *associated* into a unity. There is. they say, an idea of *a*, and also an idea of *b*. *Therefore*, they say, there is an idea of $a + b$, or of a and *b* together. Which is like saying that the mathematical square of a plus that of *b* is equal to the square of $a + b$, a palpable untruth. Idea of *a*, plus idea of *b*, are *not* identical with idea of $(a + b)$. It is one, they are two; in it, what knows a also knows *b;* in them, what knows a is expressly posited as not knowing *b;* etc. In short, the two separate ideas can never by any logic be made to figure as one and the same thing as the 'associated' idea.

This is what the spiritualists keep saying; and since we do, as a matter of fact, have the 'compounded' idea, and do know *a* and *b* together, they adopt a farther hypothesis to explain that fact. The separate ideas exist, they say, but affect a third entity, the soul. This has the 'compounded' idea, if you please so to call it; and the compounded idea is an altogether new psychic fact to which the separate ideas stand in the relation, not of constituents, but of occasions of production.

This argument of the spiritualists against the associationists has never been answered by the latter. It holds good against any talk about self-compounding amongst feelings, against any 'blending,' or 'complication,' or 'mental chemistry,' or 'psychic synthesis,' which supposes a resultant consciousness to float off from the constituents *per se*, in the absence of a supernumerary principle of consciousness which they may affect. The mind-stuff theory, in short, is unintelligible. Atoms of feeling cannot compose higher feelings, any more than atoms of matter can compose physical things! The 'things,' for a clear-headed atomistic evolutionist, are not. Nothing is but the everlasting atoms. When grouped in a certain way, *we* name them this 'thing' or that; but the thing we name has no existence out of our mind. So of the states of mind which are supposed to be compound because they know many different things together. Since indubitably such states do exist, they must exist as single new facts. effects, possibly as the spiritualists say, on the Soul (we will not decide that point here), but at any rate independent and integral, and not compounded of psychic atoms.[13]

The passion for unity and smoothness is in some minds so in-satiate that, in spite of the logical clearness of these reasonings and conclusions, many will fail to be influenced by them. They establish it sort of disjointedness in things which in certain quarters will appear intolerable. They sweep away all chance of 'passing without break' either from the material to the mental, or from the lower to the higher mental; and they thrust us back into a pluralism of consciousnesses—each arising discontinuously in the midst of two disconnected worlds, material and mental—which is even worse than the old notion of the separate creation of each particular soul. But the malcontents will hardly try to refute our reasonings by direct attack. It is more probable that, turning their back upon them altogether, they will devote themselves to sapping and mining the region roundabout until it is a bog of logical liquefaction, into the midst of which all definite conclusions of any sort may be trusted ere long to sink and disappear.

Our reasonings have assumed that the 'integration' of a thousand psychic units must be either just the units over again, simply rebaptized, or else something real, but then other than and additional to those units; that if a certain existing fact is that of a thousand feelings, it cannot at the same time be that of ONE feeling; for the essence of feeling is to be felt, and as a psychic existent *feels*, so it must *be*. If the one feeling feels like no one of the thousand, in what sense can it be said to *be* the thousand?[13a] These assumptions are what the monists will seek to undermine. The Hegelizers amongst them will take high ground at once, and say that the glory and beauty of the psychic life is that in it all contradictions find their reconciliation; and that it is just because the facts we are considering *are* facts of the self that they are both one and many at the same time. With this intellectual temper I confess that I cannot contend. As in striking at some unresisting gossamer with a club, one but overreaches one's self, and the thing one aims at gets no harm. So I leave this school to its devices.

The other monists are of less deliquescent frame, and try to break down distinctness among mental states by *making a distinction*. This sounds paradoxical, but it is only ingenious. The distinction is that *between the unconscious and the conscious being of the mental state*. It is the sovereign means for believing what one likes in psychology, and of turning what might become a science into a tumbling-ground for whimsies. It has numerous champions, and elaborate reasons to give for itself. We must therefore accord it due consideration. In discussing the question: Do Unconscious Mental States Exist?

It will be best to give the list of so-called proofs as briefly as possible, and to follow each by its objection, as in scholastic books.[14]

*First Proof.* The *minimum visible*, the *minimum audible*, are objects composed of parts. How can the whole affect the sense unless each part does? And yet each part does so without being separately sensible. Leibnitz calls the total consciousness an *aperception,'* the supposed insensible consciousness by the name of *'petites perceptions.'*

"To judge of the latter," he says, "I am accustomed to use the example of the roaring of the sea with which one is assailed when near the shore. To hear this noise as one does, one must hear the parts which compose its totality, that is, the noise of each wave, . . . although this noise would not be noticed if its wave were alone. One must be affected a little by the movement of one wave, one must have some perception of each several noise, however small it be. Otherwise one would not hear that of 100,000 waves, for of 100,000 zeroes one can never make a quantity." 15

*Reply.* This is an excellent example of the so-called 'fallacy of division,' or predicating what is true only of a collection, of each member of the collection distributively. It no more follows that if a thousand things together cause sensation, one thing alone must cause it, than it follows that if one pound weight moves a balance, then one ounce weight must move it too, in less degree. One ounce weight does not move it at *all;* its movement *begins* with the pound. At most we can say that each ounce affects it in *some* way which helps the advent of that movement. And so each infra-sensible stimulus to a nerve no doubt affects the nerve and helps the birth of sensation when the other stimuli come. But this affection is a nerve-affection, and there is not the slightest ground for supposing it to be a 'perception' unconscious of itself. "A certain *quantity* of the cause may be a necessary condition to the production of *any* of the effect,"[16] when the latter is a mental state.

*Second Proof.* In all acquired dexterities and habits, secondarily automatic performances as they are called, we do what *originally* required a chain of deliberately conscious perceptions and volitions. As the actions still keep their intelligent character, intelligence must still preside over their execution. But since our consciousness seems all the while elsewhere engaged, such intelligence must consist of unconscious perceptions, inferences, and volitions.

*Reply.* There is more than one alternative explanation in accordance with larger bodies of fact. One is that the perceptions and volitions in habitual actions may be performed consciously, only so quickly and inattentively that no *memory* of them remains. Another is that the consciousness of these actions exists, but is *split-off* from the rest of the consciousness of the hemispheres. We shall find in previous chapters numerous proofs of the reality of this split-off condition of portions of consciousness. Since in man the hemispheres indubitably cooperate in these secondarily automatic acts, it will not do to say either that they occur without consciousness or that their consciousness is that of the lower centres, which we know nothing about. But either lack of memory or split-off cortical consciousness will certainly account for all of the facts.[17]

*Third Proof.* Thinking of A, we presently find ourselves thinking of C. Now B is the natural logical link between A and C, but we have no consciousness of having thought of B. It must have been in our mind 'unconsciously,' and in that state affected the sequence of our ideas.

*Reply.* Here again we have a choice between more plausible explanations. Either B was consciously there, but the next instant forgotten, or its *brain-tract* alone was adequate to do the whole work of coupling A with C, without the idea B being aroused at all, whether consciously or 'unconsciously.'

*Fourth Proof.* Problems unsolved when we go to bed are found solved in the morning when we wake. Somnambulists do rational things. We awaken punctually at an hour predetermined overnight, etc. Unconscious thinking, volition, time-registration, etc., must have presided over these acts.

*Reply.* Consciousness forgotten, as in the hypnotic trance.

*Fifth Proof.* Some patients will often, in an attack of epileptiform unconsciousness, go through complicated processes, such as eating a dinner in a restaurant and paying for it, or making a violent homicidal attack. In trance, artificial or pathological, long and complex performances, involving the use of the reasoning powers are executed, of which the patient is wholly unaware on coming to.

*Reply.* Rapid and complete oblivescence is certainly the explanation here. The analogue again is hypnotism. Tell the subject of an hypnotic trance, during his trance, that he *will* remember, and he may remember everything perfectly when he awakes, though without your telling him no memory would have remained. The extremely rapid oblivescence of common *dreams* is a familiar fact.

*Sixth Proof.* In a musical concord the vibrations of the several notes are in relatively simple ratios. The mind must unconsciously count the vibrations, and be pleased by the simplicity which it finds.

*Reply.* The brain-process produced by the simple ratios may be as directly agreeable as the conscious process of comparing them would be. No counting, either conscious or 'unconscious,' is required.

*Seventh Proof.* Every hour we make theoretic judgments and emotional reactions, and exhibit practical tendencies, for which we can give no explicit logical justification, but which are good inferences from certain premises. We know more than we can say. Our conclusions run ahead of our power to analyze their grounds. A child, ignorant of the axiom that two things equal to the same are equal to each other, applies it nevertheless in his concrete judgements unerringly. A boor will use the *dictum de omni et nullo* who is unable to understand it in abstract terms.

"We seldom consciously think how our house is painted, what the shade of it is, what the pattern of our furniture is, or whether the door opens to the right or the left, out or in. But how quickly should we notice a change in any of these things? Think of the door that you have most often opened, and tell, if you can, whether it opens to the right or left, out or in. Yet, when you open the door, you never put your hand on the wrong side to find the latch, nor try to push it when it opens with a pull. . . What is the precise characteristic in your friend's step that enables you to recognize it when he is coming? Did you ever consciously think the idea, 'If I run into a solid piece of matter I shall get hurt, or be hindered in my progress,' and do you avoid running into obstacles because you ever distinctly conceived, or consciously acquired and thought that idea."[18]

Most of our knowledge is at all times potential. We act in accordance with the whole drift of what we have learned, but few items rise into consciousness at the time. Many of them, however, we may recall at will. All this co-operation of unrealized principles and facts, of potential knowledge, with our actual thought is quite inexplicable unless we suppose the perpetual existence of an immense mass of *ideas in an unconscious state,* all of them exerting a steady pressure and influence upon our conscious thinking, and many of them in such continuity with it as ever and anon to become conscious themselves.

*Reply.* No such mass of ideas is supposable. But there are all kinds of short-cuts in the brain; and processes not aroused strongly enough to give any 'idea' distinct enough to be a premise, may, nevertheless, help to determine just that resultant process of whose psychic accompaniment the said idea *would* be a premise, if the idea existed at all. A certain overtone may be a feature of my ,friend's voice, and may conspire with the other tones thereof to arouse in my brain the process which suggests to my consciousness his name. And yet I may be ignorant of the overtone *per se,* and unable, even when he speaks, to tell whether it be there or no. It leads me to the idea of the name; but it produces in me no such cerebral process as that to which the *idea of overtone* would correspond. And similarly of our learning. Each subject we learn leaves behind it a modification of the brain, which makes it impossible for the latter to react upon things just as it did before; and the result of the difference may be a tendency to act, though with no idea, much as we should if we were consciously thinking about the subject. The becoming conscious of the latter at will is equally readily explained as a result of the brain-modification. This, as Wundt phrases it, is a 'predisposition' to bring forth the conscious idea of the original subject, a predisposition which other stimuli and brain-processes may convert into an actual result. But such a predisposition is no 'unconscious idea'; it is only a particular collocation of the molecules in certain tracts of the brain.

*Eighth Proof.* Instincts, as pursuits of ends by appropriate means, are manifestations of intelligence; but as the ends are not foreseen, the intelligence must be unconscious.

*Reply.* Previous chapters will show that all the phenomena of instinct are explicable as actions of the nervous system, mechanically discharged by stimuli to the senses.

*Ninth Proof.* In sense-perception we have results in abundance, which can only be explained as conclusions drawn by a process of unconscious inference from data given to sense. A small human image on the retina is referred, not to a pygmy, but to a distant man of normal size. A certain gray patch is inferred to be a white object seen in a dim light. Often the inference leads us astray: e.g., pale gray against pale green looks red, because we take a wrong premise to argue from. We think a green film is spread over everything; and knowing that under such a film a red thing would look gray, we wrongly infer from the gray appearance that a red thing must be there. Our study of space-perception will give abundant additional examples both of the truthful and illusory percepts which have been explained to result from unconscious logic operations.

*Reply.* That chapter will also in many cases refute this explanation. Color- and light-contrast are certainly purely sensational affairs, in which inference plays no part. This has been satisfactorily proved by Hering,[19] and shall be treated of again. Our rapid judgments of size, shape, distance, and the like, are best explained as processes of simple cerebral association. Certain sense impressions directly stimulate brain-tracts, of whose activity readymade conscious percepts are the immediate psychic counterparts. They do this by a mechanism either connate or acquired by habit. It is to be remarked that Wundt and Helmholtz, who in their earlier writings did more than anyone to give vogue to the notion that unconscious inference is a vital factor in sense-perception, have seen fit on later occasions to modify their views and to admit that results *like* those of reasoning may accrue without any actual reasoning process unconsciously taking place.[20] Maybe the excessive and riotous applications made by Hartmann of their principle have led them to this change. It would be natural to feel towards him as the sailor in the story felt towards the horse who got his foot into the stirrup,—"If you're going to get on, I must get off."

Hartmann fairly boxes the compass of the universe with the principle of unconscious thought. For him there is no namable thing that does not exemplify it. But his logic is so lax and his failure to consider the most obvious alternatives so complete that it would, on the whole, be a waste of time to look at his arguments in detail. The same is true of Schopenhauer, in whom the mythology reaches its climax. The visual perception, for example, of an object in space results, according to him, from the intellect performing the following operations, all unconscious. First, it apprehends the inverted retinal image and turns it right side up, constructing *fiat space* as a preliminary operation; then it computes from the angle of convergence of the eyeballs that the two retinal images must be the projection of but a single *object;* thirdly, it constructs the third dimension and sees this object *solid;* fourthly, it assigns its *distance;* and fifthly, in each and all of these operations it gets the objective character of what it 'constructs' by unconsciously inferring it as the only possible *cause* of some sensation which it unconsciously feels.[21] Comment on this seems hardly called for. It is pure mythology.

None of these facts, then, appealed to so confidently in proof of the existence of ideas in an unconscious state, prove anything of the sort. They prove either that conscious ideas were present which the next instant were forgotten; or they prove that certain results, *similar* to results of reasoning, may be wrought out by rapid brain-processes to which no ideation seems attached. But there is one more argument to be alleged, less obviously insufficient than those which we have reviewed, and demanding a new sort of reply.

*Tenth Proof.* There is a great class of experiences in our mental life which may be described as discoveries that a subjective condition which we have been having is really something different from what we had supposed. We suddenly find ourselves bored by a thing which we thought we were enjoying well enough; or in love with a person whom we imagined we only liked. Or else we deliberately analyze our motives, and find that at bottom they contain jealousies and cupidities which we little suspected to be there. Our feelings towards people are perfect wells of motivation, unconscious of itself, which introspection brings to light. And our sensations likewise: we constantly discover new elements in sensations which we have been in the habit of receiving all our days, elements too, which have been there from the first, since otherwise we should have been unable to distinguish the sensations containing them from others nearly allied. The elements must exist, for we use them to discriminate by; but they must exist in an unconscious state, since we so completely fail to single them out.[22] The books of the analytic school of psychology abound in examples of the kind. Who knows the countless associations that mingle with his each and every thought? Who can pick apart all the nameless feelings that stream in at every moment from his various internal organs, muscles, heart, glands, lungs. etc., and compose in their totality his sense of bodily life? Who is aware of the part played by feelings of innervation and suggestions of possible muscular exertion in all his judgments of distance, shape, and size? Consider, too, the difference between a sensation which we simply *have* and one which we *attend to.* Attention gives results that seem like fresh creations; and yet the feelings and elements of feeling which it reveals must have been already there—in an unconscious state. We all know *practically* the difference between the so-called sonant and the so-called surd consonants, between D, B, Z, G, V, and T, P, S, K, F, respectively. But comparatively few persons know the difference *theoretically,* until their attention has been called to what it is, when they perceive it readily enough. The sonants are nothing but the surds plus a certain element, which is alike in all, superadded. That element is the laryngeal sound with which they are uttered, surds having no such accompaniment. When we hear the son ant letter, both its component elements must really be in our mind; but we remain unconscious of what they really are, and mistake the letter for a simple quality of sound until an effort of attention teaches us its two components. There exist a host of sensations which most men pass through life and never attend to, and consequently have only in an unconscious way. The feelings of opening and closing the glottis, of making tense the tympanic membrane, of accommodating for near vision, of intercepting the passage from the nostrils to the throat, are instances of what I mean. Everyone gets these feelings many times an hour; but few readers, probably, are conscious of exactly what sensations are meant by the names I have just used. All these facts, and an enormous number more, seem to prove conclusively that, in addition to the fully conscious way in which an idea may exist in the mind, there is also an unconscious way; that it is unquestionably the same identical idea which exists in these two ways; and that therefore any arguments against the mind-stuff theory, based on the notion that *esse* in our mental life is *sentiri,* and that an idea must consciously be felt as what it is, fall to the ground.

*Objection.* These reasonings are one tissue of confusion. Two states of mind which refer to the same external reality, or two states of mind the later one of which refers to the earlier, are described as the same state of mind, or 'idea,' published as it were in two editions; and then whatever qualities of the second edition are found openly lacking in the first are explained as having really been there, only in an 'unconscious' way. It would be difficult to believe that intelligent men could be guilty of so patent a fallacy, were not the history of psychology there to give the proof. The psychological stock-in-trade of some authors is the belief that two thoughts about one thing are virtually the same thought, and that this same thought may in subsequent reflections become more and more *conscious* of what it really *was* all along from the first. But once make the distinction between simply *having an idea* at the moment of its presence and subsequently knowing all sorts of things *about it;* make moreover that between a state of mind itself, taken as a subjective fact, on the one hand, and the objective thing it knows, on the other, and one has no difficulty in escaping from the labyrinth.

Take the latter distinction first: Immediately all the arguments based on sensations and the new features in them which attention brings to light fall to the ground. The sensations of the B and the V when we attend to these sounds and analyze out the laryngeal contribution which makes them differ from P and F respectively, are *different sensations* from those of the B and the V taken in a simple way. They stand, it is true, for the *same letters,* and thus mean the *same outer realities;* but they are different mental affections, and certainly depend on widely different processes of cerebral activity. It is unbelievable that two mental states so different as the passive reception of a sound as a whole, and the analysis of that whole into distinct ingredients by voluntary attention, should be due to processes at all similar. And the subjective difference does not consist in that the first-named state *is* the second in an 'unconscious' form. It is an absolute psychic difference, even greater than that between the states to which two different surds will give rise. The same is true of the other sensations chosen as examples. The man who learns for the first time how the closure of his glottis feels, experiences in this discovery an absolutely new psychic modification, the like of which he never had before. He had another feeling before, a feeling incessantly renewed, and of which the same glottis was the organic starting point; but that was not the later feeling in an 'unconscious' state; it was a feeling *sui generis* altogether, although it took cognizance of the same bodily part, the glottis. We shall see, hereafter, that the same reality can be cognised by an endless number of psychic states, which may differ *toto coelo* among themselves, without ceasing on that account to refer to the reality in question. Each of them is a conscious fact; none of them has any mode of being whatever except a certain way of being felt at the moment of being present. It is simply unintelligible and fantastical to say, because they point to the same outer reality, that they must therefore be so many editions of the same 'idea,' now in a conscious and now in an 'unconscious' phase. There is only one 'phase' in which an idea can be, and that is a fully conscious condition. If it is not in that condition, then it is not at all. Something else is, in its place. The something else may be a merely physical brain-process, or it may be another conscious idea. Either of these things may perform much the same *function* as the first idea, refer to the same object, and roughly stand in the same relations to the upshot of our thought. But that is no reason why we should throw away the logical principle of identity in psychology, and say that, however it may fare in the outer world, the mind at any rate is a place in which a thing can be all kinds of other things without ceasing to be itself as well.

Now take the other cases alleged, and the other distinction, that namely between *having* a mental state and knowing all *about* it. The truth is here even simpler to unravel. When I decide that I have, without knowing it, been for several weeks in love, I am simply giving a name to a state which previously *I have not named,* but which was fully conscious; which had no residual mode of being except the manner in which it was conscious; and which, though it was a feeling towards the same person for whom I now have a much more inflamed feeling, and though it continuously led into the latter, and is similar enough to be called by the same name, is yet in no sense identical with the latter, and least of all in an 'unconscious' way. Again, he feelings from our viscera and other dimly-felt organs, the feelings of innervation (if such there be), and those of muscular exertion which, in our spatial judgements, are supposed unconsciously to determine what we shall perceive, are just exactly what we feel them, perfectly determinate conscious states, not vague editions of other conscious states. They may be faint and weak; they may be very vague cognizers of the same realities which other conscious states cognise and name exactly; they may be conscious of much in the reality which the other states are conscious of. But that does not make them *in themselves* a whit dim or vague or unconscious. They are externally as they feel when they exist, and can, neither actually nor potentially, be identified with anything else than their own faint selves. A faint feeling may be looked back upon and classified and understood in its relations to what went before or after it in the stream of thought. But it, on the one hand, and the later state of mind which knows all these things, about it, on the other, are surely not two conditions, one conscious and the other 'unconscious,' of the same identical psychic fact. It is the destiny of thought that, on the whole, our early ideas are superseded by later ones, giving fuller and the later ideas preserve their own several substantive identities as so many several successive states of mind. To believe the contrary would make any definite science of psychology impossible. The only identity to be found among our successive ideas is their similarity of cognitive or representative function as dealing with the same objects. Identity of *being*, there is none; and I believe that throughout the rest of this volume the reader will reap the advantages of the simpler way of formulating the facts which is here begun.[23]

So we seem not only to have ascertained the unintelligibility of the notion that a mental fact can be two things at once, and that what seems like one feeling, of blueness for example, or of hatred, may really and 'unconsciously' be ten thousand elementary feelings which do not resemble blueness or hatred at all, but we find that we can express all the observed facts in other ways. The mind-stuff theory, however, though scotched, is, we may be sure, not killed. If we ascribe consciousness to unicellular animalcules, then single cells can have it, and analogy should make us ascribe it to the several cells of the brain, each individually taken. And what a convenience would it not be for the psychologist if, by the adding together of various doses of this separate-cell-consciousness, he could treat thought as a kind of stuff or material, to be measured out in great or small amount, increased and subtracted from, and baled about at will! He feels an imperious craving to be allowed to *construct* synthetically the successive mental states which he describes. The mind-stuff theory so easily admits of the construction being 'made, that it seems certain that 'man's unconquerable mind' will devote much future pertinacity and ingenuity to setting it on its legs again and getting it into some sort of plausible working-order. I will therefore conclude the chapter with some consideration of the remaining difficulties which beset the matter as it at present stands.

### Difficulty of Stating the Connection between Mind and Brain

It will be remembered that in our criticism of the theory of the integration of successive conscious units into a feeling of musical pitch, we decided that whatever integration there was was that of the air-pulses into a simpler and simpler sort of physical effect, as the propagation of material change got higher and higher in the nervous system. At last, we said (p. 159), there results some simple and massive process in the auditory centres of the hemispherical cortex, to which, *as a whole,* the feeling of musical pitch directly corresponds. Already, in discussing the localization of functions in the brain, I had said (p. 73) that consciousness accompanies the stream of innervation through that organ and varies in quality with the character of the currents, being mainly of things seen if the occipital lobes are much involved, of things heard if the action is focalized in the temporal lobes, etc., etc.; and I had added that a vague formula like this was as much as one could safely venture on in the actual state of physiology. The facts of mental deafness and blindness, of auditory and optical aphasia. show us that the whole brain must act together if certain thoughts are to occur. The consciousness, which is itself an integral thing not made of parts, 'corresponds' to the entire activity of the brain, whatever that may be, at the moment. This is a way of expressing the relation of mind and brain from which I shall not depart during the remainder of the book, because it expresses the bare phenomenal fact with no hypothesis, and is exposed to no such logical objections as we have found to cling to the theory of ideas in combination.

Nevertheless, this formula which is so unobjectionable if taken vaguely, positivistically, or scientifically, as a mere empirical law of concomitance between our thoughts and our brain, tumbles to pieces entirely if we assume to represent anything more intimate or ultimate by it. The ultimate of ultimate problems, of course, in the study of the relations of thought and brain, is to understand why and how such disparate things are connected at all. But before that problem is solved (if it ever is solved) there is a less ultimate problem which must first be settled. Before the connection of thought and brain can be explained, it must at least be *stated* in an elementary form; and there are great difficulties about so stating it. To state it in elementary form one must reduce it to its lowest terms and know which mental fact and which cerebral fact are, so to speak in immediate juxtaposition. We must find the minimal mental fact whose being reposes directly on a brain-fact; and we must similarly find the minimal brain-event which will have a mental counterpart at all. Between the mental and the physical minima thus found there will be an immediate relation, the expression of which, if we had it, would be the elementary psycho-physic law.

One own formula escapes the unintelligibility of psychic atoms by *taking the entire thought* (even of a complex object) *as the minimum with which it deals on the mental side.* But in taking the entire brain-process as its minimal fact on the material side it confronts other difficulties almost as bad.

In the first place, it ignores analogies on which certain critics will insist, those, namely, between the composition of the total brain-process and that of the *object* of the thought. The total brain-process is composed of parts of simultaneous processes in the seeing, the hearing, the feeling, and other centres. The object thought of is also composed of parts, some of which are seen, others heard, others perceived by touch and muscular manipulation.

'How then,' these critics will say, ''should the thought not itself be composed of parts, each the counterpart of a part of the object and of a part of the brain process?" So natural is this way of looking at the matter that it has given rise to what is on the whole the most flourishing of all psychological systems—that of the Lockian school of associated ideas—of which school the mind-stuff theory is nothing but the last and subtlest offshoot.

The second difficulty is deeper still. *The 'entire brain-process' is not a physical fact at all.* It is the appearance to an onlooking mind of a multitude of physical facts. 'Entire brain' is nothing but our name for the way in which a million of molecules arranged in certain positions may affect our sense. On the principles of the corpuscular or mechanical philosophy, the only realities are the separate molecules, or at most the cells. Their aggregation into a 'brain' is a fiction of popular speech. Such a fiction cannot serve as the objectively real counterpart to any psychic state whatever. Only a genuinely physical fact can so serve. But the molecular fact is the only genuine physical tact—whereupon we seem, if we are to have an elementary psycho-physic law at all, thrust right back upon something like the mind-stuff theory, for the molecular fact, being an element of the 'brain,' would seem naturally to correspond not to the total thoughts, bitt to elements in the thought.

What shall we do? Many would find relief at this point in celebrating the mystery of the Unknowable and the 'awe' winch we should feel at having such a principle to take fir charge of our perplexities. Others would rejoice that the finite and separatist view of things with which we started had at last developed its contradictions, and was about to lead us dialectically upwards to some 'higher synthesis' in which inconsistencies cease from troubling and logic is at rest. It may be constitutional infirmity, but I can take no comfort in such devices for making a luxury of intellectual defeat. They are but spiritual chloroform. Better live on the ragged edge, better gnaw the file forever!

### The Material-Monad Theory

The most rational thing to do is to suspect that there may be a third possibility,' an alternative supposition which we have not considered. Now there *is* an alternative supposition—a supposition moreover which has been frequently made in the history of philosophy, and which is freer from logical objections than either of the views we have ourselves discussed. It may be called the *theory of polyzoism or multiple monadism;* and it conceives the matter thus:

Every brain-cell has its own individual consciousness, which no other cell knows anything about, all individual consciousnesses being 'ejective' to each other. There is, however, among the cells one central or pontifical one to which *our* consciousness is attached. But the events of all the other cells physically influence this arch-cell; and through producing their joint effects on it. these other cells may be said to 'combine.' The arch-cell is, in fact one of those external media' without which we saw that no fusion or integration of a number of things can occur. The physical modifications of the arch-cell thus form a sequence of results in the production whereof every other cell has a share, so that, as one might say, every other cell is represented therein. And similarly, the conscious correlates to these physical modifications form a sequence of thoughts or feelings, each one of which is, as to its substantive being, an integral and uncompounded psychic thing, but each one of which may (in the exercise of its *cognitive* function) be *aware of THINGS* many and complicated in proportion to the number of other cells that have helped to modify the central cell.

By a conception of this sort, one incurs neither of the internal contradictions which we found to beset the other two theories. One has no unintelligible self-combining of psychic units to account for on the one hand: and on the other hand, one need not treat as the physical counterpart of the stream of consciousness under observation, a 'total brain-activity' which is non-existent as a genuinely physical fact. But, to offset these advantages, one has physiological difficulties and improbabilities. There is no cell or group of cells in the brain of such anatomical or functional pre-eminence as to appear to be the keystone or centre of gravity of the whole system. And even if there were such a cell, the theory of multiple monadism would, in strictness of thought, have no right to stop at it and treat it as a unit. The cell is no more a unit, materially considered, than the total brain is a unit. It is a compound of molecules, just as the brain is a compound of cells and fibres. And the molecules, according to the prevalent physical theories, are in turn compounds of atoms. The theory in question, therefore, if radically carried out, must set up for its elementary and irreducible psycho-physic couple, not the cell and its consciousness, but the primordial and eternal atom and its consciousness. We are back at Leibnitzian monadism, and therewith leave physiology behind us and dive into regions inaccessible to experience and verification; and our doctrine, although not self-contradictory, becomes so remote and unreal as to be almost as bad as if it were. Speculative minds alone will take an interest in it; and metaphysics, not psychology, will be responsible for its career. That the career may be a successful one must be admitted as a possibility—a theory which Leibnitz, Herbart, and Lotze have taken under their protection must have some sort of a destiny.

But is this my last word? By no means. Many readers have certainly been saying to themselves for the last few pages: "Why on earth doesn't the poor man say *the Soul* and have done with it?" Other readers, of anti-spiritualistic training and prepossessions, advanced thinkers, or popular evolutionists, will perhaps be a little surprised to find this much-despised word now sprung upon them at the end of so physiological a train of thought. But the plain fact is that all the arguments for a 'pontifical cell' or an 'arch-monad' are also arguments for that well-known spiritual agent in which scholastic psychology and common-sense have always believed. And my only reason for beating the bushes so, and not bringing it in earlier as a possible solution of our difficulties, has been that by this procedure I might perhaps force some of these materialistic minds to feel the more strongly the logical respectability of the spiritualistic position. The fact is that one cannot afford to despise any of these great traditional objects of belief. Whether we realize it or not, there is always a great drift of reasons, positive and negative, towing us in their direction. If there be such entities as Souls in the universe, they may possibly be affected by occurrences in the nervous centres. To the state of the entire brain at a given moment they may respond by inward modifications of their own. These changes of state may be pulses of consciousness, cognitive of objects few or many, simple or complex. The soul would be thus a medium upon which (to use our earlier phraseology) the manifold brain-processes *combine their effects.* Not needing to consider it as the inner aspect' of any arch-molecule or brain-cell, we escape that physiological improbability; and as its pulses of consciousness are unitary and integral affairs from the outset, we escape the absurdity of supposing feelings which exist separately and then 'fuse together' by themselves. The separateness is in the brain-world, on this theory, and the unity in the soul-world; and the only trouble that remains to haunt us is the metaphysical one of understanding how one sort of world or existent thing can affect or influence another at all. This trouble, however, since it also exists inside of both worlds, and involves neither physical improbability nor logical contradiction, is relatively small.

I confess, therefore, that to posit a soul influenced in some mysterious way by the brain-states and responding to them by conscious affections of its own, seems to me the line of least logical resistance, so far as we yet have attained.

If it does not strictly *explain* anything, it is at any rate less positively objectionable than either mind-stuff or a material-monad creed. *The bare Phenomenon, however, the Immediately known thing which on the mental side is in apposition with the entire brain-process is the state of consciousness and not the soul itself.* Many of the stanchest believers in the soul admit that we know it only as an inference from experiencing its *states.* Accordingly, we must return to its consideration again, and *ask ourselves whether, after all, the ascertainment of a blank unmediated correspondence, term for term, of the succession of states of consciousness with the succession of total brain-processes, be not the simplest psycho-physic formula, and the last word of a psychology which contents itself with verifiable laws, and seeks only to be clear, and to avoid unsafe hypotheses.* Such a mere admission of the empirical parallelism will there appear the wisest course. By keeping it to, our psychology will remain positivistic and non-metaphysical; and although this is certainly only a provisional halting-place, and things must some day be more thoroughly thought out, we shall abide there in this book, and just as we have rejected mind-dust, we shall take no account of the soul. The spiritualistic reader may nevertheless believe in the soul if he will; whilst the positivistic one who wishes to give a tinge of mystery to the expression of his positivism can continue to say that nature in her unfathomable designs has mixed us of clay and flame, of brain and mind, that the two things hang indubitably together and determine each other's being but how or why, no mortal may ever know.

## REFERENCES

1. Psychology § 62.
2. *Ibid.*, § 272.
3. *Fragments of Science for Unscientific People*, 5th ed., p. 420.
4. Belfast Address *Nature*, August 20, 1874. p. 318. I cannot help remarking that the disparity between motions and feelings on which these authors lay so much tress, is somewhat less absolute than at first sight it seems. There are categories common to the two worlds. Not only temporal succession (as Helmholtz admits, *Physiologische Optik*, p. 445), but such attributes as intensity, volume, simplicity or complication, smooth or impeded change, rest or agitation, are habitually predicted

of both physical facts and mental facts. Where such analogies obtain, the things do have something in common.

5. Psychology § 131.
6. *Nature*, as above, 317-8.
7. Nascent's is Mr. Spencer's great world. In showing how at a certain point consciousness must appears upon the evolving scene this author fairly outdoes himself in vagueness.

   "In its higher forms, Instinct is probably accompanied by a rudimentary consciousness. There cannot be co-ordination of many stimuli without some ganglion through which they are all brought into relation. In the process of bringing them into relation, this ganglion must be subject to the influence of each—must undergo many changes. And the quick succession of changes in a ganglion, implying as it does perpetual experiences of differences and likenesses, constitutes the *raw material* of consciousness. The *implication* is that as fast as instinct is developed, some kind of consciousness becomes nascent." (*Psychology* § 195).

   "Separate impressions are received by the senses—by different parts of the body. If they go no further than the places at which they are received, they are useless. Or if only some of them are brought into relation with one another, they are useless. That an effectual adjustment may be made, they must be all brought into relation with one another. But this implies some centre of communication common to them all, through which they severally pass; and as they cannot pass through it simultaneously, they must pass through it in succession. So that as the external phenomena responded to become greater in number and more complicated in kind, the variety and rapidity of the changes to which this common centre of communication is subject must increase—there must result an unbroken series of these changes—*there must arise a consciousness.*

   "Hence the progress of the correspondence between the organism and its environment, necessitates a gradual reduction of the sensorial changes to a succession and by so doing *evolves a distinct consciousness*—a consciousness that becomes higher as the succession becomes more rapid and the correspondence more complete." (*Ibid.,*).

   It is true that in the *Fortnightly Review* (n.s., vol. xiv, p. 716) Mr. Spencer denies that he means by this passage to tell us anything about the origin of consciousness at all. It resembles, however, too many other places in his *Psychology* (e.g., §§ 43, 110, 244) not to be taken as a serious attempt to explain how consciousness must at a certain point be 'evolved.' That, when a critic calls his attention to the inanity of his words, Mr. Spancer should say he never meant anything particular by them, is simply an example of the scandalous vagueness with which this sort of 'chromo-philosophy is carried on.
8. His own words are: "Mistakes are made in the sense that he admits having been touched, when in reality it was radiant heat that affected his skin. In own before-mentioned experiments there was never any deception on the entire palmar side of the hand or on the face. On the back of the hand in one case in a series of 60 stimulations 4 mistakes occurred, in another case 2 mistakes in 45 stimulations. On the extensor side of the upper arm 3 deceptions out of 48 stimulations were noticed, and in the case of another individual, 1 out of 31. In one case over the sine 3 deceptions in a series of 11 excitations were observed; in another, 4 out of 19. On the lumbar spine 6 deceptions came among 29 stimulations, and again 4 out of 7. There is certainly not yet enough material on which to rest a calculation of probabilities, but anyone can easily convince himself that on the back there is no question of even a moderately accurate discrimination between warmth and a light pressure so far as but small portions of skin come into play. It has been as yet impossible to make corresponding experiments with regard to sensibility to cold." (*Lehrbuch der Anatomie und Physiologie der Sinnesorgane* (1864), p. 29).
9. *Principles of Psychology*, § 60.
10. Oddly enough, Mr. Spencer seems quite unaware of the *general* function of the theory of elementary

units of mind-stuff in the evolutionary philosophy. We have seen it to be absolutely indispensable, if that philosophy is to work, to postulate consciousness in the nebula,—the simplest way being, of course, to suppose every atom animated. Mr. Spencer, however, will have it (*e.g., First Principles*, § 71) that consciousness is only the occasional result of the 'transformation' of a certain amount of 'physical force' to which it is 'equivalent.' Presumably a brain must already be there before any such 'transformation' can take place; and so the argument quoted in the text stands as a mere local detail, without general bearings.

11. The compounding of colours may be dealt with in an identical way. Helmholtz has shown that if green light and red light fall simultaneously on the retina, we see the colour yellow. The mind-stuff theory would interpret this as a case where the feeling green and the feeling red 'combine' into the *tertium quid* of feeling, yellow. What no doubt really occurs is that a third kind of nerve-process is set up when the combined lights impinge on the retina,—not simply the process of red plus the process of green, but something quite different from both or either. Of course, then, there *are* no feelings, either of red or of green, present to the mind at all; but the feeling of yellow which *is* there, answers as directly to the nerve-process which momentarily then exists, as the feelings of green and red would answer to their respective nerve process did the latter happen to be taking place.

12. Someone might say that although it is true that neither a blind man nor a deaf man by himself can compare sounds with colours, yet since one hears and the other sees they might do so both together.... But whether they are apart or close together makes no difference; not even if they permanently keep house together; no, not if they were Siamese twins, or more than Siamese twins, and were inseparably grown together, would it make the assumption any more possible. Only when sound and colour are represented in the same reality is it thinkable that they should be compared." (Brentano: *Psychologie vom empirischen Standpunkte*, p. 209).

13. The reader must observe that we are reasoning altogether about the *logic* of the mind-stuff theory, about whether it can *explain the constitution* of higher mental states by viewing them as *identical with lower ones* summed together. We say the two sorts of fact are not identical: a higher state *is* not a lot of lower states; it is itself. When, however, a lot of lower states have come together, or when certain brain conditions occur together which, *if they occurred separately, would produce* a lot of lower states, we have not for a moment pretended that a higher state may not emerge. In fact it does emerge under those conditions; and our previous chapters will be mainly devoted to the proof of this fact. But such emergence is that of a new psychic entity, and *is toto caelo* different from such an 'integration' of the lower states as the mind-stuff theory affirms.

It may seem strange to suppose that anyone should mistake criticism of a certain theory about a fact for doubt of the fact itself. And yet the confusion is made in high quarters enough to justify our remarks. Mr. J. Ward, in his article "Psychology" in the *Encyclopaedia Britannica*, speaking of the hypothesis that "a series of feelings, can be aware of itself as a series,'" says (p. 39): "Paradox is too mild a word for it; even contradiction will hardly suffice." Whereupon, Professor Bain takes him thus to task: "As to `a series of states being aware of itself,' I confess I see no insurmountable difficulty. It may be a fact, or not a fact; it may be a very clumsy expression for what it is applied to; but it is neither paradox nor contradiction. A `series' merely contradicts an individual, or it may be two or more individuals as co-existing; but that is too general to exclude the possibility of self-knowledge. It certainly does not bring the property of self-knowledge into the foreground, which, however, is not the same as denying it. An algebraic series might know itself, without any contradiction: the only thing against it is the want of evidence of fact." (*Mind*, xi, 459). Prof. Bain thinks, then, that all the bother is about the difficulty of seeing how a series of feelings can have the knowledge of itself *added* to *it!!!* As if anybody ever was troubled about that. That, notoriously enough, is a fact: our consciousness is a series of feelings to which every now and then is *added* a retrospective consciousness that they have come and gone. What Mr. Ward and I are troubled about is merely the silliness of the mind-stuffists and associationists continuing to say that the `series of states' is the `awareness of itself; that if the states be posited severally, their collective consciousness is *eo ipso* given : and that we need no farther explanation, or `evidence of fact.'

13A. If the sensation of *pitch* be ignorant of all such things as *tops*, what sense is there in the declaration that it consists of nothing but things that know taps exclusively?

14. The writers about 'unconscious cerebration' seem sometimes to mean that and sometimes unconscious thought. The arguments which follow are culled from various quarters. The reader will find them most systematically urged by E. von Hartmann: *Philosophy of the Unconscious*, vol. 1 and by E. Colsenet: *La Vie inconsciente de Pesprit* (1880). Consult also T. Laycock: *Mind and Brain*, vol. I, chap. V (1860); W.B. Carpenter: *Mental Physiology*, chap. VIII; F.P. Cobbe *Darwinism in Morals, and Other Essays*, essay xi, "Unconscious Cererbration" (1872); F. Bowen: *Modern Philosophy*, pp. 429-480; R.H. Hutton: *Contemporary Review*, vol. xxiv, p. 201; J.S. Mill: *An Excmination of Sir William Hamilton's Philosophy*, chap. xv; G.H. Lewes: *Problems of Life and Mind*, 3rd series, Prob. II, chap. x, and also Prob. III, chap. II; D.G. Thompson: *A System of Psychology*, chap xxxiii; J.M. Baldwin: *Handbook of Psychology*, chap. iv.

15. *Nouveaux essais*, Avant-propos.

16. J.S. Mill: *Examination of Hamilton*, chap. xv.

17. Cf. Dugald Stewart: *Elements of the Philosophy of the Human Mind*, chap, II.

18. J.E. Maude: "The Unconscious in Education," in *Education*, vol. II, p. 401. (1882).

19. *Zur Lehre vom Lichtsinne* (1878).

20. Cf. Wundt: *Uber den Einfluss der Philosophie*, etc.—Antrittsrede (1876), pp. 10-11; Helmholtz: *Die Thatsachen in der Wahrnehmung* (1879), p. 27.

21. Cf. *Uber die vierfache Wurzel des Satzes vom zureichenden Grunde*, pp. 59-65. Compare also F. Zollner's *Natur der Cometen*, pp. 342 ff., and 525.

22. Cf. the statements form Helmholtz to be found later in Chapter XIII.

23. The text was written before Professor Lipps's *Grundtatsachen des Seelenlebens* (1883) came into my hands. In Chapter III of that book the notion of unconscious thought is subjected to the clearest and most searching criticism which it has yet received. Some passages are so similar to what I have myself written that I must quote them in a note. After proving that dimness and clearness, incompleteness and completeness do not pertain to a state of mind *as such*—since every state of mind must be *exactly* what it is, and nothing else—but only pertain to the way in which states of mind stand for objects, which they more or less dimly, more or less clearly, *represent;* Lipps takes the case of those sensations which attention is said to make more clear. "I perceive an object," he says, "now in clear daylight, and again at night. Call the content of the day-perception *a* and that of the evening-perception $a^1$. There will probably be a considerable difference between *a* and $a^1$. The colours of *a* will be varied and intense, and will be sharply bounded by each other; those of $a^1$ will be less luminous, and less strongly contrasted, and will approach a common gray or brown, and merge more into each other. Both percepts, however, as such, are completely determinate and distinct form all others. The colour of $a^1$ appear before my eye neither more nor less decidedly dark and blurred than the colours of *a* appear bright and sharply bounded. But now I know, or believe I know, that one and the same real Object A corresponds to both *a* and $a^1$. I am convinced, moreover that *a* represents A better than does $a^1$. Instead, however of giving to my conviction this, its only correct, expression, and keeping the content of my consciousness and the real object, the representation and what it means, distinct from each other, I substitute the real object for the content of the consciousness, and talk of the experience as if it consisted in one and the same object (namely, the surreptitiously introduced real one), constituting twice over the content of my consciousness, once in a clear and distinct, the other time in an obscure and vague fashion. I talk now of a distincter and of a less distinct *consciousness* of A, whereas I am only justified in talking of two consciousness, *a* and $a^1$, equally distinct *in se*, but to which the supposed external object A corresponds with different degrees of distinctness," (pp. 37-38).

# 32

# The Methods and Snares of Psychology

We have now finished the physiological preliminaries of our subject and must in the remaining chapters study the mental states themselves whose cerebral conditions and concomitants we have been considering hitherto. Beyond the brain, however, there is an outer world to which the brain-states themselves 'correspond.' And it will be well, ere we advance farther, to say a word about the relation of the mind to this larger sphere of physical fact.

**Psychology—A Natural Science**

That is, the mind which the psychologist studies is the mind of distinct individuals inhabiting definite portions of a real space and of a real time. With any other sort of mind, absolute Intelligence, Mind unattached to a particular body, or Mind not subject to the course of time, the psychologist as such has nothing to do. 'Mind,' in his mouth, is only a class name for minds. Fortunate will it be if his more modest inquiry result in any generalisations which the philosopher devoted to absolute Intelligence as such can use.

To the psychologist, then, the minds he studies are *objects*, in a world of other objects. Even when he introspectively analyses his own mind, and tells what he finds there, he talks about it in an objective way. He says, for instance, that under certain circumstances the colour gray appears to him green, and calls the appearance an illusion. This implies that he compares two objects, a real colour seen under certain conditions, and a mental perception which I believe to represent it, and that he declares the relation between them to be of a certain kind. In making this critical judgment, the psychologist stands as much outside of the perception which he criticises as he does of the color. Both are his objects. And if this is true of him when he reflects on his own conscious states, how much truer is it when he treats of those of others! In German philosophy since Kant the word *Erkenntnisstheorie*, criticism of the faculty of knowledge, plays a great part. Now the psychologist necessarily becomes such an *Erkenntnisstheoretiker*. But the knowledge he theorises about is not the bare function of knowledge which Kant criticises—he does not inquire into the possibility of knowledge *uberhaupt*. He assumes it to be possible, he does not doubt its presence in himself at the moment he speaks. The knowledge he criticises is the knowledge of particular men about the particular things that surround them. This he may, upon occasion, in the light of his *own* unquestioned knowledge, pronounce true or false, and trace the reasons by which it has become one or the other.

It is highly important that this natural-science point of view should be understood at the outset. Otherwise more may be demanded of the psychologist than he ought to be expected to perform.

A diagram will exhibit more emphatically what the assumptions of Psychology must be:

| 1<br>The Psychologist | 2<br>The Thought Studied | 3<br>The Thought's Object | 4<br>The Psychologist's Reality |
|---|---|---|---|

These four squares contain the irreducible data of psychology. No. 1, the psychologist, believes Nos. 2, 3, and 4, which together form *his* total object, to be realities, and reports them and their mutual relations as truly as he can without troubling himself with the puzzle of how he can report them at all. About such *ultimate* puzzles he in the main need trouble himself no more than the geometer, the chemist, or the botanist do, who make precisely the same assumptions as he.[1]

Of certain fallacies to which the psychologist is exposed by reason of his peculiar point of view—that of being a reporter of subjective as well as of objective facts, we must presently speak. But not until we have considered the methods he uses for ascertaining what the facts in question are.

## The Methods of Investigation

*Introspective Observation is what we have to rely on first and foremost and always.* The word introspection need hardly be defined—it means, of course, the looking into our own minds and reporting what we there discover. *Everyone agrees that we there discover states of consciousness.* So far as I know, the existence of such states has never been doubted by any critic, however sceptical in other respects he may have been. That we have *cogitations* of some sort is the *inconcussun* in a world most of whose other facts have at some time tottered in the breath of philosophic doubt. All people unhesitatingly believe that they feel themselves thinking, and that they distinguish the mental state as an inward activity or passion, from all the objects with which it may cognitively deal. *I regard this belief as the most fundamental of all the postulates of Psychology,* and shall discard all curious inquiries about its certainty as too metaphysical for the scope of this book.

*A Question of Nomenclature.* We ought to have some general term by which to designate all states of consciousness merely as such, and apart from their particular quality or cognitive function. Unfortunately most of the terms in use have grave objections. 'Mental state,' 'state of consciousness,' 'conscious modification,' are cumbrous and have no kindred verbs. The same is true of 'subjective condition.' 'Feeling' has the verb 'to feel,' both active and neuter, and such derivatives as 'feelingly,' 'felt,' 'feltness,' etc., which make it extremely convenient. But on the other hand it has specific meanings as well as its generic one, sometimes standing for pleasure and pain, and being sometimes a synonym of *'sensation'* as opposed to *thought*; whereas we wish a term to cover sensation and thought indifferently. Moreover, 'feeling' has acquired in the hearts of platonising thinkers a very opprobrious set of implications; and since one of the great obstacles to mutual understanding in philosophy is the use of words eulogistically and disparagingly, impartial terms ought always, if possible, to be preferred. The word *psychosis* has been proposed by Mr. Huxley. It has the advantage of being correlative to *neurosis* (the name applied by the same author to the corresponding nerve-process), and is moreover technical and devoid or partial implications. But it has no verb or other grammatical form allied to it. The expressions 'affection of the soul,' 'modification of the ego,' are clumsy, like 'state of consciousness,' and they implicitly assert theories which it is not well to embody in terminology before they have been openly discussed and approved. 'Idea' is a good vague neutral word, and was by Locke employed in the broadest generic way; but notwithstanding his authority it has not domesticated itself in the language so as to cover bodily sensations, and it moreover has no verb. 'Thought' would be by far the best word to use if it could be made to cover sensations. It has no opprobrious connotation such as 'feeling' has and it immediately suggests the omnipresence of cognition (or reference to an object other than the mental state itself), which we shall soon see to be of the mental life's essence. But can the expression 'thought of a toothache' ever suggest to the reader the actual present pain itself? It is hardly possible; and we thus seem about to be forced back on some *pair* of terms like Hume's 'impression and idea,' or Hamilton's presentation and representation,' or the ordinary 'feeling and thought,' if we wish to cover the whole ground.

In this quandary we can make no definitive choice, but must, according to the convenience of the context, use sometimes one, sometimes another of the synonyms that have been mentioned. *My own partiality is for either FEELING or THOUGHT*. I shall probably often use both words in a wider sense than usual, and alternately startle two classes of readers by their unusual sound; but if the connection makes it clear that mental states at large, irrespective of their kind, are meant, this will do no harm, and may even do some good.[2]

*The inaccuracy of introspective observation* has been made a subject of debate. It is important to gain some fixed ideas on this point before we proceed.

The commonest spiritualistic opinion is that the Soul or *Subject* of the mental life is a metaphysical entity, inaccessible to direct knowledge, and that the various mental states and operations of which we reflectively become aware are objects of an inner sense which does not lay hold of the real agent in itself, any more than sight or hearing gives us direct knowledge of matter in itself. From this point of view introspection is, of course, incompetent to lay hold of anything more than the Soul's *phenomena.* But even then the question remains, How well can it know the phenomena themselves?

Some authors take high ground here and claim for it a sort of infallibility. Thus Ueberweg:

"When the mental image as such is the object of my apprehension, there is no meaning in seeking to distinguish its existence in my consciousness (in me) from its existence out of my consciousness (in itself)—for the object apprehended is, in this case, one which does not even exist, as the objects of external perception do, in itself outside my consciousness. It exists only within me."[3]

And Brentano:

"The phenomena inwardly apprehended are true in themselves. As they appear—of this the evidence with which are apprehended is they a warrant—so they are in reality. Who, then, can deny that in this a great superiority of Psychology over the physical sciences comes to light?"

And again:

"No one can doubt whether the psychic condition he apprehends in himself *be*, and be *so*, as he apprehends it. Whoever should doubt this would have reached that *finished* doubt which destroys itself in destroying every fixed point from which to make an attack upon knowledge."[4]

Others have gone to the opposite extreme, and maintained that we can have no introspective cognition of our own minds at all. A deliverance of Auguste Comte to this effect has been so often quoted as to be almost classical; and some reference to it seems therefore indispensable here.

Philosophers, says Comte,[5] have

"in these latter days imagined themselves able to distinguish, by a very singular subtlety, two sorts of observation of equal importance, one external, the other internal, the latter being solely destined for the study of intellectual phenomena.... I limit myself to pointing out the principal consideration which proves clearly that this pretended direct contemplation of the mind by itself is a pure illusion.... It is in fact evident that, by an invincible necessity, the human mind can observe directly all phenomena except its own proper states. For by whom shall the observation of these be made? It is conceivable that a man might observe himself with respect to the *passions* that animate him, for the anatomical organs of passion are distinct from those whose function is observation. Though we have all made such observations on ourselves, they can never have much scientific value, and the best mode of knowing the passions will always be that of observing them from without; for every strong state of passion...is necessarily incompatible with the state of observation. But, as for observing in the same way *intellectual* phenomena at the time of their actual presence, that is a manifest impossibility. The thinker cannot divide himself into two, of whom one reasons whilst the other observes him reason. The organ observed and the organ observing being, in this case, identical, how could observation take place? This pretended psychological method is then radically null and void. On the one hand, they advise you to isolate yourself, as far as possible, from every external sensation, especially every intellectual work,-for if you were to busy yourself even with the simplest calculation, what would become of *internal* observation?—on the other band, after having with the utmost care attained this state of intellectual slumber, you must begin to contemplate the operations going on in your mind, when nothing there takes place! Our descendants will doubtless see such pretensions some day ridiculed upon the stage. The results of so strange a procedure harmonise entirely with its principle. For all the two thousand years during which metaphysicians have thus cultivated psychology, they are not agreed about one intelligible and established proposition. '*Internal observation*' gives almost as many divergent results as there are individuals who think they practise it."

Comte hardly could have known anything of the English, and nothing of the German, empirical psychology. The 'results' which he had in mind when writing were probably scholastic ones, such as principles of internal activity, the faculties, the ego, the *liberum arbitrium indifferentiœ*, etc. John Mill, in replying to him,[6] says:

"It might have occurred to M. Comte that a fact may be studied through the medium of memory, not at the very moment of our perceiving it, but the moment after: and this is really the mode in which our best knowledge of our intellectual acts is generally acquired. We reflect on what we have been doing, when the act is past, but when its impression in the memory is still fresh. Unless in one of these ways, we could not have acquired the knowledge, which nobody denies us to have, of what passes in our minds. M. Comte would scarcely have affirmed that we are not aware of our own intellectual operations. We know of our observings and our reasonings, either at the very time, or by memory the moment after; in either case, by direct knowledge, and not (like things done by us in a state of somnambulism) merely by their results. This simple fact destroys the whole of M. Comte's argument. 'Whatever we are directly aware of, we can directly observe.'"

Where now does the truth lie? Our quotation from Mill is obviously the one which expresses the most of *practical* truth about the matter. Even the writers who insist upon the absolute veracity of our immediate inner apprehension of a conscious state have to contrast with this the fallibility of our *memory* or *observation* of it, a moment later. No one has emphasised more sharply than Brentano himself the difference between the immediate *feltness* of a feeling, and its perception by a subsequent reflective act. But which mode of consciousness of it is that which the psychologist must depend on? If to *have* feelings or thoughts in their immediacy were enough, babies in the cradle would be psychologists, and infallible ones. But the psychologist must not only *have* his mental states in their absolute veritableness, he must report them and write about them, name them, classify and compare them and trace their relations to other things. Whilst alive they are their own property; it is only *post-mortem* that they become his prey.[7] And as in the naming, classing, and knowing of things in general we are notoriously fallible, why not also here? Comte is quite right in laying stress on the fact that a feeling, to be named, judged, or perceived, must be already past. No subjective state, whilst present, is its own object; its object is always something else. There are, it is true, cases in which we appear to be naming our present feeling, and so to be experiencing and observing the same inner fact at a single stroke, as when we say I feel tired,' 'I am angry, etc. But these are illusory, and a little attention unmasks the illusion. The present conscious state, when I say 'I feel tired,' is not the direct state of tire; when I say 'I feel angry,' it is not the direct state of anger. It is the state of *saying-I-feel-tired,* of *saying-I-feel-angry,*-entirely different matters, so different that the fatigue and anger apparently included in them are considerable modifications of the fatigue and anger directly felt the previous instant. The act of naming them has momentarily detracted from their force.[8]

The only sound grounds on which the infallible veracity of the introspective judgment might be maintained are empirical. If we had reason to think it has never yet deceived us, we might continue to trust it. This is the ground actually maintained by Herr Mohr.

"The illusions of our senses," says this author, "have undermined our belief in the reality of the outer world; but in the sphere of inner observation our confidence is intact, for we have never found ourselves to be in error about the reality of an act of thought or feeling. We have never been misled into thinking we were *not* in doubt or in anger when these conditions were really states of our consciousness."[9]

But sound as the reasoning here would be, were the premises correct, I fear the latter cannot pass. However it may be with such strong feelings as doubt or anger, about weaker feelings, and about the *relations to each other* of all feelings, we find ourselves in continual error and uncertainty so soon as we are called on to name and class, and not merely to feel. Who can be sure of the exact *order* of his feelings when they are excessively rapid? Who can be sure, in his sensible perception of a chair, how much comes from the eye and how much is supplied out of the previous knowledge of the mind? Who can compare with precision the *quantities* of disparate feelings even where the feelings are very much alike? For instance, where an object is felt now against the back and now against the cheek, which feeling is most extensive? Who can be sure that two given feelings are or are not exactly the same? Who can tell which is briefer or longer than the other when both occupy but an instant of time? Who knows, of many actions, for what motive they were done, or if for any motive at all? Who can enumerate all the distinct ingredients of such a complicated feeling as *anger?* and who can tell offhand whether or no a perception of *distance* be a compound or a simple state of mind? The whole mind-stuff controversy would stop if we could decide conclusively by introspection that what seem to us elementary feelings are really elementary and not compound.

Mr. Sully, in his work on *Illusion,* has a chapter on those of Introspection from which we might no"' quote. But, since the rest of this volume will be little more than a collection of illustrations of the difficulty of discovering by direct introspection exactly what our feelings and their relations are, we need not anticipate our own future details, but just state our general conclusion that *introspection is difficult and fallible; and that the difficulty is simply that of all observation of whatever kind.* Something is before us; we do our best to tell what if is, but in spite of our good will we may go astray, and give a description more applicable to some other sort of thing. The only safeguard is in the final *consensus* of our farther knowledge about the thing in question, later views correcting earlier ones, until at last the harmony of a consistent system is reached. Such a system, gradually worked out, is the best guarantee the psychologist can give for the soundness of any particular psychologic observation which he may report. Such a system we ourselves must strive, as far as may be, to attain.

The English writers on psychology, and the school of Herbart in Germany, have in the main contented themselves with such results as the immediate introspection of single individuals gave, and shown what a body of doctrine they may make. The works of Locke, Hume, Reid, Hartley, Stewart, Brown, the Nulls, will always be classics in this line; and in Professor Bain's *Treatises* we have probably the last word of what this method taken mainly by itself can do-the last monument of the youth of our science, still untechnical and generally intelligible, like the Chemistry of Lavoisier, or Anatomy before the microscope was used.

*The Experimental Method.* But psychology is passing into a less simple phase. Within a few years what one may call a microscopic psychology has arisen in Germany, carried on by experimental methods, asking of course every moment for introspective data, but eliminating their uncertainty by operating on a large scale and taking statistical means. This method taxes patience to the utmost, and could hardly have arisen in a country whose natives could be *bored*. Such Germans as Weber, Fechner, Vierordt, and Wundt obviously cannot; and their success has brought into the field an array of younger experimental psychologists, bent on studying the *elements* of the mental life, dissecting them out from the gross results in which they are embedded, and as far as possible reducing them to quantitative scales. The simple and open method of attack having done what it can, the method of patience, starving out, and harassing to death is tried: the Mind must submit to a regular *siege*, in which minute advantages gained night and day by the forces that hem her in must sum themselves up at last into her overthrow. There is little of the grand style about these new prism, pendulum, and chronograph-philosophers. They mean business, not chivalry. What generous divination, and that superiority in virtue which was thought by Cicero to give a man the best insight into nature, have failed to do, their spying and scraping, their deadly tenacity and almost diabolic cunning, will doubtless some day bring about.

No general description of the methods of experimental psychology would be instructive to one unfamiliar with the instances of their application, so we will waste no words upon the attempt. *The principal fields of experimentation* so far have been: (1) the connection of conscious states with their physical conditions, including the whole of brain-physiology, and the recent minutely cultivated physiology of the sense-organs, together with what is technically known as 'psycho-physics,' or the laws of correlation between sensations and the outward stimuli by which they are aroused; (2) the analysis of space-perception into its sensational elements; (3) the measurement of the *duration* of the simplest mental processes; (4) that of the *accuracy of reproduction* in the memory of sensible experiences and of intervals of space and time; (5) that of the manner in which simple mental states *influence each other*, call each other up, or inhibit each other's reproduction; (6) that of the *number of facts* which consciousness can simultaneously discern; finally, (7) that of the elementary laws of oblivescence and retention. It must be said that in some of these fields the results have as yet borne little theoretic fruit commensurate with the great labor expended in their acquisition.

But facts are facts, and if we only get enough of them they are sure to combine. New ground will from year to year be broken, and theoretic results will grow. Meanwhile the experimental method has quite changed the face of the science so far as the latter is a record of mere work done.

The *comparative method,* finally, supplements the introspective and experimental methods. This method presupposes a normal psychology of introspection to be established in its main features. But where the origin of these features, or their dependence upon one another, is in question, it is of the utmost importance to trace the phenomenon considered through all its possible variations of type and combination. So it has come to pass that instincts of animals are ransacked to throw light on our own; and that the reasoning faculties of bees and ants, the minds of savages, infants, madmen, idiots, the (leaf and blind, criminals, and eccentrics, are all invoked in support of this or that special theory about some part of our own mental life. The history of sciences, moral and political institutions, and languages, as types of mental product, are pressed into the same service. Messrs. Darwin and Galton have set the example of circulars of questions sent out by the hundred to those supposed able to reply. The custom has spread, and it will be well for us in the next generation if such circulars be not ranked among the common pests of life. Meanwhile information grows, and results emerge. There are great sources of error in the comparative method. The interpretation of the 'psychoses' of animals, savages, and infants is necessarily wild work, in which the personal equation of the investigator has things very much its own way. A savage will be reported to have no moral or religious feeling if his actions shock the observer unduly. A child will be assumed without self-consciousness because he talks of himself in the third person, etc. No rules can be laid clown in advance. Comparative observations, to be definite, must usually be made to test same pre-existing hypothesis; and the only thing then is to use as much sagacity as you possess, and to be as candid as you can.

## The Sources of Error in Psychology

*The first of them arises from the Misleading Influence of Speech.* Language was originally made by men who were not psychologists, and most men to-day employ almost exclusively the vocabulary of outward things. The cardinal passions of our life, anger, love, fear, hate, hope, and the most comprehensive divisions of our intellectual activity, to remember, expect, think, know, dream, with the broadest genera of aesthetic feeling, joy, sorrow, pleasure, pain, are the only facts of a subjective order which this vocabulary deigns to note by special words. The elementary qualities of sensation, bright, loud, red, blue, hot, cold, are, it is true, susceptible of being used in both an objective and a subjective sense. They stand for outer qualities and for the feelings which these arouse. But the objective sense is the original sense; and still to-day we have to describe a large number of sensations by the name of the object from which they have most frequently been got. An orange color, an odor of violets, a cheesy taste, a thunderous sound, a fiery smart, etc., will recall what I mean. This absence of a special vocabulary for subjective facts hinders the study of all but the very coarsest of them. Empiricist writers are very fond of emphasising one great set of delusions which language inflicts on the mind. Whenever we have made a word, they say, to denote a certain group of phenomena, we are prone to suppose a substantive entity existing beyond the phenomena, of which the word shall be the name. But the *lack* of a word quite as often leads to the directly opposite error. We are then prone to suppose that no entity can be there; and so we come to overlook phenomena whose existence would be patent to us all, had we only grown up to hear it familiarly recognised in speech.[10] It is hard to focus our attention on the nameless, and so there results a certain vacuousness in the descriptive parts of most psychologies.

But a worse defect than vacuousness comes from the dependence of psychology on common speech. Naming our thought by its own objects, we almost all of us assume that as the objects are, so the thought must be. The thought of several distinct things can only consist of several distinct bits of thought, or 'ideas'; that of an abstract or universal object can only be an abstract or universal idea. As each object may come and go, be forgotten and then thought Of again, it is held that the thought of it has a precisely similar independence, self-identity, and mobility. The thought of the object's recurrent identity is regarded as the identity of its recurrent thought; and the perceptions of multiplicity, of coexistence, of succession, are severally conceived to be brought about only through a multiplicity, a coexistence, a succession, of perceptions. The continuous flow of the mental stream is sacrificed, and in its place an atomism, a brickbat plan of construction, is preached, for the existence of which no good introspective grounds can be brought forward, and out of which presently grow all sorts of paradoxes and contradictions, the heritage of woe of students of the mind.

These words are meant to impeach the entire English psychology derived from Locke and flume, and the entire German psychology derived from Herbart, so far as they both treat 'ideas' as separate subjective entities that come and go. Examples will soon make the matter clearer. Meanwhile our psychologic insight is vitiated by still other snares.

*'The Psychologist's Fallacy.'* The *great* snare of the psychologist is the *confusion of his own standpoint with that of the mental fact* about which he is making his report. I shall hereafter call this the 'psychologist's fallacy' *par excellence.* For some of the mischief, here too, language is to blame. The psychologist, as we remarked above (p. 183), stands outside of the mental state he speaks of. Both itself and its object are objects for him. Now when it is a *cognitive* state (percept, thought, concept, etc.), he ordinarily has no other way of naming it than as the thought, percept, etc., *of that object*. He himself, meanwhile, knowing the self-same object in *his* way, gets easily led to suppose that the thought, which is *of* it, knows it in the same way in which he knows it, although this is often very far from being the case.[11] The most fictitious puzzles have been introduced into our science by this means. The so-called question of presentative or representative perception, of whether an object is present to the thought that thinks it by a counterfeit image of itself, or directly and without any intervening image at all; the question of nominalism and conceptualism, of the shape in which things are present when only a general notion of them is before the mind; are comparatively easy questions when once the psychologist's fallacy is eliminated from their treatment,—as we shall ere long see.

*Another variety of the psychologist's fallacy is the assumption that the mental state Studied must be conscious of itself as the psychologist is conscious of it.* The mental state is aware of itself only from within; it grasps what we call its own content, and nothing more. The psychologist, on the contrary, is aware of it from without, and knows its relations with all sorts of other things. What the thought sees is only its own object; what the psychologist sees is the thought's object, plus the thought itself, plus possibly all the rest of the world. We must be very careful therefore, in discussing a state of mind from the psychologist's point of view, to avoid foisting into its own ken matters that are only there for ours. We must avoid substituting what we know the consciousness *is*, for what it is a consciousness *of*, and counting its outward, and so to speak physical relations with other facts of the world, in among the objects of which we set it down as aware. Crude as such a confusion of standpoints seems to be when abstractly stated, it is nevertheless a snare into which no psychologist has kept himself at all times from falling, and which forms almost the entire stock-in-trade of certain schools. We cannot be too watchful against its subtly corrupting influence.

**Summary**

To sum up the chapter, Psychology assumes that thoughts successively occur, and that they know objects in a world which the psychologist also knows. *These thoughts are the subjective data of which he treats, and their relations to their objects, to the brain, and to the rest of the world constitute the subject-matter of psychologic science.* Its methods are introspection, experimentation, and comparison. But introspection is no sure guide to truths *about* our mental states: and in particular the poverty of the psychological vocabulary leads us to drop out certain states from our consideration, and to treat others as if they knew themselves and their objects as the psychologist knows both, which is a disastrous fallacy in the science.

## NOTES

1. On the relation between Psychology and General Philosophy, see G.C. Robertson, *Mind*, vol. VIII, p. 1, and J. Ward, *ibid.*, p. 153; J. Dewey: *ibid.*, vol. XI, p. 1.
2. Compare some remarks in Mill's *Logic*, bk. I, chap. III, §§ 2, 3.
3. *System of Logic*, § 40.
4. *Psychologie*, bk, I, chap. I, §§ 2, 3.
5. *Cours de philosophie positive*, I, 34-7.
6. *Auguste Comte and Positivism*, 3rd edition (1882), p. 64.
7. Wundt says: "The first rule for utilising inward observation consists in taking, as far as possible, experiences that are accidental, unexpected, and not intentionally brought about.... *First* it is best as far as possible to rely on *Memory* and not on immediate Apprehension.... *Second*, internal observation is better fitted to grasp clearly conscious states, especially voluntary mental acts: such inner processes as are obscurely conscious and involuntary will almost entirely elude it, because the effort to observe interferes with them, and because they seldom abide in memory." (*Logik*, II, 482).
8. In cases like this, where the state outlasts the act of naming it, exists before it, and recurs when it is past, we probably run little practical risk of error when we talk as if the state knew itself. The

state of feeling and the state of naming the feeling are continuous, and the infallibility of such prompt introspective judgments is probably great. But even here the certainty of our knowledge ought not to be argued on the *a priori* ground that *percipi* and *esse* are in psychology the same. The states are really two; the naming state and the named state are apart; '*percipi* is *esse*' is not the principle that applies.

9. J. Mohr: *Grundlage der empirischen Psychologie* (Leipzig, 1882), p. 47.
10. In English we have not even the generic distinction between the-thing-thought-of and the-though-thinking-it, which in German is expressed by the opposition between *Gedachtes* and *Gedanke*, in Latin by that between *cogitatum* and *cogitatio.*
11. Compare B.P. Bowne's *Metaphysics* (1882), p. 408.

# 33

# The Stream of Thought

We now begin our study of the mind from within. Most books start with sensations, as the simplest mental facts, and proceed synthetically, constructing each higher stage from those below it. But this is abandoning the empirical method of investigation. No one ever had a simple sensation by itself. Consciousness, from our natal day, is of a teeming multiplicity of objects and relations, and what we call simple sensations are results of discriminative attention, pushed often to a very high degree. It is astonishing what havoc is wrought in psychology by admitting at the outset apparently innocent suppositions, that nevertheless contain a flaw. The bad consequences develop themselves later on, and are irremediable, being woven through the whole texture of the work. The notion that sensations, being the simplest things, are the first things to take up in psychology is one of these suppositions. The only thing which psychology has a right to postulate at the outset is the fact of thinking itself, and that must first be taken up and analysed. If sensations then prove to be amongst the elements of the thinking, we shall be no worse off as respects them than if we had taken them for granted at the start.

*The first fact for is, then, as psychologists, is that thinking of some sort goes on.* The word thinking is used, for every form of consciousness indiscriminately. If we could say in English 'it thinks,' as we say 'it rains' or 'it blows,' we should be stating the fact most simply and with the minimum of assumption. As we cannot, we must simply say that *thought goes on.*

### Five Characters in Thought

How does it go on? We notice immediately five important characters in the process, of which it shall be the duty of the present chapter to treat in a general way:

(1) Every thought tends to be part of a personal consciousness.

(2) Within each personal consciousness thought is always changing.

(3) Within each personal consciousness thought is sensibly continuous.

(4) It always appears to deal with objects independent of itself.

(5) It is interested in some parts of these objects to the exclusion of others, and welcomes or rejects—*chooses* from among them, in a word—all the while.

In considering these five points successively, we shall have to plunge *in medias res* as regards our vocabulary, and use psychological terms which can only be adequately defined in later chapters of the book. But everyone knows what the terms mean in a rough way; and it is only in a rough way that we are now to take them. This chapter is like a painter's first charcoal sketch upon his canvas, in which no niceties appear.

### *(i) Thought Tends to Personal Form*

*Every 'thought' is part of a personal consciousness,* personal consciousness' is one of the terms in question. Its meaning we know so long as no one asks us to define it, but to give an accurate account of it is the most difficult of philosophic tasks.

In this room—this lecture-room, say—there are a multitude of thoughts, yours and mine, some of which cohere mutually, and some not. They are as little each-for-itself and reciprocally independent as they are all-belonging-together. They are neither: no one of them is separate, but each belongs with certain others and with none beside. My thought belongs with my other thoughts, and your thought with your other thoughts. Whether anywhere in the room there be a mere thought, which is nobody's thought, we have no means of ascertaining, for we have no experience of its like. The only states of consciousness that we naturally deal with are found in personal consciousnesses, minds, selves, concrete particular I's and you's.

Each of these minds keeps its own thoughts to itself. There is no giving or bartering between them. No thought even comes into direct *sight* of a thought in another personal consciousness than its own. Absolute insulation, irreducible pluralism, is the law. It seems as if the elementary psychic fact were not *thought* or *this thought* or *that thought*, but *my thought,* every thought being *owned.* Neither contemporaneity, nor proximity in space, nor similarity of quality and content are able to fuse thoughts together which are sundered by this barrier of belonging to different personal minds. The breaches between such thoughts are the most absolute breaches in nature. Everyone will recognise this to be true, so long as the existence of *something* corresponding to the term 'personal mind' is all that is insisted on, without any particular view of its nature being implied. On these terms the personal self rather than the thought might be treated as the immediate datum in psychology. The universal conscious fact is not 'feelings and thoughts exist,' but I think' and 'I feel.'[1] No psychology, at any rate, can question the *existence* of personal selves. The worst a psychology can do is so to interpret the nature of these selves as to rob them of their worth. A French writer, speaking of our ideas, says somewhere in a fit of anti-spiritualistic excitement that, misled by certain peculiarities which they display, we 'end by personifying' the procession which they make,—such personification being regarded by him as a great philosophic blunder on our part. It could only be a blunder if the notion of personality meant something essentially different from anything to be found in the mental procession. But if that procession be itself the very 'original' of the notion of personality, to personify it cannot possibly' be wrong. It is already personified. There are no marks of personality to be gathered *aliunde,* and then found lacking in the train of thought. It has them all already; so that to whatever farther analysis we may subject that form of personal selfhood under which thoughts appear, it is, and must remain, true that the thoughts which psychology' studies do continually tend to appear as parts of personal selves.

I say 'tend to appear' rather than 'appear,' on account of those facts of sub-conscious personality, automatic writing, etc., of which we studied a few in the last chapter. The buried feelings and thoughts proved now to exist in hysterical anaesthetics, in recipients of post-hypnotic suggestion, etc., themselves are parts of *secondary personal selves.* These selves are for the most part very stupid and contracted, and are cut off at ordinary times from communication with the regular and normal self of the individual; but still they form conscious unities, have continuous memories, speak, write, invent distinct names for themselves, or adopt names that are suggested; and, in short, are entirely worthy of that title of secondary personalities which is now commonly given them. According to M. Janet these secondary personalities are always abnormal, and result from the splitting of what ought to be a single complete self into two parts, of which one lurks in the background whilst the other appears on the surface as the only self the man or woman has. For our present purpose it is unimportant whether this account of the origin of secondary selves is applicable to all possible cases of them or not, for it certainly is true of a large number of them. Now although the *size* of a secondary self thus formed will depend on the number of thoughts that are thus split-off from the main consciousness, the *form* of it tends to personality, and the later thoughts pertaining to it remember the earlier ones and adopt them as their own. M. Janet caught the actual moment of inspissation (so to speak) of one of these secondary personalities in his anaesthetic somnambulist Lucie. Lie found that when this young woman's attention was absorbed in conversation with a third party, her anaesthetic hand would write simple answers to questions whispered to her by himself. "Do you hear?" he asked. *"No,"* was the unconsciously written reply. "But to answer you must hear." *"Yes, quite so."* "Then how do you manage?" *"I don't know."* "There must be someone who hears me. *"Yes."* "Who?" *"Someone other than Lucie."* "Ah! another person. Shall we give her a name?" *"No."* "Yes, it will be more convenient." *"Well, Adrienne, then."* "Once baptised, the subconscious personage," M. Janet continues, "grows more definitely outlined and displays better her psychological characters. In particular she shows us that she is conscious of the feelings excluded from the consciousness of the primary or normal personage. She it is who tells us that I am pinching the arm or touching the little finger in which Lucie for so long has had no tactile sensations."[2]

In other cases the adoption of the name by the secondary self is more spontaneous. I have seen a number of incipient automatic writers and mediums as yet imperfectly 'developed,' who immediately and of their own accord write and speak in the name of departed spirits. These may be public characters, as Mozart, Faraday, or real persons formerly known to the subject, or altogether imaginary beings. Without prejudicing the question of real 'spirit-control' in the more developed sorts of trance-utterance, I incline to think that these (often deplorably unintelligent) rudimentary utterances are the work of an inferior fraction of the subject's own natural mind, set free from control by the rest, and working after a set pattern fixed by the prejudices of the social environment: In a spiritualistic community we get optimistic messages, whilst in an ignorant Catholic village the secondary personage calls itself by the name of a demon, and proffers blasphemies and obscenities, instead of telling us how happy it is in the summer-land.[3]

Beneath these tracts of thought, which, however rudimentary, are still organised selves with a memory, habits, and sense of their own identity, M. Janet thinks that the facts of catalepsy in hysteric patients drive us to suppose that there are thoughts quite unorganised and impersonal. A patient in cataleptic trance (which can be produced artificially in certain hypnotised subjects) is without memory on waking, and seems insensible and unconscious as long as the cataleptic condition lasts. If, however, one raises the arm of such a subject it stays in that position, and the whole body can thus be moulded like wax under the hands of the operator, retaining for a considerable time whatever attitude he communicates to it. In hysterics whose arm, for example, is anaesthetic, the same thing may happen. The anaesthetic arm may remain passively in positions which it is made to assume; or if the hand be taken and made to hold a pencil and trace a certain letter, it will continue tracing that letter indefinitely on the paper. These acts, until recently, were supposed to be accompanied by no consciousness at all: they Were physiological reflexes. M. Janet considers with much more plausibility that feeling escorts them. The feeling is probably merely that of the position or movement of the limb, and it produces no more than its natural effects when it discharges into the motor centres which keep the position maintained, or the movement incessantly renewed.[4] Such thoughts as these, says M. Janet, "are known by *no one*, for disaggregated sensations reduced to a state of mental dust are not synthetised in any personality."[5] He admits, however, that these very same unutterably stupid thoughts tend to develop memory,—the cataleptic ere long moves her arm at a bare hint; so that they form no important exception to the law that all thought tends to assume the form of personal consciousness.

### (2) Thought is in Constant Change

I do not mean necessarily that no one state of in md has any duration—even if true, that would be hard to establish. The change which I have more particularly in view is that which takes place in sensible intervals of time; and the result on which I wish to lay stress is this, that *no state once gone can recur and be identical with what it was before.* Let us begin with Mr. Shadworth Hodgson's description.

"I go straight to the facts, without saying I go to perception, or sensation, or thought, or any special mode at all. What I find, when I look at my consciousness at all, is, that what I cannot divest myself of, or not have in consciousness, if I have any consciousness at all, is a sequence of different feelings. I may shut my eyes and keep perfectly still, and try not to contribute anything of my own will; but whether I think, or do not think, whether I perceive external things or not, I always have a succession of different feelings. Anything else that I may have also, of a more special character, comes in as parts of this succession. Not to have the succession of different feelings is riot to be conscious at all.... The chain of consciousness is a sequence of *differents*."[6]

Such a description as this can awaken no possible protest from anyone. We all recognise as different great classes of our conscious states. Now we are seeing, now hearing; now reasoning, now willing; now recollecting, now expecting; now loving, now hating; and in a hundred other ways we know our minds to be alternately engaged. But all these are complex states. The aim of science is always to reduce complexity to simplicity; and in psychological science we have the celebrated 'theory of *ideas*' which, admitting the great difference among each other of what may be called concrete conditions of mind, seeks to show how this is all the resultant effect of variations in the *combination* of certain simple elements of consciousness that always remain the same. These mental atoms or molecules are what Locke called 'simple ideas.' Some of Locke's successors made out that the only simple ideas were the sensations strictly so called. Which ideas the simple ones may be does not, however, now concern us. It is enough that certain philosophers have thought they could see under the dissolving-view-appearance of the mind elementary facts of *any* sort that remained unchanged amid the flow.

And the view of these philosophers has been called little into question, for our common experience seems at first sight to corroborate it entirely. Are not the sensations we get from the same object, for example, always the same? Does not the same piano-key, struck with the same force, make us hear in the same way? Does not the same grass give us the same feeling of green, the same sky the same feeling of blue, and do we not get the same olfactory sensation no matter how many times we put our nose to the same flask of cologne? It seems a piece of metaphysical sophistry to suggest that we do not; and yet a close attention to the matter shows that *there is no proof that the same bodily-sensation is ever got by us twice.*

*What is got twice is the same* OBJECT. We hear the same *note* over and over again; we see the same *quality* of green, or smell the same objective perfume, or experience the same *species* of pain. The realities, concrete and abstract, physical and ideal, whose permanent existence we believe in, seem to be constantly coming up again before our thought, and lead us, in our carelessness, to suppose that our 'ideas' of them are the same ideas. When we come, some time later, to the chapter on Perception, we shall see how inveterate is our habit of not attending to sensations as subjective facts, but of simply using them as stepping-stones to pass over to the recognition of the realities whose presence they reveal. The grass out of the window now looks to me of the same green in the sun as in the shade, and yet a painter would have to paint one part of it dark brown, another part bright yellow, to give its real sensational effect. We take no heed, as a rule, of the different way in which the same things look and sound and smell at different distances and under different circumstances. The sameness of the *things* is what we are concerned to ascertain; and any sensations that assure us of that will probably be considered in a rough way to be the same with each other. This is what makes off-hand testimony about the subjective identity of different sensations well-nigh worthless as a proof of the fact. The entire history of Sensation is a commentary on our inability to tell whether two sensations received apart are exactly alike. What appeals to our attention far more than the absolute quality or quantity of a given sensation is its *ratio* to whatever other sensations we may have at the same time. When everything is dark a somewhat less dark sensation makes us see an object white. Helmholtz calculates that the white marble painted in a picture representing an architectural view by moonlight is, when seen by daylight, from ten to twenty thousand times brighter than the real moonlit marble would be.[7]

Such a difference as this could never have been *sensibly* learned; it had to be inferred from a series of indirect considerations. There are facts which make us believe that our sensibility is altering all the time, so that the same obtect cannot easily give us the same sensation over again. The eye's sensibility to light is at its maximum when the eye is first exposed, and blunts itself with surprising rapidity. A long night's sleep will make it see things twice as brightly on wakening, as simple rest by closure will make it see them later in the day.[8] We feel things differently according as we are sleepy or awake, hungry or full, fresh or tired; differently at night and in the morning, differently in summer and in winter; and above all things differently in childhood, manhood, and old age. Yet we never doubt that our feelings reveal the same world, with the same sensible qualities and the same sensible things occupying it. The difference of the sensibility is shown best by the difference of our emotion about the things from one age to another, or when we are in different organic moods. What was bright and exciting becomes weary, flat, and unprofitable. The bird's song is tedious, the breeze is mournful, the sky is sad.

To these indirect presumptions that our sensations, following the mutations of our capacity for feeling, are always undergoing an essential change, must be added another presumption, based on what must happen in the brain. Every sensation corresponds to some cerebral action. For an identical sensation to recur it would have to occur the second time *in an unmodified brain.* But as this, strictly speaking, is a physiological impossibility, so is an unmodified feeling an impossibility; for to every brain-modification, however small, must correspond a change of equal amount in the feeling which the brain subserves.

All this would be true if even sensations came to us pure and single and not combined into 'things.' Even then we should have to confess that) however we might in ordinary conversation speak of getting the same sensation again, we never in strict theoretic accuracy could do so: and that whatever was true of the river of life, of the river of elementary feeling, it would certainly be true to say, like Heraclitus, that we never descend twice into the same stream.

But if the assumption of 'simple ideas of sensation' recurring in immutable shape is so easily shown to be baseless, how much more baseless is the assumption of immutability in the larger masses of our thought!

For there it is obvious and palpable that our state of mind is never precisely the same. Every thought we have of a given fact is, strictly speaking, unique, and only bears a resemblance of kind with our other thoughts of the same fact. When the identical fact recurs, we *must* think of it in a fresh manner, see it under a somewhat different angle, apprehend it in different relations from those in which it last appeared. And the thought by which we cognise it is the thought of it-in-those-relations, a thought suffused with the consciousness of all that dim context. Often we are ourselves struck at the strange differences in our successive views of the same thing. We wonder how we ever could have opined as we did last month about a certain matter. We have outgrown the possibility of that state of mind, we know not how. From one year to another we see things in new lights. What was unreal has grown real, and what was exciting is insipid. The friends we used to care the world for are shrunken to shadows; the women, once so divine, the stars, the woods, and the waters, how now so dull and common! the young girls that brought an aura of infinity, at present hardly distinguishable existences; the pictures so empty; and as for the books, what *was* there to find so mysteriously significant in Goethe, or in John Mill so full of weight? Instead of all this, more zestful than ever is the work, the work; and fuller and deeper the import of common duties and of common goods.

But what here strikes us so forcibly on the flagrant scale exists on every scale, down to the imperceptible transition from one hour's outlook to that of the next. Experience is remoulding us every moment, and our mental reaction on every given thing is really a resultant of our experience of the whole world up to that date. The analogies of brain-physiology must again be appealed to corroborate our view.

Our earlier chapters have taught us to believe that, whilst we think, our brain changes, and that, like the aurora borealis, its whole internal equilibrium shifts with every pulse of change. The precise nature of the shifting at a given moment is a product of many factors. The accidental state of local nutrition or blood-supply may be among them. But just as one of them certainly is the influence of outward objects on the sense-organs during the moment, so is another certainly the very special susceptibility in which the organ has been left at that moment by all it has gone through in the past. Every brain-state is partly determined by the nature of this entire past succession. Alter the latter in any part, and the brain-state must be somewhat different. Each present brain-state is a record in which the eye of Omniscience might read all the foregone history of its owner. It is out of the question, then, that any total brain-state should identically recur. Something like it may recur; but to suppose *it* to recur would be equivalent to the absurd admission that all the states that had intervened between its two appearances had been pure nonentities, and that the organ after their passage was exactly as it was before. And (to consider shorter periods) just as, in the senses, an impression feels very differently according to what has preceded it: as one color succeeding another is modified by the contrast, silence sounds delicious after noise, and a note, when the scale is sung up, sounds unlike itself when the scale is sung down; as the presence of certain lines in a figure changes the apparent form of the other lines, and as in music the whole aesthetic effect comes from the manner in which one set of sounds alters our feeling of another; so, in thought, we must admit that those portions of the brain that have just been maximally excited retain a kind of soreness which is a condition of our present consciousness, a codeterminant of how and what we now shall feel.[9]

Ever some tracts are waning in tension, some waxing, whilst others actively discharge. The states of tension have as positive an influence as any in determining the total condition, and in deciding what the *psychosis* shall be. All we know of submaximal nerve-irritations, and of the summation of apparently ineffective stimuli, tends to show that *no* changes in the brain are physiologically ineffective, and that presumably none are bare of psychological result. But as the brain-tension shifts from one relative state of equilibrium to another, like the gyrations of a kaleidoscope, now rapid and now slow, is it likely that its faithful psychic concomitant is heavier-footed than itself, and that it cannot match each one of the organ's irradiations by a shifting inward iridescence of its own? But if it can do this, its inward iridescences must be infinite, for the brain-redistributions are in infinite variety. If so coarse a thing as a telephone-plate can be made to thrill for years and never reduplicate its inward condition, how much more must this be the case with the infinitely delicate brain?

I am sure that this concrete and total manner of regarding the mind's changes is the only true manner, difficult as it may be to carry it out in detail. If anything seems obscure about it, it will grow clearer as we advance. Meanwhile, if it be true, it is certainly also true that no two 'ideas' are ever exactly the same, which is the proposition we started to prove. The proposition is more important theoretically than it at first sight seems. For it makes it already impossible for us to follow obediently in the footprints of either the Lockian or the Herbartian school, schools which have had almost unlimited influence in Germany and among ourselves. No doubt it is often *convenient* to formulate the mental facts in an atomistic sort of way, and to treat the higher states of consciousness as if they were all built out of unchanging simple ideas. It is convenient often to treat curves as if they were composed of small straight lines, and electricity and nerve-force as if they were fluids. But in the one case as in the other we must never forget that we are talking symbolically, and that there is nothing in nature to answer to our words. *A permanently existing 'idea' or 'Vorstellung' which makes its appearance before the footlights of consciousness at periodical intervals, is as mythological an entity as the Jack of Spades.*

What makes it convenient to use the mythological formulas is the whole organisation of speech, which, as was remarked a while ago, was not made by psychologists, but by men who were as a rule only interested in the facts their mental states revealed. They only spoke of their states as *ideas of this or of that thing*. What wonder, then, that the thought is most easily conceived under the law of the thing whose name it bears! If the thing is composed of parts, then we suppose that the thought of the thing must be composed of the thoughts of the parts. If one part of the thing have appeared in the same thing or in other things on former occasions, why then we must be having even now the very same 'idea' of that part which was there on those occasions. If the thing is simple, its thought is simple. If it is multitudinous, it must require a multitude of thoughts to think it. If a succession, only a succession of thoughts can know it. If permanent, its thought is permanent. And so on *ad libitum*. What after all is so natural as to assume that one object, called by one name, should be known by one affection of the mind? But, if language must thus influence us, the agglutinative languages, and even Greek and Latin with their declensions, would be the better guides. Names did not appear in them inalterable, but changed their shape to suit the context in which they lay. It must have been easier then than now to conceive of the same object as being thought of at different times in non-identical conscious states.

This, too, will grow clearer as we proceed. Meanwhile a necessary consequence of the belief in permanent self-identical psychic facts that absent themselves and recur periodically is the Humian doctrine that our thought is composed of separate independent parts and is not a sensibly continuous stream. That this doctrine entirely misrepresents the natural appearances is what I next shall try to show.

### *(3) Within Each Personal Consciousness, Thought is Sensibly Continuous*

I can only define 'continuous' as that which is without breach, crack, or division. I have already said that the breach from one mind to another is perhaps the greatest breach in nature. The only breaches that can well be conceived to occur within the limits of a single mind would either be *interruptions, time-gaps* during which the consciousness went out altogether to come into existence again at a later moment; or they would be breaks in the *quality* or content, of the thought, so abrupt that the segment that followed had no connection whatever with the one that went before. The proposition that within each personal consciousness thought feels continuous, means two things:

1. That even where there is a time-gap the consciousness after it feels as if it belonged together with the consciousness before it, as another part of the same self.

2. That the changes from one moment to another in the quality of the consciousness are never absolutely abrupt.

The case of the time-gaps, as the simplest, shall be taken first. And first of all, a word about time-gaps of which the consciousness may not be itself aware.

On page 198 we saw that such *time*-gaps existed, and that they might be more numerous than is usually supposed. If the consciousness is not aware of them, it cannot feel them as interruptions. In the unconsciousness produced by nitrous oxide and other anaesthetics, in that of epilepsy and fainting, the broken edges of the sentiment life may meet and merge over the gap, much as the feelings of space of the opposite margins of the 'blind spot' meet and merge over that objective interruption to the sensitiveness of the eye. Such consciousness as this, whatever it be for the onlooking psychologist, is for itself unbroken. It *feels* unbroken; a waking of it is sensibly a unit as long as that day lasts, in the sense in each the hours themselves are units, as having all their parts next each other, with no intrusive alien substance between. To expect the consciousness to feel the interruptions of its objective continuity as gaps, would be like expecting the eye to feel a gap of silence because it does not hear, or the ear to feel a gap of darkness because it does not see. So much for the gaps that are unfelt.

With the felt gaps the case is different. On waking from sleep, we usually know that we have been unconscious, and we often have an accurate judgment of how long. The judgment here is certainly an inference from sensible signs, and its ease is due to long practice in the particular field.[10] The result of it, however, is that the consciousness is, *for itself,* not what it was in the former case, but interrupted and discontinuous, in the mere time-sense of the words. But in the other sense of continuity, the sense of the parts being inwardly connected and belonging together because they are parts of a common whole, the consciousness remains sensibly continuous and one. What now is the common whole? The natural name for it is *myself*, *I*, or *me*.

When Paul and Peter wake up in the same bed, and recognise that they have been asleep, each one of them mentally reaches back and makes connection with but *one* of the two streams of thought which were broken by the sleeping hours. As the current of an electrode buried in the ground unerringly finds its way to its own similarly buried mate, across no matter how much intervening earth; so Peter's present instantly finds out Peter's past, and never by mistake knits itself on to that of Paul. Paul's thought in turn is as little liable to go astray. The past thought of Peter is appropriated by the present Peter alone. He may have a *knowledge*, and a correct one too, of what Paul's last drowsy states of mind were as he sank into sleep, but it is an entirely different sort of knowledge from that which he has of his own last states. He *remembers* his own states, whilst he only *conceives* Paul's. Remembrance is like direct feeling; its object is suffused with a warmth and intimacy to which no object of mere conception ever attains. This quality of warmth and intimacy and immediacy is what Peter's *present* thought also possesses for itself. So sure as this present is me, is mine, it says, so sure is anything else that comes with the same warmth and intimacy and immediacy, me and mine. What the qualities called warmth and intimacy may in themselves be will have to be matter for future consideration. But whatever past feelings appear with those qualities must be admitted to receive the greeting of the present mental state, to be owned by it, and accepted as belonging together with it in a common self. This community of self is what the time-gap cannot break in twain, and is why a present thought, although not ignorant of the time-gap, can still regard itself as continuous with certain chosen portions of the past.

Consciousness, then, does not appear to itself chopped up in bits. Such words as 'chain' or 'train' do not describe it fitly as it presents itself in the first instance. It is nothing jointed; it flows. A 'river' or a 'stream' are the metaphors by which it is most naturally described. *In talking of it hereafter, let us call it the stream of thought, of consciousness, or of subjective life.*

But now there appears, even within the limits of the same self, and between thoughts all of which alike have this same sense of belonging together, a kind of jointing and separateness among the parts, of which this statement seems to take no account. I refer to the breaks that are produced by sudden *contrasts in the quality* of the successive segments of the stream of thought. If the words 'chain' and 'train' had no natural fitness in them, how came such words to be used at all? Does not a loud explosion rend the consciousness upon which it abruptly breaks, in twain? Does not every sudden shock, appearance of a new object, or change in a sensation, create a real interruption, sensibly felt as such, which cuts the conscious stream across at the moment at which it appears? Do not such interruptions smite us every hour of our lives, and have we the right, in their presence, still to call our consciousness a continuous stream?

This objection is based partly on a confusion and partly on a superficial introspective view.

The confusion is between the thoughts themselves, taken as subjective facts, and the things of which they are aware. It is natural to make this confusion, but easy to avoid it when once put on one's guard. The things are discrete and discontinuous; they do pass before us in a train or chain, making often explosive appearances and rending each other in twain. But their comings and goings and contrasts no more break the flow of the thought that thinks them than they break the time and the space in which they lie. A silence may be broken by a thunder-clap, and we may be so stunned and confused for a moment by the shock as to give no instant account to ourselves of what has happened. But that very confusion is a mental state and a state that passes us straight over from the silence to the sound. The transition between the thought of one object lad the thought of another is no more a break in the *thought* than a joint in a bamboo is a break in the wood. It is a part of the *consciousness* as much as the joint is a part of the *bamboo.*

The superficial introspective view is the overlooking, even when the things are contrasted with each other most violently, of the large amount of affinity that may still remain between the thoughts by whose means they are cognised. Into the awareness of the thunder itself the awareness of the previous silence creeps and continues; for what we hear when the thunder crashes is not thunder *pure,* but thunder-breaking-upon-silence-and-constrasting-with-it.[11] Our feeling of the same objective thunder, coming in this way, is quite different from what it would be were the thunder a continuation of previous thunder. The thunder itself we believe to abolish and exclude the silence; but the *feeling* of the thunder is also a feeling of the silence as just gone; and it would be difficult to find in the actual concrete consciousness of man a feeling so limited to the present as not to have an inkling of anything that went before. Here, again, language works against our perception of the truth. We name our thoughts simply, each after its thing, as if each knew its own thing and nothing else. What each really knows is clearly the thing it is named for, with dimly perhaps a thousand other things. It ought to be named after all of them, but it never is. Some of them are always things known a moment ago more clearly; others are things to be known more clearly a moment hence.[12] Our own bodily position, attitude, condition, is one of the things of which *some* awareness, however inattentive, invariably accompanies the knowledge of whatever else we know. We think; and as we think we feel our bodily selves as the seat of the thinking. If the thinking be *our* thinking, it must be suffused through all its parts with that peculiar warmth and intimacy that make it come as ours. Whether the warmth and intimacy be anything more than the feeling of the same old body always there, is a matter for the next chapter to decide. *Whatever* the content of the ego may be, it is habitually felt *with* everything else by us humans, and must form a *liaison* between all the things of which we become successively aware.[13]

On this gradualness in the changes of our mental content the principles of nerve-action can throw some more light. When studying, the summation of nervous activities, we saw that no state of the brain can be supposed instantly to die away. If a new state comes, the inertia of the old state will still be there and modify the result accordingly. Of course we cannot tell, in our ignorance, what in each instance the modifications ought to be. The commonest modifications in sense-perception are known as the phenomena of contrast. In aesthetics they are the feelings of delight or displeasure which certain particular orders in a series of impressions give. In thought, strictly and narrowly so called, they are unquestionably that consciousness of the *whence* and the *whither* that always accompanies its flows. If recently the brain-tract *a* was vividly excited, and then *b*, and now vividly *c*, the total present consciousness is not produced simply by *c*'s excitement, but also by the dying vibrations of a and *b* as well. If we want to represent the brain-process we must write it thus: *abc*—three different processes coexisting, and correlated with them a thought which is no one of the three thoughts which they would have produced had each of them occurred alone. But whatever this fourth thought may exactly be, it seems impossible that it should not be something *like* each of the three other thoughts whose tracts are concerned in its production, though in a fast-waning phase.

It all goes back to what we said in another connection only a few pages ago. As the total neurosis changes, so does the total psychosis change. But as the changes of neurosis are never absolutely discontinuous, so must the successive psychoses shade gradually into each other, although their *rate* of change may be much faster at one moment than at the next.

This difference in the rate of change lies at the basis of a difference of subjective states of which we ought immediately to speak. When the rate is slow we are aware of the object of our thought in a comparatively restful and stable way. When rapid, we are aware of a passage, a relation, a transition *from* it, or *between* it and something else. As we take, in fact, a general view of the wonderful stream of our consciousness, what strikes us first is this different pace of its parts. Like a bird's life, it seems to be made of an alternation of flights and perchings. The rhythm of language expresses this, where every thought is expressed in a sentence, and every sentence closed by a period. The resting-places are usually occupied by sensorial imaginations of some sort, whose peculiarity is that they can be held before the mind for an indefinite time, and contemplated without changing; the places of flight are filled with thoughts of relations, static or dynamic, that for the most part obtain between the matters contemplated in the periods of comparative rest.

*Let us call the resting-places the 'substantive parts,' and the places of flight the 'transitive parts,' of the stream of thought.* It then appears that the main end of our thinking is at all times the attainment of some other substantive part than the one from which we have just been dislodged. And we may say that the main use of the transitive parts is to lead us from one substantive conclusion to another.

Now it is very difficult, introspectively, to see the transitive parts for what they really are. If they are but flights to a conclusion, stopping them to look at them before the conclusion is reached is really annihilating them. Whilst if we wait till the conclusion *be* reached, it so exceeds them in vigor and stability that it quite eclipses and swallows them up in its glare. Let anyone try to cut a thought across in the middle and get a look at its section, and he will see how difficult the introspective observation of the transitive tracts is. The rush of the thought is so headlong that it almost always brings us up at the conclusion before we can arrest it. Or if our purpose is nimble enough and we do arrest it, it ceases forthwith to be itself. As a snowflake caught in the warm hand is no longer a flake but a drop, so, instead of catching the feeling of relation moving to its term, we find we have caught some substantive thing, usually the last word we were pronouncing, statically taken, and with its function, tendency, and particular meaning in the sentence quite evaporated. The attempt at introspective analysis in these cases is in fact like seizing a spinning top to catch its motion, or trying to turn up the gas quickly enough to see how the darkness looks. And the challenge to *produce* these psychoses, which is sure to be thrown by doubting psychologists at anyone who contends for their existence, is as unfair as Zeno's treatment of the advocates of motion, when, asking them to point out in what place an arrow *is* when it moves, he argues the falsity of their thesis from their inability to make to so preposterous a question an immediate reply.

The results of this introspective difficulty are baleful. If to hold fast and observe the transitive parts of thought's stream be so hard, then the great blunder to which all schools are liable must be the failure to register them, and the undue emphasising of the more substantive parts of the stream. Were we not ourselves a moment Since in danger of ignoring any feeling transitive between the silence and the thunder, and of treating their boundary as a sort of break in the mind? Now such ignoring as this has historically worked in two ways. One set of thinkers have been led by it to *Sensationalism*. Unable to lay their hands on any coarse feelings corresponding to the innumerable relations and forms of connection between the facts of the, world, finding no *named* subjective modifications mirroring such relations, they have for the most part denied that feelings of relation exist; and many of them, like flume, have gone so far as to deny the reality of most relations *out* of the mind as well as in it. Substantive psychoses, sensations and their copies and derivatives, juxtaposed like dominoes in a game, but really separate, everything else verbal illusion,—such is the upshot of this view.[14] The *Intellectualists*, on the other hand, unable to give up the reality of relations *extra mentem*, but equally unable to point to any distinct substantive feelings in which they were known, have made the same admission that the feelings do not exist. But they have drawn an opposite conclusion. The relations must be known, they say, in something that is no feeling, no mental modification continuous and consubstantial with the subjective tissue out of which sensations and other substantive states are made. They are known, these relations, by something that lies on an entirely different plane, by an *actus purus* of Thought, Intellect, or Reason, all written with capitals and considered to mean something unutterably superior to any fact of sensibility whatever.

But from our point of view both Intellectualists and Sensationalists are wrong. If there be such things as feelings at all, *then so surely as relations between objects exist in return natura, so surely, and more surely, do feelings exist to which these relations are known.* There is not a conjunction or a preposition, and hardly an adverbial phrase, syntactic form, or inflection of voice, in human speech, that does not express some shading or other of relation which we at some moment actually feel to exist between the larger objects of our thought. If we speak objectively, it is the real relations that appear revealed; if we speak subjectively, it is the stream of consciousness that matches each of them by an inward coloring of its own. In either case the relations are numberless, and no existing language is capable of doing justice to all their shades.

We ought to say a feeling of *and*, a feeling of *if*, a feeling of *but*, and a feeling of *by*, quite as readily as we say a feeling of *blue* or a feeling of *cold*. Yet we do not: so inveterate has our habit become of recognising the existence of the substantive parts alone, that language almost refuses to lend itself to any other use. The Empiricists have always dwelt on its influence in making us suppose that where we have a separate name, a separate thing must needs be there to correspond with it; and they have rightly denied the existence of the mob of abstract entities, principles, and forces, in whose favor no other evidence than this could be brought up. But they have said nothing of that obverse error, of which we said a word, supposing that where there is *no* name no entity can exist. All *dumb* or anonymous psychic states have, owing to this error, been coolly suppressed; or, if recognised at all, have been named after the substantive perception they led to, as thoughts 'about' this object or 'about' that, the stolid word *about* engulfing all their delicate idiosyncrasies in its monotonous sound. Thus the greater and greater accentuation and isolation of the substantive parts have continually gone on.

Once more take a look at the brain. We believe the brain to be an organ whose internal equilibrium is always in a state of change—the change affecting every part. The pulses of change are doubtless more violent in one place than in another, their rhythm more rapid at this time than at that. As in a kaleidoscope revolving at a uniform rate, although the figures are always rearranging themselves there are instants during which the transformation seems minute and interstitial and almost absent, followed by others when it shoots with magical rapidity, relatively stable forms thus alternating with forms we should not distinguish if seen again; so in the brain the perpetual rearrangement must result in some forms of tension lingering relatively long, whilst others simply come and pass But if consciousness corresponds to the fact of rearrangement itself why, if the rearrangement stop not, should the consciousness ever cease? And if a lingering rearrangement brings with it one kind of consciousness, why should not a swift rearrangement bring another kind of consciousness as peculiar as the rearrangement itself? The lingering consciousnesses, if of simple objects, we call 'sensations' or images,' according as they are vivid or faint; if of complex objects, we call them 'percepts' when vivid, 'concepts' or 'thoughts' when faint. For the swift consciousnesses we have only those names of 'transitive states,' or 'feelings of relation,' which we have used.[15] As the brain-changes are continuous, so do all these consciousnesses melt into each other like dissolving views. Properly they are but one protracted consciousness, one unbroken stream.

### *Feelings of Tendency*

So much for the transitive states. But there are other unnamed states or qualities of states that are just as important and just as cognitive as they, and just as much unrecognised by the traditional sensationalist and intellectualist philosophies of mind. The first fails to find them at all, the second finds their *cognitive function*, but denies that anything in the way of *feeling* has a share in bringing it about. Examples will make clear what these inarticulate psychoses, due to waxing and waning excitements of the brain, are like.[16]

Suppose three Successive persons say to us: 'Wait!' 'Hark!' 'Look!' Our consciousness is thrown into three quite different attitudes of expectancy, although no definite object is before it in any one of the three cases. Leaving out different actual bodily attitudes, and leaving out the reverberating images of the three words, which are of course diverse, probably no one will deny the existence of a residual conscious affection, a sense of the direction from which an impression is about to come, although no positive impression is yet there. Meanwhile we have no names for the psychoses in question but the names hark, look, and wait.

Suppose we try to recall a forgotten name. The state of our consciousness is peculiar. There is a gap therein; but no mere gap. It is a gap that is intensely active. A sort of wraith of the name is in it, beckoning us in a given direction, making its at moments tingle with the sense of our closeness, and then letting us sink back without the longed-for term. If wrong names are proposed to us, this singularly definite gap acts immediately so as to negate them. They do not fit into its mould. And the gap of one word does not feel like the gap of another, all empty of content as both might seem necessarily to be when described as gaps. When I vainly try to recall the name of Spalding, my consciousness is far removed from what it is when I vainly try to recall the name of Bowles. Here some ingenious persons will say: "How *can* the two consciousnesses lie different when the terms which might make them different are not there? All that is there, so long as the effort to recall is vain, is the bare effort itself. How should that differ in the two cases? You are making it seem to differ by prematurely filling it out with the different names, although these, by the hypothesis, have not yet come. Stick to the two efforts as they are, without naming them after facts not yet existent, and you'll be quite unable to designate any point in which they differ." Designate, truly enough. We can Only designate the difference by borrowing the names of objects not yet in the mind. Which is to say that our psychological vocabulary is wholly inadequate to name the differences that exist, even such differences as these. But namelessness is compatible with existence. There are innumerable consciousnesses of emptiness, no one of which taken in itself has a name, but all different from each other. The ordinary way is to assume that they are all emptinesses of consciousness, and so the same state. But the feeling an absence is *toto coelo* other than the absence of a feeling: it is an intense feeling. The rhythm of a lost word may be there without a sound to clothe it; or the evanescent sense of something which is the initial vowel or consonant may mock us fitfully, without growing more distinct. Everyone must know the tantalising effect of the blank rhythm of some forgotten verse, restlessly dancing in one's mind, striving to be filled out with words.

Again, what is the strange difference between an experience tasted for the first time and the same experience recognised as familiar, as having been enjoyed before, though we cannot name it or say where or when? A tune, an odor, a flavor sometimes carry this inarticulate feeling of their familiarity so deep into our consciousness that we are fairly shaken by its mysterious emotional power. But strong and characteristic as this psychosis is-it probably is due to the submaximal excitement of wide-spreading associational brain-tracts-the only name we have for all its shadings is 'sense of familiarity.'

When we read such phrases as 'naught but,' 'either one or the other,' '*a* is *b*, but,' 'although it is, nevertheless,' 'it is an excluded middle, there is no *tertium quid*,' and a host of other verbal skeletons of logical relation, is it true that there is nothing more in our minds than the words themselves as they pass? What then is the meaning of the words Which we think we understand as we read? What makes that meaning different in one phrase from what it is in the other? 'Who?' 'When?' 'Where?' Is the difference of felt meaning in these interrogatives nothing more than their difference of sound? And is it not (just like the difference of sound itself) known and understood in an affection of consciousness correlative to it, though so impalpable to direct examination? Is not the same true of such negatives as 'no,' 'never,' 'not yet'?

The truth is that large tracts of human speech are nothing but *signs of direction* in thought, of which direction we nevertheless have an acutely discriminative sense, though no definite sensorial image plays any part in it whatsoever. Sensorial images are stable psychic facts; we can hold them still and look at them as long as we like. These bare images of logical movement, on the contrary, are psychic transitions, always on the wing, so to speak, and not to be glimpsed except in flight. Their function is to lead from one set of images to another. As they pass, we feel both the waxing and the waning images in a way altogether peculiar and a way quite different from the way of their full presence. If we try to hold fast the feeling of direction, the full presence comes and the feeling of direction is lost. The blank verbal scheme of the logical movement gives us the fleeting sense of the movement as we read it, quite as well as does a rational sentence awakening definite imaginations by its words.

What is that first instantaneous glimpse of someone's meaning which we have, when in vulgar phrase we say we twig' it? Surely an altogether specific affection of our mind. And has the reader never asked himself what kind of a mental fact is his *intention of saying a thing* before he has said it? It is an entirely definite intention, distinct from all other intentions, an absolutely distinct state of consciousness, therefore; and yet how much of it consists of definite sensorial images, either of words or of things? Hardly anything! Linger, and the words and things come into the mind; the anticipatory intention, the divination is there no more. But as the words that replace it arrive, it welcomes them successively and calls them right if they agree with it, it rejects them and calls them wrong if they do not. It has therefore a nature of its own of the most positive sort, and yet what can we say about it without using words that belong to the later mental facts that replace it? The intention *to-say-so-and-so* is the only name it can receive. One may admit that a good third of our psychic life consists in these rapid premonitory perspective views of schemes of thought not yet articulate. How comes it about that a man reading something aloud for the first time is able immediately to emphasise all his words aright, unless from the very first he have a sense of at least the form sentence yet to come, which sense is fused with his consciousness of the present word, and modifies its emphasis in his mind so as to make him give it the proper accent as he utters it? Emphasis of this kind is almost altogether a matter of grammatical construction. If we read 'no more' we expect presently to come upon a 'than'; if we read 'however' at the outset of a sentence it is a 'yet,' a 'still,' or a 'nevertheless,' that we expect. A noun in a certain position demands a verb in a certain mood and number, in another position it expects a relative pronoun. Adjectives call for nouns, verbs for adverbs, etc. And this foreboding of the coming grammatical scheme combined with each successive uttered word is so practically accurate that a reader incapable of understanding four ideas of the book he is reading aloud, can nevertheless read it with the most delicately modulated expression of intelligence.

Some will interpret these facts by calling them all cases in which certain images, by laws of association, awaken others so very rapidly that we think afterwards we felt the very *tendencies* of the nascent images to arise, before they were actually there. For this school the only possible materials of consciousness are images of a perfectly definite nature. Tendencies exist, but they are facts for the outside psychologist rather than for the subject of the observation. The tendency is thus a *psychical* zero; only its *results* are felt.

Now what I contend for, and accumulate examples to show, is that 'tendencies' are not only descriptions from without, but that they are among the *objects* of the stream, which is thus aware of them from within, and must be described as in very large measure constituted of *feelings* of *tendency*, often so vague that we are unable to name them at all. It is, in short, the re-instatement of the vague to its proper place in our mental life which I am so anxious to press on the attention. Mr. Galton and Prof. Huxley have, as we shall see in previous chapters, made one step in advance in exploding the ridiculous theory of Hume and Berkeley that we can have no images but of perfectly definite things. Another is made in the overthrow of the equally ridiculous notion that, whilst simple objective qualities are revealed to our knowledge in subjective feelings, relations are not. But these reforms are not half sweeping and radical enough. What must be admitted is that the definite images of traditional psychology form but the very smallest part of our minds as they actually live. The traditional psychology talks like one who should say a river consists of nothing but pailsful, spoonsful, quartpotsful, barrelsful, and other moulded forms of water. Even were the pails and the pots all actually standing in the stream, still between them the free water would continue to flow. It is just this free water of consciousness that psychologists resolutely overlook. Every definite image in the mind is steeped and dyed in the free water that flows round it. With it goes the sense of its relations, near and remote, the dying echo of whence it came to us, the dawning sense of whither it is to lead. The significance, the value, of the image is all in this halo or penumbra that surrounds and escorts it,—or rather that is fused into one with it and has become bone of its bone and flesh of its flesh; leaving it, it is true, an image of the same *thing* it was before, but making it an image of that thing newly taken and freshly understood.

What is that shadowy scheme of the 'form' of an opera, play, or book, which remains in our mind and on which we pass judgment when the actual thing is done? What is our notion of a scientific or philosophical system? Great thinkers have vast premonitory glimpses of schemes of relation between terms, which hardly even as verbal images enter the mind, so rapid is the whole process.[17] We all of us have this permanent consciousness of whither our thought is going. It is a feeling like any other, a feeling of what thoughts are next to arise, before they have arisen. This field of new of consciousness varies very much in extent, depending largely on the degree of mental freshness or fatigue. When very fresh, our minds carry an immense horizon with them. The present image shoots its perspective far before it, irradiating in advance the regions in which lie the thoughts as yet unborn. Under ordinary conditions the halo of felt relations is much more circumscribed. And in states of extreme brain-fag the horizon is narrowed almost to the passing word,—the associative machinery, however, providing for the next word turning up in orderly sequence, until at last the tired thinker is led to some kind of a conclusion. At certain moments he may find himself doubting whether his thoughts have not come to a full stop; but the vague sense of a *puts ultra* makes him ever struggle on towards a more definite expression of what it may be; whilst the slowness of his utterance shows how difficult, under such conditions, the labor of thinking must be.

The awareness that our *definite* thought has come to a stop is an entirely different thing from the awareness that our thought is indefinitively completed. The expression of the latter state of mind is the falling inflection which betokens that the sentence is ended, and silence. The expression of the former state is 'hemming and hawing,' or else such phrases as *'et cetera,'* or 'and so forth.' But notice that every part of the sentence to be left incomplete feels differently as it passes, by reason of the premonition we have that we shall be unable to end it. The 'and so forth' casts its shadow back, and is as integral a part of the object of the thought as the distinctest of images would be.

Again, when we use a common noun, such as *man,* in a universal sense, as signifying all possible men, we are fully aware of this intention on our part, and distinguish it carefully from our intention when we mean a certain group of men, or a solitary individual before us. In the chapter on Conception we shall see how important this difference of intention is. It casts its influence over the whole of the sentence, both before and after the spot in which the word *man* is used.

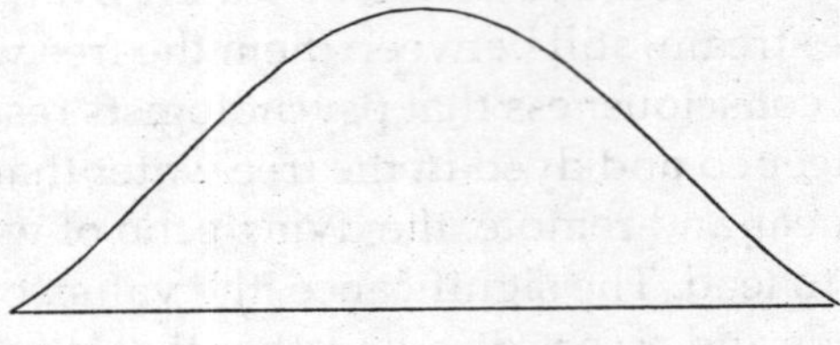

**Fig. 33.1**

Nothing is easier than to symbolise all these facts in terms of brain-action. Just as the echo of the *whence,* the sense of the starting point of our thought, is probably due to the dying excitement of processes but a moment since vividly aroused; so the sense of the whither, the foretaste of the terminus, must be due to the waxing excitement of tracts or processes which, a moment hence, will be the cerebral correlatives of some thing which a moment hence will be vividly present to the thought. Represented by a curve, the neurosis underlying consciousness must at any moment be like this:

Each point of the horizontal line stands for some brain-tract or process. The height of the curve above the line stands for the intensity of the process. All the processes are *present*, in the intensities shown by the curve. But those before the latter's apex *were* more intense a moment ago; those after it *will be* more intense a moment hence. If I recite *a, b, c, d, e, f, g*, at the moment of uttering *d*, neither *a, b, c*, nor *e, f, g*, are out of my consciousness altogether, but both, after their respective fashions, 'mix their dim lights' with the stronger one of the *d*, because their neuroses are both awake in some degree.

There is a common class of mistakes which shows how brain-processes begin to be excited before the thoughts attached to them are *due*—due, that is, in substantive and vivid form. I mean those mistakes of speech or writing by which, in Dr. Carpenter's words, we mis-pronounce or mis-spell a word, by introducing into it a letter or syllable of some other whose turn is shortly to come; or, it may be, the whole of the anticipated word is substituted for the one which ought to have been expressed."[18] In these cases one of two things must have happened: either some local accident of nutrition *blocks* the process that is *due*, so that other processes discharge that ought as yet to be but nascently aroused; or some opposite local accident *furthers* the *latter processes* and makes them explode before their time. In the chapter on Association of Ideas, numerous instances will come before us of the actual effect on consciousness of neuroses not yet maximally aroused.

It is just like the 'overtones' in music. Different instruments give the 'same note,' but each in a different voice, because each gives more than that note, namely, various upper harmonics of it which differ from one instrument to another. They are not separately heard by the ear; they blend with the fundamental note, and suffuse it, and alter it; and even so do the waxing and waning brain-processes at every moment blend with and suffuse and alter the psychic effect of the processes which are at their culminating point.

Let us use the words *psychic overtone, suffusion*, or *fringe*, to designate the influence of a faint brain-process upon our thought, as it makes it aware of relations and objects but dimly perceived.[19]

If we then consider the *cognitive function* of different states of mind, we may feel assured that the difference between those that are mere 'acquaintance,' and those that are 'knowledges-*about*' is reducible almost entirely to the absence or presence of psychic fringes or overtones. Knowledge *about a* thing is knowledge of its relations. Acquaintance with it is limitation to the bare impression which it makes. Of most of its relations we are only aware in the penumbral nascent way of a 'fringe' of unarticulated affinities about it. And, before passing to the next topic in order, I must say a little of this sense of affinity, as itself one of the most interesting features of the subjective stream.

In all our voluntary thinking there is some topic or subject about which all the members of the thought revolve. Half the time this topic is a problem, a gap we cannot yet fill with a definite picture, word, or phrase, but which, in the manner described some time back, influences us in an intensely active and determinate psychic way. Whatever may be the images and phrases that pass before us, we feel their relation to this aching gap. To fill it up is our thoughts' destiny. Some bring us nearer to that consummation. Some the gap negates as quite irrelevant. Each swims in a felt fringe of relations of which the aforesaid gap is the term. Or instead of a definite gap we may merely carry a mood of interest about with us. Then, however vague the mood, it will still act in the same way, throwing a mantle of felt affinity over such representations, entering the mind, as suit it, and tingeing with the feeling of tediousness or discord all those with which it has no concern.

Relation, then, to our topic or interest is constantly felt in the fringe, and particularly the relation of harmony and discord, of furtherance or hindrance of the topic. When the sense of furtherance is there, we are 'all right'; with the sense of hindrance we are dissatisfied and perplexed, and cast about us for other thoughts. Now *any* thought the quality of whose fringe lets us feel ourselves 'all right,' is an acceptable member of our thinking, whatever kind of thought it may otherwise be. Provided we only feel it to have a place in the scheme of relations in which the interesting topic also lies, that is quite sufficient to make of it a relevant and appropriate portion of our train of ideas.

*For the important thing about a train of thought is its conclusion.* That is the *meaning*, or, *as* we say, the topic of the thought. That is what abides when all its other members have faded from memory. Usually this conclusion is a word or phrase or particular image, or practical attitude or resolve, whether rising to answer a problem or fill a pre-existing gap that worried us, or whether accidentally stumbled on in revery. In either case it stands out from the other segments of the stream by reason of the peculiar interest attaching to it. This interest *arrests* it, makes a sort of crisis of it when it comes, induces attention upon it and makes us treat it in a substantive way.

The parts of the stream that precede these substantive conclusions are but the means of the latter's attainment. And, provided the same conclusion be reached, the means may be as mutable as we like, for the 'meaning' of the stream of thought will be the same. What difference does it make what the means are? *"Qu'importe le flacon, pourvu qu'on ait l'ivresse?"* The relative unimportance of the means appears from the fact that when the conclusion is there, we have always forgotten most of the steps preceding its attainment. When we have uttered a proposition, we are rarely able a moment afterwards to recall our exact words, though we can express it in different words easily enough. The practical upshot of a book we read remains with us, though we may not recall one of its sentences.

The only paradox would seem to lie in supposing that the fringe of felt affinity and discord can be the same in two heterogeneous sets of images. Take a train of words passing through the mind and leading to a certain conclusion on the one hand, and on the other hand an almost wordless set of tactile, visual and other fancies leading to the same conclusion. Can the halo, fringe, or scheme in which we feel the words to lie be the same as that in which we feel the images to lie? Does not the discrepancy of terms involve a discrepancy of felt relations among them?

If the terms be taken *qua* mere sensations, it assuredly does. For instance, the words may rhyme with each other,—the visual images can have no such affinity as *that*. But *qua* thoughts, *qua* sensations *understood,* the words have contracted by long association fringes of mutual repugnance or affinity with each other and with the conclusion, which run exactly parallel with like fringes in the visual, tactile and other ideas. The most important element of these fringes is, I repeat, the mere feeling of harmony or discord, of a right or wrong direction in the thought. Dr. Campbell has, so far as I know, made the best analysis of this fact, and his words, often quoted, deserve to be quoted again. The chapter is entitled "What is the cause that nonsense so often escapes being detected, both by the writer and by the reader?" The author, in answering this question makes *(inter alia)* the following remarks:[20]

"That connexion [he says] or relation which comes gradually to subsist among the different words of a language, in the minds of those who speak it,...is merely consequent on this, that those words are employed as signs of connected or related things. It is an axiom in geometry, that things equal to the same thing are equal to one another. It may, in like manner, be admitted as an axiom in psychology, that ideas associated by the same idea will associate one another. Hence it will happen, that if from experiencing the connexion of two things, there results, as infallibly there will result, an association between the ideas or notions annexed to them, as each idea will moreover be associated by its sign, there will likewise be an association between the ideas of the signs. Hence the sounds considered as signs will be conceived to have a connexion analogous to that which subsisteth among the things signified; I say, the sounds considered as signs: for this way of considering them constantly attends us in speaking, writing, hearing, and reading. When we purposely abstract from it, and regard them merely as sounds, we are instantly sensible that they are quite unconnected, and have no other relation than what ariseth from similitude of tone or accent. But to consider them in this manner commonly results from previous design and requires a kind of effort which is not exerted in the ordinary use of speech. In ordinary use they are regarded solely as signs, or, rather, they are confounded with the things they signify; the consequence of which is, that in the manner just now explained, we come insensibly to conceive a connexion among them of a very different sort from that of which sounds are naturally susceptible.

"Now this conception, habit, or tendency of the mind, call it which you please, is considerably strengthened both by the frequent use of language and by the structure of it... Language is the sole channel through which we communicate our knowledge and discoveries to others, and through which the knowledge and discoveries of others are communicated to us. By reiterated recourse to this medium, it necessarily happens, that when things are related to each other, the words signifying those things are more commonly brought together in discourse. Hence the words and names themselves, by customary vicinity, contract in the fancy a relation additional to that which they derive purely from being the symbols of related things. Farther, this tendency is strengthened by the structure of language. All languages whatever, even the most barbarous, as far as hath yet appeared, are of a regular and analogical make. The consequence is, that similar relations in things will be expressed similarly: that is, by similar inflections, derivations, compositions, arrangement of words, or juxtaposition of particles, according to the genius or grammatical form of the particular tongue. Now as, by the habitual use of a language (even though it were quite irregular), the signs would insensibly become connected in the imagination, wherever the things signified are connected in nature, so, by the regular structure of a language, this connexion among the signs is conceived as analogous to that which subsisteth among their archetypes."

If we know English and French and begin a sentence in French, all the later words that come are French; we hardly ever drop into English. And this affinity of the French words for each other is not something merely operating mechanically as a brain-law, it is something we feel at the time. Our understanding of a French sentence heard never falls to so low an ebb that we are not aware that the words linguistically belong together. Our attention can hardly so wander that if an English word be suddenly introduced we shall not start at the change. Such a vague sense as this of the words belonging together is the very minimum of fringe that can accompany them, if 'thought' at all. Usually the vague perception that all the words we hear belong to the same language and to the same special vocabulary in that language, and that the grammatical sequence is familiar, is practically equivalent to an admission that what we hear is sense. But if an unusual foreign word be introduced, if the grammar trip, or if a term from an incongruous 'vocabulary suddenly appear, such as 'rat-trap' or 'plumber's bill' in a philosophical discourse, the sentence detonates, as it were, we receive a shock from the incongruity, and the drowsy assent is gone. The feeling of rationality in these cases seems rather a negative than a positive thing, being the mere absence of shock, or sense of discord, between the terms of thought.

So delicate and incessant is this recognition by the mind of the mere fitness of words to be mentioned together that the slightest misreading, such as 'casualty' for 'causality,' or 'perpetual' for 'perceptual,' will be corrected by a listener whose attention is so relaxed that he gets no idea of the *meaning* of the sentence at all.

Conversely, if words do belong to the same vocabulary, and if the grammatical structure is correct, sentences with absolutely no meaning may be uttered in good faith and pass unchallenged. Discourses at prayer-meetings, reshuffling the same collection of cant phrases, and the whole genus of penny-a-line-isms and newspaper-reporters flourishes give illustrations of this. "The birds filled the tree-tops with their morning song, making the air moist, cool, and pleasant," is a sentence I remember reading once in a report of some athletic exercises in Jerome Park. It was probably written unconsciously by the hurried reporter, and read uncritically by many readers. An entire volume of 784 pages lately published in Boston[21] is composed of stuff like this passage picked out at random:

"The flow of the efferent fluids of all these vessels from their outlets at the terminal loop of each culminate link on the surface of the nuclear organism is continuous as their respective atmospheric fruitage up to the altitudinal limit of their expansibility, whence, when atmosphered by like but coalescing essences from higher altitudes,-those sensibly expressed as the essential qualities of external forms,—they descend, and become assimilated by the afferents of the nuclear organism."[22]

There are every year works published whose contents show them to be by real lunatics. To the reader, the book quoted from seems pure nonsense from beginning to end. It is impossible to divine, in such a case, just what sort of feeling of rational relation between the words may have appeared to the author's mind. The border line between objective sense and nonsense is hard to draw; that between subjective sense and nonsense, impossible. Subjectively, any collocation of words may make sense—even the wildest words in a dream-if one only does not doubt their belonging together. Take the obscurer passages in Hegel: it is a fair question whether the rationality included in them be anything more than the fact that the words all belong to a common vocabulary, and are strung together on a scheme of predication and relation,—immediacy, self-relation, and what not,—which has habitually recurred. Yet there seems no reason to doubt that the subjective feeling of the rationality of these sentences was strong in the writer as he penned them, or even that some reader by straining may have reproduced it in themselves.

To sum up, certain kinds of verbal associate, certain grammatical expectations fulfilled, stand for a good part of our impression that a sentence has a meaning and is dominated by the Unity of one Thought. Nonsense in grammatical form sounds half rational; sense with grammatical sequence upset sounds nonsensical; e.g., "Elba the Napoleon English faith had banished broken to be Saint because Helena at." Finally, there is about each word the psychic overtone of feeling that it brings us nearer to a forefelt conclusion. Suffuse all the words of a sentence, as they pass, with these three fringes or haloes of relation, let the conclusion seem worth arriving at, and all will admit the sentence to be an expression of thoroughly continuous, unified, and rational thought.[23]

Each word, in such a sentence, is felt, not only as a word, but as having a *meaning.* The 'meaning' of a word taken thus dynamically in a sentence may be quite different from its meaning when taken statically or without context. The dynamic meaning is usually reduced to the bare fringe we have described, of felt suitability or unfitness to the context and conclusion. The static meaning, the word is concrete, as 'table,' 'Boston,' consists of sensory images awakened; when it is abstract, as 'criminal legislation,' 'fallacy,' the meaning consists of other words aroused, forming the so-called 'definition.'

Hegel's celebrated dictum that pure being is identical with pure nothing results from his taking the words statically, or without he fringe they wear in a context. Taken in isolation, they agree in the single point of awakening no sensorial images. But taken dynamically, or as significant,—as *thought,—their* fringes of relation, their affinities and repugnances, their function and meaning, are felt and understood to be absolutely opposed.

Such considerations as these remove all appearance of paradox from those cases of extremely deficient visual imagery of whose existence Mr. Galton has made us aware. An exceptionally intelligent friend informs me that he can frame no image whatever of the appearance of his breakfast-table. When asked how he then remembers it at all, he says he simply *'knows'* that it seated four people and was covered with a white cloth on which were a butter-dish, a coffee-pot radishes, and so forth. The mind-stuff of which this 'knowing' is made seems to be verbal images exclusively. But if the words 'coffee,' 'bacon,' 'muffins,' and 'eggs' lead a man to speak to his cook, to pay his bills, and to take measures for the morrow's meal exactly as visual and gustatory memories would, why are they not, for all practical intents and purposes, as good a kind of material in which to think? In fact, we may suspect them to be for most purposes better than terms with a richer imaginative coloring. The scheme of relationship and the conclusion being the essential things in thinking, that kind of mind-stuff which is handiest will be the best for the purpose. Now words, uttered or unexpressed, are the handiest mental elements we have. Not only are they very *rapidly* revivable, but they are revivable as actual sensations more easily than any other items of our experience. Did they not possess some such advantage as this, it would hardly be the case that the older men are and the more effective as thinkers, the more, as a rule, they have lost their visualising power and depend on words. This was ascertained by Mr. Galton to be the case with members of the Royal Society. The present writer observes in his own person most distinctly.

On the other hand, a deaf and dumb man can weave his tactile and visual images into a system of thought quite as effective and rational as that of a word-user. *The question whether thought* is *possible without language* has been a favourite topic of discussion among philosophers. Some interesting reminiscences of his childhood by Mr. Ballard, a deaf-mute instructor in the National Cole at Washington, show it to be perfectly possible. A few graphs may be quoted here.

"In consequence of the loss of my hearing in infancy, I was debarred from enjoying the advantages which children in the full possession of their senses derive from the exercises of the common primary school, from the every-day talk of their school-fellows and playmates, and from the conversation of their parents and other grown-up persons.

"I could convey my thoughts and feelings to my parents and brothers by natural signs or pantomime, and I could understand what they said to me by the same medium; our intercourse being, however, confined to the daily routine of home affairs and hardly going beyond the circle of my own observation.

"My father adopted a course which he thought would, in some measure, compensate me for the loss of my hearing. It was that of taking me with him, when business required him to ride abroad; and lie took me more frequently than he did my brothers; giving, as the reason for his apparent partiality, that they could acquire information through the ear, while I depended solely upon my eye for acquaintance with affairs of the outside world.

"I have a vivid recollection of the delight I felt in watching the different scenes we passed through, observing the various phases of nature, both animate and inanimate; tho we did not, owing to my infirmity, engage in conversation. It was during those delightful rides, some two or three years before my initiation into the rudiments of written language, that I began to ask myself the question: *How came the world into being?* When this question occurred to my mind, I set myself to thinking it over a long time. My curiosity was awakened as to what was the origin of human life in its first appearance upon the earth, and of vegetable life as well, and also the cause of the existence of the earth, sun, moon, and stars.

"I remember at one time when my eye fell upon a very large old stump which we happened to pass in one of our rides, I asked myself, 'Is it possible that the first man that ever came into the world rose out of that stump? But that stump is only a remanent of a once noble magnificent tree, and how came that tree? Why, it came only by beginning to grow out of the ground just like those little trees now coming up. And I dismissed from my mind, as an absurd idea, the connection between the origin of man and a decaying old stump....

I have no recollection of what it was that first suggested to me the question as to the origin of things. I had before this time gained ideas of the descent from parent to child, of the propagation of animals, and of the production of plants from seeds. The question that occurred to my mind was: whence came the first man, the first animal, and the first plant, at the remotest distance of time, before which there was no man, no animal, no plant; since I knew they all had a beginning and an end.

"It is impossible to state the exact order in which these different questions arose, *i.e.*, about men, animals, plants, the earth, sun, moon, &c. The lower animals did not receive so much thought as was bestowed upon man and the earth; perhaps because I put man and beast in the same class, since I believed that man would be annihilated and there was no resurrection beyond the grave,—tho I am now told by my mother that, in answer to my question, in the case of a deceased uncle who looked to me like a person in sleep, she had tried to make me understand that he would awake in the far future. It was my belief that man and beast derived their being from the same source, and were to be laid down in the dust in a state of annihilation. Considering the brute animal as of secondary importance, and allied to man on a lower level, man and the earth were the two things on which my mind dwelled most.

"I think I was five years old, when I began to understand the descent from parent to child and the propagation of animals. I was nearly eleven years old, when I entered the Institution where I was educated; and I remember distinctly that it was at least two years before this time that I began to ask myself the question as to the origin of the universe. My age was then about eight, not over nine years.

"Of the form of the earth, I had no idea in my childhood, except that, from a look at a map of the hemispheres, I inferred there were two immense discs of matter lying near each other. I also believed the sun and moon to be two round, flat plates of illuminating matter; and for those luminaries I entertained a sort of reverence on account of their power of lighting and heating the earth. I thought from their coming up and going down, traveling across the sky in so regular a manner, that there must be a certain something having power to govern their course. I believed the sun went into a hole at the west and came out of another at the east, traveling through a great tube in the earth, describing the same curve as it seemed to describe in the sky. The stars seemed to me to be tiny lights studded in the sky.

"The source from which the universe came was the question about which my mind revolved in a vain struggle to grasp it, or rather to fight the way up to attain to a satisfactory answer. When I had occupied myself with this subject a considerable time, I perceived that it was a matter much greater than my mind could comprehend; and I remember well that I became so appalled at its mystery and so bewildered at my inability to grapple with it that I laid the subject aside and out of my mind, glad to escape being, as it were, drawn into a vortex of inextricable confusion. Tho I felt relieved at this escape, yet I could not resist the desire to know the truth; and I returned to the subject; but as before, I left it, after thinking it over for some time. In this state of perplexity, I hoped all the time to get at the truth, still believing that, the more I gave thought to the subject, the more my mind would penetrate the mystery. Thus, I was tossed like a shuttlecock, returning to the subject and recoiling from it, till I came to school.

"I remember that my mother once told me about a being up above, pointing her finger towards the sky and with a solemn look on her countenance. I do not recall the circumstance which led to this communication. When she mentioned the mysterious being up in the sky, I was eager to take hold of the subject, and plied her with questions concerning the form and appearance of this unknown being, asking if it was the sun, moon, or one of the stars. I knew she meant that there was a living one somewhere up in the sky; but when I realised that she could not answer my questions, I gave it up in despair, feeling sorrowful that I could not obtain a definite idea of the mysterious living one up in the sky.

"One day, while we were haying in a field, there was a series of heavy thunder-claps. I asked one of my brothers where they came from. He pointed to the sky and made a zigzag motion with his finger, signifying lightning. I imagined there was a great man somewhere in the blue vault, who made a loud noise with his voice out of it; and each time I heard[24] a thunder-clap I was frightened, and looked up at the sky, fearing he was speaking a threatening word."[25]

Here we may pause. The reader sees by this time that it makes little or no difference in what sort of mind-stuff, in what quality of imagery, his thinking goes on. The only images *intrinsically* important are the halting-places, the substantive conclusions, provisional or final, of the thought. Throughout all the rest of the 'stream, the feelings of relation are everything, and the terms related into its full sensible-image-value, under penalty of the thought being left unrealised and pale.

This is all I have to say about the sensible continuity and unity of our thought as contrasted with the apparent discreteness of the words, images, and other means by which it seems to be carried on. Between all their substantive elements there is 'transitive' consciousness, and the words and images are 'fringed,' and not as discrete as to a careless view they seem. Let us advance now to the next head in our description of Thought's stream.

### *(4) Human Thought Appears to Deal with Objects Independent of Itself; That is, it is Cognitive, or Possesses the Function of Knowing*

For Absolute Idealism, the infinite Thought and its objects are one. The Objects are, through being thought; the eternal Mind is, through thinking them. Were a human thought alone in the world there would be no reason for any other assumption regarding it. Whatever it might have before it would be its vision, would be there, in *its* 'there,' or then, in *its* 'then'; and the question would never arise whether an extra-mental duplicate of it existed or not. The reason why we all believe that the objects of our thoughts have a duplicate existence outside, is that there are *many* human thoughts, each with the *same* objects, as we cannot help supposing. The judgment that *my* thought has the same object as *his* thought is what makes the psychologist call my thought cognitive of an outer reality. The judgment that my own past thought and my own present thought are of the same object is what makes *me* take the object out of either and project it by a sort of triangulation into an independent position, from which it may *appear* to both. *Sameness* in a multiplicity of objective appearances is thus the basis of our belief in realities outside of thought.[26] We shall have to take up the judgment of sameness again.

To show that the question of reality being extra-mental or not is not likely to arise in the absence of repeated experiences of the *same*, take the example of an altogether unprecedented experience, such as a new taste in the throat. Is it a subjective quality of feeling, or an objective quality felt? You do hot even ask the question at this point. It is simply *that taste.* But if a doctor hears you describe it and says: "Ha! Now you know what *heartburn* is," then it becomes a quality already existent *extra mentern tuam,* which in turn have come upon and learned. The first spaces, times, things qualities, experienced by the child probably appear, like the first heartburn, in this absolute way, as simple *beings,* neither in nor out of thought. But later, by having other thoughts than this present one, ana making repeated judgments of sameness among their objects, he corroborates in himself the notion of realities, past and distant as well as present, which realities no one single thought either possesses or engenders, but which all may contemplate and know. This, as was stated in the previous chapter, is the *psychological* point of view, the relatively uncritical non-idealistic point of view of all natural science, beyond which this book cannot go. A mind which has become conscious of its own cognitive function, plays what we have called 'the psychologist' upon itself. It not only knows the things that appear before it; it knows that it knows them. This stage of reflective condition is, more or less explicitly, our habitual adult state of mind.

It cannot, however, be regarded as primitive. The consciousness of objects must come first. We seem to lapse into this primordial condition when consciousness is reduced to a minimum by the inhalation of anaesthetics or during a faint. Many persons testify that at a certain stage of the anaesthetic process objects are still cognised whilst the thought of self is lost. Professor Herzen says:[27]

"During the syncope there is absolute psychic annihilation, the absence of all consciousness; then at the beginning of coming to, or has at a certain moment a vague, limitless, infinite feeling—a sense of *existence and general* without the least trace of distinction between the me and the not-me."

Dr. Shoemaker of Philadelphia describes during the deepest conscious stage of ether-intoxication a vision of

> "two endless parallel lines in swift longitudinal motion...on a uniform misty background...together with a constant sound or whirr, loud but distinct...which seemed to be connected with the parallel lines... These phenomena occupied the whole field. There were present no dreams or visions in any way connected with human affairs, no ideas or impressions akin to anything in past experience, no emotions, of course no idea of personality. There was no conception as to what being it was that was regarding the two lines, or that there existed any such thing as such a being; the lines and waves were all.[28]

Similarly a friend of Mr. Herbert Spencer, quoted by him in *Mind* (vol. III. p. 556), speaks of "an undisturbed empty quiet everywhere, except that a stupid presence lay like a heavy intrusion *somewhere,—a* blotch on the calm." This sense of objectivity and lapse of subjectivity, even when the object is almost indefinable, is, it seems to me, a somewhat familiar phase in chloroformisation, though in my own case it is too deep a phase for any articulate after-memory to remain. I only know that as it vanishes I seem to wake to a sense of my own existence as something additional to what had previously been there.[29]

Many philosophers, however, hold that the reflective consciousness of the self is essential to the cognitive function of thought. They hold that a thought, in order to know a thing at all, must expressly distinguish between the thing and its own self.[30] This is a perfectly wanton assumption, and not the faintest shadow of reason exists for supposing it true. As well might I contend that I cannot dream without dreaming that I dream, swear without swearing that I swear, deny without denying that I deny, as maintain that I cannot know without knowing that I know. I may have either acquaintance-with, or knowledge-about, an object O without thinking about myself at all. It suffices for this that I think O, and that it exist. If, in addition to thinking O, I also think that I exist and that I know O, well and good; I then know one more thing, a fact about O, of which I previously was unmindful. That, however, does not prevent me from having already known O a good deal. O *per se,* or O *plus* P, are as good objects of knowledge as O *plus me* is. The philosophers in question simply substitute one particular object for all others, and call it *the* object *par excellence.* It is a case of the 'psychologist's fallacy', *They* know the object to be one thing and the thought another; and they forthwith foist their own knowledge into that of the thought of which they pretend to give a true account. To conclude, then, *thought may, but need* not, *in knowing, discriminate between its object and itself.*

We have been using the word Object. *Something must now be said about the proper rise of the term Object in Psychology.*

In popular parlance the word object is commonly taken without reference to the act of knowledge, and treated as synonymous with individual subject of existence. Thus if anyone ask what is the mind's object when you say Columbus discovered America in 1492,' most people will reply 'Columbus,' or 'America,' or, at most, 'the discovery of America.' They will name a substantive kernel or nucleus of the consciousness, and say the thought is 'about' that,—as indeed it is,—and they will call that your thought's 'object. Really that is usually only the grammatical object, or more likely the grammatical subject, of your sentence. It is at most your fractional object'; or you may call it the 'topic' of your thought, or the 'object of your discourse.' But the *Object* of your thought is really its entire content or deliverance, neither more nor less. It is a vicious use of speech to take out a substantive kernel from its content and call that its object; and it is an equally vicious use of speech to add a substantive kernel not articulately included in its content, and to call that its object. Yet either one of these two sins we commit, whenever we content ourselves with saying that a given thought is simply 'about' a certain topic, or that topic is its 'object.' The object of my thought in the previous sentence, for example, is strictly speaking neither Columbus, nor America, nor its discovery. It is nothing short of the entire sentence, 'Columbus-discovered-America-in-1492.' And if we wish to speak of it substantively, we must make a substantive of it by writing it out thus with hyphens between all its words. Nothing but this can possibly name its delicate idiosyncrasy. And if we wish to *feel* that idiosyncrasy we must reproduce the thought as it was uttered, with every word fringed and the whole sentence bathed in that original halo of obscure relations, which, like an horizon, then spread about its meaning.

Our psychological duty is to cling as closely as possible to the actual constitution of the thought we are studying. We may err as much by excess as by defect. If the kernel or 'topic,' Columbus, is in one way less than the thought's object, so in another way it may be more. That is, when named by the psychologist, it may mean much more than actually is present to the thought of which he is reporter. Thus, for example, suppose you should go on to think: 'He was a daring genius!' An ordinary psychologist would not hesitate to say that the object of your thought was still 'Columbus.' True, your thought is *about* Columbus. It 'terminates' in Columbus, leads from and to the direct idea of Columbus. But for the moment it is not fully and immediately Columbus, it is only 'he,' or rather 'he-was-a-daring-genius'; which, though it may be an unimportant difference for conversational purposes, is, for introspective psychology, as great a difference as there can be.

The object of every thought, then, is neither more nor less than all that the thought thinks, exactly as the thought thinks it, however complicated the matter, and however symbolic the manner of the thinking may be. It is needless to say that memory can seldom accurately reproduce such an object, when once it has passed from before the mind. It either makes too little or too much of it. Its best plan is to repeat the verbal sentence, if there was one, in which the object was expressed. But for inarticulate thoughts there is not even this resource, and introspection must confess that the task exceeds her powers. The mass of our thinking vanishes for ever, beyond hope of recovery, and psychology only gathers up a few of the crumbs that fall from the feast.

The next point to make clear is that, *however complex the object may be, the thought of it is one undivided stale of consciousness.* As Thomas Brown says.[31]

"I have already spoken too often to require again to caution you against a mistake, into which, I must confess, that the terms, which the poverty of our language obliges us to use, might, of themselves, very naturally lead you;—the mistake of supposing, that the most complex states of mind are not truly, in their very essence, as much one and indivisible, as those which we term simple—the complexity and seeming coexistence which they involve being relative to our feeling[32] only, not to their own absolute nature. I trust I need not repeat to you, that, in itself, every notion, however seemingly complex, is, and must be, truly simple—being one state, or affection, of one simple substance, mind. Our conception of a whole army, for example, is as truly this one mind existing in this one state, as our conception of any of the individuals that compose an army: Our notion of the abstract numbers, eight, four, two, is as truly one feeling of the mind, as our notion of simple unity."

The ordinary associationist-psychology supposes, in contrast with this, that whenever an object of thought contains many elements, the thought itself must be made up of just as many ideas, one idea for each element, and all fused together in appearance, but really separate.[33] The enemies of this psychology find (as we have already seen) little trouble in showing that such a bundle of separate ideas would never form one thought at all, and they contend that an Ego must be added to the bundle to give it unit, and bring the various ideas into relation with each other.[34] We will not discuss the ego just yet, but it is obvious that if things are to be thought in relation, they must be thought together, and in one *something,* be that something ego, psychosis, state of consciousness, or whatever you please. If not thought with each other, things are hot thought in relation at all. Now most believers in the ego make the same mistake as the associationists and sensationists whom they oppose. Both agree that the elements of the subjective stream are discrete and separate and constitute what Kant calls a 'manifold.' But while the associationists think that a 'manifold' can form a single knowledge, the egoists deny this, and say that the knowledge comes only when the manifold is subjected to the synthetising activity of an ego. Both make an identical initial hypothesis; but the egoist, finding it won't express the facts, adds another hypothesis to correct it. Now I do not wish just yet to 'commit myself' about existence or non-existence of the ego, but I do contend that we need not invoke it for this particular reason—namely, because the manifold of ideas has to be reduced to unity. *There is no manifold of coexisting ideas;* the notion of such a thing is a chimera. *Whatever things are thought in relation are thought from the outset in a unity, in a single pulse of subjectivity, a single psychosis, feeling, or state of mind.*

The reason why this fact is so strangely garbled in the books seems to be what on an earlier page. I called the psychologist's fallacy. We have the inveterate habit, whenever we try introspectively to describe one of our thoughts, of dropping the thought as it is in itself and talking of something else. We describe the things that appear to the thought, and we describe other thoughts *about* those things—as if these and the original thought were the same. If, for example, the thought be 'the pack of cards is on the table,' we say, "Well, isn't it a thought of the pack of cards? Isn't it of the cards as included in the pack? Isn't it of the table? And of the legs of the table as well? The table has legs—how can you think the table without virtually thinking its legs? Hasn't our thought then, all these parts—one part for the pack and another for the table? And within the pack-part a part for each card, as within the table-part a part for each leg? And isn't each of these parts an idea? And can our thought, then, be anything but an assemblage or pack of ideas, each answering to some element of what it knows?"

Now not one of these assumptions is true. The thought taken as an example is, in the first place, not of 'a pack of cards.' It is of 'the-pack-of-cards-is-on-the-table,' an entirely different subjective phenomenon, whose Object implies the pack, and every one of the cards in it, but whose conscious constitution bears very little resemblance to that of the thought of the pack *per se.* What a thought *is,* and what it may be developed into, or explained to stand for, and be equivalent to, are two things, not one.[35]

An analysis of what passes through the mind as we utter the phrase *the pack of cards is on the table* will, I hope, make this clear, and may at the same time condense into a concrete example a good deal of what has gone before.

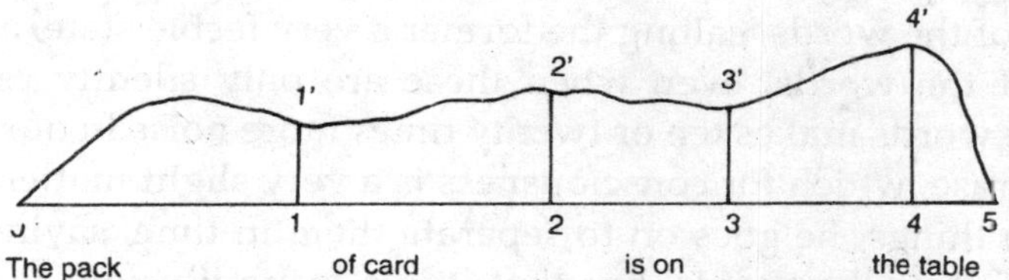


**Fig. 33.2.** The Stream of Consciousness

It takes time to utter the phrase. Let the horizontal line in Fig. 33.2 represent time. Every part of it will then stand for a fraction, every point for an instant, of the time. Of course the thought has *tame parts.* The part 2–3 of it, though continuous with 1–2, is yet a different part from 1–2. Now I say of these time-parts that we cannot take any one of them so short that it will not after some fashion or other be a thought of the whole object 'the pack of cards is on the table.' They melt into each other like dissolving views, and no two of them feel the object just alike, but each feels the total object in a unitary undivided way. This is what I mean by denying that in the thought any parts can be found corresponding to the object's parts. Time-parts are not such parts.

Now let the vertical dimensions of the figure stand for the objects or contents of the thoughts. A line vertical to any point of the horizontal, as 1–1', will then symbolise the object in the mind at the instant 1; a space above the horizontal, as 1–1'–2'–2, will symbolise all that passes through the mind during the time 1–2 whose line it covers. The entire diagram from 0 to 0' represents a finite length of thought's stream.

Can we now define the psychic constitution of each vertical section of this segment? We can, though in a very rough way. Immediately after o, even before we have opened our mouths to speak, the entire thought is present to our mind in the form of an intention to utter that sentence. This intention, though it has no simple name, and though it is a transitive state immediately displaced by the first word, is yet a perfectly determinate phase of thought, Unlike anything else. Again, immediately before O′, after the last word of the sentence is spoken, all will admit that we again think its entire content as we inwardly realise its completed deliverance. All vertical sections made through any other parts of the diagram will be respectively filled with other ways of feeling the sentence's meaning. Through 2, for example, the cards will be the part of the object most emphatically present to the mind; through 4, the table. The stream is made higher in the drawing at its end than at its beginning, because the final way of feeling the content is fuller and richer than the initial way. As Joubert says, we only know just what we meant to say, after we have said it." And, as M. V. Egger remarks, "before speaking, one barely knows what one intends to say, but afterwards one is filled with admiration and surprise at having said and thought it so well."

This latter author seems to me to have kept at much closer quarters with the facts than any other analyst of consciousness.[36] But even he does not quite hit the mark, for, as I understand him, he thinks that each word as it occupies the mind *displaces* the rest of the thought's content. He distinguishes the 'idea' (what I have called the total *object* or meaning) from the consciousness of the words, calling the former a very feeble state, and contrasting it with the liveliness of the words, even when these are only silently rehearsed. "The feeling," he says, "of the words makes ten or twenty times more noise in our consciousness than the sense of the phrase, which for consciousness is a very slight matter.[37] And having distinguished these two things, he goes on to separate them in time, saying that the idea may either precede or follow the words, but that it is a 'pure illusion' to suppose them simultaneous.[38] Now I believe that in all cases where the words are *understood*, the total idea may be and usually is present not only before after the phrase has been spoken, but also whilst each separate is uttered.[39] It is the overtone, halo, or fringe of the word, as *spoken an that sentence*. It is never absent; no word in an understood sentence comes to consciousness as a mere noise. We feel its meaning as it passes; and although our object differs from one moment to another as to its verbal kernel or nucleus, yet it is *similar* throughout the entire segment of the stream. The same object is known everywhere, now from the point of view, if we may so call it, of this word, now, from the point of view of that. And in our feeling of each word there chimes an echo or foretaste of every other. The consciousness of the 'Idea' and that of the words are thus cosubstantial. They are made of the same 'mind-stuff,' and form an unbroken stream. Annihilate a mind at any instant, cut its thought through whilst yet uncompleted, and examine the object present to the cross-section thus suddenly made; you will find, not the bald word in process of utterance, but that word suffused with the whole idea. The word may be so loud, as M. Egger would that we cannot *tell* just how its suffusion, as such, feels, or how it differs from the suffusion of the next word. But it does differ; we may be sure that, could we see into the brain, we should the same processes active through the entire sentence in different degrees, each one in turn becoming maximally excited and then yielding the momentary verbal 'kernel,' to the thought's content, at other times being only sub-excited, and then combining with the other sub-excited processes to give the overtone or fringe.[40]

We may illustrate this by a farther development of the diagram. Let the objective content of any vertical section through stream be represented no longer by a line, but by a plane figure, highest opposite whatever part of the object is most prominent in 'consciousness at the moment when the section is made. This part, in verbal thought, will usually be some word. A series of sections 1–1', taken at the moments 1, 2, 3, would then look like this:

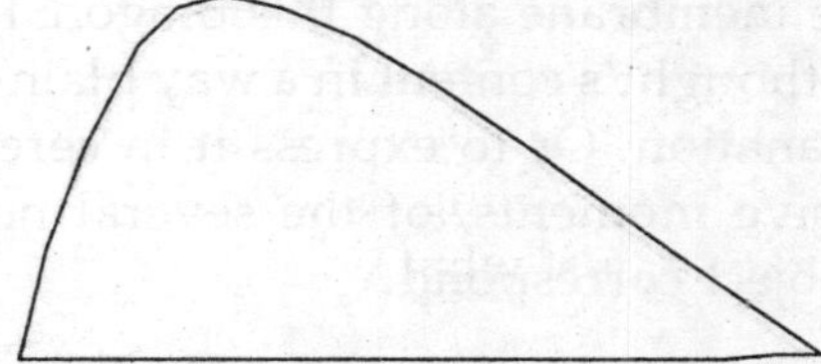

**Fig. 33.3.** The Pack of Cards is on the Table

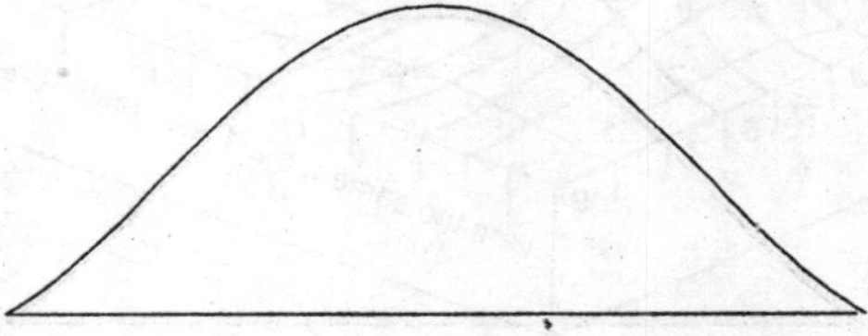

**Fig. 33.4.** The Pack of Cards is on the Table

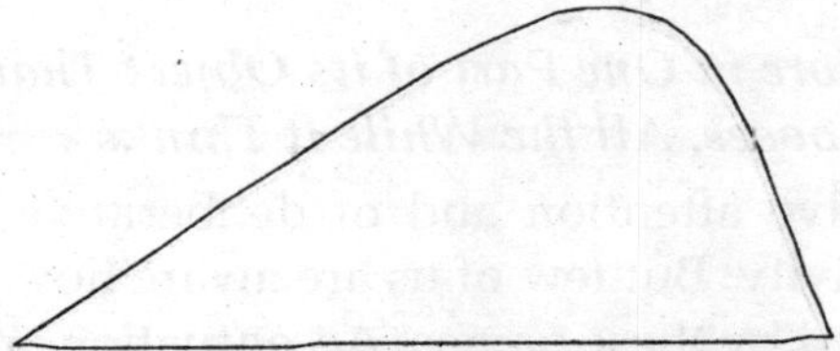

**Fig. 33.5.** The Pack of Cards is on the Table

The horizontal breadth stands for the entire object in each of the figures; the height of the curve above each part of that object marks the relative prominence of that part in the thought. At the moment symbolised by the first figure *pack* is the prominent part; in the third figure it is *table*, etc.

We can easily add all these plane sections together to make a solid, one of whose solid dimensions will represent time, whilst a cut across this at right angles will give the thought's content at the moment when the cut is made. Let it be the thought, 'I am the same I that I was yesterday.' If at the fourth moment of time we annihilate the thinker and examine how the last pulsation of his consciousness was made, we find that it was an awareness of the whole content with *same* most prominent, and the other parts of the thing known relatively less distinct. With each prolongation of the scheme in the time-direction, the summit of the curve of section would come further towards the end of the sentence. If we make a solid wooden frame with the sentence written on its front, and the time-scale on one of its sides, if we spread flatly a sheet of India rubber over its top, on which rectangular co-ordinates are painted, and slide a smooth ball under the rubber in the direction from o to 'yesterday,' the bulging of the membrane along this diagonal at successive moments will symbolise the changing of the thought's content in a way plain enough, after what has been said, to call for no more explanation. Or to express it in cerebral terms, it will show the relative intensities, at successive moments, of the several nerve-processes to which the various parts of the thought-object correspond.

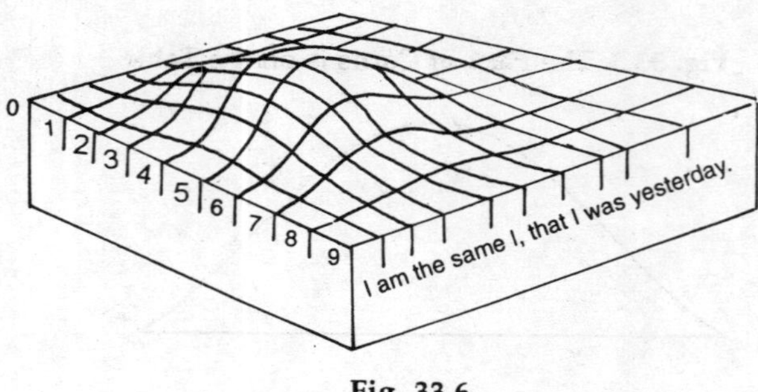


**Fig. 33.6**

The last peculiarity of consciousness to which attention is to be drawn in this first rough description of its stream is that

### *(5) It is Always Interested More in One Part of its Object Than in Another, and Welcomes and Rejects, or Chooses, All the While it Thinks*

The phenomena of selective attention and of deliberative will are of course patent examples of this choosing activity. But few of us are aware how incessantly it is at work in operations not ordinarily called by these names. Accentuation and Emphasis are present in every perception we have. We find it quite impossible to disperse our attention impartially over a number of impressions. A monotonous succession of sonorous strokes is broken up into rhythms, now of one sort, now of another, by the different accent which we place on different strokes. The simplest of these rhythms is the double one, tick-tock, tick-tock, tick-tock. Dots dispersed on a surface are perceived in rows and groups. Lines separate into diverse figures. The ubiquity of the distinctions, *this* and *that, here* and *there, now* and *then,* in our minds is the result of our laying the same selective emphasis on parts of place and time.

But we do far more than emphasise things, and unite some, and keep others apart. We actually *ignore* most of the things before us. Let me briefly show how this goes on.

To begin at the bottom, what are our very senses themselves but organs of selection? Out of the infinite chaos of movements, of which physics teaches Las that the outer world consists, each sense-organ picks out those which fall within certain limits of velocity. To these it responds, but ignores the rest as completely as if they did not exist. It thus accentuates particular movements in a manner for which objectively there seems no valid ground; for; as Lange says, there is no reason whatever to think that the gap in Nature between the highest sound-waves and the lowest heat-waves is an abrupt break like that of our sensations; or that the difference between violet and ultra-violet rays has anything like the objective importance subjectively represented by that between light and darkness. Out of what is in itself an undistinguishable, swarming *continuum*, devoid of distinction or emphasis, our senses make for us, by attending to this motion and ignoring that, a world full of contrasts; of sharp accents, of abrupt changes, of picturesque light and shade.

If the sensations we receive from a given organ have their causes thus picked out for us by the conformation of the organ's termination, Attention, on the other hand, out of all the sensations yielded, picks out certain ones as worthy of its notice and suppresses all the rest. Helmholtz's work on Optics is little more than a study of those visual sensations of which common men never become aware—blind spots, *muscae volitantes*, after-images, irradiation, chromatic fringes, marginal changes of color, double images, astigmatism, movements of accommodation and convergence, retinal rivalry, and more besides. We do not even know without special training on which of our eyes an image falls. So habitually ignorant are most men of this that one may be blind for years of a single eye and never know the fact.

Helmholtz says that we notice only those sensations which are signs to us of *things*. But what are things? Nothing, as we shall abundantly see, but special groups of sensible qualities, which happen practically or aesthetically to interest us, to which we therefore give substantive names, and which we exalt to this exclusive status of independence and dignity. But in itself, apart from my interest, a particular dust-wreath on a windy day is just as much of an individual thing, and just as much or as little deserves an individual name, as my own body does.

And then, among the sensations we get from each separate thing, what happens? The mind selects again. It chooses certain of the sensations to represent the thing most *truly*, and considers the rest as its appearances, modified by the conditions of the moment. Thus my table-top is named *square*, after but one of an infinite number of retinal sensations which it yields, the rest of them being sensations of two acute and two obtuse angles: but I call the latter *perspective* views, and the four right angles the *true* form of the table, and erect the attribute squareness into the table's essence, for aesthetic reasons of my own. In like manner, the teal form of the circle is deemed to be the sensation it gives when the line of vision is perpendicular to its centre—all its other sensations are signs of this sensation. The real sound of the cannon is the sensation it makes when the ear is close by. The real color of the brick is the sensation it gives when the eye looks squarely at it from a near point, out of the sunshine and yet not in the gloom; under other circumstances it gives us other color-sensations which are but signs of this—we then see it looks pinker or blacker than it really is. The reader knows no object which he does not represent to himself by preference as in some typical attitude, of some normal size, at some characteristic distance, of some standard tint, etc. But all these essential characteristics, which together form for us the genuine objectivity of the thing and are contrasted with what we call the subjective sensations it may yield us at a given moment, are mere sensations like the latter. The mind chooses to suit itself, and decides what particular sensation shall be held more real and valid than all the rest.

Thus perception involves a twofold choice. Out of all present sensations, we notice mainly such as are significant of absent ones; and out of all the absent associates which these suggest, we again pick out a very few to stand for the objective reality *par excellence.* We could have no more exquisite example of selective industry.

That industry goes on to deal with the things thus given in perception. A man's empirical thought depends on the things he has experienced, but what these shall be is to a large extent determined by his habits of attention. A thing may be present to him a thousand times, but if he persistently fails to notice it, it cannot be said to enter into his experience. We are all seeing flies, moths, and beetles by the thousand, but to whom, save an entomologist, do hey say anything distinct? On the other hand, a thing met only nice in a lifetime may leave an indelible experience in the memory. Let four men make a tour in Europe. One will bring home only picturesque impressions—costumes and colors, parks and news and works of architecture, pictures and statues. To another all this will be non-existent; and distances and prices, populations and drainage-arrangements, door—and window-fastenings, and other useful statistics will take their place. A third will give a rich account of the theatres, restaurants, and public balls, and naught beside; whilst the fourth will perhaps have been so wrapped in his own subjective broodings as to tell little more than a few names of places through which he passed. Each has selected, out of the same mass of presented objects, those which suited his private interest and has made his experience thereby.

If, now, leaving the empirical combination of objects, we ask how the mind proceeds *rationally* to connect them, we find selection again to be omnipotent. In a future chapter we shall see that all Reasoning depends on the ability of the mind to break up the totality of the phenomenon reasoned about, into parts, and to pick out from among these the particular one which, in our given emergency, may lead to the proper conclusion. Another predicament will need another conclusion, and require another element to be picked out. The man of genius is he who will always stick in his bill at the right point, and bring it out with the right element—'reason' if the emergency be theoretical, 'means' if it be practical—transfixed upon it. I here confine myself to this brief statement, but it may suffice to show that Reasoning is but another form of the selective activity of the mind.

If now we pass to its aesthetic department, our law is still more obvious. The artist notoriously selects his items, rejecting all tones, colors, shapes, which do not harmonise with each other and with the main purpose of his work. That unity, harmony, 'convergence of characters,' as M. Tame calls it, which gives to works of art their superiority over works of nature, is wholly due to *elimination.* Any natural subject will do, if the artist has wit enough to pounce upon some one feature of it as characteristic, and suppress all merely accidental items which do not harmonise with this.

Ascending still higher, we reach the plane of Ethics, where choice reigns notoriously supreme. An act has no ethical quality whatever unless it be chosen out of several all equally possible. To sustain the arguments for the good course and keep them ever before us, to stifle our longing for more flowery ways, to keep the foot unflinchingly on the arduous path, these are characteristic ethical energies. But more than these; for these but deal with the means of compassing interests already felt by the man to be supreme. The ethical energy *par excellence* has to go farther and choose which *interest* out of several, equally coercive, shall become supreme. The issue here is of the utmost pregnancy, for it decides a man's entire career. When he debates, Shall I commit this crime? choose that profession? accept that office, or marry this fortune?—his choice really lies between one of several equally possible future Characters. What he shall *become* is fixed by the conduct of this moment. Schopenhauer, who enforces his determinism by the argument that with a given fixed character only one reaction is possible under given circumstances, forgets that, in these critical ethical moments, what consciously *seems* to be in question is the complexion of the character itself. The problem with the man is less what act he shall now choose to do, than what being he shall now resolve to become.

Looking back, then, over this review, we see that the mind is at every stage a theatre of simultaneous possibilities. Consciousness consists in the comparison of these with each other, the selection of some, and the suppression of the rest by the reinforcing and inhibiting agency of attention. The highest and most elaborated mental products are filtered from the data chosen by the faculty next beneath, out of the mass offered by the faculty below that, which mass in turn was sifted from a still larger amount of yet simpler material, and so on. The mind, in short, works on the data it receives very much as a sculptor works on his block of stone. In a sense the statue stood there from eternity. But there were a thousand different ones beside it, and the sculptor alone is to thank for having extricated this one from the rest. Just so the world of each of us, howsoever different our several views of it may be, all lay embedded in the primordial chaos of sensations, which gave the mere *matter* to the thought of all of us indifferently. We may, if we like, by our reasonings unwind things back to that black and jointless continuity of space and moving clouds of swarming atoms which science calls the only real world. But all the while the world *we* feel and live in will be that which our ancestors and we, by 'lowly cumulative strokes of choice, have extricated out of this, like sculptors, by simply rejecting certain portions of the given stuff. Other sculptors, other statues from the same stone! Other minds, other worlds from the same monotonous and inexpressive chaos! My world is but one in a million alike embedded, alike real to those who may abstract them. How different must be the worlds in the consciousness of ant, cuttle-fish, or crab!

But in my mind and your mind the rejected portions and the selected portions of the original world-stuff are to a great extent the same. The human race as a whole largely agrees as to what it shall notice and name, and what not. And among the noticed parts we select in much the same way for accentuation and preference or subordination and dislike. There is, however, one entirely extraordinary case in which no two men ever are known to choose alike. One great splitting of the whole universe into two halves is made by each of us; and for each of us almost all of the interest attaches to one of the halves; but we all draw the line of division between them in a different place. When I say that we all call the two halves by the same names, and that those names are *'me'* and *'not-me'* respectively, it will at once be seen what I mean. The altogether unique kind of interest which each human mind feels in those parts of creation which it can call *me* or *mine* may be a moral riddle, but it is a fundamental psychological fact. No mind can take the same interest in his neighbor's *me* as in his own. The neighbor's me falls together with all the rest of things in one foreign mass, against which his own *me* stands out in startling relief. Even the trodden worm, as Lotze somewhere says, contrasts his own suffering self with the whole remaining universe, though he have no clear conception either of himself or of what the universe may be. He is for me a mere part of the world; for him it is I who am the mere part. Each of us dichotomises the Kosmos in a different place.

Descending now to finer work than this first general sketch, let us in the next chapter try to trace the psychology of this fact of self-consciousness to which we have thus once more been led.

## NOTES

1. B.P. Bowne: *Metaphysics*, p. 362.
2. *L'Automatisme psychologique*, pp. 317-18.
3. Cf. A Constans: *Relation sur une epidemie d'hystero-demonopathie en 1861*, 2me ed., Paris, 1863.—Chiap a Franzolini: *L'Epidemia di istero-demonopatie in Verzenis*, Reggio, 1879.—See also J. Kerner's little work: *Nachricht von dem Vorkommen des Bessessenseyns*, 1836.
4. For the Physiology of this compare the chapter on the Will.
5. *Loc. cit.*, p. 316.
6. *The Philosophy of Reflection*, 1, 248, 290.
7. *Populare wissenschaftliche Vortrage*, Drittes Heft (1876), p. 72.
8. Fick, in L. Hermann's *Handbuch der Physiologie*, Bd. III, Th. I, p. 225.
9. It need of course not follow, because a total brain-state does not recur, that no *point* of the brain can ever be twice in the same condition. That would be as improbable a consequence as that in the sea a wave-crest should never come twice at the same point of space. What can hardly come twice is an identical *combination* of wave-forms all with their crests and hollows reoccupying identical places. For such a total combination as this is the analogue of the brain-state to which our actual consciousness at any moment is due.
10. The accurate registration of the 'how long' is still a little mysterious.
11. Cf. Brentano: *Psychologie*, vol. I, pp. 219-20. Altogether this chapter of Brentano's on the Unity of Consciousness is as good as anything with which I am acquainted.
12. Honour to whom honour is due! The most explicit acknowledgment I have anywhere found of all this is in a buried and forgotten paper by the Rev. James Wills, on "Accidental Association," in the *Transactions of the Royal Irish Academy*, vol. XXI (1848). Mr. Wills writes:

    "At every instant of conscious thought, there is a certain sum of perceptions, or reflections, or both together, present, and together constituting one whole state of apprehension. Of this some definite portion may be far more distinct than all the rest; and the rest be in consequence proportionably vague, even to the very limit of obliteration. But still, within this limit, the most dim shade of perception enters into, and in some infinitesimal degree modifies, the whole existing state. This state will thus be in some way modified by any sensation or emotion, or act of distinct attention, that may give prominence to any part of it; so that the actual result is capable of the utmost variation, according to the person or the occasion.... To any portion of the entire scope here described there may be a special direction of the attention, and this special direction is strictly what is *recognised as* the idea present to the mind. This idea is evidently not commensurate with the entire state of apprehension, and much perplexity has arisen from not observing this fact. However deeply we may suppose the attention to be engaged by any thought, any considerable alteration of the surrounding phenomena would still be perceived; the most abstruse demonstration in this room would not prevent a listener, however absorbed, from noticing the sudden extinction of the lights.... Our mental states have always an *essential unity,* such, that each state of apprehension, however variously compounded, is a single whole, of which every component is, therefore, strictly apprehended (so far as it is apprehended), as a part. Such is the elementary basis from which all our intellectual operations commence."

13. Compare the charming passage in Taine on *Intelligence* (N.Y. ed.), I, 83-4.
14. E.g.: "The stream of thought is not a continuous current, but a series of distinct ideas, more or less rapid in their succession; the rapidity being measurable by the number that pass through the mind in a given time." (Bain: *The Emotions and the Will,* p. 29.)
15. Few writers have admitted that we cognise relations through feeling. The intellectualists have explicitly denied the possibility of such a thing—e.g., Prof. T.H. Green (*Mind,* vol. VII, p. 28): "No feeling, as such or as felt, is [of?] a relation.... Even a relation between feelings is not itself a feeling or felt." On the other hand, the sensationists have either smuggled in the cognition without giving any account of it, or have denied the relations to be cognised, or even to exist, at all. A few honourable exceptions, however, deserve to be named among the sensationists. Destutt de Tracy, Laromiguiere, Cardaillac, Brown, and finally Spencer, have explicitly contended for feelings of relation, consubstantial with our feelings or thoughts of the terms 'between' which they obtain. Thus Destutt de Tracy says (*Elemens d'ideologie,* T. Ier, chap. IV); "The faculty of judgment is itself a sort of sensibility, for it is the faculty of feeling the relations among our ideas; and to feel relations is to feel." Laromiguiere writes (*Lecons de philosophie,* IIme Partie, 3me Lecon):

"There is no one whose intelligence does not embrace simultaneously many ideas, more or less distinct, more or less confused. Now, when we have many ideas at once, a peculiar feeling arises in us: we fell, among these ideas, resemblances, differences, relations. Let us call this mode of feeling, common to us all, the feeling of relation, or relation-feeling *(sentiment-rapport).* One sees immediately that these relation-feelings, resulting from the propinquity of ideas, must be infinitely more numerous than the sensation-feelings *(sentiments-sensations)* or the feelings we have of the action of our faculties. The slightest knowledge of the mathematical theory of combinations will prove this.... *Ideas* of relation originate in feelings of relation. They are the effect of our comparing them and reasoning about them."

Similarly, de Cardaillac (*Etudes elementaires de philosophie,* Section I, chap. VII):

"By a natural consequence, we are led to suppose that at the same time that we have several sensations or several ideas in the mind, we feel the relations which exist between these sensations, and the relations which exist between these ideas.... If the feeling of relations exists in us,...it is necessarily the most varied and the most fertile of all human feelings: 1°, the most varied, because, relations being more numerous than being, the feelings of relation must be in the same proportion more numerous than the sensations whose presence gives rise to their formation; 2°, the most fertile, for the relative ideas of which the feeling-of-relation is the source.. are more important than absolute ideas, if such exist.... If we interrogate common speech, we find the feeling of relation expressed there in a thousand different ways. It is easy to seize a relation, we say that it is *sensible,* to distinguish it from one which, because its terms are too remote, cannot be as quickly perceived. A sensible difference, or resemblance.... What is taste in the arts, in intellectual productions? What but the feeling of those relations among the parts which constitutes their merit?... Did we not feel relations we should never attain to true knowledge,...for almost all our knowledge is of relations.... We never have an isolated sensation;...we are therefore never without the feeling of relation.... An *object* strikes our senses; we see in it only a sensation... The relative is so near the absolute, the relation-feeling so near the sensation-feeling, the two are so intimately fused in the composition of the object, that the relation appears to us as part of the sensation itself. It is doubtless to this sort of fusion between sensations and feelings of relation that the silence of metaphysicians as to the latter is due; and it is for the same reason that they have obstinately persisted in asking from sensation alone those ideas of relation which it was powerless to give."

Dr. Thomas Brown writes (*Lectures*, XLV, *init.*): "There is an extensive order of our feelings which involve this notion of relation, and which consist indeed in the mere perception of a relation some sort.... Whether the relation be of two, or of many external objects, or of two or many affections of the mind, the feeling of this relation...is what I term a relative suggestion; that phrase being the simplest which it is possible to employ, for expressing, without any theory, the mere fact of the rise of certain feelings of relation, after certain other feelings which precede them; and therefore, as involving no particular theory, and simply expressive of an undoubted fact.... That the feelings of relation are states of the mind essentially different from our simple perceptions, or conceptions of the objects...that they are not what Condillac terms *transformed sensations*, I proved in a former Lecture, when I combated the excessive simplification of that ingenious, but not very accurate philosopher. There is an original tendency or susceptibility of the mind, by which, or perceiving together different objects, we are instability, without the intervention of any other mental process, sensible of their relation in certain respects, as truly as there is an original tendency or susceptibility by which, when external objects are present, and have produced a certain affection of our sensorial organ, we are instantly affected with the primary elementary feelings of perception: and, I may add, that, as our sensations or perceptions are of various species, so are there various species of relations;—the number of relations, indeed, even of external things, being almost infinite, while the number of perceptions is necessarily, limited by that of the objects which have the power of producing some affection of our organs of sensation.... Without that susceptibility of the mind, by which it has the feeling of relation, our consciousness would be as truly limited to a single point, as our body would become, were it possible to fetter it to a single atom."

Mr. Spencer is even more explicit. His philosophy is crude in that he seems to suppose that it is only in transitive states that outward relations are known; whereas in truth space-relations, relations of contrast, etc., are felt along with their terms, in substantive states as well as in transitive states, as we shall abundantly see. Nevertheless Mr. Spencer's passage is so clear that it also deserves to be quoted in full (*Principles of Psychology*, § 65):

"The proximate components of Mind are of two broadly-contrasted kinds—Feelings and the Relations between feelings. Among the members of each group there exist multitudinous unlikenesses, many of which are extremely strong; but such unlikenesses are small compared with those which distinguish members of the one group from members of the other. Let us, in the first place, consider what are the characters which all Feelings have in common, and what are the characters which all Relations between feelings have a common.

"Each feeling, as we hare define it, is any portion of consciousness which occupies a place sufficiently large to give it a perceivable individuality; which has its individuality marked off from adjacent portions of consciousness by qualitative contrasts; and which, when introspectively contemplated, appears to be homogeneous. These are the essentials. Obviously if, under introspection, a state of consciousness is decomposable into unlike parts that exist either simultaneously or successively, it is not one feeling but two or more. Obviously if it is indistinguishable from an adjacent portion of consciousness, it forms one with that portion—is not an individual feeling but part of one. And obviously if it does not occupy in consciousness an appreciable area, or an appreciable duration, it cannot be known as a feeling.

"A Relation between feelings is, on the contrary, characterised by occupying to appreciable part of consciousness. Take away the terms it unites, and it disappears along with them; having no independent place—no individuality of its own. It is true that, under an ultimate analysis, what we call a relation proves to be itself a kind of feeling—the monetary feeling accompanying the transition from one conspicuous feeling to an adjacent conspicuous feeling. And it is true that, notwithstanding its extreme brevity, its qualitative character is appreciable; for relations are (as we shall hereafter see) distinguishable from one another only by the unlikenesses of the feelings which accompany the momentary transitions. Each relational feeling may, in fact, be regarded as one of those nervous shocks which we suspect to be the units of compositions of feelings; and, though instantaneous, it is known as of greater or less strength and as taking place with greater or less facility. But the contrast between these relational feelings and what we ordinarily call feelings, is to strong that we must class them apart. Their extreme brevity, their small variety, and their dependence on the terms they unite, differentiate them in an unmistakable way.

"Perhaps it will be well to recognise more fully the truth that this distinction cannot be absolute. Besides admitting that, as an element of consciousness, a relation is a momentary feeling, we must also admit that just as a relation can have no existence apart from the feelings which form its terms, so a feeling can exist only by relations to other feelings which limit it in space or time or both. Strictly speaking, neither a feeling nor a relation is an independent element of consciousness: there is throughout a dependence such that the appreciable areas of consciousness occupied by feelings, can no more possess individualities apart from the relations which link them, than these relations can—possess individualities apart from the feelings they link. The essential distinction between the two, then, appears to be that whereas a relational feeling is a portion of consciousness inseparable into parts, a feeling ordinarily so-called, is a portion of consciousness that admits imaginary division into like parts which are related to one another in sequence or co-existence. A feeling proper is either made up of like parts that occupy time, or it is made up of like parts that occupy space, or both. In any case, a feeling proper is an aggregate of related like parts, while a relational feeling is undecomposable. And this is exactly the contrast between the two which must result if, as we have inferred, feelings are composed of units of feeling, or shocks."

16. M. Paulhan (*Review Philosophique*, XX, 455-6), after speaking of the faint mental images of objects and emotions, says: "We find other vaguer states still, upon which attention seldom rests, except in persons who by nature or profession are addicted to internal observation. It is even difficult to name them precisely, for they are little known and not classed; but we may cite as an example of them that peculiar impression which we feel when, strongly preoccupied by a certain subject, we nevertheless are engaged with, and have our attention almost completely absorbed by, matters quite disconnected therewithal. We do not then exactly think of the object of our preoccupation; we do not represent it in a clear manner; and yet our mind is not as it would be without this preoccupation. Its object, absent from consciousness, is nevertheless represented there by a peculiar unmistakable impression, which often persists long and is a strong feeling, although so obscure for our intelligence." "A mental sign of the kind is the unfavourable disposition left in our mind towards an individual by painful incidents erewhile experienced and now perhaps forgotten. The sign remains, but is not understood; its definite meaning is lost." (p. 458).

17. Mozart describes thus his manner of composing: First bits and crumbs of the piece come and gradually join together in his mind; then the soul getting warmed to the work, the thing grows more and more, "and I spread it out broader and clearer, and at last it gets almost finished in my head, even when it is a long piece, so that I can see the whole of it at a single glance in my mind, as if it were a beautiful painting or a handsome human being; in which way I do not hear it in my imagination at all as a succession—the way it must come later—but all at once, as it were. It is a rare feast! All the inventing and making goes on in me as in a beautiful strong dream. But the best of all is the *hearing of it all at once.*"

18. *Mental Physiology*, § 236. Dr. Carpenter's explanation differs materially from that given in the text.

19. Cf. also S. Stricker: *Vorlesungen uber allegemeine und experimentelle Pathologie* (1879), pp. 462-3, 501, 547; Romanes; *Mental Evolution in Man: Origin of Human Faculty*, p. 82. It is so hard to make one's self clear that I may advert to a misunderstanding of my views by the late Prof. Thomas Maguire of Dublin (*Lectures on Philosophy*, 1885). This author considers that by the 'fringe' I mean some sort of psychic material by which sensations in themselves separate are made to cohere together, and wittily says that I ought to "see that uniting sensations by their 'fringes' is more vague than to construct the universe out of oysters by platting their beards" (p. 211). But the fringe, as I use the word, means nothing like this it is part of the *object cognised*,—substantive *qualities* and *things* appearing to the mind in a *fringe of relations*. Some parts—the transitive parts—of our stream of thought cognise the relations rather than the things; but both the transitive and the substantive parts form one continuous stream, with no discrete sensations' in it such as Prof. Maguire supposes, and supposes me to suppose to be there.
20. George Campbell: *The Philosophy of Rhetoric*, book II, chap. VII.
21. *Substantialism: Or, Philosophy of Knowledge*, by 'Jean Story' (1879).
22. M.G. Tarde, quoting (in Delboeuf: *Le Sommeil et les reves* (1885), p. 226) some nonsense-verses from a dream, says they show how "prosodic forms may subsist in a mind from which logical rules are effaced.... I was able, in dreaming, to preserve the faculty of finding two words which rhymed, to appreciate the rhyme, to fill up the verse as it first presented itself with other words which, added, gave the right number of syllables, and yet I was ignorant of the sense of the words.... Thus we have the extraordinary fact that the words called each other up, without calling up their sense.... Even when awake, it is more difficult to ascend to the meaning of a word than to pass from one word to another; or to put it otherwise, *it is harder to be a thinker than to be a rhetorician*, and on the whole nothing is commoner than trains of words not understood."
23. We think it odd that young children should listen with such rapt attention to the reading of stories expressed in words half of which they do not understand, and of none of which they ask the meaning. But their thinking is in form just what ours is when it is rapid. Both of us make flying leaps over large portions of the sentences uttered and we give attention only to substantive starting points, turning points, and conclusions here and there. All the rest, 'substantive' and separately intelligible as it may *potentially* be, actually serves only as so much transitive material. It is *internodal* consciousness, giving us the sense of continuity, but having no significance apart from its mere gap-filling function. The children probably feel no gap when through a lot of unintelligible words they are swiftly carried to a familiar and intelligible terminus.
24. Not literally *heard*, of course. Deaf-mutes are quick to perceive shocks and jars that can be felt, even when so slight as to be unnoticed by those who can hear.
25. Quoted by Samuel Porter: "Is Thought Possible without Language?" In *Princeton Review*, 57th year, pp. 108-12 (Jan. 1881). Cf. also W.W. Ireland: *The Blot upon the Brain* (1886), Paper x, part II; G.J. Romanes: *Mental Evolution in Man*, pp. 81-83, and references therein made. Prof. Max Muller gives a very complete history of his controversy in pp. 30-64 of his *Science of Thought* (1887). His own view is that Thought and Speech are inseparable; but under speech he includes any conceivable sort of symbolism or even mental imagery, and he makes no allowance for the wordless summary glimpses which we have of systems of relation and direction.
26. If but one person sees an apparition we consider it his private hallucination. If more than one, we begin to think it may be a real external presence.
27. *Revue Philosophique*, vol. XXI, p. 671.
28. Quoted from the *Therapeutic Gazette*, by the N.Y. *Semi-Weekly Evening Post* for Nov. 2, 1886.
29. In half-stunned states self-consciousness may lapse. A friend writes me: "We were driving back from—in a wagonette. The door flew open and X., alias 'Baldy,' fell out on the road. We pulled up at once, and then he said, 'Did anybody fall out?' or 'Who fell out?'—I don't exactly remember the words. When told that Baldy fell out, he said, 'Did Baldy fall out? Poor Baldy!'"

30. Kant originated this view. I subjoin a few English statements of it. J. Ferrier: *Institutes of Metaphysic*, Proposition I: "Along with whatever any intelligence knows it must, as the ground or condition of its knowledge, have some cognisance of itself." Sir William Hamilton: *Discussions on Philosophy and Literature, Education and University Reform*, p. 47: "*We know;* and *We knew that we know:*—these propositions, *logical* distinct, are *really* identical; each implies the other.... So true is the scholastic brocard:—'*Non sentimus nisi sentimus nos sentier.*'" H.L. Mansel: *Metaphysics*, p. 58: "Whatever variety of materials...may exist within reach of my mind, I can become conscious of them only by recognising them as mine.... Relation to the conscious self is thus the permanent and universal feature which every state of consciousness, as such, must exhibit." T.H. Green: *Introduction to Hume*, p. 12: "A consciousness by the man...of himself in negative relation to the thing that is his object, and this consciousness...must be taken to go along with the perceptive act itself. No less than this indeed can be involved in any act that is to be the beginning of knowledge at all. It is the minimum of possible thought or intelligence."

31. *Lectures on the Philosophy of the Human Mind*, Lecture 45.

32. Instead of saying *to our feeling only,* he should have said, to the *object* only.

33. "There can be no difficulty in admitting that association does form the ideas of an indefinite number of individuals into one complex idea; because it is an acknowledged fact. Have we not the idea of an army? And is not that precisely the ideas of an indefinite number of men formed into one idea?" (James Mill's *Analysis of the Phenomena of the Human Mind* (J.S. Mill's Edition), vol. I, p. 264).

34. For their arguments, see above, pp. 160-164.

35. I know there are readers whom nothing can convince that the thought of a complex object has not as many parts as are discriminated in the object itself. Well, then, let the word parts pass. Only observe that these parts are not the separate 'ideas' of traditional psychology. No one of them can live out of that particular thought, any more than my head can live off of my particular shoulders. In a sense a soap-bubble has parts; it is a sum of juxtaposed spherical triangles. But these triangles are not separate realities; neither are the 'parts' of the thought separate realities. Touch the bubble and the triangles are no more. Dismiss the thought and out go its parts. You can no more make a new thought out of 'ideas' that have once served than you can make a new bubble out of old triangles. Each bubble, each thought, is a fresh organic unity, *sui generis.*

36. In his work, *La Parole interieure* (Paris, 1881), especially chapters V and VI.

37. Page 301.

38. Page 218. To prove this point, M. Egger appeals to the fact that we often hear someone speak whilst our mind is preoccupied, but do not understand him until some moments afterwards, when we suddenly 'realise' what he meant. Also to our digging out the meaning of a sentence in an unfamiliar tongue, where the words are present to us long before the idea is taken in. In these special cases the word does indeed precede the idea. The idea, on the contrary, precedes the word whenever we try to express ourselves with effort, as in a foreign tongue, or in an unusual field of intellectual invention. Both sets of cases, however, are exceptional, and M. Egger would probably himself admit, on reflection, that in the former class there is some sort of a verbal suffusion, however evanescent, of the idea, when it is grasped—we hear the echo of the words as we catch their meaning. And he would probably admit that in the second class of cases the idea persists after the words that came with so much effort are found. In normal cases the simultaneity, as he admits, is obviously there.

39. A good way to get the words and the sense separately is to inwardly articulate word for word the discourse of another. One then finds that the meaning will often come to the mind in pulses, after clauses or sentences are finished.

40. The nearest approach (with which I am acquainted) to the doctrine set forth here is in O. Liebmann's *Zur Analysis der Wirklichkeit*, pp. 427-438.

# Bibliography


Akishige, Y. Studies on constancy problem. IIA. *Psychologia*, 1968, 11, 43-55.

Akita, K. Effect of the gradual change of distribution of practice in motor learning. *Japanese Psychological Research*, 1966, 8, 18-29.

Ando, S. Zen and Christianity. *Psychologia*, 1965, 8, 123-134.

Berrien, F.K. Values of Japanese and American students. Technical Report No. 14, Department of Defense, Office of Naval Research, Group Psychology Branch, Washington, 1964.

Brammer, L.M. Counselor education in the Republic of China: An outsider's view. *Psychologia*, 1965, 8, 220-222.

Chen, C.K. The 1963 annual psychological society. (In Chinese) *Acta Psychologica Sinica*, 1964, 8, 109-112.

Chen, D.J. How psychology can be of service to the socialistic reconstruction. (In Chinese) *Acta Psychologica Sinica*, 1959, 3, 142-145.

Chiba, T. On proper consciousness (Koyu-ishiki). *Psychologia*, 1960, 3, 65-72.

Ching, C.C. The behaviourism of J.B. Watson. (In Chinese) *Acta Psychologica Sinica*, 1965, 9, 361-374.

Chou, H.S. Analysis of mistakes made in learning resolution of factors by first grade junior middle school pupils. (In Chinese) *Acta Psychologica Sinica*, 1965, 8, 223-229.

Chu, C.S. Problems on the object of psychology. (In Chinese) *Acta Psychologica Sinica*, 1956, 1, 11-19.

Chu, H.L. Critical comments on Gestalt psychology. (In Chinese) *Acta Psychologica Sinica*, 1958, 2, 85-98.

Cohen, J., Hansel, C.E.M., and Sylvester, J.D. A new phenomenon in time judgment. *Nature*, 1953, 172-901.

Dhairyan, D. Research needs for development of psychotherapy in India. In T.K.N. Menon (Ed.), *Recent trends in psychology*. Oriental Longmans, 1961, pp. 154-161.

Doi, L.T. Morita therapy and psychoanalysis. *Psychologia*, 1962, 3, 117-123.

Dumoulin, H. Methods and aims of Buddhist meditation: Satipatthana and Zen. *Psychologia*, 1962, 5, 175-180.

Fromm, E. Psychoanalysis and Zen Buddhism. *Psychologia*, 1959, 2, 79-99.

Fujisawa, F. The psycho-physiological studies of sleep. *Japanese Psychological Research*, 1960, 2, 120-134.

Fujita, O. Studies of spontaneous alternation in rats. VIII. The effect of food deprivation, reward and intertrial interval. (In Japanese) *Japanese Journal of Psychology*, 1961, 32, 303-310.

Gardiner, H.M. Psychology in Thailand. *Psychologia*, 1968, 11, 122-124.

Hassan, F. Letter to Dr. Koji Sato. *Psychologia*, 1963, 6, 179-180.

Hirano, T. Effects of functional disturbances of the limbic system on the memory consolidation. *Japanese Psychological Research*, 1965, 7, 171-182.

Holmes, S.W. Zen Buddhism and transactional psychology. *Etc.;* 1957, 14, 243-349.

Hora, T. Tao, Zen, and existential psychotherapy. *Psychologia*, 1959, 2, 236-249.

Hundal, P.S. Organisation of mental abilities at successive grade levels. *Indian Journal of Psychology*, 1966, 41, 65-72.

Hwang, C.H. A study of the personal preference of Chinese university students by Edwards Personal Preference Schedule. *Psychology and Education*, 1967, 1, 52-68.

Ikeda, H. and Obonai, T. Studies in figural after-effects. IV. The contrast-confluence illusion of concentric circles and the figural after-effect. *Japanese Psychological Research*, 1955, 2, 17-23.

Imada, H. "Vigor" of water drinking behaviour of rats as a function of thirst drive. *Japanese Psychological Research*, 1964, 6, 108-114.

Indow, T.A. General equi-distance scale of the four qualities of tastes. *Japanese Psychological Research*, 1966, 8, 136-150.

Ishihara, I. *Psychology of Verbal Behaviour* (In Japanese) Tokyo: Kobunkan, 1960.

Ishihara, S. Growth and decay of induction. IX. Several aspects of behaviour in the semicircular apparatus. (In Japanese) *Japanese Journal of Psychology*, 1966, 37, 1-11.

Iwahara, S. Studies of the "spread of effect." V. The spread of verbal punishment and the meaningfulness of cue stimuli. *Japanese Psychological Research*, 1958, 5, 38-50.

Iwahara, S. Psychological activities at the University of the Ryukyus, the National Taiwan University and Taiwan Normal University. *Psychologia*, 1967, 10, 223-225.

Iwahara, S., and Fujita, O. Behaviourism in Japan. *Psychologia*, 1963, 4, 59-64.

Iwahara, S., Nagamura, N., and Iwasaki, T. Effect of chlordiazepoxide upon experimental extinction in the straight runway as a function of partial reinforcement in the rat. *Japanese Psychological Research*, 1967, 9, 128-134.

Iwahara, S., Takeuchi, E., and Nagamura, N. EEG patterns during natural sleep in the rat and their multivariate analyses. (In Japanese) *Bulletin of Faculty Education, Tokyo University of Education*, 1967, 13, 41-57.

Jayasuriya, D.L. Recent psychological research in Ceylon. *Psychologia*, 1965, 8, 169-174.

Joshi, M.C. Psychological researches in India. *Jalota Commemoration Volume*, 1965, 25-34.

Kakizaki, S. Binocular rivalry and stimulus intensity. *Japanese Psychological Research*, 1960, 2, 94-105.

Kaneko, T. *Science of color: Its psychophysiology.* (In Japanese) Tokyo: Misuzu-Shobo, 1968.

Kasamatsu, A., and Hirai, T. An electroencephalographic study of the Zen meditation (Zazen). *Folia Psychiatrica et Neurologica Japonica*, 1966, 20, 315-336.

Kawai, H., and Kondo, K. Discussion on Morita therapy. *Psychologia*, 1960, 3, 92-99.

Kitao, N. Effects of mediated association on paired-associate learning. VIII. About the degree of prior learning and instruction. (In Japanese) *Japanese Journal of Physiology*, 1967, 38, 137-147.

Kora, T., and Sato, K. Morita therapy: A psychotherapy in the way of Zen. Psychologia, 1958, 1, 219-225.

Krishnakanth, A., and Prasad, J.N. Socio-economic differences on a reasoning test. *Indian Psychological Review*, 1967, 3, 119-122.

Krishnan, B.A. review of contributions of Indian psychologists (1950-1960). In T.K.N. Menon (Ed.), *Recent Trends in Psychology.* Orient Longmans, 1961.

Kuraishi, S. On the reproduction of simple thought-configuration by using the method of paired comparison. (In Japanese) *Japanese Journal of Psychology*, 1937, 12, 578-602.

Kuroda, R. Stereopsychology: Its scope and method. *Acta Psychologica Keijo*, 1931, 1, 69-82.

Lagmay, A.V. Letter to Dr. Koji Sato. *Psychologia*, 1963, 6, 179-180.

Liu, I.M., and Hu, W. The cube and Weber's Law. *Acta Psychologica Taiwanica*, 1967, 9, 87-89.

Liu, K.C. *Practice on the Breathing Therapy.* (In Chinese) Hopei People's Press, 1957.

Lun, S.H. Researches in perception in Democratic Germany. (In Chinese) *Acta Psychologica Sinica*, 1958, 2, 45-52.

Matsuyama, Y., and Tsukioka, S. The intertrial-interval response in relation to amount of warning signal, and restraint time. *Japanese Psychological Research*, 1964, 6, 1-9.

Maupin, E.W. Zen Buddhism: A psychological review. *Journal of Consulting Psychology*, 1962, 26, 362-278.

Morikawa, Y. Functions of stimulus and response in paired-associate verbal learning. *Psychologia*, 1959, 2, 41-56.

Morinaga, S., Noguchi, K., and Ohnishi, A. The horizontal vertical illusion and the relation to spatial and retinal orientation. *Japanese Psychological Research*, 1962, 4, 25-29.

Morris, C.W. Comments on mysticism and its language. *Etc.*, 1951, 9, 3-8.

Motokawa, K. Retinal traces and visual perception of movement. *Journal of Experimental Psychology*, 1953, 45, 369-377.

Motora, Y. *An essay on Eastern philosophy.* Leipzig: Voigtlander, 1905.

Motoyoshi, R. Simultaneous and successive discrimination under three types of jumping platform. *Japanese Psychological Research*, 1956, 4, 50-61.

Motoyoshi, R., and Iwahara, S. Japanese studies on animal behaviour in the last decade. *Psychologia*, 1960, 3, 135-148.

Murphy, G., and Murphy, L.B. (Eds.) *Asian Psychology*. New York: Basic Books, 1968.

Ni, C.F. A preliminary criticism on the behaviourism of J.B. Watson. (In Chinese) *Acta Psychologica Sinica*, 1957, 1, 194-200.

Niimi, Y., Kubota, K., and Iwama, Y. Spontaneous variations of the sin potentials and skin potential reflexes during natural sleep in the cat. *Japanese Journal of Physiology*, 1968, 18, 190-197.

Niki, H. Response perseveration following the hippocampal ablation in the rat. *Japanese Psychological Research*, 1964, 6, 108-114.

Obonai, T. The concept of psychophysiological induction: A review of experimental works. *Psychologia*, 1957, 1, 3-9.

Ono, S. A mathematical analysis of motor learning: A control system model. *Japanese Psychological Research*, 1966, 8, 72-89.

Otsuka, N. Stereopsychology and studies on k'an by Ryo Kuroda. *Psychologia*, 1960, 3, 73-39.

Pareek, U. Psychology in India. *Psychologia*, 1957, 1, 55-59.

Rao, S. Occupational role and personality: A comparative study of a few occupational groups in India. *Indian Journal of Psychology*, 1966, 41, 59-64.

Razran, G. Psychology in Communist countries other than the U.S.S.R. *American Psychologist*, 1958, 13, 177-178.

Rogers, A.H. Zen and LSD: An enlightening experience. *Psychologia*, 1964, 7, 150-151.

Sagara, M., and Oyama, T. Experimental studies on figural aftereffects in Japan. *Psychological Bulletin*, 1957, 54, 327-338.

Sato, K. How to get Zen enlightenment: On Master Ishiguro's five-days' intensive course for its attainment. *Psychologia*, 1959, 2, 107-113.

Sato, K., and Suzuki, D.T. Zen and LSD 25. *Psychologia*, 1967, 10, 129-132.

Sen, I. Teaching of personality in Indian universities. *Indian Journal of Psychology*, 1958, 33, 129-133.

Shuh, P. China's recent research work in psychology. *Psychologia*, 1959, 2, 193-202.

Su, H.Y. Letter to Dr. Koji Sato. *Psychologia*, 1963, 6, 176.

Sugimura, T. Intradimensional and extradimensional shifts as a function of stimulus change and overtraining. *Japanese Psychological Research*, 1967, 9, 78-84.

Sukemune, S. Effects of total number of acquisition trials under partial reinforcement schedules on running speeds. *Japanese Psychological Research*, 1963, 5, 183-187.,

Suzuki, D.T. *Zen Buddhism*. Garden City, N.Y.: Anchor Books, 1956.

Takada, Y. Reaction time and information in the discrimination of length of lines. *Japanese Psychological Research*, 1960, 2, 14-24.

Takahashi, S. The present status of psychological activities in Korea. *Psychologia*, 1967, 10, 225-226.

Tanaka, Y. Status of Japanese experimental psychology. *Annual Review of Psychology*, 1966, 17, 233-272.

Thompson, R.F. *Foundations of physiological psychology*. New York: Harper and Row, 1967.

Thwin, H. Department of Psychology, University of Rangoon, Burma. *Psychologia*, 1962, 5, 107-111.

Tsai, H.J., and Liu, S.Y. Lambda waves of human subjects of different age levels. (In Chinese) *Acta Psychologica Sinica*, 1965, 8, 343-352.

Tsao, C., and Shen, Y. Developmental studies on the recognition and generalisation of Chinese characters in primary school children. III. Development of the discrimination of detail. (In Chinese) *Acta Psychologica Sinica*, 1965, 8, 135-140.

Tsao, J.C. On the fundamental viewpoints of psychology. (In Chinese) *Acta Psychologica Sinica*, 1965, 9, 101-105.

Tsao, J.C., Li, C.C., Ching, C.C., Chang, T.H., Yu, C.S., Feng, K.C., and Chu, T.H. Human factors in signal design of control room of an electric power station. (In Chinese) *Acta Psychologica Sinica*, 1966, 9, 53-58.

Umemoto, T. Japanese studies in verbal learning and memory. *Psychologia*, 1959, 2, 1-9.

Van Dusen, W. LSD and enlightenment of Zen. *Psychologia*, 1961, 4, 11-16.

Yen, F., and Cheng, F.Y. Binocular disparity, stimulus intensity, and the way of light presentation have to do with necessary stimulus duration time to produce depth perception. *Acta Psychologica Taiwanica*, 1966, 8, 85-91.

Yokose, Z. Theoretical formula of vector-field and its experimental proof. *Psychologia*, 1957, 1, 17-21.

Yoshida, M. Studies of psychometric classification of odors (5). *Japanese Psychological Research*, 1964, 6, 145-154.

Yuki, K. Experimental psychology. In A. II. Livermore (Ed.), *Science in Japan*. Washington, D.C.: American Association for the advancement of Science, 1965, pp. 335-373.

Zaidi, S.M.H. Pakistan: A society in transition. *Psychologia*, 1964, 7, 15-21.